HONEST BROKER?

Joseph V. Hughes Jr. and Holly O. Hughes Series
on the Presidency and Leadership

James P. Pfiffner, General Editor

HONEST BROKER?

The National Security Advisor and Presidential Decision Making

John P. Burke

Texas A&M University Press   College Station

LIBRARY OF CONGRESS CATALOGING-IN-PUBLICATION DATA

Burke, John P., 1953–
   Honest broker? : the national security advisor and presidential decision
making / John P. Burke. — 1st ed.
         p. cm. — (Joseph V. Hughes Jr. and Holly O. Hughes series on the
presidency and leadership)
   Includes bibliographical references and index.
   ISBN-13: 978-1-60344-098-1 (cloth : alk. paper) 7028856
   ISBN-10: 1-60344-098-4 (cloth : alk. paper)
   ISBN-13: 978-1-60344-102-5 (pbk. : alk. paper)
   ISBN-10: 1-60344-102-6 (pbk. : alk. paper)
   1. United States. Assistant to the President for National Security Affairs—
Decision making—History.   2. National Security Council (U.S.)—Decision
making—History.   3. Presidents—United States—Decision making—History—
20th century.   4. National security—United States—Decision making—History—
20th century.   I. Title.   II. Title: National security advisor and presidential
decision making.   III. Series: Presidency and leadership (Unnumbered)
UA23.15.B87   2009
355'.033573—dc22
2008034985

To the memory of my departed colleagues,

Raul Hilberg
1926–2007
and
James S. Pacy
1930–2008

But most of all for my mother,

Eleanor Sutherland Burke
1921–2007

Contents

Acknowledgments

I would especially like to thank former NSC advisors Brent Scowcroft and Anthony Lake for consenting to be interviewed on this project. Former NSC staff members and State Department officials Harold Saunders and Philip Zelikow also provided valuable input. As well, I would like to thank Fred I. Greenstein for reading an early draft of the manuscript and offering wise counsel, as did the reviewers for Texas A&M University Press. James P. Pfiffner has been an especially important source of encouragement, advice, and counsel; I am very pleased that this book appears in the Joseph V. Hughes and Holly O. Hughes Series on the Presidency and Leadership at Texas A&M University Press that he edits. I would also like to thank Mary Lenn Dixon, editor in chief of Texas A&M University Press, for her support of this project. Thom Lemmons, my immediate editor, and Scott Barker, my skilled copyeditor, worked diligently to improve upon my efforts and bring this book to fruition.

At various points, I have drawn on archival research undertaken at the Eisenhower, Kennedy, Johnson, Ford, and Carter presidential libraries, as well as the Nixon Presidential Materials Project at the National Archives in College Park, Maryland. I would like to thank the archivists there for their excellent efforts in assisting researchers such as I. Unfortunately, much of the archival material on national security matters remains closed to researchers at the more recent presidential libraries and the Freedom of Information Act process of opening materials at the post-Carter libraries has proved to be a lengthy, multiyear, and often disappointing endeavor. I would also like to thank the Oral History Project at Columbia University for granting me permission to quote from the oral history collection housed at the Eisenhower Library.

For the past three years, I have taught my seminar course at the University of Vermont on the topic of national security decision making. My students, as always, have been a source of inspiration as I have worked on this project.

This work draws on two of my previously published articles in *Presidential Studies Quarterly*, whose editor, George C. Edwards III, has done a remarkable job during his tenure in nurturing a journal that now makes a major, high-quality contribution to the field of presidency studies. Parts of this introduction and parts of the concluding chapter draw on "The Neutral/Honest Broker Role in Foreign-Policy Decision Making: A Reassessment," which appeared in June 2005. Parts of chapter 6 on Condoleezza Rice's tenure as NSC advisor draw on "Condoleezza Rice as NSC Advisor: A Case Study of the Honest Broker Role," which appeared in September 2005. Some of the material also draws on two books I have written on presidential transitions—*Presidential Transitions: From Politics to Practice* and *Becoming President: The Bush Transition 2000–2003*—as well as my study of presidential management and White House staff and advisory organization, *The Institutional Presidency: Organizing and Managing the White House, from FDR to Bill Clinton,* and my coauthored analysis of the Vietnam decision making of Eisenhower and Johnson, *How Presidents Test Reality: Decisions on Vietnam, 1954 and 1965.*

HONEST BROKER?

Introduction

The Case for the Honest Broker Role

Analysis of presidential decision making, particularly in the area of foreign and national security policy, is a critical area of research. It examines processes and dynamics that are truly consequential in their results. Its implications and findings bear great significance when put into practice.

In studying decision making, much attention has focused on a range of variables thought to have some causal impact and explanatory value: the organization and structure of decision-making processes, the impact of presidential personality, management, and leadership style, the development and effects of a White House-centered institutional presidency, the presence of bureaucratic politics and group dynamics, and the consequences of rational actors operating within institutionally defined parameters, to list just a few. However, with some important exceptions,[1] relatively little attention has been focused on how the particular *roles* of participants in presidential decision-making processes are defined and operate.

My purpose in this book is to examine the role of the National Security Council (NSC) advisor: the president's chief, in-house source of coordination and of substantive counsel on foreign policy and national security matters. But the argument of the book is also, in part, admittedly prescriptive. I am interested in how a particular definition of the role of NSC advisor—that of the honest broker—relates to effective presidential decision making. The basic notion of the role, which I will discuss in more detail below, is that the NSC advisor is not just another source of policy advice. Rather, the person in that position needs to be concerned with the fair and balanced presentation of information to the president and those advising the president (often called the "principals") as well as the overall quality of the organizations and processes that come into play in decision making. As we shall see, these elements of the broker role were central to the responsibilities of the NSC advisor—"Special Assistant to the President for National Security Affairs," as it was initially titled—when the position was created in 1953 by President Dwight D. Eisenhower. But I should also point out that the title NSC "advisor" is something of a misnomer for the position during the Eisenhower years: providing substantive policy advice was not seen as part of the advisor's role and occurred rarely.

In the post-Eisenhower years, the job evolved considerably. Eisenhower saw the NSC system and its staff as a device for effectively harnessing the relevant agencies and departments so that they would have productive input on policy options. For his immediate successor, John F. Kennedy, that system was too ossified and bureaucratic: the NSC advisor and staff, by contrast, needed to be a presidential instrument—a *presidential* staff and a direct source for *presidential* initiatives. Subsequent presidencies, as we shall see, have grappled with these two organizationally different models and the different implications they bear for the role of the NSC advisor.

The book explores this evolution, especially how many national security advisors have deviated, in various ways, from the foundational task of what I will call "brokerage." This part of the analysis concerns how other facets of the post-Eisenhower NSC advisor's role—such as providing personal advice to the president, serving as a media spokesperson, or getting involved in the implementation of policy—stand in relation to the task of brokerage as well as how they affect decision making. Is honest brokerage a thing of the past? As we shall see it is not. Can it be squared with these added duties as the job has changed over time? That is a more difficult question, and one that shall be of chief concern.

There is a strong case to be made that honest brokerage is an important and vital contributor—although not necessarily the only contributor—to effective decision making. Many NSC advisors have identified honest brokerage as an important part of the job of being an effective advisor. Some empirical studies of what makes for decision-making success identify components of the deliberative process that approximate some of the duties of the honest broker. Likewise studies of decision failures, such as the Tower Commission's report on the Iran-Contra scandal of the Reagan years, have identified problems that might have been remedied through more effective brokerage activity. The findings of the Tower Commission are also illustrative of another part of the argument: the problems that can arise when NSC advisors embrace other activities, such as secret efforts to exchange arms for hostages and the diversion of funds to the contras in Nicaragua.

At the same time, the reader should note that I recognize that honest brokerage is still *only* a piece of the puzzle—albeit an important one as we shall see—relating to what makes for an effective national security advisor or, more broadly, an effective national security decision-making process. There are tasks for the NSC advisor necessary for effectiveness that go beyond or are otherwise separate from brokerage.[2] Competent and experienced staff must be hired and morale fostered. Day-to-day staff support for the president and the other principals must be provided, to list but a few.

But brokerage, I would argue, provides a useful "lens of analysis" for understanding the job of NSC advisor. As we shall see, a strong case can be made that its presence has positive bearing on effective decision making, and its absence heightens risks of deliberative failure and policy error. Other factors and agents matter too—most notably what the president brings to the table as the ultimate decision maker. But the "lens" of the NSC advisor's role is also instructive.

The reader should also note, as I discuss below, that brokerage should not be taken to mean that the NSC advisor serves simply as some fair-minded clearing house for managing the interagency process. That is part of brokerage, but so too is the NSC advisor's concern for the quality of the deliberative process and the effective functioning of the NSC system. Post-Eisenhower NSC advisors and their staffs also often serve as a source for the development of *presidential*-level policy initiatives; Kennedy's concerns are just as relevant as Ike's. The argument of the book recognizes this: indeed its central task is to understand how brokerage might still be undertaken while taking into account this and other components of the job of a contemporary NSC advisor.

I. What is the Honest Broker Role?

The role of the NSC advisor as an honest broker has its practical origins, as will be discussed in detail in the next chapter, in the Eisenhower presidency. As a matter of academic scrutiny, attention to the role of honest broker arose in the debate, more than thirty-five years ago, concerning Alexander George's discussion of the "managerial custodian" (a particular variant of the broker role) in a lengthy 1972 article in the *American Political Science Review*. George's article merited a comment by I. M. Destler and a rejoinder by George—in the same issue—then was further explicated by George in testimony before a federal commission on the organization of foreign policy deliberations, and most importantly in his work *Presidential Decisionmaking in Foreign Policy*.[3]

George's theory of the NSC advisor as managerial custodian provides a good starting point (although it is one that the argument of the book shall move beyond a bit) in fleshing out the role of the honest broker. According to George, six tasks are required of the managerial custodian:

1. Balancing actor resources within the policy-making system
2. Strengthening weaker advocates
3. Bringing in new advisers to argue for unpopular options
4. Setting up new channels of information so that the president and other advisers are not dependent upon a single channel
5. Arranging for independent evaluation of decisional premises and options, when necessary
6. Monitoring the workings of the policy-making process to identify possibly dangerous malfunctions and instituting appropriate corrective action[4]

Although George places the managerial custodian role within a larger theory of effective structure and organization ("multiple advocacy"), the role is interesting in its own right and some parts of it may be applicable in a wider array of organizational and decision-making settings. Perhaps more significant is George's argument that it can contribute to—but not necessarily guarantee—effective presidential decision making.[5] Early empirical confirmation of the benefits of the broker role was also established by Roger Porter in his extensive examination of the Economic Policy Board during the Ford administration.[6]

The broker role has also become a common self-definition (or part thereof) of many who have occupied the position of national security advisor, as well as a point of reference for journalistic observers and political pundits. For example, the introduction to the oral history project of the Brookings Institution and the Center for International and Security Studies on the role of the NSC advisor (which included a roundtable and interviews with nine former national security advisors) observes that: "Since the Kennedy administration, the assistant to the president for national security affairs (a.k.a. 'the national security adviser') has played two roles: manager ('honest broker') of the day-to-day policy process and substantive policy adviser." The introduction goes on to note that "Presidents clearly want both, but the roles are in tension. . . . Some national security advisers have balanced these roles adroitly. Others have not, generating discord within the president's senior advisory team."[7]

As a part of political vocabulary and practice, moreover, the honest broker role has been applied to other White House positions, most notably that of the chief of staff. At the time his appointment as chief of staff was announced during the 1988 transition to office of George H. W. Bush, for example, John Sununu saw as one of his responsibilities "to be an honest broker and present the views on the various sides of the issue."[8] Once in office, however, Sununu quickly acquired the reputation of a policy advocate and a heavy-handed operative with a tough, even intimidating style.[9] In selecting a chief of staff during his 2000 transition, George W. Bush (perhaps based on his father's eventual experience with Sununu) also had the broker role in mind. According to Clay Johnson, the executive director of the transition:

> [Bush] did not want someone to be chief of staff who was over-territorial, or was a control freak, or felt like they had to control the content or the recommendations that flowed to the president. He wanted somebody who was more a facilitator, an orchestrator, and a tie breaker; as they say an honest broker. . . . The president's knowledge about the way he likes to work led him to choose Andy Card.[10]

Particular definitions and usages of the role vary. Even a terminological difference exists: sometimes it is referred to as "neutral broker," other times as "honest broker." At a very bare minimum, the brokerage role might encompass the narrow notion of a policy administrator of the sort that the NSC executive secretary played during the latter years of the Truman administration before the position of NSC advisor was created under Eisenhower.[11] The national security advisor as administrator, according to Cecil Crabb and Kevin Mulcahy, "has a low level of responsibility with regard to both implementation and policy making," and duties are restricted to "briefing the president on the international situation, representing departmental proposals and viewpoints, scheduling matters for presidential decisions, and monitoring NSC directives."[12] Neutrality rather than policy advocacy is stressed, but brokerage is also fairly limited: representing and monitoring.

In other usages, the role is more robustly defined, and, in fact, depending upon how those definitions are fleshed out, there appear to be some differences in the meaning of the terms "neutral broker" and "honest broker." The NSC advisors in the Eisenhower administration, for example, were more attentive to the quality, character, and components of the decision process and, especially, its deliberative forums than were their Truman counterparts. At the same time, they did not serve as policy advocates in their own right, or very rarely did.[13] Policy neutrality, but with a more enhanced emphasis on and actions directed toward ensuring the quality and coherence of the decision *process* was the order of the day. Arguably, George's managerial custodian represents an even more robust definition of this process-directed and quality-attentive definition of the role. In Roger Porter's view,

> The honest broker [Porter's term for the custodial role] and his staff are not intermediaries between departmental advocates and the president, like a centralized management staff, but they do more than simply insure due process. They promote a genuine competition of ideas, identifying viewpoints not adequately represented or that require qualification, determining when the process is not producing a sufficiently broad range of options, and augmenting the resources of one side or the other so that a balanced presentation results. In short, they insure due process and quality control.[14]

Beginning in the 1960s, and basically continuing to the present, policy advocacy on the part of the NSC advisor began to come to the fore, reaching its apogee under Henry Kissinger during the Nixon presidency.[15] For NSC advisors during this period, varying degrees of policy advice were tendered—ranging from outright advocacy as a member of the president's inner circle (and even beyond) to more private, one-on-one counsel. But many NSC advisors both recognized and struggled with the need to have the views of others fairly presented. Here the sense of brokerage, coupled as it was with some measure of policy advocacy on the NSC advisor's part, has been more about making sure all relevant views were fairly represented; that is, *honest* rather than *neutral* brokerage.

There can be significant variation, however, in how that notion of honest broker is more concretely defined. According to Colin Powell, who served as NSC advisor under President Reagan, members of the cabinet often represent the views of their respective institutional bureaucracies, and these views often differ. As a result, a principal role of the NSC advisor is "to *get it all out*—all the agendas, all the facts, all the opinions, all of the gray and white and black areas written down."[16] For Samuel Berger, President Bill Clinton's NSC advisor during his second term, the role has dual meaning: "One is honest broker in terms of conveying the opinions of your colleagues to the president. And the other is honest broker between your colleagues."[17]

For Anthony Lake, President Clinton's NSC advisor during his first term, being an honest broker is to avoid "surprises" and to "drive the process." Lake recognized that modern NSC advisors often present their own policy views, "but you also have to make sure that the others know what the views are so there are no surprises." At the same time, in Lake's view, the NSC advisor must be concerned that the national security system is serving the president's decision-making needs: "you have to drive the process, and you have to understand that only the NSC can do that." [18] Issues are more crosscutting than they were in the 1950s and "practically every issue now has an economic, military, political, diplomatic dimension, [making] it hard for any cabinet officer to have the absolute lead on that issue. . . . So it has to be coordinated and it has to be led from the White House."[19]

Yet as Brent Scowcroft—who served two stints on the job during the Ford and George H. W. Bush presidencies—points out, brokerage remains central, if not foundational to being an effective NSC advisor even as the needs for coordination and advocacy by the NSC advisor have increased:

> If you are not an honest broker the system doesn't work well. The first thing you have to do is to establish in the minds of all of the members of the NSC that their views will be presented honestly and straightforwardly to the president. . . . Once they are comfortable with that, they certainly expect that you will present your own views but that you will do it in a way that doesn't disadvantage theirs.[20]

Even Henry Kissinger would later become persuaded of the merits of a broker-like role. In his memoirs, he notes that he became "convinced that a president should use the national security adviser primarily as a senior administrator and coordinator to make certain that each significant point of view is heard."[21]

II. Why the Honest Broker Role Matters

Why this attention to the *honest broker* role of the NSC advisor? Should the particular way the job is defined not simply be a matter of presidential preference, that is a conception of the job that centers around what serves the *president's* advising needs, cognitive processes, and decision-making predilections? Or, perhaps the role of NSC advisor should be grounded in the particular strengths and contributions of the *person* who occupies the job? These are not unimportant concerns, and we shall return to them again. But concern for the role, with an emphasis on honest brokerage, is consequential for two reasons: evidence suggesting its positive contribution to presidential decision making and evidence indicating how that decision making might suffer in its absence. Although there has not been extensive analysis of the role per se, there have been several case studies indicating the positive value of its presence and the costs of its absence.

George himself is instructive on this matter, if a bit briefly. George notes how the managerial custodian role contributed to the positive quality of presidential decision making: Eisenhower's 1954 decision not to intervene in Indochina, and Lyndon Johnson's 1964 decision not to proceed with a multilateral force for NATO.[22]

George's limited findings, however, have been substantiated by more extensive case analysis. As Fred I. Greenstein and Richard Immerman observe, during the Eisenhower years, "The assistant for national security affairs played an active, but largely procedural part in the deliberations [at full NSC meetings]. He kept the debate on track, directed the council's attention to disagreements and ambiguities, and watched for signs of policy slippage."[23]

In her analysis of Eisenhower's national security policy making, Meena Bose found evidence of the presence of multiple advocacy and an NSC advisor acting as a managerial custodian, central parts of George's later theory of effective decision making. She also presents a convincing case of their absence during the Kennedy years.[24] Similar findings occur in Porter's analysis of the Ford administration's Economic Policy Board (EPB). According to Porter, "Multiple advocacy characterized the Economic Policy Board's structure and operation. . . . Those who viewed it most closely, including several with governmental experience spanning a number of administrations, considered the EPB highly successful, particularly compared with similar groups in the past." Porter, moreover, is quite explicit in his discussion of the place of the honest broker role in the operations of the Ford EPB.[25] Further evidence: although directed at the chiefs of staff who defined their roles as administrators/brokers rather than policy advocates, David Cohen notes the positive contribution of effective brokerage, "A chief who fails as an administrator fails not only the president but the institution as a whole. If a [chief of staff] is not a capable administrator, the administration will likely make avoidable mistakes."[26]

Comparative analysis of Eisenhower's decision not to intervene in Indochina in 1954 and Johnson's decision to significantly escalate the number of U.S. forces in South Vietnam over the summer of 1965 especially indicates the positive value of the broker role and the costs that accrue in its absence. While not the only factor that had bearing on Eisenhower's decision making, the role of NSC special assistant Robert Cutler was consequential and in a positive direction in 1954.[27] As Greenstein and I note in *How Presidents*

Test Reality, "Cutler was acting (in Alexander George's usage) as a custodian manager in the Eisenhower institutional presidency. His role was not that of a policy advocate . . ."[28] By contrast, in 1965 and absent an effective broker, "The Johnson advisory system played into the conflict-avoiding, difference-splitting political style that had become ingrained in Johnson during his career on Capitol Hill."[29]

Other analyses of presidential decision making also are indicative of the value of the process-directed and quality-attentive character of the broker role. Its components seem closely related, for example, to redressing factors in Irving Janis's analysis of ineffective decision making in small groups:

1. Incomplete survey of policy alternatives
2. Incomplete survey of policy objectives
3. Failure to examine major costs and risks of the preferred choice
4. Poor information search
5. Selective bias in processing information
6. Failure to reconsider originally rejected alternatives
7. Failure to work out detailed information, monitoring, and contingency plans[30]

Janis's criteria, moreover, have been applied empirically to nineteen national security decisions from the Truman through the Nixon presidencies. Each of these decisions was examined to determine the presence of the seven criteria, as well as an independent rating of the favorability or unfavorability of the decision outcome. What is striking in the findings is that the authors find correlations between quality of the decision process and outcomes that "were sizable and in the hypothesized direction."[31] Moreover, of the four Eisenhower-era decisions in the study, two showed no symptoms of defective decision making (Indochina 1954, Taiwan Straits 1958), one showed one symptom (Taiwan Straits 1954–1955), and one showed two (Suez 1956). Overall, the Eisenhower-era decisions had the fewest symptoms of any of the administrations in the study.[32] These findings are also confirmed in a similar study of the relationship between ten decision-making processes and policy outcomes, from the Truman through the George H. W. Bush presidencies, undertaken by Patrick J. Haney and using criteria similar to those proposed by Janis.[33] While these case studies do not resolve the causal issue of whether it was effective brokerage, organizational structure, the president's personal strengths and abilities (or, conversely, weaknesses), or some other set of factors that mattered most, they do suggest success where brokerage was present.

Conversely, a more robustly defined role for the NSC advisor—especially in the area of policy advocacy—portends difficulty. According to Destler, "it changes the staff from *mediating* between the president and senior officialdom to that of *substituting* for officialdom, reducing the president's perceived need to work with and through established channels."[34]

The Tower Commission's analysis of the decision failure of the Reagan NSC process in the Iran-Contra scandal is especially revealing when such substitution occurs. In the view of the Tower Commission's principals—Sen. John Tower (R-TX), former senator, and Carter-era secretary of state, Edmund Muskie, and former NSC Advisor Brent Scowcroft—the absence of honest brokerage was notable. Decision failures can clearly be traced to the machinations of an NSC staff and of NSC advisors out of control. As the *Tower Commission Report* on the scandal concludes,

> The Iran initiative ran directly counter to the Administration's own policies on terrorism, the Iran/Iraq war, and military support to Iran. . . . Established procedures for making national security decisions were ignored. Reviews of the initiative by all the NSC principals were too infrequent. The initiatives were not adequately vetted below the cabinet level. Intelligence resources were underutilized. Applicable legal constraints were not adequately addressed. . . . This pattern persisted in the implementation of the Iran initiative. The NSC staff assumed direct operational control. . . . How the initiative was to be carried out never received adequate attention from the NSC principals or a tough working-level review. No periodic evaluation of the progress of the initiative was ever conducted. The result was an unprofessional and, in substantial part, unsatisfactory operation.[35]

The Tower Commission's recommendations for reform are also notable in the way they echo many of the components of the broker role. "It is the National Security Adviser who is primarily responsible for managing this process on a daily basis. . . . It is his responsibility to ensure"

- that matters submitted for consideration by the Council cover the full range of issues on which review is required
- that those issues are fully analyzed
- that a full range of options is considered
- that the prospects and risks of each are examined
- that all relevant intelligence and other information is available to the principals

- that legal considerations are addressed
- that difficulties in implementation are confronted (90)

The national security advisor, moreover, has these responsibilities "not only with respect to the president but with respect to all the NSC principals." They should be "informed of the president's thinking and decisions." They should have "adequate notice and an agenda for all meetings." Decision papers should be "provided in advance." Adequate records should be kept of "NSC consultations and presidential decisions." Finally, it is the responsibility of the NSC advisor "to monitor policy implementation and to ensure that policies are executed in conformity with the intent of the president's decisions."[36]

The Tower Commission's analysis is not only relevant to Iran-Contra, but it offers a cautionary tale for other NSC advisors in other administrations. As we shall see, its analysis is also applicable—albeit in limited and varying degree—to the travails that McGeorge Bundy faced under Kennedy, Henry Kissinger under Richard Nixon, and Condoleezza Rice under George W. Bush.

III. Expanding the Broker Role?

The Tower Commission's findings and recommendations offer powerful warnings about NSC advisors who abandon brokerage and become too deeply enmeshed in policy formulation and implementation. Yet, more recent NSC advisors may have had legitimate reasons for expanding their responsibilities beyond those of their Eisenhower-era forebears. Policy advocacy, political involvement, and diplomatic and other implementation efforts have become attached to the duties of some—perhaps if not all—recent NSC advisors. These additional responsibilities signal the presence of powerful forces at work that need to be understood in making a realistic assessment of the role of the NSC advisor in the contemporary era. For our purposes, these differing conceptions of the NSC advisor role not only indicate the presence of significant malleability in how the job has been defined, but they also prompt the question whether the broker role might be complemented by these other tasks and responsibilities, without significant compromise to the broker role. George, it should be noted, is not optimistic or supportive on this score: the managerial custodian "should not be combined with becoming (1) a policy adviser-advocate; (2) a public spokesman . . . ; (3) a watchdog of the president's personal power stakes in policy issues; or (4) an implementer of decisions already taken."[37] "Role conflict" and "role overload" will likely compromise effectiveness if any or all of these duties are added.[38]

Possibly. But given the significant addition of some of these four tasks (and perhaps others as well) in practice and maybe for good reason, is it not time to again consider whether some admixture might work? Indeed, on the larger question of multiple advocacy, George is more flexible: "In stating the case for multiple advocacy, I do not mean to imply that it can or should be rigidly applied in all circumstances."[39] And, "Multiple advocacy need not work perfectly in order to be valuable. In some cases even a modest amount of multiple advocacy may suffice to highlight considerations that would otherwise be neglected or improperly appraised."[40] Let us move down this latter path in considering the honest broker role.

IV. Plan of the Book

The book will examine the roles of all of the NSC advisors from the Eisenhower years (including a brief analysis of their Truman precursors) through the George W. Bush administrations. The six sets of NSC advisors I have selected for more in-depth treatment represent important junctures in the development of the position, raise important issues concerning the broker role, and explore the impact of deviations from it. In chapter 1, the initial development of the role of the NSC advisor as well as the organization of the National Security Council and its staff during the Truman and Eisenhower presidencies is considered. The Eisenhower-era NSC advisors are an especially important area of attention in light of the explicit emphasis given to an NSC advisor who would be attentive to the fair representation of views and the organization and quality of the decision-making process. Robert Cutler's tenure in the position is of special interest, given that he served two separate stints as NSC advisor, as well as having been the chief organizer of the structure of the Eisenhower decision process. Yet his service under a president and secretary of state who were deeply informed on policy matters also bears implications concerning an NSC advisor who was deliberately restricted in his role as a policy advocate in his own right.

In chapter 2, McGeorge Bundy's role is the focus of analysis. His tenure as NSC advisor saw an important expansion in the role as a personal counselor to the president as well as the dismantling of most of the organizational structures developed under the previous administration. In many respects his tenure marks the beginning of the contemporary job of NSC advisor.

Yet Bundy's struggles with the disorganized and fragmented nature of the Kennedy decision process are instructive. As well, Bundy is one of two NSC advisors to serve under two presidents, which is interesting for purposes of comparison and also important in understanding the impact of the individual president, and a president's decision-making needs, on the NSC advisor's role.

Chapter 3 is devoted to Henry Kissinger—by far the most prominent NSC advisor and one with a highly determinative impact on the foreign and national security policies of the Nixon presidency. As we shall see, Kissinger represents a hard case for the argument in favor of the broker role: his successes are often touted. But, as I will argue, underlying them was a policy process fraught with problems, and further inspection will reveal outcomes that sometimes were less than optimal.

Chapter 4 analyzes Brent Scowcroft's role in the position. Scowcroft deserves special attention for three reasons. First, he too served under two presidents, Gerald Ford and George H. W. Bush, which like Bundy's tenure is important for comparative purposes. Second, he was one of the three principal members of the Tower Commission's report on Iran-Contra, which, as noted above, is significant for its emphasis on the importance of honest brokerage. Third, and perhaps most important, he comes closest to embracing the precepts of honest brokerage but in a context within which a contemporary NSC advisor takes on additional responsibilities, particularly private counsel to the president. How he balanced those demands is of particular interest.

In chapter 5, the six NSC advisors under Ronald Reagan are analyzed. This chapter is important, first, given the number of individuals who occupied the role—and how differently they defined their job. Second, Reagan was a president strong on policy vision but sometimes short on policy detail. Most important, of all the post–World War II presidencies, it is one where the activities of the NSC advisor almost brought this presidency down. How it recovered is especially instructive. Revitalization of the honest broker role was central to that recovery.

In chapter 6, Condoleezza Rice's tenure as NSC advisor is considered. Her role in the job is notable given the seeming strength of the George W. Bush foreign policy team but with a president with limited foreign policy exposure. At the same time, she served as a trusted personal counselor to the president and was a highly visible public figure, rivaling Kissinger in media attention. This administration also faced the most significant national security challenges since the Truman years: the response to the attacks of September 11, 2001, war against the Taliban in Afghanistan, the successful achievement of bringing down Saddam Hussein's regime in Iraq, but the continuing effort to create a democratic government in that unfortunately sectarian-divided and strife-torn nation. As we shall see, despite initial good efforts, honest brokerage declined over time, with significant effect on policy.

The NSC advisors I treat briefly in the appendix are also instructive. Walt Rostow succeeded Bundy in 1966 but was more clearly a more vigorous policy advocate with detriment to Lyndon Johnson's decision making. Zbigniew Brzezinski, to some extent like Rice, took office pledged to brokerage, but he eventually found himself forced into an adversarial and advocacy role during the Carter presidency. The two Clinton administration NSC advisors, Anthony Lake and Sandy Berger, differed a bit in their roles but struggled with a policy process that was often highly informal: effects on policy varied in their positive or negative outcome. Stephen Hadley's tenure in George W. Bush's second term offers some interesting contrasts and comparisons with his earlier role as Rice's deputy NSC advisor as well with Rice's own tenure in the post during the first term.

Within each chapter, I have attempted to follow a similar framework of analysis. First, the general contours of the decision-making process, its organization and workings are described. Second, the role of the particular NSC advisor is examined. Third, the relation of the NSC advisor's role to the decision process and its policy outcomes are explored. Analysis here will focus on key and illustrative cases of policy decision making. I do not offer a comprehensive assessment of all policy initiatives or a history of U.S. foreign policy since 1947. Instead, I will examine key cases that explore the methods and important moments of national security coordination and advising. Finally, the implications to be drawn from the experience of each NSC advisor about the contemporary applicability of the honest broker role are discussed in the concluding chapter. Analysis is offered concerning how a "broker plus" role might incorporate both honest brokerage and some of the other duties of the NSC advisor.

CHAPTER 1

THE FOUNDATION
OF HONEST BROKERAGE

Truman's Executive Secretaries, Eisenhower's Special Assistants

Thoroughhe workings of the national security policy process during the Truman and Eisenhower administrations provide important insight into the origins and early operations of the National Security Council (NSC), the broader process of policy making, and the development of the NSC advisor's role as an honest broker. The experience of the Eisenhower administration suggests that honest brokerage is practicable and can be a contributor to effective presidential decision making. At the same time, it poses challenges to the present applicability of the broker role to contemporary presidencies: it operated in a national security context now five decades past, one with different policy challenges, different political pressures, and with principals who understood—most notably President Eisenhower himself—the organizational requisites of effective decision making and came to the task substantively well-prepared to make sound policy choices.

I. The Truman National Security Process

The initial structure of the broader national security system, however, originated in the Truman administration. The lack of an institutionalized body during World War II and its immediate aftermath to routinely coordinate and integrate the policy planning and subsequent work of the military service branches, the State Department, the White House and other agencies and departments provided an important impetus. Prior to Public Law 80–253—the "National Security Act of 1947" signed on July 26—interagency interaction had been jerry-rigged and informal. Historically, periodic foreign policy crises had been managed by the president and State Department or, in the case of war, by ad hoc arrangements between the White House and the relevant cabinet-level departments of State, War, and Navy.[1]

Even during World War II, as the foreign policy responsibilities of the United States changed markedly, President Franklin D. Roosevelt, as per custom, relied on the informal coordinating efforts of Admiral William Leahy and White House aide Harry Hopkins. More formal procedures emerged late. A State Department-War Department-Navy Department Coordinating Committee (SWNCC)—operating at the assistant secretary level—was established in 1944, and the secretaries of each of the three departments held weekly meetings starting in 1945. A precursor to what would emerge as the Joint Chiefs of Staff was also established. All of this was a start, but it was in marked contrast to the more organized efforts of their British counterparts—the Combined Chiefs of Staff and the Committee of Imperial Defence—that U.S. officials had become acquainted with during the war years.[2]

Nor did the U.S. variant, developed late, work very effectively. James S. Lay Jr., who became executive secretary of the NSC under both Truman and Eisenhower, noted in a January 1953 report on the history of the NSC that the SWNCC was "overburdened" and forced to rely on an "elaborate organization of sub-committees . . . which delayed at lower levels rather than speeded up the resolution of major policy issues." Meetings of the three departmental principals—the next stage up—"had no fixed agenda and no integrated staff. The result consisted of either general discussions or ad hoc decisions." As for serving the president's needs, none of the ad hoc arrangements "recognized or assisted the role of the president as the leader and policy-maker. As a result, policies were either developed without his knowledge or consent, or he was informed after the die was cast and his principal cabinet members presented him with a single recommendation and no alternatives or background analysis."[3]

THE CREATION OF THE NATIONAL SECURITY COUNCIL

Both during and after the war, the need for more organized policy making and better coordination came to be recognized, although solutions varied considerably. The drive for change was also bolstered by the greater responsibilities of the United States in the postwar period and the looming cold war. Periodic crises and sporadic involvement—where ad hoc arrangements would suffice—were now things of the past: the United States was the leading Western power, facing continuous national security challenges. The crosscutting, interdepartmental complexity of policy issues also called for change.

As Dillon Anderson, one of Eisenhower's NSC advisors, later noted, after World War II, "decisions affecting related activities of several responsible departments could no longer be made safely on the ex parte presentation to the president by a single department head."[4] The 1947 act, after much debate and compromise, provided the beginnings of an answer with the creation of the National Security Council, a statutorily defined deliberative body to advise the president.[5]

The NSC, especially the composition of the council's membership, was also affected by the contemporaneous debate over the unification of the armed forces (which Truman favored) and the subissue of what to do organizationally about the emerging significance of air power (creation of a separate air force versus continuation of air power units within the army and the navy and no unique air force mission). While full service-branch unification did not take place—largely due to the skillful machinations of then Navy Secretary James Forrestal and his allies in Congress—an initially weak Department of Defense was created as part of the 1947 act, replacing War and Navy at the cabinet table and with the separate secretaries of army, navy, and (now) air force reporting to the secretary of defense. But, as Anna Kasten Nelson notes, to gain Forrestal's support and Senate approval for a new department of defense, Truman was forced to include the secretaries of the three service branches as statutory members of the NSC along with the secretary of defense: "The council would allow the service secretaries personally to present their points of view to the president without their inclusion in the cabinet. The council was a small price to pay for Forrestal's support of a single head for the armed services." Had Truman's initial proposal for full unification taken place, the need for the NSC would have been "obviated," there would have been a "single department with a single chief of staff" making "coordinating mechanisms" unnecessary.[6] According to White House aide George Elsey, who participated in the negotiations over the act, the compromise was necessary "to keep the Navy in the person of Forrestal from kicking over the traces."[7] (A 1949 revision of the act would eventually remove the three service secretaries from the council, leaving only the secretary of defense; the vice president was also added as a statutory member, and the Chairman of the Joint Chiefs of Staff was designated as the Council's chief military adviser, permitting him more freedom to disagree with the secretary of defense.)[8]

Another dynamic at work in the creation of the NSC was an attempt to hem in Truman's decision making, an effort undertaken both by opponents of unification and his foreign policy within the Republican-controlled

80th Congress. According to James Lay, Forrestal envisioned the NSC as a "policy forming" and not just an advisory body.[9] Initial drafts of the act alarmed analysts in the White House's Bureau of the Budget (BOB), as well as Secretary of State George Marshall: they were concerned that the proposed NSC might possess statutory power limiting the president's options and other decision-making prerogatives. According to Nelson, "rewriting a phrase here and eliminating another there, they fashioned the [then] rather precisely defined council, with statutory direction and an executive director confirmed by the Senate, into the present NSC: a group purely advisory in nature, with no authoritative functions in statute and with a staff appointed at the sole discretion of the president."[10]

Even then, a battle raged on how the council would operate and under whose direction. Newly appointed Defense Secretary Forrestal worked mightily, once the 1947 act had passed and the new council was up and running, to bring it under the control of the Pentagon. Again the Bureau of the Budget—as well as trusted Truman aide Clark Clifford—came to Truman's defense and made sure that the council was a direct presidential instrument and, especially, that its executive secretary and staff were considered part of the Executive Office of the President (Forrestal worked hard but unsuccessfully to have the NSC staff lodged within Defense). The BOB also successfully urged Truman to make the secretary of state rather than the secretary of defense the presiding officer of the NSC in the president's absence.[11]

Truman also did his part to bring the NSC under presidential control and thwart Forrestal's ambitions. At the first full meeting of the NSC on September 26, 1947, Truman told the group that they were "*his* council and that he expected everyone to work harmoniously without any manifestations of prima donna qualities."[12] Following further advice from the BOB, Truman subsequently signaled that the NSC would only be one of a number of avenues of policy advice by meeting with it infrequently. As NSC Executive Secretary Sidney Souers noted in 1949, "Both the cabinet and the Council are parts of the president's immediate official family. As such their use and operation in any particular instance are subject to the president's personal discretion and judgment. . . . The council's activities therefore are a supplement to, rather than a substitute for, the functions of the cabinet."[13]

Presidential absence from some NSC meetings also prevented the possibility—perhaps the probability—of Truman being forced to make on the spot decisions at NSC meetings or otherwise being bound by its recommendations.[14] According to the NSC's history on the White House Web site, "by not attending most NSC meetings, Truman ensured that Council members would seek him out to press their own points of view privately."[15] In fact, it would be another ten months before Truman would attend another NSC meeting, and from September 1947 until the outbreak of the Korean War in June 1950, Truman attended only twelve of the NSC's fifty-seven meetings.[16] After the Korean War broke out, the NSC met every Thursday, and Truman attended sixty-four of its remaining seventy-one meetings.[17]

Not only did Truman thwart any efforts to constrain his decision making, but, as I. M. Destler has noted, he began the process whereby the initial intention of the 1947 act "was turned on its head. The National Security Council became in practice not the powerful senior advisory forum that was envisioned, but the staff instituted under the council's name. Presidents employed this staff, not just as a link to the permanent government but also as an alternative to it."[18]

II. The Truman NSC Executive Secretaries

Truman's choice to head the NSC staff as its first "executive secretary"— Rear Adm. Sidney Souers—would be but a pale imitation, if that, of even the weaker NSC advisors in subsequent administrations. Most accounts of the history of the NSC and its staff mention Souers and his successor under Truman, James S. Lay Jr., but they are rarely included in lists of "NSC advisors," a role that begins in the Eisenhower presidency. At most they served as somewhat weak policy coordinators and staff facilitators, not sources of substantive policy advice much less embodying other aspects of the modern NSC advisor's role. Yet they were steadfast in maintaining the NSC and its staff as a presidential instrument and one that would serve at most in an advisory but not constraining capacity.[19]

In Souers's view, the executive secretary served as "an anonymous servant." He acted as "only a broker of ideas in criss-crossing proposals among a team of responsible officials." But he was not an advocate of policy in his own right: "His proper functions demand that he be a non-political confidant of the president, and willing to subordinate his personal views on policy to his task of coordinating the views of responsible officials."[20]

But even given this restricted view of their role, Souers and Lay began to assemble at least part of the foundation for what would develop later. Before the war, Souers had been a St. Louis business executive (no small geographic association in the Truman presidency) and had served in the naval reserve. Called to active duty, he served as an intelligence officer, rising to deputy chief of naval intelligence. A close friend of Truman adviser Clark Clifford (also from St. Louis), Souers was tapped after the war to serve as the first director of the Central Intelligence Group—the successor to the wartime OSS and the immediate precursor of the Central Intelligence Agency, also established in the 1947 legislation.[21] Beyond his own experience and expertise, Souers brought to the job keen bureaucratic instincts. He knew all of the major players and was trusted even by Forrestal. All the while, as Nelson notes, "he set about implementing a White House-centered NSC. . . . The implementation of the NSC process that finally took hold . . . was clearly aided by Souers's understanding of and sensitivity to the bureaucratic realities and personalities within the Truman administration."[22]

While the first NSC working paper would be delivered directly by the State Department to Truman, and only after Truman's approval was it reported to Souers, it was to be the last to take that route. Working with Clifford, Souers arranged that any NSC material would be routed through *him* first and then on to the president. Souers also developed the practice that *he* would inform NSC members of any subsequent presidential action or decision. Souers, moreover, quite shrewdly controlled the NSC's agenda. Members of the council might propose issues for discussion, but Souers personally would take the matter up with Truman for final disposition.[23]

There were weaknesses. Souers's own NSC staff was small and largely drawn from departmental detailees.[24] Initial position papers for NSC discussion were prepared either by the Defense Department or, on most occasions, by the State Department's policy planning staff (headed for a time by none other than George Kennan), rather than by NSC staff. As well, the working groups established to consider these papers—before they rose to the full Council—were drawn from the affected departments.[25]

In the view of James Lay, the significant number of staff members detailed from departments "tended to become or be looked upon as foreigners to their respective departments." But at the same time, the "consultants" from the departments who directly vetted policy papers with the NSC's executive secretary "looked upon their passive role as secondary to their heavy departmental responsibilities, [and] gave less and less attention to NSC affairs." The final product—staff reports to the NSC—"were too frequently unacceptable when they reached the Council table. It was difficult for the staff to exercise initiative in developing forward-looking policies." As a result, "more and more, individual departments preferred to send their draft recommendations directly to the Council without any staff coordination, with inevitable clashes and delays at the Council table."[26] According to the history of the NSC on the White House Web site, the planning process prior to NSC meetings "suffered from haphazard staffing and irregular meetings and was sometimes bypassed entirely. The executive secretaries of the Council had no real authority or influence beyond managing the process."[27]

Difficulties extended to the deliberations of the full Council. In the view of Walter Millis, "The effect of the NSC is not prominent; NSC no doubt considered the staff papers, debated policy and arrived at recommendations, but . . . Defense, State, the Budget Bureau, the White House, [made] independent determinations—usually on a hasty if not extemporaneous basis."[28] According to Anna Kasten Nelson, "throughout the Truman Administration the State Department refused to recognize the NSC as an important policymaking group." Secretary of State Marshall generally sent his undersecretary of state to meetings, while his successor, Dean Acheson, did not attend until Truman began regularly to do so once the Korean War began. Acheson also made sure that key committees were chaired by representatives from State.[29]

Souers's role was quite limited, especially in Truman's own mind. According to Elmer Staats, the job of executive secretary "meant whatever the President wanted it to mean . . . In practice, President Truman used Admiral Souers primarily as his liaison with the intelligence community. He used to refer to him as his . . . 'cloak-and-dagger' man."[30]

According to Lay, who detailed the problems in the Truman NSC in a January 1953 transition report, "bi-weekly meetings of the Council were not proving effective in meeting ever more difficult problems." Truman's absence now had a downside: NSC members "were expressing their views to each other rather than to their superior who was to make the final decision." Differences were "deferred or glossed over," council members were unprepared for discussion and tended to rely on staff, and "these shortcomings . . . tended to encourage individual members to take their case directly to the president, who was thus put under pressure to make decisions without full knowledge of the views of other interested departments or agencies."[31]

Another problem was the expanding number of those who attended the Council's meetings. According to Lay, "the large attendance discouraged free and full discussion by the principals."[32] Truman shared this view, and Lay included a memo from the president to him in his transition report that emphasized this point. According to a later study by Stanley L. Falk, the increasing number of persons at NSC meetings "not only made for too large a group for free discussion, but also encouraged NSC members to look to their departmental advisers and to present their departmental rather than individual views of problems."[33] Nor was there any mechanism for coordination or oversight of policy implementation. As Souers noted in 1949, "operating responsibility" was carried out as it had been "traditionally": by the departments themselves.[34] The latter problem would not be solved during Truman's presidency.

While Souers was at best a weak coordinator, he played an important role in the development of the NSC staff as a presidentially directed and institutionally loyal resource. At the same time, the fragile nature of the NSC staff and its executive secretary remained a problem. Souers's replacement in January 1950 was James Lay, Souers's deputy and a career civil servant who had served as executive secretary of the National Intelligence Authority. Lay was a competent bureaucrat but, unlike Souers according to Nelson, he "regarded himself as a servant of the NSC rather than as a staff assistant to the president. He was either unwilling or unable to assume the tasks of coordinating information and smoothing relationships that were performed by Souers."[35] But Lay's talents as an administrator were apparently valued enough that he was retained as executive secretary throughout the eight years of the Eisenhower presidency; whatever he may have lacked as an interdepartmental coordinator was complemented by the new NSC special assistant role put in place in 1953 by Robert Cutler and carried out by Cutler's successors.[36]

Yet even under Lay, the NSC was strengthened. In June 1950, Truman notified Lay that he was "cracking down" on the disorder. Attendance at meetings was now restricted—the statutory members plus the designated advisers: "No one else could be present without Truman's specific approval."[37] A new "senior staff" group, drawn from relevant departments and agencies, but under Lay's leadership as executive secretary (rather than someone from State or Defense), would also now serve as the channel for pre-NSC meeting planning.[38] As Nelson notes, "the net effect of this reorganization was to strengthen the hand of the White House at the expense of the departments."[39]

Lay's tenure set the stage for needed changes by Truman's successor. It was also an early powerful lesson that despite the constancy of one president and his needs as a decision maker, the roles—and impact—of those who might advise him can matter enormously. At the same time, it established the vital need for a presidentially controlled and orchestrated national security advising process. "There is now a place for coordinated consideration of our security problems," Souers noted in 1949, but "much remains to be done."[40]

III. The Eisenhower National Security Process

Needed organizational change came quickly. By the end of March 1953, a significantly altered national security system was in place, one which would prove to be a more orderly, highly organized, and regularly used process. It especially squared with Eisenhower's long interest in and knowledge of the organizational requisites of policy formulation and implementation and other factors bearing on the effectiveness of decision making. Concerns about the national security process and a need for reforms had also been raised by Eisenhower in the 1952 campaign.

The system was devised by Robert Cutler during the 1952 transition and the early months of the new administration. Cutler, the president of Boston's Old Colony Trust Company, was a reserve brigadier general who had served on Secretary of War Henry Stimson's staff and had briefly been on the Truman NSC Psychological Strategy Board (PSB).[41] Cutler met Eisenhower in 1948 when Secretary of Defense Forrestal asked him to assist then Army Chief of Staff Eisenhower in presenting the defense appropriation bill to Congress. In 1952, he was an early Eisenhower supporter and accompanied him on the campaign trail during the general election as a speech writer and personal assistant. Shortly before Christmas 1952, Gov. Sherman Adams—Eisenhower's designate as chief of staff and acting under his instructions—approached Cutler about heading the NSC staff and reorganizing its operations. Although Cutler was reticent about returning to Washington, he was eager to join the new administration in that capacity. Cutler met with Eisenhower at the latter's transition headquarters at the Hotel Commodore in New York City, and the deal was sealed.[42]

At a preinaugural meeting of the cabinet, Eisenhower introduced Cutler and told the group about his new job and mission. Cutler then briefed the members on the history of the NSC and its staff, and he outlined some of its problems and the need for organizational changes. He also spoke about his own conception of his position. He would not be a policy advocate, he told them, but he would be an agent of the president concerned with the quality of the deliberative process and the performance of the NSC and its staff.

By inauguration day, Cutler was fast at work analyzing the NSC operations of the Truman years and drawing up new plans. He consulted widely, including past members of the NSC and its staff, academics, and other governmental officials.[43] In February, he convened two major day-long meetings, during which the participants intensively discussed reform of the NSC system.[44] By the middle of March, Cutler had finished his work, and on

March 22, he notes in his memoirs, he met with Eisenhower to go over his recommendations. For an hour and a half the two reviewed Cutler's report, with the president asking frequent questions. According to Cutler, Eisenhower "offered a half dozen corrections and changes before noting 'D. E.' on the cover." Eisenhower informed Cutler that he had decided on a new title for his position (several had been discussed)—"Special Assistant to the President for National Security Affairs"—and Cutler's first presidential charge was to put the report into action. Cutler was instructed to draft his own appointment letter, the letters appointing members to the new Planning Board, and to prepare a cover letter on the new system that the president would sign, which would then be circulated along with Cutler's report to the other principals.[45]

The changes Cutler made closely track with the deficiencies in the Truman NSC process, especially those laid out in the January 19, 1953, memorandum to Cutler by Executive Secretary James Lay. Similar concerns were raised by Gen. George C. Marshall, who had served both as secretary of state and secretary of defense in the Truman years. A February 19, 1953, NSC document—a record of a Cutler conversation with Marshall—especially notes Marshall's concerns that "there was too much compromise before the papers came to the NSC. The papers failed to state pros and cons. The papers presented a fait accompli to be accepted or rejected or modified a little. The papers never presented alternatives to decide upon. There must be a way to get objections up before the Council if it is really to deliberate."[46] Marshall also stressed the need for active participation by the president in the NSC's deliberations. Truman, according to Marshall, "came in, sat down, went out. He was not a leader, a force at the table to bring out discussion."[47]

The most noticeable feature of the new system was the creation of what came to be dubbed "policy hill." Its organizational topography included a more regular and better organized planning operation before full consideration at NSC meetings—the NSC Planning Board. The Planning Board—the "upside" of policy hill—sought to address some of Marshall's concerns (which also echoed points made by Lay) that policy alternatives be placed before the NSC as well as the need for outlining departmental points of disagreement—so-called "policy splits."

Cutler, however, was no slavish follower of the advice he received, nor were his efforts simply confined to remedying the weaknesses in the Truman system. He rejected a proposal, which Eisenhower had made in a campaign speech in Baltimore on September 26, 1952, that outside consultants be brought in to sit with the NSC (a proposal that Lay had also made in his

January 19, 1953, memo). In a later meeting with Eisenhower, Cutler questioned the wisdom of this suggestion, especially the inclusion of persons holding other public offices, "because of the division of loyalty."[48] Cutler also took issue with General Marshall's view that "no permanent staff of the NSC can possibly take the place of staff representatives of the agencies. These Senior Staff men must be active in their agencies and in the stream of things in order to be useful."[49] In Cutler's view, *both* the departmental representatives associated with the NSC staff should be strengthened and the staff working just for the NSC should be increased (albeit moderately); each group was necessary for its effective operations. However, Cutler rejected the advice of some that an enlarged NSC staff concern itself with policy implementation.[50]

With respect to the NSC staff, Cutler retained Lay as executive secretary and S. Everett Gleason as Lay's deputy. In Cutler's view their institutional memory from the Truman years would be helpful. They are "devoted, capable, and well-informed," he told Eisenhower, "They will provide continuity, effectively operate the staff mechanism, and greatly help in the policy planning."[51]

Creation of the Planning Board, while important, was not the only alteration in process. Effective operations, as much as good organization and structure, were objects of Cutler's scrutiny and remedy. Cutler's recommendations included a strong charge—indeed "an unbreakable engagement" in his words—that NSC principals be briefed by their representatives before Council meetings. Cutler particularly stressed that every Planning Board participant "must express and stand by his honest views; those views, if substantial conflicts cannot be fairly resolved, may never be suppressed or compromised, but should be reported to the Council."[52] Indeed, the report clearly states that each Planning Board member "has the *right* to have included in any report sent up to the Council, in his own words, any disagreement on the part of his department or agency with any part of such report."[53]

Other changes in Cutler's report included better circulation of policy papers before NSC meetings, clear agendas, which would be set by Cutler, and regular briefings of Eisenhower by Cutler of agenda matters on the afternoon before NSC meetings. Cutler also included in his recommendations a clear list of his own duties as NSC advisor. Some reflected elements of brokerage: oversight of the deliberative process and power to remedy any deficiencies. Cutler had "responsibility for the rate of flow of work through the Planning Board, and the manner of presentation and quality of such work." Cutler would preside at Planning Board meetings, but he saw as his special duty— and here we explicitly see direct brokerage—to "lead the discussion in such manner as to bring out the most active participation by all present." More generally, it was Cutler's duty to bring "to the attention of the president with recommendations for appropriate action, lack of progress of an agency in carrying out a particular policy which has been assigned to it."[54]

Still other changes were regular meetings of the NSC (generally weekly, on Thursday mornings—usually two hours in length but sometimes reaching four—with Eisenhower in attendance) and the creation of "records of action" reflecting NSC deliberations and presidential decisions. These were prepared generally by the Friday after the Thursday NSC meeting, or by Monday or Tuesday of the next week at the latest. According to Gordon Gray (Eisenhower's last NSC advisor), they also offered the opportunity for "reclammas,"—dissenting interpretations put forward from time to time by departments objecting to something in the record. Eisenhower usually agreed with Gray's interpretation.[55] More generally, as Robert Bowie and Richard Immerman note, records of actions provided "insurance against an official charged with implementation misinterpreting a decision or directive."[56]

Cutler's recommendations also included Eisenhower's desire that the secretary of the treasury and the director of the Bureau of the Budget be made nonstatutory members of the NSC so that the fiscal and economic impact of national security decisions would be properly factored in. Fiscal concerns also figured in another recommendation adopted: the requirement of financial appendices to Planning Board policy options that were up for discussion by the full NSC.[57] Other ad hoc members of the Council were added as needed, such as the attorney general when matters of constitutional or legal import arose.[58]

What would come to be the "down slope" side of policy hill—the Operations Coordinating Board (OCB)—was not the product of Cutler's direct handiwork, but the result of a special advisory board, the Jackson Committee. Chaired by William H. Jackson—a businessman and former CIA official who also served as acting NSC advisor in the latter months of 1956—its purpose (much like Cutler's) was to examine and improve on the policy mechanisms of the Truman years, in this case the Psychological Strategy Board.[59] Among its more prominent members were Cutler, Gordon Gray, and C. D. Jackson, all of whom had served on the Truman PSB, with the latter two serving as its chairmen. In September 1953, the committee recommended that the PSB be abolished and replaced by the OCB. The OCB would have *as part* of its duties the development of psychological strategy aimed at the cold war propaganda. But it was given a broader mandate: it would monitor and coordinate policy implementation by agencies and departments. The Jackson Committee's recognition of the importance of this part of the policy process, however, was presaged in the advice Cutler received earlier in the year. Lay had noted problems in relying on individual departments to carry out national security policy without further oversight and coordination. General Marshall was especially instructive about later stages of the policy process when he "spoke at length about the need for policy coordination. Policy is 10% planning and 90% carrying into effect. Some one must keep constant watch to see that policies are being carried out (a follow-up)."[60] The new OCB was chaired (until January 1960) by the undersecretary of state (initially Eisenhower's wartime chief of staff, Gen. Walter Bedell Smith) and its members consisted of representatives from other agencies and departments (here much like the Planning Board) as well as Cutler from the NSC.

The formal organization of the Eisenhower NSC process was not without its critics, particularly the Senate subcommittee investigation led by Sen. Henry Jackson (D-WA) toward the close of the administration.[61] Even today, when there is greater appreciation of the inner workings of the Eisenhower presidency and of Eisenhower's leadership style, the debate continues. As Arthur Schlesinger Jr. asked as late as 2000, "Is the layered Eisenhower machinery really 'a precedent for effective national security advising'? On the record, surely not. It is wrong too in theory. Organization charts are less important than people." Moreover, according to Schlesinger, the Eisenhower model "is all the more wrong" with the onset of the digital age: "the vertical arrangements of the past are being replaced by increasingly horizontal arrangements—which is the way that presidents like FDR and JFK operated instinctively."[62] By contrast, in the view of Laurin Henry, the author of an extensive early study of presidential transitions, "The Planning Board, the NSC, and the OCB constituted an architectonic system for policy formulation, decision, and execution of which the administration was extremely proud."[63]

IV. Cutler as NSC Advisor

This debate about the merits of organization and structure is important (although I think Schlesinger is wrong about the effectiveness of the formal national security structure during the Eisenhower years and the continuing relevance of a structured and organized process). But debate about organization misses another side of the decision-making process: the roles of the participants, the "people" that even Schlesinger finds more important than "organizational charts." This aspect of the Eisenhower-era NSC process is also noteworthy and consequential: an internal organizational culture that encouraged free-flowing discussion and sought to make participants advisers to the president in their own right rather than as representatives of their respective agencies or departments. In Cutler's view, the "acid bath" of the Planning Board was especially important in washing out the "dangerous impurities" of "ex parte decisions . . . special pleading, imprecise guidance, and suppression of conflicting views."[64] The same expectations held for members of the NSC. According to Cutler, Eisenhower made clear—in the president's words—that the council was a "corporate body" in its own right, free from other influences. Its members should "seek, with their background and experience, the most statesmanlike answer to the problems of national security, rather than to attempt solutions which represent a mere compromise of agency positions."[65] At the beginning of an October 13, 1953, meeting of the NSC, Eisenhower told the group that "you come to this table as an individual in your own right, not merely to represent a department. Your background helps us all to reach a corporate decision and not merely a compromise of varying departmental positions. What we are seeking is the best solution of our problems by the corporate mind represented here." Eisenhower then went on to make it a general principle of his deliberative processes: "The concept applies also to advisory and supporting bodies such as the NSC Planning Board and the Joint Chiefs of Staff." Eisenhower closed by noting, "I am convinced that a great many meetings in Washington are nothing but meetings designed to achieve acceptable consensus. I don't want that view to prevail here."[66]

CUTLER AND THE PLANNING BOARD: UP POLICY HILL

More important, for our purposes, were expectations for the role of the NSC advisor that were close to those of an honest broker, as set within the context of these organizational arrangements and procedures. The way Cutler's role as NSC advisor was defined had important consequences for how that organizational culture and its institutional components operated to facilitate effective decision making.

Throughout the various stages of the policy process, Cutler's efforts were directed at making sure each operated effectively to enhance presidential decision making.

Cutler chaired the thrice-weekly meetings of the Planning Board, and, as noted, was attentive to the quality, fairness, and openness of its deliberations. Initial drafts of papers were usually assigned by Cutler to the lead department with primary responsibility in that policy area; its representative was encouraged if not expected to call on other departments and agencies in putting together a draft. When completed, the initial draft was circulated to the other representatives on the Planning Board for discussion, critique and alteration. Cutler (and his successors) chaired the meetings, opening them "with his own criticisms and comments based on extensive work by his [NSC] staff," according to Phillip Henderson, and "from all accounts these debates were generally spirited and rigorous." Everett Gleason, Lay's deputy executive secretary under both Truman and Eisenhower, characterized them as "informal and democratic."[67] Often several sessions were required to finalize a document, and alterations would be made throughout the process.

Most importantly, as Cutler stated in a final report to Eisenhower in April 1955, "At the Planning Board, honest effort is made to settle such differences, but never with a view to watering-down a basic split or 'sweeping it under the rug.'" In fact, according Cutler, it was a "recognized function" to "sharpen" differences and "make as precise as possible the expression of this conflict to the end that the Council can make an effective decision between the opposing views."[68] According to Karl G. Harr, a participant in the Planning Board, "You were thrown into, I think, the most realistic hopper of debate and mind-rubbing with people coming from the other national security agencies of government . . . all of these people getting together under the aegis of the Planning Board. It was wonderful."[69]

Following the work of the Planning Board and ten days before an NSC meeting, Cutler circulated an agenda to those who would be in attendance, followed three days later by Planning Board and other documents for each agenda item. This prior effort not only made for an orderly process, but it allowed the Planning Board representatives to brief their departmental principals before an NSC meeting on the topics and issues to be discussed.

Throughout the process, the operative principle was that background papers and policy options would express rather than conceal disagreements and other disputes. As Cutler notes in his memoirs, "Where there existed conflicts of opinion that could not be honestly resolved, the papers coming through the Council to the President for consideration should make clear all sides of the disputed point."[70] It was Cutler's job to make sure that they did so.

Nor were the documents prepared for NSC members of small import. As we shall see in other administrations, the paper trail was often haphazard, unbalanced in views, or simply nonexistent. For Cutler, his efforts were a point of pride and contribution: save for emergency matters where advanced preparation was not possible, "items were presented for Council deliberation on the basis of carefully staffed and carefully written documents

. . . the busy reader would always know where to find the covering letter, the general considerations, the objectives, the courses of action to carry out the objectives, the financial appendices, the supporting staff study; for they invariably appeared in this sequence in the final document."[71]

CUTLER AND NSC MEETINGS: AT THE TOP OF POLICY HILL

The next step—the day before an NSC meeting—Cutler briefed Eisenhower, especially covering "my explanations to the Council of each agenda item, giving enough background to point up the issues to be decided."[72] Then, at NSC meetings, after an opening briefing by CIA Director Allen Dulles, Cutler introduced each agenda item. This introduction was important in his view: "A clear explanation was the key to a successful interchange of views by the Council members. . . . Often I would identify in the paper and read aloud certain passages. If there were disputed points, each one would be taken up in order."[73]

Although Eisenhower presided, Cutler was responsible for the meeting's flow, and especially notable was his practice of alternatively calling upon supporters then dissenters of issues under review: "I would indicate by name the first speaker on an issue; then follow with the supporter of the contrary view and with others who evidenced by eye or hand that they wished to speak." All were given a fair chance to express their views: "Those who sat at the Council table had a right to speak; none was denied a chance. . . . As long as the managing hand was mine, people whose responsibilities entitled them to be heard by the Council were to be heard if they so requested, and nothing was to be swept under the rug or compromised or glossed over. . . . It was my responsibility . . . to assure debate by presenting differences which had not been resolved at a lower level sharply and precisely in the draft document before the Council."[74] Elsewhere, Cutler observes that "In fact it the *particular task* of the Special Assistant to the President to sharpen and make more precise and provocative any divergences that may exist so that the pros and cons can be accurately discussed and explored before the president at the Council meeting." In so doing, moreover, Cutler was sensitive to the danger of "lowest common denominator" solutions (which was often attributed to the process by critics of the Eisenhower NSC)[75]: "In devising policy under our democratic form of government, reasonable accommodation may be required, but never soft compromise."[76] Cutler also recognized the price of more formal procedures: the loss of "informal 'kicking around' of a problem at the Council meeting." Yet in his mind, "disadvantages are more than offset by the likelihood that a more sure, decisive result will be achieved if the considerations are based on an exactly prepared and commonly understood statement of facts and of recommendations."[77] At the same time, it was not a forum that was a slave to the Planning Board's work or Cutler's agenda. Participants were free to raise points or broach issues that had not been covered in the formal papers prepared beforehand.

Cutler did take a directive hand. He would quickly summarize the consensus of the Council at each point in its agenda, pausing to see if objections were raised; if objections did come the debate would recommence. Votes were never taken (as some observers at the time thought), nor was unanimity required to bring a particular matter to closure.[78] It was Eisenhower's practice to usually reserve making a final decision until sometime after the meeting was over. The NSC and its supporting system was there to advise not constrain and certainly not to bind or dictate.

As for Eisenhower, the process fit his personal decision-making predilections, both as they had come to be formed during his military career and now in his capacity as chief executive. During his presidency 366 meetings of the NSC were held, and Eisenhower presided at over 90 percent of them.[79] According to Cutler, "The President liked a good debate. . . . He wished to hear frank assertions of differing views."[80] Eisenhower "likes nothing better than the flashing interchange of views . . . Out of the grinding of these minds comes a refinement of the raw material into valuable metal."[81]

But the president was also an active participant—one of those grinding minds. As Douglas Kinnard notes, "Eisenhower was much more forceful in meetings than Truman had been and appeared more independent of [Secretary of State John Foster] Dulles than Truman had been of [Secretary of State Dean] Acheson."[82] Records of the discussions at NSC meetings document a president offering his own ideas and suggestions and actively questioning the views of others. On occasion, he seemed to settle on a course of action only later to reverse himself as the discussion wore on: meeting regularly with close associates permitted him to "think out loud" as he mulled over his policy choices. His colleagues on the Council felt free, in turn, to challenge him.

Eisenhower at times even acted as his own broker of the process. In 1954, he was not happy with a Planning Board document on a response to the deteriorating situation of the French forces at Dien Bien Phu in Indochina. He ordered it recalled and set up an alternative planning process under Undersecretary of State Smith's direction. Elmer Staats, who attended many NSC meetings, later recalled that, "one day [Eisenhower] got a little irritated with Bobby Cutler, and he thought Cutler was going on too long on a briefing session. He said, 'Dammit Bobby, bring us issues and options so we can make decisions here.'"[83]

Dillon Anderson, who succeeded Cutler as NSC advisor, would later dismiss the criticism that "a lot of compromises were made and a lot of issues were swept under the rug, and it would come in in agreed form and the President would just sit there and nod his head. . . . This is completely inaccurate. Nor did he always buy the recommendations that came in the form of the paper . . ." Moreover, according to Anderson, "if he had a notion, as he often did, that a subject had not been developed to the point it should have been and there were some things he wanted to know before he made a decision, then whether they were unanimous or not, it went back. He regurgitated it and we tried to rework it again." What transpired in NSC meetings also had effect on Eisenhower's decisions: "I don't think he ever went into the [NSC] meeting with a closed mind, and I've seen him be persuaded to a view that was different from the view that he entertained perhaps quite vehemently the day before. I've seen his mind changed or modified."[84]

According to Attorney General Herbert Brownell, NSC meetings were "lively affairs, with frank and sometimes heated exchanges among the members." Sometimes, Eisenhower "would stand back and let the debate take its course; at other times he would become an active participant." Staff papers "almost always included the presentation of opposing views." The latter, in Brownell's view, "made simple ratification impossible." It was neither "government by committee," nor did it reflect "least common denominator solutions." For his part, Brownell felt he "would not have been prepared if I hadn't attended NSC meetings," for the "most important contribution I made . . . formulation of the Formosa Resolution," at the time of the Quemoy and Matsu offshore islands crisis.[85]

At the same time, Cutler recognized that economy of deliberative time also was expected by the president: "If the meeting swept forward without a wasted minute, the President was interested and satisfied. *That was my job.*"[86] Most participants caught on to these expectations. However, Secretary of Defense Charles Wilson, the former head of General Motors, often tried Eisenhower's and Cutler's patience. His style in early meetings, according to Cutler, was "more suited to the presiding officer at a General Motors meeting than to a single Council member." But even Wilson "learned in time, occasionally prompted by direct presidential intervention."[87]

CUTLER AFTER NSC MEETINGS: DOWN POLICY HILL

Cutler's responsibilities also continued after an NSC meeting was over. He and the executive secretary of the NSC staff, James Lay, would prepare drafts of "records of actions," formal documents that set out in detail how disputed points were resolved and what decisions Eisenhower had made. These were then circulated to attendees for comment and proposed revision, then presented to the president for final approval (and on some occasion, Eisenhower's own changes). After that, a policy directive was prepared conforming to the record and circulated to those "charged with carrying out its terms and to those with a 'need to know.'"[88] Attention to *what* had been precisely decided was a piece of the policy process that some—if not many—of Eisenhower's successors would neglect—and to their detriment.

Cutler's innovations both in better planning before NSC meetings and in keeping records of action after them were also adopted elsewhere in the Eisenhower administration. As he notes, until November 1954, formal records of cabinet meetings were not kept nor was there a system for the orderly circulation of policy papers before meetings. But that month, according to Cutler, "the cabinet operation was reorganized in the pattern established by me for the Council." A secretary to the cabinet—initially Maxwell Rabb—was appointed, and "our warm friendship avoided friction between Cabinet and Council agenda. There was plenty for each to do."[89] Cordial cabinet and NSC staff relations were yet another piece of the policy process that some of their successors would neglect to their detriment.

But *what* had been decided was only part of the equation to make sure that policy was properly implemented. The so-called downside of "policy hill" was the Operations Coordinating Board (OCB), which had as its task the monitoring and oversight of how national security policy was implemented.

The OCB had arisen "like a phoenix out of the ashes" of the Truman-era Psychological Strategy Board, in Cutler's view. And it was a broader and more effective effort: the PSB was handicapped both by its limited scope in understanding the task of effective implementation—a restriction to developing psychological strategies to be waged in winning the cold war—and by its "independently existing" conception of strategy divorced from attention to the effective carrying out of the policies themselves.[90] By contrast, the Eisenhower OCB was "a coordinator and a follower-up and a progress reporter." The OCB's purpose was to "'help set the stage' by encouraging the most favorable arrangement of department and agency plans to carry out an approved security policy."[91]

Meeting usually every Wednesday, the OCB formal meeting was preceded by a lunch of the senior members without staff present, which was quite informal and allowed members to bring whatever was on their minds to the group table. Following the lunch, the regular meeting began. It had a formal agenda and the bulk of its activities concerned discussion of operational plans—devised by working groups (some thirty to forty at any one time)—and the preparation of reports and papers as well as guidelines for interagency coordination. In turn, OCB's actions, in the form of progress reports (usually every six months for a particular item), were regular features back at the top of policy hill—at NSC meetings. At least in Cutler's mind, that had a salutary effect on policy as well: "These progress reports, which turn up at almost every Council meeting, provide another source of ideas for change or modification in policy [by the president and the NSC principals]."[92] According to Karl Harr, who served as the OCB's vice chairman after 1958, "It was an extremely useful tool because it was so well-contained, in terms of security, and yet it was so broad in scope in terms of the diversified representation there. There was almost nothing of importance on the national security side of the government's business that couldn't be discussed, and discussed by the people who had operational responsibility." In addition, according to Harr, "it was essential that you did that, that you had a structure that was validly representative, genuinely representative of these certain points of view, working on the thing—keeping each other honest."[93]

CUTLER AND THE QUALITY OF THE DECISION-MAKING PROCESS

The other facets of Cutler's tenure as NSC advisor—beyond simple brokerage within the existing organizational arrangements—were his efforts to seek improvement in how various stages of the policy process worked. Cutler was especially mindful, for example, that the size of deliberative groups that had been established could have effects on their usefulness to sound decision making: "I struggled to preserve a nice balance between attendance which permitted intimate, frank, fruitful discussion and attendance which turned the group into a 'town meeting' . . . At too largely attended meetings I have seen [Secretary of State] Foster Dulles 'clam up,' with a knowing look at me across the table."[94] In a November 30, 1954, memorandum to some thirty administration officials, Cutler clearly laid out rules for attendance, especially procedures to be followed for those whose ad hoc participation might be needed. Cutler stressed that any participant "will *not* bring supporting personnel." The first item in the memo also pointed out that Cutler was acting under the Eisenhower's direction: "The President has indicated to me that he wishes attendance at NSC meetings kept to the minimum level necessary to enable free group discussion." The memo was revised and recirculated on March 30, 1955.[95] In his final report to the president on April 1,

1955—the day before he was to leave his first stint as NSC advisor—Cutler emphasized the need to keep participation to a minimum, and he noted his recommendation in his initial March 17, 1953, memorandum that "as a general rule, not more than eight persons who participate in discussions should attend Council meetings." In the April 1955 memo, Cutler also recognized the "constant pressure" by others to attend, but that "such pressure must be resisted," not just for national security reasons but so that "intimate, frank, and fruitful discussion can take place."[96]

Cutler's April 1955 report also included other suggestions for better effectiveness. He stressed again the need for NSC members to do their "home work" before meetings, especially adequate prior briefings by their subordinates on the Planning Board. Agenda items for NSC meetings should also be reduced in number from six or seven to two or three principal items. Meetings should not exceed two-and-a-half hours, and they should better facilitate the "'free talk' which the president has from time to time desired." Cutler also recommended that the NSC staff be slightly increased to ease the burden on the NSC advisor. In another document responding to criticisms of the second Hoover Commission, Cutler agreed with some of its findings that the financial appendices to NSC documents needed improvement.[97] Cutler, however, strongly dissented from its view that the NSC staff be enlarged and with a larger policy mandate; it would place it in a "policy maker" role, its lack of "operational responsibility" might make it "ivory tower and sterile, not reflecting hard realities," and it "would tend to intervene between the president and his cabinet ministers."[98] NSC staff advocacy was not in the cards for Cutler.

During Cutler's second stint as NSC advisor—from January 7, 1957, to June 24, 1958—his responsibilities increased slightly when the OCB was brought under his control and he was designated as its vice chairman.[99] The day he took office he prepared a document outlining how the NSC system might effectively serve the president. It covered much the same ground as earlier reports, emphasizing the importance of the Planning Board and the quality of NSC meetings. Cutler now further recommended that membership in the Planning Board be changed every three years "in order to bring fresh points of view" into its deliberations. Planning Board papers to the NSC "should be shortened and sharpened." As well, Cutler urged that "fresh consideration" be given to the use of outside consultants "for particular tasks"—a bit of change from his earlier opposition to outsiders. And he also urged that the number of persons authorized to attend NSC meetings be placed under consideration.

Cutler especially sought to respond to Eisenhower's wish that, in the second term, it might be possible to "open up" deliberations in NSC meetings. Now that they were beyond an "initial testing and familiarizing period," the president wanted to move from "weekly consideration by the Council of policy *documents* to more free debate on policy *issues.*"[100]

Cutler also recommended that the OCB "should be brought by executive order within the NSC structure."[101] The latter was accomplished on July 1, 1957. Once again, Cutler brought to Eisenhower's attention areas of reform. On March 20, 1957, he sent an interim report to Eisenhower on the "trial period" when he headed both the Planning Board and served as vice chair of the OCB. In his view, he was overextended and that one NSC assistant was needed for policy formulation and Council activities while another was needed for operational oversight and OCB matters. Eisenhower took Cutler's advice and appointed (at Cutler's suggestion) Frederick Dearborn, NSC special assistant to the president for security operations, as NSC representative and vice chair of the OCB. As well, Cutler suggested "further critical study" of the OCB: "While the OCB is still relatively new, there is need for independent criticism at [the] presidential level to set its pattern right." Cutler also indicated his tenure as NSC advisor would be short, and that by early 1958 he would train a deputy to succeed him.[102]

It should also be noted that Cutler's successor as NSC advisor, Gordon Gray, was more receptive to a stronger role for the NSC advisor with respect to the OCB. In January 1960, he became its chair, wearing the two hats that Cutler had found so onerous.[103] As Gray told McGeorge Bundy—his successor as NSC advisor—during the 1960 transition, "the change was an improvement both in theory and in practice for a variety of reasons, including the elimination of a situation in which a protagonist [the undersecretary of state] was also the 'impartial chairman,' and the more direct involvement of the president through his [NSC] special assistant." Gray also strongly encouraged Bundy not to abolish the OCB—as the [Sen. Henry] Jackson Subcommittee and others had advocated. In Gray's view, the OCB's functions were "vital," and it "would be unhappy waste of time and resources" to abolish it "and then find it necessary to recreate it."[104] It was not advice that Bundy would follow. Whatever the faults of the OCB, and there were certainly some—which even Eisenhower recognized in the second volume of his memoirs[105]—the absence of attention to implementation was potentially costly.

BEYOND BROKERAGE

As for other aspects of the NSC advisor's role that most post-Eisenhower occupants of the office have embraced—personal advocacy, media visibility, a direct hand in diplomatic contacts and negotiations, and the carrying out of more politically related tasks—little can be found.

In marked contrast to his successors as NSC advisor, Cutler offered little if any substantive policy advice. Policy advocacy was rarely—very rarely in fact—part of his (and Eisenhower's) conception of the role. Throughout his tenure, Cutler's concerns were directed at process rather than substance. In his view, the NSC advisor "had no independent status. When he spoke or acted, he spoke or acted for the President. Therefore I sought to be objective and impartial in presiding over the Planning Board." Cutler served two stints as NSC advisor—January 1953 to April 1955, then again from January 1957 to July 1958—and it is only in the second period he would later recollect—"and then very rarely—did I suggest an independent position before the Planning Board and carry it up to the Council, identified . . . as strictly my own suggestion."[106]

Among the limited number of instances where Cutler gingerly voiced his own views were questions dealing with whether there should be multinational financing of foreign aid programs—which Cutler favored—or unilateral and bilateral efforts, reduction in U.S. forces in Europe ("a balloon punctured" by both Eisenhower and Dulles according to Cutler), and a redefinition of the use of atomic weapons. Such was Cutler's concern about even these infrequent efforts at advocacy, that his views were typed (at Cutler's instigation) on blue paper to highlight them as the NSC advisor's personal views lest they be confused with Planning Board recommendations.[107] On another occasion—this early in the first term—Cutler and staff secretary Pete Carroll suggested to Eisenhower further efforts to get the British to bolster the tottering French government of Premier Rene Mayer. Eisenhower looked at them "quizzically," according to Cutler, and told them, "You boys think you are Assistant Secretaries of State? Go talk to [Undersecretary of State] Smith." They did, but as Cutler notes, "It was my last solo venture into State Department territory."[108] "The 'whales,' and not the 'minnow' [Cutler] . . . should be the originators of policy," in Cutler's view; "My job was to administer, to serve, to get things done, and to be trusted. Such an assignment . . . should be enough for any man."[109]

Cutler's limited conception of his role is all the more notable given his close personal relationship with Eisenhower, which might have served as a "back channel" for policy advice but did not. In the section of Eisenhower's first volume of memoirs discussing the personal friends he hunted, fished, and played bridge and golf with, the only member of the administration who is mentioned is Cutler ("one whose company I always enjoyed and who became a very close friend").[110]

Cutler especially eschewed a publicly visible presence. For Cutler, anonymity was not too strong a term: "an 'anonymous' Assistant to the President has no charter to speak for his Chief in public." And anonymity, in turn, strengthened his relation to the president. In their private meetings, Cutler recounts, Eisenhower often "seemed to be thinking out loud to test his ideas on someone whom he trusted *to keep his mouth shut.*"[111]

Few articles appeared in the press on Cutler's activities as NSC advisor. One of the few, in the *New York Times Magazine,* is telling: its title, taken from a quotation by an associate, is "'Untouchable, Unreachable, and Unquotable.'"[112] Another article, this in the *Saturday Evening Post,* was titled "The Mystery Man of the White House."[113]

Cutler's resolve to avoid the press was sorely tested when he was approached by columnist Joseph Alsop, a longtime friend of Cutler's from their Harvard undergraduate years. Alsop wanted Cutler to be a "confidant," providing background information if not exclusive material useful to the administration's public relations (and of course of great value to Alsop). Cutler turned him down, but Alsop persisted. Cutler took a letter Alsop had written him, again proposing the relationship, to Eisenhower. The president read it, "with mounting color." Cutler told him that he had refused the offer and had informed Alsop that "I could not talk again about a matter of this kind." "That goes for me, too," Eisenhower replied. Needless to say, over the ensuing years, Cutler notes, "the Alsop column had no good word for me."[114]

Although Cutler had been active in Republican politics, there is only one somewhat politically related action on his part after he joined the White House. According to Sherman Adams, Cutler was one of the "stronger enemies of [Sen. Joseph] McCarthy on our team." Early in the administration, McCarthy sent the White House a letter demanding to know its policy on British trade with the People's Republic of China. The issue was political dynamite (McCarthy, according to Adams, had been "egged on" by Democrats on his Senate investigative subcommittee) and a full account would have "required the disclosure of highly classified secret information." Cutler pressed for a public rebuttal, but Adams successfully argued against it, and the matter was dropped.[115]

More generally with respect to his role, Cutler respected the bounds set by the president; this was no bureaucrat engaged in infighting to maintain or expand his policy turf. Cutler understood why Eisenhower chose to consult others or to deviate from the Planning Board's or even the full NSC's counsel. The most important example occurred early in the administration when the president called for a basic reexamination of strategic policy. This exercise might have been undertaken solely by the Planning Board. Eisenhower, however, sought an alternative venue for its consideration—Project Solarium. Its three-team policy exercise proved especially productive. As Meena Bose notes, it was an effort of "unprecedented comprehensiveness," and "set the framework for subsequent debates on strategy, which culminated in Eisenhower's approval of the New Look [defense strategy] in October 1953."[116] Cutler along with CIA Director Allen Dulles and Undersecretary of State Walter Bedell Smith composed the working group for the project. The project's eventual reports were presented to the NSC following a summary report by the NSC staff and the drafting of a new national security policy paper—NSC 162—by the Planning Board.[117] Related studies were undertaken by the Joint Chiefs of Staff.[118]

Absence of Cutler's territorial concerns also extended to the physical domain. In what was surely a unique instance in the environs of the White House where proximity to the Oval Office is taken as a sign of power, Cutler turned down Sherman Adams's query whether he wanted an office in the West Wing (where most of his post-Eisenhower successors would choose to lodge). Instead Cutler set up shop with the rest of the NSC staff in the Old Executive Office Building next door to the White House.[119]

Cutler, as we saw, expressed concerns about increasing the size of the NSC staff: "Because such a staff is divorced from operating responsibility, its product would tend less to reflect the hard realities of the field." [120] Cutler was especially concerned that a strong NSC advisor and staff might upset the balance that Eisenhower had wanted between the cabinet members and the White House staff. The direct access of the NSC advisor and staff to the president might lead them, in Cutler's view, "to intervene between the president and his cabinet members," causing "grave damage."[121] As for the NSC advisor, Cutler worried about the effects of expanding the position's duties: "I would think it inadvisable formally to give him [the NSC advisor] greater responsibilities or formally increase his functional prestige. His existing power to speak for the president is all that any servant needs or should seek."[122] It was a prescient warning about the consequences of an overly powerful NSC adviser.

BEYOND THE FORMAL NSC SYSTEM

Cutler's role in the NSC system and the place of that system in Eisenhower's own deliberations must also be properly understood. In short, they were not the only game in town. Not only were the characterizations made by the Jackson Senate subcommittee wrong about the internal dynamics of the NSC system (overly formal, bureaucratic, and consensus prone), they misunderstood how Eisenhower made decisions and failed to notice the presence of alternative channels of information and advice.[123] In a number of instances—the Suez crisis of 1956, Quemoy and Matsu in 1955 and 1958, and Lebanon in 1958—it was informal meetings of the president's top advisers that proved decisive (although in most cases NSC meetings discussed them as well).[124]

Formal meetings of the NSC were not Eisenhower's only exposure to policy debate. After NSC meetings, the president would often invite a smaller group of key participants back to the Oval Office for further discussion. According to Cutler, this was quite customary, and Eisenhower "would arrange with me in advance to have the statutory members, and perhaps one or two others, join him in his office to discuss matters he thought as yet too sensitive for more general exposure."[125]

Cutler himself was often a participant. As Fred I. Greenstein and I note in a study of the administration's 1954 Indochina decision making, "Like a number of Eisenhower's other principal aides, Cutler participated in the informal as well as the formal side of the presidential advisory process. He frequently met with the president after hours . . ."[126] Cutler found these sessions as well as his own private meetings with the president stimulating—but more about what Eisenhower taught him than about what Cutler said to the president: "On these occasions, a chance remark or a request by me for guidance would lead the President to reflective rumination, aroused exposition, or careful explanation. . . . He seemed to enjoy sharpening the issue by exposing to me the weakness or strength of differing courses."[127]

Moreover, Eisenhower utilized a wide variety of informal contacts—beyond the bounds of his formal NSC system or even his official family—as a source of information and advice. According to Greenstein, "Eisenhower drew for advice on many White House aides, other administration members, and friends and acquaintances for what appears to have been as rich—if not as palpably contrived—a flow of face-to-face conversation, questioning, and thinking out loud as occurred under Roosevelt."[128]

Eisenhower also thought it useful to build alternative channels of advice into his regular NSC system. A group of seven outside consultants was formed at the start of the administration, and other outside advisers would be called in later on other policy matters.[129] The record here was mixed. Some, such as the scientific advisers brought in after Sputnik, worked well (and led to the creation of a permanent White House unit, the present Office of Science and Technology Policy), others such as the Gaither Committee on civil defense moved well beyond their initial mandate and proved a political embarrassment to the administration.[130] According to Bose, the development of the New Look (especially its Project Solarium component) "is perhaps the most multiple-advocacy laden process in the history of the modern presidency."[131]

Alternative channels were sometimes employed within the bounds of the administration's officialdom. During the Indochina crisis of 1954, a special committee, headed by Undersecretary of State Smith, was constituted to come up with policy alternatives. Eisenhower told Smith that his group should be "self-contained," and that "neither NSC nor OCB need be cut in." Their work was eventually brought before the NSC, but they operated outside of normal NSC policy development channels.[132]

Cutler himself was of two minds about the use of outside "civilian" consultants on national security matters. As direct participants in the NSC (especially as *regular* members, as some had advocated) he felt that they were of limited utility since they often lacked experienced-based knowledge; in his view they would be too theoretical, too much of the "ivory tower" and "might tend to dominate the Council discussions." As well they might weaken one of the chief virtues of the NSC system (in his mind), namely that it "brings to the president the views of the very officials upon whom he will later rely to carry out his national security decisions." At the same time, outside views might be of great value as ad hoc consultants at other points in the policy process or as advisers to the NSC or the president on a more limited basis: "We used such consultants on a considerable number of occasions . . . These men in no sense represented special interests. They were carefully selected because of broad and diverse backgrounds of experience . . ."[133]

It is also important to note that not everything dealing with national security matters went through the NSC system. On routine matters that did not require deliberation with other departments or involve major policy changes, the White House staff secretariat proved useful. This was another Eisenhower organizational innovation. Led through most of Eisenhower's tenure by Col. (later Brig. Gen.) Andrew J. Goodpaster, the staff secretariat provided organization and structure for this day-to-day component of coordination, with Goodpaster serving as the White House contact point with cabinet members and agency heads in the national security and foreign policy area (for other cabinet members, domestic issues were handled through Chief of Staff Sherman Adams's operation). As Kinnard notes, "if a defense issue did not involve the formulation, revision, or clarification of NSC policy, then it was not part of the NSC system. These matters were handled by the staff secretary . . . directly with the president."[134]

Defense Secretary Neil H. McElroy would later recall that "if we just wanted to clear things, in our field, not something which involved a conversation which would lead to a conclusion which was, let's say, a change or something new . . . we would do that through Andy [Goodpaster]." [135] According to Gordon Gray, the NSC staff was largely concerned with long-range planning, while Goodpaster was the "spot man for the president." Their respective responsibilities did overlap a bit—Goodpaster was liaison to the military and to intelligence agencies—but there was good will between them. According to Gray, "We avoided difficulty by keeping each other fully informed. And I think he will tell you that anything he should have known he was told by me, and anything that he knew that impinged upon my responsibilities I was fully aware of. And we saw each other, I would say, practically on a daily basis." Most of their communication was oral, according to Gray.[136] Although Goodpaster was asked to stay on for several months in the new Kennedy administration, his staff secretariat (like much of the Eisenhower NSC system) was radically altered, if not in reality abolished.

V. Cutler's Successors as NSC Advisor: Dillon Anderson and Gordon Gray

On April 2, 1955, Dillon Anderson succeeded Cutler as NSC advisor and served until September 1, 1956 (Anderson had agreed only to stay on until the start of the fall 1956 campaign). Anderson was a prominent Houston attorney at Baker and Botts, one of the city's leading law firms. During World War II, he had served in the War Department general staff on mobilization issues, working under Gen. Wilton Persons—who later headed, in the Eisenhower years, the White House congressional liaison unit and succeeded Adams as chief of staff in 1958. After the war, Anderson became the managing partner at Baker and Botts and had come to know Eisenhower during several speaking engagements in Texas. Anderson was active in the 1952 campaign,[137] and starting in 1953 was one of the outside consultants brought in to advise on national security issues. In a 1956 article in *Atlantic*

Monthly Anderson described his activities as NSC special assistant in almost the exact phrases that Cutler used: great effort to make sure that the Planning Board expressed its disagreements, yet finding common ground where possible; making sure the president and the members of the NSC were fully briefed on agendas and with the requisite background memoranda before meetings; and, during NSC meetings, making clear to all why items were on the day's agenda, how they might relate to past deliberations of the council, and then to endeavor to bring forth "what is to be decided, what the alternatives are, any divergences of views, and what action is recommended by the NSC Planning Board."[138]

In his analysis of a number of NSC meetings during Anderson's tenure, Phillip Henderson details an NSC advisor who acted much like Cutler in brokering the process, one that continues to be marked during his tenure by regular policy splits, lively interchanges, and a very active President Eisenhower.[139] Like Cutler, Anderson avoided expressing his own policy views. As he would later note in a Columbia University oral history, "I became mindful early in the game that the only way I could be of continuing service to him was to keep out of an effort to suggest policy to him. . . . I could have plugged my own views. But I felt it was not the right thing for me to try to get in between the President and his Secretary of State on foreign policy matters." As a result, Anderson "enjoyed the most cordial relations" with the other NSC principals, "because they knew that I was not trying to use my proximity to the President to end-run them on any of their subjects."[140] Following a short interim period in which William H. Jackson served as acting NSC advisor, Cutler returned to his old post on January 7, 1957.

Cutler's successor after his second stint as NSC adviser was Gordon Gray. Gray had a long and distinguished career before joining the Eisenhower administration. A lifelong Democrat from North Carolina, Gray was a prominent newspaper publisher and former member of the North Carolina State Senate. He served as assistant secretary then secretary of the army under Truman. He was appointed the president of the University of North Carolina (1950–1955) and served as the first director of the Psychological Strategy Board under Truman (1951). In 1955, he joined the Eisenhower administration as assistant secretary of defense for international security, served as director of the Office of Defense Mobilization, and succeeded Cutler as NSC advisor on June 24, 1958.[141] Gray was well familiar with the operations of the NSC. During part of his service as secretary of the army under Truman he was a statutory member of the NSC (until the 1949 reorganization). Starting in 1955 he attended NSC meetings as Defense Secretary Wilson's back-up ("all of them," according to Gray), and from 1957 until June of 1958 as head of defense mobilization he was once again a statutory member of the NSC.[142]

According to General Goodpaster, Gray like Cutler served as an "honest broker" of the process, especially during Planning Board meetings.[143] The one major expansion of the NSC advisor's job that occurred during Gray's tenure was his assumption of the chairmanship of the OCB in early 1960. Cutler had strenuously avoided wearing the two hats—policy planning and formulation *and* policy oversight—as NSC advisor: in 1957 he temporarily served as *vice* chair and found it too demanding. Not so with Gray, whose somewhat broader governmental experience may have better prepared him for both roles.

Like Cutler, Gray was attentive to the workings of the NSC process and sought improvement. But unlike Cutler, he was less wedded to its formal structure. According to Anna Kasten Nelson, when he became NSC advisor "he held a series of informal discussions with members of the administration to improve the process." Many of them "shared the view that too much time was wasted in council meetings, that there was too much document reading, that too much time and effort was spent on language changes in policy papers, and perhaps there were even too many meetings." Gray was especially concerned that the size of meetings was getting unwieldy, with the result that important matters were handled outside the NSC process.[144]

Gray also protected the prerogatives of the NSC and the workings of the process. As he later recollected,

> There were many occasions involving both Foster Dulles and the then chairman of the Joint Chiefs, whoever he was at the time, who would object to having some item on the NSC agenda. And so I would say to Foster . . . or to whoever it was, "Well, I'll take it up to the President," and the President invariably said, "Ask Dulles whose Council he thinks this is. Of course put it on the agenda." There were many occasions when Dulles didn't want to have the NSC messing in his business, as it were.[145]

It may have been tempting for Gray to expand the role of the NSC advisor. There is some evidence that he was a bit more willing to offer policy advice than Cutler had been. In an October 18, 1961, letter to John S. D. Eisenhower, the president's son, Gray notes that he often used CIA Director Allen Dulles's regular briefing at the opening of NSC meetings to make points in policy directions he favored: "I must confess now that many times I used the briefing device to get a point mentioned in the Council when I had run into resistance from one or another of the departments. . . . In advance of the meeting I would simply ask Allen Dulles to include an item."[146] According to Anna Kasten Nelson, Gray "was more policy oriented and less paper bound" compared to Cutler.[147] Gray, of course, had deeper foreign policy experience than had Cutler.[148]

Gray also faced a different context with respect to the secretary of state than did his predecessors. Dulles was a trusted presidential confidant. According to Gray, Eisenhower felt that "I know the inside of Dulles' mind as well as I know my own." His successor, former Massachusetts governor and then undersecretary of state, Christian Herter, was another matter: "He liked Herter and he had confidence in Herter." But the bond was not that close. Herter had a hearing impairment and "was not as strong as Dulles was. And the president after one miscue found that Herter didn't understand the way the President spoke."[149]

But Gray, like his Eisenhower predecessors, remained a largely invisible figure to the media and the public, this despite the fact that there were a series of other positions for which he was under consideration or declined appointment. Unlike Anderson or Cutler, Gray was clearly an (already quite accomplished) "up-and-comer" potentially slated for even higher office. In late November 1957, while Gray was still heading the Office of Defense Mobilization, Sherman Adams approached him about serving as "general manager" of the administration's civil rights program—Gray declined.[150] He was approached about serving as head of the Atomic Energy Commission by Lewis Strauss, who was not privy to his impending selection as NSC advisor. In November 1959, Gray was approached about serving as deputy secretary of defense to incoming Secretary of Defense Thomas Gates. Gray was more amenable to this offer but was also perfectly happy to remain with the NSC. A November 30, 1959, meeting with the president is particularly revealing about Eisenhower's thoughts on his NSC advisors. Eisenhower had decided to keep Gray at the NSC advisor post, because in his view "the Council was operating better now than at any time in his experience." Gray was needed to keep the NSC's "indispensable machinery moving forward in a dynamic fashion." Gray could be replaced only "for one of two other jobs in government: secretary of state and secretary of defense." In addition, Eisenhower felt that Gray's likely successor as NSC advisor, his deputy Karl Harr, "had not the background, experience or wisdom to 'lay down the law' to the secretaries of state and defense and others." Eisenhower also reflected favorably in comparing Gray to his two predecessors. Eisenhower had (in Gray's recounting of the meeting) "affection and admiration for Bobby Cutler but tension in Council meetings and related activities had largely disappeared since [his] departure." He "felt highly" about Dillon Anderson, "a superior individual but that his approach had been too legalistic." In summary, according to Gray, the president "said he liked the way things were going" even though the Defense Department "seriously needed bolstering."[151]

VI. Policy: Process, Role, and Outcome

As Greenstein and Immerman summarize, "The assistant for national security affairs played an active, but largely procedural part in the deliberations [at full NSC meetings]. He kept the debate on track, directed the council's attention to disagreements and ambiguities, and watched for signs of policy slippage."[152] According to Meena Bose's analysis of the development of the New Look strategy, the "lengthy and heated debated" at an important October 7, 1953, NSC meeting illustrates Cutler's role as an honest broker if not reaching the ideals of Alexander George's notion of multiple advocacy. Cutler outlined "the principal points of NSC 162 . . . summarizing the major differences of opinion." He "clarify[ied] points when needed, redirecting debate when it diverged, and ensuring that the council considered each area of disagreement."[153]

Sometimes Cutler went a bit further. At an early NSC meeting during the 1954 Indochina crisis, Eisenhower began to discuss giving U.S. troops a certain type of fuse bomb, but Cutler then quickly pointed out that introduction of U.S. forces had yet to be authorized. According to one analysis of the episode, "Cutler seems to have had an effect. The discussion of intervention shifted from Eisenhower's point about the equipment needed in jungle fighting and did not remain focused on tactical issues of the sort that could have led policy makers to take for granted that the broader strategic question of intervention had been settled."[154] He did something similar at the October 7, 1953, meeting, when he told the group that they were "degenerating into a debating society" and then "invited the Council to return to the nature of the threat facing the United States."[155] Also at a March 4, 1953, meeting on the budget, Cutler "interjected," according to Bowie and Immerman, that the NSC's consideration of Bureau of the Budget estimates "did not imply anyone's acceptance of either the cuts or a commitment to a balanced budget by FY 1955."[156] Bowie and Immerman also note that Cutler could come down hard on the work of the Planning Board when it failed to meet his expectations: he "reacted with a slashing attack" on a draft policy paper prepared by a special committee of the Planning Board charged with developing a major policy response to Project Solarium. Its analysis of key issues was so "watered down and obscured" and "modified and conditioned" that "they do not standout sharply and clearly for decision. . . . The paper generally may be characterized as not a new policy at all."[157]

On another occasion, Cutler recognized that expanded time for debate was needed. When Army Secretary Robert Stevens and Army Chief of Staff Matthew Ridgway were alarmed by proposed cuts in army personnel, Cutler recalls, "I arranged with the President for Stevens to speak at length and for Ridgway to have a full half hour of Council time."[158]

Sometimes Cutler was swatted down. At an October 13, 1953, NSC meeting (a follow-up to the critical October 7 meeting that Bose notes), Cutler suggested that JCS Chairman Adm. Arthur Radford provide a "clear text" for a statement on atomic weapons contained in NSC 162. Eisenhower broke in, telling Cutler, "No, we could not hope to do better than the presently agreed language."[159] At a June 24, 1954, NSC meeting, there was a deep division of view on the size of the U.S. nuclear arsenal needed. After some debate, Cutler raised the "hoary issue" that some Planning Board members felt that without further increases the Soviet Union might "nibble the free world to death piece by piece." Eisenhower strongly objected: that view was "completely erroneous . . . the more atomic weapons each side obtains, the more anxious it will be to use these weapons."[160] On still another occasion, when a tariff on British bicycles was up for discussion, Cutler (an avid cyclist) "protested, quite out of order" according to Sherman Adams. Cutler interjected that "The British make a damn sight better bicycle than we do. Leave them alone." Eisenhower jocularly replied: "You already have your British bicycle, so you shouldn't be worrying about the tariff."[161]

In the view of Dillon Anderson, "The thorough care that went into foreign policy formulation paid off": conclusion of the Korean war, dealing "calmly and firmly" with the "flare-up" over Quemoy, Matsu, and the offshore islands, the avoidance of "committing U.S. troops to a land war on the mainland of Asia; yet we yielded no prestige; we gave up no ground." The U.S. "got along with our NATO partners," and responded with "firm readiness" to the 1958 crisis in Lebanon. ". . .We consolidated the cause for world peace without retreating anywhere in the world. . . . Military strength . . . was increased markedly. And it was done without the cruel and devastating consequence of inflation."[162] More generally, as Cutler later noted, in Eisenhower's "eight years as president, the United States ended one war (in Korea), initiated no war, suffered no war to be thrust upon her, induced other countries to drop an already initiated war (at Suez), and took steps to prevent the outbreak of war in distant parts of the world."[163]

It is also important to note that the NSC system, especially meetings of the Council, was largely directed at long-range planning and did not have as its primary focus a response to any immediate crisis at hand—hence the name of its initial integrative body: the *Planning* Board. Yet as Eisenhower recognized from his own military experience, continued attention to planning facilitated an adept and effective response to immediate crisis. In a paper produced by Cutler in March 1968 and circulated to Eisenhower, the former president noted in the margins that "through this practice [of continuous planning], the members of the NSC became familiar *not only with each other but with the basic factors of problems* that might, on some future date, face the president." Furthermore, as Cutler notes in the paper, "Thus in time of sudden, explosive crisis, these men would gather to work with and for the president, not as strangers, but as men intimately made familiar, through continuing association with the character, abilities, and understandings of each colleague at the Council table. Such training and familiarity enabled them to act in an emergency, not as ciphers and not as yes-men for the president, but as men accustomed to express their own views . . ."[164]

Extensive deliberation had another purpose. Even if at times it did not alter Eisenhower's basic approach to problems and issues, as Bose observes, "it had the important effect of conveying his chosen policy to his associates and explaining to them the reasoning behind it." Moreover, Eisenhower saw a related purpose "to his highly structured process besides that of aiding decision making, namely that of team building and coordination."[165]

In April 1967, Eisenhower responded to a letter from Dillon Anderson. In his reply, the former president told him that he was "struck by the great feeling of confidence I unfailingly felt in the work of Bobby Cutler, Gordon Gray and yourself." "Personally I have the conviction," he went on, "that the absence of a similar position, occupied by a man of similar ability, was the cause of our abysmal failure at the Bay of Pigs and other errors in foreign operations." Eisenhower continued his reflections: "In recent years, the White House has been occupied by people whose important experience has been confined to legislative work. Such an experience is not calculated, I think, to develop any real understanding of the need, in complicated matters, for skillful staff work and orderly analysis of difficult problems. The lack of an efficient Planning Board, with an executive in charge of all the staff work applying to it, has been responsible for some of our difficulties. So I shall never cease to be grateful to you and the two others that occupied this critical post in my Administration."[166]

VII. Implications

The most important implication to be drawn from analysis of the Eisenhower-era NSC advisors is that the honest broker role—at least their variant of it—is practicable and not some mere ideal. My analysis of the broker role in this study is, in part, prescriptive in approach. Can the model as set out by Alexander George and others—albeit modified to take into account other facets of the job of NSC advisor—be put into practice? The Eisenhower experience suggests not only that it can be put into place but that it also contributes to effective presidential decision making. But there are a number of factors that also may set some limits on its applicability for other presidents.

THE NSC ADVISOR'S ROLE EXPECTATIONS AND HONEST BROKERAGE
Cutler's expectations for the job of NSC advisor were obviously an important part of the equation. Working under Eisenhower's direction, he clearly played a central role in not only defining what the reorganized NSC system would look like. He in effect invented for himself—and for the first time—a particular variant of the NSC advisor's broker role. Some of his inclinations are debatable: he was, at least initially, steadfast in his view that inclusion of outside consultants was not likely to be productive. But he wisely recognized the need for institutional memory by keeping on James Lay as executive secretary of the NSC staff.

Throughout his two stints as NSC advisor, Cutler was also highly concerned with the smooth and effective operations of the NSC system. He was a tough task master, yet his concern was directed at the quality of the deliberative process not his own prestige or standing with the president. The one quibble that might be raised—and it is a bit of an unknown in terms of its counterfactual consequences—is whether the OCB might have functioned more effectively if it had been brought under the NSC advisor's control earlier (which occurred in 1957 during Cutler's second tour of duty, and eventually was more direct with Gray's assumption of its chairmanship in 1960).

Cutler embraced that part of the broker role pertaining to the fair, even handed, and informed development and presentation of policy options. Yet his diligence here was accompanied by the practice of not pressing his own policy views. In part, this reflected the absence of his own deep vision on policy matters, as well as his prior experience and expertise with matters of process rather than substance. In this respect, Cutler is quite different from his post-Eisenhower successors. And, as a result, he does not offer us much in the way of practical lessons for how brokerage can be effectively meshed with policy advocacy (although the occasions when he did express his views are notable for the steps he took to make sure all understood he was speaking only on his own behalf). Nor do Cutler and his successors tell us very much about the NSC advisor taking on a more visible, public role. This was a time of a different media age, when relative anonymity could easily be practiced and when others—the cabinet secretaries most notably—could be the prime agents for feeding the media beast. Cutler's continual concern with the quality of the decision-making process, however, remains timely.

EVOLUTION OF THE NSC ADVISOR'S ROLE OVER TIME

Honest brokerage continued under Cutler's successors. The particular context of the role in this presidency may be an important explanatory factor. The presence of a highly organized policy-making and implementing process—"policy hill"—may have constrained the evolution of the NSC advisor's role. Yet, even in his second stint, Cutler recognized that some changes were needed. Gordon Gray's tenure as the last Eisenhower NSC advisor is also notable. The policy-directive role that John Foster Dulles had filled was reduced after his death. His successor, Christian Herter, did not possess Dulles's policy weight or long experience. Gray, in turn, was a bit more inclined to substantively air his advice. Indeed, his prepresidential policy experience was much richer than Cutler's.

Gray hewed to the broker role, but he was less wedded to the mechanics of the system. But here he was not alone. Eisenhower also came to recognize the need for more flexibility and more free-flowing discussion, less structured by the work of the Planning Board. Gray also recognized the need for what Cutler had resisted: NSC advisor chairmanship of the OCB. Had it occurred earlier, would the OCB have been more effective? Would its potential contributions to the policy process have been more widely understood and embraced?

PRESIDENTIAL DECISION-MAKING NEEDS, PRESIDENTIAL ROLE EXPECTATIONS

In some sense, the NSC system during this administration operated under ideal circumstances. Most notable was what Eisenhower himself brought to the table. He was deeply versed in foreign affairs, national security, and defense policy. The decision-making process was more of a reality check on his own considerable instincts and substantive vision as a decision maker. It was not an option-robust and information-rich process pouring into an empty vessel.

At the same time, Eisenhower recognized that a well-organized process could still aid his decision making. It might reveal unknown information or unexplored options. Its deliberative interchanges enabled Eisenhower to synthesize the facts and make "net judgments." Nor was this a new procedural experience to him. His unique military background and its emphasis on orderly decision, command, and control processes came profitably—and familiarly—to the fore once he became a *presidential* decision maker.

As president, he valued its written work product and was comfortable with its deliberative settings, even if at times they simply confirmed his prior views or tested his patience. In the end, of course, he recognized that he made the decisions; the more formal aspects of the process were there to assist and advise not determine. Final decisions were generally made privately, often after informal consultation with a closer group of advisers.

On May 10, 1967, when the NSC system was in disarray under his successors, Eisenhower dictated a letter to Gordon Gray from his bed at Walter Reed Army Hospital in which he told Gray, "I share your conviction that it is impossible for any President to be constantly in possession of the coordinated and analysed security information, except through a well-organized staff . . . similar to the National Security Council." Eisenhower then encouraged Gray, Cutler, or Anderson—"or all three of you together"—to "publish something that would help the public to understand the value of such an organization."[167]

Eisenhower was not just a participant in—but the orchestrator and field marshal of—what was organized and what transpired. A number of Cutler's memos dealing with organizational matters indicate he was acting under the president's direction or as a result of presidential concerns. But even prior to that, Eisenhower had spoken about the need for NSC reform during the 1952 election, and it was he during his transition to office who set Cutler to the task of accomplishing it.

Concern for the operations of the NSC system and the role of the NSC advisor, moreover, was ongoing for the president. To take just one example, in an August 7, 1957 memo to Lay, Cutler begins "While I was talking with the President yesterday afternoon . . . ," and then goes on to state that Eisenhower wanted Cutler to be more "difficult" in accepting papers for consideration by the full NSC; it was the president's view that papers only of concern to one department should not generally be brought forth for the group's consideration. According to Cutler, "he also seemed to feel that the Council might be too frequently reviewing policy papers. I intend to speak further with him about this subject."[168]

Eisenhower was especially vital to the success of the process in setting expectations about decision making, whether it was the need for prior preparation and long-range plans, the organization of a deliberative process, or the pace of discussion and the demeanor of its participants. According to Cutler, he had a "profound sense of order, delegation, and responsibility." [169]

Eisenhower also had a sense how the process, including the NSC advisor's role, not only served *his* needs but those of his associates. While cognizant of the parochial—departmentally grounded—perspectives of cabinet participants, he recognized the contribution of their experience-based, policy expertise: the NSC drew, according to Cutler, "viability" from that. Eisenhower "expected them, from knowledge derived from day-to-day experience in their assigned field, to initiate recommendations for security policy germane to the responsibilities with which he charged them."[170] But the process also fostered team work: presidential priorities were communicated, and participants were made aware of the concerns and interests of others. Most notably, Eisenhower saw benefit in the regularity of the process for times of crisis; the latter would raise the stakes and time would be pressing, but the group had already been well-prepared on where the administration stood, what its priorities were, and what options were likely available.

Eisenhower especially had expectations about the role of the NSC advisor. It came at his instigation of course. But the particulars of the role were what he thought was needed, and it fit squarely—indeed was vital to—a process he valued. According to Gordon Gray, Eisenhower did not see the NSC advisor as a regular source of substantive policy advice or in an operating role: it "was a staff job and so considered by the President and me, unlike for example, Kissinger's performance where he's an operator as well as staff. General Eisenhower never would have had, I think, anybody in that position in an operating capacity."[171]

OTHER IMPLICATIONS

One particular lesson from this period, which we will especially see as needed in subsequent presidencies, was the presence of smooth and cooperative relations between the NSC advisor and the secretary of state. As Carnes Lord notes, "Strikingly, the NSC role was virtually invisible during the Eisenhower years in spite of the high level of activity associated with the Council itself and the interagency structure supporting it. This suggests that the State-NSC conflicts of the past are at least as much a result of the *personal styles and strategies of those advisers* and (more importantly) *inadequate management* by the president as they are a reflection of enduring institutional tensions."[172] This view is shared by Greenstein and Immerman, who note that "There was a general absence of the public and semipublic feuds and cleavages that have marked a number of later presidencies, as well as the tension that existed in many later presidencies between the secretary of state and the national security adviser."[173] An underlying lesson, in turn, is that all of the participants—the NSC advisor, the president, and the other principals—play a part in making brokerage effective.

At the same time, the experience of these Eisenhower-era NSC advisors does not wholly resolve the question of how the honest broker role can be contemporaneously applied. Their brokerage was set within a particular national security structure. As Eisenhower implies in his April 1967 letter to Anderson, the work of the NSC advisor *within the Planning Board* was a key contributor to success—organizational setting was closely linked to individual role. Moreover, the Eisenhower NSC *system,* according to Greenstein and Immerman, "was also unlike that of a number of later presidencies in that it made full use of the expertise of the departments and agencies represented in the NSC."[174]

In Henderson's view, the NSC *staff*—which also had a major role in the preparation of policy papers and in briefing the NSC advisor—was a positive factor. It was largely drawn from policy professionals, a "permanent, career oriented cadre . . . charged with preserving continuity . . . [and] institutional memory."[175] The NSC staff also had the advantage of serving as, according to Clark and Legere, "an independent source of analysis of departmental recommendations,"[176] one not tied to a particular bureaucratic perspective.

But the relation of the system to the role—whatever the positive features of the former—also poses a problem. The Eisenhower NSC—within which the advisor role was set—was historically bound in both the policy challenges and the political context of the 1950s. Whether it can be adapted in whole or in great part to a contemporary presidency has divided those who have studied it. Some, such as Greenstein and Immerman are optimistic. Writing during the 2000 election, they note: "even if the next and future presidents do not adopt the Eisenhower system in toto, they may want to adapt features of it to their own needs."[177] Others, such as Anna Kasten Nelson, caution that while meritorious at the time, the present-day timeliness of national security decision making and "White House hegemony" doom the applicability of such a lengthy, heavily department-involved, and dependent process: "the Eisenhower NSC process, like his policy, will never again be emulated."[178] The particular debate need not be resolved here, but it raises an important question that will be addressed as we examine subsequent presidencies and the roles of NSC advisors. Can brokerage operate in different organizational settings or in quite different political and policy contexts?

Both the NSC advisor's role and the broader NSC system also were dependent on other actors in the process, Secretary of State John Foster Dulles most notably. Dulles clearly emerges as the dominant figure (aside from the president) in NSC meetings. Dulles also clearly guarded those policy areas that he felt were the prerogative of the secretary of state and his department. Moreover, as Nelson notes, the system worked precisely because Eisenhower recognized that Dulles "would have to *dominate* certain parts of it." But, that said, as Nelson also points out, "the lack of conflict between Dulles and [the NSC advisors] . . . was due both to Eisenhower's confidence in Dulles *and to the perception of the role*" of NSC advisor developed by Cutler, Anderson, and Gray.[179] The impact of this particular secretary of state meshed well with the particular roles of these NSC advisors. But can an *expanded* brokerage role mesh well with another strong secretary of state and achieve a relatively harmonious and productive relationship?

The presence of Dulles and Eisenhower, who were both deeply and substantively informed across a range of policy issues, raises another twist for the present-day application of the honest broker model. Can it be applied when the principal actors—especially the president and the secretary of state—do not have the background and expertise of an Eisenhower and Dulles? Here the Eisenhower experience provides a bit—but only a bit—of reassurance. First, Dulles's successor, Christian Herter, possessed fewer preformed policy views and was less dogged in asserting them. Yet the system—including the role of Gordon Gray as NSC advisor—continued to work, perhaps even better than before. Second, Eisenhower's two defense secretaries until June 1959—Charles E. Wilson and Neil McElroy—were business executives who lacked prior experience or substantive knowledge and expertise in even defense matters much less broader national security issues.[180] They were brought on board as managers of the Pentagon, reflecting their respective experience as the heads of General Motors and Procter & Gamble. Again, like Herter, to no serious detriment to the process (although in this case, Eisenhower was uniquely positioned far beyond any recent president to fill any substantive breaches on defense matters).[181]

Finally, the brokerage of the Eisenhower-era NSC advisors was limited. They clearly moved beyond the limited coordination undertaken by their Truman-era predecessors. They were especially active in ensuring that the Planning Board—their variant of the interagency process—operated reasonably effectively: consensus where possible, differences made clear. They also were a force at NSC meetings in making sure deliberations were effective, and they were attentive to the effectiveness of the broader NSC system. Yet in other ways they were not like most of their successors. They rarely advocated their own policy views. They worked in an era where print journalism was dominant, the media was relatively docile, and there was certainly no round-the-clock news cycle—they could be invisible. On these and other matters, their successors would operate quite differently. Indeed, on some measures they had to operate quite differently. Can the positive elements of the brokerage of Cutler et al. be retained, while at the same time expanding the job to include other activities that have come to be embraced by their successors?

CHAPTER 2

The Decline of Honest Brokerage

Bundy as NSC Advisor

The appointment of McGeorge Bundy as John F. Kennedy's NSC advisor marked an important watershed in the evolution of the role of the NSC advisor. Under his early direction much of the organizational apparatus of the Eisenhower-era national security system was dismantled. The role of honest broker as the center point of the NSC advisor's responsibilities was eclipsed. In its place emerged an NSC advisor who was a powerful figure in his own right, often acting as a policy advocate. Bundy's tenure in the position set the stage for even more powerful NSC advisors to follow him. According to Andrew Preston, the history of the NSC advisor's role "must be divided into 'B.B.' and 'A.B.'—Before Bundy and After Bundy—such was his influence."[1]

Two years younger than JFK, Bundy had a quick rise in his academic career at Harvard, becoming dean of the Faculty of Arts and Sciences in 1953, at the age of thirty-four. Earlier, Bundy had cowritten the memoirs of Henry Stimson, former secretary of State (under Hoover) and War (under Taft then FDR and briefly Truman).[2] Bundy served as a consultant to Richard Bissell on the Marshall Plan (his and Bissell's path crossed once again during the Bay of Pigs debacle). In 1952, his major work, *The Pattern of Responsibility*, was published; it was based on Secretary of State Dean Acheson's speeches, hearings testimony, and public statements, with interspersed commentary by Bundy. In 1952, he was appointed executive secretary of the State Department's Oppenheimer Panel on nuclear disarmament, and he drafted its report.

Bundy first met Kennedy as fellow elementary students at the Dexter Lower School in Brookline, Massachusetts; they became better acquainted as adults when JFK joined the Harvard Board of Overseers in 1956. Although nominally a Republican, Bundy developed a comfortable—although before the presidency not a particularly close—relationship with JFK. Their personal bond eventually proved much closer than that experienced by the Eisenhower NSC advisors.

I. The Kennedy National Security Process

Both Kennedy and Bundy harbored deep distrust of the formal national security structure that had been developed by their predecessors. In part, this reflected a recognition that a less formal and less hierarchical process would better fit Kennedy's own style as a decision maker. In a September 4, 1961, letter responding to a query by Sen. Henry Jackson (D-WA) concerning NSC operations in the new administration, Bundy noted that the changes made to date fit Kennedy's intention to develop a close relation with his secretaries of state and defense and his own predilection for small group deliberative settings. Kennedy, according to Bundy, "has made it clear that he does not want a large separate organization between him and his Secretary of State." Nor, Bundy continued, "does he wish any questions to arise as to the clear authority and responsibility of the Secretary of State, not only in his own department . . . but also as the agent of coordination in all our major policies toward other nations."[3]

Both Kennedy and Bundy were adherents to the criticisms that the Jackson Subcommittee had leveled against the Eisenhower NSC process—in fact, Jackson had been a close friend of Kennedy since entering the Senate together in 1953. As JFK himself noted on December 31, 1960, in announcing Bundy's appointment as NSC advisor:

> I have been much impressed with the constructive criticism contained in the recent staff report by Senator Jackson's Subcommittee on National Security Policy Machinery. The Subcommittee's study provides a useful starting point for the work that Mr. Bundy will undertake in helping me to strengthen and simplify the operations of the National Security Council.[4]

Once in office, Bundy and Kennedy quickly dismantled the Planning Board and the OCB, despite the entreaties made to keep them largely intact by members of the Eisenhower administration during the transition, including President Eisenhower himself.[5] An especially notable voice of caution was Eisenhower staff secretary Gen. Andrew Goodpaster, who was asked to temporarily stay over in the new administration. Bundy and Kennedy, however, wanted immediate change. Reform of the OCB, which the Jackson subcommittee had particularly criticized as overly bureaucratic and ineffective, had no support among the Kennedy team; it was quickly abolished. Nor was there any recognition of the utility of the Planning Board; it was seen as a consensus seeking producer of overly broad, watered down policy papers. Goodpaster defended the Eisenhower policy process but to no avail. As Bundy himself later noted, "Neither Kennedy nor his principal cabinet advisers, Secretary of State Dean Rusk and Secretary of Defense Robert McNamara, believed in general policy papers as a way of producing specific results."[6] Ironically, Kennedy had explicitly criticized the absence of effective planning in the 1960 campaign; in his view, there was "the lack of long-range preparation, the lack of policy planning, the lack of purposeful national strategy backed by strength."[7]

As well, meetings of the NSC were fewer and less important. According to Theodore Sorensen, Kennedy's chief White House adviser, they were used—when they were used—for "minor decisions" or "major ones actually settled earlier." Kennedy "strongly preferred to make all major decisions with far fewer people present." During and after crises, the NSC was often convened, but for the purpose of getting everyone on record and to "silence outside critics."[8] As Kennedy himself observed in an NBC television interview in April 1961, meetings of the NSC are "not as effective" as smaller decisions groups: "it is more difficult to decide matters involving national security if there is a wider group present."[9]

These organizational changes allowed Bundy to reduce the size of the NSC staff, from seventy-four to forty-nine according to estimates.[10] Yet they also increased the power of the NSC staff and the NSC advisor. Abolishment of the Planning Board and OCB eliminated staff positions involved in *interdepartmental* coordination of the policy-making and implementation process. But in their place, the NSC staff became more directly involved as the authors of national security policy. Bundy organized the remaining staff according to regional or functional portfolios.[11] In place of the OCB, Bundy and his staff took on the job of issuing National Security Action Memorandas (NSAMs) informing recipients of policy directives.[12] With all these changes, the NSC staff—and the NSC advisor—were thus potentially placed in a greater policy advocacy role, eclipsing any initial hope for a return to State Department dominance.

Bundy's power and influence grew accordingly. The possibility for honest brokerage was now attenuated. First, interagency coordination lacked organization and suffered as a result. Second, the absence of routine and regular methods of bringing departmental and agency views and positions to the presidential level would create a vacuum for policy likely be filled by advocacy from the NSC advisor and staff. Bundy's response to Senator Jackson noting a reduced staff role between the president and the secretaries of state and defense was misleading. It failed to acknowledge that, absent the organizational strictures of the Planning Board and its method of fostering interdepartmental coordination, vetting of policy would be ad hoc and more potentially subject to the interests and proclivities of Bundy and his staff. It also failed to acknowledge that Bundy and his staff would have unfettered entrée for policy advocacy in the Oval Office. Sound organization had been replaced by conditions that were not conducive at all to the sort of State Department-centered process that Jackson or Kennedy—at least initially—favored.

Not surprisingly, Kennedy quickly became dissatisfied with State's role in his policy making. According to Sorensen, he "was discouraged with the State Department as soon as he took office." Kennedy failed to realize the bureaucratic forces at work: "He felt that it too often seemed to have built-in inertia which deadened initiative." State was subject to "excessive delay. It spoke with too many voices. . . . It was never clear who was in charge, who was clearly delegated to do what, and why his own policy line seemed consistently to be altered or delayed."[13] According to Arthur Schlesinger Jr., Kennedy "earnestly hoped that the State Department would serve as his agent of coordination." Yet "it was a constant puzzle to Kennedy that the State Department remained so formless and impenetrable." Kennedy once told Schlesinger, "Damn it, Bundy and I get more done in one day at the White House than they do in six months at the State Department. . . . They never have any ideas over there."[14] But Kennedy may have been a bit disingenuous: he may have wanted—in appointing a weak, institutionalist figure like Rusk—to be his *own* secretary of state all along, with Bundy as chief deputy and brains trusts.

II. Bundy as NSC Advisor—Kennedy

Also not surprisingly, Bundy filled the breach and began to provide substantive advice to Kennedy, unlike his Eisenhower predecessors, in his frequent memoranda to Kennedy. Problems initially emerged in his access to the president (as I will discuss below). But unlike some of his successors, notably Henry Kissinger, he tried to keep Rusk and McNamara informed. According to Rusk, Bundy and Walt Rostow, his successor as NSC advisor, were "very good" about not "coming between the President and a cabinet officer without the cabinet officer's knowledge." If the NSC advisors provided their own policy advice, Rusk notes, "they would also inform the cabinet officer so that the cabinet officer would have a chance to comment on those proposals from his own point of view."[15] Nor, according to another account, did cabinet members complain "that Bundy used his influence and proximity to the president to undue advantage."[16]

Yet Bundy's memos to JFK lacked the rigor of the Eisenhower deliberative process: they were directed at "action" rather than "planning," on "what was happening at the moment."[17] According to Roger Morris, while Bundy assembled a staff of "exceptional talent," he did not see his job "as a critical adversary on behalf of the presidential interest in provoking the widest spectrum of discussion."[18]

On the positive side, unlike Kissinger under Nixon, Bundy did not attempt to monopolize his access to the president. NSC staff members often accompanied Bundy to his meetings with Kennedy. According to Carl Kaysen, Bundy's deputy, "We were few enough so the president had some idea of who we were and what we were doing."[19]

Although Bundy characterized his role as a mere "traffic cop—to see what gets forwarded to the president," in actuality he began to assume greater power. As Bundy biographer Kai Bird notes, "very early in the new administration, it became clear that Bundy's shop was running circles around Rusk's. Bundy had daily access to the president; Rusk did not." Bundy was labeled in the press as a "shadow secretary of state"—a far cry from Senator Jackson's hopes or Kennedy's initial intentions. Dean Acheson, Truman's secretary of state, was asked what he would have done under the circumstances. "Resign," was Acheson's terse reply.[20]

Bundy's role as a personal adviser to the president not only expanded considerably, he also was the daily conduit for intelligence information and briefings. Whereas meetings of the NSC and other informal settings enabled CIA Director Allen Dulles to provide Eisenhower (and, in NSC meetings, the other principals) with intelligence material (as well as the opportunity to discuss it), Kennedy's dislike of NSC meetings effectively ended that venue. Despite General Goodpaster's advice that the CIA should provide the daily intelligence briefing, Bundy took on the responsibility himself.[21] It was another change that brought problems. By May 1961, even Bundy acknowledged the briefing arrangement was problematic: it was "currently not well done by either Clifton or me (we can't get you to sit still, and we are not really professionals)."[22]

Related changes also increased the power of the NSC advisor. Where Staff Secretary Goodpaster had been an important conduit of foreign policy information and national security intelligence within the Eisenhower White House (in addition to CIA Director Dulles) that job now devolved upon Bundy.[23] In addition, the NSC advisor and staff, with the creation of the White House Situation Room after the Bay of Pigs fiasco in April 1961, directly received cable traffic and other information. They no longer had to rely on what was forwarded (or might not be forwarded) from State, Defense, and the CIA. After the Bay of Pigs, office space for the NSC advisor and a small number of staff was also provided on the ground floor of the White House, near the Situation Room—a location in the West Wing that Cutler had assiduously avoided.[24]

The abolition of the Planning Board enhanced Bundy's role. Bundy, his deputy (Rostow then Kaysen), and the NSC staff directly undertook policy development, sometimes on their own, sometimes in interagency task forces.[25] Other changes portended a greater involvement in operations, particularly after the abolishment of the OCB. Absent the organizational divide between planning and operational coordination, the NSC advisor and staff were potentially placed in a more direct operational role; the organizational "check" of departmental and agency participation on the OCB (and the fact that it was chaired by a representative from State though most of the Eisenhower presidency) was eliminated. According to Inderfurth and Johnson, another facet of the NSC staff's involvement in operations was "a procedure known as 'cross-hatching' . . . requiring White House clearance for important outgoing State Department cables."[26] On many occasions, the NSC staff not only cleared those cables but initiated them.[27]

The field was open for the NSC advisor to assume a more operational role. As Bundy himself acknowledged in his letter to Jackson, they had "deliberately rubbed out the distinction between planning and operations."[28] But at what cost and with what consequences?

BUNDY: SOME BROKERAGE CONCERNS

As we shall see in detail, the Bay of Pigs and Cuban missile crisis deliberations do not provide evidence of Bundy fulfilling the central mission of the broker role—testing policy options, pushing hard on assumptions, exploring implications, making sure a full range of alternatives is on the table. Yet Bundy was not without concern for another important part of the broker role: how the advising process was operating, whether it was organized effectively, and he did bring deficiencies to Kennedy's attention.

On May 16, 1961, in a memo to Kennedy, Bundy outlined some of his concerns about the decision-making process: "We need some help from you so that we can serve you better." Although the White House was in Bundy's view (and in accord with Kennedy's preferences) a "center of energy,"

> we do have a problem of management; centrally it is a problem of your use of time and your use of staff. You have revived the government, which is an enormous gain, but in the process you have overstrained your own calendar, limited your chances for thought, and used your staff incompletely. You are altogether too valuable to go on this way; with a very modest change in your methods you can double your own effectiveness and cut the strain in half.

Bundy then proposed several correctives. One suggestion was that the president try to stick to his schedule. A second was more regular and focused meetings with Bundy. Kennedy needed a "real and regular time each day for national security discussion and action." For the past several weeks, Bundy noted, "I have succeeded in catching you on three mornings for a total of 8 minutes." Moreover, Bundy continued, those meetings often consisted of Kennedy's queries about news items rather than substantive matters from Bundy needing presidential attention: "6 of the 8 minutes were given not to what I had for you but for what you had for me from [journalists] Marguerite Higgins, David Lawrence, Scotty Reston, and others. . . . You must not stop reading the papers," but regularly scheduled meetings were needed: "After lunch? Tea? You name it. But you have to mean it, and it really has to be every day." In Bundy's view, regular meetings

> can save you a lot of time . . . [and] can give your staff a coordinated sense of what you want and it can give everyone who needs it a time of day when they can reach you through an easy channel [i.e., Bundy himself]. It also gives you a way of keeping track of your own tremendous flow of ideas. Right now it is so hard to get to you with anything not urgent and immediate that about half the papers and reports that you personally ask for are never shown to you because by the time you are available you clearly have lost interest in them. If we put a little staff work on these and keep in close touch, we can be sure that *all* your questions are answered.

Yet the meetings Bundy had in mind—at least at that point in time—were not the more structured deliberations of the Eisenhower-era, but rather more "face time" with Bundy himself. Later in the memo, Bundy recognized the need for better "staffwork . . . We need to be sure we are doing what you want." But Bundy offered little analysis, in this post–Bay of Pigs assessment, of how a better deliberative process might be crafted that would better develop and vet policy options. Rather, he framed his concerns in the more limited terms of watchfulness over the foreign policy bureaucracy and the need to stimulate problem solving:

> You are entitled to feel confident that a) there is no part of government in the national security area that is not watched over closely by someone from your own staff, and b) there is no major problem of policy that is not out where you can see it and give a proper stimulus to those who should be attacking it.

"With your stimulus and leadership," Bundy concluded, "we'll do the job."[29]

To some extent—but only to some extent—Kennedy's procedures began to change. Bundy met more frequently with the president. He also convened morning staff meetings.[30] In a June 22, 1961, memo to the president, Bundy noted some of the changes made and their positive contributions. More were suggested, such as the appointment of a senior military adviser (a post that Gen. Maxwell Taylor—former army chief of staff under Eisenhower but a critic of its New Look policy—soon occupied).[31]

Although Bundy did not envisage a return to the recently abandoned Planning Board, he did recognize that a more formal and better organized system of policy analysis was needed: "there should be a more clearly defined pattern for preparation for new policy papers, and reporting on crisis areas. . . . Much could be ordered that is now somewhat haphazard. . . . Timing and rules of procedure for the NSC itself need improvement. The NSC should probably meet more regularly—though not more often—and at fixed times. . . . This would require a presidential acceptance of routine that might be dull. But meetings that are called suddenly, or suddenly called off, make staff work hard." Bundy also recognized deficiencies in policy coordination after decisions had been made. Interdepartmental coordination on the other side of the "policy hill" should be "carefully, but sparingly increased." Eisenhower's OCB went too far in Bundy's view (and was "dangerous"), "but in the first months we have probably gone too far the other way." More generally, Bundy recognized that Kennedy wanted a department or task force-based, rather than a White House centered, coordination process. The former should be "the agency of daily action." But, in Bundy's view, more White

House coordination and oversight was needed: "I am proposing . . . weekly meetings to ensure that somewhat more formal processes are followed."[32]

But the effort proved fitful. According to Elmer Staats, who had served as executive director of the OCB for four years and was then deputy director of the BOB under Kennedy, "There were meetings which tended to be in the nature of substitutes for the OCB, that is, regular luncheon meetings held in Mr. Bundy's office [or elsewhere]." However, "they were never formalized, and as time went on, even these have fallen into disuse." Commenting in 1964, Staats noted that "there are now staff meetings which Mr. Bundy has of his own staff" to which others are invited "to exchange information and ideas, etc."[33]

Others also experienced poor coordination. One day Gen. Earle Wheeler (then serving as chief staff officer for the JCS—he later became chairman of the JCS under Johnson) was handed NSAM #22. Wheeler was baffled at first, then he realized that the last one he had been given was #4. Numbers 5 through 21 had not been forwarded to his office, yet these represented important national security orders of the president. "The lines of control have been cut," Wheeler told his Pentagon associates, "But no other lines have been established."[34]

In October 1961, Bundy proposed to Kennedy another change that harkened back to the Eisenhower years: regular meetings of the NSC. In a memo on October 10, Bundy indicated that Kennedy himself had brought up the possibility: "You mentioned on the way to Dallas that you would like to have regular meetings of the National Security Council." Bundy "very strongly" agreed with this plan: "There are lots of kinds of business which ought to be transacted relatively formally, and which we can dispose of more efficiently if meetings are regularly scheduled, and their times set in advance. Calling such meetings on short notice, in the past, has produced incomplete staff work and given unreasonable difficulty to members of the Council and their staffs. . . . If you approve this general plan . . . it probably will not bore you more than one time in four." Bundy also noted that Fred Dutton, the White House secretary to the cabinet, "feels the same way about the Cabinet, and would like to have its meetings scheduled on alternate Thursday mornings."[35]

But frequent meetings of the NSC did not occur. Whereas the NSC usually met weekly under Eisenhower, only twelve meetings of the NSC were convened in 1962; the last three (on October 20, 21, and 22) concerned the Cuban missile crisis. Another twelve were convened in 1963.[36] At the presidential level, Kennedy and Bundy continued to hew in favor of more collegial and flexible arrangements, especially with the creation of the Executive Committee of the National Security Council (ExCom), which provided the administration's chief deliberative forum during and after the Cuban missile crisis instead of the NSC.[37] Forty-two meetings of the ExCom were convened from October 1962 through March 1963, compared to the slim number of NSC meetings held. Subcommittees of ExCom were also established to deal with issues that emerged after the October resolution of the crisis.

Bundy's concerns for a better system of policy development and vetting below the level of the principals, which he had raised in his June 22, 1961, memo, also took shape. In January 1962, a standing group of largely second-level White House and department officials was constituted, and its aim was "to organize and monitor the work of the National Security Council and to take up such matters as may be presented to the Group by the members [of the NSC]."[38] The group met fifteen times from January 1962 through August 1962. According to Bromley Smith—the executive secretary of the NSC under Kennedy and Johnson—over its eight months in existence "its usefulness varied." In particular, "lack of driving support from the State Department representative resulted in a rather desultory life."[39]

It was not until the spring of 1963 when concerted attention was finally paid to developing a planning mechanism below the level of the NSC or the ExCom principals. In an April 2, 1963, memo to the president, Bundy noted that "as you know, there has been considerable discussion in recent months of the need for strengthening interdepartmental planning and coordination on major national security issues." Bundy regarded the creation of ExCom as a good first step and "a good instrument for major interdepartmental decision." But it was "not so good for lesser matters of coordination." In his view, ExCom "has not proved effective at all, except during the extraordinary week of October 16–22, in the process of forward planning."

The committee would be parallel in membership to the NSC but without the president, vice president, and secretaries of state and defense. In his memo, Bundy was particularly attentive to the dynamics of small group deliberative settings. The secretaries of defense and state were excluded because as senior principals representing the two main foreign policy-related departments, "neither can speak in committee without engaging the whole weight of a great advisory department." Bundy might also have had in his mind Secretary of State Rusk's reluctance to express his views and concerns in any type of group setting, as well as Secretary of Defense McNamara's ability to voice his points of view sharply and directly, perhaps foreclosing the willingness of others to express dissent. As to the other members of the group, Bundy advised that they "should attend as individuals, not as representatives of agencies." "If a man cannot come," Bundy added, "no one automatically comes in his place."[40] On April 15, the president approved the creation of what was now named the "NSC Standing Group," and its first meeting was held the next day.[41] But it too proved ineffective; as Bromley Smith observes, "As once before, the Group meetings declined in number and its work was taken over by informal ad hoc committees."[42]

Although the effectiveness of the procedures and structures that Bundy successfully urged upon Kennedy cannot be assessed given the short time span until Kennedy's assassination, they do indicate efforts on Bundy's part that recognized Kennedy's collegial deliberative preferences. At the same time, they were cognizant of the deficiencies that had been manifested and attempted to insert more organized and orderly correctives. Bundy especially appears to have had in mind a structure that would combine some of the functions of the Eisenhower-era Planning Board and OCB but without what he and others in the Kennedy administration perceived as their excessive formalism.

But there were two issues that were potentially problematic. While Bundy served as an able critic of process and procedure, he did not recognize the impact of his own role in the process, especially serving as an honest broker in deliberations rather than as just another advocate at the table. Bundy also did not successfully come to terms with the relationship of the NSC staff to those in other departments and agencies. He thought that planning work could be undertaken without an extensive staff of his own. Yet, archival evidence indicates that his own staff began increasingly to provide the background papers, including the outline and analysis of policy options and recommended courses of action that were then presented to the Standing Group.[43]

III. Policy: Process, Role, and Outcome

The two most significant national security decisions of the Kennedy presidency—the Bay of Pigs invasion and the Cuban missile crisis—are especially revealing about Bundy's role as an honest broker in internal deliberations. Here the departure from his predecessors under Eisenhower is most clear. He is at times clearly a policy advocate. But each episode also reveals even a Bundy, at points, cognizant about the need for a broker role as deliberations unfold.

THE BAY OF PIGS FIASCO

The downside of the changes in the NSC planning system and Bundy's role as NSC advisor quickly became apparent in April 1961 with the Bay of Pigs invasion fiasco. Designed as an anti-Castro Cuban invasion force that would precipitate a mass uprising in Cuba and the installation of a provisional anti-Castro government, the effort proved a complete failure.

A preinvasion attack on Castro's air force, crucial to the success of the plan, failed—Castro was prepared for, if not tipped off about, what would transpire. In the original plan, U.S. planes were assigned the mission.[44] However, in an effort to conceal U.S. involvement (at President Kennedy's explicit direction), unmarked and obsolete World War II vintage B-26s were used, and they proved ineffectual against Castro's superior air power and his ability to conceal his planes from attack. A planned second air attack was canceled (again under Kennedy's direction), since it might reveal U.S. involvement and endanger relations with Latin American and European powers as well as possibly sparking a Soviet response. A brigade of 1,400 anti-Castro Cuban exiles—who had been training in Guatemala—succeeded in landing, but they were quickly overpowered by Castro's army and bombings by his air force. On the first day, two of four supply ships were sunk, the other two fled away. By the second day, the brigade was surrounded by over 20,000 of Castro's troops. By the third day, the remaining 1,200 were captured and imprisoned. Their escape was also compromised by a recent White House decision to move the landing site from a spot near the city of Trinidad, which was nearer the Escambray Mountains where they were to conduct guerilla operations. Kennedy and his advisers feared the Trinidad site would attract too much attention. Unfortunately, the Bay of Pigs site was eighty miles from the Escambray and surrounded by swampy terrain, making escape more difficult.[45] The Bay of Pigs invasion is commonly cited as a textbook case of a presidential decision-making fiasco.

One interpretation of the episode—and it was one that Bundy held[46]—puts the blame on the Eisenhower presidency and the failure of the new Kennedy administration to have the will, fortitude, and wisdom to stop a flawed but ongoing plan so early in a new presidency. Yet that interpretation ignores where Eisenhower himself stood on the plan. The CIA proposal was developed in 1959 and came before Eisenhower in the summer of 1960. According to Goodpaster, Eisenhower saw it only as a "contingency" if Castro's regime collapsed or was overthrown. The concept was "to create a Cuban military unit" that could become "the core of a post-Fidel Cuban army." It was "not to invade Cuba. No invasion, no provocations." After Richard Bissell, head of the CIA's directorate of plans, briefed Eisenhower, Goodpaster warned him, "Mr. President if you don't watch it, that plan will take on legs of its own." "Not while I am president," Ike replied.[47]

Of course Eisenhower's remaining tenure in office was short. And his successor had boxed himself in during the 1960 campaign by vowing to be more aggressive toward the Castro regime. When the CIA plan was presented to Kennedy, the predicate of a Cuban revolt *beforehand* was apparently and conveniently dropped by the CIA briefers. Other alterations by the new administration further weakened its possibilities for success.

This was not simply acquiescence to a precooked CIA plan. As the documents in the *Cuba, 1961–1962* volume of the *Foreign Relations of the United States* indicate, there was significant evolution in the plan over the first three months of the new administration. Moreover, it was an evolution marked by a series of high-level meetings, as well as significant "tasking" for alterations in the plan by the Pentagon, the JCS, the State Department, and others. Most notable were Kennedy's efforts to reduce direct U.S. involvement. In a meeting of the principals on February 8, 1961, Kennedy, "pressed for alternatives to a full-fledged 'invasion,' supported by U.S. planes, ships and supplies."[48] But it was Kennedy, not Bundy, who had "pressed."

In a memo to Kennedy on March 15, 1961, a month before the invasion, Bundy emphasized the need to remove Castro's air force as a critical part of plan. Bundy recommended one air strike by six to eight B-26s "some time before the invasion." Kennedy eventually doubled the number: one air strike two days before the invasion and the other the morning of it.[49] The first strike proved unsuccessful and Kennedy decided to call off the second air strike but not the invasion. It was a political and not a military decision.

The decision to invade and the logistics surrounding it were not done in haste. Although there was some pressure to consider an invasion before June 1961, when it was thought that Castro's air force and air defenses would be much stronger, some eighty days passed between the briefing Bissell gave Kennedy on the plan eight days after his inauguration and the April 17 invasion. Although planning was kept in strict secrecy, Kennedy convened an ad hoc group of civilian and military advisers who held numerous meetings on the planned invasion. Those analyzing their deliberations have come up with a number of explanations for failure, including Irving Janis's emphasis on the presence of "groupthink," Theodore Sorensen's on a communications gap between the president's military and civilian advisers and the dangers of such a major effort so early in a new presidency, and Arthur Schlesinger Jr.'s on the near unanimity of Kennedy's senior advisers—many of whom, in the CIA and military, Kennedy did not know—as well as excessive secrecy that blocked needed challenges to the CIA plan from experts with different views.[50]

But what filters through most accounts is how faulty were the assumptions underlying key facets of the planned invasion. Irving Janis details six major assumptions that led to miscalculation:

1. "No one will know that the United States was responsible for the invasion."
2. "The Cuban air force is so ineffectual that it can be knocked out completely."
3. The anti-Castro brigade has "high morale" and will carry out the invasion without U.S. ground troops.
4. Castro's army "is so weak" that the "brigade will be able to establish a well-protected beachhead."
5. The invasion will set off "sabotage by the Cuban underground and armed uprisings," probably leading to the "toppling of the Castro regime."
6. If the brigade does not succeed, it can retreat to the Escambray and reinforce anti-Castro guerilla forces.[51]

Janis's attribution of decision failure to groupthink is in part correct. There were signs of "concurrence-seeking": uncritical thinking, group cohesiveness that led to premature closure on the invasion plan, failure to adequately assess the plan and probe its assumptions, and an overly optimistic assessment of possible outcomes. But also problematic were broader organizational processes that might have prevented the pathologies of small-group deliberations from emerging. As Theodore Sorensen later recalled, "the new administration had not yet fully organized itself for crisis planning." In particular, Kennedy "had not yet geared the decision-making process to fulfill his own needs, to isolate the points of no return, to make certain he was fully informed before they passed, and to prevent alternatives from being presented to him too late to start anew." Organizational difficulties, in turn, affected the abilities of participants: "only the CIA and the Joint Chiefs had an opportunity to study and ponder the details of the plan." Memoranda detailing the plan and other written materials, according to Sorensen, "were distributed at the beginning of each session and collected at the end, making virtually impossible any systematic criticism or alternatives."[52] According to Gen. Maxwell Taylor, who was charged by the president with conducting a postmortem study of the episode's deliberative failures, meetings "were held without a prepared agenda. . . . No records were kept of meetings. . . . Hence there was always doubt in the minds of participants in the planning as to where the plan stood at any given moment."[53]

BAY OF PIGS: A NEED FOR BROKERAGE

Yet the decision making leading up to the ill-fated invasion was more fluid and open than either groupthink or broader organizational dysfunction might suggest. Individual actors—and how they defined their roles—mattered in the process. Their deliberations were consequential. As General Taylor later noted, key participants were eager "to carry it through and to obtain approval"; moreover they "*accepted* restrictions on their operations without explaining their implications clearly to the President and the senior officials."[54] In his testimony before Taylor's committee, Bundy especially singled out "military planners" who "became *advocates* rather than *impartial evaluators*." More generally, "many people were reticent in their representations to the President."[55]

Problems stemming from the absence of honest brokerage on Bundy's part must also be factored in. As Taylor's and Bundy's assessments indicate, brokerage was called for: it is precisely directed at altering the conditions and behaviors they single out. So too with the problematic assumptions that Janis notes. Honest brokerage seems especially directed at breaking the hold of several of the central tendencies conducive to groupthink: the illusion of unanimity, suppression of personal doubts, and the presence of mind-guards and an unbalanced playing field among advisers.

Moreover, as Janis observes, "In retrospect, the president's advisers could see that even as they first began to debate the plan, *sufficient information was available* to indicate that their assumptions were much too shaky."[56] And it is precisely an honest broker's chief role to ensure that such information is available and brought forward. Moreover, as Janis notes, that information might have corrected false assumptions, "if at the group meetings they had been more critical and probing in fulfilling their advisory role."[57] But again, "critical and probing" during meetings seems central to the honest broker's tasks.

Bundy largely failed at those brokerage responsibilities. But what is also of special interest is that brokerage was not wholly absent, at least at the early stages. On February 3, Bundy called Rusk and discussed the diverging views about the merits of the invasion plan:

[Bundy] said the Pres has been saying re Cuba that he has the feeling *he has heard different arguments* from different kinds of people and he wonders if [Adolph] Berle [head of the administration's Latin American policy task force] is going to be involved in that kind of problem and wants him to if it is all right with the Sec [Rusk]. The Sec said yes—he is in charge of the total Latin American task force . . . B[undy] said if there is a serious difference of view he would like the people to come over and argue with him. R[usk] confirmed that Berle is fully informed. B said he got an extremely instructive lecture from Mann and there is a divergence of his view and the Agency's [CIA] view. *If there is a real divergence it will help Mann's view to have it argued out direct with the Pres.* R is not concerned as [Assistant Secretary of State Thomas] Mann's view is Berle's . . . B said it may be important given the level of that feeling—*the Pres is ready to listen*—otherwise he is assuming it is going all right.[58]

On February 8, Bundy alerted Kennedy that "there is a divergence of view between State on the one hand and CIA and Defense on the other. Defense and CIA now feel quite enthusiastic about the invasion from Guatemala—at the worst they think the invaders would get into the mountains, and at the best they think they might get a full-fledged civil war in which we could then back the anti-Castro forces openly. State Department takes a much cooler view." Moreover, Bundy noted, "This divergence of view has not been openly and plainly considered in recent task force discussions, as I understand it."[59]

Bundy's efforts continued, at least for awhile. On February 18, 1961, Bundy presented Kennedy with two divergent position papers on what to do about Cuba: one by Richard Bissell, the architect of the military invasion plan, and the other by Thomas Mann, the assistant secretary of state for Inter-American affairs, who was a critic of the CIA's proposals. As Bundy notes in his cover memo: "Here, in sharp form, are the issues on Cuba. Bissell and Mann are the real antagonists at the staff level." Also, Bundy placed Bissell's memo on top of Mann's: "Since I think you lean to Mann's view." Brokerage was thus present both in alerting Kennedy to the presence of divergent views as well as making sure that the president was first presented with an option paper that, at least in Bundy's mind, ran against Kennedy's inclinations.

But at the same time, in that very cover memo, Bundy also offered his own take and a possible resolution: creation of a government in exile and a trade embargo against Castro—in part embracing some of Mann's sugges-tions—then at some future point pursuit of Bissell's military options under "the color of civil war."[60] Advocacy quickly reared its head. But a review of dissenting views did not occur. Mann later said that his memo "was like a stone falling in water."[61] Although Bundy's suggestions were not followed, Kennedy, apparently hewing to his own sense of personal caution, cut down Bissell's plan so that direct U.S. involvement was (seemingly) not so appar-ent. But it was a move that ultimately would make the invasion's success much less likely.

As the deliberative process continued to unfold, others still had concerns. However, Bundy was not the broker who would bring them to the table. At a crucial meeting on April 4, Sen. J. William Fulbright (D-AR) strongly op-posed the plan; lesser reservations were expressed by Rusk. However, others with a variety of concerns acquiesced. Most notably, Mann, whom Bundy undoubtedly knew had very deep reservations, ended up joining with the others in supporting the plan: "As everybody present expressed support, I did the same."[62] Bundy's own initial concerns about the operation evaporated. Perhaps it was group pressure or perhaps he was lulled into a false sense of security by the arguments and stature of Richard Bissell, its chief proponent. Bissell, after all, had been Bundy's mentor: he had taught him economics at Yale and after the war had brought him into the planning operations for the Marshall Plan.

In February 1961, Bundy also missed an opportunity to present before the president the rather considerable reservations that the military had about the CIA's plan. A special committee, led by Brig. Gen. David Gray, had been constituted to study the invasion plan, and he reported to the Joint Chiefs that it had a "fair chance" for success, which Gray defined as about 30 percent.[63] After reviewing Gray's report, the Joint Chiefs offered "tepid ap-proval," according to one account. Gen. David Shoup, commandant of the Marine Corps, was especially skeptical about the small size of the invasion force and its training. Adm. Arleigh Burke, chief of naval operations, felt the plan was "weak" and "sloppy," but gave his approval nonetheless. While this internal dissent might have provoked some caution at the White House, it did not: on February 8, Bundy informed Kennedy that the Pentagon and the CIA were enthusiastic, and he argued that the invasion would likely spark an insurrection against Castro.[64]

After the failed invasion, Bundy continued to maintain that the Joint Chiefs favored the plan in a memorandum to Gen. Maxwell Taylor, as part of the latter's postmortem study. According to Bundy, "it was clearly understood that they [the Joint Chiefs] approved the plan and favored the operation on this revised basis. I base this statement upon the fact that the President repeatedly asked for the opinion of representatives of the Defense Department including members of the Joint Chiefs, and was invariably informed that the Defense Department favored the operation. I do not think this was merely a matter of 'concurrence by attendance.' The military certainly wanted the operation to proceed."[65] However, in Taylor's view, the Joint Chiefs' "defense was that it had been impossible to follow the development of the Cuban plan because of the way matters were conducted . . . the Joint Chiefs of Staff were in a position of looking over the shoulders of the officials of the CIA, trying to keep abreast of the status of the plan but apparently unable to react in time to be able to apply effective influence in its shaping."[66] Had Bundy been a broker willing to convey the JCS's reservations, Kennedy might not have ordered the invasion. Indeed, Kennedy blamed both the CIA and the military for the failed effort. With respect to the latter, as he told journalist Ben Bradlee, "The first advice I am going to give my successor is to watch the generals and to avoid feeling that just because they are military men their opinions on military matters were worth a damn."[67]

Other evidence also points to Bundy's advocacy as a problem. Marcus Raskin, a former congressional aide who joined the NSC staff in April 1961, suggested to Bundy that the White House consider a Brazilian offer to broker a deal with Cuba. "Oh, no," Bundy told him, "It'll take just one detachment and [Castro will] be out of there."[68] Raskin quickly found himself frozen out. During a postinvasion staff meeting, Bundy walked in and told the group, "Well I guess Che learned more from Guatemala than we did." (Che Guevara had been in that country during the CIA-led overthrow of the Arbenz government in 1954.) Raskin then asked, "What have we learned from Cuba?" The room got silent, and Bromley Smith, the NSC executive secretary, remarked, "There should be no recriminations. There must be loyalty." Later that day, Raskin got a call from a Bundy aide who told him, "Mac would appreciate it very much if you did not go to any more staff meetings." In terms of his effectiveness, Raksin later recalled, "I was done after two days."[69]

Other potential critics were also frozen out once Bundy felt that Kennedy was prepared to go forward with the revised invasion plan. At one breakfast meeting shortly before the invasion, Richard Goodwin, a close aide to JFK, warned Bundy that even if the invasion were successful and a provisional government set up, the U.S. would be asked to intervene, "And if we agree it'll be a massacre. . . . We'll have to fight house-to-house in Havana." Bundy replied, "Listen, Dick, I have a good idea. Why don't you go over to see Rusk." According to Bird, "Only afterwards did Goodwin realize that Bundy had shunted him out of the way," knowing that Rusk "had no inclination to change the president's mind."[70]

In fact, it would not have been too difficult a task for Bundy to have acted more robustly as an honest broker and taken steps to reveal the miscalculations in the invasion plan. Kennedy seems at times a bit dodgy in his support of plan—especially, as Janis notes—of the assumption that it would lead to a wider uprising.[71] Kennedy was particularly concerned that U.S involvement go undetected, yet the absence of strong support by the JCS for the plan went largely unexplored at the presidential level.

Interestingly, early on Kennedy had fundamental questions about the planned invasion. In a February 4, 1961, memo, for example, Kennedy told Bundy,

> It is my understanding that there is a sharp difference of opinion between the defense [department and] CIA on what we should do about Cuba . . . Can you find out if the differences of view have been settled, or if they continue. I believe we should have an opportunity to have them placed before me and have them argued out again. Would you let me know right away on this.[72]

The next day, Kennedy raised the issue again with Bundy:

> Has the policy for Cuba been coordinated between Defense, CIA (Bissell) and Man[n] and Berle? Have we determined what we are going to do about Cuba. What approaches we are going to make to Latin American governments on the matter. If there is a difference of opinion between the agencies I think they should be brought to my attention.[73]

On February 8, Kennedy told his advisers that he wanted "alternatives to a full-fledged invasion, supported by U.S. planes, ships and supplies."[74]

Kennedy's queries indicate not only his unsettled mind about the invasion plan, but it was also an invitation for Bundy to serve as broker of a troubled decision process. There were *some* efforts: on February 8, as we saw, Bundy confirmed JFK's sense that there were differences of opinions, and on February 18, he forwarded the Mann and Bissell memos to him. Yet Bundy does not seem particularly robust in his brokerage, especially in pushing for a more organized examination of the invasion plan among Kennedy's advisers.

What did take place was an effort to scale back the plan and conceal direct U.S. involvement, but not one that questioned its basic assumptions. Kennedy's concerns remained. As late as March 11, he informed some of his senior aides that "he could not endorse a plan that put us in so openly, in view of the world situation. He directed the development of a plan where U.S. assistance would be less obvious and would like to meet again within the next few days."[75]

Although Bundy told Kennedy on March 15, that "I have been a skeptic about Bissell's operation," the revised plan—which sought to conceal U.S. involvement—placed them "on the edge of a good answer." In Bundy's view, "They have done a remarkable job of reframing the landing plan so as to make it unspectacular and quiet, and plausibly Cuban in its essentials."[76] But as Robert Dallek notes, as planning went forward, Kennedy "remained hesitant, and even a little distraught about what to do." According to Dallek, Kennedy was especially distressed about Adm. Arleigh Burke's assertion that "the plan was dependent on a general uprising in Cuba, and that the entire operation would fail without such an uprising."[77]

Revelations about imperfections in the invasion plan might have tilted Kennedy's calculations of the political costs away from appearing to be weak on Cuba and toward an assessment of the political repercussions of a failed invasion and what would happen—and did happen—to Soviet-Cuban relations. Specific assumptions might also have been easily challenged. As Janis notes, the presumption that Castro's army was weak was "directly contrary" to the reports of experts in the State Department and in British intelligence.[78] The CIA "had no intelligence that the landing would touch off widespread revolt." Nor had its intelligence branch "been asked to estimate the chances of an invasion being supported by the resistance movement or by popular uprisings behind the lines." Experts on the Cuban desk of the State Department, "who kept a daily surveillance of political activities in Cuba," also were not asked for their judgments.[79]

Some Kennedy aides had reservations. A number of memoranda, critical of the invasion plan, from Arthur Schlesinger Jr. to Kennedy can be found in the State Department's *Foreign Relations of the United States* volume dealing with Cuba in 1961.[80] Rusk was also a potential critic—and indeed a very powerful one had he chosen to voice his concerns. In meetings at the State Department, according to Roger Hilsman, director of State's intelligence and research staff, Rusk "asked penetrating questions that frequently caused us to reexamine our position." But at the White House, Rusk's demeanor was different; he failed to press his concerns.[81] Rusk and Schlesinger also met privately a week before the invasion: "Rusk, surprisingly offered no arguments against Schlesinger's objections. He said he had been waiting for some time to draw up a balance sheet of the pros and cons."[82] In his memoirs, Rusk acknowledges that he had reservations about the plan: it violated international law and was unlikely to spawn a popular uprising. Rusk, who had been chief of war plans in the China-Burma-India theater during World War II, also thought the invasion force was too small and "did not stand a snowball's chance in hell of success." Yet, while apparently telling Kennedy of some of his concerns, Rusk "never expressed my doubts explicitly in our planning sessions. . . . I wish I had pushed my reticence aside."[83]

Chester Bowles, Rusk's undersecretary of state and a strong critic of the invasion plan, sometimes attended White House meetings in Rusk's absence. But Bowles was forbidden by informal protocol from airing his concerns unless asked to do so by the president (who did not). But on March 31, Bowles sent Rusk a lengthy memo. In it, he told the secretary of state, "During your absence I have had an opportunity to become better acquainted with the proposal, and I find it profoundly disturbing." After laying out his considerable objections, Bowles advised Rusk, "If you agree after careful thought that this operation would be a mistake, I suggest that you personally and privately communicate your views to the President. It is my guess that your voice will be decisive."[84] According to Janis, "Rusk told Bowles that there was no need for any concern, that the invasion plan would be dropped in favor of a quiet little guerilla operation." Rusk may have been heartened that the more ambitious CIA plan initially proposed had been significantly scaled back. But as Janis notes, "at subsequent White House meetings he must have soon learned otherwise." Bowles's warning might have "reinforced Schlesinger's concerns" and "jolted some in Kennedy's in-group, if not Kennedy himself, to reconsider the decision."[85] But Kennedy never saw Bowles's memo—a flawed process again reared its head. According to Rusk, "I reported Bowles's opposition to Kennedy, but I did not give him the memorandum . . . since Kennedy had let us all know he didn't like having a bunch of memos shoved at him."[86]

At least one potential critic of the invasion plan, U.N. Ambassador Adlai Stevenson, was only told about it one week before it occurred. In fact, Stevenson was only informed the day after a *New York Times* article revealed the existence of secret training facilities for the Cuban exiles. Even then, Stevenson was made privy to only part of the plan and was reassured that it was largely an undertaking by exile groups.[87]

Vice President Lyndon Johnson was another potential critic of the plan but was not always part of the deliberative process. According to Rusk, LBJ "appeared skeptical about the operation, but he didn't attend many of our meetings on it; he seemed to think the invasion was a harebrained scheme that could not succeed."[88]

Concerns about the military wisdom of the plan were often forwarded to McNamara by the Joint Chiefs. As early as January 27, 1961, the JCS informed McNamara that the current plan, "does not assure the accomplishment of the above objective nor has there been detailed follow-up planning to exploit that plan if it succeeds or for any direct action that might be required if the plan is found to be inadequate."[89] On January 22, 1961, at a meeting of the principals (without the president), JCS Chairman Lyman Lemnitzer warned of the strength of Castro's forces: he "estimated that the Revolutionary Army had 32,000 [troops], the Revolutionary National Police 9,000, the Militia over 200,000. *He said that Cuba was an armed camp.* They had received more than 30,000 tons of arms and equipment over the past five or six months." At the meeting, Rusk specifically asked CIA Director Dulles about the estimated strength of the resistance then in Cuba; Dulles "said we could count on about 1,000."[90] Chief of Naval Operations Arleigh Burke was also a skeptic. On March 16, 1961, when asked by Kennedy what the chances of success were, he gave Kennedy "a probability figure of about 50 percent."[91]

Indeed, some weighty dissent broke through, but without wider consequences on Kennedy's decisions. In late March, Kennedy asked former Secretary of State Dean Acheson his views on the invasion. Acheson's response, after Kennedy explained the plan, was "Are you serious?" Told that Castro could mass 25,000 troops against the 1,500-member brigade, Acheson replied, "It doesn't take Price-Waterhouse to figure that fifteen hundred aren't as good as twenty-five thousand."[92]

Problems in how meetings were conducted might also have benefited from brokerage. At the crucial April 4 meeting that Senator Fulbright attended, Kennedy began to conduct an informal straw vote; unfortunately, the discussion got off track before it came time for Schlesinger to weigh in or for a fuller debate about Fulbright's reservations about the invasion. According to Janis, "Of course, one or more members could have prevented this bypassing by suggesting that the group discuss Senator Fulbright's arguments and requesting that Schlesinger and the others who had not been called upon be given the opportunity to state their views. But no one made such a request."[93] It was precisely the type of occasion where one of Eisenhower's NSC advisors might have made an effort to bring the discussion back on track. But it was not an effort that Bundy either recognized was needed or was willing to undertake.

In addition to Bundy's role in this episode, the Bay of Pigs deliberations are also a powerful reminder that brokerage operates in tandem with good deliberative organization. Dissent and the questioning of assumptions might have made its way to the principals, just as the policy "splits" emerged from the Planning Board to the full NSC under Eisenhower. But dissent lower down failed to come forward; poor organization worked in tandem with poor brokerage. Hilsman, for example, had heard of the invasion plan from Dulles early on, warned Rusk of the dangers, and requested he allow the Cuba experts at State to scrutinize its assumptions; Rusk told him no, "this is being too tightly held."[94] Failure here—with Bundy as a fitful broker, some of the other participants thwarted in their dissent, and a broader delibera-tive process that failed to register either their concerns or the unexamined assumptions of the proponents of an invasion—was clearly consequential. As Schlesinger concludes, "Had one senior adviser opposed the adventure, I believe that Kennedy would have canceled it."[95]

Kennedy was clearly shaken by the failure of his first major national se-curity decision. As Ernest May and Philip Zelikow note, the episode "had effects on Kennedy's style of decision making. Afterward, he recognized that he had not only listened to too few advisers but that he had given the is-sues too little time." Bundy, "whose offer to resign Kennedy rejected, also counseled that he become more deliberative." Indeed, as May and Zelikow point out, Eisenhower had subjected Kennedy "to a staff school quiz" before bestowing his support after the fiasco: "Mr. President, before you approved this plan did you have everybody in front of you debating the thing so that you could get the pros and cons yourself and then [make] the decision . . . ?" Kennedy acknowledged that he had not.[96]

But there was one major change made in the aftermath of the Bay of Pigs: the creation of the White House Situation Room in the basement of the West Wing, where Bundy would now have an office. It served as a central source for information, especially cable traffic from other departments and agencies, which Bundy had recognized as crucial for his own and the NSC staff's operations.[97] The situation room increased a needed flow of informa-tion to the NSC advisor. But it also brought with it an expansion in his role: with information comes power.

THE CUBAN MISSILE CRISIS

Although Kennedy remained reluctant to turn to NSC meetings as his chief deliberative forum or to create the more formal structures of his predecessor, which fostered a planning process that would better serve the deliberations of the principals when crisis arose, changes were made in how the Kennedy advisory system operated. Kennedy put more trusted associates in charge of intelligence and the military. Dulles and Bissell were replaced at the CIA, and Gen. Maxwell Taylor became a personal military adviser and then chairman of the Joint Chiefs. Sorensen and brother Robert Kennedy, the attorney general, were brought more directly into the deliberative process, and they were charged with making sure that the errors of the Bay of Pigs invasion were not repeated (Bobby often chaired meetings in JFK's absence during deliberations at the time of the Cuban Missile Crisis in October 1962.) By that point, what was now dubbed the Executive Committee—ExCom—was operating more effectively. Kennedy also occasionally brought in outside advisers such as Acheson, Robert Lovett, and John McCloy, the foreign policy "wise men" of the time.

In early September 1962, when increased Soviet naval shipments to Cuba were noticed and some type of military buildup was apparently occurring, Kennedy convened his chief advisers. Bundy's position was that a "turning point" would only be reached if surface-to-surface missiles, which would be capable of firing nuclear weapons, were introduced. But even then, according to Max Frankel, Bundy caught JFK's drift, and he initially felt that counter action might not be required. U.S. missiles would still outnumber those of the Soviet Union by fifteen to one, and a few more missiles in Cuba might not radically change the overall nuclear equation.[98] (The supposed "missile gap," which had played such a part in the 1960 election, was now a thing of the past.)

The crisis came to head the morning of Tuesday, October 16, when Bundy notified JFK of the missile sites detected by U-2 flights over the previous weekend. It would essentially end on Sunday, October 28, following Khrushchev's pledge to remove the missiles, Kennedy's pledge not to invade Cuba, and a secret agreement to remove outdated U.S. missiles from Turkey.

As part of Kennedy's efforts to improve his decision-making effectiveness, one might expect that Bundy would have been charged with serving as a stronger honest broker. Yet, Bundy's role in the deliberative process during the missile crisis eludes easy or simple classification. At times, he clearly is an advocate, although his advocacy ranged across the spectrum of options. On other occasions, his comments reflect brokerage: clarifying options, probing assumptions, avoiding premature closure in favor of a particular course of action.

Bundy's frequently changing position—if not advocacy—is especially evident in the early days of the crisis. At the first meeting of the principals on the morning of October 16, Bundy favored a limited air strike against just the missile sites, not destruction of Cuba's "whole air complex," which the JCS had advised.[99] Bundy also sided with Treasury Secretary Douglas Dillon, who pointed out that a quick strike might give the Soviet Union a chance to back off, and in Bundy's view, a slower effort to build NATO and OAS support might lead to pressure that the United States could live with the missiles.[100] Bundy also noted "a substantial political advantage in limiting the strike in surgical terms to the thing that is in fact the cause of action."[101] Later, again entering the debate against a broader air strike, Bundy told the group that "politically" a more limited operation "makes it as easy for him [the Soviet Union] as possible," an "enormous premium" when set "against the hazard of going after all the operational airfields becoming a kind of general war."[102] But Bundy also agreed with the point that U.S. allies might react negatively to military action, whether broader or more limited, especially if it led to a Soviet response in Berlin or elsewhere; if the Europeans can live with Soviet medium range ballistic missiles, "why can't we?"[103]

Another meeting was held at 6:30 P.M. that same day. According to Frankel, Bundy's position shifted again: he acknowledged Kennedy's warning of the "gravest consequences" if missiles were placed in Cuba, but he again reiterated a point he had made in September, before the missiles were actually discovered, that their introduction might not change the overall strategic balance.[104] Now, he made the point again, and queried McNamara about whether the missiles changed the equation: "How gravely does this change the strategic balance?" Bundy asked, rapping the table with his knuckles. McNamara replied that his personal view was "not at all." General Taylor then argued they made a great deal of difference. According to Sheldon Stern's interpretation of the meeting tapes, Bundy condescendingly countered with a laugh, "'Oh I asked the question with an awareness of the political realities."[105] But Bundy also reiterated his position in favor of a limited attack: more limited air strikes have "political advantages," and "the punishment fits the crime." If they launch air attacks against the United States (Cuban air bases still intact), "then *they* have made a general war against Cuba of it, which then becomes much more their decision."[106]

Yet it was McNamara, not Bundy, who was the person during the course of the meeting to sharpen the consideration of the options before the group, which he defined as three: 1) a political approach of negotiation; 2) the extensive air strike plan put forward by the JCS, which would "almost certainly" lead to a Soviet military response; and 3) a plan between a political and military approach that involved a naval blockade, accompanied by an announcement that there would be a U.S. attack if Cuba began any offensive actions. "Attack who?" Bundy asked. "The Soviet Union," McNamara replied.[107] Later in the meeting, Bundy also raised other possible responses, including a list of sabotage options.[108] Bundy specifically asked whether international waters should be mined or whether it would be more advisable to restrict mines to Cuban waters.[109] Kennedy pointed out that Soviet missiles in Cuba would be "just as if we suddenly began to put a major number of MRBMs in Turkey. Now that'd be goddamn dangerous, I would think." It was Bundy who informed him, "Well, we did, Mr. President."[110] After Kennedy left, but with the tape system still running, McNamara told the remaining participants that a blockade with a threat of nuclear reprisal "doesn't seem to be a very acceptable one. . . . But wait until you work on the others!" "That's right," Bundy said in agreement.[111]

After the meetings held on October 17, JFK came to the same conclusion as Bundy had the morning of the sixteenth: our allies might conclude that we should just live with the missiles. Kennedy privately taped his own observations about what had transpired so far, concluding—oddly, since Bundy had taken a number of positions—that Bundy did not favor any action and feared a Soviet response against Berlin if air strikes occurred.[112]

By Thursday the eighteenth, Bundy had shifted again, suggesting the need to bomb Cuba and offer an exchange of the outdated Jupiter missiles in Turkey. Later that evening, he shifted again, urged by his wife to choose the least violent course of action.[113] "Somewhat to everyone's surprise," according to Sorensen, "Mac Bundy urged that we not overlook the justification of no action at all." But, "everybody jumped down my throat," Bundy later recalled.[114] The next day, Bundy was back to an air strike and queasy about the success of the blockade. By now, according to Frankel, Kennedy was becoming irritated at Bundy's frequent change in position. It was "Bundy's third change of heart in three days. Having begun the week in favor of an air strike, then switched to supporting a blockade, then shifted again to favor doing nothing until the Soviets actually threatened Berlin, Bundy had decided overnight to rejoin the air attack faction. Kennedy indulged him, telling him to keep all options open."[115] But, in Sorensen's view, Kennedy was "a bit disgusted." As Bird notes, "he needed a consensus and he expected Bundy to guide the ExCom meetings toward that consensus. Instead here was Bundy prolonging the debate, giving the hawks a chance to revive their arguments on behalf of an airstrike." In Sorensen's view, "it was not one of Bundy's best weeks," and JFK "didn't like it."[116]

CUBAN MISSILE CRISIS: ADVOCACY OR BROKERAGE?

Whether Bundy strategically shifted position in order to keep Kennedy's options open or whether his own preferred course of action changed is a question that is difficult to answer. According to Stern, it is hard to categorize Bundy's role in the ExCom's deliberations: "Bundy initially urged military actions against the missiles alone because of concern about Soviet reprisals in Berlin. However, he was always eager to stand up for his personal policy choices and sometimes irritated the president. Bundy eventually supported extensive air strikes in Cuba and, in later meetings, forcefully resisted JFK's willingness to 'trade' Soviet missiles in Cuba for U.S. missiles in Turkey because he believed this choice would divide the NATO alliance and undermine American credibility."[117] According to Bird, in the first week, Bundy "managed to make the argument for all three options: diplomacy, blockade, and bombing. . . . To put it generously, he was still exploring all options; to put it less generously, Bundy was confused and deeply conflicted." For Bobby Kennedy, Bundy "did some strange flip-flops."[118]

In the view of May and Zelikow, "Bundy is unsettled during the first week about what to do, offering many questions but few answers, but seems to become stronger and more focused as the crisis develops."[119] Yet as May and Zelikow also note, "Bundy is the clarifier—the person who frames in precise language the issue that the President must decide."[120] As Bundy himself commented during one of the meetings, "Our principal problem is to try and imaginatively to think what the world would be like if we do this, and what it will be like if we don't."[121]

Frankel takes Bundy further toward brokerage: Bundy "justified his constant shift of views as a duty to keep all options before the president."[122] Frankel's interpretation is bolstered by Bundy's later recollection that the "testing" of options was an important part of the deliberative process during that first week. According to Bundy, JFK's "instant conclusion" at the outset of the crisis was "tested" by McNamara on Tuesday morning and by Bundy himself on Thursday evening; "It was also tested by the president himself."[123]

In 1988, Bundy recalled his position taking as an effort to encourage Kennedy to further explore the merits of various options:

> On Friday morning, still uneasy with the blockade, I turned in the other direction and told the president that I thought the preference he had expressed for the blockade at the end of the discussion Thursday should not become final without further review. He also heard renewed arguments that morn-

ing from the Joint Chiefs of Staff. If he was annoyed by these arguments, as Sorensen has reported, he did not show it to me, and my own belief is that in part of his mind he welcomed the prospect of a further test of options.[124]

For Bundy's part, he felt "Bobby was trying to impose a consensus where there was none. . . . I thought I was getting paid to keep the argument going and make sure we got it right."[125] Moreover, with respect to the air strike, Bundy wrote (in a 1964 memorandum for his private files) that he kept that option open under Kennedy's explicit instructions. In addition, Bundy saw the danger of Soviet escalation with both the air strike and blockade options.[126] In the end, Bundy cast his lot with the blockade as the less provocative course of action.[127]

Based on his careful listening to the tapes made of ExCom meetings, Stern emphasizes the tension between Kennedy and Bundy and that Bundy's comments may have been more personal advocacy. The claim Bundy later made that he was a devil's advocate in order focus the discussion "simply fails to convincingly account for the compelling evidence on the tapes."[128] Stern concedes, however, that Bundy "correctly assumed that JFK did not wish to be surrounded by ciphers. He spoke his mind freely and seemed to genuinely enjoy the intellectual challenge of these high-stake discussions."[129]

But there was much advocacy nonetheless. According to Stern, Bundy "sometimes seemed to forget that *he* was not the President and his self-centered tone and repeated admonitions about what 'I myself' would do frequently strained JFK's patience."[130] While the tapes clearly show that Bundy had no reservations about challenging Kennedy, at times Bundy's comments appear to limit rather than enhance discussion. At an October 22 meeting, Kennedy emphasized to the group that all the missile bases might not be destroyed by U.S. air strikes. Bundy replied, "*Entirely true,* Mr. President. But I *don't* think the next few days is the time to talk about it." According to Stern, Kennedy "responded with unmistakable annoyance, 'Well, I know, but I want everybody to understand it, Mac, if you don't mind!'"[131]

Sometimes brokerage and advocacy seem to blend for Bundy. At a crucial meeting on October 24, Bundy clashed with Kennedy's position that the Soviet tanker *Bucharest* be allowed to pass the blockade line unchallenged. According to Bundy, "there is a *real* case to be made, which has perhaps not been presented as strongly this morning . . . as it *could* be, for *doing* it and *getting* it done." Bundy pressed the point further: "It is *important* for you to know, Mr. President, . . . that there is a *good,* substantial argument and a lot of people in the argument on the other side." Bundy then called on Assistant

Secretary of Defense Paul Nitze, who shared Bundy's position. Nitze argued for full enforcement of the blockade "against everybody, not selecting ships or the type of ships." "That's correct," Bundy added. However, Kennedy was not persuaded: "We don't want to precipitate an incident."[132] The *Bucharest* was allowed to pass unchallenged.

Bundy took a similar tack on October 27, after Khrushchev's two messages had reached Washington. The first, a more rambling and personal letter had essentially proposed the removal of missiles in exchange for a U.S. pledge not to invade Cuba—it offered a potential way out of the crisis. The second message, a public one (likely with Politburo input) came over Radio Moscow the next day. It contained additional, more controversial terms: a public "trade" of the missiles in Cuba for U.S. missiles in Turkey. Kennedy argued "strenuously for the Turkish option," according to Stern. To the president, the missiles were obsolete anyway and had been scheduled for removal. Bundy saw things quite differently, and he repeatedly and vociferously argued the danger to the NATO alliance of an explicit and essentially forced trade. The United States would be, in Bundy's view, "in real trouble . . . we *should* tell you that that's the *universal* assessment of everyone in the government that's connected with these alliance problems." But Bundy also noted they would loyally follow Kennedy if he chose otherwise: "we'll *all* join in doing this if this is the decision." [133]

Later in the meeting, Kennedy returned to a piece of the issue (bringing the missile trade before the NATO Council immediately), and Bundy again pressed his opposition. According to Stern, Kennedy "ignored Bundy's objection and changed the subject." Following a forty-five-minute absence from the ExCom meeting, Kennedy again returned to the issue. Bundy "intrepidly pointed out again" his opposition: "we have *really* to agree on the *track,* you see, Mr. President, and I think that there's a *very* substantial difference between us." According to Stern, Kennedy was willing to discuss their differences, even though his mind was made up.[134] The impasse was resolved when the Soviets, through personal mediation between Bobby Kennedy and Soviet Ambassador Anatoly Dobrynin, agreed to a more private withdrawal of the missiles in Turkey over a period of four to five months.[135] The terms were quite agreeable to Bundy and ExCom.

Even Bundy himself acknowledged flaws in the deliberative process. In discussing the air strike option, which Bundy initially supported, he notes the differences between Acheson's position of a limited air strike against just the missile sites and a much larger bombing operation that the military favored, as well as his own role as an advocate: "I know how inadequate this exploration [of the differences] was because for about twenty-four hours I was its straw boss. I was wary of the blockade . . ."[136] On Thursday, Bundy later recollected, "I reopened the question of a diplomatic course, but with no success whatever."[137]

Late Friday, while Kennedy was out campaigning for the upcoming mid-term elections, two working groups were created, at Rusk's suggestion, to further explore the blockade versus air strike options.[138] Bundy was clearly not a broker but rather, in his words, the "manager of the air-strike group."[139] However, Acheson, one of his key allies in favor of a more limited effort, bowed out from participating, and the group focused on the enlarged military plan. Late Saturday, following JFK's hasty return to Washington under the cover that he had a cold, the two options were again debated before the group with the president in attendance. McNamara presented the blockade plan, Maxwell Taylor—not Bundy—presented the air strike option. By the end of the meeting, according to May and Zelikow, Kennedy was "midway between the 'hawks and the doves'": no negotiation, a blockade coupled with the demand to remove the missiles, no immediate air strike but continued preparation if the Russians failed to comply.[140]

In the end, at a crucial point in the group's early deliberations that led to the blockade, Bundy was not an honest broker testing the merits of each of the plans. That job fell to others. As Janis observes, it was Robert Kennedy and Sorensen, "the two men whom the President trusted most," who were given the role of "intellectual watchdogs." "These two men were told to pursue relentlessly every bone of contention in order to prevent errors arising from too superficial analysis of the issues."[141] Indeed, if anyone emerged as a broker it was JFK himself. As Bundy himself later noted, based on his own listening to the tapes of the period, "The man at the dramatic center of these tapes is a man expecting and encouraging the open and honest advice of others . . ."[142]

But even here Frankel offers a cautionary warning about the presumed quality of the decision process and Bundy's role in it. Kennedy's encouragement to Bundy late the first week to keep all options open was "playacting": Kennedy had already told his brother and Sorensen to "pull the ExCom to a consensus in his absence," a consensus around the blockade option.[143] Frankel, moreover, detects further problems in the process, especially its fragmented and disorganized character: "not even the presence of the president gave the meetings structure; they became a babble of digressions and interruptions, with little regard for rank or responsibility." Between meetings team members conferred informally, but without the benefits of research staff; the deliberative circle was tightly constrained.[144] Kennedy "used the group [ExCom] to test his instincts. But most often he nudged the discussion toward consensus and endorsement of the actions he came to favor."[145]

But Bundy did play one *very* important role in the deliberative process, and here his advocacy had benefit. On Saturday morning, October 27, when Khrushchev's second, more demanding proposal became known, it was Bundy who first urged the president to ignore it and respond to the first one Khrushchev had sent. Kennedy was initially reluctant, but Bundy's view prevailed in the end. The second message demanded an explicit trade of Soviet missiles in Cuba for U.S. missiles in Turkey. Bundy argued that Khrushchev had backed off the "purely Cuban context" of the first letter, but that there was "nothing wrong with our posture in sticking to that line." Kennedy was concerned about "what he is *now* proposing." Bundy countered that Khrushchev is "in a difficult position to change it overnight, having sent *you* a personal communication." "Well let's say he has changed it, and this is his latest position," Kennedy replied. "I would answer back," Bundy replied ("testily" according to Stern's transcription of the White House tapes), "saying 'I would prefer to deal . . . with your interesting proposals of last night.'" According to Stern, "Someone egged Bundy on, whispering, 'Go for it!'"[146]

A Presidential Burden: Kennedy as His Own Broker

Lacking an organized advisory system, and without a chief of staff on the domestic side or a full-fledged honest broker in foreign and national security policy, a tremendous burden was placed on the president, which in turn had implications for the administration's policies. Numerous memoranda at the Kennedy Library illustrate Kennedy at the center of the action, at times micromanaging the White House paper flow and parceling out assignments to his aides and cabinet officials.[147] These instructions and other memos and notes to staff members clearly show Kennedy on top of the situation—issuing instructions, calling for relevant information, and demanding timely briefings. Yet they also show a president serving as his own quality control officer, monitoring closely the flow and detail of the policy-making process.

Kennedy's memos at times show his concern about weaknesses in policy processes and procedures, especially failures to inform him fully about matters that he felt required his attention. For example, in a memo to Bundy on the question of differences in how aid was provided to India and Pakistan, Kennedy wrote, "As I understand it some of the economic aid that we give to India is used to purchase military equipment while we give the military equipment directly to Pakistan." Kennedy then, perhaps somewhat impatiently, added: "Perhaps someone who is informed about all of this could talk with me sometime."[148] On the question of opposing mainland China's admission to the United Nations, the president posed a number of queries and issues to Bundy: "What is the latest word from [U.N. Ambassador Adlai] Stevenson? Do we have a strategy? Is it going to be successful? We can't permit ourselves to get beaten. If we are not going to be able to win it on this basis we better think of another one. Would you speak to me about this?"[149] With respect to a report on Cyprus, Kennedy indicated to Bundy that if the situation was as desperate as depicted, "we can not continue to rely upon our policy of hoping that the guarantor powers shoulder the principal share of the Western burden. Shouldn't we have this more carefully reviewed?"[150]

Kennedy also raised issues that an honest broker might have been directly concerned about. As we saw, his memos of February 4 and 5, 1961, as planning for the Bay of Pigs invasion was underway, raised concerns about differences of opinion and called for them to be brought to his attention and argued out.

Kennedy's perceptions of difficulties were not confined to Cuba policy, but extended to Vietnam as well. For example, on April 14, 1961, he sent the following memo to Bundy:

1. I believe that you, General Taylor and Walt Rostow were all dissatisfied with our organizational set up in Southeast Asia.
2. An example of this is a military mission going to Southeast [Asia], the purpose of which is rather vague in our minds.
3. Should we not propose to the Secretary of State a more precise organizational set up with specific missions to do the kind of job that was done by Dean Acheson?
4. Who should we get to do it?[151]

On Middle East policy, Kennedy voiced his concerns rather sharply: "I want a report from the State Department. I asked Secretary Rusk about this [*sic*], on whose idea it was for me to send the letters to the Middle Eastern Arab leaders. The reaction has been so sour I would like to know whose idea it was, what they hoped to accomplish and what they think we have now accomplished."[152]

Kennedy's memos to Bundy not only indicate a president who may have been overburdened by his desire to be the collegial center of his advisory network, they also are indicative of some degree of failure on Bundy's part to have brokered these policy matters before they reached the president's desk.

IV. The Johnson National Security Process

Bundy is the only NSC advisor, in addition to Brent Scowcroft, to serve under two presidents. While his tenure under Kennedy was longer, he served as Lyndon Johnson's NSC advisor until the end of February 1966, when he left the administration to become president of the Ford Foundation. Bundy's years under LBJ deserve as much attention as does his service during the Kennedy presidency. He was a central figure in the steps Johnson took that led to a significant U.S. military commitment in South Vietnam, as well as other foreign policy initiatives such as the dispatch of marines to the Dominican Republic in May 1965 to quell what was perceived to be a pro-Communist rebel insurgency. Andrew Preston's *The War Council* provides an excellent, book-length analysis of Bundy's role in LBJ's Vietnam decision making, and Greenstein and I offer a comparative analysis of the differences between Eisenhower's Indochina decision making in 1954 and Johnson's in 1965. The latter may be particularly useful in understanding not just the differences in policy outcome but the differences in their respective decision-making organization and processes and the differing role of their NSC advisors. Here, I will simply more briefly sketch some of the major facets of Bundy's service under Johnson, particularly in relation to the Kennedy period and Johnson's early Vietnam decision making.

As far as the decision-making context in which Bundy now operated, meetings during the Johnson period were even more disorganized than those under Kennedy. Although Eisenhower and Kennedy used different advisory arrangements, their respective participants were generally constant. For Johnson, by contrast, there was a changing cast of characters. He began by holding frequent NSC meetings, twice a month on average during his first eleven months in office, but they were short in duration and consisted largely of briefings.[153] Johnson, however, was suspicious of leaks that might emanate from a large group. From October 1964 through January 1965, no meetings of the NSC were convened, although Johnson did hold meetings with some of the principals, and it was a time of significant evaluation about what to do about the deteriorating situation in South Vietnam. In February 1965, a period in which the administration considered air strike reprisals on North Vietnam after a major Viet Cong attack against the U.S. military base at Pleiku, Johnson consulted more widely but haphazardly. From early March through May, a crucial period in which particular reprisals to attacks evolved into a pattern of continuing air strikes against North Vietnam (Operation Rolling Thunder) and the first marine battalions were introduced into South

Vietnam in what would quickly become a direct combat role for the first time, Johnson's contact was largely limited to Bundy, McNamara, and Rusk, whom he met in twelve Tuesday lunches over that three-month period. The lunches, however, were poor forums for sustained, analytic discussion. Agendas were brief, largely unstaffed, and poorly prepared; no common records were kept of proceedings, and feedback to subordinates was haphazard.[154] Assistant Secretary of State for Far Eastern Affairs William Bundy, who attended some of them and was McGeorge's brother, found them "time wasting." "Johnson would tee-off" at perceived critics; "There was a lot of blowing steam and his sense of focusing on an issue was not acute."[155] As Greenstein and I note, "Johnson's insulation from the rest of the national security community, including the JCS chief, his successive CIA directors and all second-level officials is particularly noteworthy."[156] Even as Bundy's stature grew, the NSC staff, which had enjoyed access to Kennedy, was now cut out of contact with Johnson.[157] Fewer National Security Action Memoranda were issued under Johnson than had been the case for Kennedy.[158]

More generally as Greenstein and I also note, "The Johnson policy process had some of the qualities of an unassembled jigsaw puzzle. There was much information and analysis, but nowhere within the national security apparatus were the various pieces assembled, posing the president and his aides with coherent proposals and counterproposals."[159] For his part, LBJ was willing to immerse himself in policy matters and, at least in the view of some associates, wanted an array of options placed before him. His long-time friend, Supreme Court Justice Abe Fortas, once described Johnson as a "pack rat for information."[160] According to Rusk, Johnson "never objected to people putting forward views that were contrary to his own inclinations. . . . He wanted all points of view brought forward."[161] And, "He was willing to listen to anything they had to say before the decision was made."[162]

Nor was Johnson restricted to organizational channels for information: he was an inveterate user of the telephone, calling a range of individuals, in and out of government.[163] Johnson's problem was not the absence of conflicting advice, as Kennedy had faced during the Bay of Pigs.[164] Rather, a range of advice was present but its organization into a sustained and effective process of deliberation was poor.

The Johnson process especially calls attention to the two aspects of the honest broker role: a broker concerned with the organization and quality of the process and a broker concerned with the full and fair presentation of the options, positions, and analysis of the participants in the process. Bundy, however, was largely remiss on both dimensions.

V. Bundy as NSC Advisor—Johnson

Bundy's role as NSC advisor remained a powerful one as it had been under Kennedy. Yet Bundy also adapted it to the president he served. Whereas Bundy was willing to make suggestions to Kennedy on how to improve the deliberative process, a similar effort was much rarer under Johnson. Broader changes in organization were not discussed, although Bundy would sometimes encourage efforts to clarify what had been decided (itself a symptom of problems in process) but often without follow-up or further consequence.

On the second aspect of the broker role, Bundy was not the honest broker to "assemble the pieces of the jigsaw puzzle." Nor did he consistently endeavor to pose before Johnson a coherent set of policy options and analysis of their strengths and weaknesses, as might have occurred under Cutler and the Planning Board during the Eisenhower presidency. As Greenstein and I note, Bundy often did at times bring "differences of viewpoint to Johnson's attention. But because he was also a policy adviser, in advancing his own views he sometimes failed to do justice to the views of others."[165]

According to Preston, from Kennedy's assassination through the summer of 1964, Bundy "self-consciously" limited "his role to that of an adviser. He would steer policy in a certain direction, but always the one in which Johnson himself ultimately wanted to travel." However, after the Gulf of Tonkin incidents, with Johnson more indecisive and the situation in South Vietnam deteriorating, Bundy "pressed vigorously for more drastic measures. . . . He had undergone the transformation from adviser to advocate." Starting in the fall of 1964, Bundy "began his own campaign to convince the president of the need for military escalation."[166]

On occasion, that advocacy meant stifling dissent. Early in the Kennedy administration, Bundy succeeded in marginalizing Undersecretary of State Chester Bowles.[167] He did the same with Bowles's successor, George Ball, an important critic of further escalation in South Vietnam. During 1964 on at least two occasions, according to Preston, Bundy "used the election campaign to justify the stifling of any internal opposition" on the part of Ball, telling him to keep his dissent to himself.[168] In October 1964, Ball composed a sixty-seven-page memorandum that was sharply critical of the assumptions underlying further intervention in South Vietnam. McNamara, Rusk, and Bundy met with Ball on November 7, after Election Day, to discuss the memo, but they were "dead set" against it, according to Ball, and "uninterested in the point-by-point discussion" Ball hoped to provoke. Bundy did not forward the memo to Johnson. However, on February 26, 1965,

Johnson received the memo from aide Bill Moyers (who had learned about the memo at a recent lunch with Ball). Moyers later told Ball that Johnson "found it fascinating and wanted to know why he had not read it before."[169] Ball was the most notable of dissenters, but not the only one. In Preston's extensive study of Bundy and Vietnam, he observes that "Bundy and the NSC staff moved quickly and effectively to squash dissent and limit the president's choice of action to a very narrow one of how and when, rather than whether, the United States should wage war in Vietnam."[170]

Johnson, in fact, appears to have been highly reliant on Bundy's memoranda to him, more so than Kennedy, given the sometimes restricted nature of the Johnson process. In those memos, Bundy generally set out the policy options that were expressed in the attached policy papers by others, but he also put his own spin on them and advanced his own policy views. The memos to LBJ differed from those Bundy had sent Kennedy—Bundy's covering letters to Kennedy were generally shorter in evaluation and more like an index. For Johnson, they were more extensive and often laden with emotional language likely to rouse powerful feelings. Sometimes they had a gossipy or cutting tone: Sen. Mike Mansfield (D-MT), the majority leader, exhibited a "somewhat mousey stubbornness;"[171] Sen. Joseph Clark (D-PA) was "a man who has plenty of convictions but not quite enough courage to give them full expression."[172] The press corps was gossiping, Bundy wrote Johnson, "that you are lonely in Hawkville with no beautiful doves like Roger Hilsman to keep you straight."[173]

VI. Policy: Process, Role, and Outcome—Vietnam 1965

The Johnson administration's deliberations over escalation in Vietnam in 1965 particularly illuminate Bundy's role as NSC advisor and its effects on policy deliberations and outcomes. Bundy frequently provided his own interpretation of the merits of the advice of others he forwarded to the president, as well as offering his own take on issues and sometimes acting as broker by raising hard questions. One of the most notable of Bundy's missives was what has come to be termed the "fork in the Y" memo of January 27, 1965. In it Bundy expressed his and McNamara's pessimistic assessment of the situation in South Vietnam and the inadequacies of present policy. Bundy outlined two alternatives: the use of direct military power or a track of negotiation. Acting as a broker, he stated that "both should be carefully studied and the alternative programs should be argued out before you." At the same time, Bundy outlined Rusk's position, who wanted to stick with the present course. Bundy then deprecated Rusk's view: "This would be good if it was possible. Bob and I do not think it is": in effect isolating Rusk from the two other principals.[174] Nor would Bundy put into practice the reexamination and further debate he called for. No study groups were assembled, no second-level officials brought in, no additional analysis or memos called for—Bundy's memo was it—and it is notable that the views of Johnson's two other principals reached the president through Bundy and with his gloss.

Based on an analysis of Johnson's daily appointment diary, Greenstein and I found that there is little evidence that extensive examination subsequently occurred among the principals. On January 27, the three principals—Rusk, McNamara, and Bundy (later joined by Moyers and Ball) did meet with Johnson for an hour and fifteen minutes. But as we note, "If Rusk's reservations were examined, they can have been considered only briefly and only in the restricted circle of Johnson and his top three advisers."[175] Rusk left the next day for Winston Churchill's funeral and then journeyed to Florida to recover from influenza.[176] In the interim, Johnson embarked on air strikes against North Vietnam, which very quickly evolved into a sustained bombing campaign and marked a major turning point in the war. An NSC meeting was held on February 1, which neither Rusk nor McNamara attended. The primary topic was Bundy's impending trip to South Vietnam, not policy alternatives. Bundy also told the group that no major policy changes were likely to occur as a result of his visit.[177]

But major changes did occur. At Maxwell Taylor's suggestion (Taylor was U.S. ambassador to South Vietnam at the time) Bundy was sent to Saigon in order to take a fresh look at the situation; it was a crucial point in time when Johnson was on the verge of finally carrying through on his policy of air strikes in response to Communist attacks. During Bundy's visit, the U.S. air base at Pleiku was attacked. Immediately, Bundy was in contact with Johnson's assembled advisers at the White House, and he proposed a two-step response (which had been discussed in December[178]): immediate retaliation for attacks then a graduated response of air strikes not tied to any specific attack. Johnson immediately approved the retaliatory air strike, which he had been reluctant to do on the occasion of earlier attacks.[179] Records of the meeting indicate that those in Washington were responding to impressions of Bundy and his traveling party on unfolding events and their on-the-spot advice.[180] The time for debate was over, Bundy reportedly told them.[181] Those traveling with Bundy noted how the normally staid Bundy was emotionally moved— if not a bit unhinged—when he visited the site of the attack. According to one, "it was during Pleiku that [Bundy] sort of caught religion on Vietnam." In the view of Gen. William Westmoreland, the U.S. military commander in South Vietnam, once Bundy "smelled a little gunpowder he developed a field marshal psychosis."[182] According to Vice President Hubert Humphrey, soon to be excluded from the circle of Johnson's Vietnam advisers, at Pleiku, Bundy became "an advocate."[183]

When Bundy returned to Washington, he immediately forwarded to Johnson a memorandum urging a shift to the second phase—sustained bombing. Within days, on February 13, Johnson convened his advisers and approved the new policy.[184] But Johnson was also troubled by the consequences a public signal of a shift in policy might entail, and some of his principals, McNamara most notably, began to question whether Johnson had in fact signed on to a program of sustained bombing of the North. On February 17, Bundy sent a memo to Johnson stating that "there is a deep seated need for assurance that the decision has in fact been taken. . . . McNamara repeatedly stated that he simply has to know what the policy is so that he can make his military plans and give his military orders." Bundy then noted that perhaps the problem, especially on Bundy's part, was a confusing of two questions: one was the firmness of Johnson's decision to order bombing, the other was a public declaration of a change in policy. Bundy proposed that Johnson be clear to the principals, Ambassador Taylor, and others that a change in policy had occurred, but that Johnson leave it to Rusk or the U.N. ambassador to make any public statements and that a "loud public signal of a major change" not come from the White House.[185] That neither Bundy nor McNamara (and perhaps even LBJ himself) were clear about where policy stood is troubling. Bundy as broker had untangled the confusion, but Bundy as political strategist had also proposed a pattern of concealment and downplay that would bedevil Johnson from that point until the end of his presidency.

Underlying escalation was also a peculiar shift in its logic. Whereas in 1964 a stable political situation in South Vietnam was taken as a precondition for further military effort, by early 1965 further military intervention was seen as fostering political stability. As George Ball notes in his memoirs, "it was classic bureaucratic casuistry."[186] And Bundy was one of its chief practitioners.

Bundy also played an important role in the introduction of U.S. forces in an official combat role. Once air strikes were underway from the U.S. air base at DaNang, General Westmoreland requested two marine battalions to guard the airbase, a request that was approved by Johnson on February 26 without any discussion among the principals or with civilian staff analysis (two more battalions were added over the next several weeks, and other air bases that needed guarding were added). Ostensibly in place for base security, the marine units were soon actively "patrolling": first within a ten-mile perimeter, then at thirty miles, and finally by June 1 at fifty miles.[187] The U.S. ground war in South Vietnam was under way, but with little prior deliberation.

Ambassador Taylor strongly opposed the introduction of ground forces, fearing that the South Vietnamese would slacken their efforts and the United States would be placed in an inhospitable combat setting.[188] In a late-March visit back to Washington, he thought he had an agreement to quash a new Westmoreland request for at least two U.S. divisions to be placed in the central highlands of South Vietnam. But on returning to Saigon, he found out—via JCS cable traffic—that the 173rd airborne brigade had been approved for deployment. Taylor fired off several cables, which Bundy answered in a conciliatory way. Bundy also sought to calm the waters by telling Johnson that more direct orders to Taylor "would be very explosive right now because he will not agree with many of them and he will feel that he has not been consulted." Bundy felt, however, that they could win over Taylor—at that point the most vocal critic against ground troops: "I am sure we can turn him around if we give him just a little more time to come aboard."

While his comments about Taylor indicate an NSC advisor bent on smoothing dissent (yet another Bundy function), Bundy also took on a broker role in that very same memo. Toward the end he added, "I am *not* sure that you yourself currently wish to make a firm decision to put another 10,000–15,000 combat troops in Vietnam today. As Taylor says, we were planning when he left to use the Marines already on the scene in combat roles and see how that worked. It is not clear that we now need all these additional forces."[189] In other memos, Bundy sought to clarify U.S. goals in Vietnam.[190] In late March, he urged that at an upcoming NSC meeting "it would be helpful at this point for all present to take a deep breath and listen to each other for about half a half hour in review of the situation as it now stands."[191] Notes of the NSC meeting, however, indicate that the discussion got sidetracked into why the press had become so negative; Bundy's intended brokerage did not occur.[192]

The administration was at a crucial point and at the edge of a major military commitment that would complement its new air campaign. Yet, major steps were taken without a full examination of policy alternatives, underlying assumptions, and future implications. Additional deployments were temporarily suspended but then resumed following a meeting of Taylor, McNamara, JCS Chairman Earle Wheeler, and other military commanders and civilian advisers in Honolulu on April 19 and April 20. Bundy did not attend, but the results were consequential: Taylor threw in the towel and an increase to 82,000 military personnel was recommended; they would operate from additional "coastal enclaves," and their mission now included more extensive, offensive "search and destroy" operations. Taylor later recounted in his memoirs that he felt he had been misled. He had not realized that Johnson had made up his mind on the bombing campaign and the introduction of the marine battalions, which were "only the first on the list." He was under the impression that Johnson was "exercising restraint," but "I soon sensed that, having crossed the Rubicon, [Johnson] was now off for Rome on the double."[193] The Honolulu meeting is interesting not only in its curb on Taylor but also for its dynamics. McNamara was the only principal there; many of the other participants were the military brass. As George McT. Kahin notes, Taylor faced a "Macedonian phalanx" bent on further intervention.[194]

In contrast to what Taylor confronted, Bundy accommodated a degree of dissent within his own staff. NSC aides such as Chester Cooper and James Thomson were permitted to develop internal studies dealing with a negotiated settlement, détente with North Vietnam, and nonmilitary initiatives to win over the South Vietnamese populace.[195] According to Preston, this latitude may have reflected Bundy's realization by May 1965 that sustained bombing of North Vietnam was not working. While still in favor of a U.S. commitment to South Vietnam, Bundy became more of a "soft hawk," unsure about his previous advice.[196]

In early June, the White House received a request from Westmoreland for more troops, which would bring the force level of U.S. and allied troops up to 200,000—the so called forty-four-battalion request. Through June and into July, Johnson conducted extensive discussion with his civilian and military advisers, congressional leaders, and others. Scholarly analysis is divided over how genuine were Johnson's intentions and whether and at what point his mind was made up to approve Westmoreland's request.[197] But Johnson did receive a range of advice. Again, Bundy played a crucial role. In a July 1 memo, for example, he forwarded to Johnson four key position papers, one by McNamara in favor of the troop increase, another by Ball urging negotiation and a face-saving withdrawal, a short paper by Rusk that advanced no real proposal but emphasized the stakes involved, and a fourth, by William Bundy, which urged a "middle course." As he had in the "fork in the Y" memo, Bundy summarized each but offered his own gloss: urging

Johnson to reject Ball and then move to a more narrow consideration of the McNamara and William Bundy proposals. And again, as he had done earlier, he posed a series of sharp questions (a number were prescient on the implications of further military involvement—e.g., "If we need 200 thousand men now . . . may we not need 400 thousand later?"). He also proposed a meeting of the group for a "sharpening of the issues." The meeting took place, but it was not what Bundy had hoped for. Johnson plucked ideas from each of the papers, such as sending Averill Harriman to Moscow and McNamara and JCS Chair Wheeler to Saigon to report on Westmoreland's request. Ball was assigned the job of further analysis of negotiation steps.[198] But that was the end of the process, no follow-up occurred at what would mark a major turning point in the administration's Vietnam deliberations.

Not surprisingly, McNamara's report from Saigon was favorable, and, even before he returned to Washington, Bundy outlined for Johnson steps that needed to be taken to put it into effect. The "soft hawk" had once again become a "hard hawk" and any reservations he had about more ground troops dropped away; McNamara's escalation plan, which Bundy had seen in late June as "rash to the point of folly," was now his preferred course of action.[199] He urged Johnson not "to give the *appearance* of great haste in reaching a decision" but warned that too much delay would create "too wide a gap between McNamara's return and the point of decision."[200] While in Saigon, McNamara had received a cable from his deputy, Cyrus Vance, who had met with Johnson three times, indicating that it was Johnson's "current intention" to approve Westmoreland's request.[201]

Johnson's consultations in late July, after McNamara's return, were extensive. The meetings were orchestrated and led by Johnson, with Bundy as a very secondary actor and surely no broker forcing a more effective process. On July 21, Bundy especially took on Ball's reservations and made easy work of them.[202] Bundy did ask some more probing questions—akin to Ball's concerns—at a meeting on July 22, but it occurred in the final minutes of a long session and did not generate a discussion of them.[203] Throughout the late-July consultations—which were extensive but plagued with a number of problems in terms of their quality as a deliberative exercise[204]—Bundy in no way lived up to an honest broker role. Perhaps he knew that Johnson's mind was made up? Johnson did, however, ignore advice Bundy gave him when he announced his decision on July 28. Bundy had counseled an address to Congress or a televised fireside chat. Instead, Johnson down played what had been decided and made his announcement at a midday press conference, along with the nominations of Abe Fortas to the Supreme Court and network newsman John Chancellor as head of the U.S. Information Agency. Johnson also did not fully reveal the troop levels he had in fact authorized (only an immediate increment was announced) nor did an expected call up of reserves occur. Only cryptically did the president indicate that Westmoreland would be given what troops he needed. Not stated, was Johnson's decision that the U.S. commitment had now become open-ended.[205]

BEYOND BROKERAGE AND ADVOCACY

Bundy's expansion of the role of NSC advisor beyond honest brokerage or even advocacy was also problematic at times. Bundy became a more visible public figure than his predecessors, but not always to the administration's benefit. His name appeared in the *New York Times Index* over his five-year tenure more often than his Eisenhower predecessors combined.[206] In 1965, "Operation Target: College Campus" was organized by the White House to try to win over increasing opposition to escalation; White House aide Jack Valenti and the NSC staff ran it jointly. Former Dean Bundy was eager to engage his academic colleagues on the war. He initially refused an invitation to speak at a forum on the war at Washington University in St. Louis. He accepted an invitation to debate at a teach-in in Washington, D.C., in May, but Johnson forced him to cancel the appearance at the last minute. In June, he spoke to students at Harvard and later that month appeared in a televised debate with Hans J. Morgenthau, a prominent University of Chicago professor of international relations. The forum was of Bundy's choosing—a one-on-one debate, no gaggle of academic critics at a teach-in.[207] Although Bundy technically "won" the debate, "his aggressive debating tactics came across as mean spirited," according to Preston, especially when he brought out a list of Morgenthau's past erroneous predictions. Moderator Eric Severeid even intervened, saying "this has become something of a personal confrontation." Bundy's experiences during these appearances, according to Preston, marked "a particularly sour moment" in his tenure as NSC advisor, and they "struck blows to the administration's credibility."[208] The debate did not help his relations with the president either: LBJ had not given Bundy permission to appear, was livid at his defiance, and even temporarily told aide Bill Moyers that he was going to fire Bundy.[209] Bundy's picture on the cover of *Time* and a lengthy, favorable article that week did not help matters.

Bundy's efforts with the press were also often perceived as ham-handed. He gave a highly optimistic press briefing following his return to Washington after the Pleiku incident. But the media reception hardly reflected his optimism. An editorial in the *Washington Post* criticized Bundy's attempts to "sidetrack" reporters' questions, and saw it as part of a recent pattern in which the administration had "deliberately sought to misinform the public."[210] But throughout his tenure as NSC advisor, Bundy developed close relations with the press, particularly such luminaries as the columnists Walter Lippmann and Joseph Alsop, Ben Bradlee of *Newsweek* and the *Washington Post,* and reporters from the *New York Times.*[211] These contacts were in marked departure from his press-shy Eisenhower predecessors (recall Cutler's dealings with Alsop), but they set a foundation that would be followed by his successors. Johnson, however, kept a wary eye on Bundy's dealings with reporters and had him report to him personally on any press contacts. On one occasion, Johnson refused permission for Bundy to appear on NBC's *Meet the Press;* Bundy was disappointed, telling Johnson, "I admit I enjoy this kind of thing."[212]

Although Bundy was usually not directly involved in politics, there were occasions when he did so. Over the summer of 1964, Johnson had used him as a political conduit to Robert Kennedy in an effort to persuade him to take his name out of consideration as Johnson's running mate. Bundy also drafted a memo to Johnson laying out a strategy for an electoral appeal to the Eastern Establishment wing of the Republican Party.[213]

Bundy also made forays into public diplomacy. During the Dominican crisis in May 1965 (which involved the introduction of 24,000 U.S. troops), Bundy was dispatched by Johnson to negotiate the establishment of a coalition government once a cease-fire had been achieved.[214] According to Rusk, "I was skeptical about McGeorge Bundy's selection to this team, as I would have been about any member of the White House, because his presence involved the White House directly in the outcome."[215] Part of Johnson's motivation may have been to get Bundy out of town when he was scheduled to appear at one of the academic teach-ins. But Bundy's experience in the Dominican Republic was also rocky. According to Preston, it began to show the waning of his influence with Johnson, who preferred to deal the State Department's representative on Bundy's mission, Thomas Mann. The deal that Bundy thought he made with the contending parties also collapsed— Bundy had been warned by Mann of its problems and Rusk had reservations. According to Preston, "the Dominican crisis marked the beginning of the end of Bundy's tenure as Johnson's Special Assistant."[216] Nor had Bundy's demeanor been especially crisp in the other mission he performed for Johnson during this period: the fact-finding trip to Saigon at the time of the Pleiku incident. Bundy's reaction—sustained bombing—in effect sent the Johnson war train down the tracks. In Preston's view, Bundy and his staff "were largely responsible for the ultimate decision to wage war instead of peace."[217]

VII. IMPLICATIONS

Bundy's tenure as NSC advisor under both Kennedy and Johnson presents a mixed picture. There was a clear change from the Eisenhower years, but not for the better. The power of the NSC advisor clearly rose, but it was not equally matched by effective performance. Nor was the job of NSC advisor generally operative within a decision-making system that facilitated that performance.

THE NSC ADVISOR'S ROLE EXPECTATIONS AND HONEST BROKERAGE

Bundy's initial expectations as NSC advisor are largely reactive. Both he and Kennedy rejected the formal structure that Eisenhower and Cutler had set up—it was ossified and overly bureaucratic in their view. Their initial rhetoric—and it may only have been rhetoric—signaled a return to State Department dominance of the policy process. Given Rusk's operating style, however, that was not to be. Bundy was dismissive of the need for policy planning, and the interagency vetting process, now much more informal, was weak if not haphazard at times. Dismantlement of the Eisenhower-era system, coupled with an action rather planning-oriented focus plus Rusk's reticence, strengthened the role of Bundy and his staff. Although not by deliberate design, for better or worse, they became more clearly and directly a presidential instrument rather than one serving the needs of a deliberative process. It would mark an important watershed in the development of the role of NSC advisor.

Bundy was an advocate at times, and here we see a marked departure from his predecessors. In the deliberations over the Bay of Pigs invasion and the Cuban missile crisis, Bundy was one among a number of vocal actors. At times, his efforts appear guided by brokerage, especially in the later days of the Cuban missile crisis debate (and often to Kennedy's irritation). On other occasions, he seems merely to be one among many at the table expressing his own policy views. Nor were those views always consistent and firmly grounded: during the first week of the missile crisis Bundy appears all over the lot in terms of what course of action to take. During the Bay of Pigs, it was Bundy who falsely reassured Kennedy that the military thought the invasion plan would succeed. By the time of the missile crisis, in many ways, McNamara had a more decisive impact in sharpening and "righting" the process, as did Kennedy himself.

At the same time, while the abolishment of the Eisenhower system fit Kennedy's predilections, Bundy came to recognize the problems that ensued.

At times he embraced the second side of the honest broker role: concern for the organizational quality of the deliberative process. Adoption of his recommendations, however, was mixed at best and late in coming. Some of Bundy's actions were also ill-advised, particularly the weakened briefing role of the CIA and Bundy's own increasing role as a conduit for intelligence matters. As Goodpaster later recollected, "raw intelligence . . . should not come to the president. You can give the president too much . . . not even McGeorge Bundy, as brilliant as he is, can do a job of analysis for the staff over in CIA and DIA."[218]

EVOLUTION OF THE NSC ADVISOR'S ROLE OVER TIME

Attention to Bundy's tenure as NSC advisor is of particular import given that he served under two, often very different presidents. Bundy adjusted his role to Johnson; his memoranda were both more substantive in their policy analysis and recommendations, and they were more personal in tone than had been the case with JFK. At one level this provides important and positive insight on the emphasis on *role,* which structures the argument of this book. Even though the actor—Bundy—remained a constant, his activity and behavior were subject to change. Malleability of role, at the level of the individual, has largely been unexplored, yet clearly it is of great importance.

At another level, however, the substance of that change in role raises a caution. Bundy's "adjustments" may have fit Johnson's needs too closely, offering too much emotional reassurance and interjecting too much political calculation. Bundy raised concerns at times about what needed to be decided and whether something had been decided—facets of the broker role—but there was less concern raised about the overall quality of the problematic Johnson process than had been the case under Kennedy. Where advice by Bundy was tendered on the need to have options more fully explored, there was little follow-up. As one of the three main principals in the restricted Johnson inner circle, Bundy's power as an advocate was greater and had more impact. Yet it did not seem to have more positive effect on Johnson's decision making.

PRESIDENTIAL DECISION-MAKING NEEDS, PRESIDENTIAL ROLE EXPECTATIONS

Bundy's service under both Kennedy and Johnson is revealing. Who is president clearly matters. Kennedy was attentive to the substance of foreign policy issues, as his central role in the debate during the Cuban missile crisis attests. The deliberative process matched his predilections: a fast-paced collegial system. Bundy as NSC advisor largely fit Kennedy's needs: a smart, close, and trusted aide there to look out for the president's interests.

One might argue that the Kennedy experience belies the notion that the NSC advisor should act as an honest broker. John F. Kennedy was his own honest broker it might be claimed, one who needed a loyal and effective agent if not enforcer as NSC advisor. It is in part true, moreover, that Kennedy did at times serve as his own honest broker. Yet, in response, it should be noted that the presence of *presidential* brokerage need not exclude brokerage on the part of the NSC advisor. There were occasions when even Eisenhower, operating in a brokerage-rich environment, stepped into that role. But more to the point, even an astute Kennedy needed more. He clearly was no broker during the Bay of Pigs: the process moved far too quickly and fitfully, deliberative forums were flawed, and available information that the plan was highly problematic went unexplored. Exclusively presidential brokerage is also likely to be impaired if problems exist deeper in the policy process and fail to rise to a presidential level of attention—recall the false reassurances given Kennedy about the military's estimate of the success of the invasion plan.

Brokerage by the president alone might also be difficult, especially if a president is set on a course of action. Even during the "success case" of the missile crisis, some accounts indicate that Kennedy was less a broker than a president too eager for consensus and closure and too prone to accept a public trade of missiles sites as a way out of the crisis, an option that Bundy strenuously opposed. It was Bundy, moreover, who pressed Kennedy to respond to Khrushchev's first rather than second message. Finally, Kennedy's efforts put considerable burden on his time and attention; as we saw, he often exhibited considerable pique in having to sort out what was placed before him. Indeed, Kennedy himself recognized—at least in a general sense—that he needed good staff work. As he noted in a BBC interview in April 1961, the NSC staff should "make sure that these important matters are brought here in a way which permits a clear decision after alternatives have been presented," rather than providing "prearranged agreement."[219]

The Bundy case study more broadly provides evidence why a simple and close fit of the NSC's advisor's role with presidential needs is not fully wise. Not only was additional brokerage needed in the deliberations of Kennedy's team, Bundy's struggle for a better process of decision making is notable. Kennedy's work ways, in fact, were the initial object of Bundy's concern: more time with the president, more regularity of meetings. As time wore on, Bundy's attention turned to other problems of process, yet it was an area that Kennedy either resisted or was unconcerned about. Bromley Smith is notable on this last point:

> We used several devices to try to coordinate the White House. We worked toward some kind of a system for President Kennedy, even though he didn't think he needed much of a system. We had to have more than he really wanted in order to the job he wanted done.[220]

Under Johnson, organization and process were even worse; there was no Bay of Pigs to send an early signal of needed change. The mixed signals in the Gulf of Tonkin attacks might have served as such, but they did not. Johnson, who had less foreign policy experience or interest than Kennedy, was more beholden to his advisers. Honest brokerage was clearly needed, yet it often was not provided.

While needed, would Johnson have tolerated more brokerage? He clearly paid attention to Bundy's advocacy, but there are signs he might have been more receptive to brokerage. He was an impulsive decision maker at times and could be domineering. Yet he was also cautious. The course he chose to take on Vietnam (and how he got there) notwithstanding, Johnson often expressed deep worry about committing U.S. forces. He also paid deep attention to what was brought before him or argued about in his presence. "Johnson, more so than anyone I have worked with, wanted to hear different points of view," his longtime friend and confidant Abe Fortas recollected. Johnson's mind "was a perfectly fantastic machine. . . . He was a pack rat for information and more particularly for points of view."[221] Others, such as Rusk, shared that assessment.

Other aspects of Johnson's decision-making style also called for brokerage. He was dependent on the advice of his key advisers, perhaps too dependent. As Rusk observes, "He was prepared to make a decision." Yet he valued consensus before it reached the presidential level: "He was impatient about the inability or the unwillingness of senior colleagues to agree among themselves. He disliked the role of refereeing among senior colleagues." As a result, according to Rusk, a "special effort" was made to "reach a common conclusion." Johnson might not accept it: "He had views of his own, but he wanted to have the best effort of his colleagues invested in the problem before the President himself came to a final result."[222] "Consensus," "common conclusion," prior "best effort," and a president disinclined to personally referee, however, suggest a policy process likely to benefit from the reality testing provided by an honest broker.

OTHER IMPLICATIONS

Whatever their problems appear to have been in hindsight, Bundy's efforts garnered little resentment among his colleagues. He was often perceived as intellectually and personally confident. But he managed to achieve largely cordial relations with those with whom he worked. Even George Ball had good things to say about Bundy: he found him helpful at times, neither arrogant nor a bureaucratic in-fighter.[223] Rusk was of similar mind. In his memoirs, Rusk observes that no one was "more competent than Bundy," and he was a "man of great ability." Moreover, "In our relationship he always dealt honorably with me, and I never detected any backbiting, behind-the-scenes maneuvering, or trying to influence decisions without my knowledge."[224] As we shall see, few of Rusk's successors were able to say the same of the NSC advisor during their tenure. Bundy was powerful, but any frictions may have been smoothed over by Bundy's general agreement with and respect for McNamara, Rusk's own reticence and avoidance of bureaucratic in-fighting, and the close bonds Bundy was able to establish—albeit it in different ways—with both Kennedy and Johnson.

One general lesson of Bundy's tenure under both presidents is that serving as an honest broker stands in uneasy tension with other aspects of the post-Eisenhower role of NSC advisor, especially policy advocacy. Bundy's tenure also begins to reveal tensions with other activities that his successors grappled with: public visibility, attention to political matters, and involvement in diplomatic and other implementation efforts. With respect to the latter, would the decisions made at the time of the Pleiku attacks and the quick but unexamined leap to the introduction of combat battalions have occurred if Bundy had been in Washington rather than Saigon? Nor were Bundy's efforts in the Dominican Republic all that successful; Johnson eventually turned to the State Department's representatives rather than Bundy for guidance toward a solution.

With respect to the NSC advisor as a public figure, we see here another marked departure from the Eisenhower years. Bundy was clearly a more effective spokesperson in the Johnson years than the more placid Rusk. Yet his efforts sometimes were overbearing and aroused controversy. They also began to grate on a media-attentive and distrustful Johnson.

Another lesson is the importance of honest brokerage not just in the give-and-take of discussion and deliberation but also as directed to the organization and quality of the broader system or process in which deliberations are set. Kennedy and Johnson each needed help on both fronts.

Finally, there is the issue of fit with individual presidents. Kennedy was more attentive to how information and advice came to him; advocacy could be balanced against the advice of others. Johnson is a case study in how too close a fit can contribute to decision-making problems and flawed policy outcomes. Yet even the closely fit Johnson system could change: his decision in March 1968 to bar further escalation and seek negotiation resulted from a changed advisory process. That change, however, came from the efforts of his new defense secretary, Clark Clifford, and not his NSC advisor and Bundy's successor, Walt Rostow.

CHAPTER 3

The Costs of Absent Brokerage

Henry Kissinger as NSC Advisor

E xamination of Henry Kissinger's tenure as NSC advisor presents both
a hard and an easy case for the notion that some conception of the
honest broker role, albeit expanded, ought to be central to the NSC
advisor's position. The easy case is made by critics, such as Seymour Hersh
and Christopher Hitchens among others, whose accounts portray him in a
highly negative light. The title of Hitchens's work, *The Trial of Henry Kissinger,* conveys the author's negative assessment; indeed, Hitchens modestly describes his project as having been *"confined . . .* to the *identifiable* crimes that
can and should be placed on a proper bill of indictment."[1] For Hersh, the
summary title is *The Price of Power.*

But criticism traduces across the ideological spectrum. The critiques
some conservatives raise with what some regard as the singular foreign policy
achievements of the Nixon presidency are also notable. Indeed, they turn
these putative successes on their head: détente and strategic arms agreements
with the Soviet Union that prolonged the existence of that communist state,
rapprochement with the People's Republic of China that unnecessarily placed
Taiwan in a precarious international position, and military disengagement in
South Vietnam and a peace treaty with North Vietnam that created the conditions for military defeat. For liberals, the administration's efforts in Chile,
East Timor, expansion of the Vietnam War into Cambodia and Laos, plus
needless delay in the peace negotiations with North Vietnam point to failed
policy—at least from their perspective.

I. The Nixon National Security Process

Yet there is a harder case for honest brokerage that Kissinger presents when
thinking about the role of the NSC advisor, one that turns less on one's

normative assessment of the policies the Nixon administration pursued and focuses instead on its operations and its contributions to the quality of the decision-making process. The role of NSC advisor that Kissinger came to define was not purely of his own making. It had the stamp of a president who wanted a strong Kissinger-like figure and a White House-centered national security process. Moreover, it was a period during which President Nixon had very clear policy aims and purposes. According to Elliot Richardson, who assumed a number of cabinet posts in the Nixon presidency, "Nixon was, from the outset, the principal architect of a foreign policy resting on a series of quite strategic aims."[2] Even more trenchantly, as one NSC aide later explained, what precisely a president wants is crucial:

> If the president says "What do I do?" that's a very different situation from the president saying, "I want to *do* this, help me make it happen." And clearly what you had under Nixon and Kissinger was a president who knew what he wanted to do, and he used the NSC mechanism to make it happen.[3]

To phrase it a bit differently, the process of policy development may be less consequential than the successful effort to build support and effectively implement policies that have already been largely presidentially set and determined. Brokerage by this reasoning *might* be less needed if policy choices have already been basically decided upon.

The organizational processes in which Kissinger operated also make it a harder case. The errors that Bundy made in dismantling the Eisenhower NSC system—but then belatedly struggled to put in place better routines—did not bedevil Kissinger and Nixon. Both recognized and quickly moved toward better organization. But it was organization with a particular stamp and purpose: one that would place control of foreign and national security policy making in their hands.

The "hard case" for brokerage notwithstanding, the process of policy development and the deliberative process at its apex still mattered in this presidency. Centralization did occur, but it also had effect on what policy course was chosen. In short, as we shall see, a need for honest brokerage remained.

Kissinger's selection by Nixon as NSC advisor appears odd in some respects, but, working together, they both embraced the need for White House control and direction of U.S. foreign policy. Their motives may have differed, as did their backgrounds. An émigré from Nazi Germany in 1938, Kissinger worked in a shaving-brush factory while attending high school at night. He initially attended the City College of New York, until he was drafted into the army in 1943. He served as an interpreter in the Counter Intelligence Corps, witnessed the worst of Nazi atrocities in the liberated concentration camps, and was valued for his service in ferreting out Gestapo and other Nazi officials in the immediate postwar period. After the war, the GI Bill enabled him to attend Harvard, where he received his B.A. degree in 1950 and his doctorate in 1954. During the remainder of the 1950s and through 1968, he taught in Harvard's Government Department, was director of its Defense Studies Program and its International Relations Seminar, both of which brought contact with a wide array of foreign policy experts and his increasing prominence as an authority on national security issues. He was a consultant to an array of private and governmental foreign policy efforts.

In the mid-1950s Kissinger came within Nelson Rockefeller's orbit. In 1968, he was Governor Rockefeller's chief foreign policy adviser in his failed quest for the Republican presidential nomination against Nixon. During the GOP convention, he and Richard Allen, his counterpart for Nixon, privately brokered an agreement on foreign policy differences between the two candidates, especially on Vietnam, so that no internal division or "floor fight" would occur over the party's platform.[4] There would be no repeat of the 1960 "Compact of Fifth Avenue," when Nixon was perceived to have caved to Rockefeller's political demands.

During the general election campaign of 1968, Kissinger privately provided policy advice to Vice President Hubert Humphrey, the Democratic nominee. But he worked both sides of the political fence. According to both Richard Allen and H. R. Haldeman, Kissinger conveyed information he had obtained to the Nixon camp about what was going on at the Paris peace talks between the United States and the North Vietnamese.[5] After the election, Allen—who was a bit junior at the time—encouraged Nixon to appoint Kissinger as NSC advisor. Despite Nixon's distrust of Rockefeller and Harvard intellectuals, Kissinger was offered the post.

At their first postelection meeting late in November, Kissinger recalls that Nixon was "painfully shy," with a "show of jauntiness that failed to hide an extraordinary nervousness." Two days later, meeting again, Nixon even provided the names of Duke University professors (Nixon had attended law school there) who would vouch for his foreign policy credentials.[6] As Nixon notes in his memoirs, he had a "strong intuition about Henry Kissinger, and I decided on the spot that he should be my National Security Adviser."[7]

Yet, despite their lack of prior familiarity, Kissinger was an apparent good match to what Nixon wanted. As H. R. Haldeman, the White House chief of staff, explains,

Kissinger had a lot of parallel views to Nixon . . . vis-à-vis the importance of the President versus the State Department. Nixon needed a man with credentials and ability and a mentality to cope with all of that, who shared his views. Kissinger fit all of these requirements.[8]

Organizational Centralization

The NSC system that Nixon and Kissinger created marked a return in some respects to what had prevailed under Eisenhower, but only in some respects. It was more highly organized than under Kennedy and Johnson. But, unlike during the Eisenhower era, it was a White House-centered process, with the NSC advisor in a strong advocacy role. Indeed, Kissinger's appointment as NSC advisor was announced before that of William P. Rogers, a former attorney general under Eisenhower and a Nixon confidante, as secretary of state.

Change happened quickly. During the 1968 transition, Nixon partially embraced but also departed from the NSC process in which he himself had participated in as vice president: he wanted more and better organization but without, as Kissinger notes, "lowest common denominator" recommendations or single choices.[9] Based on recommendations by Kissinger, former Harvard colleague Morton Halperin, and Gen. Andrew Goodpaster,[10] a new system was devised during the transition that, while more formally structured, would centralize control of policy in Nixon's—and Kissinger's—hands. The Johnson-era Senior Interdepartmental Group (SIG)—where State played a major role—was abolished, in part on the advice of former President Eisenhower who felt that it encouraged "end-runs" or "counterattack by leaking" by the Defense Department. Nixon's distrust of a State Department-dominated process that would likely produce one precooked option was another factor in its demise.[11] Nor were there to be the more informal Tuesday lunches to work out differences among the principals. Instead, an NSC Review Group was created, below meetings of the full NSC, as well as an NSC Ad Hoc Under Secretary's Committee, below the NSC Review Group, and a variety of interagency regional groups.[12] Key committees were chaired by Kissinger himself, not by departmental representatives. Most important among these latter groups was the interagency Washington Special Action Group (WSAG), set up in April 1969 to deal with crisis situations. Another was the Review Group, where Kissinger approved papers going to Nixon and the NSC members and was able to control the latter's agenda.

The written record of policy options and deliberations was also strengthened with the creation of National Security Decision Memoranda (NSDM)—

which reflected Nixon's policy choices—and background analyses, done on an interagency basis, titled National Security Study Memoranda (NSSMs). Some 165 NSSMs were produced during the first term alone.[13] The NSSMs, ordered by Kissinger, allowed him to conduct his secret negotiations and other tightly held policy matters, while receiving departmental input but without departmental knowledge of what he was precisely up to. According to Kissinger, "It enabled me to use the bureaucracy without revealing our purposes."[14]

The new system was approved by Nixon shortly after Christmas 1968, even before Nixon held his first meeting with those who would be his foreign policy principals, save of course for Kissinger. On December 28, 1968, at Key Biscayne, Nixon told William Rogers, his designate for secretary of state, and Rep. Mel Laird (R-WI), his designate for secretary of defense, of the organizational changes. According to Kissinger, "Like so many meetings in the Nixon administration the Key Biscayne session had its script determined in advance."[15] Rogers and Laird later raised objections, but Nixon resisted any alterations.[16] It was a harbinger of Nixon's and Kissinger's determination to dominate the process and a signal of little tolerance of departmental concerns or perspectives. And it would have costs.

Interestingly, Nixon had a long personal association with Rogers—the latter had been at his side during the "secret fund" scandal and the ensuing Checkers Speech in the 1952 campaign—and Rogers had been a supportive voice as a congressional legal staff member during the Alger Hiss hearings. Yet Nixon did not envision him as a source of policy advice on the order of a John Foster Dulles, or even for that matter a Dean Rusk. According the Haldeman, Nixon "saw Rogers as being a negotiator . . . [while] foreign policy would be established at the White House by the President. The President would be in effect his own secretary of state."[17] However, it was not a division of labor that Nixon managed effectively or that came to fruition as he envisioned. Four years later, Nixon told Haldeman that Rogers was "completely captive to the foreign service."[18]

The system that was developed to express Nixon's hoped-for White House dominance gave some deference to interagency input, at least on paper. But, as it turned out, it was one in which Kissinger and his staff—but not necessarily Nixon—had the upper hand in controlling the agendas, chairing key committees, and providing much of the staffing for the various groups. According to Richard Allen, Kissinger's top aide the first year, "Henry had converted the NSC [staff] from an advisory position into a policy originator and driver of policy."[19]

But there was a potential tension here: Kissinger's dominance of the process sat uneasily with Nixon's own strong interests in key policy areas. According to General Goodpaster, who knew Nixon well having served as staff secretary for most of the Eisenhower presidency and as a close Nixon adviser on NSC operations during the transition, it was not just White House control; in fact, Nixon "was going to *do* foreign policy. He was going to direct it, he was going to engage himself in it. He clearly had in mind major initiatives."[20]

There was also another dynamic at work. As Walter Isaacson notes, the White House-centered system developed to accomplish those initiatives may not have yielded the "conflicting options" that Nixon wanted. It was also "destined to be overshadowed by the related demand that Nixon made: as much power as possible be shifted from the State and Pentagon bureaucracies to the NSC staff." As a result, while it may have been more suited for "bold new approaches, secrecy, surprise, and tactical maneuvering . . . it was not well suited for building a bureaucratic and public consensus for major policies, nor for creating institutional checks on a defiant president who was prone to act on impulse."[21]

WEAKENING OF THE COUNCIL

The system also continued to weaken the significance of the full NSC as a deliberative body and a resource for decision making, while strengthening Kissinger's influence as NSC advisor. Johnson's Tuesday lunches had displaced the NSC. Nixon eliminated the lunches but the NSC was still placed in an after-the-fact role.

Kissinger would open NSC meetings with an outline of items for consideration, the principals would discuss, and then Nixon would summarize and highlight key issues. At some point later, Nixon's decision would be distributed in a NSDM, if appropriate. As JCS Chairman Adm. Thomas H. Moorer observes, following Kissinger's opening briefing, "the president would go around the room, asking each participant his views. He would never make a decision at the meeting, but would go back to the Oval Office and later—at about two in the afternoon—I would get a memorandum, called a presidential decision memo, that would say the president had decided on option two or three . . ."[22] However, what Moorer misses, as one high-level NSC staffer points out, is that while Nixon never made a decision at a meeting, he would meet privately with Kissinger afterwards, where they would decide "what they ought to be doing."[23]

Moreover, while the NSC members received the various position papers, Nixon and Kissinger kept to themselves any summary memos or recommendations, which Kissinger had prepared.[24] Kissinger and his staff also prepared talking points for Nixon. These included likely comments and positions that Rogers, Laird, or others might take and suggested responses by Nixon to their possible objections.[25]

Not only may the real deliberative process have occurred in Nixon's private meetings with Kissinger, some decisions may have been made before the NSC had in fact met. According to Helmut Sonnenfeldt, another key Kissinger deputy, sometimes decisions were made before NSC meetings, with the meetings merely providing a "paper trail" indicating that discussion had taken place and no one had been bypassed.[26] According to William Hyland—a NSC Soviet specialist and later deputy NSC advisor under Brent Scowcroft—"it was a heady experience to be asked to draft presidential decisions before NSC meetings had even been held."[27]

That the meetings of the full NSC did not matter is important: the Council was essentially the only place in the Kissinger structure where the cabinet secretaries met as a group with the president (and Kissinger). Departments were represented on the other committees by subcabinet members, and that is where the real action took place, "not the NSC itself," according to one participant. Recommendations from these groups to the president "did not include the secretaries"—at least directly. So, "It was a very clever way of keeping the secretaries from participating in the decision-making process until it reached the National Security Council, by which time the President had pretty well made up his mind."[28]

By June 1969, Nixon found even these infrequent, scripted NSC meetings tiresome. He told Haldeman to cut their frequency, and in their place, as Haldeman's diary notes indicate, "[Nixon] decided no more NSC meetings. Result of leak . . . will make decisions privately with K [Kissinger]."[29] NSC meetings continued to be convened periodically, but largely as a formality: ensuring consensus on decisions Nixon and Kissinger had already made.

Open-ended oral debate, which Nixon disliked but which was an essential part of the Eisenhower-era process, was thus avoided. Policy differences—and objections—were relegated to a written level. As aide John Ehrlichman later observed, Nixon "didn't want meetings around the cabinet table with passionate advocates pounding away at each other . . . He was not comfortable with face-to-face contact."[30] Kissinger saw a Nixon who made "decisions in solitude on the basis of memoranda or with very few intimate aides. He abhorred confronting colleagues with whom he disagreed and he could not bring himself to face a disapproving friend."[31] According to Scowcroft, "Nixon didn't particularly like meetings; he didn't like listening to oral arguments. Instead he preferred to take all the papers into his office, study them and then just ask questions."[32] For Goodpaster, "Nixon was never a man who welcomed open controversy."[33]

II. Kissinger as NSC Advisor

The new national security system was a recipe for a major enhancement of the role of the NSC advisor, far beyond what either Bundy or Rostow had achieved. As Winston Lord—who served on the NSC staff and later became U.S. Ambassador to China (among other appointments)—observes, a committee process that the NSC advisor largely chaired and his staff orchestrated was crucial to Kissinger's dominance: "You set the agenda, you run the meeting, and you write the follow-up memo to the president. So I think Kissinger was very conscious about chairing most of the key committees, and having his staff people essentially run them."[34]

GATEKEEPER?

Kissinger was also the conduit—if not gatekeeper—for the NSC staff, and access to Nixon was carefully controlled—and limited—by Kissinger. During the first week of his presidency, Nixon convened a meeting of top NSC staff members. But, Nixon was generally uncomfortable in a group setting and it was not repeated.[35]

From that point on, staff contacts were few. According to Marshall Green, who served in the State Department, "Kissinger wouldn't tolerate anyone else having the president's ear."[36] In the view of Winston Lord, Kissinger kept the "staff from having access." Unlike Rostow, who would bring aides along to meetings with President Johnson, "it was really just Henry and the president."[37] In Lord's view, "It reflected his [Kissinger's] tremendous mixture of ego and insecurity."[38] For Sonnenfeldt too, the practice was a "manifestation of his insecurity."[39] Hyland recalls that Kissinger "monopolized the president . . . and shielded him from access by the NSC [staff]." Contact with Nixon was "vicarious"—through his comments on memos.[40]

Even Al Haig, Kissinger's later deputy and a skilled bureaucratic operator, treaded gingerly when access to Nixon was involved. Prior to Haldeman's resignation, press secretary Ron Ziegler told Haig that "the president wants to know what you think" about the unfolding Watergate crisis. According to Haig, "I wasn't close to the president then. Henry made sure of that; nobody who worked for him was close to the president—I don't mean that to be as nasty as it sounds."[41] On July 12, 1971, while Kissinger was on his first secret visit to China, Nixon asked Haig to brief Rogers on Kissinger's secret Paris meetings with the North Vietnamese, Haldeman reports, "so Rogers will be completely up to date on all the missions Henry's been on. . . . Haig was very concerned about this and told me he thought that it will probably permanently break it off with him and Henry, but that he would go ahead and do it anyway."[42]

Kissinger's concern for limiting access also had broader organizational repercussions.[43] Kissinger did not return to the Eisenhower-era practice of having a powerful staff secretary who would monitor and watch over the paper flow and handle daily intelligence matters, the job that General Goodpaster had so skillfully and effectively undertaken for Eisenhower. Kissinger appointed Richard M. Moose to undertake some of the staff secretary's duties, but not the daily contact with the president that Goodpaster had enjoyed. Moose's tenure was short-lived; he left by August 1969.[44] Kissinger also left vacant the post of NSC executive secretary, which had dated to the inception of the NSC in 1947. Bromley Smith, who had held the job during the Kennedy and Johnson presidencies, "was basically sent packing." Kissinger didn't want to fill the post of someone who was a presidential appointee because it "could somehow be a threat to him," according to Robert Kimmitt, who served a stint in that position during the Reagan administration.[45]

Clearances on NSC cables had to come from Kissinger directly, whereas in the Johnson NSC system, others had been deputized to perform that task. The result was that staff members wasted time waiting to see Kissinger personally.[46] According to Sonnenfeldt, "In the first year it was like a Moroccan whorehouse, with people queuing up outside his door for hours."[47]

The logjam on Kissinger's desk caught the attention of the ever watchful Haldeman and Ehrlichman. As Haldeman notes in an October 13, 1969, diary entry, "K is getting heat for his staff inefficiency, which is really just bottlenecking."[48] For Ehrlichman, it led to a tense exchange with Kissinger on July 24, 1971. As Haldeman observes, it started with Ehrlichman criticizing Kissinger for not showing up for a staff meeting on the Defense budget, which in turn, "was causing them to shift their plans around etc. . . . So I asked Henry to come in and join us. Ehrlichman then jumped on him pretty hard, on not only that, but also the intelligence thing . . . and the fact that Henry piles stuff up and is not available to sign off on it himself and won't let anyone else sign off on it. Ehrlichman says that since we have this logjam, there is nothing he can do but go around Henry. . . . At this point, Henry blew and said as long as he's here, nobody's going to go around him, and he is not going to permit anybody to sign off for him." Ehrlichman then got rougher; Kissinger said he "couldn't talk to him that way." Kissinger then "stalk[ed] out of the meeting." [49]

Another contributor to the backup and delay was Kissinger's initial reluctance to have a high-powered aide serve as deputy NSC advisor, (as Bundy but not Rostow had done). There was a distinguished line of likely deputies. The first was Richard Allen—who had been Nixon's initial chief foreign policy adviser during the campaign, had been instrumental in bringing Kissinger into the Nixon camp, and had lobbied for his appointment as NSC advisor. Allen held the deputy title but was not well used during his brief tenure.[50] Others were Lawrence Eagleburger, Morton Halperin, Helmut Sonnenfeldt, and Alexander Haig. It was Haig who proved to be the more skillful bureaucratic in-fighter, but it took until June 1971 for him to secure both the deputy title and the responsibilities to go along with it.[51]

Other levels of the NSC staff were clearly talented. As then NSC staff member Harold Saunders observes, "Henry assembled an NSC staff that was astutely put together. He had a lot of people who were really top people in the bureaucracies, CIA, the military, Defense and State, and that made for a very good NSC staff because they knew how the machinery of government worked."[52]

Yet there is some question whether lower levels of the staff always performed effectively. Kissinger's primary interest was in control not management. Staff were discouraged from informal contact with their opposite numbers in agencies and departments (although some ignored that directive). Kissinger instructed the staff that they were only to have contact with the press on his instructions, although as we shall see his own press contacts were a source of consternation to Nixon and Haldeman.[53] Kissinger even removed the White House mess privileges from the staff, which they had enjoyed during the Johnson years. According to Lord, he didn't want the NSC staff "fraternizing" with other White House aides.[54]

The size of staff grew. By September 1969, according to one count, 114 were on-board, twice the size of the NSC staff under Kennedy and then Johnson. About thirty of these were professionals, but that was about equal in number to the *entire* NSC staff at the end of the Eisenhower administration, professional and administrative.[55] At the same time, staff turnover was significant. By September 1969, 40 percent of the top thirty or so original staff members had left, including key aides Eagleburger and Halperin. By the summer of 1971, only seven of the original group remained.[56] Kissinger's role as a tough, demanding task master was a prime source of staff dissatisfaction, as were his efforts at gatekeeping and control.[57] Richard Allen, for example, "Found that I was basically being cut out of a lot of things." Nixon had directed him to be his "listener." Nixon "didn't want to see a lot of people. He wanted me to do that." Allen did so but became disillusioned, "writing the stuff up and finding it never got to him. It would be headed off."[58]

POLICY TILT?

The question of how much Kissinger sought to bias or tilt the written policy material that went to the paper-consuming and information-voracious Nixon is elusive. Clearly, Kissinger weighed in with his own considerable views on policy matters. But were alternatives also presented and appropriately vetted? For some, Kissinger's and the NSC staff's dominance over the policy process had its source in, and met, Nixon's expectations. According to Sonnenfeldt, Nixon "didn't want to have precooked decisions that were bargained out in the bureaucracies and among Cabinet officers in such a way that he could only accept or reject them."[59] According to Saunders, Nixon worried that a more interagency-reliant process, dominated by the State Department as it was under Johnson, would encourage the bureaucracy to come to one recommendation. Nixon likely concluded that "I won't have any real choices." With that in mind, according to Saunders, the interagency "review process . . . was moved back to the White House under Kissinger."[60]

In Saunders's view, moreover, Kissinger was something of an honest broker of that process, at least early on:

> Kissinger in the early days of his tenure was really quite scrupulous about doing the positive things . . . making sure that all reasonable options had been laid out dispassionately and the advantages and disadvantages of each had been fairly stated. I would say that if you went back to the files of that first year of Kissinger's NSC you would probably find some of the best analytical staff work in a policy context that you could find anywhere. The first year of the Nixon administration was a real effort by Henry to make sure all points of view were fairly laid out with all of their advantages and disadvantages, and that was the job of the basic level of the NSC system and it was the job of the NSC staff to capture that in memos we did for the president.[61]

Yet, others discerned problems. According to Ivo Daalder, Morton Halperin, who had been one of the key players in devising the system during the 1968 transition, felt it "worked wonderfully" at the start, but after 1969 "it fell apart for a variety of reasons."[62] Saunders also notes that "later on Henry assumed more of a policy role. I think in some ways that got skewed as we got on into the administration."[63]

Others felt that the interagency memoranda process may have had bureaucratic purposes beyond simply a search for sound policy alternatives. According to Winston Lord, there was "a whole flood of NSSMs" at the start of the administration. In part, they were "a genuine search for intellectual depth, analysis and preparation of options for policy by the various agencies." But they also had another purpose: "to put so much work on the bureaucracy and keep them so busy that the president and Kissinger could get on with running American foreign policy."[64] According to Sonnenfeldt, "there really wasn't a whole lot of faith in most of these [early] NSSMs. . . . It was assumed the State Department would be its old self and [present] . . . two extreme options and a middle option which was their preferred option."[65] Moreover, like Lord, Sonnenfeldt felt that the "utility of a NSSM is right, and the make-work role of the NSSM . . . is also right. In fact, it tied up people who might have smelled a rat if they hadn't been so busy doing the NSSMs."[66] James Schlesinger—who was deputy director of the OMB, chair of the Atomic Energy Commission, director of the CIA, secretary of defense and then, under Carter, secretary of energy—felt that Nixon "had less patience with the staff system" and used it "to push over his ideas rather than to listen to anyone else's."[67]

In 1971, journalist John Leacacos observed in an article in *Foreign Policy* that Kissinger himself "rated many of the early NSC studies no better than 'C'—barely passing." Indeed, in Leacacos's view, the presumed goal of providing Nixon with a broader range of options may have been more hype than fact: "One sometimes wonders, while prowling the White House basement, whether often repeated phrases like 'keeping the options open,' and 'the president's spread of options' don't have more a liturgical than an intellectual significance."[68] By 1971, Leacacos also noted that the more formal, presumably more Eisenhower-like organizational system, had less impact. The committee structure, in particular, had become less relevant save for those Kissinger chaired: "Crucial issues have been maneuvered to committees chaired by Kissinger, thence directly to the president." As for the Under Secretaries Committee, one of the few chaired by a representative from State and designed largely to implement policy, "its actual importance (never very great) continues to lapse." It suffered from "ineffectiveness" and was "moribund." As for the NSC, its full meetings diminished: thirty-seven in

1969, twenty-one in 1970, and ten in 1971 (through September).[69] Yet, as Saunders cautions, the policy task changed over time: "Later on you had the administration get its basic policy review finished and then it gets into lines of action, so you have a different set of needs. The president is very familiar with certain issues, so that you tend to be presenting options for some fairly limited actions rather than large policy."[70]

Not only may some have regarded the NSSMs as busy work and the initial organizational structure in decline, but Kissinger had an enormous impact on what options were finally presented to Nixon. All eventually filtered through Kissinger, whether as key committee chair, NSC advisor controlling the agenda, or in his private meetings with the president. Kissinger was the gatekeeper for work coming from his own staff. According to Allen, "I found myself thwarted at almost every level. My memos were ostensibly going to the President, but Henry organized the National Security Council in such a way that no one could write to the President, and [Kissinger's] name went on the memoranda that were prepared by others."[71]

Even Nixon registered concerns, especially about how Kissinger handled meetings. In a June 24, 1970, diary entry, Haldeman notes that Nixon "went into this whole problem this afternoon at EOB with me, especially re. K's [Kissinger] horrible way of handling a meeting and giving all the feeling that they have no part except to follow his orders. P [President] worries about how to overcome this and concludes he has to meet privately with Laird and Rogers more often, and handle them himself instead of through K, but this will just get K up all the tighter, so!?"[72]

The written product that went to Nixon may also have been skewed: it was always Kissinger who would write the final memo to Nixon, the one that sat at the top. According to Ehrlichman, Nixon told him that he much preferred the formal options papers Kissinger presented him to the contentious meetings he faced in domestic policy: "Henry always brings me nice neat papers on national security problems and I can check the boxes. Nobody badgers me and picks on me."[73] Yet Ehrlichman also later observed that Kissinger once told him that memoranda to Nixon could be structured to bias Nixon's selection. Nixon usually selected option two among the three Kissinger would present: "You people are very foolish to give him more than three options. You must also arrange it so that the one you favor is the second one," Kissinger reportedly told Ehrlichman.[74]

The character of Kissinger's personal meetings with Nixon remains elusive. Some of the taped recordings of Nixon's private conversations—which started in February 1971—provide evidence of a Kissinger pliant to Nixon's diatribes, slurs, and sometimes outlandish statements. However, many White House tapes, undoubtedly with more substantive discussions, remain classified for national security reasons. But there is some evidence that his quest for dominance may have clouded the advice Kissinger gave the president. In the view of Marshall Green, "Kissinger was brilliant in his own way, but he was self-seeking, self-aggrandizing. I don't think the president got the best kind of support this way."[75] According to White House aide Charles Colson, Nixon "recognized that Henry could be a sycophant at times, which he was, and never disguised very well."[76] Gerald Ford recalled that Kissinger was often "coy . . . Dear friend. First-class secretary of state. But Henry always protected his own flanks."[77] In Ehrlichman's opinion, Kissinger "was obsequious naturally. He would lard things unbelievably. Nixon would make an outrageous statement . . . Kissinger would eagerly rumble in with, 'Yes Mr. President, your analysis is absolutely correct and certainly very profound.' I would cringe."[78]

EXCLUSION

Kissinger's control of the national security process also led to the attenuation of influence of those outside the NSC staff. On the positive side, according to Philip Odeen, who served on the NSC staff from 1971 to 1973, departmental views were not shut out. But it was a process in which Kissinger and his staff had a determining and not just coordinating role: "We [NSC staff] were expected very much to drive the agenda, to make sure our alternatives were considered." "We were not just coordinating" and "our role was to [make sure] that the right people . . . addressed the issues that Henry wanted addressed. There was not much question who was in charge."[79]

Others saw problems. Even Kissinger's top aide, Sonnenfeldt, felt that White House control went too far at times: "When I discovered the extent to which President Nixon wanted to have policy making and even policy execution concentrated in the White House . . . I had even more misgivings."[80] According to Kenneth Rush—Nixon's old law professor at Duke, who served as U.S. ambassador to West Germany, then deputy secretary of defense, and then state—"Henry wanted everything to go through him."[81] In October 1974, as he was to begin his tenure as the first U.S. diplomatic liaison to China, George H. W. Bush noted in his diary that "people at the State Department seem scared to death about our China policy." Kissinger, now serving as both secretary of state and NSC advisor, "keeps the cards so close to his chest that able officers . . . seem unwilling to take any kind of initiative."[82]

One of the most serious repercussions of Kissinger's dominance of the policy-making process was the almost total exclusion of Secretary of State William Rogers. Rogers brought little in the way of substantive foreign policy knowledge or experience to the position.[83] Yet his exclusion also weakened the impact of his department in policy formulation. Rogers's situation was well known and open to full view. One senator remarked at the time that Kissinger had become "secretary of state in everything but title" (this was, of course, before he formally held that position). According to another, "They let Rogers handle Norway and Malagasy, and Kissinger would handle Russia and China and everything else he was interested in."[84] In the view of Kenneth Rush, "Bypassing the State Department was a deliberate pattern."[85] According to William H. Sullivan, U.S. ambassador to Iran, "Henry was very aggressive; he did cut Bill [Rogers] out."[86]

Exclusion of Rogers may have certainly reflected Nixon's own distrust of the State Department and his hopes to bypass it, rather than being solely a result of Kissinger's efforts. But Kissinger clearly fueled the negative relationship with his disdain for Rogers. In the first volume of his memoirs, *White House Years,* Kissinger reports—mincing few words—that "few secretaries of state have been selected because of their president's confidence in their ignorance of foreign policy. . . . I tended to view [Rogers] as an insensitive neophyte who threatened the careful design of foreign policy. . . . I tried to bypass him as much as possible." Rogers's efforts to make himself and State more relevant "endangered coherent policy . . . I believed that Rogers had no grasp of the geopolitical stakes." Nor was it just a Kissinger-Rogers feud; it permeated through their respective staffs: "The result was a bureaucratic stalemate," according to Kissinger, "in which the White House and State Department representatives dealt with each other as competing sovereign entities."[87]

Nor was exclusion confined to Rogers. During the initial stages of the planning of the Cambodian invasion of 1970, while discussions were held with JCS Chair Admiral Moorer, both Rogers *and* Defense Secretary Laird were kept away under the guise that it was just a military briefing.[88] In a memo to Nixon on April 26, 1970, Kissinger reminded him that while the U.S. military in Saigon had been preparing to send troops into Cambodia, "up until now Secretary Laird has not been aware of the likelihood of its being approved and opposition can be expected from him as well as the Secretary of State."[89] While both were eventually brought into the picture at a hastily convened Sunday evening NSC meeting, according to Isaacson, Nixon and Kissinger went into it "with a decision already made and tried to maneuver around those officials they had cut out." Moreover, they used the military briefing gambit again: the meeting was just to discuss a variety of options, "Laird and Rogers said little." After the meeting was over, Nixon summoned Kissinger and signed the invasion order.[90]

Difficulties persisted. The administration's initial NSDM assigned the Kissinger-led WSAG "implementing authority" for the operation.[91] Laird protested, with success, that this violated the military chain of command. Laird may also have suspected that there had been communications between the White House and the military that had occurred without his knowledge and that also violated the statutory chain of command.[92]

MANAGING KISSINGER

Kissinger's relations with Rogers and others in the administration were a frequent topic of discussion and posed problems that Nixon, Haldeman, Ehrlichman, Attorney General John Mitchell, and others were forced to deal with repeatedly. In Haldeman's view, "Henry saw a lot of ghosts in the dark out to get him all the time."[93] Most prominent, Haldeman's diaries are full of numerous entries where Kissinger's battles with Rogers are noted, and they frequently came to Nixon's and not just Haldeman's attention:

August 29, 1969: E [Ehrlichman], K [Kissinger], and I had a long session, primarily about Rogers problem.[94]

March 10, 1970: I learned from Haig this morning that K had real battle with Rogers on phone yesterday about Laos, and the whole deal is really building up.[95]

June 23, 1970: K in for a long talk, about his worries about very adverse stories about his dating [actress] Jill St. John. He thinks Rogers is planting them to try to destroy him.[96]

July 13, 1970: K in to see me for his periodic depression about Rogers. This time he's found Rogers is meeting with Dobrynin. . . . K's temptation is to confront Bill [Rogers] and insist they have it out with P [President], or else one will have to leave. Thinks he can scare him out. I urged against it on grounds he might not scare out and P can't follow through, especially before [midterm] elections. Actually it would be counterproductive for K, and hurt him badly with P, and solve nothing.[97]

July 15, 1970: K is building up a new head of steam re. Rogers . . . K still feels this is all part of a plan to do him in and take over foreign policy by State from W[hite] H[ouse]. Talked to me several times—trouble is he's almost psycho about it—and keeps repeating his charges and complaints but has no real alternative except to fire Rogers, which isn't very likely. I agreed to try to get Haig in with P to discuss the whole problem.[98]

August 6, 1970: [Kissinger] just obsessed with conviction that Rogers is out to get him and to sabotage all our systems and foreign policy.[99]

Sept 10, 1970: K got me at end of staff meeting to plead that Rogers be kept out of meeting with Golda Meir next week, on grounds he's most hated man in Israel and would be a disaster.[100]

Nov 11, 1971: Henry . . . thinks that Rogers has declared total war on him and is maneuvering to sabotage him on all fronts except Vietnam.[101]

Others in the administration were also subject to Kissinger's complaints:

Jan 22, 1970: K called all disturbed because Laird is skipping the NSC meeting tomorrow where he's supposed to hit the hard line on ABM; wants to be able to say he wasn't present when decision was made to go ahead. Dedicating a nuclear frigate instead. K really mad.[102]

Nov 11, 1971: Henry thinks that Laird has sabotaged us as usual on the troop withdrawal announcement.[103]

Kissinger's behavior often came up in Haldeman's conversations with Nixon. Despite his distrust of the State Department, Nixon was often displeased with Kissinger's effort to exercise near total control over foreign policy, and he was concerned about his effectiveness as NSC advisor. Haldeman frequently describes these conversations as "long," often ending with instructions by Nixon on how to deal with Kissinger, especially in attempting to defuse his conflicts with Rogers and Laird:

October 9, 1969: [Haldeman and Nixon met for lunch] long talk about things in general. Esp. K's concern about Rogers and his [Kissinger's] obsession with *total* compliance and perfection, which needs to be modified somehow. [Nixon] wants me to work with K and try to keep him on an even keel, and stop his worrying.[104]

October 11, 1969: [Nixon is] concerned about K's attitude and wants to be sure we keep him upbeat. Can't let him overact to each little aberration of Rogers or Laird. K argues you have to maintain tight discipline in the little things or you can't control the big ones. P feels that you should lose the ones that don't matter and save your strength and equity for the big battles that really count.[105]

October 13, 1969: Another long introspective talk at the end of the day. I sense a growing intolerance of K's attitudes and habits [by Nixon]. He overreacts and bothers the P. Tendency now more and more to keep him out—and K senses this, which builds up his frustration and accelerates the overreacting.[106]

Following an NSC meeting in mid-October 1969, Nixon met privately with Rogers and Laird. According to Haldeman, "apparently this uncovered all their problems with Kissinger." Nixon told his chief of staff that "he'll have to bring Mitchell in more" because Kissinger can't deal with Rogers and Laird, "has problems communicating with them, and has become an issue. Wants me to make it clear to K, hard to do."[107] But problems persisted.

October 27, 1969: The K problem came to a head today. [Nixon] got into problem of K vs. State, and especially Rogers, which we had discussed last week and which K had churned up more over the weekend in phone calls with P. [Kissinger then arrived and after Nixon left, raised his concerns about Rogers.] [Kissinger] wanted me in the noon meeting because he had to get into the Rogers' problem with [Nixon]. I took him into my office and tried to point out the fallacy of his technique, regardless of merits of case. I think he saw it a little at least. [Later, Haldeman and Nixon met.] [Nixon] called me in to re-state his concerns with this as latest example. *Feels K is impairing his usefulness, and is obsessed beyond reason with this problem.* Later P called Mitchell and me in to discuss further and asked Mitchell to have a talk with K.[108]

Haldeman's diary entries are confirmed by Ehrlichman's recollections. Nixon at first tolerated Kissinger's complaints about Rogers "as the price of doing business with Henry, but before long the President was complaining . . . of Henry's tendency to waste great blocks of the President's time in childish and petty complaints against Rogers."[109]

NIXON'S CONCERNS WITH KISSINGER'S ROLE

Although Kissinger's role as a strong NSC advisor had Nixon's endorsement, it is also important to note that Nixon was not always happy with other aspects of Kissinger's performance in the job, as Haldeman's diary entries clearly attest. Following the mid-October meeting of Nixon with Rogers and Laird, Haldeman noted in his diary that the problem is Kissinger's "insistence on perfection and adherence to the line in every detail. Also injects himself too much into everything, between P and Cabinet officers, and they just won't buy it, so he becomes ineffective even at getting them to do what they already were ready to do."[110] On February 10, 1970, Nixon discussed staff performance with Haldeman and the need for top staff members to deal with problems with "great confidence." In Haldeman's view, this was "obviously a reaction to K's incessant hand-wringing."[111] Kissinger's frequent contact with Nixon was sometimes a source of irritation to the president. On January 19, 1970, Haldeman noted that Nixon "had me keep K out all day again, doesn't want to get distracted."[112] Nor was Nixon unaware of Kissinger's dealings with the NSC and White House staffs: on March 9, 1970, while Kissinger was on one of his secret trips to Paris, Nixon "called me at home tonite to have me call K to tell him not to nitpick [press secretary Ron] Ziegler and Haig's work while he was gone."[113]

Nixon himself was sometimes critical of Kissinger's work product. On October 13, 1971, Nixon felt that Kissinger's briefing book on China was "brilliant, but [Nixon] now wants a brief memo that tells, first . . . what are our goals, and, second, what will the Chinese want . . . that we have to resist. . . . He wants the book boiled down to its essentials, to come directly to the point, and cut out the BS on historical processes and everything and get it buttoned down." Later, Haldeman reports that Kissinger was "somewhat upset by the critique."[114]

During the India-Pakistan crisis in December 1971, Kissinger told reporters that Nixon was thinking about canceling the upcoming summit with the Soviets unless they put more pressure on India. The White House press secretary later told reporters that Kissinger was in error and cancellation was not under consideration. "I blew it, I was just damn stupid," Kissinger told one reporter. Nixon response was to limit his contact with Kissinger. Meetings with Kissinger were canceled, and Nixon refused to take Kissinger's phone calls.[115]

Nixon was also concerned that Kissinger kept things from him. In December 1971, Nixon was irritated that Kissinger never told him about the discovery that the Joint Chiefs of Staff had placed a spy in the White House: he "was particularly concerned because Henry and Haig had not raised it with him, although it was such a clear security problem. He can't figure out why they didn't do this when they do know at least some of the particulars."[116]

Nixon was sometimes dissatisfied with Kissinger's advice. Following an April 1, 1970, meeting with Rogers, Nixon told Haldeman that he had to have more of them without Kissinger present. In his diary, Haldeman notes that Nixon "feels K doesn't give him an accurate picture of Laird's and

Rogers' view. Always puts it in black and white. P. talked a long time with E and me about this problem, trying to figure out how to handle this. Basically, it's impossible because of the characters, especially K."[117]

Nixon's distrust of Kissinger apparently reached such a point that Nixon wanted material he had sent Kissinger removed from Kissinger's office files. As Haldeman notes on November 20, 1972 (an interesting date given the collapse of peace talks with North Vietnam), Nixon "wants to be sure that I get from Kissinger's office all the files and memoranda from and to the President and get them into the President's files, especially all of his handwritten stuff, the originals, physically move it into the President's files now."[118] Nixon may just have been concerned that the records appear in his own presidential files for historical purposes. But on January 7, 1973, Nixon again raised the issue in an interesting context: a "discussion of his Kissinger concerns again. Made the point that Haig has got to . . . totally level with him on the Kissinger problem. . . . Then he raised concerns about the Kissinger papers, and all the President's papers on national security that Kissinger is holding including Henry's phone calls, and conversation memos and cables and so on, which he wants to be sure we get a hold of and stay on top of as much as possible."[119] Nixon's concerns were not unfounded. According to Isaacson, when he was thinking of resigning in early 1973 Kissinger secretly sent thirty crates of documents to be stored in the bomb shelter at the Rockefeller estate in Pocantico Hills, New York. When Kissinger decided to stay on, the documents were returned to the White House.[120] Nor, during this period, was it entirely clear on Nixon's part what role Kissinger might have in a second term or even if he would be asked to stay on in some capacity. Hence, control of presidential records was important from Nixon's point of view. Nixon might also have been concerned about what Kissinger's version of events might be concerning peace talks with North Vietnam.

BEYOND BROKERAGE: SECRET DIPLOMACY

Another potentially problematic aspect of Kissinger's role as NSC advisor was his frequent use of secret, back-channel negotiations to achieve policy ends or to lay the ground work for them. Such activity is explicitly rejected by Alexander George in his conception of the managerial custodian role; it undermines perceptions of the NSC advisor's integrity with the other principals, and it involves the NSC advisor too heavily in operational activities. Back-channel efforts also depart from traditional methods of diplomatic contact through the State Department. They prevent interagency input on policy matters and could lead to confusion about administration priorities and policy positions.

For a less strict conception of the honest broker role, secret efforts by the NSC advisor also pose dilemmas but in an opposite way: foreign powers may be more comfortable with direct contact with the White House rather than the more porous State Department (as was the case for the Soviet Union). In addition, presidents may prefer that the NSC advisor conduct such negotiations—often to signal direct presidential involvement and priorities—and some foreign policy goals may be achievable only through such secret channels.

As we shall see when we get to particular policy outcomes, Kissinger's secret diplomatic efforts were mixed in their benefits, some aided policy goals but others generated difficulty for the administration. Even with what is regarded as the most successful effort—opening of relations with the People's Republic of China—where secrecy seemed most necessary, Kissinger may have gone too far at times and some difficulties ensued as the State Department was cut out.

BEYOND BROKERAGE: PUBLIC VISIBILITY AND THE PRESS

Another marked departure from George's prescription of the managerial custodian role was Kissinger's public visibility. He was hardly the anonymous figure of a Robert Cutler, Dillon Anderson, or Gordon Gray. During his tenure, and for decades later, Kissinger was a recognized public figure. Few today, and few then, could recall who had been Nixon's secretary of state. During his first two years, Kissinger was low-key, and he was rarely mentioned in the media. But later, after China, Kissinger became a celebrity. Even his dating habits became the subject of intense media speculation.

Kissinger relished his contacts with the press and the attention they brought him. They were undoubtedly a useful channel for getting the Nixon administration's views across. In the view of Nixon aide Raymond Price, Kissinger "was very good at handling the press." But Price also acknowledges that "he leaked a little more than I would have preferred."[121] Kissinger's frequent press contacts may have been one reason why he was often behind schedule.[122] They also ratcheted up tensions with State. According to Kenneth Rush, Kissinger "was a master at manipulating the media through leaks," and "leaks from Henry [were] attributed by President Nixon to State or Defense."[123]

Haldeman found Kissinger obsessive about press coverage of him. At a March 1973 meeting with Nixon and Haig (on Kissinger's bad treatment of Haig and his accusations of disloyalty), Haldeman told of the time when Kissinger "even hit me on parking his airplane in the wrong place" on return from one of his secret trips. Kissinger "was furious because he didn't get any press coverage on his return arrival, blaming me for parking his plane in such a way that the press couldn't cover him."[124] As Haldeman later recalled, "Kissinger was loving the limelight . . . and he became concerned with his own limelight."[125]

Kissinger's visibility had other downsides, especially when he was subject to press criticism. As former President Ford recalled in an interview with Bob Woodward (released after Ford's death), Kissinger had "the thinnest skin of any public figure I ever knew." "I think he was a super secretary of state," Ford said, "but Henry in his mind never made a mistake, so whatever policies there were that he implemented, in retrospect he would defend." Sensitivity, in turn, affected his relationship with the president. According to Ford, "Any criticism in the press drove him crazy." Kissinger would come in and say: "I've got to resign. I can't stand this kind of unfair criticism." Such threats were routine, "I often thought, maybe I should say: 'Okay, Henry. Goodbye,' 'But I never got around to that.'"[126]

NIXON CONCERNS ABOUT KISSINGER'S PRESS RELATIONS

Haldeman's diaries reveal numerous occasions when Nixon was concerned about Kissinger's contacts with the press, especially the amount of time consumed. On January 14, 1970, Haldeman notes that Nixon was concerned "about use of K's time, especially with the press. Wants me to take over his schedule, guidance for public and PR things, get him to see the right press people and not waste time on the unwinnables."[127] At the same time, Nixon was also the early impetus in encouraging Kissinger's press contacts; he was especially concerned that the White House handle press relations on foreign policy matters rather than the State Department.[128]

However, Nixon grew increasingly frustrated with Kissinger's media contacts, especially after Kissinger's secret diplomatic missions. Nixon recognized that they worsened the situation with Secretary of State Rogers. So Nixon specifically instructed that Kissinger was not to provide background interviews to reporters, as the following Haldeman diary entries note:

> June 29, 1970: Some more talk about press-handling technique. [Nixon] especially does *not* want K giving superlong backgrounders.[129]
> July 10, 1971: [Nixon] made the point that when Henry gets back [from his first visit to China], he'll be the mystery man of the age, and he'll kill the whole thing if he has one word of backgrounder to any press people. So there are to be no backgrounders whatsoever. He has to quit seeing anyone from

the *Times* or *Post* on any basis. [Moreover, Nixon added] Rogers is easier to handle if Kissinger doesn't background."[130]

On July 13, 1971: [Kissinger returned and wanted to deal with the press. Nixon] made the point that Kissinger was *obsessed* with doing something with the press. I agree with Rogers on this, but that's going to be hard to do because Henry really is determined to do it.[131]

But Kissinger was not above disobeying Nixon's explicit instructions. On August 11, 1971, following an article in the *New York Times* by James Reston that was critical of Nixon, Haldeman records that Nixon "has ordered that Henry not see Reston at all."[132]

A month later, in a late-night telephone call to Haldeman, Nixon told him that Kissinger had said that Reston "was in to see him or that Henry had talked to Reston and Reston had asked for an interview with the President." According to Haldeman, "It's completely incredible, because several weeks ago, in President's office . . . President then made the point loud, clear, and solidly to Henry that under no circumstances would he see Reston at any time, ever . . . that we knew he would be coming around trying to get an interview. . . . The next thing we know, Henry's back and is talking with him."[133]

Despite Kissinger's promise that he would not talk to reporters about his China trip, Nixon grew incensed over stories about Kissinger's trip in the newspapers. Nixon dispatched John Scali—a former diplomatic reporter for ABC News who was now working for Nixon as a foreign policy and media adviser—to find out who was talking to the media. Using White House meeting and telephone call logs, Scali reported back to Nixon that Kissinger had held twenty-four sessions with reporters; twenty-two of them had written stories about Kissinger in China.[134] Also, during the China trip, Kissinger had managed to disobey Nixon's explicit instructions—this time that his name not appear on the mission's joint communiqué. "Repeatedly I received instructions," Kissinger later acknowledged, but he ignored them and the document began "Premier Chou En-lai and Dr. Henry Kissinger . . ."[135]

On at least two occasions, Kissinger was caught lying to Haldeman about press contacts. A Haldeman diary entry of December 14, 1972, notes: "Got into the press thing, and it was really quite hysterical because he flatly told me that he had not talked with [*New Republic*'s] John Osborne . . . and didn't understand why we didn't trust him when he says he doesn't talk to these people. Then I read him direct quotes from the story, and after hemming and hawing a bit, he said, well, I talked to him on the phone but I didn't meet with him."[136] Kissinger offered the same excuse when it was discovered that Kissinger had once again talked to James Reston of the *New York Times* for a column titled "Nixon and Kissinger," which portrayed the latter as opposing the resumed bombing of North Vietnam over Christmas 1972. Kissinger denied talking to him, but White House phone records revealed that he had. He later told Haldeman that it was only over the phone. [137]

Kissinger's favorable press coverage sometimes irritated Nixon, especially when reports suggested that Kissinger not Nixon was the architect of the administration's foreign policy successes. On October 8, 1971, Nixon raised the issue with Haldeman about an article in the *Washington Star* "that implied that Henry was dominating the making of all foreign policy. The President was quite concerned about it, first because it's not true, particularly the China initiative, for instance, was not Henry's. Second it would drive Rogers up the wall. . . . [Nixon] thinks this results from the way Henry does his briefings."[138]

On other occasions, Nixon was worried that Kissinger was grabbing the limelight. On February 15, 1973, following his return from successful peace negotiations with North Vietnam, Kissinger wanted to hold a press conference. But, according to Haldeman, Nixon "was disturbed because he feels that he has to make the first statement on the aid to North Vietnam question. . . . He feels there is a real problem with the Kissinger news conference on return . . . making the point that we have the toughest sale we ever had on aid to North Vietnam and that the President has to do it." Nixon was "also concerned about the fact that Henry didn't submit the communiqué to him before he put it out . . . and he was wondering about that. I hadn't seen it either, which I also found surprising."[139]

Nixon also sometimes viewed the substance of Kissinger's comments to the press as self-serving. In March of 1973, Nixon even ordered Haldeman to disseminate a story on Kissinger's weaknesses. Nixon felt "that Kissinger's trying to cover his left flank. . . . Wants me to talk to Safire and get our story out on Vietnam. Point out the truth regarding Kissinger panicking on Cambodia, Laos, and Pakistan while the President always had to buck him up. Show him Kissinger's frenetic messages from Paris and tell him that side of the story. Also building Haig as the unsung hero, like a rock in all of this."[140]

AN OBSESSION WITH LEAKS

Kissinger's press relations were problematic in still another way. Although Kissinger felt little compunction to limit his own access to the press, access of his own staff was another matter. Early on, Kissinger had notified his staff that they were only to have contact with the press under his instruction. Yet

Kissinger's own leaks may have encouraged unauthorized leaks by others.[141] According to Richard Allen, "leaks were coming, frankly, from the NSC staff. . . . These people all became accomplished leakers."[142] Not surprisingly, Kissinger became quite concerned.

Not only were the leaks problematic in their own right in tipping the administration's hand, they had wider repercussions. Haldeman realized early on in the administration that Kissinger seemed preoccupied about leaks. As he notes in a June 16, 1969, diary entry, he was "worried about K's overreaction to leaks in his office."[143]

Perhaps more consequentially, the issue of leaks from the NSC staff quickly led to the wiretapping of NSC officials suspected of leaks, a pattern of response that may have encouraged the wider behavior that eventually led to Watergate.[144] According to Haldeman, "unintentionally and unknowingly an important precedent for Watergate had been established." [145]

Kissinger's response to the leaking of the classified *Pentagon Papers,* a Defense Department study of the history of U.S. involvement in Vietnam through the Johnson years, may have had more direct linkage to Watergate. The *Papers* were leaked by a sometime associate of Kissinger, Daniel Ellsberg, who by 1971 had become an outspoken critic of the war. Kissinger was reportedly enraged by the leak. According to Ehrlichman, the *Pentagon Papers* were "Lyndon Johnson's problem" and "embarrassed [Nixon] in no way . . . there was not a word about Richard Nixon in any of the forty-three volumes." However, they "caused Henry Kissinger deep concern; the episode touched him in many ways . . . Kissinger fanned Richard Nixon's flame white-hot."[146] According to Haldeman, Kissinger told Nixon, "It shows you're a weakling, Mr. President." [147] Within a month the White House "Plumbers Unit" was created to deal with leaks, and it would soon be involved in a range of illegal activities, including the Watergate break-in at Democratic Party headquarters.

Concerns about Kissinger's loyalty may even have led Nixon to start taping his conversations. On taking office, Nixon had dismantled Lyndon Johnson's taping system. But in February 1971, he ordered it reinstalled. According to Haldeman, the main reason was to get on record where Kissinger stood on the invasion of Cambodia, and "to pin down the opinions of Henry Kissinger and other advisers who often seemed to come up with their own versions of both their own and the President's positions."[148]

The other effect of leaking may have been further secrecy on Nixon's part. Not only may this have created a climate of isolation, but it may have generated bureaucratic counter efforts. The most notable—and extreme— was the attempt by the Joints Chiefs of Staff to use a military aide on Kissinger's

NSC staff as a spy within the White House.[149] But the most extensive were Defense Secretary Laird's efforts. Unbeknownst to Kissinger, Laird arranged with the National Security Agency—under Pentagon jurisdiction—to receive "my own copy of every back-channel message Henry sent. . . . Sometimes you have to do these things and play someone else's game against them." Laird also obtained copies of the communications from the North Vietnamese negotiators in Paris back to Hanoi. Laird had access to all CIA cable traffic (through the NSA). When the seemingly wily Kissinger used the military rather than the diplomatic cable system (to prevent State from learning what he was doing), Laird obtained reports. Even when Kissinger was in the White House, Laird got reports from the Army Signal Corps, which ran the secure White House telephone system.[150]

III. Policy: Process, Role, and Outcome

The national security system that Kissinger dominated had a number of major effects on policy: one resulting from its internal dynamics, another from the frequent exclusion of departmental input and Kissinger's running battles with Rogers and Laird, still more from Kissinger's secret diplomacy.

Effects of Internal Dynamics

Kissinger's relationship with his own NSC staff represents a mixed picture. Kissinger did hire talented aides who went on to play prominent roles in foreign policy making for the next thirty years: Lawrence Eagleburger, Anthony Lake, Al Haig, Brent Scowcroft, John Negroponte, Richard Holbrooke, Robert McFarlane, and Winston Lord to name but a few. Moreover, as Isaacson points out, despite Kissinger's "petulant tantrums and tyrannies," aides found his staff a place "where independent thinking was prized and sycophancy was not." Kissinger "liked to be challenged on substance, and he enjoyed a solid analytic argument. . . . He did not seal himself off like Nixon, but instead sought out the most assertive minds on his staff."[151]

Kissinger also could be an analytically tough taskmaster with his subordinates, one who insisted on quality. Harold Saunders recalls that analytic rigor

> was an hourly posture on [Kissinger's] part really. I can remember him looking at a memo I did while I stood there in his office, looking down at the pros and cons that I had stated for some option or another. And he said "Look, you have a much longer statement of the pros than you have of

the cons, what are you trying to put over on me here." That almost sound mechanistic, but it was designed to get really to the bottom of the arguments we were laying out. And to make sure that the real motives behind them were surfaced. That was his normal way of working and it took the practical form of many memos coming back for redo. That was almost a standard experience.[152]

Compared to Kissinger's predecessor, Walt Rostow, Saunders found that "it was just much more rigorous under Kissinger. Walt certainly in my field was no less concerned to get the best possible thinking for the president, but the demands for analytical rigor were not nearly as strong then as under Kissinger."[153]

Part of those differences stemmed from the different decision-making styles of the presidents they served. Johnson preferred to talk things through, so the memoranda process was less important. Nixon was highly reliant on the written advice coming from the NSC system as he worked through policy issues in private. While the NSC staffs under Rostow and Kissinger were "more similar than not" in terms of organizational culture and day-to-day work ways, according to Saunders, and Rostow was not "sloppy . . . I would say that there were significant differences in culture. Because of Henry's demands and ways of doing things, the staff was just much more on its toes."[154]

Yet some discerned problems. Even Saunders notes that Kissinger's rigor occurred most strongly in "the first year or maybe two."[155] According to Richard Allen, Kissinger staffed the NSC "with a group of people who could best be described as Nixon critics and at worse as Nixon haters . . . I was in the NSC, the number two man, alive in a sea of hostility. It was amazing."[156] Sometimes key staff members were kept in the dark about what Kissinger was up to. One member of the NSC East Asian staff, for example, was surprised to learn—from the Indonesian ambassador, of all people—of a possible Nixon visit to Jakarta. Kissinger had undertaken the planning but without informing his own area staff.[157] More generally, policy was "very much a matter of a small circle of individuals," according to Sonnenfeldt. NSC staff "were not directly involved except to the extent that Kissinger, who was very much involved directly with the President, sought our advice and used our expertise to buttress his own arguments."[158]

Bureaucratic infighting also sometimes erupted within the NSC staff as a result of Kissinger's actions. Who was in charge of NSC planning for the Strategic Arms Limitation Talks (SALT) with the Soviet Union was unclear for a period. Two different top staff members thought they had been assigned the job: Mort Halperin, who had been involved in SALT issues, and Lawrence E. Lynn Jr., director of the NSC's Office of Program Analysis. They jockeyed for control of the program, and both became disillusioned with the operations of the NSC staff system.[159] The end result was that Kissinger established a Verification Panel, chaired by himself, with staff support by Lynn and his group. Kissinger was the ultimate victor.

The 1970 decision to invade Cambodia was especially controversial within the NSC staff. Although several staff members were able to write position papers against the invasion, their efforts had little effect. On occasion, their opposition appears to have especially led to personal anger on Kissinger's part, telling one aide that "your views represent the cowardice of the Eastern Establishment," and referring to others as a "bleeding hearts club."[160] Two top aides, Anthony Lake (a future NSC advisor himself) and Roger Morris, resigned in protest; others left the NSC staff as well.

Kissinger's domination of the policy process had other effects. At times, President Nixon registered strong concerns about his NSC advisor's priorities, especially when they conflicted with presidential instructions. In late April 1972, Kissinger made a secret visit to Moscow, the purpose of which was to discuss Nixon's upcoming summit, the SALT treaty, and—for Nixon—Soviet pressure on North Vietnam, especially in light of its recent spring offensive in the South. Nixon was reluctant to let Kissinger make the trip, and later reflected that in his diary that "Henry, with all of his many virtues, does seem too often to be concerned about preparing the way for negotiations with the Soviets."[161] But Nixon relented. However, he instructed Kissinger—despite the latter's desire for flexibility—to bring up Vietnam first and not move on to other issues unless Soviet leader Leonid Brezhnev agreed to put pressure on North Vietnam.[162] Failing that, Kissinger was told to "just pack up and come home."[163] Kissinger brought up Vietnam first, as instructed, but received little encouragement from Brezhnev; the meeting then moved on to the SALT treaty—where the Soviets offered some important concessions—and Nixon's upcoming visit.

But the White House was not pleased. On April 22, 1972, Haldeman notes in his diary that "apparently [Kissinger] hasn't followed instructions from the President as to what he is to be negotiating. He's spending his time on the Soviet Summit agenda rather than on getting Vietnam settled. The President was clearly disturbed by what information he had received from Henry last night." According to Haldeman, Nixon had expected a message from Kissinger, but Kissinger had delayed sending it because he was "determined to have a three-day meeting and he's managed to do it."[164]

For Nixon, Soviet help on Vietnam was to be "linked"—Kissinger's favorite tactic—to arms control and the summit. "It seems to me that their primary purpose in getting you to Moscow to discuss the summit has now been served," he wrote Kissinger, "while our purpose of getting some progress on Vietnam has not been served." "There were sharply worded cables," Nixon later recalled. "I wanted Henry to know that it was vitally important to see our priorities taken up first . . . Vietnam had to be front and center. It was my belief that it was vital to link progress on things that the Soviets wanted, such as arms control, with progress on what we wanted."[165]

Nixon and Haldeman also were concerned that in the wake of the achievements in dealing with China, Soviet Union, and North Vietnam, that Kissinger would seek even bolder foreign policy initiatives that were both self-serving and at odds with Nixon's priorities. On February 6, 1973, Haldeman notes that he and Nixon "got into quite a long. . . discussion of Henry's whole situation, making the point that he's made all his big plays now and he's trying to look for ways to maintain the momentum, which is essentially impossible." Kissinger, moreover, was not content with more mundane work: "Henry's obviously not interested in taking the time to work out the details of the [Vietnam peace] agreement, etc., which must be done, but doesn't really interest him at this point."[166]

A small point, but perhaps significant: according to Ehrlichman, Nixon had to *order*—Ehrlichman's emphasis—Kissinger to attend senior White House staff meetings: "Nixon was concerned that Henry was drifting off in his own direction. He was too independent. The rest of the staff should have a chance to gather him in each morning."[167]

EFFECTS OF EXCLUSION

Perhaps of even more importance in its effect on policy was Kissinger's attempt to exclude others from the deliberative process. In Richard Allen's view, the system Nixon and Kissinger established "was largely responsible for a lot of misdeeds in foreign policy. They made a decision early on, which I opposed then and would oppose even today, to isolate and humiliate the Department of State."[168]

The exclusion of Rogers and others was not without cost. As Kenneth Rush observes, "When they went to Moscow and Beijing, Bill Rogers was treated very badly, and there were acrimonious clashes between Rogers and Kissinger in both places."[169] So too with Middle East policy according to Saunders: "I can only state from my primary experience of working on Arab-Israeli diplomacy at that time, I think it was very real. I think there was genuine contempt on Henry's side for Rogers and the State Department. . . . The talk about the feud or whatever you want to call it was not for the most part overdone I don't think."[170]

Marshall Green, then assistant secretary of state for Far-Eastern and Asian Affairs, recalled his difficulties during Nixon's 1969 visit to President Ferdinand Marcos in the Philippines. Nixon and Kissinger met with Marcos, while Rogers (and Green) met with the foreign minister, Fidel Ramos. Yet Green was expected to report to the assembled media, some 200 strong, about the main summit: "of course, everybody could tell that I hadn't been there; it was very difficult—very embarrassing. . . . I do think that the secretary of state should have been at that meeting. I think that Henry Kissinger was imputing too much to his position. This was the beginning of a problem I had to live with during the next three or four years, when I was assistant secretary." Not only was Nixon distrustful of State, according to Green, but "Kissinger did all he could to play on the president's prejudices to enhance his own position." In Green's view, exclusion of State also negatively affected relations with Japan. Yet Green does acknowledge "had he looked to the bureaucracy completely for the opening to China, we would never have done it because we didn't know it could go that far."[171]

The one area where Rogers and the State Department were able to exercise some influence was on Middle East policy. By 1970, as the "Rogers Plan" was in development, Kissinger became especially antagonistic toward the secretary of state, and both Haldeman and Nixon spent time trying to calm Kissinger down and defuse tensions.[172] Several of Haldeman's diary entries note Nixon's frustration with Kissinger on Middle East policy, even including Nixon's doubts about his continued usefulness as NSC advisor. March 1970 was an especially crucial point at which Kissinger began to press Nixon and Haldeman on Rogers's efforts.[173]

March 10, 1970: [Haldeman received a call] saying K had to see P, new break in Mid East. P won't see him, K very upset. Problem continues. P wants me to try to untangle him too.[174]

March 17, 1970: Biggest problem of the day came via phone from P after I got home. . . . K had apparently hit him again on the Rogers problem. Said Rogers is out to get him and takes a stab 2–3 times a day. Probably comes from Rogers having a meeting with P yesterday while K in Paris. P trying as usual to stay out of it, and K as usual obsessed with discussing it in detail. P wants me to try and get him turned off.[175]

March 18, 1970: [At a meeting with Nixon, we] finally get to the real point, Kissinger. He's really worried about his psychopathic obsession with the idea that Rogers is out to get him, *and even more by his [Kissinger's] inability to stay out of the Israel problem. Talked about how we could help by trying to get K. to stick to priorities, etc.*[176]

August and September 1970 saw another flare-up in Kissinger's concerns about Rogers and the Middle East. Haldeman especially notes Nixon's increasing frustration with Kissinger's maneuvering.

August 16, 1970: Monumental flap with K, who called accusing P and me of playing games with him yesterday about boat ride, etc, to cover up plan to have Rogers up to Camp David [with Nixon but without Kissinger]. Incredible . . . He made reference to several early A.M. phone calls from P yesterday, with quick hang-ups. Very hard to figure, but has to be cleared up. He called me again at home, but I didn't quiet him much.[177]

August 17, 1970: I told [Nixon] about the flap, which K had continued today. [K] still convinced we were playing games with him. He's really very bitter and uptight, and when I totally refuted his claim, he backed off. . . . *All of this really worries P because it created doubts about K's reliability on other recommendations, and gets in the way of doing his work P realized K's basically jealous of any idea that is not his own,* and he can't swallow the apparent early success of the Mideast plan because its Rogers.' In fact, he's probably actually trying to make it fail for just this reason. Of all people, he has to keep his mind clean and clear, and instead he's obsessed with these weird persecution delusions. [Haldeman also recognized the toll on Nixon]: I'll have to talk to K some more because *this will prey on P's mind until something settled, but I don't think it is curable. P said several times that K may have reached the end of his usefulness.*[178]

August 18, 1970: [In a meeting the next day, Nixon and Haldeman] got into K problem again. [Nixon] wants me to let K know that we caught him on his bluff on this one, he's building up a monstrous story that does him no good.[179]

September 21, 1970: [Rogers and Kissinger blow up following an important principals' meeting with Nixon on the Middle East crisis, where Rogers accused Kissinger of withholding information from Nixon. Kissinger tried to be conciliatory, but Rogers] feels K trying to force P to rash decision. All this from K . . . The whole struggle went on through the day, K and Haig dropping in to my office three or four times to report the latest. K really disturbed that Rogers will win out. . . . [Nixon] had me go into K's office with him, to get updating and K started in again . . . P okayed K's plans but cut him short on complaints. [Later, Nixon told Haldeman], "*he's about come to conclusion can't tolerate any longer, either K or Rogers has to go, no other solution.*"[180]

According to Saunders, whose portfolios on the NSC staff and later at the State Department centered on the Middle East,

> I think the tension at the beginning of the period was that Henry wasn't comfortable with the Middle East. He knew a lot about Soviet affairs and arms control and a whole bunch of other things but he really never had to deal with the Middle East. I think he was trying to get control of it, of policy toward the Middle East, but here was Rogers coming out with the Rogers Plan; it wasn't Henry's way of doing things, so he pushed back.[181]

But Kissinger was able to win out over Rogers on the Middle East in the end, particularly after the 1973 war. In other areas, the invasion of Cambodia particularly marked the further ascendance of Kissinger's impact over foreign policy.

EFFECTS OF SECRET DIPLOMACY

Kissinger's back-channels and secret diplomacy were hallmarks of his tenure as NSC advisor. They represent the core of the "hard case" that Kissinger presents to some notion of the honest broker role: secret missions involve exclusion in policy input from other sources, strained relations with others in the interagency process, and the possibility of freelancing advocacy. Moreover, secret efforts occurred in a number of important policy areas for the Nixon presidency: dealings with the Soviet Union especially in the SALT negotiations, with North Vietnam in achieving a peace settlement, and in the opening up of relations with the People's Republic of China.

With the respect to the Soviet Union, Nixon himself had wanted a direct connection to the Soviets, and Kissinger's efforts served as an important channel of communication—bypassing the State Department—on a variety of foreign policy issues.[182] Kissinger began to establish back-channel discussions with Soviet Ambassador Anatoly Dobrynin starting in February 1969. They took on policy substance. In April 1969, Kissinger signaled to Dobrynin his willingness to bypass the stalled Paris peace talks with the North Vietnamese by himself engaging in direct but secret meetings with their representatives in Paris. These clandestine efforts began in August 1969, and they proved to be the crucial channel for an eventual settlement. Other secret negotiation efforts on Kissinger's part were central to the opening of relations with the People's Republic of China, an effort that Nixon himself clearly originated but that Kissinger secretly carried out, leading to Nixon's historic February 1972 visit to the PRC.

Some have argued that secrecy and back-channel efforts were needed especially in the case of China, the Soviet Union, and Vietnam. According to Winston Lord, each involved Communist powers and each "lent themselves to secrecy and tight control." Each also involved sensitive matters where Nixon and Kissinger, fearing leaks, "didn't want a lot of people in on it."[183] Moreover, in Lord's view, "These talks involved politically risky moves by both sides. Thus, you could make the case for secrecy in each case."[184]

But were there some costs to Kissinger's efforts? Did they go too far and go on for too long? In Isaacson's view, "handling the negotiations in secret from the State Department did not make the SALT outcome sturdier, the China opening smoother, or the Vietnam settlement any speedier." Secrecy took a toll on Kissinger's staff. They often had to prepare several sets of briefing papers and memoranda: one for those in the know, one for those somewhat in the know, and one for those completely out of the loop. According to Anthony Lake, "The levels of knowledge and duplicity were like a Mozart opera in complexity." In general, according to Lake, "Some secrecy in government is necessary, but Henry crossed the line from secrecy to deceit." [185] There were, moreover, broader effects on the policy process. Once suspicions about Kissinger's activities registered at State or Defense, compromise flew by the wayside. As Kissinger himself concedes, if their "pristine position was not achieved, the agencies were not responsible."[186]

STRATEGIC ARMS LIMITATION TALKS

Let us now consider some specific cases of Kissinger's diplomatic efforts. With respect to SALT, although the United States and the Soviet Union had been engaged in formal negotiations since 1969 in Helsinki and Vienna over nuclear arms limitations, it was Kissinger's private talks with Dobrynin that were crucial in laying the foundation for a treaty. Critics, however, have held that Kissinger might have been able to press the Soviets for a better deal.[187]

One issue was the failure to include in the treaty a ban on multiple independently targetable reentry vehicles (MIRVs), an omission that led to a dramatic increase in the number of warheads on a single missile. According to Kissinger aide William Hyland, refusal to ban them "was the key decision in the entire history of SALT. . . . It was a truly fateful decision that changed strategic relations, and changed them to the detriment of U.S. security."[188] Kissinger understood the impact that MIRV deployment would have, but he felt inclusion would be "more than the traffic would bear" and favored other arms limitations options.[189] In April 1970, Nixon approved two of several negotiating packages. One package included a ban on MIRVs, but Kissinger attached two conditions that made it a nonstarter with the Soviets. One was a requirement for onsite inspections—a provision only the Pentagon favored and the Soviets were likely to turn down. The second condition was a loophole permitting the *production* of MIRVs but not their testing or later deployment. Since the United States had already undertaken successful testing and the Soviets had not, it too was a nonstarter. An agreement banning MIRVs was off the table; when it was presented to the Soviets, they did not regard it as a serious proposal.[190]

Kissinger then proposed the second package: high ceilings on the number of existing missiles plus the limitation of antiballistic missile (ABM) sites to one at each nation's capital. The Soviets jumped at the proposal, but it proved to be a "first-class blunder," as Kissinger himself later acknowledged.[191] A capital-based ABM system had not been discussed by the NSC, and it ran counter to a congressionally approved ABM proposal that would protect two U.S. missile sites in the West, not Washington, D.C. According to Isaacson, Kissinger "would spend the next year trying to extricate the U.S. from this position."

Kissinger also botched linkage of reductions in offensive missiles to limits on ABM sites, an important bargaining chip. In March 1970, Dobrynin had asked whether the United States wanted a comprehensive agreement or one limited to ABM defense systems (which the Soviets favored). According to Isaacson, "Kissinger did not realize the distinction Dobrynin was making." Either approach was suitable, he told Dobrynin. When Dobrynin later came back with a proposal for an ABM-only agreement, Kissinger told him Washington would consider it.[192] But here too Kissinger blundered. When Gerard Smith, the chief U.S. negotiator in Vienna, learned of the offer in July 1970, he immediately cabled Kissinger and told him that the ABM was "our strongest bargaining counter," and thus any constraint on our ABM sites should be linked to constraints on Soviet offensive missiles, in one negotiation package.[193] According to Isaacson, here too "it would take Kissinger a year to undo this mess."[194]

While an agreement on ABMs and offensive missiles was eventually achieved in 1972, Kissinger's initial blunders may have weakened the U.S. bargaining position. Moreover, other blunders occurred along the way. Chief arms negotiator Smith later faulted Kissinger for not including submarine-based missiles in the 1971 "breakthrough" with Dobrynin, an offensive technology where the Soviets were behind but rapidly catching up. According to Smith, "There is no evidence to indicate that this major change in SALT policy was ever considered in advance by anyone except Kissinger—and perhaps not even by him. It may well have been a random answer [to Dobrynin] of a fatigued and overextended man [Kissinger] who did not realize the immense significance of his words."[195] In 1972, the Soviets conceded on the submarine-based missiles, although the agreement allowed them considerable modernization and a high ceiling on the number of missiles; a second ABM site was also permitted under the final treaty.

As discussions between Kissinger and Dobrynin wore on, SALT negotiators were often kept in the dark about Kissinger's efforts. Indeed, the U.S. delegation was at a negotiating disadvantage due to Kissinger's secret talks: their Soviet counterparts were kept abreast of the Kissinger/Dobrynin talks but they were not.[196] According to Helmut Sonnenfeldt, "it was three minutes before the public announcement in Moscow and Washington that it was shown to the SALT [negotiating] team and to the Secretary of State, who had tremendous problems with it."[197] Even after the agreement was reached and publicized, the SALT negotiators were kept in the dark on certain issues: when Paul Nitze, a delegate to the SALT talks, came to the White House in search of more information, only excerpts of some records were made available to him.[198]

In chief negotiator Smith's view, a better SALT agreement might have been achieved through normal channels: "Was it necessary to pursue such duplicitous diplomacy?"[199] Kissinger "was a one-man stand, a presidential aide against the resources of the Soviet leadership."[200] Kissinger, moreover, "was often acting as a principal, not an agent . . . [he] had too much influence."[201] Yet influence did not always equate with adeptness. Kissinger was especially at a disadvantage as the final details of the treaty were being worked out during Nixon's May 1972 summit in Moscow; the U.S. SALT negotiators remained in Helsinki until just hours before it was publicly announced. Kissinger and his aides were on their own. Furthermore, Kissinger's "Lone Ranger," secretive style may have, as Isaacson points out, "undermined future support for SALT by his trickiness in dealing with some of the details."[202] That view has some merit. As President Carter later recalled, "Kissinger in effect pulled the proposals out of his hip pocket, and a lot of those discussion points were secret even from Gerry Smith, our chief negotiator, and the Joint Chiefs of Staff, and certainly, from the American public."[203] It put Carter's own arms reduction efforts, SALT II, in a tougher spot.

CHINA

With respect to Kissinger's mission with China, the case for secret negotiation seems especially strong given the politically charged nature of the White House's efforts and the damage that publicity might have entailed. Yet even here there may have been costs. Winston Lord, a member of the secret traveling party, acknowledges that "the secretary of state and the State Department and the Defense Department didn't even know what the policy was."[204] And secrecy may have had negative repercussions for the success of the effort.

One cost was that it exacerbated existing tensions with State. Rogers's complete lack of knowledge of Kissinger's secret mission and the possibility of a tectonic change in U.S.-China policy were important contributors to his increasing rift with Kissinger. Rogers was finally officially informed on July 8, 1971, while Kissinger was abroad.[205] For Kissinger, a June 28, 1971, *New York Times* story that speculated that Kissinger would be going to China led him to accuse Rogers of being the source of the leak and was the occasion (once again) of efforts by Nixon and Haldeman to calm Kissinger down. According to Haldeman, "Henry's convinced that Rogers leaked this on purpose in an attempt to try to stop Henry as the negotiator with the Chinese, and to try to break off his relations with Dobrynin. The same story had a number of accurate reports on changes in ambassadorial assignments, which Henry feels were just put in to validate the other points. The President told me to talk to Haig about keeping Henry calmed down, because there's nothing we can do."[206]

Another cost was that Kissinger's penchant for not even informing the secretary of state or other high-level officials may have had some detrimental effect on his own efforts. As Lord acknowledges, "you could have brought in a couple of key State people on each of these issues and sworn them to secrecy and used their expertise and had more bureaucratic support in a crunch . . . I don't think it was foreordained that everything had to leak. . . . We would have had more expertise."[207] According to Richard Solomon, a senior NSC staffer, exclusion especially of the CIA meant that Kissinger could not even turn to them to gather information about senior Chinese leaders. Solomon had to develop his own back-channel to the CIA "despite Henry's efforts to compartmentalize the process."[208]

Problems would especially emerge, during Kissinger's secret October 1971 trip, in the drafting of what became the Shanghai Communiqué. The Chinese rejected an initial U.S. draft, and each side agreed to draft its own language and then locate areas of convergence. This forced Kissinger's team to work alone; as Lord notes, "We drafted the whole damn thing over night

. . . essentially it was done without State at all."[209] But difficulties continued to persist even when the final version of the communiqué was approved by both sides during Nixon's trip to China in February 1972.

The status of U.S. treaties with Taiwan in the communiqué was the issue. Although Rogers and other officials from State were part of Nixon's traveling party, Kissinger and his staff still had the largely exclusive upper hand. According to Lord, Kissinger and two other aides (one was Lord himself) negotiated the Taiwan issue, "while the State Department was off talking about claims and assets and economics and exchanges, and they weren't even involved."[210] However, as Marshall Green of the State Department observes, "The Shanghai Communiqué could have been a disaster. It had been approved by Nixon and Chou En-lai . . . but it excluded reference to our treaty obligations to Taiwan." When State was finally informed of the details, it was forced to remedy the errors. As Green recalls, "Kissinger was very mad at me for finding the mistake in the communiqué, because I put him in an embarrassing position vis-à-vis the president. He had bound Nixon to a document that was open to criticism from the right wing."[211] Moreover, as Isaacson points out, the lack of reference to the Taiwan treaty was an odd omission. The communiqué noted other treaty commitments with nations in the region, but not the most central one: "Rogers finally got through to Nixon with this and a host of lesser criticisms."[212]

VIETNAM

Other of Kissinger's secret efforts were sometimes problematic. In Isaacson's view, Kissinger might have been more effective had he been more public in his negotiations with the North Vietnamese: "As he later discovered when he used such an approach on his Middle East shuttles, the resulting drama and world attention can create a momentum and be conducive to a settlement, rather than an obstacle." Plus, it might have "calmed some of the anger of the antiwar movement."[213] The North Vietnamese, moreover, had not insisted on secrecy—that was Kissinger's doing. Once the meetings were made public in early 1972, "Hanoi was put on the defensive for a change," Isaacson notes.[214]

Nor, perhaps, were Kissinger's peace negotiations all that skillful. Kissinger boldly moved forward in an attempt to reach an agreement, even though both Nixon and South Vietnam's president, Nguyen Van Thieu, posed difficult obstacles. Kissinger's skills as a bargainer were formidable, especially in papering over and fudging disagreements. But those same strengths proved weaknesses in achieving an agreement, not just with North Vietnam but with Nixon and Thieu, with whom he often failed to appropriately consult. His messages to Nixon were vague: "there has been some definite progress," he informed Haldeman in "cryptic" (Kissinger's word) fashion.[215]

Nixon was at odds with Kissinger on the latter's attempts to secure a settlement before the before the 1972 election. This strategy was the opposite of Nixon's own political view; he felt a strong electoral mandate, against a weak antiwar candidate like George McGovern, would get a better deal from the North Vietnamese. A preelection settlement, moreover, might open him up to political criticism.[216] As Haldeman observed on September 28, 1972, it was Nixon's view that "Henry was trying to get a settlement before the election for the value to us politically, which the President feels is negative rather than positive."[217] Kissinger's efforts here also raise questions about the merits of the NSC advisor serving as a "political watchdog," especially since it ran counter to Nixon's own rather considerable political instincts.[218]

There is also some evidence—again—that Kissinger went beyond Nixon's authority in trying to secure an agreement before Election Day. According to Ehrlichman, "twice he cabled the North Vietnamese in the president's name to accept their October proposal. . . . Henry did that over Al Haig's strong objections and beyond any presidential authority."[219] On November 29, Haldeman met with Haig who felt that "basically the screw-up was Henry's fault, in that he committed to a final negotiation and settlement before he really should have."[220] Meeting with Haig on December 10, 1972, Nixon told him that "the problem is that we pushed so hard on the settlement before the election," which Nixon opposed, and "that put us in a bad spot. We're still trying to dig out from that."[221] According to Dallek, "Kissinger functioned as a surrogate president, making all the negotiating decisions without seeking Nixon's direct approval."[222]

As it turned out, Thieu balked at the terms of the agreement in late October 1972. It was not until late January 1973, following a massive bombing campaign against the North, continued pressure on Thieu, and a secret agreement to support South Vietnam militarily if the North launched an offensive, that a deal was ultimately reached. Even then, Nixon had concerns that Kissinger might grab too much of the credit, and he ordered Haldeman and Ziegler to develop a press plan "so we can control Kissinger."[223] Nixon also ordered that all of Kissinger's telephone logs be checked and monitored to see which people in the press he was talking to.[224]

In Nixon's view, Kissinger comments to the press in late October that "peace is at hand" made the U.S. bargaining position more difficult: "That's why they've shifted to a harder position," he told Ehrlichman in December.[225]

As for the final agreement in January, it proved to be an empty promise to Saigon; neither Nixon nor Ford was in any position to come to the future aid of South Vietnam. As John Negroponte, then a diplomat involved in the negotiations, told one of Thieu's aides: "We really screwed you guys."[226]

CUBA

Sometimes Kissinger's relationship with Dobrynin had negative repercussions. In the fall of 1970, U-2 reconnaissance photographs revealed the apparent existence of a Soviet submarine base at Sienfuegos, Cuba, a possible violation of the JFK-Khrushchev agreement of 1962. The evidence and its implications for U.S.-Soviet relations were extensively discussed at the highest levels of the principals. But information was tightly held, and Kissinger's meetings with Dobrynin and his personal negotiations over the definition of "base" proved crucial in defusing the crisis. That would prove of positive merit, at least in the short-run. But on the other hand, Kissinger had once again gone solo. Moreover, as Dallek notes, the British ambassador to the United States, John Freeman, felt that Kissinger "had exaggerated the Soviet danger" at Sienfuegos, way beyond CIA information about the base.[227]

The lack of proper institutional memory about what Kissinger had privately negotiated arose in the Carter presidency when it acquired evidence of Soviet use of the port.[228] It especially contributed to the stalled ratification of the SALT II treaty and the end of détente with the Soviet Union.

NIXON'S CONCERNS ABOUT SECRET DIPLOMACY

Although Kissinger's secret missions were a hallmark of this administration's foreign policy, Nixon himself was sometimes aware of their potential negative consequences. In September 1971, Nixon raised concerns with Haldeman about Kissinger as a secret emissary to North Vietnamese representatives in Paris—Nixon was especially troubled by "Henry's delusions of grandeur as a peacemaker."[229] In mid-October 1972, as Kissinger appeared close to an agreement with the North, Haldeman noted that Nixon's view was that "Henry is strongly motivated in all this by a desire for personally being the one to bring about a final peace settlement."[230] In November 1972, press coverage of Kissinger's secret negotiations and the sense they conveyed of him as the chief architect not just instrument of the administration's foreign policy considerably irritated Nixon. "We've got to stop paying the price for K [Kissinger]," he told Haldeman.[231] "We've got to leash Henry more than we have up to now," Nixon told Haldeman on November 20.[232] The next day, Nixon said he "can't tolerate

Henry's increasing problems," and instructed Haldeman to "bring him back to earth."[233]

With respect to the opening of China, Nixon was initially reluctant to send Kissinger, knowing the impact it would have on the State Department. As Haldeman noted on April 28, 1971, "there was a long discussion . . . primarily the question of selection of an emissary, with the President ruling out himself or Rogers and then ruling out Kissinger because that would break all the china with State."[234]

Although Kissinger was operating under Nixon's instructions during the mission, the degree of secrecy that Kissinger insisted upon sometimes posed problems for Nixon. With respect to secret efforts with the Soviet Union, Haldeman notes on December 28, 1970,

> [Nixon] asked me to have a talk with Haig because he's concerned as a result of his conversation with Rogers yesterday, that Rogers is aware of what Henry's doing with the Russians. While Henry thinks he's operating secretly, he's not really. The President feels that Henry's got to open up the fact of his secret channel so that Rogers knows about it and we have some more candor in this whole thing . . . [it] poses a very bad situation for the President. . . . There's a good chance that this will come out, which would be a very embarrassing thing. The President feels Henry's got to realize he's not a secret-type person, that the things he does do come out.[235]

The problem of informing Rogers festered for another five months. On May 13, 1971, Kissinger and Haldeman met with Nixon and "got into the problem of Rogers and the SALT agreement, since that's now set . . . The problem is how to fill Rogers in ahead of time without his feeling that it's been maneuvered behind his back, which of course it has. The President is very sensitive to this, but doesn't seem to have any fixed ideas on how to deal with it."[236] On May 18, 1971, Haldeman notes: "The President is still extremely worried about how to tell Rogers, and went back and forth on that, frequently, on and off during the rest of the afternoon, but we locked him in for a 9:00 appointment and he's going to have to face up to it now."[237] Following that meeting, Nixon told Haldeman that he "had the feeling that there was very much of a problem." Haldeman then spent an hour with Rogers at the State Department: "He was very clearly very upset. His basic point was, 'Why didn't you tell me that you were doing this? There's no need for me to be involved, but I do have to be informed.'" Rogers offered to resign, but "I didn't really respond to that. . . . He made the point that if the

President doesn't trust him, he can't do his work." Rogers then reiterated his complaints against Kissinger for not posting him on his dealings with Dobrynin and other matters. Nixon later called Rogers to smooth things out, and "right after he hung up *the P heaved a deep sigh, looked out the window, and said it would be goddam easy to run this office if you didn't have to deal with people.*"[238] It was telling commentary not just about Kissinger, but also about this president.

Nixon, according, to Haldeman, became "horrified" at some of Kissinger's proposed secret missions. On July 21, 1971, shortly after Kissinger's secret trip to China, he told Nixon he would like to do the same with North Vietnam: "The President was horrified by a proposal Kissinger made to go on a secret trip to Hanoi after he leaves Peking on the next trip. *The President's point being that Henry is now getting carried away with his secret diplomacy, and going too far.*"[239] In fact, Nixon appears to have been quite fed up with Kissinger's efforts and was actually considering dropping him as NSC advisor. At a November 21, 1972, meeting on second-term transition issues, Haldeman notes that "Kissinger's problems came up a number of times in conversations during the day. *President thought Henry ought to forget about the fetish of secret meetings. . . . President really feels he should leave by midyear.*"[240] In December 1972, Nixon shared his concerns with then Deputy Secretary of Defense Kenneth Rush, who was under consideration to replace Rogers at State: Nixon "told me he didn't know whether he was going to keep Henry or not."[241]

Other foreign policy episodes present a mixed picture concerning Kissinger's diplomatic efforts. He is generally lauded for his work during the 1973 Israel-Egypt war.[242] But his actions in the CIA's efforts in overthrowing the government of Salvador Allende in Chile and in tilting the United States in support of Pakistan during its 1971 war with India have been criticized.

IV. Implications

The "hard" case that Kissinger's expansive role as NSC advisor presents to an alternative, honest broker conception of the position is a bit less hard than it seems at first glance. Although Kissinger and Nixon had policy successes, some policy errors and failures can be traced to how Kissinger carried out the job of NSC advisor. As Rothkopf observes, Kissinger and Nixon created together "the smallest, most powerful, most brilliant" team. But it was sometimes the "most dysfunctional inner circle of all."[243]

The NSC Advisor's Role Expectations and Honest Brokerage

Kissinger's pregovernmental experience offered little in the way of forming a sense of what he hoped to embody in the role of NSC advisor. Like Bundy, he was an academic, although Kissinger had much more extensive experience serving as an outside consultant during the Eisenhower, Kennedy, and Johnson administrations. But if his sense of the role of the NSC advisor and what processes and procedures might structure effective decision making were a bit nebulous, he did bring two things that would figure importantly to the job. One was a mastery of bureaucratic politics, albeit one honed in the environs of Harvard rather than Washington. The other was his deep familiarity with—and strong positions in—many areas of national security policy as well as a clearly honed sense of cold war geopolitics.

The latter predisposed Kissinger to be a policy advocate. But it was not his advocacy, per se, that was problematic. *How* Kissinger filled that advocacy role was at times the issue. Kissinger clearly was no honest broker—aiming always and above all to get all views fully aired before the president in an honest and fair way. Given their agenda, Kissinger—and Nixon—were in part justified in their concerns about the bureaucratically embedded positions and slow response of State and Defense. Yet, Kissinger's battles to exclude Rogers, Laird, and others went way beyond what was needed. They were time consuming, distracting, and weakened morale. Moreover, their persistence often blocked relevant input from departments in the policy process. Kissinger's gatekeeping may even have extended unnecessarily to blocking input from his own staff and at times may have compromised its performance.

The problem was compounded by other aspects of Kissinger's role as NSC advisor, especially his penchant for secret diplomacy. While at times such efforts may have been necessary—and China is the good example here—there is also the risk of an addiction to the bureaucratically unfettered world that secret negotiation allows. There is also high risk of policy error—and here China is also a good example, as were the secret strategic arms negotiations with the Soviets and dealings with the North Vietnamese. Absence of departmental expertise has a price: "flying solo" carries risks.

Kissinger's visibility as NSC advisor also was problematic at times. Not so much that he was a well-known public figure (although that troubled Nixon), but rather in the way it led to a preoccupation with press coverage. Not only did Kissinger spend much time and effort in dealing with the press—now part of the job of the NSC advisor—but he worried about how *he* was being portrayed, and his maneuvering with the press played a part in bureaucratic one-upsmanship with Rogers and Laird. His own press leaks may have created a culture of leaks from elsewhere. And it appears to have generated an attempt to stop leaks that led to the creation of the Plumbers' Unit and other efforts, such as the resumption of secret taping, that would lead to the downfall of this presidency.

Both Kissinger's secret diplomacy and his media visibility also generated concerns for Nixon. The China initiative was clearly Nixon's in origin,[244] and it was Nixon in the end who decided to send Kissinger on the mission. But Kissinger sometimes went beyond, if not on some occasions directly against, Nixon's instructions on his diplomatic missions. Kissinger's relations with reporters especially garnered Nixon's outrage, particularly when contacts were made against explicit presidential order. Kissinger's antics took up the president's time, as Haldeman's diary entries repeatedly attest.

The issue of whether these activities "beyond brokerage" are fundamentally problematic or whether the problems that emerged stem from Kissinger's own idiosyncratic and at times excessive practices is difficult to untangle. Other NSC advisors will begin to provide the answer. Yet Kissinger provides cautionary signals concerning the merits of an overly robust role for the NSC advisor.

EVOLUTION OF THE NSC ADVISOR'S ROLE OVER TIME

Kissinger's role as NSC advisor clearly evolved over time, but not in the direction of balanced brokerage. Rather it was Kissinger's power, control, prestige, and visibility that increased over time. Prior to his secret missions to China and to North Vietnamese negotiators in Paris, Kissinger was not particularly a visible public figure. But as time went on, two key aspects of his NSC advisor's role fed upon each other: secret diplomacy fueled media interest in Kissinger, which may have fueled Kissinger's interests in even more diplomacy—which Nixon would eventually have concerns over. Kissinger's preoccupation with leaks, and the responsive actions that followed, was another consequence of an NSC advisor seeking control internally and concerned about external perceptions.

Kissinger insisted on good staff work, to his credit; he didn't want "precooked decisions," or ones "bargained out in the bureaucracies."[245] Yet the quality of that NSC staff work also appears to lessen over time, in part as a consequence of Kissinger's own activities as NSC advisor. Many of his aides seem to regard the early years, particularly before the Cambodian invasion, as a kind of golden age, but the quality of advice may have been downhill from then on.

Kissinger gets more than passing marks for his efforts to attract a skilled and experienced staff, many of whom went on to further prominence. Yet staff attrition was high, the toll on key staff from wiretaps and then Cambodia was considerable. His inability to settle on a deputy is troubling, as was the reluctance to appoint an NSC executive secretary. Unlike for Bundy and Rostow, there was no Bromley Smith to provide institutional memory, so too for James Lay under Eisenhower.

PRESIDENTIAL DECISION-MAKING NEEDS, PRESIDENTIAL ROLE EXPECTATIONS

Nixon's selection of Kissinger is a bit of a cipher. There was no extensive prepresidential association; this is odd, given Nixon's preoccupation with personal loyalty. Yet they somehow clicked. But there were tensions—and suspicions—from the start. "I don't trust Henry, but I can use him," Nixon told a rival of Kissinger early in his presidency.[246]

What Nixon wanted and needed in an NSC advisor does need to be factored in. He did not want predetermined policy options; this was a lesson he drew—perhaps erroneously—from his vice presidential experience under Eisenhower. But he sometimes disliked what Kissinger did, even coming close to firing him on several occasions. Nixon too created the conditions for what transpired. How the NSC advisor's role was defined was both Nixon's and Kissinger's doing. And that is an important lesson in its own right: both the president and the NSC advisor matter in how the job gets fleshed out.

Nixon's penchant for delegation especially contributed to Kissinger's power and prominence as NSC advisor. Nixon only wanted to focus on the key foreign policy issues he was interested in; the rest would be up to Kissinger. In a lengthy March 1970 memorandum to Kissinger, Haldeman, and Ehrlichman, Nixon clearly sets out what he felt he should attend to and what should be delegated to his assistants. In the part of the memo dealing with foreign affairs, he instructed Kissinger that the only policy areas he wanted brought to his attention were those dealing with East-West issues, the Soviet Union, China, Eastern Europe (but only where it affected relations with Russia), and Western Europe (but only where NATO issues were involved). As for the rest, Kissinger was instructed "to farm out as much of the decision making" as possible.[247]

No mechanisms of presidential oversight were part of Nixon's delegation practices. No procedures were established to ensure that those entrusted with authority acted appropriately and abetted a sound deliberative process. Nor had Nixon much concern to encourage teamwork and other strategies—

which were central to Eisenhower's management style—that aimed to make the staff work effectively. In fact, Nixon may have matters even worse. For a president with a penchant for isolation, delegation without more concern for management and oversight might have exacerbated the problem.

"Managing Kissinger," moreover, rose frequently to the presidential level, yet Nixon was an ineffective manager, generally willing to pawn problems with Kissinger off to Haldeman and others. Still, as speechwriter Raymond Price observes, "The care and feeding of Henry was one of the greatest burdens of [his] presidency."[248] As Haldeman noted on March 2, 1971, Nixon, *"made the point several times that the price he has to pay to Kissinger in terms of emotional drain on himself is very great."* In Haldeman's view, "Most of the fault in all of this is chargeable to Henry . . . his almost psychopathic concern with everything Rogers does. He almost acts like a little kid. And we don't seem to be able to find a way to overcome this."[249] Paradoxically, Kissinger's continued grasp for greater power and control would sometimes lead to presidential reaction as problems resulted, and Kissinger's influence with Nixon would wane.

Nixon's own idiosyncrasies also come into play. According to Lawrence Eagleburger, "Kissinger and Nixon *both* had degrees of paranoia. . . . They developed a conspiratorial approach to foreign policy management." According to Issacson, "To get anything done, Kissinger quickly learned, required catering to Nixon's prejudices." In Ehrlichman's view, "If you bucked Nixon on his petty biases and idiosyncratic pronouncements, he'd cut you dead. He wouldn't see you or return your memos."[250] Presidential proclivities must be factored in, but the Nixon-Kissinger relationship also suggests that they need to be checked and counterbalanced, as I noted in the introductory chapter.

The problem of too close a fit with presidential needs is problematic in the Nixon-Kissinger relationship in another way. It was a close and tight one, not easily penetrable by others with divergent views. In some policy decisions, however, Nixon's instincts would sometimes err, and he was prone to quick decisions. Kissinger would balk at times. Yet Nixon largely lacked an early and consistent brake, which an honest broker might have provided at various points in his deliberations.

Other Implications

The penultimate measure of Kissinger's power was his ability to retain the NSC advisor role when Nixon appointed him secretary of state on August 22, 1973. According to Rothkopf, President Ford later felt that forcing Kissinger out as NSC advisor in November 1975 was his "most important contribution" to the national security decision process. Ford was trying "to restore Henry to the role of an adviser, not 'the adviser.' I think he had the sense that the national security system called for giving the president a range of views, and what had happened was that Nixon sank into the depths and Henry assumed greater power, that there was far too much judgment in the hands of one person who wasn't the president."[251] Ford later told journalist Bob Woodward, "Why Nixon gave Henry both secretary of state and head of the NSC, I never understood," Ford said, "Except he was a great supporter of Kissinger. Period." But Ford viewed Kissinger's dual roles as a conflict of interest that weakened the administration's ability to fully air policy debates: "They were supposed to check on one another."[252] But problems were not just confined to the period of Kissinger's dual jobs, they emerged earlier when Kissinger wore only one hat.

Kissinger's tenure as NSC advisor also bears lessons about the relationship of role and organization. Unlike Bundy, who operated with a greater degree of freedom in the organizationally fluid Kennedy process, Kissinger had put in place a more formally structured operation. Yet that process was usually quite malleable to Kissinger's own ends, and it was rarely an impediment to what he sought to achieve. In part, this may have reflected his own skill in crafting a structure that maximized his own power and control. As Goodpaster observed, the system "offered the power to Henry and Henry availed himself of it."[253] But Kissinger's tenure is also indicative of the importance of individual roles and the impact they can exert. An important lesson here is that roles clearly matter, even if organizational structures are designed to channel and constrain.

Kissinger might have especially reflected on his own earlier writings in this regard. As he observed in 1966, the statesman "is suspicious of those who personalize foreign policy, for history teaches him the fragility of structures dependent upon individuals."[254]

CHAPTER 4

The Benifits of Balanced Brokerage

Scowcroft as NSC Advisor

Analysis of Brent Scowcroft's role as NSC advisor is particularly important in understanding how a modern, post-Eisenhower occupant of that role can meet some of the requirements of honest brokerage, yet at the same time take on—judiciously—other tasks such as serving as personal counselor to the president or acting as a diplomatic channel. Scowcroft's tenure as NSC advisor is also important given that he—along only with Bundy—served in the position under two presidents. Indeed, Scowcroft not only served as NSC advisor to Presidents Gerald R. Ford and George H. W. Bush, he also served under Nixon as Henry Kissinger's deputy after Al Haig left that position. His widely recognized ability to perform well as NSC advisor is yet another factor. During the Nixon and early Ford presidencies, as deputy, he had to navigate through the waters of a secretary of state (Kissinger), who had long dominated foreign and national security policy making, and a secretary of defense (James Schlesinger), who was a potent rival to Kissinger and another skilled academician. After Scowcroft became Ford's NSC advisor, the Kissinger phenomenon would remain but Schlesinger's replacement, Donald Rumsfeld, was a powerful actor in his own right with considerable White House, congressional, and bureaucratic experience. In the George H. W. Bush presidency, the interpersonal calculus was a bit different and more collegial. Yet Scowcroft still dealt with a secretary of state with close ties to the president, a wealth of Washington experience, and bureaucratic savvy (James A. Baker III), a secretary of defense also with broad governmental experience, drive, and intellect (Richard Cheney), and a JCS chairman who had himself had significant NSC staff experience and his own record as NSC advisor (Colin Powell). In both presidencies, it was a talented but potentially tough crew.

I. The Ford National Security Process

A graduate of West Point, Scowcroft initially planned a career as an Air Force fighter pilot. But those hopes were dashed when his P51 Mustang fighter malfunctioned and crashed on a training flight, injuring him severely. He then earned a masters degree in international relations at Columbia, later followed by a doctorate. He taught Russian history and politics both at West Point and the Air Force Academy. He became fluent in both the Russian and Serbo-Croatian languages—the latter during a stint as military attaché at the U.S. embassy in Belgrade. Returning to Washington, he served on the policy planning staff of the JCS, then became military aide to President Nixon. While in the White House, he came to Kissinger's attention. Kissinger was impressed by his background in Soviet studies but also because he had seen him stand up to White House Chief of Staff H. R. Haldeman.[1] Hiring Scowcroft was, according to Kissinger, "one of the best decisions I have ever made."[2] "I needed a strong person as my deputy, who would be willing to stand up to me if necessary. . . . Not every day," Kissinger added, "but to stand up for what he thought was right."[3]

KISSINGER'S DEPUTY NSC ADVISOR

Although it would not be until November 3, 1975, that Scowcroft was elevated to the NSC advisor position, his influence as Kissinger's deputy was great. The deputy post was especially influential once Kissinger became secretary of state in August 1973 but retained the NSC job. Despite his considerable talents, Kissinger sometimes found it difficult to serve as both NSC advisor and secretary of state. How could he provide objective advice to the president if it was his own advice he was commenting on as NSC advisor?

According to Winston Lord—as key aide, first on the NSC staff then at State—"After all, when he wore two hats, he could send himself a memo then approve it, which was ridiculous. Even Henry in a candid moment would tell you it was kind of a weird system."[4] According to the White House Web site's *History of the National Security Council,* "Kissinger later admitted . . . that the union of the two positions did not work. Department of State representatives were his subordinates while he wore his Secretary of State hat. When he chaired a meeting, they had to represent his point of view or else all interdepartmental matters would be outside his control. Kissinger indicated he was in an inherently absurd position of either pushing his Department's views as chairman or dissociating himself from his subordinates."[5] Kissinger—already overworked as NSC advisor, as we saw in the previous chapter—became even more overloaded with two important and time-consuming jobs. His NSC aides reportedly attempted to get him to deal with the backlog of paperwork by putting memos in folders with enticing labels—sure to catch Kissinger's interest—such as "Scowcroft Conversations with the President."[6]

In the muddle, Scowcroft's stature as a skilled deputy rose as Kissinger became more deeply enmeshed in his duties as secretary of state. According to Ford, when Scowcroft was deputy to Kissinger, he was the first person to see the president, usually at 7:30 A.M.[7] According to Kissinger, Scowcroft attended his morning briefings with Ford. During Kissinger's not infrequent absence from Washington, Scowcroft would brief the president.[8] Scowcroft's role as deputy was more powerful than usual. Scowcroft in effect often took Kissinger's place as NSC advisor. According to Harold Saunders, "You couldn't be that close to the president and not perform certain functions. Once Henry was secretary of state, his functions were vastly different, in some ways a lot broader and a lot more demanding of his time in terms of the detail he had to cope with. So I don't think he would have time to do very much of the NSC type of stuff. Brent was a wonderful deputy."[9] Even the usually modest Scowcroft later acknowledged that he was serving as de facto NSC advisor when Kissinger held both jobs.[10]

We also see the emergence of Scowcroft's role as an honest broker during this period. As Scowcroft later related, Kissinger's dual rule "made things very different and lopsided. . . . So in a way I had to lean over backwards with Defense to make sure that the system ran in a more or less balanced way."[11] Moreover, Scowcroft generally got along well with Kissinger. As he later recalled, "I had a good working relationship."[12] He was loyal yet knew his boss's strengths and weaknesses. He also was more of a calming influence with both Kissinger and the other members of the NSC staff than the more excitable Haig. According to Saunders, "I think of the two of them in terms of an electrical apparatus: one piece of the apparatus takes a current and steps it up and another takes the current and steps it down. Haig was the first and Scowcroft was the second."[13] In terms of the day-to-day workings of the staff, "it was a change in the way of doing business with the deputy. Brent was a lot smoother . . . than Haig was. It was more that kind of change. I don't think the quality of the work changed very much."[14]

When Scowcroft replaced Haig in the deputy position in early 1973, Nixon wanted him to pass on information about Kissinger's activities, which Haig had done. Haldeman was assigned to approach Scowcroft, but Scowcroft did not rise to the bait: "Haldeman talked in general terms about how I worked for the president and not Kissinger. But it was an indirect conversation and it never went anywhere."[15] Scowcroft also knew his boss's strengths and weaknesses. When a reporter complained to Scowcroft that Kissinger would not see him. Scowcroft told him to write something critical, "He'll call." According to Isaacson, "the reporter did, and Kissinger did."[16]

Scowcroft's tenure as military aide to Nixon undoubtedly provided him with a good interpersonal lay of the land. Moreover, as Scowcroft was about to assume the deputy position, Nixon told Haig to bring him up to speed on the hazards of dealing with Kissinger. According to Haldeman, Nixon "made the point that Haig's got to fill Scowcroft in completely and totally level with him on the Kissinger problem. So that he knows how to go at this."[17]

But even the diplomatic Scowcroft could get crosswise of Kissinger. In July 1975, written remarks prepared for the president's departure at Andrews Air Force Base to attend the Helsinki conference included a line that the United States had never recognized the Soviet Union's incorporation of the Baltic States. This had long been U.S. policy, but Kissinger took it as an unnecessary slap at the Soviet Union and "blew up at Scowcroft and [presidential counselor Robert] Hartmann in the hallway just outside the Oval Office as other aides watched startled." "You will pay for this!" Kissinger yelled. "Heads will roll." Although Scowcroft had cleared the line, it was deleted from Ford's spoken remarks but still appeared in the written text given to the press. The one line garnered considerable media attention, as well commentary on how Kissinger was attempting to "muzzle" Ford.[18]

In early 1974, Scowcroft was one of the few top White House aides who envisioned the possibility that Nixon might be impeached or otherwise forced to resign his presidency. According to Robert McFarlane—then Kissinger's military assistant on the NSC staff (and himself a future NSC advisor under Reagan)—Scowcroft began to meet for an hour or so each week with Vice President Ford: "In each of these meetings, he would present the Vice President one of a series of 30 or 40 papers he had tasked the staff to prepare on the top national security issues of the day, in order to bring Ford up to speed on what he would presumptively face if he became president. It was clear that Brent thought that was what was going to happen."[19]

Ford and Scowcroft began to develop a close relationship. Both were unassuming in their ways, and their demeanors and interpersonal styles were in sharp contrast to those of Nixon and Kissinger. According to Ford, "Scowcroft hardly fit the Hollywood stereotype of a fighting man." Short, thin, and balding, according to Ford, "he never raised his voice. . . . If he was really upset about something, he might say 'Gosh.'"[20]

For his part, Scowcroft was attentive to fulfilling Ford's particular needs and expectations as a decision maker. Scowcroft recognized that, unlike the more solitary and reclusive Nixon, Ford operated differently. "Ford liked to make his decisions after listening to his advisers argue the issues back and forth," Scowcroft later noted. "He liked the give and take of personal debate. He was a voracious reader but he rarely made decisions based only on his reading of the documents." Honest brokerage, under Ford, required adjustment in Scowcroft's view: "advisers must learn to respond to the way in which a president wants information."[21]

Scowcroft's elevation to NSC advisor was not a sure thing. Kissinger notes that Defense Secretary Rumsfeld had pushed for Arthur Hartman for the NSC position—Hartman was then serving as assistant secretary of state for Europe and had been a friend of Rumsfeld's during the latter's post–chief of staff service as ambassador to NATO. In the third volume of his memoirs, Kissinger describes a meeting with Ford and Rumsfeld over the appointment as "a brief crossing of swords." Kissinger recommended Scowcroft, "believing him to be the best qualified and also the person most comfortable with existing procedures . . . [Ford] selected Scowcroft shortly afterward."[22]

The transition to Scowcroft's tenure as NSC advisor also proceeded smoothly. According to Kissinger, the end of his dual roles "had the potential of turning into a difficult transition, but Scowcroft's tact and integrity averted any tension."[23] In Scowcroft's view, the transition "was very smooth. I had a good working relationship with Kissinger. I had been his deputy for about three years. He was not insecure having me in that job."[24]

II. Scowcroft as NSC Advisor—Ford

Kissinger remained a dominant force in his now sole capacity as secretary of state. Yet change did occur in the national security process with Scowcroft now officially at the helm of the NSC staff. Following Scowcroft's appointment, the other principals became influential once more.[25] It is worth noting that, unlike the first volume of his memoirs, which is replete with accounts of battles with others in the Nixon administration, Kissinger's comments about Scowcroft are few in the third volume, *Years of Renewal,* which covers the Ford presidency. Moreover, what is said is quite laudatory about Scowcroft's performance as NSC advisor:

I had total confidence that he would represent my views fairly to the president, the president's views accurately to me, and his own views precisely to both of us, whether we liked them or not. . . . He gave Ford his independent judgment in dealing with foreign policy issues without ever giving me the feeling that he was competing with my responsibilities as secretary of state. Scowcroft acted as the balance wheel of the national security process, and he has remained a national asset and personal friend.[26]

In the second volume of his memoirs, *Years of Upheaval,* Kissinger comments that Scowcroft was an "outstanding example" of an NSC advisor adept at "the preparation of options, which is in the main what interdepartmental machinery does." This work "should be the province of a security adviser chosen for fairness, conceptual grasp, bureaucratic savvy, and a willingness to labor anonymously."[27]

The marked change from Kissinger's own difficulties as NSC advisor with Secretary of State Rogers and others compared to his assessment, now as secretary of state, of Scowcroft's performance may in part reflect their own shared history: a chief whose trusted deputy eventually takes on his former job. But it also reflects Scowcroft's conception of the role. He did not try to cut Kissinger's access to the president, as Kissinger had attempted—usually successfully—with Rogers. According to the White House's history of the NSC, Kissinger retained, on the one hand, "Ford's confidence and unlimited access." On the other, "both men exchanged ideas constantly. . . . Scowcroft was content to operate in a quiet, unobtrusive way. He took seriously the NSC obligation to present the President with clear analyses and options for decision."[28] Nor, it must be added, did Scowcroft come to the job with an overarching theory of global politics and a policy defining vision, as Kissinger had done. There was no major clash of opposing ideas and differing foreign policy world views.

Nor was there a battle of clashing personalities. Kissinger and Scowcroft retained a strong, positive personal relationship. According to Scowcroft,

We had a good relationship and by the time I assumed his job, I knew him very well. I knew how to get around the difficult side of him and appeal to the easy side of him.

It was pretty smooth, but he had had one of his jobs taken away from him and he was used to being the whole thing. So there was something of an adjustment, but I think it was quite smooth.[29]

Scowcroft's interpersonal style and adeptness was probably a large measure of the successful equation: "Henry Kissinger had worn two hats for a couple of years—that was a hard adjustment for him—*and I took account of that.*"[30] In fact, their relationship was such that after leaving office, they remained friends and Scowcroft joined Kissinger at his consulting firm, Kissinger Associates.

Yet as NSC advisor, Scowcroft was no pushover. He recognized their respective roles, including protecting his own power and prerogatives as NSC advisor. Scowcroft was his own man. While by no measure an aggressive advocate, Scowcroft did put his imprint on NSC operations. Kissinger's confidence in Scowcroft's comfort with "existing procedures" is not quite accurate. According to one account, his role as deputy "placed him near the center of Kissinger's NSC operation, and he apparently did not like what he saw." Kissinger achieved some successes, "but in the process subverted the NSC system, creating friction in the executive branch and committing some spectacular errors."[31] Organizational changes followed under Scowcroft's leadership. As the White House's NSC history notes, "Many of the most aggressive members of Kissinger's NSC team also made the move to State, allowing Scowcroft to fashion a staff that reflected the new relationships."[32] Scowcroft reduced the NSC staff back to forty-five professionals. He appointed William Hyland as his deputy, and he willingly divided up the work with Hyland. Most importantly, Scowcroft worked hard to develop smoother relations between NSC staff and the cabinet-level principals and their deputies. Meetings of the full NSC also became more frequent.[33]

SCOWCROFT AS HONEST BROKER

But in addition to organizational savvy, Scowcroft exhibited an interpersonal and management style that was a much needed improvement over the mercurial temperament, bureaucratic competitiveness, and sometimes desultory interest in organizational matters of his predecessor. According to one account, "Scowcroft did not seek to draw attention to himself or awe others with his intellect. . . . He was cool under pressure, and while unfailingly polite, he could be blunt and forceful." Scowcroft "won high marks in Washington," and he "smoothly managed the NSC machinery, making sure that all the major agency heads got their say on key policy issues."[34] According to David Gompert, who served in the State Department during this period, Scowcroft "had to play pretty much the opposite of the role that Kissinger had played. . . . He had to be the mediator, the soother, the occasional medic to deal with all the breakage that Henry caused in the State Department."[35]

Honest and fair brokerage was central to Scowcroft conception of the NSC advisor role. He would give his own advice but also appropriately relay the views of others. As he later recalled:

> When I was part of the National Security Council, we would handle big decisions by doing a substantial study in which we would include the recommendations of the interagency groups, etc. As national security adviser, I would attach to that a memorandum of no more than three pages in which I summarized the issues to the extent that I knew them, the views of his other senior advisers, and then my own judgments regarding the pros and cons of the different options and recommendations. I tried not to give the President lengthy reading materials. I summarized everything I sent to him with the documents behind the summary in the event that he wanted to go over them.[36]

Scowcroft recognized that other NSC advisors "have done it differently. . . . Zbigniew Brzezinski, for example, told me that he ordinarily gave President Carter between one hundred and one hundred and fifty pages of reading every night." But in Scowcroft's view, "that is a burden one cannot impose on a president; he doesn't have time to do things like that. He should focus on the forest and not on the trees."[37]

Scowcroft was a crisp taskmaster, but on some occasions even he would relent. During Kissinger's spring 1976 journey to Africa, Scowcroft apparently wanted messages to the president bereft of unnecessary "travel-log" filler. According to Kissinger, "reacting to Scowcroft's stricture that we spare the president our description of local color," Winston Lord sent an attenuated report: "Next we went to see a cultural performance. It was interesting; since this is a poor country, some of the girls only had half a costume, but I don't want to bore you with color or tell you what half was missing since this would needlessly excite you." According to Kissinger, "Fortunately, Scowcroft, who had been right in the first place, has a good sense of humor and spiked the abbreviated version."[38]

BEYOND BROKERAGE

Scowcroft's tenure as NSC advisor is also of importance because while serving as an honest broker he was able to incorporate some of the additional responsibilities taken on by his post-Eisenhower predecessors and successors. And he did so without apparent injury or negative effect. Compared to Kissinger tenure in the position, Scowcroft operated out of the political and media limelight. "I kept a very low profile as national security adviser," Scowcroft recollected. "In fact, the White House staff kept saying that you got to start going on television more." Scowcroft, who talked the matter over with President Ford, preferred to remain low key: "I did not want to appear to be competing with Henry Kissinger." Moreover, "that helped" keep his relations with Kissinger on a smooth and even keel.[39] More generally, "managing" Kissinger remained an issue as it had in the Nixon years. According to Scowcroft, "[President Ford] used to talk about the care and feeding of Henry Kissinger all the time."[40]

Scowcroft did occasionally involve himself in political matters. In 1976, Ronald Reagan was able to mount a serious challenge to Ford's nomination that went down to the wire. At the 1976 Republican convention, as part of that challenge, Reagan's forces attempted to push through a foreign policy plank to the party platform titled "Morality in Foreign Policy." It was an implicit attack on Kissinger: it criticized détente with the Soviet Union that granted unilateral favors, secret diplomacy and agreements, and the White House's treatment of Soviet dissident Alexander Solzhenitsyn. Vice President Nelson Rockefeller and Scowcroft argued for strong opposition to the plank at the convention; James Baker (Ford's chief delegate strategist) and Chief of Staff Richard Cheney urged caution. Ford was initially inclined to fight but began to realize it might provide Reagan with momentum. When the convention finally took the matter up, Baker's political instincts prevailed when he realized that it was getting late in the evening and there were likely to be more Reagan delegates than Ford delegates in the convention hall. Opposition to the plank was strategically dropped.[41] According to Ford, Scowcroft was also involved in the selection of Sen. Robert Dole (R-KS) as his vice presidential running mate in 1976.[42]

Over the summer, according to Ford, both Kissinger and Scowcroft advised him that seeing Alexander Solzhenitsyn "would be unwise," even though it would improve Ford's standing with conservatives. According to Ford, "In the end, I decided to subordinate political gains to foreign policy considerations."[43]

During the general election campaign, Scowcroft and Cheney were forced to do damage control in the wake of Ford's gaffe, during one of his debates with Carter, when he said that Poland was not under Soviet domination. As Ford said it, Scowcroft turned to campaign consultant Stuart Spencer and said, "You've got a problem." Spencer asked why, and Scowcroft replied that there were Soviet troops stationed in Poland. Ford meant to say we do not *accept* Soviet domination.[44] Scowcroft and Cheney had difficulty handling the gaffe. Scowcroft tried to clear it up at a postdebate press briefing: "I think what the president was trying to say is that we do not recognize Soviet dominance of Europe." But the impact of the remark lingered. Ford resisted the notion that he was in error, and it took another week before he acknowledged that he might not have expressed himself clearly enough.[45]

III. POLICY: PROCESS, ROLE, AND OUTCOME—FORD

Scowcroft's relatively short stint as NSC advisor—from November 3, 1975, until January 20, 1977, a bit over fourteen months—does not provide an extensive record linking his role as NSC advisor to the policy initiatives of the waning Ford presidency. Plus, Kissinger retained an active role as the guiding force for policy. But Scowcroft's service earlier in the Ford administration provides some evidence of his impact on policy. He was technically Kissinger's deputy, but as he himself acknowledged, given the burden on Kissinger, he was at times de facto NSC advisor.

Scowcroft's performance as deputy played a major role in his promotion to NSC advisor. Ford also later recollected that Scowcroft's ability to provide counsel that balanced Kissinger was a major factor in his appointment:

> When Kissinger had both State and NSC, there was not an independent evaluation of proposals, and I never liked that arrangement that I inherited. And when the time came to make some [other] changes at the Pentagon and CIA, it was logical to tell Henry, "I'm gonna just leave you as secretary of state and upgrade Brent Scowcroft."[46]

Scowcroft's performance on the job, especially during crises, also was a major factor. According to John Robert Greene, Scowcroft was promoted because Ford felt he "had distinguished himself during the evacuation of Saigon and the *Mayaguez* incident."[47] During the *Mayaguez* crisis, Scowcroft was a strong advocate for a military response.[48] The crew of the merchant vessel had been seized by the Khmer Rouge off the Cambodian coast; it was the first post-Vietnam test of U.S. national security resolve. Ford's advisers were divided. Defense Secretary James Schlesinger favored no air strikes. Vice President Rockefeller wanted B-52 strikes against the Cambodian mainland. Scowcroft and Kissinger wanted a strong response, but by carrier-based planes, not a full-blown B-52 bombing run. Ford agreed. A marine assault on the offshore island where the ship's crew was believed to be held was also added.[49]

Was the operation a success? Ford's approval ratings went up eleven points, and according to Greene, "the press and the administration presented the crisis as an example of strong presidential decision making."[50] Yet, the marines encountered stiffer resistance than anticipated, and their casualties were higher than the number of crew they sought to rescue. During the operation, the Cambodian rebels released the crew, and the marine assault may not have been necessary. Other analysts of the incident have felt that bombing the Cambodian mainland was too punitive. According to a report undertaken by the General Accounting Office, the attack had been done prematurely.[51] Scowcroft favored a forceful response but also a more measured operation.

During the late April 1975 evacuation from Saigon, "Operation Frequent Wind," the effort was in large measure directed by Scowcroft from the White House Situation Room. Here the positive merits of Scowcroft's actions are clearer. Some 7,000 Americans and South Vietnamese were evacuated from the U.S. embassy site alone.[52]

Scowcroft also at times defended the prerogatives of the NSC staff. At the Helsinki Accords conference in 1975, for example, there was tension between the White House speechwriting staff—under then Chief of Staff Rumsfeld's control—and the NSC speechwriters under Kissinger and Scowcroft. The political stakes were high, and the White House group refused to give the NSC speechwriters a copy of Ford's departing remarks. Scowcroft gave Ford an alternative draft, and he detailed his concerns about what the White House speechwriters had prepared. Ford delivered Scowcroft's version.[53]

Once he became NSC advisor, Scowcroft was a bit more proactive but still within the bounds of the honest broker role. While Kissinger remained the driving intellectual force behind foreign policy in the Ford presidency, Scowcroft stood his ground—albeit in gentlemanly Scowcroft fashion. In President Ford's view, he used both Kissinger and Scowcroft "as they should have been used under the law that was passed in 1947." Kissinger was "the primary promoter" of foreign policy positions. But "I was the final determining person in making a judgment." Kissinger "made recommendations. . . . And if I wanted additional background, I would turn to Brent."[54]

IV. The George H. W. Bush National Security Process

Like Nixon, George H. W. Bush was an active president in foreign affairs, interested in immersing himself in the detail of issues. But, unlike Nixon, he relished hearing the different views and ensuing debates of his advisers. As he observes in *A World Transformed* (cowritten with Scowcroft, but with separate sections identifying their own contributions on a variety of foreign policy topics—the closest we have to a Bush presidential memoir), "I intended to be a 'hands-on' president." From the start, "I wanted the key foreign policy players to know that I was going to involve myself in many of the details of defense, international trade, and foreign affairs policies."[55] According to Colin Powell, "President Bush was much more involved than President Reagan. He wanted to hear the fights; he wanted to hear the debates. . . . Bush very much enjoyed listening to us all bat away."[56]

At the same time, Bush recognized that he could not learn all the details of policy matters, was unwilling to micromanage, and needed to rely on a strong group of principals who would work as a team.[57] The emphasis on debate, teamwork, and delegation led Bush to select Scowcroft as his NSC advisor. Bush had worked closely with him when he was director of the CIA in the Ford presidency, and he knew him further from the various boards and commissions on which Scowcroft served during the Reagan years. Bush initially toyed with the idea of a position at Defense or CIA for Scowcroft. But the fit was better with what Bush wanted from his NSC advisor. Honest brokerage was first and foremost in his mind: Scowcroft's "reputation," "deep knowledge," and "prior experience" was such, according to Bush, that there could be "no doubt he was the *perfect honest broker.*" According to Bush, Scowcroft would not try to isolate cabinet members from the president, and his appointment—and reputation—would signal that "the NSC's function was to be critical in the decision-making process." At the same Bush recognized that Scowcroft's counsel and advice were important to the mix in filling in Bush's own weaknesses: "[I] had a vision of the world I wanted to see, but I had no fixed 'ten-point plan.'" Scowcroft would fill in the details. Although expected to serve as an honest broker, "I also knew he would give me his own experienced views on whatever problem might arise."[58]

In addition to Scowcroft, Bush assembled a talented national security and foreign policy team, many of whom had worked together before in the Nixon, Ford, and Reagan presidencies: Secretary of State James Baker, Secretary of Defense Richard Cheney, JCS Chairman Colin Powell, and Robert Gates, who served as Scowcroft's deputy and, later, as CIA director.[59] According to Powell, "look at the team that came in—Scowcroft, Cheney, Baker, Powell, and Bob Gates. We had all worked for or with each other in some capacity before; we were all the best of friends and the best of adversaries. By that I mean that we all knew each other, we knew how we fought, and we knew each other's strengths and weaknesses."[60]

They were strong personalities with strong views and wise in the ways of bureaucratic politics. Bush recollected in *A World Transformed* that "Brent and Jim did get moderately crosswise, but very rarely." Bush understood the institutional forces at work. On the one hand, Baker "worried he might be excluded from a decision that affected his department. As a former chief of staff, he knew how a strong-willed presidential adviser, if backed by the president, can easily isolate a cabinet member," Bush noted. On the other hand, Scowcroft and the NSC staff "were also concerned about what State might be up to." The management and interpersonal challenges were recognized, and usually successfully dealt with: "We tried very hard, and I think successfully, to keep all the participants informed and eliminate personality clashes which could undermine policy-making as well as effective diplomacy."[61] In Baker's view, they were a group of "experienced, collegial peers who had worked together in one capacity or another and who liked and respected one another . . . we trusted one another." Policy differences were sometimes present. Cheney and Scowcroft were more cautious than he was about changing policy, according to Baker. But these differences never led to the "backbiting of the Kissinger-Rogers, Vance-Brzezinski eras or the slugfests of our national security teams during the Reagan years."[62]

In Cheney's opinion, "None of these conflicts occurred in the Bush administration." First, "Bush wanted it that way." Second, their prior relationships, especially in the Ford administration, "helped enormously." "Intensive differences did occur at times," according to Cheney, "but everyone knew that they could speak openly in the councils of government and tell the president what they thought with their colleagues present. Even if something foolish was said during those meetings, everyone knew that it would not appear in the *Washington Post* the next day." Moreover, the president was instrumental in this: "He would not have tolerated anyone leaving a meeting and then leaking something that was said to the press."[63]

The interpersonal dynamic of the group was key to its success. For Scowcroft, "There was a deep camaraderie among us . . . I think this quality set apart the Bush administration from any other I knew. . . . These were strong personalities, yet egos did not get in the way of the nation's business. A genuine sense of humor made jokes and respectful kidding part of the daily routine, and eased even the most difficult crises. It was an informal—but, at the same time, deadly serious—crowd."[64]

The turmoil in the national security process of the Reagan years undoubtedly offered negative lessons that Bush, Baker, and Powell wanted to avoid. In the view of Dennis Ross, who directed policy planning at State, "When

Bush came in, he wanted to unlearn the lessons of the Reagan administration. He hated the leaks. . . . He wanted people who were in key positions to be able to work together, and he wanted them to know that he expected their staff to work together."[65]

Not only had most worked together before, there was also the unique situation that some had served in the other's position. Both Baker and Cheney had been White House chiefs of staff, and thus could understand things from that perspective. Powell had served in Scowcroft's role as NSC advisor, indeed, he was his immediate predecessor under Reagan. Even President Bush could claim some institution-based perspective, having served not only as vice president but also as CIA director, U.S. ambassador to the U.N., and as U.S. liaison in Beijing.

Although Scowcroft was not a member of the Reagan team, he had co-chaired the Tower Commission, which was charged with examining the history of the Iran-Contra scandal, understanding how the NSC staff had gotten so out of control, and proscribing remedies. Chief among them was an understanding of the proper role of the NSC advisor. Once in office, Scowcroft's conception of his position and the operations of the NSC staff system were critical to the generally smooth and productive relations among the principals. In Baker's view, one of the greatest achievements of the Bush presidency was that the national security system "worked the way it is supposed to." That was important, moreover, in effectively managing the "historic changes"—especially the end of the cold war—that occurred during Bush's term in office.[66]

V. Scowcroft as NSC Advisor—Bush

Central to making that national security apparatus work well was Scowcroft's conception of the NSC advisor's role. Under Bush, Scowcroft continued in his belief that the NSC advisor must serve as an honest broker, yet coupled to that was a stronger role as a personal adviser to the president than had been the case in the Ford administration.

THE HONEST BROKER "PLUS"
The most important lesson to be drawn from Scowcroft's second stint as NSC advisor was his ability to be a broker and to expand beyond it. As Scowcroft recalled, brokerage remained important, if not in some sense foundational: "If you are not an honest broker the system doesn't work well. The

first thing you have to do is to establish in the minds of all of the members of the NSC that their views will be presented honestly and straightforwardly to the president." If this occurs, more becomes possible: "Once they are comfortable with that, they certainly expect that you will present your own views but that you will do it in a way that doesn't disadvantage theirs."[67] In a similar vein, shortly after Secretary of State Cyrus Vance resigned in his feud with NSC Advisor Zbigniew Brzezinski in 1980, Scowcroft observed, "I think it is important that the national security adviser should have the confidence of all agency heads involved in the process. Otherwise the process will be stifled and the agency heads will go around him to the president, making for poor policy."[68]

Scowcroft met daily with Bush, following the president's CIA briefing (which Scowcroft, Gates, Chief of Staff John Sununu, and—once or twice a week—CIA Director William Webster attended). Scowcroft took special care that these *not* be occasions for presidential decision making without the knowledge and participation of the other principals. "The president can make a decision anytime he wants," Scowcroft notes. But, mindful of what had transpired at points between Reagan and his NSC advisors during Iran-Contra, "when that happened and the president said 'I think we ought to do this,' I said, 'Fine, we'll do that; but let me check with my colleagues and see if there are any problems we haven't thought about.' So I would call around to them and say, 'The president wants to do this, do you have a problem with it?'"[69] In addition, Scowcroft had Gates, his deputy, attend in order to make sure that what transpired was interpreted properly; the same went for meetings of the NSC as well.[70] In Scowcroft's view, they were all part of the honest broker role.[71]

In Bush's view, "Brent always made sure the views of every 'player' were understood by him and by me. If he could not resolve the impasse separately, then the principals would sort it out with me. . . . He took a lot of pressure off me by keeping an open, honest approach to the NSC job. He was one of the reasons why we had a really cohesive and sound policy-making process: key decisions were well vetted ahead of time."[72]

Bush also understood his own responsibilities in making Scowcroft's role work: "To preserve Brent's brokering role, I was careful to make sure that he was informed and not taken by surprise, especially on substantive important decisions." "Brent would generally be in the room," according to Bush, but when he was not "I never failed to inform Brent or share material with him. Usually any request to get me on the phone regarding security or foreign policy would come through Brent anyway."[73] At the same time, Bush recognized that everything was not always perfect: "It was an imperfect system at times, but it worked."[74]

From his perspective, Scowcroft recognized that the NSC advisor should be a counselor, "a confidant to the president," able to examine issues "solely from the perspective of the president without having a separate constituency that he must serve or must lead."[75] According to one account, "Scowcroft is not hesitant to state his own opinions on matters—Bush wants to hear them—but he does not exploit his access to consistently push his own agenda, as Kissinger and other national security advisers have done. Instead, Scowcroft serves as an evaluator of the president's ideas and as a repository of knowledge and insight on which Bush can draw . . . a confidential adviser without a bureaucratic stake."[76]

According to Secretary of State Baker, "Brent would sometimes remain silent when I spoke rather than present a countervailing view on a foreign policy issue. It wasn't because I was the president's close friend or out of timidity—Brent had forceful opinions and was never shy about disagreeing with colleagues—but rather out of respect for the way the system was supposed to work. Brent saw himself as a coordinator."[77]

BEYOND BROKERAGE

But Scowcroft also was not averse to bringing forth his own views if he felt the questions under discussion or the options before the principals were not adequate—this aspect of his role would be especially important in the early days following Saddam Hussein's invasion of Kuwait. As Richard Haass, the NSC staff director for Near East and South Asian affairs at the time, observes, "the national security adviser has to have two hats . . . the first has to be the management hat, and everyone has to feel the process is legitimate." But there is also a second hat: "he's also got to be willing to put forward his own agenda if he thinks the consensus from the whole is wrong, or that no one is saying the right thing. . . . he can still have his own voice so long as everyone around there has confidence that he doesn't get so persuaded by his own voice that he's no longer a legitimate broker. . . . Brent did this very well"[78]

According to Roger Porter, who headed the Bush economic and domestic policy staffs, it really involves "two crucial elements of what I've described as dispensing due process and exercising quality control. And Scowcroft embodied that in a truly unusual and remarkable way." In a tribute to Scowcroft that Porter organized, he found that Presidents Nixon, Ford, and Bush, as well as colleagues Baker, Powell, Cheney, and Kissinger "kept emphasizing in slightly different ways his capacity to play both of those roles. They did not view him as just a dispenser of due process. They viewed him as someone who had ideas, who actively exercised what I like to call quality control, who added to the discussion when it seemed appropriate. He is a model that others could usefully emulate."[79]

Yet for Scowcroft, as we saw, being an honest broker came first and was foundational to his sense of the job: "If you are not an honest broker the system doesn't work well. . . ."[80] Scowcroft's view of the role of the NSC advisor, moreover, was both informed and supported by the report of the Tower Commission—of which he was one of the three principal members—in its examination of the Iran-Contra scandal. Its diagnosis of the Reagan-era national security system and its recommendations for reform read like pure Scowcroft—which they largely might well have been. The NSC advisor should be "an 'honest broker' for the NSC process. He assures that issues are clearly presented to the president; that all reasonable options, together with an analysis of their disadvantages and risks, are brought to his attention; and that the views of the president's other principal advisers are accurately conveyed." Policy advocacy by the NSC advisor may occur—and indeed may need to occur—but its risks need to be recognized: "To the extent that the national security adviser becomes a strong advocate for a particular point of view, his role as an 'honest broker' may be compromised, and the president's access to the unedited views of the NSC principals may be impaired." Public visibility also poses dangers: the NSC advisor should "generally operate off-stage."[81]

Scowcroft walked a fine line, and by most accounts he was generally successful. He clearly avoided becoming too overt a policy advocate as some of his predecessors, Kissinger most notably, had become. But he also did not confine his role to that of a managerial custodian, eschewing policy advice. In fact, he apparently felt freer to offer Bush counsel than he had during his tenure under Gerald Ford. Scowcroft spent more time with Bush than any other senior official in the administration, and the comments above plus other reports indicate that he also freely expressed his views to the president, but made it clear to Bush when he was doing so. As Kevin Mulcahy notes, he "actively guard[ed] the president's interests in the policy-making process," but he also advocated "personal policy preferences, if convinced that a department proposal is inimicable to the president's interests." Scowcroft was "a full partner" with the other principals, "but without usurping their departmental prerogatives or presuming to be the sole instrument of the president's will."[82]

With respect to public and media visibility, Baker rather than Scowcroft was the usual public face of the Bush administration. When he became NSC advisor, Scowcroft told both Bush and Baker, "'I will only go on radio and television and so on after I have talked with Jim Baker and we have agreed that I should do it.' We did that for about three or four months, and then I called him one day and he said, 'You don't have to call anymore. I don't have any problem with you going on anytime you want.'"[83] But Scowcroft rarely took advantage of that invitation. Baker and Scowcroft, according to one report, "got along well in part because Scowcroft let Baker speak for the administration."[84]

Nor was Scowcroft much involved in the political efforts of the Bush administration. In fact, involvement in politics during the Bush years seems even less than the couple of instances where it occurred during the Ford presidency. However, Scowcroft was available to defend the administration when called on.[85]

Although there were occasions when Scowcroft might be involved in policy operations, they were far, far less than those that Kissinger had undertaken and were authorized by the president and with the knowledge of the secretary of state. According to Scowcroft,

> I got involved when we wanted to underline the president's personal involvement. When I undertook missions to other countries, it was to underscore that this is the president's interest, not the institutional Department of State, for example. So we used it very sparingly. But to run operations, like Iran-Contra, is not the job of the NSC. We can't do that because we don't have the people, the expertise, to run an operation.[86]

It was determined, for example, that Scowcroft rather than the more prominent Baker was the appropriate person to undertake a secret trip to China following the Tiananmen crackdown of 1989.

Scowcroft would also have contact with foreign diplomats, but only if it had been deemed necessary in consultation with the president or the secretary of state. According to Scowcroft, sometimes it is necessary for the NSC advisor to be the point of contact with representatives of foreign governments, but problems arise "if the national security advisor does that on his own and the secretary of state thinks he ought to be the one to do it. . . . Kissinger-Rogers and Brzezinski-Vance were the two cases where things really got crossed."[87] According to Scowcroft, "I bent over backwards not to appear to be repeating, frankly, what Henry Kissinger did," and he always kept Baker informed of any diplomatic contacts.[88]

But Scowcroft's "honest broker plus" role was not without its costs. Much of the day-to-day management of the NSC staff fell to his deputy NSC advisor, first Robert Gates then Adm. Jonathan Howe. According to one account, when Scowcroft returned to his own desk, "often at the end of the day, paperwork can be piled high. . . . Some staff members often complain that Scowcroft has too little time for them and often fails to stay on top of unfolding events."[89] According to another account, some also complained that Scowcroft paid "too much attention to his personal relationship with the president than to organization, turning the security council [staff] from a well-spring of policy initiative to a lesser clearinghouse of information."[90] Other accounts, as we shall see, stress that the NSC deputies, especially Gates, effectively took up any of the slack.

ORGANIZATION AND DECISION MAKING: THE "SCOWCROFT MODEL"

The national security system under Scowcroft is often lauded as a model of effectiveness. It alerts us to the importance of brokerage directed not just to the fair presentation of advice and information but the structures and processes through which that advice is channeled.

A major contribution of Scowcroft's tenure during the Bush presidency was the creation of what has come to be termed the "Scowcroft model" of the NSC advisory system. Central to it and at its apex is the use of the principals' committee—the main members of the NSC—chaired by the NSC advisor. The group's chief purpose was to work through policy issues and options before meeting with the president. It worked well and was adopted by both the Clinton and George W. Bush presidencies. According to Scowcroft, it had special merit because "what it did was save a lot of the president's time." Moreover, "we were able to agree frequently without taking his time."[91] Of additional importance, in Scowcroft's view, was that the NSC advisor chaired the committee, not the secretary of state, who had done so in other administrations. According to Scowcroft, "you can't work that way because no cabinet officer will work for another cabinet officer."[92]

Scowcroft had developed the new arrangement during the 1988 transition—but it can be traced back to advice he gave his predecessors Frank Carlucci and Powell after Iran-Contra. And unlike the fait accompli for cabinet members that Kissinger's organizational changes entailed in the 1968 Nixon transition, Scowcroft circulated his proposal to Baker and Sen. John Tower (R-TX), who was then Bush's nominee for secretary of defense. According to Scowcroft, "I had to convince [Baker] in the beginning because it was new.

It hadn't been done before, and he was wondering whether that cut into his prerogatives. But I convinced him. It was a collegial operation."[93]

Although Baker's predecessor, George Shultz, refused to attend any meeting at which someone other than the president or himself presided, Baker had no problems with Scowcroft chairing the principals in the president's absence. Even though "I was junior to them all," Scowcroft later recalled, "there wasn't that kind of problem. It worked beautifully."[94]

It was an important historical development in the organizational workings of the NSC system. Kissinger's dominance of the Nixon committee system had presaged it, but at the price of organizational subterfuge and exclusion. Here, Scowcroft was able to bring all of the principals productively and cooperatively together. Moreover, it recognized the place of the NSC advisor's position as the only one where the crosscutting pieces of national security policy could come together; rarely does a department representative have a clean claim on policy dominance. In Scowcroft's view, "It may be the only way it will work."[95] In Powell's view, the Scowcroft system was crucial to effective decision making: Scowcroft used a model where you could have "these kinds of open debates and discussions."[96]

As he had done during the Ford administration, Scowcroft sought to revive the NSC's interagency coordination process, continuing the post-Iran-Contra changes—again recommended by Scowcroft himself[97]—made by Carlucci and Powell. In some ways, Scowcroft was able to revive a process that harkened back to the Eisenhower Planning Board, but without its more cumbersome formality. Here Scowcroft's effort focused on the importance of the deputies' committee, drawn from the major departments and agencies, but chaired by Scowcroft's own deputy, Robert Gates. A Soviet specialist with a doctorate from Georgetown University, Gates had risen through the ranks of the CIA, served on the Ford NSC staff, then returned to the CIA where he eventually became deputy director to Bill Casey. He also became director of the CIA later in the Bush presidency, and, after serving as president of Texas A&M University, replaced Rumsfeld as George W. Bush's secretary of defense. According to one account, the deputies' group "would meet as often as everyday, and its principal task would be to debate and reach agreement on narrowed policy options that could be brought to Bush and his top national security aides for final decision. A chief goal of the set-up was to reduce the gap that too often existed between the middle level of government where detailed policy was developed, and the top level, where decisions are made. A committee of deputies bridged this gap because its members would be trusted by the top level yet be in a position to communicate easily with the lower level."[98] Many in the deputies' group also had the advantage of having a shared experience in the Reagan presidency. They not only knew each other, but, like the principals, understood the weaknesses of the Reagan national security process. According to Richard Haass, that familiarity was extensive:

> A lot of us knew each other from beforehand . . . Almost all of us, not just at the top level, but at a level or two down also knew each other from in and out of government. . . . I think there was something about the tone that the president and others set, that you didn't get the feeling that this was an administration where food fights would be tolerated for long. . . . The work-to-bullshit ratio was better in this administration than any other I've ever seen, and less of your calories went into the bureaucratic game in this administration. There was also less concern about leaks than in any other administration.[99]

Gates's role as Scowcroft's deputy was also crucial. Not only did he run the interagency process, but he also served as its honest broker and effective manager. According to Philip Zelikow, NSC staff director for European and Soviet affairs at the time,

> What Gates did was to push down the process of initial policy papers and the breaking out of issues so that that occurred as much as possible and in as rigorous a way as possible at the assistant secretaries' level below the deputies' committee. So by the time you got to the deputies' meeting with Gates, very often the particular issues were already identified with some crispness. And then the quality of the analysis on those issues was correspondingly higher and more focused. By the time something would come to the principals, it was defined even better still.[100]

In addition to emphasizing sound and thorough policy analysis, Gates managed the NSC staff, freeing Scowcroft up to serve as counselor to the president. According to Zelikow, there was an effective "division of labor between Scowcroft and Gates":

> Scowcroft was the partner of the president, and he was in effect the White House chief of staff for all foreign matters. . . . The real operation of the machine was Gates's job. . . . Gates was the person who had to make the machine really run and stay sharp. It was Gates's job to get things to Brent's

attention and frame issues so that Brent could operate in the most effective way. One needed the other to reach their full potential, which is often the case. In a good managerial system, you want to hire people to offset your weaknesses, and vice versa. The Scowcroft-Gates combination was an exceptional team in that way.[101]

Gates took the initiative, for example, based on CIA reports questioning the survival of the Soviet Union as it then existed, to set up a small, secret working group to explore contingency planning in the event of its collapse or other major changes. Chaired by Condoleezza Rice, then serving as an NSC staff Soviet specialist, it began work in September 1989, two years before the Soviet Union's eventual demise. Among its findings, according to Gates, was the strong possibility that the Soviet Union would in fact collapse.[102] According to Scowcroft,

> [Gates] was very central. The deputies' committee worked so well because of Bob Gates. Before every meeting, he would come in and say, "Here's the subject." And then he would say, "Where do you think we want to end up?" I would say what I thought. He gave everybody their head at the meeting. But in the end, we would have either a decision or a split down clearly defined lines. He was extremely effective. He was terrific.[103]

At the third level of the NSC process were eight (initially, more would be added) Policy Coordinating Committees (PCCs). These groups examined and developed policy proposals. Yet the effectiveness of the work undertaken at this level—dubbed National Security Review (NSR) papers—seems mixed, especially those undertaken early in the new administration. NSR-3, on policy toward the Soviet Union, came before Bush in mid-March 1989, but it yielded no major changes from the Reagan years and was characterized as "status-quo plus."[104] According to Scowcroft, "it was disappointing . . . short on detail and substance," and lacked "imaginative initiatives." In its place, Scowcroft asked Condoleezza Rice to draft an alternative think piece, which was much better in Scowcroft's view and evolved into a new approach for dealing with Gorbachev.[105]

NSR-12, on basic national security policy, suffered delay, and by May 1989 only sections of an early draft had been produced, and Scowcroft even felt they were inadequate.[106] Slow work ran against the deadline for a NATO summit meeting, and Scowcroft himself took the lead in fashioning a conventional arms reduction proposal for the meeting. It was an initiative that was warmly greeted by the NATO allies and led to a conventional forces treaty with the Soviet Union that was much to U.S. advantage. In Baker's view, these early policy reviews were handicapped by the fact that many Bush subcabinet appointees were still not in place and, as a result, Reagan holdovers—more averse to examining their own policies—played a major role. Existing bureaucracy produced the papers, rather than fresh sources who did not have a vested interest in prior policies. The result was "least-common-denominator thinking, with every potentially controversial—that is, interesting—idea left out in the name of bureaucratic consensus. In the end, what we received was mush," in Baker's opinion. [107]

Additional problems existed at the third level: working groups were headed generally by departmental assistant secretaries not NSC staff (although an NSC official served in the capacity of "executive secretary" of each group).[108] According to Richard Haass, "one of the real weaknesses of the PCC level is that it was periphery-chaired. It's very hard to have any player be both a player and the referee. The assistant secretary of state comes to the meeting to chair it and to represent the State Department. This puts him in an extremely difficult position." Moreover, according to Haass, Baker's reliance on a tight-knit circle at the top of the State Department generated distance from the assistant secretaries from State who might chair these committees: "I think this problem was compounded in the Baker State Department, because for the most part assistant secretaries were somewhere north of Siberia. And quite honestly, they weren't the players."[109]

In 1989, as Baker notes, the effort at a basic policy review may also have been handicapped by the delays recent presidents have faced in getting subcabinet appointees confirmed. Departmental secretaries are generally confirmed quickly, their subordinates may take several months. If the organizational structure mandates department-led efforts, the team of political appointees charged with that undertaking at State, Defense, or elsewhere may still be thin or, even if confirmed, encumbered with the tasks of learning their basic departmental responsibilities.

In Scowcroft's view, these efforts at long-range planning were important but difficult to achieve in practice: "I always thought that the NSC, as the agent of the president, ought to have a long-range planning function. I tried it both times and it never worked satisfactorily. Either nobody had time to pay attention to it or you had to grab them when a fire broke out. That was one of the most frustrating things to me. Nobody else is in a position to do the broad, long-range thinking that the NSC is, but I don't know how you do it."[110] At the same time, Scowcroft sought a lean NSC staff operation. He cut the professional staff by about 20 percent from what it had been under Reagan. It was his view that duplication of departmental work should be avoided if possible.[111]

INFORMAL DELIBERATIONS

It is also important to note that informal channels of information and advice were important in this presidency and they coexisted with the more formal processes of the Scowcroft system. President Bush himself was notorious for "Rolodex diplomacy," and other personal contact with a wide range of political leaders and policy experts, both in the United States and abroad (his frequent telephone calls earned him the nickname "the mad dialer"[112]). He also engaged in frequent contact with his principals outside the structure of the NSC system.

According to John Bolton, who served in the State Department during these years—and later served in the George W. Bush presidency both at State and as U.N. ambassador—the president's "personal approach to decision making was typified by the weekly breakfast, sometimes a lunch, attended by Jim Baker, Dick Cheney, and Brent Scowcroft." Moreover, according to Bolton, "If at any point an issue had trouble being resolved through the regular bureaucratic process—for example, through interdepartmental meetings or the deputies' committee system—the staff knew that the weekly breakfast group could be decisive."[113] Bush also held regular twice-weekly meetings with Baker. According to Baker, these sessions were extremely useful. They were freewheeling discussions, where the assumptions and concepts underlying policy were questioned: "We would also think out loud, and I am convinced this helped me in many cases to know almost instinctively where the President would come out on a given issue."[114]

Informal deliberations among the principals proved crucial even during Bush's transition to office when he called together a group—Baker, Scowcroft, Treasury Secretary Nicholas Brady (who continued on in that post under Bush), Federal Reserve Chairman Alan Greenspan, and OMB director-designate Richard Darman—to quickly develop a plan for dealing with an impending debt crisis in several Latin American countries. Dubbed the "Brady plan," it was one of the early successes of the Bush presidency.[115] Informal deliberations also proved crucial in the immediate aftermath of Saddam Hussein's invasion of Kuwait. The principals quickly resolved on a

U.S. response. Details, however, would be worked out within the deputies' group.[116]

Informality—but with some structure and regularity—was also present in the administration's other foreign policy deliberations. In April 1989, as they were set to consider a policy review on Europe, Scowcroft raised with Bush the idea that "a full-blown NSC gathering was not always the place for a no-holds barred discussion among the president's top advisers. Some might be inhibited from expressing themselves frankly with staff present and the constant possibility of leaks." Scowcroft suggested that a more limited group start the deliberative process—Bush, Scowcroft, Vice President Dan Quayle, Baker, Lawrence Eagleburger (Baker's deputy), Cheney, Sununu, and Gates. Bush liked the idea, it worked according to Scowcroft, and set a new pattern for top-level meetings—the "core group." Formal NSC meetings continued to be held, but the core group became the predominant forum for deliberations at the presidential level.[117] In Bush's view, "I liked the uninhibited and informal debate the 'core group' stirred up, which is why I approved using the gatherings more often in the future. I was stimulated by the ideas going back and forth between Cheney, Baker, and Scowcroft."[118] During the Persian Gulf crisis, the core group became the "gang of eight" (the list above, minus Eagleburger).

Scowcroft also took informal steps to make sure the other principals understood each others' positions and operated, as best they could, as a team. According to Baker, the Wednesday breakfasts that Scowcroft hosted were useful to the president's three top advisers. Scowcroft and "Cheney and I compared notes to make sure we were all singing from the same hymnal." Oftentimes, when their respective staffs were at war over an issue, Baker notes, "we'd read our prepared talking points to one another, and discover in the process just how much the State, Pentagon, and NSC bureaucracies distrusted each other." Above all, Scowcroft "went out of his way to be collegial."[119] In Scowcroft's view,

> The primary usefulness was not on big issues, which were worthy of a meeting between us or something, but all the little things that crop up . . . little irritations that came up, to chat over what we were doing, and what the problems were. It was a chance to relax and exchange notes. It was very useful, although it wasn't always easy to do because one of us was usually traveling. It was very useful because it was totally informal.[120]

VI. Policy: Process, Role, and Outcome—Bush

Did the Scowcroft NSC process and his role as broker *and* counselor yield sound policy? The question cannot be answered simply, since much depends on a normative assessment of the Bush administration's foreign policy as well as recognition of the rapidly changing, eventual post–cold war context in which they operated. It was a unique foreign policy watershed, unmatched since Truman's challenges after the end of World War II. The following will explore but a few of the administration's most important responses.

ARMS REDUCTION: EUROPE AND THE SOVIET UNION

The principals' initial challenge was handling the politically charged issue of modernizing U.S. short-range nuclear forces (SNFs) in Europe as well as responding to a Gorbachev proposal to reduce conventional forces. The effort led to the 1990 agreement on the reduction of U.S. and Soviet conventional forces in Europe.[121] The chief diplomatic obstacle was that NATO countries were deeply divided over the presence of SNFs in Europe, while the United States and Britain recognized that SNFs, with a range of 500 miles, were essential to a deterrence strategy against much larger Soviet conventional forces. Gorbachev compounded the problem with an offer to unilaterally withdraw 500 Soviet SNFs within a year followed by complete withdrawal if the United States was willing to make further, radical cuts. Although politically popular, Gorbachev's proposal was still lopsided: the Warsaw Pact had some 1,400 missile launchers to NATO's 88.[122]

The May 1989 NATO summit proved crucial to resolving these differing perspectives among the NATO allies, strengthening NATO unity, obtaining a conventional arms control initiative in Europe (CFE), and regaining the public relations initiative from Gorbachev. According to Philip Zelikow, "I'm sure that Bush and Scowcroft both thought that the May 1989 summit experience, the conventional arms control initiative, was an unequivocal success. Here they had developed a large multinational initiative, totally in secret, successfully sprung a surprise that had been overwhelmingly adopted, and it received unanimous acclaim."[123]

The key was the administration's effort to secure an agreement that would substantially reduce Soviet conventional forces with lesser reductions by the United States (through—as initially proposed—an equal troop ceiling for both sides[124]), and once that agreement was in place the parties would enter into negotiations over a reduction of nuclear forces in Europe (given that the Soviet conventional force advantage had been removed).[125] When East Germany collapsed, the equation changed. Again the principals were divided on what force reduction to propose, but a common position was finally reached. According to Scowcroft,

> This decision, and the process by which it was made, was typical of the way national security issues were worked through in the Bush administration—strong men, expressing their views forcefully, under a president who joined the debate but sought to draw out the various arguments, not stifle them. Underlying it all was a sense of camaraderie that kept the discussion within bounds. When the president made the decision, debate ended immediately and attention turned to executing it.[126]

There were divergent views, the process worked, and the outcome was positive. But there was one glitch, according to Scowcroft. The sublimits—195,000 in the "central zone" of Europe and 30,000 troops elsewhere for the United States—were binding, making it difficult for the Pentagon to move troops around. According to Scowcroft, this was "not an insurmountable problem, but not a model way to make foreign policy. Integration and coordination of policy making was my responsibility, and I was not happy with such a messy outcome."[127]

How to deal with the perestroika (economic restructuring) and glasnost (openness) reforms of Gorbachev posed a particular challenge. Scowcroft and Gates were initially pessimistic about whether he was a true reformer, but they were not as pessimistic as Cheney or Vice President Quayle. Baker was the most optimistic, with President Bush somewhere in the middle: more sanguine than Scowcroft or Gates about Gorbachev's intentions, but still sharing some of their worries that the United States was dealing with a "ticking time bomb."[128] During a four-day trip to Europe in July 1989, it was Bush, in the end, who pushed for a meeting with Gorbachev in Malta in December 1989. Scowcroft, however, privately developed the secret plan to meet aboard ships off the coast of Malta—something more akin to a private meeting rather than a full-fledged ceremony-laden summit—so that "we might be able to develop some way to choreograph a session which would avoid at least some of the pitfalls of a summit without specific agreements to conclude." [129] The weather was inclement and transit between ships difficult at times, but in the end, Scowcroft notes, Malta worked better than he had hoped. No agreements resulted, but it did "renew the impetus to move ahead on START [strategic arms reduction talks] and CFE and toward an interim agreement on chemical weapons." Expanded trade was proffered and

the prospect of most favored nation status was dangled. Frank exchanges occurred on a range of issues: "This gave us a much more reliable indicator of
the perils and opportunities we faced." [130] Scowcroft's concerns in opposing
a summit were not realized, perhaps largely due to his own efforts.

At the start of the Bush administration, Scowcroft counseled a go-slow
policy on the START negotiations, and it took until August 1991 for the
Bush administration to signal final agreement with the treaty. [131] Yet, the time
taken may have worked to U.S. advantage. As part of the new agreement, the
Soviet Union—now on the eve of its own dissolution and with the Warsaw
Pact gone—agreed to delink the U.S. strategic defense missile initiative from
the START arms reduction package. The latter was of less importance to
George H. W. Bush and his advisers, who were somewhat skeptical about
the Reagan SDI initiative. [132] But it would later prove important to George
W. Bush, who embraced it.

GERMAN REUNIFICATION

The administration also carefully handled the issue of German reunification
following the collapse of East Germany. Again, the principals were divided.
Scowcroft was cautious: a united Germany might prove troublesome in the
future. [133] Yet as Scowcroft notes, Bush was the first in his administration and
the first among Western leaders to back reunification. [134]

Still, the administration played a careful game, fearful of destabilizing
Gorbachev's increasingly difficult position in the Soviet Union. According
to Richard Melanson, it was the administration's "two-plus-four" process
that led to reunification. Negotiations were first held between East and West
Germany, then reviewed by the four World War II occupying powers. The
approach was "Bush's idea. Bush handled this sticky situation very gracefully
and very well." [135]

In actuality, "two-plus-four" was the result of extensive debate among
the principals and their staffs. Scowcroft and the NSC staff favored a more
all-German approach; Baker and State stressed the involvement of the four
occupying powers, albeit in a more indirect way. [136] Scowcroft put aside his
reservations and went along with Baker. [137] Deliberations were highly informal. The issue had not been raised in an NSC meeting, which Scowcroft
acknowledges "was probably my fault for not scheduling." [138]

Baker worked hard to gain general acceptance for the formula at the
Ottawa Conference of NATO and Warsaw Pact nations in February 1990,
but not, in his view, without some NSC staff opposition. [139] Once elections
were held in East Germany in March 1990 and won by the pro-reunification

Christian Democrats, the two Germanys were well on their own way to becoming one. However, it took months of careful diplomacy by Bush, Baker, and Scowcroft to secure a final Allied and Soviet agreement. Germany was reunified and, most importantly, despite Gorbachev's efforts, it remained a member of NATO.

The administration walked a fine line. On the one hand, according to Bush, "I am convinced that had the United States sat on the sidelines, the results might have disastrous." On the other, in Scowcroft's view, the administration's low-key efforts also helped: "Our policy of refusing to exult over events . . . or to talk in terms of victory for 'us' and defeat for 'them,' helped to reassure [Gorbachev] that we looked at events not as a zero-sum game but rather as one in which there were only winners."[140] According to Beschloss and Talbott, the way Bush "guided and cajoled Gorbachev" into accepting reunification and Germany's continued membership in NATO was "perhaps the single most important accomplishment in Bush's overall handling of the Soviet Union."[141]

COLLAPSE OF THE SOVIET UNION

Although the administration dealt successfully with Gorbachev and the disintegration of the Soviet Union, its approach was cautious. As noted earlier, Scowcroft initially distrusted Gorbachev's bona fides as a reformer, although others in the administration were more positive. Scowcroft would come to change his assessment, and according to Kenneth Walsh: "It was Scowcroft who reinforced Bush's belief that Gorbachev was the best hope for stable U.S.-Soviet relations." But at the same time, "it was Scowcroft who raised the harshest doubts about Boris Yeltsin's reformist impulses, even after the Russian president performed so bravely during the coup"[142]

Some missteps also occurred. As John Judis notes, "In August 1991, two weeks before the coup and three months before the dissolution of the Soviet Union, Scowcroft played a major role in writing a speech that Bush gave in Ukraine [dubbed the "Chicken Kiev" speech] vigorously supporting Gorbachev's plan for a federation and warning that the independence movements risked a 'hopeless course of isolation.'"[143] Scowcroft later claimed that the speech had been misinterpreted by critics; the reference was not to the independence movement in Ukraine but elsewhere.[144] Yet for Bush and Scowcroft, caution may have been wise. The Soviet military was unhappy with Gorbachev's reforms and the weakening of the Soviet state, as the coup attempt against him—albeit failed—clearly attests. The response to the coup was critical but measured. "The president's inclination was to condemn it outright, but if it turned out to be successful, we would be forced to live with the new leaders," Scowcroft later wrote. Bush publicly supported Yeltsin's call for a return to the legal government. But as Bush noted in a diary entry on August 19—a day on which Gorbachev's fate still hung in the balance—"If we had pulled the rug out from under Gorbachev and swung towards Yeltsin you'd have seen a military crackdown far in excess of the ugliness that's taking place now."[145]

CHINA AND TIANANMEN SQUARE

Scowcroft was instrumental in taking a measured response in the wake of the Chinese government's crackdown on pro-democracy forces at Tiananmen Square; his hope was to preserve cordial U.S.-China relations. Scowcroft even twice traveled to Beijing (the first time quite secretly) to assure their government of continued good relations as well as to relate U.S. concerns over what had occurred.[146] The first visit was an effort that Bush, who had far more China experience than either Scowcroft or Baker, personally instigated. Baker agreed but asked that a representative from State (Baker's deputy, Lawrence Eagleburger, as it turned out) accompany Scowcroft, registering Baker's concerns about what can happen when the NSC advisor goes "operational."[147] When news of the secret trip became known, the administration was roundly criticized for not being sufficiently supportive of the pro-democracy movement, despite Bush's measured but favorable public rhetoric.

For his part, Scowcroft saw the effort as positive in outcome, especially in light of the huge ideological divide between the two nations: "They were focused on security and stability. We were interested in freedom and human rights." The Chinese government was resentful about foreign "interference" but the purpose of the trip was not negotiations "but an effort to keep the lines of communication open with a people inclined to isolate themselves. . . . For me, it was a great example of the president's instinct and touch on the important issues of foreign policy. Looking back on the meetings, I think this was a case in which personal relationships had cultivated a degree of trust by each side in the motives of the other—at least keeping open a door, as the president had hoped, even if we did not agree on how to move on."[148]

Scowcroft's second visit—to inform the Chinese about what had happened at the December 1989 Malta summit with Gorbachev—was not designed to be secret, only low-key. The press was not informed in advance, so it was a bit of a surprise. The Chinese government made sure, however, that there was extensive media coverage once Scowcroft arrived. He faced a diplomatic dilemma: what to say during the traditional round of banquet toasts?

The problem was compounded by the fact that the Chinese government televised the event. He could refuse to toast and put relations in jeopardy, or he could be seen toasting leaders touted in the media as the "butchers of Tiananmen Square." He chose the latter and became "to my deep chagrin an instant celebrity—in the most negative sense of that term." Scowcroft later conceded that he "made a mess of it" in trying to keep the visit at a very low profile.[149]

PANAMA INVASION

Panama was perhaps the most problematic foreign policy effort, at least with respect to the quality of the deliberative process. Bush stepped up the effort, begun in the late Reagan years, to overthrow Panamanian dictator Gen. Manuel Noriega. In October 1989, the commander of a guard battalion at the headquarters of the Panamanian Defense Forces requested U.S. assistance in a coup against Noriega. Noriega was briefly held, but the requested assistance was not fully provided and the plot failed. According to Douglas Brinkley, "Powell advised the president not to support the plan," and Defense Secretary Cheney and General Maxwell Thurman, head of the Southern Command, concurred.[150]

The coup was poorly planned, and it is not clear if more U.S. assistance would have made a difference. But the administration's deliberative process did not function well, especially since Noriega had been on the radar screen for some time. According to Peter Rodman, then a top-level member of the NSC staff, Panama was "a process that wasn't working well."[151] As Elizabeth Drew notes, "this most experienced of administrations . . . was utterly unprepared for a fairly predictable crisis and stumbled its way through." "Even if the administration came out at the right place," Drew continues, "in deciding not to use force to help the coup succeed or to nab . . . Noriega while he was being held by the rebels, it got there by a very strange route."[152] According to another account, Bush handled the crisis "in a characteristic manner—informally, with only a small circle of trusted senior advisers, sometimes just talking with them on the telephone." According to one administration source, "For ten months they've had this collegial, informal atmosphere. They just continued as they had. They took the facts as they needed them. They shut out the bureaucracy. The flow of information into them should have been more organized. There should have been a central collection point."[153] In Scowcroft's view, "Our performance was spotty."[154] According to Baker, "It's an understatement to say that administration decision making was less than crisp."

But it was also an occasion for honest brokerage on Scowcroft's part, now directed at better organization and procedure:

> What I found was on the first real crisis . . . that State, Defense, CIA all had a lot of information channels going to Panama, back up to their principals. But there was no cross-cutting operation. So everyone had a different view of the problem. What I did was establish the deputies' committee as a *line* committee and it proved—maybe even more than the principals' committee—to be an effective operation. The deputies, the ones who really operate their departments, would sit down and talk over what they were doing and where we ought to go. That was the innovation that made the most difference.[155]

Baker also notes the change in procedures. The entire crisis-management process was revamped, including the enhanced role of the deputies' committee: "These changes stood us in good stead later during the Persian Gulf crisis."[156]

The eventual invasion of Panama in December 1989, following the killing of an unarmed marine by Panamanian troops and other provocations, was made by a smaller group of the principals. December 17 was the key date. At an emergency meeting of the principals, Powell and Cheney told Bush that a large invasion force was needed rather than a smaller, secret operation, which Bush had seemed to favor. Bush polled his advisers one by one. According to Baker, the meeting was anticlimactic, with little if any debate over the merits of invading Panama: "'This is just going on and on,' the president said. We all agreed."[157] Overall, the invasion was a success. But, at times, it was plagued by failures in intelligence gathering and communication (and embarrassment in not being able to locate Noriega for several days), which might have been corrected had better procedures been in place.[158] But as Douglas Brinkley points out: "Bush accomplished all three of his objectives: Manuel Noriega was imprisoned in Miami, Guillermo Endara was installed as president, and the Panama Canal was secure."[159]

WAR IN THE PERSIAN GULF

The Bush administration's most ambitious foreign policy initiative was its response to Saddam Hussein's invasion of Kuwait on August 2, 1990. It was an effort that enlisted the support of the world community, including such unlikely allies as Syria and the Soviet Union. The U.S. and allied military presence at the height of the war exceeded 540,000 ground, sea, and air forces. It succeeded in thwarting and ultimately defeating, at least militarily, the Iraqi regime.

The White House was largely unprepared for the invasion, despite intelligence reports that the Iraqis were massing a large military force on the Kuwait border.[160] In mid-July, JCS Chairman Powell, on learning of an Iraqi troop buildup, commissioned U.S. Central Command—led by Gen. H. Norman Schwarzkopf—to develop a two-option plan for a U.S. response in case of an invasion; one tier was defensive, the other retaliatory.[161] By August 1, when Iraqi forces reached 100,000 troops, Powell was highly concerned and wanted Cheney to inform the White House so that Bush might warn Saddam of the dangers of invasion. Yet "Cheney wasn't alarmed. He didn't take the CIA or DIA [Defense Intelligence Agency] warnings as absolutes," Bob Woodward reports.[162]

Prior to the invasion, diplomatic pressure was put on Saddam both by the United States and other Arab nations, including a critical meeting between Saddam and U.S. Ambassador to Iraq April Glaspie during which he promised diplomatic cooperation in his border dispute with Kuwait. Some have taken her comment during the meeting that "we don't take positions on territorial disputes" as a signal to Saddam that the United States would not take action should he invade. Others have interpreted her remarks differently. According to President Bush, it was "standard State Department language that we do not take positions on the merits of a boundary dispute, but expect it to be settled peacefully." Her comment "has been grossly misconstrued as implying we would look the other way."[163]

Although surprised by the invasion, Bush and the principals decided to intervene militarily. Notified at 8:20 P.M., Bush ordered Scowcroft to schedule a meeting of the NSC the next morning.[164] That night, Scowcroft convened the deputies' group, according to Bush, "to review the situation and to begin the recommendation process." Moreover, "it was the start of a critical, and often overlooked, role he was to play in what followed in the coming months. Much of the subsequent original planning and careful thought was done with him at my side, probably more than history will ever know."[165]

Bush's first public comments the next day to reporters were "not felicitous," according to Scowcroft. Choosing his words carefully since a course of action had yet to be decided, Bush nonetheless said, "We're not discussing intervention." The first NSC meeting that day was chaotic. Baker was absent (he was returning from a trip to Mongolia) and Scowcroft "was frankly appalled at the undertone of the discussion, which suggested resignation to the invasion. . . . The remarks tended to skip over the enormous stake the United States had in the situation." Later, Scowcroft took action that reflected his dual role as counselor and broker: "I asked [Bush] if in the next meeting, I could depart from custom in NSC meetings and speak first, outlining the absolute intolerability of this invasion to U.S. interests." Bush counterproposed that he make such an opening statement. But Scowcroft "told him I thought that would stifle discussion, and we agreed I would go first."[166]

In the interim between the two meetings, Bush gave a speech at Aspen, Colorado, in which his public rhetoric against the invasion was much stronger than earlier in the day. During the flight, as they rewrote Bush's remarks according to Scowcroft, "it became obvious to me that the president was prepared to use force . . . if it became necessary, although he did not explicitly say so."[167]

The NSC meeting the next day proved more successful in Scowcroft's estimation: "The tone of the discussion was much better than the day before. We had established our case. Had the president taken his cue from the earlier meeting, our policy would have been vastly different, focusing on controlling the damage rather than reversing it."[168] According to one official present, it was Scowcroft's presentation "that made clear what the stakes were, crystallized people's thinking and galvanized support for a very strong response."[169] Yet the discussion also revealed that logistics and diplomacy would be daunting. At the end of the meeting, Bush requested that military options be fully presented to him the next day, August 4, at Camp David.

The Camp David meeting was a broad discussion; not only were the principals present, but Cheney had instructed Schwarzkopf to bring key commanders from each of the services.[170] In the short term, logistics dictated an air campaign against target-rich Iraq, General Schwarzkopf told the group. A deterrent force of 200,000 to 250,000 troops in the region would take seventeen weeks to put in place; an offensive force of 150,000 troops in Saudi Arabia would take eight to twelve months. Cheney raised concerns about the success of just an air campaign, which Schwarzkopf acknowledged. Scowcroft thought the plan was "air heavy" and that ground forces would signal a clear commitment to Saudi Arabia. Baker was worried about the political repercussions of bombing Baghdad. Cheney said the United States should respond strongly to Iraq only if the nation were prepared to see it through. Scowcroft felt that the U.S. public would support intervention; Cheney was doubtful of that over the long run. Economic sanctions and a blockade were also discussed. Baker warned of losing international support with a blockade; Scowcroft disagreed. Bush was worried that the Saudis would "bug out" and accept the invasion; he suggested trying a blockade.[171] Fair to say, it was a lively exchange of divergent views.

While no direct course of action had been decided upon, a range of military and nonmilitary options and their pros and cons had been discussed. Bush's advisers argued them freely; the difficulty of the situation was recognized by all. Yet Bush also limited his hand. Returning to Washington on August 5, Bush again attempted to be judicious in his comments to reporters. Were we going to respond militarily? "Just wait. Watch and learn," he replied. "I am not going to discuss what we're doing in terms of moving forces, anything of that nature." Bush continued in this vein, but at the end of his remarks he noted, "This will not stand, this aggression against Kuwait." The last remark, as Powell told him, felt like a declaration of war against Iraq. In Bush's view, "it was still too early to make that call"—that military forces would be used. "On the other hand, I certainly felt that force *could* be necessary. I had decided that it was up to Saddam."[172] An hour later, Bush approved the first deployment of U.S. forces: the dispatch of components of the 82nd Airborne Division and two squadrons of aircraft fighters—forty-eight jets—to Saudi Arabia. They were sent in case Saddam decided to invade that country as well. Bush also told Cheney, who was in Saudi Arabia seeking approval for the U.S. forces on their soil, that the U.S. would then begin a larger deployment.[173]

Yet the deliberative process may have been a bit less than perfect. According to an account by the *Washington Post,* Bush had decided to intervene "despite the lack of a detailed war plan for fighting Iraq."[174] According to James Pfiffner, decisions were made "after hasty meetings in an atmosphere of crisis rather than a systematic process of consultation with his military advisers. The president had publicly committed the United States to a course of action that it could not easily reconsider."[175] According to Woodward, Powell "was unable to pinpoint precisely when the president had decided that this major deployment was what he wanted to do. There had not been a piece of paper that laid out the decision or the alternatives, or implications. There had been no clear statement about goals."[176] Yet, time had been pressing, and the quick introduction of U.S. forces may have caused Saddam to pause in any contemplated move against Saudi Arabia, which if successful would have been catastrophic. Others, moreover, thought the administration did the best it could under the circumstances. According to Richard Haass, who served on the deputies' committee, "I don't think it was policy making on the fly, I don't think it was unthought through, we had been talking about defending Saudi Arabia, everything up to that from the U.N. resolutions to the freezing of assets to the public comments to the military preparations to the private diplomacy."[177]

At the same time, Bush may have limited his hand in dealing with Saddam by publicly stating that the invasion "will not stand," making a partial Iraqi withdrawal from Kuwait as a basis for a negotiated settlement difficult for him to accept at a later date. On August 8, Bush addressed the nation, announcing the deployment of the troops and airpower to Saudi Arabia, as well as outlining the principles that would guide future policy. "A line has been drawn in the sand," Bush said. While the "mission of our troops is defensive," the goal was the "immediate, unconditional, and complete withdrawal of all Iraqi forces from Kuwait." By the end of August, 80,000 U.S. troops had arrived in Saudi Arabia under what was now dubbed Operation Desert Shield.

At what point Bush decided that the defensive Desert Shield should become an offensive military move against Iraq, Operation Desert Storm, is unclear. Even Bush notes in his memoirs that "I don't know exactly when I became resigned to the fact that it would come to war," although Scowcroft dates it to mid-October.[178] Yet Bush seemed eager for action much earlier. While fishing with Scowcroft off the Bush family compound in Kennebunkport on August 23, "I asked him impatiently when we could strike," Bush recounts, "I wanted to know what we could do with our air power." Yet Bush's advisers remained divided; some such as Baker were "reluctant to contemplate" the use of force, according to Bush, "and believed strongly that diplomacy and sanctions should be given every chance to get the job done."[179] Bush's advisers could also stand up to him. In late August, Bush told them he wanted to visit U.S. troops in Saudi Arabia. "It went over like a lead balloon," Bush reports, "No one was in favor of it."[180]

Alternatives to an offensive use of military force do not appear to have been fully explored. Powell felt that containment and economic strangulation were working: 95 percent of commercial business traffic into and out of Iraq had been halted. Powell tried to press Cheney in early October to stay with a containment strategy, but Cheney was skeptical. Containment still left Saddam in Kuwait, which was not the outcome Bush wanted. Powell also pressed Baker, who told him that his staff was preparing an analysis on the advantages of containment.[181]

Scowcroft's counsel to the president was central. Not only had he successfully urged a hard line against Saddam's invasion, but he had a good sense how it would play out. According to one account, while on that fishing trip with Bush, "Scowcroft suggested the strategy Bush would pursue over the following year, predicting that sanctions would fail to oust Saddam Hussein from Kuwait, that war would be necessary, but that the U.S. should not expand its objective to include Saddam's removal from power."[182] When Powell went to see Scowcroft about the containment option, Scowcroft told him that Bush "is more and more convinced that sanctions are not going to work." According to Woodward, Scowcroft was "reinforcing the president's inclinations. As a national security adviser, it was his job." But Scowcroft also "had responsibility to make sure the range of alternatives was presented." Powell was "disenchanted," according to Woodward. Scowcroft, in his view, was failing to coordinate properly.[183]

Yet for Scowcroft, the utility of economic containment may have been a settled matter. Both he and Bush, "early came to the conclusion that sanctions were unlikely to be on our side." "It was going to be a very difficult thing to keep that coalition together and that it would very likely collapse before Saddam's ability would collapse," he later recalled. "I never had any faith in sanctions and I don't think the president did either. I think he made up his mind early on that if Saddam did not withdraw of his own accord that we would force him out." A military offensive, however, was always contingent on Saddam's actions: "There was never a point at which we said 'There's nothing else that can happen, we're going to use force' right up until except maybe 48 hours ahead of time."[184]

Powell, however, had his day in court. Cheney arranged for Powell to meet privately with Bush a short time later. Powell made the case for a fuller discussion of options—including containment—to Bush, Cheney, and Scowcroft. Powell said he could live with either option. But "no one, including the President, embraced containment. If only one of them had, Powell was prepared to say that he favored it. . . . No one asked him for his overall opinion."[185] (Interestingly, he found himself in the same position in 2002, when war with Iraq emerged in the George W. Bush presidency; he would also undertake the similar back-channel efforts to press his concerns.)

By this time, even Baker had come to realize that "politically . . . it was unlikely sanctions would ever work to force Saddam out of Kuwait." At best, in Baker's view, "sanctions, coupled with the threat of military force, might persuade Saddam to leave Kuwait."[186] Powell and Baker met, they agreed that existing policy was "drifting." They discussed options. The first was "just keeping options open, which would perpetuate the drift." The second was "consciously opting for a policy of declared containment." The third was "building a deliberate offensive capability sufficient to eject Iraq from Kuwait if necessary." According to Baker, "We favored the third course. 'We have the capability to put together a real offensive force,' Powell said. This should persuade Saddam Hussein we were serious."[187] Powell had apparently caved in or otherwise had been persuaded.

The discussion got Baker thinking about a date requiring Saddam's withdrawal, after which military force would be used. It also signaled that Powell had come around in his thinking. It is possible that he either realized that it was now strategically useless to press for just the continuation of economic containment (Baker was his last possible ally among the principals), or he had come to the conclusion that it was time for a tougher stance. There is some evidence for the latter: Powell would later note that by the end of October, "it was clear that sanctions were not going to work in any kind of reasonable time." But Powell himself offers a third possibility—*he* was acting as an honest broker in the intervening months, concerned that all options were fully aired: "I had no preferred option at that time. . . . Some people think [sanctions] was the only policy I was pushing at that point but I would take issue with that. I felt it was important that the president hear all sides and meanwhile, while he was hearing all sides, I was doing everything I could to put in place, with Schwarzkopf, a powerful, powerful force that would win decisively if that's what the president wanted."[188]

Plans for attacking Iraq were clearly being developed, and they came before the president and the principals. One, which Schwarzkopf developed, was presented in early October; it was seen as uninspired and potentially having excessively high losses with its strategy of a direct, frontal attack on Iraqi forces in Kuwait. Scowcroft "was appalled with the presentation and afterwards I called Cheney to say I thought we had to do better. Cheney shared my concern." President Bush felt that "the briefing made me realize we had a long way to go."[189] After the meeting, Scowcroft immediately approached Cheney, telling him "if this is what we're going to get then we'll just have to find a different way to do military planning." Scowcroft offered to talk to Powell, although he "always wanted to be careful . . . so that I didn't get in between the military chain of command." Cheney responded that *he* would talk to Powell.[190]

Later in the month, Schwarzkopf presented a revamped plan; it called for a doubling of troops to over 500,000, and a military sweep around Kuwait and into Iraq, which might then encircle and cut off Iraqi forces. Bush accepted the troop increase at a crucial meeting with the principals on October 30. Powell did not press on the issue of containment versus an offensive operation; he simply laid out what the latter would entail.[191] On November 8, shortly after the midterm congressional elections, Bush publicly announced that the increase was needed in order to create an "offensive military option."[192]

In October, Scowcroft was also an influential voice in recognizing that a ground campaign might be needed but that an early attack, which Prime Minister Margaret Thatcher had been pressing, was ill advised. "I still thought we could simply devastate Iraq's military with all our air power after a provocation," Bush later recalled, "but Brent warned that we might eventually have to follow through with ground troops to liberate Kuwait, and if we pounded from the air too soon, before our forces were ready, there could be public pressure to stop all fighting . . . That might leave Saddam in Kuwait— and us without a military option. . . . Brent's point was good . . . there was still a lot of military, and political, preparation ahead of us before I would feel comfortable that I had the answers I needed."[193] More generally, according to another account, "In the six months leading to the war, Scowcroft became indispensable to Bush, subjecting war planners to sharp questioning and debating those opposed to intervention."[194]

Scowcroft made another valuable contribution. At the critical meeting on October 30, he opened the session by telling the group that "we are at the fork in the Y."[195] He then laid out three options. One option was to continue to see if sanctions would work. The second involved the use of force, including whether to ask for a U.N. resolution specifying a specific date for an Iraqi withdrawal. The third involved reacting to or creating an Iraqi provocation that would trigger a military response. Although no decision for war was made, not only did Bush agree to the troop increase, but Baker was sent to consult with coalition leaders about a U.N. resolution that would set a firm deadline for Saddam to withdraw from Iraq to be followed by a military response if he failed to do so.[196] Baker's efforts—plus a heavy dose of the president's personal lobbying—proved successful, and on November 29 the U.N. Security Council agreed to a resolution, with the date of compliance set at January 15.

According to Scowcroft, a full range of options had been explored. Commitment to a course of action was incremental and responsive to circumstances:

> The first strategy was to get forces into Saudi Arabia, to dissuade Saddam of any notion that he could keep on and seize Saudi oil fields. So after we had a satisfactory buildup in Saudi Arabia, [the issue was] should we stop or continue to prepare ourselves for the contingency that we might have to liberate Kuwait. That was a decision point. And it was slightly divisive within the NSC.[197]

Containment through economic sanctions "was discussed," Scowcroft later recollects,

> but we had not really made a decision. I don't know whether it was at that meeting, but right on [after], we wanted to explore—if we had to use force—whether we could get the Congress and the United Nations to go along. So I argued we needed to continue the buildup so that we had the *capability* to use force if we wanted to. . . . By that time we had determined we had to get them out of Kuwait certainly, but not necessarily by the use of force. As the buildup continued, I—and I don't know at what point—I decided that we had no other option but the use of force. Because in the end we had 500,000 troops there. And if Saddam had said, "I will agree to a slow withdrawal," we couldn't keep those troops there. We would have had to withdraw, and then putting them back in again, if it went wrong, would have been almost impossible. So I came to the conclusion somewhere in November, I think, that we did not have any options left, we had to use force.[198]

Whatever the president's final choice of action, Scowcroft was prepared. In the fall, he had asked the deputies' committee and the NSC staff to "review our war aims beyond what was set out in the resolution." They focused "on reducing Saddam's military might so that he would no longer be a threat to the region." They recommended air strikes beyond Kuwait, particularly directed at Saddam's elite Republican Guard. They discussed removing Saddam, but came to the conclusion that it could not be "formally" done within the U.N. resolutions without splitting the coalition. They warned of an "indefinite occupation of a hostile state" and the difficulties of "nation-building." According to Scowcroft, "these aims (and limits) were established well before the end of the year." The committee's review "became the basis of the directive the president would sign in January setting Desert Storm in motion."[199]

According to other accounts, various tiers of the NSC staff were actively involved in a range of planning activities for both Desert Shield and Desert Storm. As noted earlier, the deputies' committee was especially active in the immediate aftermath of the invasion. Their work continued: "They gathered and evaluated the mass of information on the crisis that hit them each day . . . [they] identified solutions that made sense across agencies and departments."[200] Their work was informed by earlier meetings in the day held by Policy Coordinating Committees, and a smaller group of the deputies attended a meeting with Gates, who in turn was a member of the core "group of eight" principals. According to Haass, during the Gulf crisis, "Brent and I, or Brent, Bob Gates, and I used to gather in Brent's office." It was a time to step back and do some advance planning, to discuss what they were working on, to ask what they were "not thinking of," and by necessity "to do that to stay one step ahead of events."[201]

As it turned out, Bush's strategy in pursuing sanctions but also demanding Iraq's complete withdrawal from Kuwait and its acceptance of all U.N. resolutions paid off. The air campaign began on January 16, 1991, and prepared the way for a ground assault on February 23. In less than one hundred hours, Iraq faced defeat. Thousands of Iraqi troops were killed (20,000 by some estimates), 50,000 to 100,000 were captured, and its equipment and military infrastructure were almost totally destroyed. U.S. causalities were light: 105 were killed during Desert Shield, 148 were killed during Desert Storm, including fifty in noncombat-related incidents.[202]

Yet, as Greene observes, questions remained: "Perhaps the biggest controversy arising from the Gulf War revolved around Bush's decision as to when it would end."[203] There was no dissent, especially from Powell or Schwarzkopf, to end the war before the Iraqi army had been completely encircled and defeated. A march to Baghdad and full defeat of the Saddam regime went beyond U.N. mandates, Bush and Scowcroft later noted. Both were especially concerned that occupation of Iraq and the overthrow of Saddam Hussein would isolate the United States from other coalition allies, and draw the United States into a situation where it had "no viable exit strategy." Prophetically they note, "Had we gone the invasion route, the United States could conceivably still be an occupying power in a bitterly hostile land."[204]

But Scowcroft also remained vigilant. When General Schwarzkopf permitted the Iraqis to keep their helicopters (without prior Washington approval), Scowcroft tried unsuccessfully to reverse the decision: "it gave [Saddam] a great loophole."[205]

Further questions remain. Were Bush and his principals too confident that Saddam Hussein would be overthrown in the aftermath of defeat? In the view of Paul Nitze—one of the successors to the foreign policy "wise men" of the 1950s and 1960s—"After it was clear Saddam Hussein's forces were not going to turn on him . . . the president should have changed his decision. He was ill served by his national security adviser."[206] Yet, as Bush himself notes, it was a multilateral effort: "In Desert Storm I hope we set positive precedents for future responses to international crises, forging coalitions, properly using the United Nations, and carefully cultivating support at home and abroad for U.S. objectives."[207]

It is also noteworthy that Bush's last comments in the chapters dealing with the Persian Gulf War in *A World Transformed* are about Brent Scowcroft, drawn from a diary entry of February 28, the last day of the war. After noting the strengths of his other advisers and military commanders, Bush ends with his NSC advisor: "Then of course Brent Scowcroft . . . He takes the burden off of the President, tasks the bureaucracy, sorts out the differences and never with credit for himself. He's always quiet but always there and always dependable."[208]

VII. Implications

Brent Scowcroft's role as NSC advisor is of special importance for three reasons. First, it clearly illustrates that honest brokerage can be a viable if not central part of the job. Brokerage is not just some dated relic of the Eisenhower years, superseded by the policy activism of a Bundy or a Kissinger. Brokerage remains relevant and was practiced by a more recent NSC advisor. Second, both of the elements of the honest broker role—a concern for the fairness of the deliberative process and a concern for the quality of the organizational channels that precede and then structure debate among the principals—were embraced by Scowcroft. His organizational concerns were especially enduring and outlasted his time as NSC advisor: the "Scowcroft model" of NSC operations was largely adopted by his successors, both in Democratic and Republican administrations. In some sense, Scowcroft was able to revive interagency planning below the level of the principals, but without the perceived over formality of the Eisenhower-era Planning Board. Third, Scowcroft's tenure provides evidence that the NSC advisor can add additional duties to the job beyond brokerage and still remain effective as an honest broker. Scowcroft, especially under George H. W. Bush, was a policy advocate at times, yet not to the detriment of a fair, balanced, probing, and otherwise full consideration of alternative views. While not a Bundy or Kissinger in terms of a visible media presence, he did not relegate himself to the invisibility of his Eisenhower forebears. He took his cue from what Kissinger and then Baker—but above all what Presidents Ford and Bush—wanted of him. So too with Scowcroft's infrequent diplomatic efforts and contacts. In short, he offers a case study of honest brokerage—"brokerage plus," if you will—adjusted and tempered to the other job demands of more contemporary NSC advisors.

The NSC Advisor's Role Expectations and Honest Brokerage

Scowcroft's tenure is especially revealing about the importance of the NSC advisor's expectations about the job. Like Bundy and Kissinger, he had cut his academic chops; he was Dr. and Professor Scowcroft as well as General Scowcroft. But he was no mere academic, as they were, with little prior government service. As *General* Scowcroft he had JCS staff experience, service as military aide in the White House, and most importantly time as Kissinger's deputy NSC advisor. Like Cutler, he came to the job with clear expectations of what he wanted his role to be. But unlike Cutler, who served two stints under one president (and with more limited prepresidential experience), Scowcroft's NSC service spanned three: Nixon and Ford as deputy, Ford and Bush as NSC advisor. The Nixon and Ford presidencies were likely important incubators in developing a sense of what contributed to or detracted from an effective national security process and an effective NSC advisor. The Reagan years offered opportunities for service on presidential commissions, none more educational about the role of the NSC advisor than Scowcroft's central efforts on the Tower Board, its diagnosis of organizational error, and its recommendations for reform.

Scowcroft's expectations and how he undertook the demands of the job are really one of a piece. So too is the persona. His firm but easygoing personality helped; the general proved a better a manager of the process and a balanced and fair voice among the principals than the Harvard dean or the Harvard professor. Scowcroft's ability to serve as a policy advocate is especially important: he offered counsel to the president, often private at times, in such a way as to not compromise his ability to fairly express the views of others. Nor was he tempted to stack the deck in debate among the principals. He also recognized the importance of establishing confidence in him among his colleagues. Scowcroft's meetings with Bush were not times for secret, private *decision making* but rather of policy exploration. Indeed, he was cognizant, from his study of Iran-Contra as a member of the Tower Commission, of the problem of private meetings with the president as a venue for quick decision making. Both Bush and Scowcroft also recognized the need for communication with the other principals of their private contacts so that they were all, as Baker phrased it, "singing from the same hymnal."

Evolution of the NSC Advisor's Role over Time

Here the issue is not so much the evolution in Scowcroft's role within either the Ford or Bush presidency. There is not much evidence of significant alteration *within* each presidency, as best as I can detect. Rather the important point is that brokerage was present, but it was adjusted to the differing presidents and decision contexts that Scowcroft faced. Scowcroft was an honest broker under both presidents. Under President Ford, however, the task was more difficult. He needed to—and succeeded in—fulfilling that task while at the same time maintaining smooth working relations with Kissinger. The "care and feeding of" Kissinger was a more ongoing concern than Scowcroft faced with Jim Baker or Dick Cheney. Another evolution was advocacy. During the Ford years, Kissinger largely filled the space of policy advice and vision. Under Bush. Baker provided a heavy dose of political strategy, but there was more "space" for Scowcroft's own substantive views. So too with media visibility. What is different from one presidency to another is Scowcroft's ability to craft a more effective model of interagency coordination under Bush in which the NSC advisor was able to take the clear lead, and, as noted, provide an enduring organizational template that still persists.

PRESIDENTIAL DECISION-MAKING NEEDS, PRESIDENTIAL ROLE EXPECTATIONS

The needs and expectations of the presidents under whom Scowcroft served is also an important factor bearing on how Scowcroft defined his own job. Ford wanted balance to Kissinger, and Scowcroft provided it. Scowcroft also clearly recognized that Ford operated differently than Nixon—he valued the give-and-take of open debate *and* he also was a voracious reader.

Bush was quite explicit in his recognition that he wanted a source of private counsel but also someone who was an honest broker. Presidential recognition of the contours of the NSC's advisor's role is clearly an important lesson from both periods of Scowcroft's tenure. But the lessons from the Bush presidency are especially important. Bush was cognizant, from his many prior governmental positions, of the interpersonal and organizational dynamics potentially at work: the bureaucratic politics of State and Defense, battles between State and the NSC staff, and interpersonal conflict and rivalry among the principals. He recognized that it was a *presidential* responsibility to set the organizational tone and define personal expectations. It was *his* responsibility to communicate to Scowcroft, Baker, or Cheney if he had met privately with one of them so that all would share in the president's thinking. Above all, he recognized that it was his job to pick the right people: advisers who would offer their unvarnished views but also operate as a team.

OTHER IMPLICATIONS

The cast of characters with whom Scowcroft interacted suggests some positive factors for brokerage but also some cautionary limits. Under Ford, Kissinger was the driving policy force providing the policy vision. Like Dulles under Eisenhower, a strong secretary of state may have made brokerage for the NSC advisor easier, since advocacy was less needed. "Handling" the bureaucratically wily and adept Kissinger, however, was a more daunting task than that faced by Cutler et al. in dealing with Dulles.

The Bush team was an especially battle-tested group, with prior experience in previous administrations and in many cases prior working relations with each other. There was no steep learning curve here—perhaps they recognized decision-making dangers and knew what to avoid. At the same time, they were tough, bureaucratically skilled characters. Scowcroft was not operating within an easy context, yet he successfully operated nonetheless. The degree of trust among the principals and their willingness to cooperate, despite policy differences at times, seems an especially important ingredient to a relatively successful process. Scowcroft was an honest broker but also a full partner with the other principals when time came to express his own policy views.

As part of that expression of views, moreover, it is especially notable that Scowcroft's policy positions and advocacy did not always prevail. Sometimes he was on the losing side, as were the other principals at times. Yet there was no jockeying for power, no one-upmanship, no recriminations, and no loss of face as a result of losing out. It was all in a day's work; all was taken in stride.

But there may be limits in the applicability of the Scowcroft case to other presidencies. Much day-to-day management of the NSC staff and system was delegated to the deputy NSC advisor, and, by all measures, Robert Gates performed well. The lesson here is that as the NSC staff has grown in size and as the demands upon it and the NSC advisor have expanded, internal management and the selection of skilled personnel have now become increasingly important. In particular, the post of deputy NSC advisor now figures strongly as part of the equation for a successful policy process and for an effective NSC advisor.

Counterfactual situations may also pose problems or limit the applicability of the Scowcroft role. Will brokerage still work under a president with less foreign policy experience and interest than George H. W. Bush? Can brokerage work under a president who is not cognizant of an honest broker's contribution to the policy process—a Lyndon Johnson say? Can the role that Scowcroft practiced operate as effectively if the other principals lack the shared experiences and the prior working relationships that we see especially during the Bush administration? Can brokerage still work if the other principals do not have the respect for the NSC advisor that we see here or if there is an absence of interpersonal trust in each other and with the process? Part of the answer may reside in attention to who are selected for key positions—again the importance of the presidential transition to office rears its head.

The sometimes secretive, tightly held nature of the Bush presidency is also an issue. Scowcroft's visits to China, the Panama effort, and the planning for a major summit with Gorbachev in Malta also signal the efforts of this administration to proceed in secret if possible, with a smaller group of advisers in the know. Leaks were an obvious concern, especially with Panama. Bush's own extensive experience in foreign affairs, his innate caution and concern to avoid mistakes, plus the experience of his principals may have compensated for any narrowing of the foreign policy advisory net. Yet even simple things were sometimes missed. The stormy weather Bush encountered at the Malta summit—the meetings were held on ships and transit between them was somewhat perilous—might have been anticipated if better staff work had been done concerning Malta's normal weather patterns that time of year. Apparently neither Cheney nor CIA Director Webster were informed that a summit was in the offing. Likewise, Chief of Staff Sununu and press secretary Marlin Fitzwater were kept in the dark about Scowcroft's first visit to China in the aftermath of the Tiananmen Square crackdown; both, however, had to deal with its political repercussions when knowledge of the visit became public.[209]

Unresolved questions: Even if the process was effective in some sense, were the outcomes the best that could have reasonably been achieved? It is a bit of a mantra among those who study presidential decision making that good decision-making processes do not necessarily guarantee optimal policy outcomes. The response to the aborted coup in Panama was clearly a problem and handled "less than crisp" (as Baker himself phrased it; "spotty" in Scowcroft's view). Success, of course, did eventually come. More difficult: Was the "measured" response to the crackdown at Tiananmen Square a squandered opportunity for encouraging nascent democracy in China? Or was it wise diplomacy? Was the military attack on Iraq premature, before sanctions had a time to work? After the successful reconquest of Kuwait and invasion of southern Iraq, did the decision not to move on to Baghdad and topple Saddam Hussein and his government lead eventually, under son

George W. Bush, to a prolonged and bloody U.S. involvement in Iraq? Or was it the best that could be achieved under existing U.N. mandates, thereby avoiding the possible political collapse of the allied coalition and the costly commitment of the United States to a possible civil war in Iraq? The historical counterfactuals are not available to us, unfortunately.

By the same token, the collapse of the Warsaw-bloc Eastern European countries was handled cautiously—and I suspect history will say well. The collapse of the Soviet Union was handled a bit more fitfully at points, but the outcome was advantageous in the end. What other historical example exists for the disappearance of one's prime enemy in the absence of a major war effort? At a minimum, the challenges Bush, Scowcroft, and their associates faced were great; they met them reasonably well. Scowcroft's role in crafting an NSC decision process, in acting as an honest broker, and in judiciously advancing a bit beyond brokerage were part of an overall and largely successful policy equation.

CHAPTER 5

Weak Brokerage, Insurgency, and Recovery

The Reagan NSC Advisors

The six NSC advisors who served over the eight years of the Reagan presidency provide an interesting set of cases about how that role can be defined so differently, especially under one president. Some, such as Richard Allen, were largely coordinators. Others such as Frank Carlucci and Colin Powell were more honest brokers. Some, such as John Poindexter, became involved in policy implementation, and in Poindexter's case with disastrous results in the Iran-Contra affair. Some were fairly visible public figures, such as William Clark; others, such as Robert McFarlane, were less so. The six put to the test the notion that the advisory system and the particular roles of its participants must closely mesh with the decision-making needs and predilections of sitting presidents: their roles as NSC advisors were defined in very different ways yet all served under one president. Their individual effectiveness also varied enormously, reaching a nadir under Poindexter. Improvement came only in the last two years, under Carlucci and especially Powell, following reforms undertaken in the wake of the Iran-Contra scandal.

I. The Reagan National Security Process

Unlike the other presidencies that we have considered, it is difficult to find broad generalizations that characterize the decision-making process throughout the Reagan years. Each of the NSC advisors had significant impact on the process, and that impact differed. There are also significant differences in the early Reagan presidency, when Secretary of State Alexander Haig sought to exert great influence over foreign policy, compared to the remaining years when George Shultz occupied that office. At the same time, Schultz was no wall flower and was a strong secretary of state. Indeed, his practice of not attending meetings chaired by anyone but the president—or himself—had a significant impact on the process. So too did the relationship between Shultz and Secretary of Defense Caspar Weinberger. They were "natural rivals," according to Reagan biographer Lou Cannon, "burdened by ancient animosities and a competing view of U.S.-Soviet relations."[1] Although no love fest, Shultz had much better relations with Weinberger's replacement at the Pentagon, Frank Carlucci.

The one constant was Ronald Reagan. But it was a constant that had both strengths and weaknesses. On the positive side, those around Reagan recognized early on the need to develop a strong, formal system that would guide policy deliberations. This was one of the tasks that Edwin Meese, Reagan's longtime aide, took on during the 1980 presidential transition. In domestic and economic policy it led to the development of a series of cabinet councils in a range of policy areas. Meese's goal was to replicate Reagan's decision making as governor of California, where he interacted directly with the heads of the state's departments and agencies, but with the realization—unlike Jimmy Carter—that consultation with the full cabinet would prove unwieldy. Meese's cabinet councils were also designed to give the White House a strong measure of control: their agendas were set there and policy staffing largely came from there as well. The cabinet councils, however, proved a mix bag; some were successful, others proved mere window dressing for decisions made in the White House.[2]

On national security and foreign policy matters, of course, the NSC served as the existing cabinet council vehicle. The major organizational change was the creation of three senior interagency groups (SIGs) that were closely tied to the departments. State took the lead in the SIG on foreign policy, the Pentagon on defense matters, and the CIA on intelligence. A fourth SIG was created a year later on international economic policy, and Treasury was the lead agency. Below the SIGs, interdepartmental working groups—chaired by a representative from the lead department—were charged with developing options to be presented to the SIGs.[3]

At least at the start of the Reagan presidency, the cabinet secretaries and the director of the CIA played a major role in their respective SIGs. As we shall see, also at the start, the NSC advisor was in a comparatively weaker position. Yet, the SIGs proved less important over time, and were replaced by a stronger NSC advisor and a staff-directed process.[4]

Although amiable, thoughtful, and personally kind to subordinates, Reagan was not a president who took on the job of managing the system around him. That task was delegated to others. But it was a task that often went unmet, or at a minimum depended on the vicissitudes of those to whom much was delegated. The politics of the well-placed and self-serving leak to the press, bureaucratic competition, and intrigue were rife in this administration. For his part, Reagan trusted.[5] As Donald Regan—treasury secretary in the first term, and chief of staff at the start of the second—notes, "Reagan seldom criticized, seldom complained, never scolded." But it was a trust that "was betrayed in shocking fashion."[6] Especially in the area of national security, Weinberger observes, "I think the president trusted his security advisors, and from the Tower Commission's point of view perhaps he gave them too much leeway or didn't keep a close enough view on them."[7]

Perhaps more problematic was the fact that delegation of the details of policy making was characteristic of this administration. Reagan did provide a broad policy vision and it would prove decisive at times: rebuilding of U.S. military capacity, the change in view of Gorbachev's bona fides as a reformer, Reagan's interest in arms control, especially in the strategic defense initiative (SDI), to take just some of the more important instances. Reagan also dutifully did his homework, reading what work was brought before him.[8] Yet he did not personally reach out in search of additional information and advice. He often asked hard questions, but without the sustained doggedness of a Kennedy. In some ways, the formal system on which he relied was the actualization of the misplaced criticism directed at the Eisenhower system in the 1950s. Moreover, while informed in a broad sense, Reagan lacked Nixon's deep substantive knowledge of foreign policy detail. In the Reagan system, presidential involvement was limited and largely confined to the final stage. There were no established mechanisms for making sure that disagreements were brought to the presidential level—save for the importuning of those who had "lost out" at lower levels. The emphasis was on producing consensus below when possible, precisely the recipe for the "lowest common denominator" options that critics have thought characteristic of formal decision-making arrangements.

In the view of Martin Anderson—another longtime Reagan associate and later head of the White House Office of Policy Development—"there were three basic ways to participate in the policy process of the Reagan administration. The first was to talk to him personally and directly. . . . This was the most effective, but opportunities were limited. . . . The second was to write and send memoranda. That was not very effective given the way Reagan liked to work. That left the third way—meetings."[9]

But meetings were at times problematic. As Donald Regan, then serving as secretary of the treasury, observed, it was a "baffling system in which the President seldom spoke, while his advisers proposed measures that contradicted his ideas and promises, created uncertainties in a situation that cried out for action." Reagan had set a broad vision. Regan thought he "understood the President's philosophy. But how did he want it carried out, if at all? Casual exchanges in Cabinet meetings and other large gatherings were not enough to give the necessary guidance."[10] As chief of staff, Regan would make the process even worse. First, he reduced the number of those who had "walk-in rights" to see Reagan. Second, he attempted to take a lead role in national security policy himself, despite his own lack of background in that area save what he learned on international economic policy as the head of Merrill Lynch and as treasury secretary.

In his memoirs, President Reagan notes that it was his practice to encourage "cabinet members to speak frankly" and that he would refrain from debate so as "not to tip my advisors off."[11] But as Don Regan indicates, more direction by the president was needed. Indeed, President Reagan notes in his memoirs the "special vantage point" of his cabinet members grounded in the responsibilities and expert knowledge of their home departments.[12] Bureaucratic politics, in his view, was actually a good thing.

Reagan, in a way like George W. Bush as we shall see, was "process dependent." When the process worked, he was well served. When it failed, he was hostage to its results. Given that process highly mattered, brokerage of that process was clearly needed. But in Reagan's case, effective brokerage proved elusive, almost to the end of his presidency—and almost at the cost of his presidency.

II. The Reagan NSC Advisors

Over the eight years of the Reagan presidency, six men served in the position of NSC advisor. Their definitions of the role varied, as did their performance. But each had significant impact on the administration's national security decision making, some for better, some for worse.

RICHARD V. ALLEN

Early decisions strongly affected foreign and national security policy making—and the role of the NSC advisor. Three in particular stand out. The first was the selection, as secretary of state, of Al Haig, who had publicly and privately touted himself as Reagan's "vicar" of foreign policy. The second was the appointment of Richard Allen as NSC advisor. Allen, as noted earlier, had been Nixon's chief foreign policy adviser during the 1968 campaign, and he had served briefly on the Kissinger NSC staff. He later served on Nixon's Commission on International Trade and Economic Policy and as a deputy assistant to the president on international economic affairs in 1971–1972.

In 1980, Allen served again as chief foreign policy adviser during the campaign, this time for Ronald Reagan. His efforts were laudable. By April 1980, he had enlisted some seventy defense and foreign policy experts to provide advice. By October, their number had grown to 132, and they were organized into twenty-five working groups.[13] After Election Day, Allen was placed in charge of one of three policy teams; his group encompassed all foreign and defense policy issues.[14]

Allen's role in the campaign and during the transition seemed to portend a strong role for him as NSC advisor. That was not to be. A third decision, organizational, placed Allen in the weakest position of any of the NSC advisors to date (and indeed since). As part of his broad responsibilities as "counselor to the president," Ed Meese was given supervision and control of both domestic *and* foreign policy; Allen and his NSC staff would not directly report to the president but through Meese. Nor would Allen have cabinet rank, as Zbigniew Brzezinski had enjoyed under Carter. The first floor, corner West Wing office that the NSC advisor had occupied since Kissinger's days was taken over by Meese. Allen was sent downstairs to a smaller basement office near the Situation Room.

The selection of Haig as secretary of state was essentially Reagan's own doing. Reagan's "kitchen cabinet" had favored George Shultz—the former director of OMB and past secretary of both Labor and Treasury—for the job. However, the fact that Shultz and Weinberger (already tapped for Defense) were both executives at the Bechtel Corporation worked against him. Reagan personally sounded out Shultz for the job first. But he never explicitly offered Shultz the position; the conversation apparently got confused and Shultz thought Reagan was calling about serving as treasury secretary, a position he did not want again. Next on the list was Haig, who may have been Reagan's choice all along. Haig had been recommended by Nixon. But some on the transition team were worried about his ability to be a team player, his activities as chief of staff during the Watergate period, and his future presidential ambitions. Haig met with William Casey and Meese, the two chief directors of the transition, as well as James A. Baker, soon to be chief of staff, and Pendleton James, who headed the transition's personnel operations. Apparently their talks removed concerns about Haig, who got the position.[15] But they had been forewarned about him.

Problems began on Inauguration Day when Haig sought to assert firm control over the policy process. He had devised a memorandum, which he hoped Reagan would immediately sign, that created a policy-making structure in which the secretary of state would have clear dominance. It immediately raised concern among Reagan's top aides—the "troika" of Meese, Baker, and his deputy, Michael Deaver—that it constituted a "power grab" by Haig.[16] They persuaded Reagan not to sign the document, and Meese instructed Haig to work with other agencies and departments involved in foreign policy to devise a more balanced substitute.

On February 26, 1981, Meese unveiled the basic structure of the national security and foreign policy process that the Reagan administration would use. Haig's responsibilities were less than he had initially tried to assert.[17] Haig lost the battle to be placed in charge of crisis management; that assignment was given to Vice President George H. W. Bush.[18] Haig reportedly read about the Bush assignment in the *Washington Post*.[19] State gained control over only one of the three new SIGs. The State Department's hand also was weakened as other SIGs and interdepartmental working groups were created at later points in the Reagan presidency. Some twenty-two SIGs were eventually created with over two hundred working groups, some meeting only once on a particular project.[20] However, it would not be until William Clark became NSC advisor in January 1982 that a formal National Security Decision Directive (NSDD) was signed by Reagan authorizing a national security policy process.[21]

The NSC advisor and his staff played a secondary role in the new setup. Allen not only reported through Meese, but departmental representatives, rather than the NSC's staff, took the lead in the new committee structure below the level of the principals and the SIGs. However, Meese and Allen would decide what issues fell within the jurisdiction of which particular interdepartmental committee, not a small matter.

Allen's role clearly departed from the pattern set by his immediate predecessors. Allen was more a subordinate part of a departmentally dominated apparatus. For Allen, his role model was Gordon Gray of the Eisenhower years rather than Bundy, Kissinger, or Brzezinski, who had used their positions, access to the president, and NSC staff to put their own imprint on policy development. Nor would Allen chair any significant committees as Kissinger, Brzezinski, and even Scowcroft had done; "Not if I can avoid it," he told one reporter. [22]

According to Inderfurth and Johnson, the NSC advisor's job "reverted to a staff function, with no mandate to engage in policy advocacy or formulation, as his predecessors had done before him."[23] According to Kevin Mulcahy, Allen "did not have a background . . . as a scholar or conceptualizer on foreign affairs. Allen consistently endorsed a low profile, facilitator conception of his job . . . and he asserted that he had no intention of making policy." The NSC staff, in Mulcahy's view, "was downgraded from a policy making and control group to a conduit for departmental proposals. More significantly, Allen and his staff did not involve themselves either in the day-to-day operations of foreign policy or in independently formulating policy initiatives." [24] As Allen himself put it, "We're not going to fight for control of policy. Policy is going to be made in a collegial way."[25] "If you're looking for the high voltage action and the big visibility and all the other perks," Allen told his staff, "don't come to this NSC."[26] Finally, selling policy and other public relations activities, in Allen's view, were the "White House press secretary's job, not mine." [27] He "adhered to his pledge to maintain a low profile. His contact with the press remained on a background basis, with only occasional on-the-record appearances."[28] According to some former NSC staff members, "the system's been emasculated. Allen isn't going to be able to coordinate policy."[29] Even his one point of regular contact with Reagan—the president's daily morning briefing—was reduced to written form in order to cut back the president's busy schedule.[30]

While Allen may have modeled himself after Eisenhower-era NSC advisors, he operated in a White House that lacked the smooth machinery and orderly processes of the Eisenhower NSC system. As Lou Cannon notes, based on an interview with Allen, "Much of Allen's time was spent vainly trying to shove decision documents and position papers through the funnel-like management system that Meese had created to spare Reagan from decision-making." Allen's paperwork ended up on Meese's desk or in his infamous briefcase "and too many of them stayed there. At one point in Allen's year-long tenure, fourteen separate papers requiring presidential decisions were blocked by the Meese bottleneck."[31] According to Allen, when he learned that he would be reporting through Meese—*after* he had accepted the position—he initially thought it might be advantageous. Meese had a "lot of clout" and might be a "two-ton blocking back, running blocking back ahead of us, doing whatever we asked him to do." But "it turned out for me that he became a two-ton elephant in the door jamb, because he could not get himself out of the mire and the muck of the paper."[32]

At one point, early in the administration, Robert McFarlane—who was Haig's counselor at State and eventually Reagan's third NSC advisor—approached Allen about the need for an interdepartmental system to provide for better policy planning, especially to deal with urgent issues that were languishing. Allen listened "noncommittally," then he told McFarlane that he did not think a lot of planning was needed; instead, they would respond to events with thoughtful and timely decisions. In McFarlane's view, it was "an amazing expression of ignorance" of international politics.[33] The result, according to McFarlane, was that during the first year of Reagan's presidency, policy was "made ad hoc, often by the last person who spoke to the president, and seldom written down." It was a "theater of chaos" and "guerilla warfare." With no coherent interagency process for developing policy, "each cabinet officer tried to put his personal agenda in front of the president."[34]

By October, reports indicated that Allen and his assistants, "now play a clearly secondary staff role and not the traditional role of adjudicators and coordinators of different departmental views. . . . With some exceptions, Mr. Allen's staff is seen by other officials as bureaucratically unskilled and highly ideological." Nor was Ed Meese much help. According to Leslie Gelb: "Meese is said to have veto power and to be a kind of traffic policeman. . . . but he does not have the background, the time or the staff to run the system on a day-to-day basis. However, they say he will not delegate the power to anyone else."[35]

With no strong NSC staff and with groups largely under departmental rather than NSC staff control, issues moved immediately from the interdepartmental groups to the full Council for deliberation. In July, Meese sought to bridge the gap by creating a National Security Planning Group (NSPG). Its aim was to create a forum for the free discussion of national security issues, similar in purpose to the NSC but without the presence of the chairman of the Joint Chiefs of Staff or any staff aides. Members were Haig, Weinberger, Bush, Meese, Baker, and CIA Director William Casey, with Reagan presiding. Allen's role was described as that of "note-taker." There was no memorandum formally establishing the group, and its operations were likened to a larger scale version of Johnson's Tuesday lunches. According to one member of the NSC staff, "Since no one is in charge, everyone has to be there." [36]

All told, Gelb reported in the *New York Times,* "The system is pictured as a highly informal, word-of-mouth one, riddled with somewhat more than the usual number of personality conflicts but with somewhat less than the usual differences over philosophy. . . . Preparations for meetings at the White House are described as erratic. Sometimes there are papers prepared, sometimes not, and sometimes the papers are prepared no more than 12 hours in advance of the meeting." In July, the NSPG met to discuss terrorism, but the option paper they had been given had not even been approved by the relevant assistant secretaries. According to Gelb, "As participants tell it, this means that White House meetings often occur without agreed papers by key aides and experts on the issues, the facts and the alternatives." After meetings, "subordinates rarely see minutes of what has been discussed or a memorandum of decisions. The net effect, according to virtually all those interviewed, is that the participants often return to their departments with more than the usual number of conflicting interpretations of what happened and what was decided."[37] As late as October 1981, the administration had only issued twelve national security decision documents and had yet to review almost all standing decisions from prior administrations on a broad range of foreign policy matters. Brokerage was clearly needed to address these organizational and policy-making defects, but Allen was in no position to provide it.

In fact, according to Inderfurth and Johnson, Allen was often blamed for the mess: "Critics said that Allen and the NSC staff had become mere conveyor belts for policy papers from the departments . . . with no attempt to provide independent analysis or options for the president's consideration." More damaging, in their view, was that "Allen was an ineffectual coordinator and failed to play the traditional adviser's role of adjudicating different departmental views or trying to iron out policy differences."[38] According to Haig, Allen was "regarded by his colleagues as irrelevant. I am sorry to say, I came to regard him in that light too."[39]

Although Reagan had hoped to avoid some of the turf battles and infighting over foreign policy of the Carter years, his administration seems to have fared much worse. Haig continued to be a source of irritation, not just to others in the foreign policy circle, but to other cabinet members, key White House staff members, and eventually the president himself. Even Haig and Allen battled. On November 5, 1981, Reagan reportedly called Haig and Allen into a private one-hour meeting in the Oval Office and ordered them to end their feuding.[40]

In December 1981, it was Allen's turn to face the political heat. Reports surfaced that in January, shortly after the inauguration, he had received $1,000 from three Japanese journalists—a custom in that country—following an interview with Mrs. Reagan. In fact, Allen had intercepted the journalists just as they were about to give the First Lady a stack of prior issues of their magazine. On his way back to his office, he discovered in the stack an envelope with the cash in it. Recognizing it would be inappropriate to give her the money, Allen instructed his secretary to dispose of it appropriately (Allen thought she would send it to the White House legal counsel's office). Instead she placed the cash in his office safe, where it was later discovered.[41] A full FBI investigation then took place. It also came to light in December that Meese had ordered a management review of the NSC apparatus, fueling speculation that Allen's departure was imminent and that major changes were planned. Although the investigation cleared Allen of wrongdoing, the expected shakeup in the NSC did take place, and he was forced to resign his position on January 4, 1982. According to Meese,

> Policy differences and personal conflicts occurred far more than expected. *Somehow,* the "roundtabling" that had served Reagan in California and in other areas of his administration didn't seem to work so well when it came to foreign affairs and national security. In frustration, the President decided that a change of players was necessary.[42]

According to Allen, "it wasn't '*somehow*,' it was because of the way they created the system, and the inefficiencies that were built into it." Foreign policy was on the back burner, in Allen's view, "until the economic program passed and then, even then, I couldn't get a National Security Council meeting."[43]

WILLIAM P. CLARK JR.

Allen's replacement was William P. Clark Jr. Clark had been serving as Haig's deputy at State (where he was presumably placed in order to have a Reagan loyalist keep an eye on the volatile secretary of state).[44] But while he was yet another longtime Reagan associate, he had no prior foreign or national security policy experience. He had been Meese's predecessor as Reagan's gubernatorial chief of staff and had been appointed by Reagan to the California State Supreme Court. Yet Clark was in a better position than his predecessor. Press reports of his appointment were favorable, largely due to his success as Haig's deputy.[45] The reporting process through Meese was ended and Clark was given direct access to Reagan, including the perk of being able to see the president personally when needed and off-schedule, which he immediately exercised much to Deaver's dismay.[46] More importantly, he was a trusted member of Reagan's team of California loyalists. Clark, who came from a pioneer California ranching family, frequently went horseback riding with the fellow-rancher president.[47]

According to the NSC's own history, "Clark took a very active role in co-ordination of policy among the agencies in such areas as intelligence and the protection of classified security information. He replaced a number of senior NSC staff members and reorganized his office to create three 'clusters' to deal with political, military, and intelligence matters." Clark also insisted, presumably to Haig's detriment, that "the role of the president as the final arbiter on matters of foreign policy be kept in front of the public." He was successful in asserting "NSC staff jurisdiction over long-range policy review, formerly a Department of State function."[48] He undertook a number of policy planning reviews. More than twice as many NSDDs were issued in his first year as NSC advisor than had been issued under Allen.[49] Clark produced concise presidential daily briefings for Reagan. According to Reagan biographer Edmund Morris, he also "saw to it that plenty of CIA and Defense Department documents were delivered to the White House."[50] Relations within the NSC staff were harmonious during his tenure. According to one staff member, "You felt you were working with [Clark] not for him. . . . I have never seen such loyalty by a staff to their leader."[51]

With respect to his press activities, according to the NSC history, "Clark emerged as a major spokesman for Reagan administration foreign policy, particularly with the Congress." Clark reinstated the post of NSC press spokesman, which had been discontinued under Allen.[52] He also created an Office of Public Diplomacy to handle broader communications efforts in foreign countries.[53] Major public announcements by State, Defense, and the CIA were now cleared through Clark and the NSC staff.[54]

Clark's tenure as NSC advisor also saw the NSC staff move back once again into the area of operations, often over State's opposition. According to the NSC's own history:

> The NSC [staff] frequently disagreed with the Department of State over the management of daily U.S. foreign relations problems. One observer called the NSC a "bee hive of activity." An NSC-chaired group took over arms control responsibilities from a State-chaired group . . . and ramrodded [a] tough negotiating position. . . . Deputy National Security Adviser Robert McFarlane replaced Philip C. Habib as the chief U.S. Middle East negotiator in July 1983, and the National Security Adviser became directly involved in the operations of foreign policy. It led to a major change in how the NSC system worked.[55]

Clark and McFarlane—whom he had brought over with him from State— also established a Crisis Pre-Planning Group, which McFarlane chaired.

The purpose was to undertake crisis planning at the deputy level, which would then report to the crisis management group chaired by Vice President Bush. According to McFarlane, the group "turned out to be one of the most productive schemes ever established in the 1980's." It undertook a number of studies, such as the possible shutoff of oil from the Persian Gulf by the Iranians.[56]

Clark and McFarlane also were centrally involved in the development of the SDI missile shield proposal. Although both had some doubts as to its technical feasibility, it might prove a valuable bargaining chip with the Soviets in their view. Announced in a major speech by Reagan on March 23, 1983, "Star Wars," as it was dubbed, was a proposal initially kept tightly held, even from Shultz, in order to prevent both leaks and opposition.[57] Clark also signaled U.S. flexibility in the sensitive issue of intermediate nuclear forces (INF) in Europe and had parts of an "open letter" from Reagan inserted in a speech Vice President Bush delivered in West Berlin proposing INF talks with the Soviets.[58]

Although Clark's relationships to Reagan and to Haig, as well as his reputation as a mediator, were thought to bring stability to the Reagan foreign policy system, difficulties persisted. While serving as Haig's deputy, Clark had worked diligently to smooth the troubled waters between Haig and the White House staff. But frictions remained. [59] According to Weinberger, Haig "was obsessed with the idea that people were trying to undermine him. He was very worried about perquisites and his own primacy as foreign policy advisor. He disliked intensely anybody else commenting on foreign policy matters in the presence of the President. . . . He kept getting angrier and angrier. He threatened to resign several times."[60]

Reports now surfaced of Haig's feuds with Clark, even including shouting matches between the two.[61] According to one White House aide, "It's untenable to have a Secretary of State who feels the president's role is subordinate to his." For his part, Haig told his own aides that he was "tired of having four or five people running foreign policy" and intended to "straighten things out" or quit.[62] Friction especially developed during the intense debates within the administration over how the United States should act in the Lebanon crisis in the spring of 1982 following the Israeli invasion.[63] According to McFarlane, Haig publicly preempted the president's authority on several occasions. He issued instructions, on one occasion, to the Middle East envoy without getting Reagan's prior approval.[64] He also dispatched an envoy to Fidel Castro without informing the president.[65] Haig sought to bolster his position with the White House by yet another resignation threat. Apparently unbeknownst to Haig, Reagan was ready to accept his resignation letter.[66] In a surprise statement on June 25, 1982, the White House announced Haig's resignation and his replacement by George Shultz.

In Weinberger's view, "We didn't have any tension at all with Bill Clark."[67] Clark's relationships with Shultz and the State Department also proved somewhat smoother than had been the case with Haig. According to Mulcahy, the "incessant warfare" abated—"There was no Clark-Shultz feud." Both were "personally loyal to Reagan," and although Clark was inclined to be a bit more hawkish, they "shared a nearly identical feeling about the role of the United States in world affairs." According to Jim Baker, however, Clark "got caught up in the idea . . . that Shultz and the State Department were not carrying out the Reagan agenda."[68] Shultz's memoirs, *Turmoil and Triumph,* also contain a number of references to clashes with Clark, including incidents where he felt that the NSC advisor had overstepped his authority or had pressed to undo decisions already made.[69] In late July 1983, Shultz expressed his discomfort with his relations to Clark and the NSC staff in a private meeting with the president. Shultz was especially incensed over reports of a possible blockade of the Sandinista regime in Nicaragua, undertaken without his knowledge, as well as McFarlane's trips to the Middle East. Shultz threatened to resign.[70] The secretary of state stressed the need for regularly scheduled discussions with the president, plus the NSC advisor. Reagan responded, "Let's try it with just the two of us first." Thereafter, when possible, Shultz regularly met with the president on Wednesday and Friday at 1:30.[71] Shultz would brief Clark after the meeting, but he eventually suggested again that Clark be allowed to attend but that "he's not to say anything." Reagan finally "relented," according to Shultz.[72]

Clark increasingly became a source of irritation to some of the other key players, and he began to fall from Reagan's favor. He especially incensed Nancy Reagan when he was featured in a *Time* magazine cover story.[73] The resignation of Interior Secretary James Watt created an opportunity for Clark's foes and was a nice fit for the Western rancher. But the story of his departure was more complex. According to Edmund Morris, Clark resigned due to the "unceasing hostility of Deaver, Schultz, and Nancy Reagan."[74] According to Shultz, toward the end of Clark's tenure, "The president was uneasy with Clark and Nancy [Reagan] . . . viewed Clark as a liability and wouldn't even talk to him."[75] In Baker's view, the NSC advisor was at fault: "Bill Clark was just not comfortable with a lot of the subjects in his job. When he would come in to brief the president in the morning, he would have the briefing done by an expert in a particular area."[76]

More damaging in Baker's view—who frequently did clash with Clark—was that Clark was too inclined to run his own national security operation, cutting out others in the Reagan inner circle.[77] Baker felt that Clark lacked political sensitivity, nor was he willing to communicate with those who handled such matters—Baker's own shop. Clark and Deaver reportedly refused to return each other's telephone calls, and both Baker and Deaver resented his private access to Reagan.[78] Reagan's foreign policy apparatus, according to Baker, "was often a witches' brew of elbows, egos, and separate agendas. From day one, the level of suspicion and distrust was utterly out of control among many of the major players. I can't remember any extended period of time when someone in the National Security cluster wasn't at someone else's throat." Even in cases where Reagan had "decided a major policy issue, his subordinates would ignore his wishes and pursue their own policy schemes. . . . The chaos and backbiting served him and the country poorly."[79] Other accounts, however, note Clark's closeness to Reagan, his strong allegiance to his agenda, and his efforts to carry through Reagan's foreign policy views.[80]

Baker especially had to engage in damage control following a leak about U.S. policy in the Lebanon. Clark—with Meese's support—prevailed upon the president to order an FBI investigation, including polygraph tests of everyone present at a recent NSC meeting. Normally, the White House legal counsel's office had the authority to recommend polygraph tests, and that office was within Baker's domain. Clark had bypassed Baker, and Shultz was particularly irate at facing the prospect of a polygraph, again even threatening to resign. Baker interrupted a lunch meeting of Reagan, Shultz, and Bush when he found out about the order. All three seemed surprised, with a "troubled" Reagan conceding that "Bill shouldn't have done this" (even though Reagan had signed the order for the investigation). Following an acrimonious meeting of Bush, Clark, the troika, the attorney general, and Reagan, the decision was reversed.[81]

In Clark's view, Baker and Deaver were the culprits. Both, according to McFarlane's account of Clark's complaints, "would perform end-runs around him, going in to the president after decisions had been made and persuading him to reinterpret or even reverse his decisions." Deaver, according to McFarlane, felt that Clark was damaging Reagan politically and he had to go.[82] Clark, the loyal soldier, recognized that it was time to leave as NSC advisor.

At the time of Clark's appointment as secretary of the interior, Baker and Deaver even concocted a plan to move Baker into the NSC advisor slot and Deaver to the chief of staff position. According to Baker, the aborted plan was an "effort to inject some sanity and cohesion into the national security process." [83] They even thought they had Reagan's assent to the move, but at the last minute others in the Reagan inner circle—with Clark as ring leader—met with Reagan and blocked the shift. [84] In Baker's view, "Predictably, it was torpedoed by some of the very same principals whose small bore behavior had given rise to the proposal in the first place."[85] In Baker's view, moreover, had his appointment gone through, "the president might have well avoided the Iran-Contra scandal in his second term."[86] Deaver would also come to the same view: if he and Baker "had gone to that meeting, none of this would have happened. Iran wouldn't have happened."[87]

But the problem was not just Clark. Shultz and Weinberger feuded with alarming regularity. The discord did not end until Weinberger's resignation in 1987. Moreover, Reagan, the skilled rancher while on the range, was loath to ride herd on his two longtime friends and associates.

ROBERT C. MCFARLANE

Robert McFarlane, Clark's deputy, became NSC advisor on October 17, 1983. McFarlane, unlike Clark, had a strong background in military and national security affairs. While a lieutenant colonel in the marines he had been on the NSC staffs of both Kissinger and Scowcroft. Returning to civilian life he served on the staff of the Senate Armed Services Committee, and then he served a stint as a counselor to Secretary of State Haig before becoming Clark's deputy.

McFarlane's challenges as NSC advisor began immediately. During his first week on the job, the terrorist attack on the marine barracks in Beirut took place, killing over 240 personnel. McFarlane, however, did not develop the close rapport with Reagan that Clark enjoyed. He had direct access to the president, but his daily briefing was limited to fifteen minutes.[88]

Like Clark, McFarlane sought to resolve policy disputes and deal as best he could with the battles between Shultz and Weinberger. Yet, according to David Abshire—who was U.S. ambassador to NATO and then was brought in as special counselor to the president to deal with the aftermath of Iran-Contra—McFarlane "was unable to move the State and Defense Departments and the NSC into a unified effort. He became as frustrated as Clark."[89]

McFarlane does get good marks in many accounts of his service as NSC advisor, for at least *attempting* to deal with the tensions between State and the Pentagon. In order to try to end the discord between Shultz and Weinberger, a regular "Family Group Lunch" was set up with them and CIA Director Casey. For McFarlane, it provided a needed venue where he endeavored to work out disagreements. According to McFarlane, "we would have lunch in the family dining room of the Residence as often as we were all in town, once a week was the target—there were no note-takers and no subordinates there."[90] McFarlane took unresolved issues to Reagan for a decision.[91] McFarlane also continued another forum for deliberation that had begun under Haig: a regular Wednesday morning breakfast staff meeting, held at either Defense or State, with McFarlane, Shultz, Weinberger, and their immediate staffs.[92]

Despite his efforts, the feuding between Shultz and Weinberger continued and permeated down the chain of command in their respective departments. After the 1984 election, McFarlane even privately offered his resignation to the president in hopes that someone better might be found to end the discord. Reagan turned down McFarlane's request—he was "indispensable." Reagan explained that Shultz and Weinberger were both his friends, adding about the two that there was "always this thing" between them. Reagan did not know why it existed, hoped they would get along better, but recognized that "at my age and their age, people don't change much." Reagan's comments indicated to McFarlane that the president was not prepared to intervene and that four more years of "guerilla government" was ahead.[93]

In fact, Reagan was so unwilling to deal with tensions among his chief principals that he even tolerated insubordination. Following the attack on the marine barracks in Lebanon, the CIA determined that a radical Shiite group, linked to the Iranian Revolutionary Guards, was responsible. The National Security Planning Group convened and a retaliatory air strike on their base of operations was approved by the president. When all was ready, the commander of the U.S. Navy's Sixth Fleet requested final permission for the attack, but never received it. Weinberger telephoned McFarlane and told him he had denied the request because he did not think it was the correct response. McFarlane was dumbstruck and outraged: Weinberger failed to carry out the president's order. McFarlane then told Reagan about what had happened, stressed there was no justification for Weinberger's action, and that Reagan ought to make that clear to his defense secretary. "Gosh, that's really disappointing," Reagan replied ("evasively" according to McFarlane). It was clear to McFarlane that Reagan was not going to call Weinberger or deal with his insubordination. In McFarlane's view, Reagan's inability to discipline his friends was "destructive" and "damaging."[94] Meanwhile, marine lives were "at risk" and U.S. Middle East policy was in jeopardy.[95]

McFarlane was also proactive in establishing groups where existing interdepartmental efforts, usually chaired by the lead department, were ineffective. He established an Arms Control Support Group at the deputy level to try to hash out departmental differences or present differing options in an orderly way before they rose to the principals' level. The latter became important for both the INF and START treaties.[96]

Sometimes, McFarlane convened outside advisory panels. With respect to Central America, McFarlane felt that the State Department-led group was "dropping the ball." The representative from State failed to convene meetings or, when they were held, they became mired in disagreement with the Defense Department's representatives. "Stalemate," in State's view, "was preferable to defeat." It was "typical bureaucratic gamesmanship," but it created paralysis and harmed policy.[97] As a consequence, McFarlane took control and created a bipartisan commission—led by Kissinger—to make recommendations for policy improvements.[98] McFarlane had used the same approach while serving as Clark's deputy to resolve other State-Pentagon impasses. In December 1982, he was instrumental in the creation of the Scowcroft Commission as a response to Weinberger's inability to successfully develop a defensive missile basing system.[99]

In his own view, McFarlane felt that the NSC system, while he was advisor, struck a good balance between cabinet input and NSC coordination. The process allowed the principals to present their "views and recommendations directly to the president . . . while still providing an adequate level of central policy control and guidance." As for the role of the NSC advisor in McFarlane's view, "He must be an honest broker of advice coming to the president from outside the White House." As a fair and honest broker: "He must be able to present the views of each department to the president so that the president appreciates the substantive nature of debates within his administration and so that the departments will have confidence that their positions are being considered." At the same time, "he must be an independent advisor and policy manager for the president." [100] Weinberger, however, felt that McFarlane, of all the NSC advisors he worked with, unnecessarily restricted his access to Reagan. McFarlane "did not want my input to the president to interfere with his own agenda."[101]

According to Abshire, McFarlane was instrumental in a number of policy successes: "the Caribbean Basin Initiative, the Kissinger Commission on Central America, and the finely honed 1985 Geneva Summit." But there was one major area of error: "the Middle East and his misjudgment of people that were to do him in."[102]

McFarlane was especially attentive to the need for long-range planning, especially on strategic issues and initiatives for a second Reagan term. In his view, Clark's efforts were at best perfunctory. While serving as his deputy, McFarlane had periodically urged Clark to nudge State, Defense, and Treasury, but "more often than not, these memos stopped at Clark's desk and never reached the president." In early 1984, McFarlane managed to get Shultz's support and gained approval for a series of studies to be conducted by experts both in and out of government. The roster of the latter, according to McFarlane, read "like a who's who of foreign affairs analysts and brilliant academic minds." In McFarlane's view, their eventual work was "uniformly excellent and impressive." The effort was supposed to lead to further deliberations and some prioritizing at the highest levels. But when McFarlane presented them to Reagan, his response was, "Gee, I've looked this over, Bud, and I think these are just terrific ideas. Let's do them all!" [103]

McFarlane played an important role in privately dealing with Congress and with the press. But he was no seeker of the media limelight, in the mold of a Kissinger, Brzezinski, or even Bundy. According to the NSC's own history, he "stepped back from the previous high profile in policy enunciation, but became more involved in the direct management of key areas of foreign policy."[104]

But, while less visible as NSC advisor, there was one major area where McFarlane moved considerably beyond the broker role: a strong presence in *implementing* policy through secret diplomacy. In 1983, while serving as deputy to Clark, he was dispatched on a secret mission to Syria to enlist its support in trying to find a solution to the civil war in Lebanon. The mission was unsuccessful, largely because the White House had no clear plan. McFarlane, however, subsequently made other trips to the region and even set up an office in Rome as a base camp.[105] McFarlane's initial mission (he was later made a special envoy), however, caused great tension with Shultz. In later testimony before the Congress's joint committee (Inouye-Hamilton) investigating Iran-Contra, Shultz acknowledged that while he and McFarlane "worked very effectively together," the deputy NSC advisor's initial secret trip to the Middle East—without Shultz's knowledge—had caused him (yet again) to submit his resignation to Reagan. Reagan refused Shultz's offer and promised it would not happen again.[106] But Shultz was vigilant, and in his memoirs he comments on the "incessant free-lance style of Bud McFarlane . . . and the NSC [staff's] obsessive desire for an operational role [that] would result in a disaster sooner or later." McFarlane "yearned to make things happen through his own secret diplomacy."[107] In Weinberger's view, "McFarlane had a lot of adventures that he wanted to get into . . . [he] was always trying to develop something . . . that would be a huge breakthrough."[108] Shultz's and Weinberger's concerns proved prophetic.

McFarlane's diplomatic activism as NSC advisor sowed the seeds of policy misadventure, eventually leading to the Iran-Contra scandal. Indeed, it was McFarlane's effort to open an initiative to Iran, his decision to send NSC consultant Michael Leeden on a private mission to Israel, and McFarlane's own subsequent meetings with David Kimche—the director general of the Israeli foreign ministry, who offered the positive assessment that moderates in the Iranian government were eager for U.S. support and could possibly help to free the hostages—that laid the foundations for an arms-for-hostages initiative.[109] The Leeden trip especially raised Shultz's consternation. According to McFarlane, "It was a piece of brashness that later cost me an angry phone call from George Shultz who saw Ledeen as having acted at my express behest to undercut State on the foreign policy stage."[110] Had McFarlane not engaged in private diplomacy through Ledeen or had there been prior consultation with Shultz about the trip, Iran-Contra likely would not have happened.

McFarlane too fell victim to the interpersonal politics and tensions within the Reagan team. In his case it was with Chief of Staff Donald Regan, who had replaced Baker at the start of the second term when the two swapped positions. Regan, Reagan's self-touted "prime minister," sought to exercise dominance over not just domestic policy, but foreign policy as well, including participation in the principals' national security meetings and in McFarlane's private meetings with Reagan.[111] Early in his tenure as chief of staff, Regan berated McFarlane for failing to inform him of the killing of a U.S. military officer who was on an inspection mission in East Germany. The incident happened over night and McFarlane assumed that the Situation Room had contacted Regan. The next morning, McFarlane tried to apologize. Regan's response was that he would not tolerate this kind of "insubordination," and that McFarlane did not "seem to realize that you work for me." McFarlane told him that he worked for the president. "The hell you do!" Regan shouted, "You work for me and everything you do will come through me or you'll be out of here." McFarlane told him he would be out of his office by the end of the day and left.

Regan later telephoned and the two patched things up a bit. McFarlane promised that he would keep Regan informed, and if time was not a constraint he would pass material through Regan to the president. But he also stood some ground, noting that there were times when his job required him to deal directly with Reagan and "I intended to keep doing that. Regan was never happy about this, but he learned to live with it."[112] Regan's efforts to control access to the president through the chief of staff's office as well as his penchant for directing blame on others in the administration were a particular sore point for McFarlane. In Shultz's view, not naming names, McFarlane "left in part out of frustration to get the administration's national security people to work together as a team. . . . No decision could be regarded as final or implemented with confidence as policy." Also, "His relations with Don Regan were tense and strained."[113] In early December 1985, a beaten-down McFarlane called it quits.

After leaving the NSC advisor post, McFarlane still retained an association with its operations.[114] In May 1986, he was placed in charge of two planeloads of weapons to be delivered to Iran. McFarlane and his traveling party failed to meet with any high-ranking Iranian officials, which should have been a tip-off that something was amiss. When the first planeload did not yield any Iranian pressure for the release of U.S. hostages in Lebanon—which had been promised—he ordered the second shipment canceled.[115]

The mission was important in another way. As they were leaving Iran, Lt. Col. Oliver North—then serving on the NSC staff where he was essentially in charge of the initiative—told McFarlane the arms sales were not a total waste; even if no hostages were released, profits from the deal were being used to fund the anti-Sandanista contras in Nicaragua. It was the first time that McFarlane learned about the second half of Iran-Contra: the legally questionable diversion of the funds from the arms sales to the contras.[116] The mission was also revealing about the precarious vetting and approval of the arms-for-hostages part of the operation. McFarlane had wanted it shut down toward the end of his tenure as NSC advisor, but Vice Adm. John Poindexter had resumed it when he replaced McFarlane as NSC advisor. Before embarking on the mission, the cautious McFarlane had asked whether Shultz and Weinberger were on board, presumably recalling their earlier opposition. Poindexter told him they were "against the arms component of it," but that they had been "involved in this decision" and in the "preparations" of McFarlane's instructions; the operation, moreover, had Reagan's approval.[117] His response was less than truthful. Earlier that month, Shultz had heard rumors that arms-for-hostages was operational again. He confronted both Poindexter and Casey, who told him that it had been shut down.[118]

In 1988, McFarlane pleaded guilty to four misdemeanor counts of withholding information from Congress on Iran-Contra. He was placed on probation and given a $20,000 fine. He was pardoned in 1992, at the end of the George H. W. Bush presidency, along with several others caught up in Iran-Contra.

JOHN M. POINDEXTER

The selection of Poindexter to replace McFarlane was a somewhat curious choice. He had been the chief military aide to Allen and Clark and then deputy NSC advisor to McFarlane, but his substantive expertise in national security and foreign policy was somewhat limited. Poindexter was clearly smart—he had graduated first in his class at the Naval Academy and later earned a doctorate in physics at Cal Tech. But as Inderfurth and Johnson point out, he "was seen as a low-key administrator, skillful in handling operational matters (especially those related to military activities or computers), but certainly not a policy maker." Moreover, they note, he lacked the stature or influence with Reagan to act as a mediator in resolving policy disputes or tensions among some of the principals.[119] According to another account, Poindexter "was quickly catapulted from a role as a junior aide to one of the administration's most senior positions. And he did so without sitting on the interagency committees, without having to cement relations with Congress and without having to talk to reporters—in short, without gaining the broad political and public relations experience most accomplished officials need before becoming senior members of an administration."[120] Retaining his active duty status in the navy also complicated his relations with Defense Secretary Weinberger—one of his bosses of a sort—making brokerage even more difficult. Reportedly, Brent Scowcroft had warned McFarlane that Poindexter was not a good fit for the job.[121]

Shultz, Weinberger, and Bush remained powerful actors. But along some dimensions—especially operational matters as we shall see—the NSC advisor and staff became more assertive, although not necessarily more effective. The first-term SIGs were, by Reagan's second term, more strongly under NSC staff control yet of limited impact. Writing in 1986, Colin Campbell observed that "only the SIG on intelligence remains active."[122]

Poindexter's tenure as NSC advisor—without factoring in the Iran-Contra scandal—was rather mixed. In the aftermath of his resignation, a number of negative reports surfaced. According to the *New York Times,* there was "turmoil on the NSC staff, distrust of Capitol Hill and a desire to conduct most affairs of the NSC in an envelope of secrecy so secure that the Congress, the State Department, the Pentagon, the White House and most of his own staff members were not aware of some developments, including many related to the Iran-Contra affair."[123] During the summer and fall of 1986, according to Shultz, "the stock of the NSC staff around town dropped. The media . . . began to characterize the NSC staff as ineffectual and Poindexter as not up to the job. . . . Since the departure of Jim Baker, Mike Deaver, and

Ed Meese from the White House, the situation there had gone downhill. There was increasing insularity and less political savvy. . . . Don Regan and John Poindexter had never really been involved in politics."[124] Once news of the Iran-Contra scandal broke, Regan and Poindexter sought to circle the wagons.[125] Shultz was appalled, and even at one point he urged Chief of Staff Regan to have Poindexter fired. Shultz even proposed temporarily serving as NSC advisor for a month: "I would clean house, and then turn the job over to whoever would be permanently appointed."[126]

McFarlane also had prior reservations: "That John was caught in this mess I saw as partly my fault . . . asking him to be the National Security Adviser, a position requiring different skills, had been an injustice to him. It was like asking Edward Teller to run HUD." Poindexter applied his skills to the new job, but they were not a good fit in McFarlane's view: "discipline, loyalty to the boss, disdain for Congress and the press."[127] According to Powell, Poindexter told him he read neither the *New York Times* nor the *Washington Post*.[128]

Poindexter's strong suit, his operational abilities, sometimes served him well: he successfully planned and managed the operation that intercepted an Egyptian airliner carrying the hijackers of the Italian cruise ship Achille Lauro.[129] But operations would also enmesh him in the most serious scandal that any NSC advisor, before or since, has faced.

III: Policy: Process, Role, and Outcome—Iran-Contra

The Iran-Contra affair provides strong evidence of the increased power—if not at times subterfuge—of the NSC advisor and staff. The first part of it would develop, under McFarlane, into a plan for the Israelis to sell military equipment to Iran, which would then be replenished by the United States. The hope was that Iran would use its influence with Hezbollah to secure the release of hostages of U.S. citizenship in Lebanon and elsewhere. Emissaries from Israel and Iranian intermediaries, who were presumed to be close to moderate elements in the Iranian government, had proposed the deal to McFarlane, who thought it worth pursuing given the failure of other efforts to secure the hostages' release. The second part, the aid to the Nicaraguan contras, emerged much later, in early 1986, when Poindexter was NSC advisor. In James Baker's view, "From the beginning to end, Iran-Contra was wrong, a textbook example of what can happen when the White House 'goes operational.'"[130]

McFarlane and Poindexter overrode the strong objections of Shultz and Weinberger to any exchange of arms-for-hostages. McFarlane's view was that it might open better relations with Iran, curb Soviet influence in the region, and gain the release of the U.S. hostages, whose welfare was a special concern of the president. Reagan thought the initiative deserved a chance and reportedly told McFarlane that he was "all for letting the Israelis do anything they wanted" in dealing with Iran.[131] In Shultz's view, it confirmed his suspicions of McFarlane: "Bud always gave me the impression that as national security adviser he wanted to be like Henry Kissinger, to do dramatic things *secretly*. As Henry brought off 'the opening to China,' so Bud had the idea of an 'opening to Iran.' McFarlane had hoped to bring off this coup, run secretly out of the NSC staff." But there was a crucial difference between Kissinger and McFarlane. Kissinger dealt with real Chinese officials and did not violate the law, in Shultz's view, "this operation with Iran, on the contrary, was conducted with disreputable arms merchants and shady operators."[132]

As for Weinberger, he too opposed the plan—one of his few areas of agreement with Shultz. In the margin of a June 17, 1985, "eyes-only" NSC study document outlining an early version of the plan, he scrawled, "This is almost too absurd to comment on."[133] Not only did Weinberger and Shultz feel that there were no moderates left to deal with in Iran, it violated the administration's own boycott of arms sales to Iran and its efforts to get other countries to do likewise.[134] According to Weinberger, he and Shultz "regarded the McFarlane proposal as perfectly absurd and dangerous, and said so many times. I believed we'd convinced the President in two meetings, but in the third meeting on it, it became quite apparent that we did not."[135]

Despite the opposition of the two most powerful principals, McFarlane continued to pursue the plan. Matters came to a head in early July when a high-level Israeli emissary, David Kimche, met with McFarlane and indicated a possibility that the Iranians might secure the release of the hostages in exchange for "something to show . . . probably weapons." McFarlane informed the president of his conversation with Kimche within days.[136] Ten days later another emissary from Israel arrived, indicating the Iranians were interested in a "good faith" show of support from the United States by allowing them to purchase 100 TOW antitank missiles from Israel, an indirect third-party transfer that proved crucial to the deal. McFarlane again brought the plan to Reagan's attention on July 18, 1985, while the president was in a hospital bed recovering from cancer surgery. According to some accounts, Reagan approved the plan.[137] In his memoirs, Don Regan (who was at the meeting) states that the president only approved a vague "political dialogue."[138] McFarlane's memoirs indicate the Reagan was "cautiously supportive" but worried about dealing with unknown individuals.[139] President Reagan himself later told the Tower Commission that he had "no recollection" of the meeting with McFarlane.[140]

McFarlane then convened a meeting of the National Security Planning Group, after Reagan returned to the White House, to further brief the president. Additional meetings of the principals were held over the next few days, according to McFarlane.[141] According to Shultz, who argued against the proposal, "I thought that the president agreed [with me], though reluctantly."[142] So too did Weinberger.[143]

According to McFarlane, his one ally was CIA Director Casey, who viewed the initiative as legally sound and good policy.[144] Unfortunately, Casey failed to inform McFarlane or the other principals, that the chief Iranian "middleman"—Manucher Ghorbanifar, with whom the CIA had prior dealings—was a risky and untested character. McFarlane later faulted Casey for not alerting him to problems with Ghorbanifar.[145]

According to McFarlane, he eventually got Reagan's final approval of the plan, despite Shultz's and Weinberger's opposition. Over the weekend of July 27 and 28, 1985, while Reagan was at Camp David, the two had a telephone conversation during which McFarlane says he pointed out their opposition. "I know," Reagan told him, "but I look at it differently. I want to find a way to do this."[146]

Another meeting of the principals was held on August 3; again the pros and cons were aired, and Weinberger voiced his strong opposition (as had the absent Shultz in a telephone conversation with McFarlane). The discussion was spirited and forceful, McFarlane recalled. According to Abshire, McFarlane, while favoring the initiative, "wanted the NSC to provide the president with all opinions related to the situation"[147]—it was a small smidgen of brokerage in an otherwise deeply flawed process. A little after noon, Reagan called McFarlane into the Oval Office. McFarlane recalls that he again laid out the proposal. Reagan reflected for a few moments, then told McFarlane it was the "right thing to do." McFarlane again reminded him of Shultz's and Weinberger's opposition. "Yes, I understand how they feel," Reagan said, "But I have to think about what's at stake here. I believe it's the right thing to do."[148]

But this is McFarlane's versions of events. Had Reagan in fact given his approval? And if he had, what to—a mere opening up of contacts? Replenishment of the Israeli weapons? An exchange of arms that might lead to the release of the hostages? Reagan, for his part, later reportedly became "upset" when he learned about the arms shipments, and he again told the Tower Commission that he had no recollection of approving them.[149] Others, such as Don Regan and Weinberger, questioned McFarlane's account of the president's approval.[150] The Tower Commission, based on its interviews with the principals, concluded at a minimum that it was "unclear what exactly was under consideration at this time. No analytical paper was prepared for the August discussions and no formal minutes of any of the discussions were made."[151]

The three shipments of arms by Israel proved unproductive.[152] Only one of the hostages was released in the fall of 1985. McFarlane later conceded that "the real blame . . . is my own, because I knew that Reagan was a humanitarian and vulnerable [on the issue of the hostages]. . . . And knowing that, when I saw it go wrong, I should not have let the administration go on, because there was nobody he trusted more than me. Never did Ronald Reagan do something that I said, 'Don't do [it].'"[153]

Yet, according to McFarlane's memoirs, he did eventually tell the president to shut down the operation. In his last daily briefing, he claims, he told Reagan that the operation was not working and urged him to convene the other principals, which they did on December 7. Shultz and Weinberger again raised their strong concerns, indeed their opposition. Reagan replied, according to McFarlane, "I just don't see it that way . . . we're trying to reach opponents of Khomeini, and I'm willing to defend it on that basis. We're not dealing with terrorists."[154] In Shultz's recollection of the meeting, however, Reagan's comments are not noted; moreover, Shultz states, "No decision was made . . . But my sense was that the point of view that Cap [Weinberger] and I argued had won the day."[155] Later that day, however, Poindexter told Shultz, "the president did not want to disengage."[156]

McFarlane's other regret was in designating Lt. Col. Oliver North—who had been detailed to the NSC staff to work on terrorism issues and Central American policies—to work on the operation. McFarlane later testified that he clearly instructed North not to violate the law.[157] When he was leaving the NSC, McFarlane also warned Poindexter about North and urged him to send him back to regular duty.[158] (In fact, earlier, McFarlane had unsuccessfully urged North to leave the White House and get a field command.)[159] McFarlane also urged Poindexter, in June 1986 after McFarlane's secret mission to Tehran, to get rid of North: "But if John heard me, he didn't listen." McFarlane "suspected that [North] probably found it easier to bully John [Poindexter] than me." Poindexter had "no experience in combat, which probably made him more susceptible to North's occasionally cockamamie ideas . . . the combination of a more freewheeling North and a National Security Adviser who didn't like Congress or the press was going to put the president in a very vulnerable position."[160]

When the deal became public in November 1986, Reagan initially confirmed the arms sales but denied they were made in exchange for hostages. In his memoirs, Shultz recalls telling the president at the time, "Mr. President you are not fully informed. You must not continue to say we made no deals for the hostages. You have been deceived and lied to. I plead with you, *don't* say that Iran has let up on terrorism." "You're telling me things I don't know!" Reagan replied. "Mr. President," Shultz said, "if I'm telling you something that you don't know—I don't know much—then something is terribly wrong here!" According to Shultz, "I could see I had not convinced him."[161] According to McFarlane, as the scandal became public, President Reagan became convinced by Regan that he had not approved the deal, and he ended up not remembering much about what had transpired.[162]

That there had been no arms-for-hostages deal was a position Reagan would not publicly retract until a press conference on March 4, 1987, after the release of the *Tower Commission Report,* which clearly linked the arms sales to the release of hostages. Not only would Iran-Contra plunge the administration into crisis after its details came to light, operatively it was a failure. Only two hostages were released from its inception in 1985 through November 1986, when it was shut down; in the interim, in fact, five more hostages were kidnapped in Lebanon.[163]

Poindexter was enthusiastic about the operation. In late November 1986, the CIA sent now NSC advisor Poindexter a private "presidential finding" on the effort for Reagan's signature; it was post hoc, since it covered McFarlane's earlier shipments.[164] Casey urged Poindexter to keep it from the other principals, which he did. The finding was subsequently destroyed, apparently by Poindexter or his minions, when information about Iran-Contra became public in November 1986.[165] Poindexter later criticized McFarlane for not preparing the finding much earlier.[166]

Despite the opposition of Shultz and Weinberger and the failed effort during McFarlane's tenure as NSC advisor, the "snake would not die," Shultz later observed.[167] Reagan remained interested in any initiative that would free the hostages. As Reagan rationalizes in his memoirs, "It's the same thing as if one of my children was kidnapped and there was a demand for ransom. Sure, I don't believe in ransom, because it leads to more kidnapping. But if I find out there's somebody who has access to the kidnapper and can get my child back without doing anything for the kidnapper, I'd sure do that."[168]

Although Shultz and Weinberger thought they had put a stop to the operation, according to Shultz, "when McFarlane left, it started again . . . [Poindexter] went back to the president."[169] By early January, Poindexter persuaded Reagan to resume the shipments and steps were taken to set up private channels for *direct* shipments, rather than through the Israelis. Accounts vary of whether there was a timely meeting of the principals. According to Shultz and the Tower Commission, a new presidential finding had been signed on January 6, 1986, the day before the principals met with Reagan in the Oval Office to discuss a new arms initiative. Shultz later stated that he did not know until a year later about the January 6 finding, but he had an "uneasy, uncanny feeling that the meeting [on January 7] was not a *real* meeting, that it had all been 'precooked.'"[170] At the meeting, according to Shultz, he and Weinberger once again vigorously argued against the initiative, but "no one else did. Cap and I were isolated."[171] According to the Tower Commission, the "January 7 meeting had earmarks of a meeting held after a decision had already been made. Indeed, a draft Covert Action Finding authorizing the initiative had been signed by the president, though perhaps inadvertently, the previous day."[172] On January 17, 1986, Reagan signed a revised finding (with some changes from the January 6 version), resuming the arms sales but through the new channels.[173]

Most importantly, it was under Poindexter's watch that the use of proceeds from arms sales would be directed to the contras in Nicaragua. According to a Senate Intelligence Committee report, in November 1985, Poindexter persuaded CIA Director Casey not to discuss the legality of the diversion of funds with the White House counsel's office; Poindexter was apparently worried about the possibility of a leak.[174] In Poindexter's view (arguably), diversion was legal since the Boland Amendment prohibiting lethal funding applied to the departments, not to the NSC staff or other White House aides.[175] In testimony before Inouye-Hamilton Committee, Poindexter revealed that in February 1986, North came to him with a proposal to use the funds from the arms sales to aid the contras, legally in North's view.

Poindexter kept much of the details of operations, especially the transfer of funds earned on the arms sales to the Nicaraguan contras, from presidential approval or scrutiny. Nor were the other principals informed, with the apparent exception of CIA Director Casey. Most importantly, Poindexter testified before Congress that he had not informed President Reagan of the diversion of funds to the contras: "I made the decision; I felt I had the authority to do it. I thought it was a good idea. I was convinced that the President would in the end think it was a good idea. But I did not want him to be associated with the decision."[176] From Shultz's perspective, "There isn't any doubt that the president signed on as far as the arms sales were concerned. I don't think anyone knew—as far as I can find out—about the diversion of funds. The president didn't know; I don't believe the vice president knew. This was all done within the circle of Poindexter and Casey and North."[177]

It was Poindexter who allowed North essentially a free and unsupervised hand in dealing with the contras in Nicaragua. The NSC's political-military affairs directorate, the normal oversight unit, was specifically told not to get involved in matters dealing with North.[178] According to Meese, North "took it upon himself to do a lot of these things. Poindexter should have had a shorter leash on him—staff people should never be given operational authority—but [Poindexter] was overworked himself and didn't understand the political ramifications."[179] By contrast, when he was NSC advisor, "Clark kept North on a very short leash, believing that North was effective only for certain assignments."[180]

Top-level supervision of the NSC staff on a day-to-day basis was also hampered by the early 1986 hospitalization of Poindexter's chief deputy, Donald Fortier, who eventually died of cancer in August. According to one account, during Fortier's illness, "North quickly filled the role of principal adviser to Admiral Poindexter on Central American policy and was left free to roam almost at will, former staff members said."[181]

The *Tower Commission Report* especially singled out the flawed nature of the deliberative process, which should have been of concern to the NSC advisor:

> The Iran initiative ran directly counter to the Administration's own policies on terrorism, the Iran/Iraq war, and military support to Iran. This inconsistency was never resolved. . . . The [Tower] Board believes that failure to deal adequately with these contradictions resulted in large part from the flaws in the manner in which decisions were made. Established procedures for making national security decisions were ignored. Reviews of the initiative by all the NSC principals were too infrequent. The initiatives were not adequately vetted below the cabinet level. Intelligence resources were underutilized. Applicable legal constraints were not adequately addressed. [182]

McFarlane, according to the report, "was caught between a president who supported the initiative and the cabinet officers who strongly opposed it. While he made efforts to keep these cabinet officers informed, the Board heard complaints from some that he was not always successful."[183]

As for Poindexter, he "on several occasions sought to exclude NSC principals . . . from knowledge of the initiative. Indeed on one or more occasions, Secretary Shultz may have been actively misled by [him]." As for the diversion of funds, Poindexter "failed grievously." He "knew that a diversion had occurred, yet he did not take the steps that were required given the gravity of that prospect. He apparently failed to appreciate or ignored the serious legal and political risks represented."[184]

Iran-Contra also offers important lessons about what happens when the NSC advisor and staff get involved in the direct implementation of policy. According to the Tower Commission:

> The NSC staff assumed direct operational control. The initiative fell within the traditional jurisdictions of the Departments of State, Defense, and CIA. Yet these agencies were largely ignored. . . . How the initiative was to be carried out never received adequate attention from the NSC principals or a tough working-level review. No periodic evaluation of the progress of the initiative was ever conducted. The result was an unprofessional and, in substantial part, unsatisfactory operation.[185]

But as the Tower Commission and others also note, Poindexter was not the only one at fault. A good measure of the problem can be attributed to Reagan's lax management practices. According to the Tower Commission, "The President's management style is to put the principal responsibility for policy review and implementation on the shoulders of advisers." Reagan's concern for the hostages "may have been conveyed in a manner so as to inhibit the full functioning of the system." Given the high stakes and risks, "the president should have ensured that the NSC system did not fail him. He did not force his policy to undergo the most critical review of which the NSC participants and the process were capable. At no time did he insist upon accountability and performance review." By contrast, "Had the president chosen to drive the NSC system, the outcome could well have been different."[186]

Revelation of the Iran-Contra affair led to Poindexter's resignation on November 25, 1986, only eleven months on the job. The smoking gun, found by Attorney General Meese's initial investigation, was an April 4, 1986, memo from North to Poindexter outlining the diversion of fund's operation.[187] In 1990, Poindexter was convicted of a number of counts relating to Iran-Contra. The convictions, however, were later overturned due to legal technicalities.

IV. Recovery

The final two NSC advisors, Frank Carlucci and Colin Powell, each had short tenures in the position. Yet their time in office was an important one. As Brent Scowcroft has noted, as honest brokers "Powell did a fine job, Carlucci did a fine job."[188] The change in nature of the NSC advisor's role mattered, and it was central to the recovery of the national security process in the wake of Iran-Contra. How it emerged is also telling: not through presidential direction or efforts to mold a process to presidential needs, but through the Tower Commission's attention to what makes for an effective decision process and the efforts of these two NSC advisors to put that advice into practice.

FRANK C. CARLUCCI III AND COLIN POWELL

Carlucci was on the job for less than a year: he was appointed December 2, 1986, and resigned on November 23, 1987, when he succeeded Weinberger as secretary of defense. Powell took the NSC job that day, and was there until the end of the Reagan presidency. Carlucci had extensive background at the federal level. A roommate of Donald Rumsfeld at Princeton (both were also on the wrestling team), Carlucci later joined the Foreign Service. He served under Rumsfeld at the Office of Economic Opportunity, as deputy director of OMB, and then undersecretary of HEW (both under Weinberger) during the Nixon years. Later, he was ambassador to Portugal, deputy director of the CIA from 1978 to 1981, and then deputy defense secretary under (again) Weinberger through the end of 1983, when he became president of Sears World Trade.[189] After Poindexter resigned, Carlucci was unexpectedly summoned to the White House and asked to serve as NSC advisor by the president himself. Reagan told him, "you're the only person that George and Cap can agree on."[190]

A Vietnam veteran (awarded a Purple Heart), Powell's ascent in Washington began when he was selected for a prestigious White House Fellowship and was assigned to the OMB, headed at the time by Weinberger and his deputy, one Frank Carlucci. Powell then held a number of army command and Pentagon posts before becoming senior military assistant to Weinberger in 1983. During the administration's arms-for-hostages effort, Powell was asked to provide information concerning the weapons requested and how they might be replenished by the U.S. He complied, but questioned the operation in writing, noting the legal obligation—under the Arms Export

Control Act—to inform Congress of the arms transfer.[191] In June 1986, now Lieutenant General Powell returned to regular military command in Germany, but six months later he was back at the White House as Carlucci's deputy at the NSC.[192]

Although their tenures were short, both had an important impact on the Reagan presidency and the reform of its national security decision making. With Donald Regan's resignation as chief of staff and his replacement by the diplomatic and politically skilled Howard Baker, the former Republican leader of the Senate, smoother relations with the White House staff ensued. Baker stayed out of national security affairs, and Carlucci had direct and unfettered access to the president. A consummate manager, Carlucci assembled a transition team to recommend changes in the staff he was about to take over.[193] Carlucci also made sure before taking the job that he was empowered to make those needed personnel and organizational changes.[194]

The reforms and practices suggested by the Tower Commission strongly informed Carlucci's and Powell's efforts. As Scowcroft later recollects, "I actually drew up a model for reform of the NSC system, and I guess I gave it to Carlucci but really Colin Powell."[195] According to Powell, "The Tower Report became our owner's manual. We did what it recommended."[196] The NSC committee structure had burgeoned and become unwieldy under their predecessors; at the same time Iran-Contra revealed much that was clandestine and highly problematic. As a result, early in his tenure as NSC advisor, Carlucci submitted NSDD 276 on organizational reform to the president. In effect, it was an early attempt to put the "Scowcroft model" into practice.

At the top of the new system was a Senior Review Group, chaired by the NSC advisor. Below that were several Policy Review Groups, which Powell, as deputy NSC advisor, chaired. NSC control of these committees avoided the department-led groups that had often bogged down the development of policy options earlier in the administration. The new system also prevented "many issues leap-frog[ing] from lower level working groups to full scale NSC meetings, where intense disagreement by the principals often precluded presidential decisions."[197] They also guaranteed an inclusiveness that was absent under Poindexter; other parties would not be kept in the dark about what the NSC staff was up to. As Powell noted at the time, "I am not a great believer in restricting attendance that much. . . . I'm not a great slammer of doors."[198] Powell, moreover, served as Carlucci's chief deputy—a shift from the multiple deputies of the Poindexter tenure.[199]

Carlucci's efforts did not come easily. The Tower Commission's recommendations notwithstanding, Shultz was alarmed at the prospect of a resurgent NSC staff, especially the prospect of attending meetings that Carlucci chaired. Shultz was ready for battle; in his mind, the proposed structure expanded "the powers of the very entity whose uncontrolled powers had brought us the Iran-Contra fiasco in the first place." The NSC advisor's job, in Shultz's view, was a staff position; he told Carlucci that he was "was not a member of the NSC. . . . You are the staff of the NSC. You serve the principals of the NSC." Carlucci replied that he "had just been trying to do what the Tower Commission recommended." Tower has "already been forgotten," Shultz told him, "Stop chewing on that nail." Shultz put his objections in writing. But Carlucci "did not yield," according to Shultz. "Forgive my annoyance," Carlucci told him, "but I did not return to government in order to be an executive secretary."[200] Shultz had asked to discuss the NSDD with Reagan, "but that had not occurred," the directive was signed on March 31, 1987.[201] In a letter responding to Shultz's critique of the NSDD, Reagan emphasized that the new committees chaired by Carlucci and Powell were intended as "feeder systems for the NSC and NSPG which I chair." Shultz says in his memoirs that he "decided that he was encouraging my instinct simply to ignore the directive" (yet another sign of Reagan's continued laxness in dealing with his principals).[202] The battle between Shultz and Carlucci over the role of the NSC advisor and staff in the decision-making process had its price. According to Shultz, "Frank Carlucci was unhappy with his job and my opposition to his NSDD 276 played a big part in that feeling."[203] Perhaps unfortunately, Reagan's directive was no where to be found in Shultz's bureaucratic calculus.

But Shultz was supportive of other parts of NSDD 276. These included the creation of an NSC legal counsel unit to monitor the staff's activities and provide the legal guidance that Poindexter had feared in approaching the regular White House legal counsel's office for advice. Carlucci told his new legal counsel: "You have access to all meetings in this organization. You report to me and only to me."[204] The NSC's own history on the White House Web site notes that Carlucci replaced "more than half of the professional staff within three months." It also notes that "Carlucci largely withdrew the NSC from its operational roles, but in the matter of Nicaragua, NSC continued to exercise the coordination that was not forthcoming from any of the agencies."[205] All covert operations underwent a "sweeping review."[206] In Carlucci's view, "the NSC should exploit its competitive advantage. It should not be doing things that other agencies normally can do . . . Certainly it shouldn't be doing covert action."[207]

Shultz, however, still had concerns that the NSC staff was involved in operations and back-channel contacts: Carlucci "had initiated a pattern of meeting with the Soviet ambassador and other ambassadors as well without the State Department's knowledge, which gave an inestimable advantage to those governments to play one side of the U.S. administration against the other. . . . Every week I would learn of some NSC staff private channel that had been kept from me."[208] Shultz's relationship with Carlucci also got rocky following Shultz's tough and candid public testimony—which was perceived by the White House as too critical and insufficiently supportive—before the congressional committee investigating Iran-Contra. "My relations with Frank Carlucci did not get easier," Shultz reports. Carlucci told him: "You have been stirring up a State Department war with the NSC."[209]

"I knew I had a problem with George Shultz," Carlucci reflected, "George was traumatized by the NSC [staff] and he wanted to reduce the NSC [advisor and staff] in effect to an executive secretariat. I told him I wouldn't do that. He didn't want me to see ambassadors, he didn't want me to travel, he didn't want me to chair meetings." Their "tense relationship" was an important factor in Powell's selection as deputy: "I needed someone who I knew could get along with George. Somebody George would be taken by. And I thought Colin was that kind of person."[210]

Carlucci by most accounts was fair and even-handed in transmitting the views of State or Defense to the president. Yet he did not shy away from expressing his own views when warranted. As he relates, "there were occasions when I told the president that Cap [Weinberger] was wrong." Weinberger especially was over optimistic in telling Reagan when SDI could be deployed. According to Carlucci, "After he'd meet with Cap, I'd say, 'Mr. President, this thing is nowhere near being deployed.' I could tell Ronald Reagan that Cap was wrong, and he would accept that. He wouldn't accept everything that Cap said unquestionably."[211]

Carlucci also promised more openness and transparency in the NSC staff's operations—at least to the extent it was feasible. Carlucci, according to one report, "made peace overtures to Congress . . . and opened the doors of his office to fellow White House staffers and to the press." Yet Carlucci also recognized the deference due to the secretaries of state and defense. According to one report, his preference was to speak on background, while it was the principals "who ought to be out front publicly."[212] Public appearances were done only at the request of the White House press office.[213] Powell was also attentive to the problem of "press disinformation" of the Poindexter years: "I will keep secret that which needs to remain secret and

I'll tell you to your face that I'm not going to tell you something," Powell told reporters, "But when it's appropriate, I will be as available as the circumstances dictate."[214]

Tensions notwithstanding, Shultz was one of Carlucci's chief supporters to become secretary of defense when Weinberger resigned in October 1987. Shultz was opposed to Carlucci's efforts as NSC advisor to be in "operational charge of important diplomatic and cabinet-level interagency groups." But Weinberger's former deputy "was able and experienced and straightforward. . . . Frank would make an excellent secretary of defense." Shultz also recommended to Reagan that Powell be promoted to NSC advisor.[215] Carlucci's substantive policy views were certainly closer to Shultz's than Weinberger's had been. In particular, Carlucci was perceived as less hard-line on the Soviet Union—policy agreement trumped bureaucratic politics.

With Powell as NSC advisor and Carlucci at Defense, the national security process was the most effective at any point during the Reagan years; unfortunately only a little over a year remained. According to the NSC's own history, Powell "directed an NSC that strived to provide balanced coordination of major foreign policy presentations for the president." As well, it notes, "Powell conducted an NSC process that was efficient but low key. There were no longer free-lancers operating out of the NSC staff."[216]

Powell was especially effective in conducting meetings of the Policy Review Group during his tenure as deputy. He controlled the agenda, which was distributed ahead of time, and no one was allowed to alter it once a meeting—usually an hour in length—began. According to Powell, "The first five minutes and the last ten minutes belonged to me. In those first five minutes, I reviewed why we were meeting and what had to be decided by the end of the session." Participants were then allowed twenty minutes to state their views, "uninterrupted." Following that was a "free-for-all" discussion. Towards the end of the hour, Powell took five minutes to summarize "everyone's views as I understood them." Participants could take one minute to voice any disagreement with Powell's summary, then "in the last four to five minutes, I laid out the conclusions and decisions to be presented as the consensus of the participants. . . . This approach seemed to work."[217] Powell's effectiveness continued when he chaired the principals' meetings now as NSC advisor.

Relations between State and Defense also improved once Weinberger was out of the picture. Shultz's earlier contretemps with Carlucci notwithstanding, the secretaries of state, defense, and the NSC advisor got along reasonably well. Their efforts at coordination were unprecedented. Meetings were held not weekly but daily. The three met every morning when it was possible in Powell's office. According to Shultz, whose idea it was, there was "no agenda, no staff, no nothing . . . So the troops would get the idea that the bosses were getting along, so they'd better get along . . . it worked well, it was good."[218] According to Carlucci, "just the three of us, no agenda, no substitutes. We worked through the day's events, trying to forge agreement."[219] Overall for Carlucci, "Those meetings were the key to the effective functioning of foreign policy in the last year and half of the administration."[220]

In general, according to Shultz, "with Colin everything worked sort of by the book, was good."[221] Powell's military background, in Shultz's view, was important because "in the services I think people get trained about roles. They understand when you're a general in charge and when you're advising . . . It's part of their training to see if you're in this role, you do this, if you're in that role you do that. So it came much easier for him."[222]

As Powell notes in his memoirs, *My American Journey,* a good NSC advisor is "an honest broker"—and of all the six Reagan NSC advisors, he came closest to it.[223] But at the same time, Powell recognized that the personal views of the NSC advisor also have their place, as long as there is fair and balanced representation of the other principals' positions: "The national security adviser may well bring a point of view that is not just the result of his staff work but are his own personal feelings about it. 'Yes, my staff's wrong and so are these other guys. And this is what you ought to do.' Put it in there."[224] According to his biographer, Karen DeYoung, it was Powell's view that he should try to guide his colleagues to consensus when possible. But "if consensus could not be reached, cabinet officers were free to make their own Oval Office pitches." At the same time, however, "Powell reserved the right to tell Reagan why he thought they were wrong. If they ended up mad at him, so be it."[225] But the latter proved rare. According to Carlucci, Powell handled them deftly, and "he'd bounce us back and forth with good humor."[226] Powell had no problem with Shultz's twice-weekly meetings with Reagan. But Powell always exercised caution when he met privately with the president; he would invite someone else along and make sure that someone was taking notes.[227] Perhaps it was his innate caution, perhaps he sought to avoid misunderstandings with the other principals, or perhaps it was a lesson he drew from Iran-Contra.

Powell departed from the pristine conception of the honest broker in another important way: he was a highly visible White House figure and understood the value of the press in getting the administration's message out. According to DeYoung, "While other senior officials spoke only rarely to reporters, and then usually under strict guidelines, Powell's strategy was to overwhelm the media with access to him and his point of view." It was not spin control or deception, in Powell's view, but "helping the American people understand the major issues that are out there by being accessible to the press."[228]

Although the administration was winding down, policy success improved in the aftermath of Iran-Contra: "Under Powell's direction, the president and his chief advisers weathered the Persian Gulf crisis in 1987, the wind-down of the Nicaraguan Contra effort, and the Reagan-Gorbachev relationship culminating in the Moscow Summit of June 1988—the smoothest ever seen by observers at the time."[229] Like Carlucci's relationship with Chief of Staff Howard Baker, Powell enjoyed excellent relations with Baker's successor, Ken Duberstein; according to Powell, "he had run the smoothest, most congenial operation I had seen during the Reagan years."[230]

Yet both Carlucci and Powell were sometimes disturbed by Reagan's passiveness. At their daily briefings, as Powell relates, Reagan "listened carefully and asked a few questions, but gave no guidance. . . . We would lay out the contrasting views . . . and wait for the president to peel them back to get at underlying motives." Carlucci would present his recommendations, but was often unclear of Reagan's decision: "Was that a yes?" he would later ask Powell. "The president's management style placed a tremendous burden on us," according to Powell.[231] When Powell took over as NSC advisor, Reagan "never spoke to me about the job, never laid out his expectations, never provided any guidance."[232]

V. Implications

The travails of the first four of Reagan's NSC advisors support the argument on the merits of an honest broker role, even if largely by negative evidence. Brokerage was often absent or ineffective, and the policy-making process was flawed. Other facets of the NSC advisor's role sometimes came to predominate, but not to positive effect. Iran-Contra is obviously the most important example of the latter. Poindexter's involvement in both the arms-for-hostages exchange and in the subsequent transfer of funds to the contras provides clear evidence of an NSC advisor deeply enmeshed in an operating role that proved dangerous to this presidency and almost brought it down. McFarlane's earlier effort to establish the arms-for-hostages part of the operation is no less problematic. Although McFarlane later attempted to shut the operation down, the earlier opposition of Shultz and Weinberger and the way Reagan was consulted and his approval apparently obtained should have signaled a process that was amiss and an effort that was likely to go awry. The Tower Commission's report is especially notable: the NSC advisor failed to secure a policy-vetting process that was effective, and he involved his staff inappropriately in clandestine operations. Moreover, honest brokerage was clearly needed, the report also emphasized, to prevent the recurrence of serious policy error.

Reagan's last two NSC advisors provide more positive evidence for brokerage. They sought to rebuild a more effective NSC system. And, following the recommendations of the Tower Commission and Brent Scowcroft, they embraced honest brokerage and put in place a better-organized and more effective policy process.

THE NSC ADVISOR'S ROLE EXPECTATIONS AND HONEST BROKERAGE

But Iran-Contra was not the only problem besetting the Reagan national security set-up. Expectations by each NSC advisor on how they might define the job were also consequential. Allen's role is also interesting in the way he at least attempted to model it after an Eisenhower-era NSC advisor. But simple coordination or policy facilitation was not enough. His experience provides some indicators that a more expansive conception of the broker role is needed, that we must move beyond the more limited conception of that role in the Eisenhower years. Allen's experience also provides evidence of the need for linkage of successful role to an effective *organizational* context. That the NSC system required Allen to report through Meese—who had responsibilities across the whole range of domestic, economic, and foreign policy—remains inexplicable. Not only was Meese an overburdened and poor manager, but the NSC system he devised, with SIGs headed by departmental representatives, struck a poor balance in bringing in the resources and voice of the NSC's own staff to bear on policy matters. Early meetings of the principals were poorly staffed, and policy review and feedback was weak. More attention was clearly needed to correct any deficiencies in process. Ironically, here a Bobby Cutler or Gordon Gray might have actually been needed.

Allen's apparent effort to avoid making his own policy recommendations may have been Cutler-like, but given the context of the *principals* in which he operated, a fair and balanced measure of advocacy may have been more useful. This is especially so in light of Haig's efforts to put his considerable stamp on things as the administration's self-styled "vicar" of foreign policy.

And it alerts us to the importance of those with whom the NSC advisor must interact as factors that affect what the NSC advisor can do and how the cast of characters can affect the process and its outcomes. What would the early foreign policy of the Reagan presidency have looked like if Shultz rather than Haig had been initially selected as secretary of state? What would have been the quality of the policy process if the tense relationship between State and Defense had been avoided had someone other than Weinberger been selected?

Clark operated in a better-organized environment, especially once Meese's oversight was eliminated. The *process* improved, in part due to Clark's attention, and the NSC staff took a more active role. But did the quality of its deliberative outcomes also improve? Clashes with State lessened once Haig was out of the picture. But there was still a strong element of interpersonal tension—with Baker now in the mix—that remained unaddressed, even when it was brought to President Reagan's attention. Clark's loyalty and long association with Reagan was a plus, but his own lack of substantive expertise in foreign and national security policy left him ill-equipped and generated difficulties with the other, better informed principals. Baker's comment about a "witches' brew of elbows, egos, and separate agendas" is revealing.

McFarlane brought to the job the expertise that Clark lacked and he was cognizant of the need to address the tensions among the principals. But here the problem was that he could not do it alone. Divisions festered on, sharp elbows remained pointed out. But it was not all context: the NSC advisor's efforts in secret diplomacy would lead down the slippery slope of policy misadventure, if not extreme danger, under his successor, John Poindexter. Although one of the personally brightest of NSC advisors, Poindexter was a poor fit for the position. He had operational skills (which unfortunately served him well in Iran-Contra). But he lacked, despite his prior service as McFarlane's deputy, the interpersonal, organizational, and broader substantive knowledge needed in an NSC advisor. Even McFarlane later came to regret his role in Poindexter's appointment; the job required "different skills" and was "an injustice to him."

EVOLUTION OF THE NSC ADVISOR'S ROLE OVER TIME

Evolution is clearly apparent during the Reagan years. But it was not in a positive direction for most of the first six years. There was little in the way of learning behavior among the first four NSC advisors. Clark and McFarlane did try, but the stage became set for the Iran-Contra debacle.

The post-Iran-Contra advisors, Carlucci and Powell, provide the silver lining and the positive lessons. The "owner's manual"—as Powell phrased it—of the *Tower Commission Report* provided a roadmap to a more balanced role for the NSC advisor: honest brokerage in the deliberative process but not restricted to the more limited Eisenhower model. As well, the report recommended changes in the system's organization. Much was put in practice by Carlucci and Powell, exemplifying the other component of the broker role: attention to the quality of the deliberative process. Context improved too: Howard Baker and then Ken Duberstein were more managerially attentive and interpersonally effective chiefs of staff, largely unwilling to meddle in foreign policy. Carlucci and Powell continued to interact with a tough cast of principals, but at the very least they handled matters more successfully than their predecessors. The situation especially improved for Powell once Carlucci replaced Weinberger at Defense.

PRESIDENTIAL DECISION-MAKING NEEDS, PRESIDENTIAL ROLE EXPECTATIONS

The Reagan years are especially instructive about the impact of the president, especially one so prone to delegate and thus so dependent on process. Reagan provided a broad policy vision, and at key points—such as his dealings with Gorbachev, his continual push for a strategic defense initiative, and his goal of rebuilding the military—he was a guiding force and a decisive actor. But on other matters, it was up to others. Moreover, the national security system for handling such matters was molded around his needs not through his own efforts but by what *others perceived* were his needs. These perceptions were often problematic. Meese was especially instrumental in setting up the flawed reporting system and poorly organized interagency process that Allen faced. Clark thought he knew the harder-line policies that his old friend favored, the pursuit of which sometimes led to end runs around the process and caused tensions with Shultz and Baker. McFarlane took the first steps toward Iran-Contra based in part on his beliefs about the president's deep concern for the hostages. Poindexter kept the diversion of funds to the contras secret, but he was convinced that Reagan would approve it in the end. The lesson: too much adaptation to what are perceived as presidential needs might be just as problematic in some instances as the failure to factor them in.

Not only was the system and the roles of the NSC advisors flawed, but presidential attention to and management of the process remained elusive. As Shultz later noted, Reagan did not like "to bang heads together particularly. Clark went. McFarlane went. Poindexter went. Carlucci went. He acted, but it took a while."[233]

Reagan was unwilling to step in, leaving even occasions of insubordination by some of the other principals, Weinberger most importantly, unaddressed. *Presidential* attention to the process and *presidential* management of the players—including a more hyperinvolved chief of staff in Don Regan at the start of the second term—are also contextual matters of great import.

The system in the end righted itself—largely with a good push from Scowcroft's efforts in crafting the Tower Commission's recommendations, then Carlucci's and Powell's efforts to put them into practice. The early effort to "fit" a system to Reagan's needs was well intended. But it might have been more successful from the start not only had it been better structured—including a more effective role for the NSC advisor—but also if that fit had been the subject of Reagan's own ongoing direction and concern.

The absence of effective brokerage for Reagan's first four NSC advisors and its return and positive effects for his remaining two is an important lesson from the Reagan years. But, as the Tower Commission clearly set out, so too were the president's responsibilities to maintain watchfulness over the people and process involved in what is surely the most crucial area of presidential decisions, those concerning national security. The Tower Commission also offers another important lesson: while decision-making arrangements need to "fit" presidential needs, they must also be structured to ensure an *effective* decision process and one in which the NSC advisor plays a central broker role.

CHAPTER 6

The Costs of Failed Brokerage

Rice as NSC Advisor

Analysis of the broker role in the George W. Bush presidency is important for a number of reasons. First, the rhetoric, if not at times the practice, of serving as an honest broker was, at least initially, embraced by Condoleezza Rice when she took over as NSC advisor. The broker role was also in George W. Bush's mind when he picked Rice for the post in December 2000; she was, in his words, "both a good manager and an honest broker of ideas."[1] Yet as we shall see, Rice's activities as a broker varied enormously during her tenure in that position. At some decision points the degree of brokerage was high. At others, it was low or absent.

Second, Rice's role as NSC advisor went considerably beyond simple brokerage. Like most of her recent predecessors, Rice took on additional duties, especially in serving as a private counselor to the president and as public spokesperson. These additional tasks are often seen as weakening brokerage. Analysis of Rice's activities thus offers an important test of whether and how much the NSC advisor's role can be expanded beyond brokerage.

Third, brokerage seems especially to have been needed in the deliberations of this presidency. George W. Bush, unlike his father, had little foreign policy expertise or experience. Finally, this administration faced a string of difficult and at times unique national security issues: the response to the terrorist attacks of September 11, war in Afghanistan and Iraq, and then the difficulties surrounding Iraq's postwar pacification and reconstruction.[2] Decisions made were highly consequential but, as we shall see, sometimes fraught with error.

I. The George W. Bush National Security Process

Like Carter and Clinton, Bush came to the presidency with little background in foreign affairs, this despite the strengths in that area his own father brought to his presidency. But unlike Carter or Clinton, Bush was no micromanager, bent on immersing himself in policy detail. September 11 changed that to some extent, and his presidency was faced with the most difficult of national security issues, to which he would most certainly respond. Yet, both before and after September 11, Bush was a decision maker prone to delegate. As a result, he was highly "process dependent." Like Reagan, much would depend on the advice given him and the quality of the deliberative process that produced it. And like Reagan again, it was a context that especially called for an honest broker.

An effective process was especially needed given Bush's proclivities as a decision maker. Delegation especially carried risks given Bush's deliberative style. As Fred I. Greenstein has noted, Bush showed "little intellectual curiosity, and appears not to have been drawn into the play of ideas."[3] In Hugh Heclo's view, "Bush learns quickly and becomes deeply informed about what he is interested in. But this sort of learning capacity turns into a liability when it comes to things that should interest him but do not."[4]

What percolated up through the advisory system and eventually made its way to the president was thus especially crucial to decision-making success. As Bruce Buchanan has observed, Bush is "not a policy wonk, so he has to rely on people who are." But that reliance can create vulnerability to error: "Bush's biggest weakness is that he may not be in a position to discern the credibility of the options his advisers lay out for him."[5] Similarly, in the view of Donald Kettl, the success of the Bush decision-making process "depends critically on his staffers' skill in boiling complex issues down to their essence. If they miss important facts, they risk blinding Bush to things he ought to know. . . . The process, then, risks making the president especially vulnerable to what he and his staff don't know—or don't know to ask."[6] Bush relied on a formal advisory system of the sort present in the Eisenhower, Nixon, and Reagan presidencies. Indeed, it is fair to say he was highly reliant on that formal process, as Reagan was. Yet, unlike Eisenhower, he did not have a sense for the need of vigilance over the process. Unlike Nixon, he lacked sure knowledge of and deep familiarity with foreign policy. Unlike Reagan, his broader foreign policy "vision" was developed on the fly. What percolated up would matter; indeed, in some ways it would be decisive, but not a guarantee for the better.

Bush was also a highly collegial decision maker, akin to some of his Democratic predecessors.[7] His key principals were an impressive group. All served in past presidencies: former chief of staff, defense secretary, and now Vice President Richard Cheney; former chief of staff, NATO ambassador, past and present Defense Secretary Donald Rumsfeld; and former NSC advisor, chairman of the Joints Chiefs of Staff, and now Secretary of State Colin Powell. CIA Director George Tenet was carried over from the Clinton administration; Rice herself had served before on the NSC staff of George H. W. Bush as a Soviet specialist, and Chief of Staff Andrew Card—who became part of the "war cabinet" after 9/11—had been deputy chief of staff then secretary of transportation under the elder Bush, as well as serving in several White House posts in the Reagan years. More notably, both Bush and a number of his chief advisers had observed first-hand the strengths and weaknesses of his father's presidency.

On the positive side, the awareness of the inner workings of a presidency was thus high and in marked contrast to the learning curve that Jimmy Carter, Bill Clinton, or even Ronald Reagan faced upon taking office. Notably, most of the George W. Bush foreign policy team had been in office during his father's deliberations over the first Persian Gulf War. War in the Middle East—and against Saddam Hussein—had already been on their policy table. On the negative side, the strengths of Bush's inner circle were also a potential weakness. They had been there before, were confident in their views, and—in the case of Cheney, Powell, and Rumsfeld—had reached the end of their political careers; the latter three had no further ambitions to serve as a potential check on their policy positions. They were, moreover, skilled bureaucratic and political operatives, often holding strong policy positions, and thus perhaps especially in need of a heavy dose of brokerage.

Yet Bush was no wallflower in the midst of his principals. Numerous accounts portray him as an active participant in discussions—here differences with Reagan in his "process dependence" are evident. "One of my jobs is to be provocative, seriously to provoke people into—to force decisions, and to make sure in everybody's mind where we are headed," he told Bob Woodward.[8] Yet there were also personal nuances to Bush's involvement, some of which may signal problems. According to one account, "Bush generally prefers short conversations—long on conclusion, short on reason."[9] According to another report, "Bush is not disengaged, but there are clear signatures to the way he engages. His questions at meetings, say participants, usually focus on practicalities: What coalitions back a particular bill? Has someone or other been consulted? Bush's curiosity has an almost tactile quality to it."[10]

For Colin Powell, Bush's practical perspective was also of import. Unlike his father who was attuned to "a more deliberate process," George W. Bush "is guided more by a powerful inertial navigation system than by intellect. He knows what he wants to do, and what he wants to hear is how to get it done."[11] Still other accounts point not just to the absence of policy reasoning but the reliance on ideological faith: "Occasional outsiders brought into the Bush Bubble have observed that faith, not evidence, is the basis for decision making."[12]

That said, others have found Bush's pattern of interpersonal engagement of positive benefit. According to Clay Johnson, who was a close aide both before and during his presidency, Bush "encourages people to push. He is interested in good ideas and to give people confidence to have a dialogue with him, to have that exchange of ideas and difference of opinion."[13] And even in Powell's view, Bush "allows his principal advisors freedom to present all sides of an argument . . . he encourages us to discuss with one another, debate with one another, and disagree with one another. And he then works hard to draw out the best ideas from everyone."[14]

Yet was Bush fully engaged when his advisers wanted to raise issues outside of his immediate agenda or perhaps even in challenge of it? After September 11, Bush was clearly an even more active participant than he had been before. There was a continual cycle of NSC and other meetings, and accounts of them portray a process of vigorous give-and-take between the president and his advisers.[15] According to one aide, "From the very beginning the president decided he wanted to chair the NSC meetings . . . because I think he didn't want a process where options were coming up to him, where we had to say 'A thinks this, B thinks this, the consensus should be this' . . . In the earliest phases, he chaired and we had our intellectual discussions about strategy—everybody, with the president there. It was great."[16]

Problems in collegial deliberations, however, mounted once Iraq was on the front burner. The problem *was not* that Bush was a passive participant. As planning progressed, according to one account, "Aides said he questioned whether the plan was too conventional, what the Iraqis might have learned from the 1991 Persian Gulf War, and he constantly asks what can go wrong with the plans and how ready the generals are if something does go wrong." Once the war was underway, Bush continued to press questions about Iraqi troop strengths, coalition troop morale, and the effectiveness of U.S. media communications with the Iraqi people.[17] According to Rumsfeld, Bush would often interrupt briefings, asking "What about this? What about that? If this occurs, what would the approach be?" Bush "pushes people to think about things he does not know."[18] According to CIA Director Tenet, "The president never became the action officer, but there was no doubt the leader was in the trenches with us. If you told him about an imminent operation on Monday, you could be certain after a few days he would ask about it, if we had not provided the necessary follow-up."[19]

But, two notable areas of possible omission emerged after the war was over: Had the president pressed his inner circle with sufficient vigor concerning the reliability of some of the evidence on which the case for war was based? Had the political, economic, and military situation in a postwar Iraq been sufficiently anticipated, and had Iraq's pacification and reconstruction been adequately planned for?

More generally, the challenge for this presidency was whether Bush was able to reap the benefits of hierarchy and formal structure—closer to the Eisenhower experience—or whether he fell victim to its weaknesses—more akin to the isolation and its consequences that beset Nixon. Likewise, were his collegial deliberations closer to those of Kennedy during the Cuban missile crisis, or were they more analogous to the decision-making fiasco of the Bay of Pigs invasion?

Other aspects of the advisory process were potentially problematic. Loyalty and discipline, particularly of the staff but also the cabinet, was another hallmark of this presidency. Few of Bush's recent predecessors were so attentive to the need for teamwork and for staying on message, while avoiding the infighting and backbiting that often plagued his predecessors. Yet as time wore on did discipline go too far, particularly in stifling dissent or in equating disagreement with disloyalty? At the same time, although discipline may have been strongly felt lower down the policy food chain, did sufficient discipline extend to the top levels of the Bush inner circle, especially such heavyweights as Rumsfeld and Cheney? Larry Wilkinson, Powell's chief of staff, felt that Cheney and Rumsfeld operated as a secretive "cabal." When asked about Wilkinson's characterization, Powell would not share the "cabal" label, but he did note that "very often maybe Mr. Rumsfeld and Vice President Cheney would take decisions to the president that the rest of us weren't aware of. That did happen, on a number of occasions"[20]

Another issue is whether there was a sufficient diversity of views within the administration. Powell clearly differed from a Cheney or a Rumsfeld, but did he possess sufficient leverage to force an honest debate? According to Colin Campbell, there was a high degree of "unrestrained ideological entrepreneurship." The administration has a "surfeit of doctrinaire players," and one consequence is that it "invests very little structure or effort in ensuring that policy initiatives receive intense collegial scrutiny."[21] Perhaps the problem is summed up best in Bush's own words: "I . . . want to make sure that the people are *there for a cause* as opposed to themselves."[22] Wariness of self-interest may be laudable, but perhaps the emphasis on "there for a cause" proved too overbearing.

One check on an advisory system that may be fraught with some problems—whether stifled access, poor coordination, problems in delegation, and too heavy a dose of loyalty and ideology—is the ability of a president to move beyond formal channels in search of information and advice. Important examples include Eisenhower's wide circle of business friends and former military associates as sources of counsel, as well as Kennedy's penchant for contacting lower-level officials and also expanding the membership of ExCom to include the "wise men" of the foreign policy establishment at the time of Cuban missile crisis. Indeed, Bush's own father was an inveterate user of the telephone, reaching out to a wide range of contacts, both at home and abroad. Moreover, even if an advisory system is relatively open and functioning well, a president may still benefit from reaching out beyond his *formal* set of advisers in search of further information and advice or to test that which his staff provides him—Alexander George's theory of multiple advocacy.

Here Bush's decision-making instincts and practices are less positive. He gave lip service to "access."[23] But a number accounts have noted that Bush sometimes operated within a "bubble" or an "echo chamber." Treasury Secretary Paul O'Neill felt that Bush "was caught in an echo chamber of his own making, cut off from everyone other than a circle around him that's tiny and getting smaller and in concert on everything." Bush lacked a "disinterested perspective about what's real and what the hell he might do about it."[24] According to one *Newsweek* account (in an article titled "Bush in the Bubble"), "Bush may be the most isolated president in modern history, at least since the late-stage Richard Nixon." Bush's outside contacts are largely social, with old friends: "He calls them all the time—but the talk is usually comforting and jocular, of sports and old days. They rarely dispense pointed political advice or brace him with bad news."[25] Yet other accounts have indicated that outside sources of advice—such as historians, political scientists, philosophers, and theologians—were periodically brought in to meet with the president. Following the 2006 midterm elections, Chief of Staff Joshua Bolten convened presidential meetings with critics of the administration's Iraq policy, which according to one White House source involved "a lot of hard discussion."[26] Were these efforts intellectual window-dressing—deliberate but stacked with like-minded and policy-reinforcing experts with little impact on Bush's thoughts and deliberations? Or was it a genuine effort to break out of any putative "bubbles" or "echo chambers"?

Whether George H. W. Bush was a powerful source of outside advice remains a mystery. Yet given that this son of a former president had unprecedented access to a range of former officials in past Republican administrations (Reagan's as well as his father's), the lack of reported extramural contact is noteworthy.[27] It would make Rice's role as NSC advisor all the more important.

II. Rice as NSC Advisor

Bush's choice of Condoleezza Rice was consequential. Many of the early accounts of her work as NSC advisor emphasized that she was acting as an honest broker. This proved no surprise. She was a veteran of the elder Bush's NSC staff where she had been mentored by Brent Scowcroft, whose stints as NSC advisor most closely approximate a broker role. Media accounts, especially during the administration's first year, often portrayed her as an honest broker. She was not seen as undercutting Powell or engaging—at least in public view—in the kind of bureaucratic battles that some of her predecessors waged against the secretary of state. According to Powell, "It isn't threatening to me. She's not supposed to be in my corner. She's not supposed to be in Rumsfeld's corner. She's supposed to be in the president's corner, and she is, and she enjoys his confidence."[28] According to Treasury's O'Neill, a later critic of Bush, the verdict on Rice is more positive: "She doesn't drive to consensus. Rather she drives toward clarity. Then he [Bush] decides what the consensus is."[29]

 At least initially, President Bush's confidence in her also appeared to have enhanced Rice's ability to execute her job. Although he did not vest her with cabinet rank, it was Rice (rather than Cheney or Powell) who chaired the meetings of the foreign policy principals, an assignment laid out in Bush's first National Security Presidential Directive, issued on February 13, 2001. The "Scowcroft model" once again prevailed. The NSC advisor would chair meetings of the principals in the president's absence—although apparently to the consternation of Vice President Cheney, who had initially lobbied to lead them.[30]

President Bush also clearly signaled his high regard for Rice's counsel in announcing her appointment: "I want Condi to come to every cabinet meeting," adding that "I will be seeing her on a daily basis."[31] Early press reports also noted her close relationship to Bush during the campaign, when she in effect served as his foreign policy "tutor," as well as their continued closeness once he was in office. As Elisabeth Bumiller observes in her biography of Rice, calls between the two were frequent, and she "found herself in the Oval Office six and more times a day. Often it was just she and Bush, talking about whatever was on the president's mind. He was her client and a demanding one." According to Card, the president "used to look forward to seeing Condi."[32]

But Bush's apparent strong reliance on Rice's counsel also raises some issues about the brokerage role in this presidency. Assuming, for purposes of argument, that she was an *honest* broker, she was hardly a *neutral* one. Instead, she felt free to offer her advice to Bush, much as Scowcroft had done in his role as broker *and* counselor to his father. At the same time, Rice was discreet concerning her advisory role to the president: "Rice wants people to think of her as an enigma. She has often said that she is 'determined to leave this town' without anyone outside Bush's tight inner circle ever figuring out where she stands on major issues." And if she does on occasion advise the president, she never shares that, "not even with her closest aides."[33] Rice's private advice giving likely aided her brokerage than if she had engaged in more widely known advocacy.[34]

After the September 11 terrorist attacks, Rice's role as NSC advisor seemed to evolve. Some brokerage continued.[35] But as we shall discuss in more detail below, problems emerged as the administration turned toward war with Iraq. Other aspects of Rice's performance did not escape criticism, particularly her role in managing the flow of information and making sure that all sides to an issue or a dispute were fairly and fully presented and their assumptions probed—activities at the core of the broker role. Rice is a "yes man," according to one former government official, "She thinks her job is just to figure out what the president is trying to say and say it more articulately."[36] In the view of one White House adviser, however, "Rice challenged Mr. Bush a lot more behind the scenes than Mr. Powell did, but that such disputes were kept safely within the family."[37]

Criticisms also were directed at the policy process. Problems were perceived at lower levels in the deliberative process, stages crucial for analyzing information, testing assumptions, and defining options that later made their way before the principals. At lower-level interagency meetings, according to one report, "the Defense Department sometimes doesn't even bother to show up."[38] According to *several* reports, some State and Defense Department officials complained that the situation had become "dysfunctional": "Decisions go unmade at the deadlocked deputies' meetings or get kicked back or ignored by the president's principals, his top advisers."[39] Other accounts, it should be noted in fairness, discerned a more effective process, especially through the efforts of Rice's deputy (and eventual successor as NSC advisor) Stephen Hadley.[40] But Hadley also was subject to the criticism that deputies' meetings were too inconclusive and Hadley too compliant with Defense's bureaucratic tactics.[41]

Effective brokerage especially was an issue at the level of the principals. According to one account, the principals "tend to revisit unresolved issues or reopen decisions already made by the president."[42] Interpersonal tensions among the principals also were noted, although accounts of the degree of tension vary.[43] Some reports indicated that disagreements "have been allowed to spin out of control."[44]

Some examples:

> Rice and her deputies have often failed to achieve consensus.[45]
>
> She will generally avoid driving an issue to a particular conclusion unless Bush has privately directed her to float a concept and see how other key actors react to it.[46]
>
> Throughout the first term, policies on such crucial issues as dealing with North Korean and Iranian nuclear programs have remained mired in disagreement, and officials said Rice never seemed to drive the process to a resolution. Officials on both sides of the administration's debate over North Korea fault Rice for failing to fashion a coherent approach to dismantling North Korea's nuclear program.[47]

Managing the sources that produce disagreement so that they do not pose longer term impact on the decision process also appears to have been problematic:

> Ms. Rice's critics have complained that she failed to adequately manage the competing feuds of the Pentagon and State Department.[48]
>
> Even after agreement has supposedly been reached, ideological warfare continues behind the scenes, undermining policy.[49]
>
> As impressive as she is on the public stage, she has been an oddly unimposing figure where it counts a lot more: in the internal decision-making processes of this administration. . . . Why did she define her role as national security adviser in the narrowest possible fashion? . . . Why the reluctance to mix it up with the likes of Cheney and Rumsfeld?[50]

Officials who have left the administration have said she was a loose administrator, allowing disputes to fester within the National Security Council.[51]

Her inability to rein in other powerful advisers, critics say, has helped lead to little planning for the occupation in Baghdad, stalled negotiations between the Israelis and Palestinians, and no success in stopping North Korea from making nuclear weapons.[52]

Many experts consider her one of the weakest national security advisers in recent history in terms of managing interagency conflicts.[53]

To the extent these problems existed, they should have been fodder for an effective broker role.

Rice's relations with Rumsfeld appear especially problematic. According to one former senior NSC staff member, in Rice "you've never really had a national security adviser who's ready to discipline the process, to drive decisions to conclusions and, once decisions are made, to enforce them. . . . [in particular] she will never discipline Don Rumsfeld. . . . Never any sanctions. Never any discipline. He never paid a price."[54] According to still another account, "critics say that more often than not she simply has settled into orbit around the real power centers"—Cheney and Rumsfeld.[55]

According to Powell biographer Karen DeYoung, Rice "was a frequent source of exasperation to Powell . . . at times Rice seemed willfully blind to the damage being done by these intramural disputes. More dangerously, in Powell's view, she tended to echo back to the president what she thought he wanted to hear rather than what he needed to know."[56] It was not the tight ship that Powell himself had run as NSC advisor; not only was Rumsfeld a problem but so too was Cheney.[57]

Rice's style, however, may have been more subtle and indirect. In meetings of the principals (especially when Bush was present), she was reported to ask "pointed questions" but "rarely takes an open stand." The other principals were often clear about her positions from private conversations. But in interactions with them she held the reins more "lightly": "She wants the president's other advisers to believe that she doesn't play favorites or whisper in the president's ear. By seeming above the fray she preserves her ability to influence decisions, however subtly."[58]

Rice's approach, on this reading, may have avoided the problem of an NSC advisor who undermines brokerage by too much personal advocacy in front of the other principals. But in holding the reins "lightly," did she miss important opportunities to act as an honest broker, "pointed questions" notwithstanding?

Yet to be fair to Rice, others have felt that she handled the situation well, especially in dealing with a tough and experienced cast of characters. In the view of Vice President Cheney, "This is not a shy, retiring group, but that's good. The challenge for Condi and the task that she handles very well is to referee that group and that process and deliver to the President their best thinking and see to it that everyone gets an opportunity to be heard."[59] So too for Treasury Secretary O'Neill, according to his biographer: "He liked Rice and trusted her. She was clearly doing her best to be an honest broker in foreign affairs—a role desperately needed in economic affairs and domestic policy."[60] Karen Hughes, Bush's top media strategist, recalls one conference call, lead by Rice, regarding a presidential speech on the Middle East. "It was a fascinating discussion," according to Hughes, "tough, smart, experienced people talking it through, what Condi calls 'working it,' letting the principals chew on the issue until the process resulted in consensus, or at least, clearer lines of disagreement."[61] Others have noted that Rice could be an effective manager and sometimes a presidential enforcer. Even Cheney felt the heat, following his VFW speech of August 26, 2002, which was perceived as too hawkish, especially his remark that return of U.N. inspectors to Iraq would give "false comfort that Saddam was somehow back in his box." According to one account, "It was time for someone to have a quiet word with Cheney," which Rice then did. She was "friendly and low-key. Cheney's speech, she blandly suggested, had been 'interpreted' by the press in a way that might 'limit the president's options.' Rice waited for Cheney himself to suggest a solution," which he did in a speech several days later. The media noted the change in Cheney's tone, "but Rice's intercession did not leak."[62]

Beyond Brokerage

As we have seen, policy advocacy poses a special danger to honest brokerage: it can compromise perceptions of fairness and objectivity and make the NSC advisor a competitor to the other principals. Yet advocacy on Rice's part does not seem to have had these effects. She clearly served in a "counselor" role to the president, tendering private advice to him. Yet the way she undertook that job offers important lessons about how it might be squared with brokerage: a general reluctance to express her own *substantive* policy views when in the company of the other principals coupled with a fairly strict personal policy of not revealing, more widely, what she advised the president in private.[63] According to "administration insiders," she "rarely tipped her hand during internal debates."[64] According to another, "If she states a position, she will announce to the gathering that she is stepping out of her role as national security adviser."[65]

Rice was especially careful not to tip her private hand in public. In Rice's own words, "I have a very strong view about this, which is that the President does not need to read my views in the newspaper. Our discussions about my views are private."[66]

She was, moreover, empowered rather than weakened by this modus operandi: "She has managed to become probably the highest-profile national security adviser since Henry Kissinger without ever employing the Kissingerian maneuver of letting it be known that her views hold sway within the Administration. Somehow she's able to convey importance without conveying content."[67]

But there were occasional exceptions. One area where she (as well as Powell, although on opposite sides) publicly weighed in was the debate over use of race in undergraduate and graduate admissions at the time that two University of Michigan affirmative action cases were under litigation before the federal courts. Drawing on her academic experience, Rice felt it appropriate to use race as one of a number of factors in determining admissions but not the point system that Michigan used at the undergraduate level (Powell supported Michigan's affirmative action practices). She "took a rare central role in a domestic debate within the White House" and held a "series of lengthy one-on-one meetings with Bush."[68] The U.S. Supreme Court eventually held in favor of Rice's position.

Nor did such visibility as a spokesperson for the administration seem to affect her other duties. In addition to her closeness to Bush as an adviser, "What most distinguishes Rice from her predecessors is her visibility and her talent in selling the Administration's foreign policy program."[69] Rice was almost universally regarded as a particularly articulate and effective public advocate. Rice's public presence may also have been enhanced by the attentiveness of this White House to media communications and its strategic implications, as well as its strong recognition of internal discipline and efforts to ensure all were speaking "on message."[70]

But Rice paid a bit of a price for her public efforts during her confirmation hearings as secretary of state. Her prior public statements (especially about Iraq's possession of aluminum tubes as an indicator of a nuclear capability—"we don't want the smoking gun to be a mushroom cloud") came under intense scrutiny and provided fodder for critics of the administration and its war policies.[71]

Rice also faced criticism (but again with apparently little impact on her role) for what was perceived to be overly partisan involvement in Bush's reelection effort. In the weeks leading up to the November 2004 election, she made nine speeches outside Washington, D.C., many in "battleground" states (Ohio, Pennsylvania, Florida, Michigan, Oregon, Washington, and North Carolina). According to one report, "Although she does not mention Democratic challenger John F. Kerry and avoids answering overtly political questions, the target of her speeches is not lost on local audiences. . . . Rice frequently supplements her speeches with interviews with local media, generating positive coverage." In contrast to Rice's visible role, "the White House has said that Bush ordered Defense Secretary Donald Rumsfeld and Secretary of State Colin Powell to avoid getting enmeshed in the campaign."[72] White House officials defended Rice's activities: "part of the job today of national security adviser is to discuss our nation's national security policy. Dr. Rice has continued the nonpolitical tradition of the post, but being nonpolitical does not mean being non-accessible," according to James Wilkinson, her communications adviser at the time. Yet Rice's level of speechmaking during the general election was in marked contrast to her predecessors: in 1980, Zbigniew Brzezinski gave two speeches; in 1988, Colin Powell gave one; in 1992, Brent Scowcroft gave none; in 1996, Anthony Lake gave two, both in Washington, D.C.; and in 2000 Samuel Berger gave one, also in Washington, D.C. Of Rice's appearances, according to Brzezinski, "That is certainly politicizing the job. I can't speak for the other national security advisers, but my recollection is we viewed the job as not a highly political one, to the extent that's possible being that close to the election."[73]

Another recognized danger is overly direct involvement in implementing national security policy; this was one of the chief lessons from the Iran-Contra affair during the Reagan years. Yet, the occasions when Rice was directly involved in diplomatic efforts do not appear to have affected her other duties as NSC advisor. In August 2001, for example, Rice not only was the first Bush official to undertake a diplomatic mission to Moscow, she also was the first senior American, including Secretary of State Powell, to meet with Russian President Vladimir Putin. According to Ivo Daalder, "Her mission to Moscow was unprecedented" since the Kissinger era.[74] Her aim was to impress upon him the U.S. case for its SDI missile defense system and the need to abrogate the 1972 ABM treaty, decisions which the Russians eventually accepted. In June 2003, during a diplomatic visit to Palestine and Israel in her capacity as the president's "personal representative," she directly confronted Prime Minister Ariel Sharon and his cabinet on the route of the proposed barrier between the two countries, asking that it be redrawn in order to show greater sensitivity to the Palestinians.[75] According to one tally, "White House records show that Rice made six [foreign] trips by herself in the first term—three that included stops in Moscow, one to London, one to Asia and the one to the Middle East."[76]

III. Policy: Process, Role, and Outcome

The Bush administration's foreign policy after the terrorist attacks of September 11, 2001, offers a very important series of episodes in understanding Rice's role as NSC advisor. In the immediate response to the attacks and as war in Afghanistan developed, Rice often acted as an honest broker of the deliberative process. Yet, once war with Iraq was on the table, brokerage became attenuated. By the time Iraq's postwar stabilization and reconstruction were under consideration, her role as honest broker was weak if almost nonexistent.

AFTER SEPTEMBER 11: WAR IN AFGHANISTAN

Developing a response to terrorism, especially military operations against the Taliban regime in Afghanistan, preoccupied the president and his advisers after September 11. As for Rice, she continued to preside over the meetings of the principals in the president's absence. Some of her activities as NSC advisor carried over from her conduct of the job before September 11. As Woodward notes, she normally saw as part of her job "to coordinate what Defense, State, the CIA and other departments or agencies were doing by making sure the president's orders were carried out." In meetings of the principals, "She was a coordinator. If pressed hard after the president had heard the views of others, she would give her opinion, but only then."[77] "It was her style not to commit herself unless the president pressed."[78] But Rice also continued to offer private counsel to Bush: "to act as counselor—to give her private assessment to the president, certainly when he asked, perhaps if he didn't."[79]

BROKERAGE AND THE QUALITY OF THE DELIBERATIVE PROCESS

But while acting as coordinator and a counselor, Rice also engaged in some brokerage activities. Indeed, her role as a broker comes into sharper relief in the period following September 11. As James Pfiffner observes, "Rice's role as NSC advisor had expanded during the months after 9/11. Beginning the administration as junior to the other principals in age and experience, she demonstrated her skill in her role as neutral broker as well as enforcer of the president's wishes."[80]

Rice sometimes expressed concern, for example, about the general quality of the deliberative process. At one Camp David session, the weekend after September 11, she felt that the morning meeting had started off well, but (in Woodward's words) it had "become repetitious, unusually freewheeling." She then convened the other principals, without the president in attendance, where "she expressed her concerns. We need to bring more discipline to the discussion in the afternoon, she said, urging them to be more specific."[81] Similarly, at a meeting on September 30, again with the president absent, Rice stressed the need to keep the president better informed: "What's the first 24, 48, 72 hours of this operation going to look like? We need to get back to the president on that." As well, she added, "it needs to be briefed to this group." Later, meeting with Bush, Rice told him the process was coming along but the principals had not reached closure. "What's the problem?" Bush asked. She summarized the discussion, then added, "You might want to press about that on Monday."[82] More generally, as Alexander Moens notes, "When matters were unresolved [at morning NSC meetings], Rice often called another meeting in the afternoon with only the principals in order to be better prepared for the next morning."[83]

Rice sometimes acted to keep the principals on the agreed-upon policy track. For example, shortly before military action commenced against the Taliban, some questioned whether they really needed to wait until the expiration of the president's declaration requiring the Taliban to close terrorist camps and turn over the Al Qaeda leadership. "Look," Rice told them, "we are going to stick to what you asked from the Taliban in your speech the other night." "Yup," Bush replied, "we've got to stick to what we've asked."[84] She also sought to tighten their considerations of options. At a meeting on October 29 (without the president present), Rice told the group, "We can't afford to lose. The Taliban proved tougher than we thought."[85] At the end of the meeting Rice returned to the immediate military situation on the ground and, according to Woodward, "suggested they go back and try to examine three options: 1. Go for Mazar. 2. Go for Kabul. 3. What if they could do neither?"[86] The timing of her intervention here was particularly important. Progress in the war was slow up to that point. On October 26, U.S. warplanes began bombing Taliban frontline forces in the north for the first time rather than just limiting attacks to its military and political infrastructure, largely in the south. On October 30, a large-scale air offensive, using B-1 and B-52 bombers, against the front line began and continued into early November. The air campaign, plus an increase in the number of Special Forces assisting the Northern Alliance, proved crucial to the quick collapse of the Taliban regime following the capture of Mazar-i-Sharif and then the fall of Kabul.[87]

Sometimes, Rice acted under the president's instructions. At an October 16 meeting of the NSC, Bush was concerned about the lack of cooperation between Defense and the CIA; they were, according to Woodward, "talking past each other." Bush instructed Rice to "get this mess straightened out." After the meeting, Rice took Rumsfeld aside and told him: "Don, this is now a military operation and you really have to be in charge." Rumsfeld replied that he was concerned about usurping the CIA's role in covert operations. Rice then said, "One person's got to be in charge of this, and that is you." "Got it," Rumsfeld answered.[88] Rice's deputy, Stephen Hadley, also was concerned about the lack of coordination between the CIA's covert operations and Rumsfeld's military ones. Rice told him to take his concerns to Rumsfeld, which Hadley did: "Mr. Secretary somebody needs to pick this up and design a strategy. Quite frankly, it's yours for the taking." "Then I'll take it," Rumsfeld replied.[89]

Rice's efforts also extended to the deputies' group in the immediate aftermath of September 11. She felt they were not making sufficient progress in developing plans and were too concerned about developing an ideal solution. In her view, the focus needed to be on immediate, short-term measures, especially in taking steps to prevent another attack. "Make sure the best is not the enemy of the good," she told them, "Do what you can right now to help reduce the risk to the United States. . . . Don't wait for the long studies. We'll have time enough to do studies."[90] Hadley also was concerned about the quality of their deliberations. "I don't think we're really on top of this," he told her about covert operations in Afghanistan. "At least I am not on top of it in the way I want to be. . . The deputies and I are going out to the CIA and sit down with George [Tenet] and his people."[91]

BROKERAGE AND ADVOCACY

To the extent that Woodward's account of the administration's deliberations is an accurate one, the occasions when Rice would stake out direct policy positions of her own during meetings of the principals appear infrequent. They did sometimes occur. For example, at a meeting of the principals before Bush's September 20 address to Congress, Rice and Powell argued in favor of toning down the language in the speech and giving nations who harbored terrorists the opportunity to change their ways.[92]

More often, her contributions to discussion, while in part reflecting personal concerns, broadly related to improving deliberations. On occasion, she would challenge assumptions, raise warning flags, and attempt to keep the range of options open. In one of the early meetings at Camp David, for example, she was concerned that an attack on Afghanistan might replicate the trouble the British had there in the nineteenth century or cause difficulty with Pakistan. As well, she raised the issue of launching military operations elsewhere in case efforts in Afghanistan went badly.[93] At a meeting (without the president present) on September 30, Rice emphasized the need for coalition participation: "The Aussies, the Canadians, the Germans want to help . . . . We ought to try to use them."[94]

Some of her comments related to possible consequences of policy choices that had yet to be aired. At an NSC meeting on September 24, she raised the point that an immediate and direct attack against the Taliban might unite the Afghan people. When the discussion then turned to gaining Uzbekistan's support, Rice cautioned against committing to that government's struggle with Islamic fundamentalists: "we have to make sure we know what we're buying into." At a meeting of the principals on October 8, the issue of how to deter Bin Laden from using weapons of mass destruction (WMD) came up. "They may not be deterrable," Rice said, "but we can discourage others who would support him in it and incentivize them to turn on him." At a CIA briefing of the principals on October 11, discussion focused on the Northern Alliance entering Kabul. In Rice's view, "We need a vision of Kabul. The vision of Kabul is important to avoid alienating the Pashtuns."[95]

She made efforts to incorporate humanitarian aide into deliberations that often seemed restricted to military issues. On September 27, for example, during a discussion of military strategy against the Taliban, Rice repeatedly pointed to the need for consideration of the nonmilitary consequences of the action. "We need to develop a humanitarian campaign and get in the swing next week," she told the group. Similarly, at a meeting of the principals on November 12 to discuss the impending advance on Kabul, Rice asked, "What's the humanitarian situation?"[96]

Finally, she also sought to get the principals to think beyond military victory and consider what postwar developments might look like. At an NSC meeting on October 12, Rice told the group, "Look we need not just a solution for Kabul, we also need to start thinking about the Afghan government."[97] Interestingly, her concern here came up after the president himself had raised the issue at an NSC meeting on October 4. "Who will run the country?" Bush asked. In Woodward's words, "We should have addressed that, Rice thought. Her most awful moments were when the president thought of something that the principals, particularly she, should have anticipated. No one had a real answer, but Rice was beginning to understand that that was the critical question. Where were they headed?"[98] It was an important warning sign that should have flashed again when war talk turned from Afghanistan to Iraq. Interestingly, Bush, not Rice, had initially brought it up.

BROKERAGE, PRIVATE COUNSEL, AND THE PRESIDENTIAL "FIT"

Rice also recognized the need to better link the views of the principals with the expectations of the president, especially on some occasions to slow down a bit the president's eagerness for a decision and ensuing action. On September 27, according to Woodward, "her soundings of some of the principals" indicated some "queasiness" on their part: "When the president had said he wanted a decision on Friday, tomorrow, everyone had seemed to salute, Yes, sir. But she knew there were doubts." Later she told the president, according to Woodward, that "the key on Friday is to try to figure out the way forward, not to try to make a decision." She then called Rumsfeld, warning him, "Don, I think tomorrow you need to be able to tell the president what the real timeline looks like, because I think his expectations are not in line with what you're going to be able to say. I think he will be all right with that, but it is important that he really now have a clear view of how long we are talking about."[99]

Her efforts bore fruit. Later, at the meeting, Bush told the group, "We need to reassess the timing and strategy for military operations. We may need more time."[100] As Bush later reflected, "I'm ready to go." But Rice's braking was welcomed by the president: "Sometimes that's the way I am—fiery. On the other hand, [Rice's] job is to bear the brunt of some of the fire, so that it—takes the edge off a little bit. And she's good at that. . . . I was growing a little impatient. I can be an impatient person."[101] Asked by Woodward why he backed off a bit on a more hurried time table, Bush replied, "That's the Rice influence there, you know. Who says she isn't powerful. I'm a realistic person . . ."[102]

Rice did it again once military operations in Afghanistan were underway, when she sensed that some of the other principals were concerned with the slow progress, perhaps even the wisdom of the basic strategy. She took her concerns directly to Bush. "You know, Mr. President," she told him, "the mood isn't very good among the principals and people are concerned about what's going on." There was some hand-wringing. "I want to know if you are concerned about the fact that things aren't moving," she asked, "Do you want to look at alternative strategies." In Bush's view, "It hasn't been that long." Was Rice concerned that the strategy wasn't working? She "did not really answer," according to Woodward. But she did advise him to raise the issue at the NSC meeting the next day: express confidence in the plan or raise the issue of doing something else. "I'll take care of it," Bush told her, which he did in the much reported meeting where Bush went around the table asking if all were still in agreement on the original plan.[103] For Bush, his earlier discussion with Rice was "memorable," according to Woodward, "Rice's job was to tell him things. Sometimes he liked to hear them, sometimes he didn't."[104] According to Moens, Rice "lived up to her job as guardian of the president's decision-making process."[105]

While we do not fully know the extent and content of Rice's private counsel to Bush (her substantive policy advice, per se, to him is noticeably absent from Woodward's account), there is some evidence that her role as private counselor to the president complemented her role as a broker rather than detracting from or otherwise undermining it. For example, shortly before military action began in Afghanistan, Bush privately asked her about the timing. "Would it be ready early next week?" he queried. "I really don't know," she carefully responded. She then directed the president back to the principals for an answer: "It's a question you should put before the group."[106] More generally, in Bush's own words, some of her private advice was couched in a broker manner: "That's the nature of her job . . . to help, you know, kind of say, well, Mr. President I appreciate that point of view, [but] I think you probably ought to think this way a little bit."[107]

Rice's role as NSC advisor during this period, whether as broker or beyond, is also interesting in the way it both positively fit with the president's expectations and work ways, but also compensated for some possible weaknesses. With respect to the former, as Bush himself observed, "I can be totally unscripted or unrehearsed with Condi."[108] With respect to the latter, Rice was sensitive to the president's penchant for quick action. According to Woodward, "Rice knew this characteristic. Yet doubt could be the handmaiden of sound policy. Careful reconsideration is a necessary part of any decision-making process. Rice felt it was her job to raise caution flags, even red lights if necessary, to urge the president to rethink."[109]

But it is also important to note that Rice operated during this period in tandem, facing new challenges, with a president who also was concerned about the quality of the information and advice he was receiving.[110] It was Bush himself, for example, who in the immediate days following September 11 recognized, according to Woodward, that the "war cabinet had not had sufficient time to really debate and evaluate their course of action, consider the options and plans." Meetings were too short, and the president's other duties sometimes consumed his time. Bush proposed that they retreat to

Camp David for more sustained deliberations over the weekend. Once there Bush told them, "Everything is on the table. Look at the options." Moreover, Bush emphasized, "We need to plan as if things won't go well."[111] Bush later told Woodward that he wanted to examine worst-case scenarios because

> I think my job is to stay ahead of the moment. A president . . . can get so bogged down in the moment that you're unable to be the strategic thinker that you're supposed to be, or at least provide strategic thought. And I'm the kind of person that wants to make sure that all the risk is assessed . . . a president is constantly analyzing, making decisions based upon risk, particularly in war, risk taken relative to . . . what can be achieved.[112]

Those were the president's thoughts then. But what would happen if his concerns drifted away? If achieving the goal—regime change in Iraq—clouded over proper assessment of risk? And would Rice or others either recognize the danger or be able to act if indeed there was recognition of danger on their part?

IV. A Breakdown of Brokerage? War in Iraq

While contentious debate may have been the usual order of the day among Bush's foreign policy principals in the aftermath of September 11 and in the steps that led to the war against the Taliban, the decision process that led to the war with Iraq raised the opposite concern: that a decision to go to war had been made—"slipped into"—with deliberations quickly turning to issues of "how" and "when," not "why" or "whether."

Iraq, moreover, was not some late blooming, post–September 11 target. The issue of what to do about Iraq had emerged early in the administration; the Defense Department had been at work developing new military plans, and the NSC staff was scrutinizing strategic options.[113] In the aftermath of September 11, Iraq was raised again, by Rumsfeld and, especially, his deputy Paul Wolfowitz, who favored going after Saddam Hussein immediately.[114] At later meetings, Powell clearly opposed such a move, noting the lack of evidence linking Iraq and the 9/11 attacks.[115] He was joined by CIA Director Tenet and Chief of Staff Card. Even Vice President Cheney agreed: "we would lose our rightful place as good guy." However, he did not rule out going after Saddam at some future point.[116] On September 16, Bush told Rice that "we won't do Iraq now. We're putting Iraq off. But eventually we'll have to return to that question."[117]

By November 2001, Bush had spoken—confidentially—to both Rice and Rumsfeld about Iraq as a possible next step in the war on terror. Following an NSC meeting on November 21, Bush privately met with Rumsfeld and instructed him to work in secret with Gen. Tommy Franks, head of U.S. Central Command (CENTCOM), in developing a new set of military plans.[118] Bush neglected to tell Rumsfeld that he had spoken to Rice about the matter that very morning. As for Rice, according to Woodward, "9/11 had put Iraq on the back burner. The president did not explain to her why he was returning to it now, or what triggered his orders to Rumsfeld."[119] Two years later, Bush told Woodward that he wanted to proceed secretly because a leak would lead to "enormous international angst and domestic speculation. I knew what would happen if people thought we were developing a potential or a war plan for Iraq. . . . It would look like I was anxious to go to war. And I'm not anxious to go to war. War is my absolute last option."[120] Bush wanted Rumsfeld to "show me what you have in place *in case* something were to happen. . . . I want to know what the options are. A president cannot decide and make rational decisions unless I understand the feasibility of that which may have to happen."[121] But the president also recognized that his instructions to Rumsfeld might be the first step to war: "Absolutely," Bush told Woodward.[122]

Over the next year, Rumsfeld and Franks were fast (and often contentiously) at work developing a war plan for Iraq. Accounts in Woodward's *Plan of Attack,* Franks's memoirs, *American Soldier,* and other sources not only depict the process at play within the Pentagon and at CENTCOM but also frequent briefings and vettings by the president and the principals. Yet at no point is there evidence of a thorough and sustained debate about the merits of the case against Iraq and the evidence and assumptions underlying it. According to one administration official, "There was absolutely no debate in the normal sense."[123] Tenet later wrote that "there was no serious debate that I know of within the administration about the imminence of the Iraqi threat. . . . Nor was there ever a significant discussion regarding enhanced containment or the costs and benefits of such an approach versus full-out planning for overt and covert regime change."[124] According to Woodward, Bush never even directly asked Rumsfeld whether he recommended going to war against Iraq.[125] Nor had Bush asked Powell or Cheney: "I could tell what they thought. I didn't need to ask . . ."[126] For Powell especially, Woodward notes, "in all the discussions, meetings, chats and back-and-forth, the president never once asked Powell, 'Would you do this? What's your overall advice? The bottom line?'"[127]

Bush's sense of wanting "to know what the options are," especially "rational" decision making based on understanding "the feasibility," are perhaps indicative of a president interested in a variety of "hows" (differing military options) rather than the "why" or "whether" (the case for war). Yet there is also evidence that Bush had yet to reach a final decision. For example, following a teleconferenced meeting of the war cabinet on December 28, 2001, where General Franks laid out in detail his planning to date, Bush later recalled that "we weren't ready to execute then," but it was his feeling that "Saddam's a threat. This is an option."[128]

More telling is that a year later, on December 21, 2002—when the U.N. inspection process was well underway—Bush himself felt the assumptions about Iraq's possession of WMD were less than compelling, at the very least in terms of marketing them to the public as a key part of a case for war. The occasion was a briefing by CIA Director Tenet and his deputy, John McLaughlin, of "The Case" (as Woodward labels it) for Saddam's possession of WMD. In addition to the president, Cheney, Rice, and Card attended but not the other principals. At the end of the presentation, Bush was underwhelmed: "Nice try. I don't think it is quite—it's not something that Joe Public would understand or would gain confidence from." Turning to Tenet, Bush asked, "I've been told all this intelligence about having WMD and this is the best you have got?" Tenet replied that "it's a slam dunk case!" Bush again pressed: "George, how confident are you?" Again, Tenet told him, "Don't worry, it's a slam dunk case." Bush cautioned Tenet (several times according to Woodward), "Make sure no one stretches to make our case." But the "case" itself was not put under scrutiny; rather, Bush told the group, "Needs a lot more work. Let's get some people who've actually put together a case for a jury."[129] The point apparently was to make the case more convincing rather than to question the validity of the evidence. Tenet, it should be noted, later took issue with Woodward's account of this meeting, arguing that his "slam dunk" comment related to the public presentation of the case, not to the quality of the intelligence underlying it.[130]

LIMITED BROKERAGE

Yet such questioning of evidence is at the heart of the broker role. Rice was there and heard the president's response, yet no action on her part was forthcoming. In general, unlike her concerns for the quality of the deliberative process following September 11 and in planning for war in Afghanistan, Rice's brokerage was far more limited once Iraq came to the fore. As Bush's own uncertainties suggest, opportunities for questioning occurred from time to time. But the questions and issues Rice raised seem largely within the parameters of the military options under discussion, never reaching the more fundamental issue of the merits of the case for war and the assumptions underlying it.

This is not, however, to suggest that what Rice brought up was insignificant. During preparations for the State of Union address in 2002, for example, Rice and Hadley suggested adding other countries to the "axis of evil." In their view, singling out Iraq alone, in Woodward's words, "would appear a declaration of war." But, as Woodward notes, part of the motivation here was that Rice also may have wanted to protect the secret war planning for Iraq.[131]

At a May 11, 2002, meeting of Bush and the other principals, at which General Franks once again reviewed war plans, Rice (as well as Card) raised concerns about a "Fortress Baghdad" scenario "with Saddam hunkering down and forcing ugly urban fighting." Bush then expressed his concerns about that possibility. According to Woodward, "Franks thought that the president . . . had been almost prompted to ask about it."[132] The concerns raised here led Rumsfeld later in the month to order Franks to more fully plan for that possibility. As well, "Rumsfeld through the JCS ordered planning for Phase Four stability operations in Iraq after combat operations."[133] Phase Four would serve as the template for U.S. action in a postwar Iraq. As we shall see, its vetting too proved problematic.

In October 2002, following a meeting of Bush and the military service chiefs, Rice "intensif[ied] her questions about munitions availability, supply lines, contamination protection for civilians and urban warfare."[134] In March 2003, right before the war was scheduled to begin, both Rice and Hadley raised concerns about the reliability of intelligence reports of Saddam's presence at his Dora Farms compound; however, they went along with the rest of the principals in supporting a "decapitation strike" against him.[135]

There is evidence of two clearer broker activities on Rice's part, both dealing with Powell. In early January 2003, as it became clearer to Rice that the inspection process was failing and the president was close to deciding (if not already having decided) on war, Rice told Bush that Powell needed to be informed: "Mr. President, if you're getting to a place that you really think this might happen, you need to call Colin in and talk to him." Bush did so on January 13.[136] That brokerage was needed here is especially revealing about problems in the deliberative process: not only was Powell not yet informed of where Bush stood, but the president needed to be prompted to bring him back into the loop. In fact, Prince Bandar bin Sultan, the longtime Saudi ambassador and Bush family confidante, had been personally informed by the president of his decision even before Bush's own secretary of state was told of the news.[137]

Rice's second (and earlier action) was particularly consequential. By the summer of 2002, Powell was frustrated both by his lack of a good personal relationship with the president[138] and by a decision-making process that seemed to focus only on war plans with Iraq but not the case for war itself, its consequences, or alternative ways of dealing with Saddam Hussein. He took his concerns to Rice, who arranged a private meeting with Bush (with Rice sitting in). Powell's concerns are particularly telling about problems in the deliberative process: "I really need to have some private time with him to go over issues that I don't think he's gone over with anyone yet." And it was at a two-hour meeting on August 5 that Powell pressed his case for asking for a U.N. resolution resuming inspections and strongly warned the president of the postwar consequences if Iraq was invaded: the so-called Pottery Barn rule: "You break it, you own it."[139]

Powell was successful in getting a U.N. resolution back on the table, and in early September, the war cabinet held spirited and open discussions (especially between Powell and Cheney) on its merits. According to Woodward, "Powell realized that he, the president and perhaps the rest of the world were traveling a road that would come to a fork. One fork would be a new U.N. resolution, weapons inspection and no war. The other fork would be war. It seemed almost that simple."[140]

In the end, Powell prevailed. Yet Powell missed a fork that had already been passed by: one that might have challenged the premises of the case for war and taken a different route. Nor could he anticipate that the U.N. path would prove a political and diplomatic dead end, and that the language of the resolution that the administration ultimately negotiated for and agreed to would force the United States to seek a second resolution, an effort that ultimately failed. The U.N. path was taken, but it would lead back to war, but one not waged under U.N. auspices. By March 2003 there was little ability to backtrack further—U.S. troops were now in place, the gauntlet thrown down. As Woodward observes, "For his larger, ultimate purposes of avoiding war . . . [Powell] may have done too well with the resolution."[141]

The way the debate unfolded in September 2002—unilateral U.S. intervention versus a U.N. resolution and an inspections process—may also have been constrained by the way Powell's concerns initially entered: Rice's arrangement of *private* meetings with the president. Had Powell *initially* pressed his case not privately but with the other principals present, would the case for war and other issues (such as postwar reconstruction) have been more directly joined and debated? We cannot know of course.

Other opportunities to raise critical questions and challenge assumptions were also missed. At a September 6, 2002, NSC meeting, General Franks told the group that he did not have any hard intelligence on the location of Iraqi SCUD missiles, and thus had no ability to attack or bomb specific sites. According to Woodward, it was another missed opportunity to raise the general issue of the reliability of intelligence reports, especially concerning WMD: "it could, and should, have been a warning that if the intelligence was not good enough to make bombing decisions, it probably was not good enough to make the broad assertion, in public or in formal intelligence documents, that there was 'no doubt' Saddam had WMD. If there was no doubt, then precisely where were they?"[142] There was no honest broker to ask.

A MIND MADE UP?

As for Rice, as the inspection process went on, according to Bush, "I would constantly talk to Condi." Once again, we do not know much about the private counsel she tendered, but we do know that by late December 2002, her views became firmer. Although Bush never directly asked Powell, Cheney, or Rumsfeld about whether he should go to war, he did privately ask Rice. "Yes," she replied. "To let this threat in this part of the world play volleyball with the international community this way will come back to haunt us some day. That's the reason to do it." But no further discussion or inquiry occurred, according to Woodward, "Bush didn't respond."[143]

In fact, there is some evidence that the case for war against Iraq was a closed issue for Rice much earlier. Richard Haass, director of policy planning in the State Department, recalled a meeting with Rice in the first week of July 2002 when he raised the issue of whether Iraq should be the focus of concern in the war on terrorism: "she said essentially, that the decision's been made, don't waste your breath."[144]

BROADER PROBLEMS

While Rice largely failed to act as a broker questioning the case for war, it is also important to note that sources of error may have run deep in this administration, perhaps beyond the ministrations of the NSC advisor. A number of accounts have noted a breakdown in the intelligence vetting process as a source of the faulty assumptions about Iraq's capabilities. Some believe it is attributable to raw intelligence that was "stovepiped" to Cheney and Rumsfeld, improperly vetted by the CIA.[145] Others blame CIA Director

Tenet for being over confident, too eager to be a team player, and not sufficiently protective of established vetting procedures.[146] Responsibility might also be located at the very top. As Pfiffner notes, "While President Bush made few untrue statements in his arguments for war, the real problem was his broader claims."[147] Moreover, as Pfiffner sets out, errors, faulty inferences, exaggerations, and misplaced assumptions ranged across the administration's case for war: links between Iraq and Al Qaeda; claims about Iraq's nuclear capabilities; its attempts to acquire "yellowcake" uranium ore; its efforts to purchase aluminum tubes for centrifuges used in uranium enrichment; its use of mobile weapons labs; its continued possession of chemical and biological weapons; and its presumed fleet of manned and unmanned aerial vehicles to deliver them.[148]

AN ABDICATION OF RESPONSIBILITY?

The causal chain of error is complex here. Rice was not only caught within it, but she also stood near the apex of the process as NSC advisor. Indeed, as honest broker she should have been the guardian of that process. As one former White House official observed, "Maybe the Secretary of Defense and his people are short-circuiting the process, and creating a separate channel to the Vice President. Still, at the end of the day, all the policies have to be hashed out in the interagency process, led by the national security adviser." Instead, there was "a real abdication of responsibility by Condi."[149]

Could an honest broker have realistically and practically encouraged the principals and the president to more carefully consider the assumptions underlying the case against the Iraqi regime? After all, the administration was not alone in its presuppositions. Most Western intelligence agencies, including the French and Germans, believed that Saddam possessed WMD; some, such as the British, thought the case for a nuclear weapons capability in the foreseeable if not imminent future was strong; and others had uncovered evidence of links between Al Qaeda and Baghdad (although no direct evidence of Iraqi participation in the attacks of September 11). And claims about Iraq's possession of chemical and biological weapons were clearly and widely held in the U.S. intelligence community during the Clinton years.[150]

The opportunities—or openings—for questioning were there: Bush's own "Nice try" reservations at Tenet's December 21, 2002, briefing on the "The Case" against Iraq and, earlier in September, General Franks's lack of information about SCUD sites might have been warning signs. As well, as James Fallows notes, the initial consideration of Iraq as a target in the days after September 11, Powell's August 2002 private meeting with Bush, and some of

Rumsfeld's concerns shortly before the attack on Iraq began were also points where deeper questions about the case for war might have been raised.[151]

Opportunity aside, was the evidence credibly questionable? This is a more difficult issue given shared assumptions both in the White House and abroad. Brokerage is not about grasping at imagined straws that only hindsight can reveal whether they were real or illusory. But credible warning signs, perhaps calling for brokerage, were there: Bush's own personal reaction at the Tenet briefing, the various reservations expressed by some parts of the intelligence community in the National Intelligence Estimate (NIE) issued in October 2002 (perhaps the most important prewar assessment of Iraqi weapons programs), as well as Powell's concerns about the reliability of some intelligence reports as he constructed the case for war in his speech before the United Nations on February 5, 2003.[152] In Woodward's view, moreover, "Well-placed officials in the administration were skeptical about the WMD intelligence on Iraq—among them Armitage [Powell's chief deputy at State], some senior military officials and even the CIA spokesman Bill Harlow. . . . This skepticism apparently did not make it in any convincing form to the president. The unambiguous pronouncements of the heavyweights Tenet, Cheney and Rumsfeld prevailed."[153] Armitage's concerns were apparently so strong that he initially demurred at White House efforts to get him involved in a public relations campaign to press the case against Saddam. He finally gave a speech, but at the price of no White House clearance of its contents— a near unprecedented concession (certainly for a deputy secretary of state), if Woodward's account is correct.[154]

It might have taken some digging—perhaps by a skilled broker interested in the quality of information—to accomplish the task. In the account that James Risen provides in his book *State of War,* CIA intelligence presented to the president concealed both its limitations (outdated evidence, questionable sources) and reservations about it held by analysts at lower levels in the agency: "If someone had spoken up clearly and forcefully, the entire house of cards might have collapsed. A little bit of digging might have revealed the truth."[155]

Finally, even if the heart of the administration's case for war was regime change in Iraq—the threat Saddam posed in the region and his potential aid to terrorist groups rather than WMD and nuclear capabilities per se— brokerage might have encouraged the administration to soften or qualify its public claims about what Saddam possessed or, in the case of nuclear weapons, was near to possessing. For it was those overly bellicose public claims that would later come back and haunt them.

THE URANIUM PURCHASE FIASCO

The most telling occasion where honest brokerage might have occurred but did not concerned the charge that Iraq had tried to purchase uranium "from Africa" for its nuclear weapons program and whether the administration had properly heeded CIA warnings about that claim. Initially, CIA Director Tenet took the blame for allowing the reference to the uranium purchases, based on questionable foreign intelligence, to appear in the president's 2003 State of the Union address.[156] But further investigation revealed that Tenet had personally intervened with Deputy NSC Advisor Stephen Hadley to prevent a similar reference in Bush's October 7, 2002, speech, a major address in Cincinnati on the rationale for war against Iraq.[157] Moreover, Hadley had received two memos from the CIA in October warning against claims about uranium purchases. On July 22, 2003, Hadley accepted blame for not remembering the CIA's counsel during the drafting of the State of the Union address.[158] But other sources indicate the situation might have been more complex than a simple memory lapse. Some reports suggest that the NSC staff had alerted the CIA to the reference in the State of the Union address; the CIA then warned again of the problem, and compromise language apparently was ironed out: reference to "Africa" rather than "Niger," and to British rather than U.S. intelligence as the source.[159]

The controversy directly raised questions about Rice's knowledge of a crucial part of the case for war, her management of the NSC staff, and her hands-on effectiveness as coordinator of the decision process. One of the CIA's October warnings listed her as a recipient, although she later claimed that she did not know of the CIA's concerns then. CIA concerns were also raised in the October 2002 NIE. The CIA's reservations were, according to some accounts, contained in an annex to the ninety-page report.[160] In July 2003, a senior administration official, asked if Rice had read the report replied that she may not have fully read it: "We have experts who work for the national security adviser who would know this information." As for the annex, she "did not read footnotes in a ninety-page document. . . . The national security adviser has people who do that." Nor had Hadley discussed with her the removal of the reference to uranium purchases in the October speech: "there was no need," he told reporters. As for the CIA memo listing her as a recipient, "I can't tell you she read it. I can't tell you she received it," Hadley noted.[161] It was not a good day for honest and attentive brokerage.

In June 2003, Powell and Rice labeled the charges as "revisionist history" (a phrase which Bush would also later use), with Rice noting that "successive CIA directors" in "successive administrations" had drawn the same conclusions as had Bush's foreign policy team.[162] However, the issue raised the question whether the administration had based its decision to go to war on faulty evidence or had overexaggerated or otherwise misinterpreted the evidence it did have.[163] By early July 2003, the White House publicly acknowledged that it should not have included the claim about uranium purchases in Bush's State of the Union address.[164] In the view of Sen. Pat Roberts (R-KS), chairman of the Senate Intelligence Committee, the error indicated that "the process was broken" and was a sign of "sloppy coordination between State and CIA and the NSC and the White House."[165] The President's Foreign Intelligence Advisory Board, following a study requested by President Bush, was also reportedly critical of how the claims and evidence about uranium purchases were evaluated. The board, chaired by former NSC Advisor Brent Scowcroft, reportedly briefed Bush in early December 2003, and, according to one report, raised concerns that "there was no organized system at the White House to vet intelligence, and the informal system that was followed did not work in the case [of Bush's State of the Union address]."[166]

The issue especially raised questions about Rice's role as advisor and broker. As she noted on July 11, 2003, "if there were doubts about the underlying intelligence in the NIE, those doubts were not communicated to the president . . . if there was a concern about the underlying intelligence there [in the NIE], the president was unaware of that concern, *as was I.*"[167] As Pfiffner observes, however, "If, as Rice said, no one communicated any of these reservations about something as crucial as nuclear weapons in Iraq to the president, the president was not being well served."[168] Not only was there a failure of brokerage, there was a failure to acquire the basic information about issues and problems that would set brokerage in motion. At a minimum the weakness in the case for uranium purchases should have served as a red warning flag.

More general criticism of the administration's case for the war in Iraq also emerged as no WMD were discovered. On July 24, 2003, former CIA Director John Deutch, in testimony before the House Permanent Select Committee on Intelligence, said that the failure to find WMD in Iraq would signify "an intelligence failure . . . of massive proportions." It would mean that the "leaders of the American public based support for the most serious foreign policy judgments—the decision to go to war—on an incorrect intelligence judgment."[169] In late September 2003, the House Intelligence Committee issued an interim report, based on four months of study, in which it took the administration to task for building its case against Iraq on evidence that was "circumstantial," "fragmentary," overly reliant on "past assessments" dating before 1998, with only some new "piecemeal" evidence, all of which was "not challenged as a routine matter."[170] Administration officials, however, immediately disputed the claims; according to Rice, "there was an enrichment of the intelligence from 1998 over the period leading up to the war."[171]

V. An Absence of Brokerage? Postwar Reconstruction

If the decision to go to war against Iraq erred in its assumptions about WMD and nuclear capabilities, deliberations about and preparations for the postwar reconstruction of the country may have been more deeply flawed, and Rice's role as broker even more attenuated. As James Fallows observes, "Exactly what went wrong with the occupation will be studied for years—or should be. The missteps of the first half year in Iraq are as significant as other classic and carefully examined failures in foreign policy, including John Kennedy's handling of the Bay of Pigs invasion, in 1961, and Lyndon Johnson's decision to escalate U.S. involvement in Vietnam, in 1965."[172] In the view of Michael E. O'Hanlon—a senior specialist at the Brookings Institution on military issues—"The post-invasion phase of the Iraq mission has been the least well-planned American military mission since Somalia in 1993, if not Lebanon in 1983, and its consequences have been far worse than any military set of mistakes since Vietnam."[173]

As Woodward notes, President Bush "wanted an outcome—Saddam out and the weapons of mass destruction eliminated."[174] And, in a sense, Bush got what he wanted: Saddam was out, and, ironically, WMD were not a problem because there were no weapons found. What Bush and his top advisers did not anticipate was the internal strife in Iraq in the postwar period and the difficulties that reconstruction would bring. Regime change occurred, but the new regime was not the one they had anticipated or planned for.

OPTIMISM AND INATTENTION

Some of the difficulties that developed arose from the differing bureaucratic cultures and ensuing competition between Defense and State. Other explanations point to tension between the civilians at Defense and military planners whose efforts were "innovative and solid for the invasion phase of the war yet negligently incomplete for the aftermath,"[175] Perhaps these divisions and the problems that issued from them were so deeply embedded as to be beyond the reach of the brokerage of the NSC advisor.

Yet plans for reconstruction were routinely brought before the principals, beginning in late December 2001.[176] In May 2002, Rumsfeld formally ordered planning for what became "Phase Four" of the military's plans: stabilization operations after major combat had ended.[177] These plans evolved over time, yet Woodward's reconstruction of the principals' deliberations reveal limited probing and questioning; attention focused on combat operations. At a crucial August 5, 2002, meeting, where General Franks presented his new "hybrid plan," Phase Four simply stated "stability operations of unknown duration." Toward the end of the meeting, discussion finally turned to the postcombat, occupation phase. The emphasis was on the number of troops needed, not the broader issues of what occupation of Iraq might entail.[178] As Franks recalls in his memoirs, the final chart on Phase Four "was the most important." Rumsfeld emphasized that "we will want to get Iraqis in charge of Iraq as soon as possible." "Heads nodded around the table." Franks made some more brief comments, heads again nodding, "And then Condi Rice tapped her watch; we were out of time."[179]

The date of August 5 is also notable, for later that evening Powell's private discussion with the president in which he warned about the dangers of occupying Iraq took place. Bush later told Woodward that he understood Powell's message that he would own Iraq, and that "we better have a strong understanding about what it's going to take to rebuild Iraq." In Woodward's view, "as I listened I glimpsed what Powell had apparently seen—uncertainty that the president fully grasped the potential consequences."[180] But Powell's concerns notwithstanding, optimism prevailed. On January 10, 2003 (a date close to the point at which the president had decided on war or was near to deciding), Bush and Cheney met with a group of Iraqi dissidents. Cheney saw the need for just a "light hand" in the postwar period; there was no discussion that an insurgency might erupt or that reconstruction might be more difficult.[181] On January 15, Bush met with the war cabinet: postwar Iraq was on the agenda, but it was mainly a discussion about food relief and other humanitarian efforts.[182]

UNHEEDED WARNINGS, BUREAUCRATIC POLITICS

Warnings of how difficult the situation in postwar Iraq might prove to be went unheeded. A January 2003 study by the National Intelligence Council (an advisory body to the director of the CIA) indicated that reconstruction might be difficult and opposition might develop ("a long, difficult and probably turbulent process").[183] The CIA's findings were briefed at an NSC meeting in February 2003.[184] According to O'Hanlon, a February 2003 study by the Army War College "underscored the importance not only of providing security but also of taking full advantage of the first few months of the post-Saddam period when Iraqi goodwill would be at its greatest."[185] The report itself warned that "suspicion of U.S. motives will increase as occupation continues," and "liberators can rapidly be relegated to the status of invaders should an unwelcome occupation continue for a prolonged time." Occupation problems would be "especially acute" if the U.S. bore the bulk of the burden rather than an international force.[186] Some Iraqi dissidents who had met with administration officials also warned of possible disorder in the postwar period.[187] In early 2003, former Joint Chiefs Chairman Gen. Hugh Shelton, at a Pentagon meeting, voiced concerns about an insufficient number of troops; similar concerns were raised by Gen. Eric Shinseki, then the Army Chief of Staff, in testimony before the Senate Armed Services Committee.[188]

Even Hadley, Rice's deputy, had concerns. Since November 2002, the NSC deputies' committee, which he chaired, had undertaken some oversight of postwar planning. In Hadley's view, Franks's "stability operations" needed further definition. The goal was democracy not just pacification.[189] Hadley's concerns, however, did not resonate upward.

Especially important was the State Department's "Future of Iraq" project, which had been at work since October 2001 and had produced thirteen volumes of reports and recommendations from a variety of experts.[190] Powell sent the study to Rumsfeld, along with the names of seventy-five State Department experts who might be involved in postwar operations.[191]

The response is a stunning example of bureaucratic friction at work. Thomas Warrick, who supervised the study, and Meghan O'Sullivan, a sanctions expert, were sent over to Defense to coordinate and work with the Office of Reconstruction and Humanitarian Assistance (ORHA), the unit that retired Lt. Gen. Jay Garner and then Paul Bremer eventually headed (and which later became the Coalition Provisional Authority). Although Garner wanted the pair, Rumsfeld reportedly kicked them out of the Pentagon, "ordering them to leave by sundown." The White House was forced to intervene, allowing O'Sullivan back in but not Warrick.[192] In Rumsfeld's view, State could not be trusted. According to Woodward, Rumsfeld felt that reconstruction should be done by those committed to the effort, not those "who have written or said things that were not supportive." It took another week to resolve the status of another seven; five were eventually allowed to participate in ORHA.[193] According to several reports, Garner was told to simply ignore the "Future of Iraq" project.[194]

A FAILURE OF EFFORT AND OVERSIGHT?

Starting in January 2003, much of the nonmilitary, postwar planning fell to the Defense Department, especially its Office of Special Plans—a unit created in 2002 by Douglas Feith, Rumsfeld's deputy for policy.[195] Feith successfully pressed the case for putting postwar planning *and* implementation under the control of Defense.[196] Although State had taken the lead in the postwar reconstruction of Afghanistan,[197] Powell raised no objections to the proposal, and it soon led to the establishment of ORHA (under the authority of the Defense Department) on January 22, 2003, by presidential directive.

In his memoir, *War and Decision,* Feith denies he was given direct authority over postwar planning—that remained General Franks's and CENTCOM's job—he was there to advise and provide analysis. Yet, Feith played a central role in devising ORHA and in developing postwar plans.[198] Planning was problematic, whether at Defense or CENTCOM. In the view of Thomas White, secretary of the army until April 2003 when he was fired, "You got the impression in this exercise that we didn't harness the best and brightest minds in a concerted effort." The issue for the Defense Department was "'we've got to control this thing'—so everyone else was suspect." Feith's group "had the mind-set that this would be a relatively straightforward, manageable task, because this would be a war of liberation and therefore reconstruction would be short-lived."[199] On February 21 and 22, 2003—less than a month before the onset of the war—some 200 officials gathered for a "rock drill" of the plans made so far. "Plans for running the country's ministries were rudimentary; ORHA had done little research," according to one account, "The drill struck some participants as ominous." In the view of one ORHA member, "I got the sense that the humanitarian stuff [Garner's specialty] was pretty well in place, but the rest of it was flying blind."[200]

But Feith's efforts—whether just advice or more authoritative—made their way upwards, and thus before Rice among others, largely without challenge. He made Power Point briefings on reconstruction and a proposed structure for Iraq's postwar government at an early March meeting of the principals and a few days later before the full the NSC with Bush presiding, just weeks before the war began. According to Woodward, "Feith displayed his organizational charts. It was a lot of abstract political science." According to Feith it was a full debate of the pros and cons.[201] Feith also presented plans for dismantling the Iraqi intelligence service, the Special Republican Guards, and the Fedayeen Saddam special militia. The regular Iraqi army might remain intact and be used "as a reconstruction force." Yet, according to Woodward, "What they didn't plan for was the possibility that hundreds of thousands of soldiers would just go home, that the workforce to rebuild the country would just melt away."[202] According to O'Hanlon, they "assumed that much of the regular Iraqi army would survive and be available to play a large role in keeping postwar order." Basic tasks, moreover, such as "policing the streets, guarding huge weapons depots, protecting key infrastructure, maintaining public order were simply not planned for." "Such planning as there was," conducted out of Feith's office, "was reportedly unfocused, shallow, and too dependent on optimistic scenarios."[203]

Where Was Rice?

Although Rice did not see her role in the Iraq war and its aftermath as "operational," she and the other principals had been briefed about and then signed off on postwar plans, however unfocused, shallow, or optimistic.[204] Rice's own NSC military aides had prepared a report for her in early 2003 titled "Force Security in Seven Recent Stability Operations." While each situation was unique, they noted, if Iraq was like Kosovo, 480,000 peacekeepers would be needed; if like Bosnia, 364,000; but if like Afghanistan, only 13,900.[205]

Perhaps Rice was comfortable with the assessments the military presented to the president on the troop force needed. Or perhaps she felt comfortable that the issue had been appropriately dealt with. As she later acknowledged in an interview, the *president* did press on the issue: "I can't tell you how many times he asked, 'Do you have everything that you need?' The answer was, these are the force levels we need." Yet, according to one account, senior military officials later acknowledged that while they did not push for more troops, "some said they would have been more comfortable with a larger reserve."[206] Could brokerage on her part have tipped the balance, especially in creating an opening for a more critical analysis of Rumsfeld's belief in a leaner troop commitment?[207] Could it have led to a better recognition of the difficulties to be encountered in an occupied Iraq, not the rosy scenarios being presented?[208]

Not only was Rice a participant at top-level meetings where reconstruction was raised and aware of the troop-level projections from her own aides, she and the NSC staff also had a hand in the reconstruction process. While not *directly* "operational," she was involved in operations nonetheless. An NSC Executive Steering Group had been created in August 2002 by Rice and Hadley to oversee and coordinate reconstruction efforts, and it was headed by Frank Miller. Yet Miller's experience signaled trouble—information and analysis was not moving forward. Not only was cooperation between Defense and the NSC staff problematic, but the civilian and military sides of the Pentagon were not communicating well. Miller was forced to convene an informal meeting each week with Card, Rice, Hadley, and I. Lewis ("Scooter") Libby, the vice president's chief of staff, to try to work out problems.[209] Perhaps the best summary of the latter is General Franks's earthy characterization of Feith: "the f**king stupidest guy on the face of the earth."[210]

Rice also appears to have played a passive role in the decision to abandon the plan to use the remnants of the Iraqi regular army as a peacekeeping force, a move that Garner viewed as a mistake and Franks as a "miscalculation." The decision was announced by Bremer on May 23, shortly after he took over in Baghdad. According to one account, "The role of top Bush administration officials in approving the plan is unclear." Some sources indicate extensive consultations between Bremer and senior officials in the Defense Department. Another source, Lawrence Di Rita, Rumsfeld's press spokesman, indicated it was not taken up by cabinet-level officials, including Rumsfeld. According to Rice, although the White House had no objections, the idea did not come from the NSC: "the whole structure had been set up so that some of those decisions could be made in the field or through the Pentagon chain."[211] It was a critical decision with enormous consequences, someone had made it, but the buck stopped elsewhere.[212]

A later incident is particularly revealing about Rice's role as NSC advisor and her difficulties in coordination and oversight. In August 2003, while at the president's Texas ranch, Bush and Rice decided to exert greater White House control over the occupation of Iraq.[213] In October, Rice was placed in charge of a new "Iraq Stabilization Group," designed to put that into effect. That the new group was needed is telling in its own right, particularly about perceptions of the effectiveness of the Defense Department's efforts in Iraq. But its public announcement as a "major restructuring" (by "a senior administration official" quoted in the *New York Times*—likely Rice) also led to some testiness on Rumsfeld's part. According to reports, Rumsfeld had only recently learned of the new group via a memo sent from Rice. Pressed by reporters, he seemed to indicate that not much was new here: such coordination was "what the responsibility of the NSC is and always has been, which is what's been going on." Pressed further, Rumsfeld told them he had "no idea" why the new arrangement was needed and to ask Rice why the changes were necessary.

Not only were Rumsfeld's responses to press queries a bit testy, the incident also raised the issue of the extent to which Rumsfeld had been involved in the decision to create the new group. Rumsfeld's own comments seem to indicate that he had learned of it only from Rice's one-page memo. White

House press secretary Scott McClellan later told reporters that Rumsfeld had been "very involved" in the change, a statement he seemed to retract a few days later when he told the press, "Maybe I should not have characterized it that way."[214] Other White House aides indicated that the creation of the new group had been discussed by members of the NSC, including Rumsfeld, as recently as the week before; Feith, however, disputes this account.[215] Whatever the level of Rumsfeld's knowledge of and participation in the creation of the new group, Rice's and the NSC's mandate had clearly been expanded. Whether she and the NSC staff would be able to assert control over the process and achieve better coordination and compliance remained the open questions.[216] By that point, the horses were already out of the barn: decisions made and actions taken regarding reconstruction would be difficult to undo or alter.

In sum, as Garner, the first head of ORHA, later reflected, few "had their head in the postwar game. The Bush administration did not. Condi Rice did not. Doug Feith didn't. You could go brief them, but you never saw any initiative come out of them. You just kind of got a north and south nod. And so it ends with so many tragic things."[217] According to Tenet, "The president was not served well, because the NSC became too deferential to a postwar strategy that was not working . . . the NSC did not fulfill its role. The NSC avoided slamming on the brakes to force the discussions with the Pentagon and everyone else that was required in the face of a deteriorating situation."[218]

VI. Implications

Condoleezza Rice's tenure in the post is of interest on a number of fronts concerning the possibility of an NSC advisor serving as an honest broker, yet adding to that some of the additional duties of her recent predecessors. She was smart, talented, and experienced. She served as counselor to a presidential candidate largely unfamiliar with the details of foreign policy, and she had her own take on a range of policy matters. At least initially, she recognized the importance of the honest broker role yet, like many of her recent predecessors, also moved beyond it. Most notable, she was a source of private advice to Bush and an effective public spokesperson for the administration. Yet why did brokerage fail when it seemed most needed: the decision to go to war against Iraq and the planning for that nation's postwar stabilization, reconstruction, and democratization? The answer is not easy here, and a number of explanations are plausible.

THE NSC ADVISOR'S ROLE EXPECTATIONS AND HONEST BROKERAGE

Rice came to the job under the prior tutelage of Brent Scowcroft. This would suggest a first-hand experience with honest brokerage but in the context of balancing that off against the other components of an NSC advisor's job, which Scowcroft generally managed effectively. At least publicly, she embraced the value of the honest broker role. Alex George—the academic "father" in many ways of the role—was her colleague at Stanford, with an office only three doors down. According to one fellow faculty member, "they talked often about their respective work."[219]

Once in office, she operated among a group of principals with long experience and what seemed at the time a diverse range of views. The private counsel she provided the president was undertaken discreetly. Its details still remain largely unknown. She was no Kissinger or Brzezinski aggressively pushing her views among the other principals. She gained initial control of the interagency process and chaired meetings in the president's absence, despite Cheney's efforts to do so. Early reports seemed to indicate that she coordinated with an effective hand.

But there were early warning signs. One organizational choice, made at the start of the administration, was that Rice and the NSC staff would stay "out of what she termed 'operational matters.'"[220] Here the concern was that the NSC needed more strategic focus, not replication of the efforts of other departments and agencies. As Hadley noted in a pre–September 11 interview, "There are a lot of things we don't do at the NSC staff because leaving them in the hands of a government agency is perfectly fine. We don't try and reproduce the State Department or the Defense Department. We try to get out of the way to let them handle the things they do. We don't want to reproduce the stovepipes that appear across the government."[221] It was a division of labor that seemed to make sense in the early days of the Bush presidency, but in the wake of 9/11 and an unforeseen war on terror, did it leave Rice and her staff ill-equipped and out-gunned to perform a coordinating role when it was most needed?

EVOLUTION OF THE NSC ADVISOR'S ROLE OVER TIME

Evolution—or perhaps more correctly devolution—in Rice's role as NSC advisor is one of the most interesting facets of this case study. Brokerage on her part failed in the end. In fact, it was a failure in the most consequential of presidential decisions: whether to go to war against another nation. One possibility is that the ebb and flow of Rice's role as an honest broker is attributable to other aspects of her job as NSC advisor. Policy advocacy, public visibility, and involvement in policy implementation and politics are generally thought to weaken brokerage. Yet for Rice, the effects on brokerage of these other components of the job do not seem the source of the problem.

In Rice's case, a number of these other tasks she undertook do not generally appear to be the source of her difficulties in fulfilling the broker role. At the most general level, brokerage appears to have declined over time as the administration moved from its immediate post-9/11 deliberations to its later decisions on war with Iraq and then its reconstruction. Yet this decline is not matched by any appreciable increase in other tasks that might have undermined brokerage.

But what was problematic were efforts to exercise legitimate monitoring and oversight over the implementation efforts of others. These tasks *do fit* with the broker role. In the case of the planning for and execution of the postwar reconstruction of Iraq, the impact of Rice's and the NSC staff's efforts were problematic at best, incompetent at worst. The creation of the NSC's Iraq Stabilization Group in October 2003 was particularly a case of too little, too late.

While, as I have argued, brokerage can fit with a number of different advisory arrangements and structures, particular patterns of decision-making organization and management practices can have both positive and negative effect. This is true at the presidential level, but what this case study also illustrates is that it is true for the NSC advisor. In Rice's case, there was a heavy reliance on delegating the unfamiliar to others. As one account notes, Rice "created a hierarchical, corporate style in which she delegated policy development to others . . . preserv[ing] time to concentrate on issues more familiar to her, to tutor Mr. Bush and to translate his instincts and decisions into policy."[222]

This arrangement is not per se problematic, but it can lead to problems if those to whom much is delegated fail at their tasks—as was the case, for example, in claims about Iraq's African uranium purchases. The interagency coordination process—heavily dependent on the work of the deputies' group—also was problematic at times (the "dysfunctional" comments noted above).[223]

The organizational choice made at the start of the administration not to replicate the efforts of State or Defense also was consequential. Through the first eight months of the new administration, this seemed benign, if not wise. But in the aftermath of September 11, particularly in the deliberations leading up to war with Iraq and its subsequent reconstruction, did it leave the NSC staff ill-equipped to perform its role effectively, lacking its own "stovepipes" (recall that Cheney and Rumsfeld had them) that might have better questioned intelligence? Did it leave Rice and her staff too prone to "get out of the way" as Hadley himself phrased it? Did it overly empower some of the principals—Cheney and Rumsfeld in particular—and make effective coordination and brokerage on Rice's part even more difficult?

Related to this is the issue of whether Rice lacked some of the knowledge or skill to challenge assumptions and preconceptions. And if greater skill and knowledge were present, would Powell have found an ally that might have created a more level playing field and allowed him to more forcefully and effectively present his reservations? As Moens notes, "it became more difficult for people in the State Department's intelligence branch to argue caution about intelligence analysis." This not only "took the critical edge off the debate," but it created "an atmosphere in which Bush and his advisers began to bolster their arguments about what Saddam Hussein allegedly possessed." In addition, "It may also have created a mild climate of 'groupthink' in which critical thinking is suppressed for fear of upsetting the predominant view. Had there been tougher debate on the intelligence, the president's comments could have remained more 'hedged,' which in turn would have insulated him somewhat from the harsh public criticism when no weapons were found in 2003."[224]

The dynamic among the principals has also been noted as problematic, and Rice may have operated (or have been forced to operate) with too light a hand. If basic organization and management were problematic at times, the far more difficult task of brokerage among this particular group of principals was likely to be more even more challenging. As Bumiller notes, "Armitage and Powell had come to the view that Rice was more of an enabler for Bush's combative instincts and not enough of a counterweight."[225]

Presidential Decision-Making Needs, Presidential Role Expectations

The problematic issue of the NSC advisor's "fit" with presidential needs and expectations comes before us again. It is clear that Rice matched well with Bush's preferences. At the start of this presidency that seemed favorable. Bush, looking back at his father's administration, wanted an honest broker—both he and Rice spoke about honest brokerage at the time her appointment was announced. Initial assessments once she was NSC advisor were also favorable. "Ms Rice herself insisted that she saw her role as ensuring that the president received a broad range of advice and options, not taking sides or shutting off debate," one account noted.[226] According to then Treasury Secretary O' Neill, "She will know when we are not going to agree. She'll say 'Let's sharpen the debate, put it on paper, and let the boss decide.'"[227] "That's the way the president wants it," according to another account, "Bush is suspicious of bureaucracy and does not want to be fed decisions that have been pre-cooked, watered down or papered over by his advisers." Rice's job "is to sharpen arguments, not squelch them or flatten them out."[228] In Karen Hughes's view, "The president insists on this, prodding and asking questions of his team until he is confident that he has considered the widest range of debate, the broadest possible information, the most thoughtful analysis."[229]

Rice initially seems to have embraced the role these accounts suggest. She even acted as a brake on the president in the period right after 9/11, as we saw. Yet when attention turned to Iraq, her perceptions of what Bush wanted from his NSC advisor seem to change. Brokerage certainly waned—"it's a done deal" prevailed. Something more than just a fit with what the president wanted was needed.

In the end, the burden was on President Bush. Did he meet the test? As we have seen, some of the principals—such as Powell—wondered whether he understood the full implications of his policy choices. He was surely confident as a decision maker. As we have seen, there were occasions when he raised issues about the deliberative process, the options before him, and the assumptions underlying them. Yet, Bush was highly dependent on the advice he received from others, especially in foreign and national security affairs.[230] When they failed, he failed.

At the same time, as Tenet's "slam dunk case" response indicates, some were too eager to reassure him. But here too we also find a presidential task: why are some self-assured in the midst of presidential doubts? It is also the president's responsibility to set the tone among the principals and to facilitate a process that will yield sound policy advice.

Nor was this president, who was normally so insistent on staff discipline and internal order, able to achieve it among some of his top principals. In the view of one former *Republican* cabinet secretary, "In a situation where there are Cabinet-level divisions, something's got to give. That's where I fault the president."[231] In the end, moreover, it was Bush himself who was lulled into the false assessments and rosy scenarios of some, but he failed to grasp the perils realized by others. Thus, some problems may be less Rice's fault than the president's. Indeed, as we have seen in a number of administrations so far, ensuring effective brokerage is a presidential responsibility, not just one for the NSC advisor to undertake. That is perhaps the most important point of all.

Conclusions

The role of the NSC advisor has evolved significantly since the Eisenhower years, a period of time when being a "neutral broker" occupied center space in how Robert Cutler and his two successors defined their jobs. Policy advocacy and increasing public visibility—and sometimes diplomatic efforts and political involvement—are components of the job for many recent NSC advisors. One might well argue that the role of the NSC advisor is now simply to serve as the principal foreign and national security adviser to the president—stop, print. The particulars are just a matter of presidential predilection or whatever the NSC advisor happens to bring to the deliberative table. He or she is simply one of a number of actors in an ever evolving policy process.

Yet the argument of this book suggests that this perspective is plainly wrong. It fails to factor in the full significance and impact of the NSC advisor on the decision making of a president. And it fails to take into account how deliberative processes might be consequential in the selection of better—or, of course, worse—policy choices. Honest brokerage thus matters, but the nature of that role must be squared with the increasingly complexity of national security policy in the post-Eisenhower years and the expanding responsibilities of the NSC advisor. How to resolve the conundrum?

I. Why the Role of NSC Advisor Matters

With respect to the relevance of taking seriously the role of the NSC advisor in presidential decision making, the argument is straight forward. These case studies of the role of the national security advisor suggest that the impact of the NSC advisor on presidential deliberations has been significant. To put it simply, role matters. It is surely not the sole determinative factor. As noted in the introduction, a range of factors has causal impact on the process of policy choice: the organization of the decision process, the expertise and experience brought to the table by the other principals, the dynamic of interpersonal relationships, and of course the knowledge, skills, and vision of the president. But it is in the activities of the NSC advisor that the various pieces and parties generally come together, for better or worse.

Part of that impact is organizational. NSC advisors often play a crucial role in how the decision-making process is organized, most especially with regard to the NSC staff and interagency venues. Cutler's efforts in almost single-handedly creating the Eisenhower-era system were notable, as were Bundy's efforts to disband them and then struggle to find an effective substitute. Kissinger created a committee structure that he came to dominate. The "Scowcroft model" was a balanced solution that asserted White House control but with due respect for departmental participation and input. Poindexter's time as NSC advisor provides warnings when formal processes are ignored and subterfuge is substituted; Rice's when the interagency process proves ineffective.

NSC advisors are also part of the deliberative process. They serve as coordinators of the process and as participants; sometimes they serve as facilitators, other times as gatekeepers of the information and advice reaching the principals. They have a crucial role in setting the tone of the interpersonal relationship among the principals—sometimes for better, sometimes for worse. Their proximity to the Oval Office makes them a daily barometer of presidential inclination, intention, and policy will.

More importantly, these case studies indicate that *how* that role is defined can have significant impact on the quality of national security decision making. Here, the emphasis on the honest broker role becomes important given its attention to the question of how the various parts of the decision process operate in contributing to effective decision making. The aim is not to simply match, as some analyses have emphasized, presidential expectations or "fit"—that is not unimportant as I note below. Rather, it is a broader concern that seems to matter most: attention to the character of the decision process itself. How that process operates and is organized can be consequential. Concern for organizational matters was an ever present priority for Cutler and Gray during the Eisenhower years, so too with Carlucci and Powell in the aftermath of Iran-Contra, and for Scowcroft during the George H. W. Bush years. It would even dawn on Bundy that there was much value in the organized work ways of the Eisenhower years, and organizational problems were frequent issues he brought to Kennedy's attention, albeit with mixed results.

Brokerage becomes especially important in the NSC advisor's role as a participant in policy debate and deliberation. Where brokerage is largely absent and where the national security advisor acts as the dominant source of advice to the president, the risks for error are great, especially as exclusion of other voices and views comes about. Even NSC advisors as skilled and knowledgeable as Kissinger encountered problems as other channels for advice were shut out. Direct involvement in policy implementation can be problematic, whether Kissinger's secret diplomatic missions or Poindexter's sub rosa efforts in Iran-Contra. Too much public visibility has its costs in its negative effects on good relations with the other principals and their sense of trust and cooperation. Likewise, too much partisan involvement can weaken the NSC advisor's stance as an objective source of policy advice.

By contrast, the presence of honest brokerage facilitates an informed and balanced deliberative process. The Eisenhower-era advisors provide early evidence of this. Lessons to be drawn from their tenure are important in terms of facilitating a fair and representative consideration of policy views. But a simple return to the practices of that era is likely ill-advised, given that they did not give voice to their own policy views. Among contemporary NSC advisors, where the demands of the job have expanded especially in the area of private counsel to the president, Scowcroft's two stints in the position indicate that "brokerage plus" can work. So, too, do the efforts of Carlucci and Powell in wake of Iran-Contra. Rice's early experiences also suggest its positive merits, although her later role in the Iraq war deliberations provides evidence of what happens as brokerage wanes.

II. Is the Broker Role Outdated?

Although the merits of the broker role appear strong, has the job of the NSC advisor changed so markedly since the Eisenhower years that a broker role is now outdated or largely inapplicable? As Bert Rockman observes, "The variability of presidents notwithstanding, the overall thrust since Eisenhower seems fairly clear: more White House centrism in foreign policy making, and an enlarged NSC role. . . . While the water has both risen and receded, the watermark is a good bit higher now than it was then." Presidents, in Rockman's view, "find their political and policy needs better served from within the White House. From this vantage point, the departments sooner or later are perceived as representing interests that are not those of the president." Nor, according to Rockman, can the secretary of state serve as both foreign minister and chief policy advocate: "To be both, foreign minister (representing departmental perspectives) and leading foreign policy maker has within it increasingly the seeds of an insoluble role conflict."[1]

The presence of oft-distrusted bureaucratic interests and the institutional forces at work that drive toward a White House-centered policy process clearly are powerful.[2] Moreover, they do seem to set expectations and demands on the role of the NSC advisor that are different from those of the Eisenhower era. The nature of foreign and national security policy problems has grown more complex and requires crosscutting inputs from a variety of agency and departments. As Anthony Lake explains,

> There are systemic reasons why it is almost inevitable that there will be increasing emphasis on the national security advisor . . . getting more involved . . . the fact is that in a world in which practically every issue now has an economic, military, political, diplomatic, etc., dimension, it is very hard for any cabinet officer to have the absolute lead on that issue. This is so because the other cabinet officers increasingly have equity on those issues and they are simply not going to follow that lead. So it has to be coordinated and it has to be led from the White House, and while presidents can do that in making general decisions, it can only be done on a day-to-day basis out of the NSC staff.[3]

A State Department-centered system under a John Foster Dulles would likely prove a poor fit for the realities of policy today. Nor would the type of brokerage of a Robert Cutler or a Gordon Gray, eschewing substantive counsel, serve to bring the policy pieces satisfactorily together for a contemporary president. But that said, brokerage remains relevant: a fair representation of views is needed and the quality of the decision-making process matters. The trick is to square it with the more recent demands on the NSC advisor's role.

While the "watermark" for the role is now higher, it also has "risen and receded" from one presidency to another, even within the tenure of a particular administration (Reagan most notably).[4] The Kissinger model did not set the job in cement for his successors. Not only has the influence of NSC advisors varied, but the ways their roles are defined have been noticeably different.

The presence of bureaucratic forces that can drive the positions of participants who come from departments and agencies is arguably strong: "Where you stand depends upon where you sit."[5] And for many presidents, in search of presidential rather than bureaucratic governance, this might lead to an activist and advocacy-laden role for the NSC advisor, or so conventional wisdom would have us believe. At the same time, it might also be the case that a departmental position is the right one. It may not always be true, as Charles Dawes once put it, that cabinet members "are the president's natural enemies."[6] Some are the president's men (and women), allegiant to the president's agenda and at battle with bureaucratic forces. One advantage of brokerage is that it provides a test for substantive merits, whether from a White House or departmental source.

Indeed, the experience of the Eisenhower administration remains notable on this general issue. Its national security process sought to ensure that departmental positions and concerns were appropriately brought to bear. As Greenstein and Immerman observe, the Eisenhower NSC system was "unlike that of a number of later presidencies in that it made full use of the expertise of the departments and agencies represented in the NSC."[7] But it was also a process—including the role of the NSC advisor—that counterbalanced the negative effects of bureaucratic politics and tested for substantive merits. It also was an arrangement that dampened conflict and avoided centralization of policy making in a powerful NSC advisor: "There was a general absence of the public and semipublic feuds and cleavages that have marked a number of later presidencies, as well as the tension that existed in many later presidencies between the secretary of state and the national security adviser."[8] According to Carnes Lord, "Strikingly, the NSC role was virtually invisible during the Eisenhower years in spite of the high level of activity associated with the Council itself and the interagency structure supporting it."[9] Note also, in a more contemporary context, how the case study of the George H. W. Bush national security process—where Scowcroft's role as honest broker was high—indicated less bureaucratic infighting compared to its Reagan predecessor even though the principals were skilled, experienced, and had well-developed policy views.

A final point: if honest brokerage contributes to effective decision making, the NSC advisor is the best participant to undertake that role. Perceptions of bureaucratic interests are fewer. And effective brokerage may dampen feelings of exclusion and mistrust.

III. EXPANDING AND RECONSTRUCTING THE BROKER ROLE

Perhaps the strongest argument against the broker being outdated is the possibility that it can serve as the *foundation* for the NSC advisor's role but with *some* modification to take into account the added tasks of more contemporary NSC advisors. Brokerage need not be restricted to the particular practices of Cutler, Anderson, and Gray in the Eisenhower years as long as the chief activities of being an honest broker remain. Can the NSC advisor take on other tasks and responsibilities, such as policy advocacy or serving as a public spokesperson for the administration, without significant compromise to the broker role?

As I noted in the introductory chapter, Alexander George is not supportive on this score: the managerial custodian's job should not be expanded to include advocating policy, serving as a public spokesman, guarding political interests, or implementing decisions.[10] But George seems too restrictive, especially given how the NSC advisor's role has evolved over time. Instead, a different approach is needed, as I have argued: let us acknowledge the strengths, advantages, and contributions of the broker role as a kind of foundation to the job of NSC advisor, but then let us explore whether and to what degree these additional tasks and expectations can be added to it.[11] That approach, I should note, may have some merit not just given the previous discussion of the positive benefits of the broker role, but it also comports with how some NSC advisors have reflected about the job they once occupied. According to Anthony Lake, while he increasingly expressed his own policy views, "I tried at the same time to absolutely be an honest broker, because if that doesn't happen the whole system collapses. I am positive I never blocked any information or access by anybody else."[12]

Destler advances another important argument by pointing out that additional roles might bolster the NSC advisor's primary management and broker role: "It seems unlikely that [the NSC advisor] can be effective in managing the process of presidential choice—of insuring the broadest canvassing of possibilities and the most fruitful analysis and debate of these possibilities—if that is the only role he has." He (or she) needs additional duties to "establish his value to the president" and "give him a sufficient feel" of the president's mind: "Such roles should be chosen with an eye to reinforcing his presidential relationship while limiting the danger properly emphasized by George and Hall—that of distorting the 'custodian's' role by compromising his objectivity."[13]

POLICY ADVOCACY

The degree to which the NSC advisor serves both as broker of the process and as a policy advocate in his or her own right is significant in the post-Eisenhower development of the role. At the same time, brokerage and advocacy present a difficult and combustible mix. Personal advocacy may compromise the perception of the NSC advisor's fairness among the principals, which is central to effective brokerage. It may lead to the perception of the NSC advisor as a competitor with other participants. It may tempt the NSC advisor to relax vigilance over the process in favor of advancing his or her own policy views and positions.[14]

Bundy, as we saw, often put his own spin on the policy options of others in the memos he forwarded to Johnson (yet other times he listed hard questions for Johnson to ponder). Bundy sometimes sought to marginalize critics of policies he favored, often important figures such as Bowles and Ball (although he was sometimes willing to tolerate a range of policy analysis on Vietnam but within his own NSC shop).

Kissinger provides the strongest case of the dangers of too much and too exclusionary advocacy. Even Nixon would complain at times that he wanted to hear the views of Rogers and Laird. He was concerned that Kissinger was not representing their views accurately to him.

William Clark's advocacy antagonized James Baker, who felt it at odds with existing Reagan administration policies. Brzezinski's advocacy hurt his relations with Secretary of State Vance. His strong role in pushing for the Iran-hostage rescue attempt led to Vance's resignation.

Some limited forms of advocacy, however, appear inherent even in the broker role. As Roger Porter observes, advocacy may be necessary "if the discussion is not sufficiently balanced and the president needs to hear an underrepresented point of view. He needs to reach for advocacy as an instrument of brokerage rather than undertaking brokerage because he is told to do so."[15] Richard Allen's tenure as NSC advisor provides another twist: too little brokerage and too little advocacy, more akin to the executive secretaries of the Truman years than a Gordon Gray whom he sought to emulate. While not usually advocates in their own right, the Eisenhower-era NSC advisors were at least attentive to bringing forth underrepresented views and facilitating the balanced decision process that Porter outlines.

Advocacy may also be needed given the increasingly crosscutting nature of policy issues; in a sense it is only through the NSC advisor that the pieces all come together. And that unique position may require advice rather than mere coordination. As Joseph Sisco—who served in the State Department from Truman through Ford—notes: "It is very important to have an NSC advisor who thinks conceptually and strategically, because it is at that coordinating point that all of the arguments, resources, and intelligence assessments have to be put together and synthesized and, on that basis, one has to make a recommendation."[16]

Many NSC advisors believe that advocacy should be more robust. Honest brokerage is fundamental to the NSC advisor's role in the view of many of them, but it can coexist with policy advocacy. However, there are conditions required to make the mixture work. Especially notable is the need for interpersonal trust among participants and a shared confidence in the integrity of the decision process. They issue from successful brokerage but also create an environment in which the NSC advisor's own policy views are not seen as threatening or as unfairly excluding the views of others. According to Scowcroft,

> If you are not an honest broker the system doesn't work well. The first thing you have to do is to establish in the minds of all of the members of the NSC that their views will be presented honestly and straightforwardly to the president. . . . Once they are comfortable with that, they certainly expect that you will present your own views but that you will do it in a way that doesn't disadvantage theirs.[17]

Scowcroft is an especially interesting case in that the views he advocated, whether among the principals or in his private counsel to the president, did not always prevail. He was much more cautious in reaction to developments in the Soviet Union, first with respect with Gorbachev then with Yeltsin. Baker's differing position on German reunification proved the wiser course. President Bush remained a decisive voice, however, whatever the positions of his chief lieutenants. Yet Scowcroft proved a key player in the endgame with Saddam Hussein. At the start, he recognized that a strong response was necessary, and he advised that steps be taken for a military response should sanctions prove ineffective. All the while, however, Scowcroft's role as broker persisted.

There may be limits to the exercise of advocacy. For Frank Carlucci, Reagan's fifth NSC advisor, it is the right of others to appeal. Carlucci would present Shultz's and Weinberger's views to Reagan, as well as his own take. However, "They always had the right to appeal and they exercised that right."[18]

For Colin Powell, it is avoiding the perception that the NSC advisor and staff are pushing their own agenda. The NSC advisor should express his or her own point of view, according to Powell. However, once the Pentagon or the State Department "sense the staff has its own agenda, then all kinds of funny things start to happen and cooperation breaks down."[19]

For Anthony Lake, an NSC advisor may "need to take a more active role, both in pushing views that can be more than either the least common denominator recommendation of the principals' committee as a whole or just reflective of those of a president who is trying to find a consensus as presidents tend to do."[20]

Some of the case studies we have examined indicate other efforts to make sure that the NSC advisor's advocacy is properly bounded, without damage to the advice coming from others. Bundy, for example, regularly forwarded his missives to Kennedy to Rusk and McNamara, and he maintained good personal relations with both of them. Even Walt Rostow—a strong policy advocate—recognized the need to "separate clearly his own view from his exposition of the problem and of alternative possible actions in response to it." As well, "he must be able to present another man's case as well as the man himself could."[21] According to Mulcahy, "Rostow was free to pitch an idea to the President as long as [Secretary of State Rusk] received a copy so as to be able to comment on it if Johnson should wish his view."[22] Both Bundy and Rostow also avoided serving as the only point of contact with the president. Unlike Kissinger, who sought to keep NSC staff away from Nixon, both often brought NSC staff members into meetings with the president when it was relevant to the issue at hand.

But Bundy also started a practice that may serve a president less well: *he* conducted the daily intelligence briefing rather than the CIA director or a CIA representative. Some subsequent presidencies reverted to the Eisenhower arrangement of a direct CIA briefing.[23] Others, such as Clinton, relied on a written statement, leading CIA directors to feel they had been cut out of needed access.

In sum, according to the Tower Commission, "To serve the president well, the national security advisor should present his own views." While "not the president's only source of advice . . . he is perhaps the one most able to see things from the president's perspective." But "he must at the same time represent the views of others fully and faithfully to the president."[24] Here, the Tower Commission both advances beyond the Eisenhower-era in recognizing the unique, presidency-centered rather than departmental-centered perspective of the NSC advisor as an advocate; yet at the same time it embraces the earlier emphasis on the importance of honest brokerage.

For academic observers, such as Destler, striking the right balance may provide a solution: "discreet advice or advocacy" is permissible in moderation, but "strong, visible internal advocacy (except of already established presidential priorities)" is not.[25] Destler's position is echoed in the conclusions of the *Tower Commission Report:* "To the extent that the national security adviser becomes a *strong* advocate . . . his role as 'honest broker' may be compromised and the president's access to the unedited views of the NSC principals may be impaired."[26] For Carnes Lord, counterbalancing bureaucratic interests may call for advocacy, "for there can be no guarantee that agency heads will in all cases subordinate their own interests and perspectives to the strategic perspective represented by the [NSC] adviser." In fact, for Lord, that "strategic perspective" offers special entrée for advocacy: "The [NSC] adviser should be considered to have the right to provide advice *in his capacity as strategic planner.*" Presidents may choose to embrace the "tactical, political, or personal factors" of others, but only the NSC advisor "can be relied on to keep the strategic perspective within presidential view."[27]

In sum, policy advocacy may be appropriate if

- bureaucratic positions fail to cover the full range of options or opinion
- effective brokerage has generated trust and confidence in the process
- competing views are fairly and fully represented
- participants have a right of appeal
- the NSC advisor is not perceived as pursuing a wholesale policy agenda
- advocacy is not overbearing and others are aware of what the NSC advisor has advocated
- advocacy represents the unique perspective of the NSC advisor on crosscutting issues
- advocacy is an expression of the president's unique, broader strategic interests

VISIBILITY

Like policy advocacy, public visibility as a spokesperson for the administration has emerged with the post-Eisenhower development of the NSC advisor's role—it occurred almost immediately starting with Bundy's tenure in the job. Yet unlike advocacy, its presence is more variable. Some NSC advisors such as Kissinger and Brzezinski were highly visible if not their administration's chief foreign policy voice. Others, such as Scowcroft and Lake, had public presences more akin to their predecessors under Eisenhower.[28]

As with policy advocacy, some proponents of the broker role have argued that activity as a spokesperson should be avoided. Alexander George is clear on this score: it should not be part of the custodial role.[29] For Porter, it is a matter of comparison with less being better: "The honest broker is less visible, less public than the advocate."[30] For the Tower Commission, the NSC advisor should operate offstage, out of the eye of the media and the public: "Ideally, the national security adviser should not have a high public profile. He should not try to compete with the secretary of state or the secretary of defense as the articulator of public policy. . . . While a 'passion for anonymity' is perhaps too strong a term, the national security advisor should generally operate offstage."[31] For Cutler, Eisenhower's first NSC assistant, anonymity was not too strong a term: "an 'anonymous' Assistant to the President has no charter to speak for his Chief in public." And anonymity, in turn, strengthened his relation to the president. In their private meetings, Cutler recounts in his memoirs, Eisenhower often "seemed to be thinking out loud to test his ideas on someone whom he trusted to keep his mouth shut."[32]

On becoming NSC advisor, Carlucci was surprised to learn that staff meetings began with a report on press stories about the administration. After asking why, he was told that it was "important." No, Carlucci instructed, any press report would come at the end of the meeting: "Once you start worrying about the press, you'll let it drive you. I wanted us to be driven by the substance of the issues." As for his own visibility, Carlucci did some "weekly backgrounders," under the advice of his press officer. But as for more public appearances, "I very seldom volunteered. I would only go on television when the White House press office said something like, 'We need a coordinated effort this Sunday. Everybody should go on television and make these points.'"[33]

The price to be paid for visibility, unlike advocacy, has not been well explored. However, a number of effects seem possible: competition and bruised relationships with other principals, the possibility of public pronouncements "locking in" the NSC advisor (and by implication the White House) to set positions and commitments, perceptions of a personal agenda and questions about fairness that might detract from the broker role, and perhaps even the time taken away from other duties. For Lake, "I tried to make my getting more involved easier by being less visible publicly . . . in general [NSC advisors] should not be very public."[34] Moreover, for Lake, the wishes of the other principals also need to be factored in: Secretary of State Christopher "didn't like it much when I did public work, and that was one of the reasons I didn't."[35] According to Samuel Berger, "I never went out without checking with the State Department . . . I think the secretary of state should have the right of first refusal on the public role."[36] Scowcroft was highly sensitive to the views of both Secretaries of State Kissinger and Baker concerning when he should step out publicly.[37] Such coordination is likely to reduce the predictable tensions between the NSC advisor and State or Defense.

Too much visibility can cause problems. Bundy's public efforts to defend the Johnson administration's Vietnam escalation were not seen as effective, plus they generated occasional anger on LBJ's part, not gratitude. Nixon often became piqued that Kissinger's public activities and press contacts might bolster his NSC advisor's reputation among Washington insiders and boost his standing with the public, perhaps at Nixon's expense. Kissinger also relished his contacts with the press, but many in the Nixon White House felt that he became too preoccupied by press coverage, especially when he was its main subject. Kissinger even disobeyed explicit instructions that he not talk to reporters or to the representatives of particular media outlets such as the *New York Times.* Kissinger's obsession with the press, in turn, led him to be preoccupied with leaks by others, which bred a culture of suspicion and isolation in the Nixon presidency. A more general problem has been noted by Bromley Smith: the NSC advisor "should be pretty anonymous lest he become a lightning rod and enemies attack the president by attacking him."[38]

Yet, under some circumstances, Smith's argument might be turned on its head: perhaps there are occasions when it is useful for the NSC advisor to serve as a lightning rod, directing criticism away from the president. The absence of visibility, moreover, is not without costs. As Lake acknowledges, "I think the president and I probably paid a price for how little I did."[39] A similar point might be made concerning Richard Allen's low visibility; it left the public stage open to the more voluble and at times volatile Al Haig.[40] We have seen secretaries of state who are either somewhat reluctant voices for their administrations—Vance—or not particularly effective ones—Rusk, or perhaps Christopher. The expansion of the cable news media and other outlets also may require a more visible presence by the NSC advisor than in the past—there is simply so much media space now that needs to be filled.

But a media presence also requires an NSC advisor who is an effective public spokesperson for the administration. And as the number of those involved in getting the administration's point of view across expands, an effective communications strategy is needed and discipline must be imposed so that all are speaking "on message." In George W. Bush's presidency, Rice was an effective spokesperson and "on message"; it was Vice President Cheney who often used public pronouncements to advance his own policy views, sometimes less effectively. But the public statements of both would come back to haunt them in the years after Saddam's downfall when no weapons of mass destruction were found, no active development of a nuclear capability had been underway, and postwar reconstruction of Iraq was not the easy transition to freedom and democracy that they had envisioned. As the Tower

Commission admonishes, "the secretary of state has traditionally been the president's spokesman on matters of national security and foreign affairs. To the extent that the national security adviser speaks publicly on these matters . . . the result may be confusion as to what is the president's policy."[41]

Public visibility appears more fraught with negative consequences than advocacy. But there are some indications that it may be appropriate to some degree if

- the secretaries of state and defense are the administration's principal spokespersons
- the other principals are comfortable with the NSC advisor's public role
- the NSC advisor is an effective public presence
- public activities are carefully orchestrated within a broader communications strategy and the NSC advisor is not freelancing or flying solo

POLITICAL WATCHDOG

Borrowing from Richard Neustadt's notion that recognizing and protecting the president's "power stakes" is critical to effective leadership, but reaching an opposite conclusion for the NSC advisor, George argues that serving as a "political watchdog" for the president should not be part of the broker role. Political calculation belongs to others. Here reservations about adding to the broker role appear greater than in the case of policy advocacy or public visibility. Political calculation may compromise effective brokerage to a greater degree. In the view of Lake, "the national security adviser should avoid taking partisan positions. It can diminish his or her credibility, and only adds to the distrust and divisions between the Executive and Congress."[42] Moreover, according to Lake,

> Another thing I think you can do to be an honest broker, while having views and even pushing them, is to keep, as much as possible, the NSC out of politics. There are two reasons for that. One is that career officials on the staff bring with them a certain expertise and that's hard when it is highly politicized. It is the case also that if the national security advisor is perceived as being political or, worse, offering advice to the president on political grounds, it shakes confidence in the administration, which in itself is bad politics.[43]

For the Tower Commission, politics may enter, but not through the NSC advisor: "While the chief of staff or others can usefully interject domestic political considerations into national security deliberations, they should do so as additional advisors to the president."[44]

As with advocacy and visibility (but perhaps to a greater degree), there is little attention in the academic literature on how the interjection of political advice and calculation by the NSC advisor might have an impact on effective decision making. On the one hand, it may be important in a decision process, especially given the president's predilections. As William Newmann notes, "the president's policy choices are deeply dependent on his overall political beliefs, goals, and fortunes at any given point."[45] Furthermore, political calculation might play an important role, given that policy and politics cannot be neatly separated and are in fact deeply intertwined: Which policy positions will gain greater congressional support? Which will enlist the cooperation of allies, especially in light of their respective domestic situations? How will political forces cause adversaries to react? Many of these seem to be questions that the NSC advisor might be in a position to answer or at least contribute to during deliberations. They have bearing both on the substance of national security policy as well as the feasibility of one option over another. To take but one example: Bundy's advice that Kennedy respond to Khrushchev's first, more personal letter of compromise rather than the second, more Politburo-reflective communication proved wise politically and reflected his understanding of the politics and personalities in the Kremlin.

More generally, as Harold Saunders notes from his long governmental service, the interagency process (and presumably the NSC advisor) sometimes had a role "to inject a political perspective—and say, well, you got six options here, they are all intellectually reasonable options, but given what the president has promised publicly or what the Congress has said, option one really isn't realistic so we are going to drop that, or maybe options three and four got merged into three and a half or four and a half, or some thing like that."[46]

On the other hand, other senses of political calculation, more akin to that of watchdog, seem more problematic: Which policy option will prove popular with the public or aid the president's broader political standing? Here a "too political" NSC advisor might endanger the broker role.

Kissinger's efforts to secure a peace agreement with North Vietnam before the 1972 election raises further concerns: an NSC advisor gearing negotiations apparently to secure partisan advantage. The Kissinger case is especially interesting given that he was also apparently operating against the president's wishes. In fact, Nixon saw greater negotiation advantage after the election, when it was likely that he would have secured a significant victory over an antiwar candidate.

Yet Scowcroft's efforts to prevent planks critical of the Ford administration's foreign policy into the Republican Convention platform in 1976 do not seem of great concern. But then again, Baker's calculations against opposition to those planks proved more strategically correct. Scowcroft was, however, a voice of wisdom in urging Ford to put his debate gaffe about Poland and its communist domination quickly behind him; had Ford done so, he might have won the close 1976 election.

Where political calculation is interjected into the deliberative process also bears scrutiny. For the Tower Commission, for example, it belongs to others, such as the chief of staff. But this also bears a price: unless the chief of staff (or some surrogate) is part of the *national security* deliberative process (including the critical meetings of the principals), politics will likely be introduced after the fact and absent their scrutiny. And, as a result, it may figure more heavily in the final choice made by the president than if it were part of a more level playing field to be balanced off against the substantive merits of particular policy options. At the same time, it should be noted that starting with Haig in the Nixon White House, some chiefs of staff have become deeply involved in foreign policy deliberations. Donald Regan, Reagan's second chief of staff, was made a nonstatutory member of the NSC, for example, and Leon Panetta, Clinton's second chief of staff was also a nonstatutory member, attended the president's national security briefings and was a member of the principals' committee as was Andrew Card after the September 11 terrorist attacks.[47]

Political or partisan *involvement* rather than political advice raises a separate set of role-related concerns. In the minds of some NSC advisors, some forms of involvement are reasonable, others are not. According to Carlucci, "I think defending the president's position is perfectly legitimate, but actively engaging in and organizing political activity is inappropriate."[48] Rice's strong involvement in the 2004 election, as we saw, was the subject of criticism at the time and would come back to haunt her during her confirmation hearings for secretary of state.

Politicization of the NSC advisor's role compromises the ability to carry out brokerage tasks. If advocacy is problematic, perceptions of pursuing a political agenda or becoming a partisan figure are even more so. Yet the interjection of political considerations into the policy process by the NSC advisor might be in occasional order if

- the NSC advisor is uniquely positioned to offer certain forms of political counsel (e.g., domestic politics of foreign governments)
- issues dealing with political impact are not adequately presented in the counsel coming from other principals (potentially part of the broker role)
- more public activities are directed at explaining or defending the administration's positions, while perceptions of a partisan political agenda and direct political involvement are avoided

IMPLEMENTATION, DIPLOMACY, AND OPERATIONS

The final area that George argues should not be part of the custodial role is that of "implementer of decisions already taken."[49] Again, the recommendations of the Tower Commission are in agreement, especially in light of the operational activities of the NSC advisor and staff during Iran-Contra. According to the Tower Commission, the NSC advisor "should focus on advice and management, not implementation and execution. Implementation is the responsibility and the strength of the departments and agencies." The NSC advisor and staff "generally do not have the depth of resources for the conduct of operations." As well, involvement in operations risks "compromising their objectivity."[50] So too with the practices of post-Iran-Contra NSC Advisor Carlucci: "I came in with the firm idea that we shouldn't be involved in operational matters, least of all running covert action programs, that our fundamental mission was policy coordination, policy oversight, and seeing that the president's policies were implemented, not necessarily implementing them ourselves."[51]

Yet involvement in operational matters has become more frequent. NSC advisors are sometimes involved in diplomatic and other efforts that are more benign than those the Tower Commission investigated or that loomed over Carlucci's time in the position. Back-channel negotiations and a range of secret and sometimes not-so-secret diplomatic missions are not uncommon among the NSC advisors we have examined.

But even here there are dangers. Bundy's efforts in the Dominican Republic crisis of 1965 indicate one early warning of the risks when the NSC advisor takes on an operational role. Even his fact-finding mission to South Vietnam, during which the Pleiku attack occurred, raises potential concern. A degree of overreaction and miscalculation seems apparent in both.

Kissinger's penchant for personal diplomacy fit Nixon's proclivities, as well as matching the interests of foreign powers, whether the Soviet Union, China, or North Vietnam. Yet, as Isaacson points out, no matter how great

Kissinger was "as a gunslinger, the lone cowboy cannot build a policy based on tending to various complex alliances unless he is willing to share information and authority with the bureaucracy." Kissinger launched an "age of bombshell diplomacy." However, "In the long run this trend will probably prove more exciting than wise."[52] In the short run of the Nixon presidency, Kissinger's efforts to keep his diplomatic efforts secret enraged Secretary of State Rogers and were a central source of tensions between State and the NSC advisor and his staff that festered for years. It was a problem that would vex Nixon personally, test his patience, and take up much time (but not his management attention). Kissinger's secret diplomacy also at times had a negative impact on policy: errors in arms control proposals and negotiations with the North Vietnamese, and even serious glitches in communiqués with Beijing as other, knowledgeable sources were cut out of the action.

Chief arms negotiator Gerard Smith's analysis of Kissinger's back-channel efforts in the SALT negotiations is especially notable. Smith had served all NSC advisors going back to Cutler in 1954. Yet he especially singles out Kissinger's efforts as problematic. While all NSC advisors, he notes, "had different styles," and "all presumably served the president in the manner he wanted," Kissinger

> was the only one who as a matter of *general practice* engaged in diplomatic operations usually handled by the secretary of state. The problem with this practice is that the [NSC advisor's] *main function is to see that the president has all points of view.* When he becomes a negotiator, he has a personal position to present to the president. In the nature of things, it is bound to take on a different nature than the positions of other government officials not so directly in contact with the president.[53]

The result, in Smith's view, was an agreement that proved less than ideal and was fraught with tactical error.

Even Scowcroft's mission to China in the wake of Tiananmen Square—a smoothing over of rough relations and not a major policy initiative in its own right—posed problems. It was presidentially mandated and perhaps wise diplomacy. But it created a public relations predicament once it became public knowledge.

Yet, as in the case of policy advocacy, the broker role may also call for some degree of involvement in operations, especially monitoring and oversight of decisions that have been made but not direct participation in implementation. In fact, such a role was part of the structure of the Eisenhower-era process: an Operations Coordinating Board charged with monitoring implementation (but not carrying it out).[54] But, even here, also recall that Cutler, while chairing the Planning Board, was only a member of the OCB during his first stint as NSC advisor. He was a reluctant vice chair of the OCB during his second stint on the job, and he was eager to give up that position—which he quickly did. It was only in 1960 that Gordon Gray assumed the chairmanship of both the Planning Board and the OCB.

There is also implied agreement by the Tower Commission with this added function of watching over how policy is carried out. According to the Commission, the NSC staff's objectivity in its legitimate oversight functions is compromised when it becomes directly operational: "They can no longer serve *as impartial overseers of the implementation,* ensuring that presidential guidance is followed, that policies are kept under review, and that results are serving the president's policy and the national interest."[55]

There also may be some operational duties beyond monitoring and oversight. Several NSC advisors have acknowledged their involvement in other areas, regarded it positively, but under certain conditions. As we have seen, foreign governments—especially the Soviet Union in the cold war years—have sometimes requested more private diplomatic contact with the White House through the NSC advisor or to have the NSC advisor serve as an emissary on sensitive missions. Such needs must be accommodated.

Unique circumstances may dictate the involvement of the NSC advisor in operational matters, as was the case with Kissinger's negotiations on normalizing relations with China. As Robert McFarlane observes, had normal processes been used, the effort would have failed: "You had to be able to find out if the Chinese were even interested—secretly. Once we confirmed that they were, if you had brought in Democrats and bureaucrats throughout the government, it would have leaked and quickly been aborted."[56]

Yet, as with policy advocacy, diplomatic freelancing by the NSC advisor can be counterproductive, and the other principals need to be informed about and in agreement with the NSC advisor's activities—trust and confidence remain the order of the day. According to Lake, "I would always coordinate in advance and I never went without both Secretary Christopher's knowledge and his approval." Yet, as Lake also notes, "Sometimes, frankly, that took a while."[57] For Scowcroft,

Ideally, from the country's standpoint, diplomats ought to use the national security adviser when it is useful to use him. Sometimes you want to be able to call an ambassador into the White House, not the State Department, if you really want to nail something down. But the problem arises if the national security adviser does that on his own and the secretary of state thinks he ought to be the one to do it. That's where personality comes in . . . . Kissinger-Rogers and Brzezinski-Vance were the two cases where things really got crossed.[58]

Another factor in diplomatic activity is an effort to emphasize a president's personal interest and concern in a foreign policy issue. According to Lake, "The secretary of state should be the chief diplomatic officer of the United States government. But sometimes it can be more effective for the White House to do it." "In those cases," according to Lake, efforts were undertaken "without burning the bridge, turning it into a Vance and Brzezinski, Kissinger and Rogers."[59] Recognition of a familiar refrain.

That said, concerns still may remain, particularly as an operational role may commit the NSC advisor to policies and positions that then later render him or her unable to objectively advise the president.

Involvement in policy implementation and ongoing operations appears to be the riskiest expansion of the NSC advisor's role. Indeed the difficulties are quite apparent in the semantics of the job title: NSC *advisor* rather than bureaucratic operative. Yet some limited activities may be feasible if

•they are directed at monitoring and oversight
•they result from special circumstances, such as the expectations of foreign governments or as signals of a particular presidential concern or direction, rather than serve as routine practices
•they avoid "freelancing" and the other principals are informed about and in agreement with them
•they are carefully weighed against any negative consequences for the broker role

Above all, they must be the result of presidential mandate and—we hope—subject to careful presidential direction and oversight.

IV. A Broader Contextual Fit?

Application of the broker role must also be considered in light of contextual factors that have bearing upon presidential decision making. How does it fit with presidential needs and expectations? How does it mesh with different types of advisory systems, structures, and networks? Does it provide the NSC advisor with internal clout and bureaucratic leverage?

THE BROKER ROLE AND PRESIDENTIAL NEEDS AND EXPECTATIONS

One contextual factor is the fit of the broker role with the president's own desires and expectations as a decision maker. The paramount position that the president's personal needs serve in considering how decision-making processes, structures, and organizations are crafted and how the particular roles of those involved in them are defined is well recognized. In general, it would be poor practice to set out an advisory system that did not fit well with a president's decision-making style.[60] Nixon, for example, would have been ill-served by a fluid, collegial system, given his discomfort with adversarial meetings and his penchant for working off of paper in a solitary setting and in close consultation with NSC Advisor Kissinger. FDR and Clinton, by contrast, would have been comfortable if not delighted by such arrangements.

With respect to the national security decision process, the need for fit appears especially strong. According to Colin Powell, "At the end of the day, the duty of the National Security Council staff and the assistant is to mold themselves to the personality of the president."[61] More generally, according to the Tower Commission, "Because the system is the vehicle through which the president formulates and implements his national security policy, it must adapt to each individual president's style and management philosophy."[62] Scowcroft, a member of the Tower Commission, particularly emphasizes that "advisers must learn to respond to the way in which a president wants information; otherwise they will either frustrate the president or the president will go around the system to get his own information."[63]

But that noted, for most recent presidents, the various components of the broker role do not seem to be impediments for establishing a working fit with presidential needs. Clearly, some tailoring for good fit might be required. For the Kennedys, Johnsons, and Clintons—who were comfortable in a more open and collegial group setting—it might take the form of active steps in meetings to ensure that brokerage is brought to bear on deliberations.[64] As Meena Bose notes with respect to Kennedy, he "could never have tolerated 'policy hill' Eisenhower style," yet

> shorter yet regular meetings of top advisers whom Kennedy trusted and respected might well have been possible, particularly if his national security staff had assumed responsibility for running the meetings according to Ken-

nedy's preferred style. In other words, the staff could have ensured that policy questions were clearly laid out, participants were prepared to make their arguments without digressions, and participants would be ready to answer the president's likely questions.[65]

For presidents who are more comfortable in a more hierarchical and formal setting, brokerage still remains applicable, but again with some tailoring. Nixon is something of a seeming hard case for brokerage, given his reclusive style. Yet brokerage should not be confined to the conventional sense of it just as operative within some open deliberative setting, with advisers arguing their positions orally before the president. It might be tailored to the more private decision maker like Nixon. The latter might involve the NSC advisor's use of the *memoranda process* to explore unpopular options, balance advocacy, and examine decisional premises and assumptions. It might also involve the NSC advisor, in private meetings and conversations with the president, in undertaking brokerage activities to make sure balanced and well-thought-out information and advice is brought to the president's attention. In fact, the Nixon and Kissinger relation is revealing on this score. Nixon's yellow pads notwithstanding, he frequently met with Kissinger to hash out matters—indeed, as a more restricted setting, it suggests a context where a type of brokerage on the NSC advisor's part might be most needed and useful.

As we saw, Eisenhower valued a well-organized policy-vetting structure, yet this was coupled with the weekly group meetings of the NSC. Both served as settings for brokerage by his NSC advisors. Given Eisenhower's deep knowledge of national security matters plus the role of Secretary of State Dulles, however, less policy advocacy was required on Cutler's part. Still, it is also interesting how Gordon Gray's role expanded a bit under Dulles's successor, Christian Herter.

Also, whatever the presidential predilection, good brokerage is not just the fair and balanced presentation of *views* before the president, whether at a Tuesday lunch for Johnson or a private meeting with Kissinger for Nixon. It is also concerned with the effective organization and workings of the *process* that comes before it. Those processes may differ from one administration to the next, but they exist in all modern presidencies, and they are just as consequential as how presidents choose to operate at the final stage of decision making. Again, as to the question of fit, note the recent adoption of the "Scowcroft model" of interagency coordination and its organization, but note also the very different preferences and styles of George H. W. Bush, Bill Clinton, and George W. Bush.

It should also be borne in mind that there are downsides to a perfect fit, as some personal predilections may be sources of decision-making weaknesses. As Carnes Lord observes, "presidents should expect to pay severe penalties for indulging quirks of their personalities . . . at the expense of institutional arrangements that reflect the basic logic of the presidential office."[66] As Bowie and Immerman point out, for example, Nixon "perverted the entire system to serve his own and Henry Kissinger's penchant for secrecy and deviousness."[67] Catering to Nixon's prejudices ultimately proved costly—not so much to Kissinger but to Nixon and his presidency. Bundy, as we saw, meshed well with JFK, yet his adjustment to the Johnson persona may have been too close a fit for a president with strong emotions and weak decision-making instincts. Reagan's emotional commitment to freeing the hostages in Lebanon encouraged McFarlane to devise the arms-for-hostages operation, and it was an operation whose implications Reagan did not fully grasp at the time. Reagan's loose management and reliance on delegation provided an opportunity for Poindexter to take it upon himself to add the diversion of funds to the Nicaragua contras piece of it, which ultimately proved so damaging. Poindexter's defense, however, was that he thought Reagan would have approved had he known about it.

Likewise, changes in organization and work ways that challenge the presidential fit or run against its grain may be beneficial. At least during the war in Afghanistan, Rice sometimes acted as a brake on Bush's desire for quick action. Bush was "ready to go." Asked by Woodward why he backed off a bit on a more hurried time table, Bush replied, "That's the Rice influence there, you know. Who says she isn't powerful. I'm a realistic person . . ."[68] When it came to war in Iraq, however, further deliberations were not needed in Rice's view, much less a tap on the brakes—it was a done deal.

On the domestic front, Clinton's decision making began to improve once personnel changes were made in June 1993 and with the tighter management practices Leon Panetta introduced when he became chief of staff a year later.[69] The "fit" with Clinton was closer before, but the result was better once more decision-making order was established. In Clinton's national security policy making, the picture was bleaker, according to Bose, especially due to the "lack of structure or discipline" and "the absence of a custodian-manager to guide the process." Clinton heard from many sources,

> But hearing from advisers may not always provide the president with the range and analysis of information that more structured sessions can provide, in which someone such as the national security adviser ensures the compre-

hensive presentation and review of policy options . . . in all cases the national security adviser should first and foremost make sure that the president hears and participates in carefully monitored debates on policy options . . . a president's advisory system should compensate for his weaknesses, and Clinton's process did not serve him well in this respect.[70]

Carter's situation is especially striking: he initially wanted multiple advocacy, yet lacked the range of policy alternatives to make it feasible.[71] He ended up with a powerful NSC advisor in Brzezinski. Kennedy's informal leadership style, according to Bose, "lacked means of winnowing information, he risked being overloaded with detail . . . he did not have channels in place for processing the information he received."[72]

Paul Kowert explores the question of fit and advisory system in another way: not only the possibility (as conventional wisdom often notes) that leaders must guard against too little advice but also the possibility that some leaders must guard against too much. For Kowert some presidents are "open leaders" who thrive on information and advice (e.g., Eisenhower in his analysis), others are "closed leaders" who are comfortable in a more restricted setting (e.g., Reagan in his analysis). While open leaders "are generally more capable of learning and improving the quality of their decision making over time," each type can also suffer if placed in the wrong organizational setting.[73] Open leaders in a closed advisory structure experience information deficit and the emergence of pathologies such as groupthink. Closed leaders in a more open setting confront information overload and often face decision deadlock.

Kowert has a good point. It is important to note, however, that the broker role is largely concerned with the *quality* of information rather than the sheer *amount* of information, which is of central concern to Kowert. Furthermore, just as it might be expanded to include policy advocacy and other activities, the specifics of the broker role might be tailored to the temperaments of either the open or closed leader and to the workings of the organizational settings that fit them best. The broker role also may fit with the general problem of any leader, which is, Kowert observes, "to distribute power among advisers in a way that optimizes the upward flow of useful advice."[74]

Finally, it is useful to return to another lesson from the Eisenhower years. The national security structure and process that Eisenhower and Cutler put in place matched the president's needs as a decision maker. Yet for Eisenhower, above and beyond that was recognition of the requisites of *effective decision making* as the prime focus of concern. As Bowie and Immerman note, "Eisenhower took office convinced that process and product were in-separable and interdependent, and the failure to recognize this symbiosis was a major source of the Truman policy disarray." Eisenhower recognized that good process "could not guarantee good policies." But he also "believed that careful and integrated planning, systematic exposure to diverse points of view and the broadest range of available information, methodical review, and effective teamwork and coordination were essential."[75]

THE BROKER ROLE AND TYPES OF ADVISORY STRUCTURES

Presidents enjoy unusual degrees of freedom in organizing the White House staff (including that of the NSC), in determining the degree and means through which the cabinet and others might be incorporated into their deci-sion making, in establishing whether there will be outside channels of infor-mation and advice, in deciding their own settings for making policy choices, and even whether organizational structures and processes have much bearing on their own final decisions. Differences clearly are present among modern presidents, especially whether they embrace a more formally defined and hierarchical advisory process or the more informal, group-centered collegial model.[76] The hierarchical and collegial patterns are not either/or alterna-tives—most presidents utilize some combination of both. The effectiveness of their common use also varies, especially as result of presidential personal-ity, cognitive and other needs, and managerial expertise.[77] Most presidents also utilize informal channels of information and advice in addition to their preferred formal or collegial systems.[78] It is also worth noting, as Karen Hult and Charles Walcott have argued, that the formal/collegial schema may be less useful and that, starting in the Nixon presidency, a "standard model" of White House organization may be emerging, albeit with some variation from administration to administration.[79]

Particular types of organizational structures and processes have strengths and weaknesses. More formally organized and hierarchical arrangements can screen out and distort information and analysis as it percolates up; collegial and small group arrangements can generate pathologies such as groupthink,[80] leader domi-nation, and strategic politicking and side-deals among participants. Tailoring and fine tuning the elements of the broker role, therefore, are likely needed to take account of these differences. But one advantage of focusing on roles rather than broader organizational arrangements (such as multiple advocacy) is that it is at a level of analysis—the individual role—that is potentially operable within and malleable to a variety of broader organizational settings. Institutions, structures, and organizations matter but so too do the roles of individuals within them.

In general, the prognosis for applying the broker role in different types of advisory systems looks quite positive. While the broker role originated and developed in the more formally organized Eisenhower presidency, it is applicable to more informal, collegial systems as well. Indeed, significant elements of the brokerage activities of the Eisenhower-era NSC advisors occurred in group settings such as meetings of the NSC or more informal venues: keeping debate on track, bringing out ambiguities, and highlighting disagreements. Janis's particular variant of the broker role provides evidence of its applicability to more collegial settings, attentive as it is to the pathologies of small decision-making groups.[81]

The introduction of the broker role is no panacea, however. As Patrick Haney notes, presidential-level efforts powerfully operate in determining effectiveness: "what does emerge from the evidence is that a president needs to select a management strategy that fits his or her style and work to emphasize the strengths and minimize the weaknesses of that model." Eisenhower preferred organization, delegation, and hierarchy, for example, "but he also incorporated competitive elements into his decision-making management to overcome the potential information screening of a hierarchical system."[82] And as I have noted more generally, effectiveness can vary greatly among presidents who use the same model: significant differences in effectiveness among formalists (Eisenhower versus Nixon) as well as among the collegialists (Kennedy versus Johnson).[83]

The case studies do suggest, however, that some organizational requisites do facilitate effective brokerage. The Eisenhower system is the obvious case in point, especially given the interagency process that was institutionally embedded in the Planning Board. The organizational routines surrounding meetings of the NSC were equally beneficial. The OCB is more of a mixed picture, but its performance improved when it was brought under NSC staff control in 1957, during Cutler's second stint as NSC advisor, and especially when it was chaired by the NSC advisor during Gordon Gray's tenure. Scowcroft developed an effective system for interagency coordination suited to the realities of a more contemporary national security process. Carlucci and Powell put in place an early formulation of it by adopting the changes recommended by the Tower Commission and its organizationally attentive principal, Scowcroft.

Absence of organizational requisites likewise has negative impact on brokerage. Bundy was largely a participant and player in Kennedy's ExCom, not a broker. Kennedy often served as his own honest broker. The Bay of Pigs fiasco provides an especially illustrative example of poor brokerage operating in tandem with poor decision-making organization. Johnson's Tuesday lunches were a poor venue for effective policy deliberation. Richard Allen was plagued by his lack of a direct relationship to Reagan and the reporting line through Ed Meese, which proved a bottleneck. The early years of the Reagan presidency also suffered from the lack of an organized venue for discussion among the principals short of a full NSC meeting. The National Security Planning Group that Meese set up in the summer of 1981 was an organizational nightmare with its lack of effective staffing, poor policy review, and an absence of feedback to subordinates.

Yet the presence of good organization is no guarantee of effectiveness. Kissinger had a talented staff and a more formalized policy process than had existed under Kennedy and Johnson, yet they failed to check his more excessive practices. Early changes in the Reagan national security process failed to curb tensions between Clark and Baker, Shultz and Weinberger. The Scowcroft model was in place under Rice, yet her role as broker dwindled over time. The deputies' committee during her tenure was especially plagued by dysfunction. The importance of effective brokerage—*especially as it relates to the quality of the decision-making process*—comes to the fore once again.

THE BROKER ROLE AND "PERSONALITIES"

While the broker role's relation to organizational arrangements is important, so too is the interpersonal dynamic at the level of the individual. As Lake notes, "A lot of it depends upon personalities. Always."[84] According to Scowcroft, "It's all personality. . . . I think you need to always be conscious of the interplay of personalities."[85] In Carnes Lord's view, "the State-NSC conflicts of the past are at least as much a result of the personal styles and strategies of those advisers and (more importantly) inadequate management by the president as they are a reflection of enduring institutional tensions."[86]

Making the various personalities work effectively together clearly contributes to a better advisory process. As Joseph Sisco, observes, "I think it would have been a much easier relationship if Henry had cooperated more fully with Bill Rogers and if there had been much greater sensitivity about the personal relationship. Henry admits this in his book."[87]

NSC advisors, like Kissinger, who "don't play well with others" can generate antagonism and tension. The latter not only fracture relationships, they can forestall needed information and advice coming from a variety of channels. Nor is the burden just on the NSC advisor. A secretary of state like Haig, who is overbearing and overly conscious of his own turf, can cause equal damage.

Part of the equation is also presidential, and what he or she brings to the table. As Scowcroft observes, "President Bush Sr. was probably unique among our presidents in having looked at the system—the whole foreign policy system—from a variety of viewpoints." His service at the U.N., in China, and as director of the CIA provided a wide organizational and foreign policy background: "Then he was vice president so he watched how it worked under a different kind of president. So by the time he was president, he pretty much knew how it had worked under different presidents, how he wanted it to work." But this experience was not just about organization, it was also about people, according to Scowcroft:

> what kind of people made it work. And I think that influenced his choice of people for the job. It is not that we didn't have vigorous debates, but at the end of the day we were all facing in the same general direction. . . . That was, I think, due to his skill in assembling a group that could give him what he wanted and work as a team rather than as a bunch of separate egos.[88]

As Scowcroft's latter comments attest, part of the equation has to do with personnel choices. This is not, however, just a matter of presidential knowledge and skill, it also has a temporal dimension. These personnel choices are first made during the transition to office. Presidents-elect and their transition advisers make a variety of calculations in selecting key appointees. In the area of national security, how those individuals are likely to work together—not just their merits qua individuals—especially needs to be factored in.

Not only is what a president brings to the table important, so too is prior knowledge and experience on the part of the NSC advisor. But the missing factor here is not familiarity with policy substance so much, but with what makes for good process. Again, Scowcroft's recollections are instructive.

> I was lucky enough to be partly in the same way [as having President Bush's broad pre-presidential experience]. Because when Kissinger started off in the White House I was over in the Pentagon. I saw how the Pentagon, one of the agencies he coordinated, reacted to the way he did business. . . . Then in the Ford administration I learned what worked and what didn't work. Then I was on the Tower Board and I looked at what had gone wrong in the Reagan administration to have allowed Iran-Contra to happen. . . . I had a lot of seasoning, which helps.[89]

More generally, according to Scowcroft,

> One of the problems with our system is that most presidents and, indeed, most cabinet officers—members of the NSC—don't have that kind of seasoning. They come in fresh. They don't understand how it works. They don't understand what makes it work and what doesn't work. That is one of the drawbacks of the system we have. Unlike a cabinet system [in a parliamentary form of government] we are not used to working together when we come into office.[90]

LEVERAGE, EFFECTIVENESS, AND PRESIDENTIAL RESPONSIBILITY

One important criticism of the broker role has been that an NSC advisor who adopts it will operate within a decision-making environment lacking "bureaucratic leverage" to manage effectively. It is a point Destler emphasized in his initial critique of George's formulation: the duties of a managerial custodian are broad, but it is a range of roles—including proximity to the president and policy advocacy—that makes the NSC advisor a powerful actor able to carry them out. The NSC advisor would be reduced to "an isolated spokesman for rationality" and likely bypassed as "ad hoc decision-making procedures would arise which the 'custodian' could neither change not control."[91] Similarly, Rockman concludes, "this super-custodian presumably would be akin to the director of the Office of Management and Budget, but without the capacity to pass judgment upon departmental requests—in other words, largely powerless. I am not the first to point out that in Washington those with status but without power quickly become worked around rather than through."[92]

These points are well taken, especially as directed at the pristine conception of the managerial custodian role that George sets out. However, the enhancement of the broker role and its tailoring to particular organizational settings and advisory systems might address some of these concerns: an appropriately expanded role might confer more power, while a fine-tuned one might limit the tasks to which the exercise of power is directed. Presence of an honest broker, in fact, might curb some of the pathologies that occur when departmental interests and perspectives are dominant: advice giving as a function of bureaucratic skill and the presence of "back-channel" advising.

But I think there is another, perhaps more important counterpoint: the broker role does not reside in a vacuum. The president's response and support, as well as the organizational culture pervading the process also have bearing on the NSC advisor's effectiveness. As David Hall notes, "the fundamental determinant of bureaucratic leverage is the Chief Executive's will and behavior. Ambiguous statements regarding a White House assistant's authority to shape the policy-making process will not long remain untested by other policy advisers."[93] In George's view, the president "will have to provide the 'custodian' with a strong presidential mandate and continuing support for his efforts." Presidents also have responsibilities to "equalize resources among his chief advisers," develop certain "rules of the game" to ensure "due process and fair competition," and to fulfill "the task of maintaining and supervising the competitive nature of policy making."[94] For Porter, "the honest broker's effectiveness requires that he enjoy the president's confidence. The other participants must perceive him as close to the president." And that perception, in turn, means that others "will participate in its activities and contribute to the development of policy."[95]

Nor are these just academic speculations. According to the Tower Commission, "A president must at the outset provide guidelines. . . . If his advisors are not performing as he likes, only the president can intervene. . . . The president is ultimately responsible for the operation of this system. If rancorous infighting develops . . . only he can deal with them."[96] Presidential responsibility in these areas is important according to those who have served as NSC advisor. In the view of Walt Rostow, "My point is that it takes a very strong president to insist that these people get along. It's only with a very strong president that these clashes you have described can't happen."[97] For Colin Powell, if the president "finds himself not getting the right advice, then he ought to fix the people or the processes that are at work. I have not seen an administration come in which did not find the need to change its processes as a group."[98]

As we have seen, presidents with problems in their decision-making procedures and in the performance of their NSC advisors have often been remiss in seeking correctives. Nixon, not just Kissinger, was the architect of how he wanted his foreign policy processes to work; he as much as Kissinger created a system that centralized control in the White House and in a powerful NSC advisor. Yet when Kissinger's own power proved problematic, Nixon was reluctant to take the needed steps. He would occasionally cut off Kissinger's access to him, vent his concerns with Haldeman, Ehrlichman, and Attorney General John Mitchell, and even muse with them about firing him. Yet he could not bring himself to rein Kissinger in.

Reagan was equally remiss. He finally accepted Haig's resignation, but he lacked the management skills to make the system work in its aftermath. Success depended upon the actions of those to whom much was delegated.

Iran-Contra was as much the result of presidential neglect as it was the machinations of Poindexter, Casey, and Oliver North. The system righted itself not as a result of Reagan's efforts, but through the efforts of Carlucci and Powell. They came to that delegated power with different, more beneficial aims: implementation of many of the reforms recommended by the Tower Commission.

Finally, the proximity to the president also may operate as a factor continuing to bolster the broker as a major player rather than a procedurally obsessed bystander. As Samuel Popkin notes with respect to chiefs of staff who chose to define their roles more narrowly as administrators,

> Although a chief's power is derived from his boss's power, it is, of course, patently false that these men, despite their loyalty, exercised no independent power. Even if they never sought to directly influence their bosses by giving advice, their management of the traffic in and out of the Oval Office enabled them to exert a direct influence on decisions.[99]

And that "traffic management" is an important part of the NSC advisor's duties in the national security arena. Similarly, David Cohen notes that a chief of staff has the potential "to be the most important and trusted of any presidential adviser" because the chief of staff "is in the president's company more than anyone else and subsequently has a captive audience."[100] So too, I think, even for an NSC advisor who is allegiant to the broker role as the foundation of his or her duties.

V. Final Points

The place of the broker role in presidential decision making deserves serious analysis and reexamination. Absence of effective brokerage is clearly notable—and detrimental—in some of these case studies of NSC advisors we have examined. Presidents may want NSC advisors to serve as counselors or visible spokespersons, but where brokerage is absent or too limited, the decision-making process suffers.

Evidence of the positive contribution of honest brokerage to effective decision making seems compelling, as the empirical work of Porter, Moens, Haney, Bose, Burke and Greenstein, and Herek, Janis, and Huth in part suggest.[101] Most of these studies framed their analysis in terms of George's theory of multiple advocacy or Janis's correctives to groupthink. Yet embedded within them is evidence of the positive significance and impact of the broker role. As we have seen in the case studies, some of the NSC advisors, not just the Eisenhower progenitors but more contemporaries—such as Scowcroft, Carlucci, and Powell—provide further evidence that brokerage works.

The applicability of the broker role in practice requires update and adaptation beyond its particular definition as a managerial custodian, which George offered over thirty years ago. Presidential and institutional demands since the Eisenhower years have led to significant expansion of the NSC advisor's responsibilities, often for good reason. The discussion and analysis offered here indicate that the broker role might be expanded to some degree—what I have termed "brokerage plus"—but brokerage activities should serve as the foundation of the NSC advisor's basic duties as well as setting constraints on what additional tasks are added. Effective brokerage especially establishes conditions of interpersonal trust and confidence in the integrity of the decision process that may permit the introduction of some forms of policy advocacy, public visibility, and other additional activities. But the latter must be carefully weighed against their effects on the broker role.

Also important for the argument in favor of honest brokerage is its flexibility *qua* role, which may allow more nuanced definitions. The latter permits adaptation to differing presidential predilections, and it allows brokerage to operate within differing advisory systems and organizational arrangements.

At the same time, the NSC advisor, however skilled in brokerage, does not stand alone in his or her efforts. Also notable is the place of presidential support and concern in making the broker role work, especially in empowering the NSC advisor with leverage and clout. As James Pfiffner observes, "It is the *president's responsibility* to create an atmosphere in which the White House staff and cabinet officers give the president all of the relevant evidence to help him make an informed decision. If they bend their advice to suit his preconceptions, they are not serving his best interests, nor the country's."[102] According to the Tower Commission, "the president bears a special responsibility for the effective performance of the NSC system. . . . If his advisers are not performing as he likes, only the president can intervene."[103]

Here the president comes into play, as we have seen. Although Cutler was the "architect," it was Eisenhower who was the "client" setting specifications. Bundy, by contrast, raised concerns about imperfections in the process, yet Kennedy was reluctant to address them. Later on, Kennedy was forced to step in as his own honest broker during deliberations of his ExCom. Nixon was vexed by the constant reassurances that Kissinger demanded, but Kissinger adapted his role to what he thought Nixon wanted. Poindexter thought he was carrying out Reagan's intent. Rice reflected where she thought Bush was headed. Scowcroft, by contrast, thought about process, options, and outcomes in their own right and with reference to effective decision making. And that is what George H. W. Bush wanted in his NSC advisor—an honest broker.

The broker role is no cure all, and it may not be applicable to all presidents or all decision-making contexts. Other factors and forces can have powerful effects on decision-making processes and their outcomes. Even where operative, the presence of an honest broker is no guarantor of success. As many observers of (and even participants in) presidential decision making commonly acknowledge, a "good" decision process does not assure the correct policy choice. But absent an effective process, of course, the probabilities of sound decisions are likely greatly lessened.

Here we return to the central emphasis of this book. Participants in that process also matter, and their roles have an impact on the equation of what contributes to policy success or failure. With respect to the latter in foreign and national security policy, the NSC advisor increasingly stands front and center; that is at least clear. That role is now ever more significant. But how that role is defined is of most import and matters even more. *Quis custodiet ipsos custodes?*, as Juvenal once prescriptively—and perhaps prophetically—phrased it.

Assistants to the President for National Security Affairs (NSC Advisors), since 1953

Stephen Hadley: January 26, 2005–January 20, 2009
Condoleezza Rice: January 22, 2001–January 25, 2005
Samuel R. Berger: March 14, 1997–January 20, 2001
W. Anthony Lake: January 20, 1993–March 14, 1997
Brent Scrowcroft: January 20, 1989–January 20, 1993
Colin L. Powell: November 23, 1987–January 20, 1989
Frank C. Carlucci: December 2, 1986–November. 23, 1987
John M. Poindexter: December 4, 1985–November 25, 1986
Robert C. McFarlane: October 17, 1983–December 4, 1985
William P. Clark: January 4, 1982–October 17, 1983
Richard V. Allen: January 21, 1981–January 4, 1982
Zbigniew Brzezinski: January 20, 1977–January 21, 1981
Brent Scowcroft: November 3, 1975–January 20, 1977
Henry A. Kissinger: December 2, 1968–November 3, 1975 (served concurrently as Secretary of State from September 21, 1973)
Walt W. Rostow: April 1, 1966–December 2, 1968
McGeorge Bundy: January 20, 1961–February 28, 1966
Gordon Gray: June 24, 1958–January 13, 1961
Robert Cutler: January 7, 1957–June 24, 1958
Dillon Anderson: April 2, 1955–September 1, 1956
Robert Cutler: March 23, 1953–April 2, 1955

Source: History of the National Security Council, White House, www.whitehouse.gov

The Others

Rostow, Brzezinski, Lake, Berger, and Hadley

I. Lyndon Johnson: Walt Rostow

On April 1, 1966, Walt Whitman Rostow succeeded McGeorge Bundy as NSC advisor. Oddly, Bundy had favored Bill Moyers for the job, one of Lyndon Johnson's closest advisers but a policy generalist and speechwriter without deep expertise in national security affairs.[1] A second competitor was Robert Komer, a White House assistant who was a strong hawk on Vietnam.[2] However, Jack Valenti, another close aide to LBJ, lobbied on Rostow's behalf and he was chosen.[3]

Rostow brought impressive credentials to the job, perhaps even exceeding those of Bundy. The son of Russian Jewish immigrants, Rostow won a scholarship to Yale for students of New Haven high schools, where the family then resided. He graduated from Yale at nineteen and won a Rhodes scholarship to Oxford, where he studied at Balliol College. Rostow developed an early interest in economic history and its relationship to political and economic development. This interest led to a doctorate when he returned to Yale, and it became the basis for his subsequent—and prolific—academic research.[4] During the war years he served in the Office of Strategic Services (the wartime precursor of the CIA), with much of his work dealing with bombing target selection—an early career experience that later served him in good stead. After the war, he was assistant head of the German-Austrian economic division in the State Department. He later served as assistant to Gunnar Myrdal—the then executive secretary of the Economic Commission for Europe—where Rostow was involved in the Marshall Plan. In 1946, Rostow taught for a year as Oxford's Harmsworth Professor of American History. In 1949, he was at Cambridge as the Pitt Professor of American History, both prestigious appointments for someone so early in an academic career. In 1950, he was appointed professor of economic history at MIT, where he served until 1961.[5] During the Eisenhower years, he was called upon as an outside consultant;

he played an especially important role in the 1955 Open Skies proposal and as an adviser to then White House aide Nelson Rockefeller.

In 1961, Rostow, by now a member of the Kennedy inner circle,[6] was initially tapped to serve as Bundy's deputy at the NSC. In December 1961, however, he was moved over to the important post of chair of policy planning in the State Department, George Kennan's perch during the Truman years.[7] Kevin Mulcahy raises the point whether the "overly garrulous," "idea-a-minute" Rostow was a poor fit for the more focused Kennedy White House. "We have to play with a narrow range of choices," Kennedy told him, "We can't do long-range planning; it has to be done over there [at State]."[8] Was it a brush-off on Kennedy's part, after a failed test run? "Temperamentally," Kai Bird notes, Rostow "was hardly the kind of man to serve as [Bundy's] deputy. Rostow was voluble, exuberant and full of good and sometimes foolish ideas."[9] Bundy was reportedly "dumbfounded" when he learned that Rostow had been appointed to succeed him; Bundy thought Rostow the kind of person who decides an issue "before he thought about [it]."[10]

Given his ties to the Kennedy presidency, his appointment as NSC advisor in 1966—when many of the Kennedy loyalists had by then left the Johnson administration—was "something of a mystery," as Larry Berman notes.[11] In bringing him back to the White House, Johnson certainly did not register any concerns for the problems that Kennedy and Bundy had perceived. Rostow and Johnson developed a close, if not at times a too close and symbiotic relationship. As Johnson noted, Rostow is "my intellectual. He's not your intellectual. He's not Bundy's intellectual. He's not Schlesinger's intellectual. He's not Galbraith's intellectual. He's going to be my Goddamn intellectual."[12] Indeed that bond of "my intellectual" proved long: Rostow's entire post–White House career was spent, until his death in 2003, in an endowed chair at the LBJ School of Public Affairs at the University of Texas.

Yet there were nuances in the LBJ-Rostow relationship. I. M. Destler notes that "Rostow seems not to have had as strong a mandate as Bundy." There were also differences between LBJ's two NSC advisors. Bundy was "an exceptional administrator-operator," while Rostow was "primarily a thinker and more than a bit of an ideologue who tended to view particular events in terms of the broader theoretical constructs he was most adept at developing."[13]

THE JOHNSON NATIONAL SECURITY PROCESS—ROSTOW

In terms of its organization, the Johnson national security process remained largely the same as it had under Bundy. Tuesday lunches continued to be the main venue of discussions among the principals, although starting in 1966 the JCS chairman and the director of the CIA also attended. Rostow would check with the other main principals on Monday in order to develop a rough agenda. There was a bit more order: Rostow would record any presidential decisions or requests for action, and, starting in late 1966, Tom Johnson, deputy press secretary, began to keep records of the group's discussions— although these were done for historical purposes and were not transmitted back to the principals and their deputies.[14] According to Bromley Smith— who continued to serve as the NSC's executive secretary—"Rostow was quite good in getting back to the various departments with the decisions that had been made."[15]

Formal meetings of the NSC were less frequently held, and Rostow came to see them as useful for review of issues that might be forthcoming but not as a context for immediate, pressing decisions or, on the other hand, periodic policy reviews serving broader planning needs.[16] According to Smith, "by then the machinery was so rusty. . . . There was no machinery to put together papers worthy of the president's attention." For his part, according to Smith, "Rostow was convinced that the Council should not be a place where decisions were made."[17]

The interagency coordination process below the level of the full Council was also more formalized in March 1966, based on a report by Gen. Maxwell Taylor. By presidential order, the secretary of state was given "authority and responsibility . . . for the overall direction, coordination and supervision of interdepartmental activities . . . overseas."[18] A Senior Interdepartmental Group (SIG) was created, chaired by the undersecretary of state, to carry out those responsibilities. According to Harold Saunders, who served on the NSC staff during this period,

> When Johnson came in, he was uncomfortable with what he regarded as the somewhat chaotic NSC operation under Kennedy. So he set up the NSC with a middle level . . . at the assistant secretary level, which is charged with coming up with all reasonable options. . . . Johnson moved the middle-level review over to the State Department under the deputy secretary there. I picture him as saying to Rusk and McNamara, "Look, you guys are smart fellows, you understand my responsibility, I want you to talk through these problems and come up with a recommendation to me as to what I should do. I want one recommendation. Then over the Tuesday lunch, we will take it apart, talk about it, you can air your differences, and so on. But help me figure out what a reasonable course of action might be."[19]

A few Interdepartmental Regional Groups (IRGs) were also established, and the groups were usually chaired by a regional representative from State. A special group on Vietnam was established (chaired by the undersecretary of state) as well as a principals' level group on arms control (chaired by Secretary of State Rusk).[20] The State Department-led process, however, harkened back to the weak system under Truman and ultimately proved less than effective.[21]

Johnson's informal contact with a range of former government officials, old friends and political associates, members of Congress, and foreign leaders was another important side to the deliberative process. But despite the fact that Johnson was an inveterate consumer of information and that the new SIG process strengthened State's impact over policy to the detriment of the NSC staff, Rostow's own role as NSC advisor remained strong. There was no return to the pre-Bundy definition of the job. In fact, Rostow expanded its duties beyond what Bundy had staked out.

Rostow was especially concerned to meet Johnson's decision-making expectations. According to Saunders, the written memoranda process was "much more rigorous under Kissinger." Given Johnson's emphasis on personal interaction rather than the kind of near-solitary (plus Kissinger) digestion of memoranda that Nixon favored,

> Walt tended to talk things through a lot with staff and try get to the bottom of things. Of course, Johnson is a fairly different president. He didn't sit up there with his yellow pad, scoring the options as Nixon did. He himself wanted to talk things through. The Tuesday lunch was not an accident, that's the way he made up his mind. Walt was thinking more in terms of how to respond to the questions he knew that Johnson would ask.[22]

Moreover, according to Saunders,

> I would never say that the work under Walt was sloppy, but it probably was a lot looser than it was [under Kissinger]. And that is again the character of the administration, the difference between somebody who made up his mind from paper and somebody who made up his mind from talking to people. Two very different human beings, Richard Nixon and Lyndon Johnson.[23]

Although Rusk later noted that there were not many substantive changes from Bundy to Rostow, Bundy "was a somewhat more skilled draftsman than Walt Rostow." Rostow "was a little prolific in his words, was not as succinct as McGeorge Bundy." Yet Rusk thought he improved over time.[24]

Procedures were also, not surprisingly, problematic. According to Bromley Smith, "Some officers would send memoranda . . . to the president without going through Rostow. Then President Johnson would say, 'Walt, what do you think of this?'" To Rostow's credit, he "was relaxed in that he didn't care who wrote memoranda to the president as long as all memos came downstairs to him before being acted on." But there was a downside: "when someone comes forth with an idea that looks great but can't be done, you have to handle it with some care lest you become a 'no can do' staff."[25] And Johnson was notoriously intolerant of a "no can do" staff.

ROSTOW AS NSC ADVISOR

In *Diffusion of Power*, Rostow explained his NSC advisor role as fourfold. First, it involved laying "before the president the widest range of options" and providing "terse, lucid, dispassionate analysis." Second, he had the task of ensuring that a "president's decision is executed." Third, the NSC advisor had a part in "in-house" foreign policy business, such as assistance in drafting presidential speeches, informal press briefings, and preparing for presidential trips abroad. Finally, he saw his role as providing advice, although here Rostow also recognized the need to "separate clearly his own view from his exposition of the problem and of alternative possible actions in response to it." As well, "he must be able to present another man's case as well as the man himself could"—an element of honest brokerage.[26]

At the same time—not mentioned by Rostow—he embraced other of the more expanded duties of the NSC advisor. He sometimes gave political as well as policy advice. He urged Johnson, for example, to give a "Gettysburg"-like speech at Notre Dame University in order to rally the nation, and he emphasized the need for a central theme linking a variety of domestic, economic, and foreign policy initiatives going into the 1966 midterm elections.[27]

Rostow, even more than Bundy, was a one-man show. He chose to serve, for example, without a deputy NSC advisor. Nor was it always an effective show. Some criticism even emerged that the quality of the NSC staff was less under Rostow than it had been under Bundy, although Mulcahy argues that it is debatable.[28] In Destler's view, "Most of the exceptional Bundy group departed well before the end of the Johnson era." As for Rostow, he "tended to save his influence for Vietnam, and the lack of bureaucratic confidence in him as an 'honest broker' made him unable to act as an across-the-board coordinator . . ."[29]

Yet Rostow's relationship with his secretary of state was by most accounts a positive one. According to Mulcahy, Rostow was "deferential to Rusk" and respectful of State's role in the policy-making process. For his part, Rusk recognized Rostow's role as a policy advocate and personal counselor to the president as long as Rusk "received a copy" of his memos to Johnson and was in the position to comment on them. But Rostow controlled the information flow: what went to the president went through him.[30]

It is debatable who was more influential—Bundy or Rostow. Prados sees Rostow as more inclined to push his own policy views and proposals than Bundy had been, "not only bringing proposals up from the bureaucracy, but taking positions from a very early stage and then fighting the proposals up through the NSC structure."[31] Mulcahy observes that no NSC advisor, before or since, was better prepared for the job than Rostow.[32] Inderfurth and Johnson, in contrast, see Bundy as more influential, and that is perhaps true over a wide range of policy matters.[33] According to Roger Morris, Rostow "saw himself as one more enthusiast at the Tuesday lunch. His cover memos on most issues were a dry rephrasing and seconding of bureaucratic recommendations."[34] But with the Johnson presidency's most important foreign policy effort—the Vietnam War—Rostow was the more direct as a policy advocate, although in the end not effective in achieving his personal policy aims.

Effects on Policy: Rostow and Vietnam

Rostow's activities in advising Johnson on Vietnam provide an important case study—and test—of his particular definition of the NSC advisor's role. The initial hope that this Yale, Columbia, Oxford, Cambridge, MIT academic might somehow move the Johnson administration to disengage from Vietnam and be a source of countervailing views to its existing policies proved particularly ill-prophetic. In fact, Rostow proved to be an enthusiastic hawk in his advice to LBJ concerning the U.S. effort in Vietnam.

One area where Rostow had a major impact was in supporting the optimistic assessments of enemy troop strengths coming from Gen. William Westmoreland's Military Assistance Command, Vietnam (MACV) in Saigon. According to Berman, "Over time, Rostow became excessively optimistic for the case of military victory by the strategy of attrition."[35] In March 1967, Rostow assured Johnson that "if victory is not in sight, it is on the way."[36]

Rostow was an important internal ally in supporting Westmoreland's analysis of North Vietnam's "crossover point"—the point at which troop attrition would exceed troop infiltration and replacement.[37] Earlier, in January, Rostow informed the president that there was, since 1960, "for the first time a net decline" in enemy forces in South Vietnam.[38] Although the military's "order of battle" analysis would generate controversy and suspicion by the CIA and even among some of the civilian officials in the Pentagon, Rostow was an advocate for the optimistic numbers Westmoreland produced for Washington. In September 1967, according to Berman, "Rostow's preference for MACV's new numbers was evident, and he pushed MACV's case to President Johnson."[39] In February 1968, following the unexpected Tet Offensive, where 80,000 enemy troops attacked over 100 South Vietnamese cities and the U.S. embassy in Saigon, Rostow still supported Westmoreland's rosy numbers; one CIA analyst, however, viewed them as a "monument of deceit."[40] But it was not a monument that Rostow as advocate rather than broker was willing to challenge; indeed, it was in his view apparently a monument worth defending. For Rostow, Tet was a failed gamble on the enemy's part: "if we all on our side do their job well," he told Johnson, "the net effect could be a shortening of the war."[41]

ROSTOW AS STRONG ADVOCATE AND BEYOND

Rostow was confident in his views and felt no compunction to hold back as a policy advocate. He was a strong proponent of taking steps to cut off North Vietnamese supply lines through the Ho Chi Minh trail—even if it meant military engagement in Laos. He had reservations about the restrictive "rules of engagement" the White House set on the military.[42] In May 1967, as Defense Secretary McNamara grew increasingly pessimistic about stepping up the air campaign and adding more troops, Rostow urged Johnson "not [to] take the heat off."[43] In another memo, Rostow warned Johnson that there are "dangerously strong feelings in your official family which tend to overwhelm the strictly military factors." But these disagreements were not for Rostow a signal to examine their causes or merits; rather, he saw the task as finding "a scenario" that "can hold our family together." Indeed the substance of the memo concerned reservations about bombing Hanoi and Haiphong by Rusk, McNamara, and JCS Chairman Earle Wheeler—a not inconsiderable triumvirate. As Bundy had done before, Rostow deprecated their views a bit: "In a curious way, all three are arguing negatively. . . . So much for sentiments."[44]

Rostow was the voice of optimism not critique or questioning, and it was an optimism that needed to be sold. At a gathering of the wise men in early November 1967—which Rostow had organized and during which most participants were supportive of the administration's Vietnam policy—Rostow told the group that "there are ways of guiding the press to show the light at the end of the tunnel."[45] After the meetings were over, Johnson asked Rostow to summarize and contrast the still relatively hawkish views of Bundy versus those of the increasingly pessimistic McNamara, who now favored a policy of stabilization in force levels and a reduction in the air campaign against the North. Rostow added his own gloss on the debate, emphasizing that McNamara's position would be seen by Hanoi "as a sign of weakness." With luck and a stable South Vietnamese government, he told Johnson, "the evidence of solid progress will become increasingly clear to one and all."[46]

For Rostow, the problem was not progress in the war itself—in his view progress was occurring—but the *perception* of lack of progress among opinion makers and the public. Not only had he emphasized as much to the wise men, but he also took active steps to make that point among the other principals. In late September 1967, he cabled Westmoreland and U.S. Ambassador Ellsworth Bunker in Saigon urging them to produce better news from the war front. Rostow also created an interagency task force to develop new ways of measuring that progress.[47] Also in September, he was part of an administration effort that sought to create "information teams" that would travel across the country to get a more favorable message across; in Rostow's view, one of the prime emphases should be that "the war is being won; no 'stalemate.'"[48]

Rostow was especially cognizant of the increasingly negative press coverage of the war. In 1967, he organized a Vietnam Information Group, which would meet weekly and plan strategy for more favorable coverage of the administration's war efforts. Ironically, the effort may have succeeded all too well: its drumbeat of success rang particularly hollow with the Tet Offensive.[49] In the aftermath of Tet, Rostow still plowed forward, urging Westmoreland and Bunker to make daily authoritative comments to counter the growing tide of media criticism. For his part, Rostow appeared on ABC's Sunday morning program *Issues and Answers*—it was part and parcel of his own public visibility as NSC advisor.[50] In March, Rostow urged Johnson to rally the country by demanding a maximum response to the enemy's attacks.[51]

In his advocacy, Rostow may have gone too far on some occasions. He sometimes overstated his position to Johnson, for example. In August 1967, Rostow emphasized to the president that "*all* of the evidence" indicated that bombing the North cut down on their infiltration into South Vietnam. As Berman observes, "There certainly was evidence to suggest otherwise, but Rostow, choosing to give Johnson only optimistic reports, said 'all' not 'some' of the evidence."[52] That same month, Rostow also informed LBJ of a conversation he had with Sen. Fritz Hollings (D-SC), in which Rostow emphasized that "in military terms we were making good progress; we could see a process that really gave light at the end of the tunnel . . . we were on a winning track if we had the capacity to sweat it out."[53] In September 1967, following a fact-finding visit to South Vietnam by Gen. Omar Bradley, a five-star military luminary from World War II, Rostow "couldn't wait to send" Bradley's report to LBJ, according to Berman. In his memo, Rostow emphasized that Bradley "emerged with a sense of great optimism," "the war is not stalemated," and "we were well on the way to winning."[54] Following a November 1967 briefing by Westmoreland, Rostow further sought to reassure Johnson that the war was going well, noting Westmoreland's assessment "of a U.S. troop withdrawal within two years," as the South Vietnamese army built its strength.[55]

According to George Ball, Rostow

> took a position very early on and spent a good deal of time defending it. . . . he was a terrible influence on the president. He played to Johnson's weaker side, always creating an image of Johnson standing against the forces of evil. He used to tell him how Lincoln was abused by everybody when he was at a certain stage of the Civil War, and "this is the position you are in, Mr. President." He spent a good deal of time creating a kind of fantasy for the president.[56]

Rostow also deflected some of Johnson's efforts to expand the range of advice. In January 1967, LBJ asked Rostow to convene a secret committee that would explore alternatives to the bombing policies then being advised and pursued by the Joint Chiefs. Rostow told Johnson such an effort would be "unsettling and possibly explosive" if revealed and would signal the president's lack of confidence in the JCS and McNamara.[57]

But Rostow later rejected the view that he sought to bias the information Johnson received: "Any man who tried to distort the flow of information to President Johnson would not have lasted two weeks in his job. . . . My objective was not to determine the President's view but to make sure he had available the widest flow of information possible—a kind of intelligence ticker, if you like."[58]

There were some signs of brokerage on Rostow's part. These efforts were less in brokering the particulars of policy options or expanding their range, but more in providing Johnson with further information. Rostow's support of Westmoreland's order of battle estimates proved ill-advised. But starting in late November 1967, Rostow felt that captured documents indicated a possible upcoming attack. Rostow arranged to have the documents sent to the

White House, and he talked with Johnson about a possible enemy offensive in the coming winter or spring.[59] It was an early warning sign of the Tet Offensive in January.

Rostow's own comments are a bit elusive on how he saw his role during this period. He notes at one point in his 2003 memoirs, *Concept and Controversy*, that he "stayed with Johnson to the last day, while steadily but quietly opposed to the way the war was being fought"—too restrictive and limited in Rostow's view. But a page later he writes, "Having failed to convince President Johnson of my notion of how the war in Vietnam should be fought, I did not campaign for my view inside or outside the government."[60] Rostow's continued advocacy belies otherwise.

Elsewhere Rostow emphasizes his policy advocacy as a response to LBJ's explicit instructions: "I started off sending the memoranda to Johnson without any recommendations by myself. After three weeks he said, 'I don't want you ever to send me a piece of paper without your own view. I'll expect you to represent the departments fairly when they have differences of opinion.'"[61]

TET OFFENSIVE: CHANGE NOT OF ROSTOW'S MAKING

The Tet Offensive began to change even the most hawkish of Johnson's outside advisers. Tet especially marked a turning point for Clark Clifford, who had periodically been brought in as an outside consultant and adviser. Now as McNamara's replacement at Defense, Clifford began a slow process to change Johnson's view of the war and urge him to seek greater efforts for peace. Former Secretary of State Dean Acheson is also especially notable as someone whose views markedly shifted. Meeting with Johnson in March 1968, Acheson told the president that he was "being led down the garden path." Explaining his position to Rostow, Acheson later recalled that "Walt listened to me with the bored patience of a visitor listening to a ten-year-old playing the piano."[62] This was an odd response given Acheson's stature and his hawkish views when called upon for advice since the early Kennedy years.

The key debate in late February and March 1968—between those who sought a fundamental change in policy through negotiations and a reduction of military effort versus those who sought to stay the course if not step up efforts—saw Rostow not as a neutral facilitator but as a strong partisan and advocate of the latter.[63] The precipitant was a report by JCS Chairman Wheeler calling for an additional 205,000 troops in Vietnam. According to Herbert Schandler, following a meeting of the principals, Rostow did not forward his own views to Johnson, but told the president the request "raised many questions to which you ought to have clear answers before making a final decision."[64] Yet as a task force under Clifford began to consider the troop request, Rostow was an advocate not a broker of the process. He expressed his support for giving the military those forces that could currently be added, while further studying how and whether larger numbers should be granted.[65] During this period of crucial deliberation, Rostow increasingly became a strong voice against Clifford's efforts to get Johnson to change his Vietnam policy.[66]

Indeed, Rostow told Johnson that the North could not sustain its present troop levels and was facing mounting losses. Rostow was also ready to mine North Vietnamese ports and call up the reserves to meet Westmoreland's request for more troops. He also initially opposed a cessation of bombing above the 20th parallel, which other advisers were advocating as a gesture toward peace.[67] In his view, that path to peace was fruitless, because "the enemy still wants war."[68] Only after an effort that showed North Vietnam that their prospect for winning was illusive, Rostow later recalled, would a peace effort and a bombing halt be feasible.[69]

Clifford proved successful in his efforts and was able to turn Johnson around.[70] The opposition to further expansion was strengthened by the negative assessment rendered by the wise men, who were once again called to the White House but now at Clifford's, not Rostow's, behest. Not only had Acheson shifted, so too did many of his colleagues. Rostow was disappointed and later remarked that they were "not focusing on Vietnam, but on the political situation in the United States."[71] The wise men had also been briefed before meeting with Johnson by State and Defense officials, allies of Clifford's efforts, who were hostile toward further escalation and pessimistic about the course of the war. During the sessions with the wise men, moreover, the briefers were subject to Clifford's careful, pointed, but leading cross-examination. According to Rostow's military aide, had Rostow done the briefing, the outcome might have been different.[72] According to Clifford, "Rostow would tell people later, 'I smelled a rat.'"[73]

As Johnson's views began to change, Rostow saw it as his duty to follow the president's lead, even if he had strong reservations. He later recalled that, by the end of March, the time had come to insert a proposal for a bombing pause north of the 20th parallel in a speech Johnson would soon deliver.[74] That speech, delivered on March 31, 1968, marked a major change in policy, as well as the president's announcement that he would not seek another term in office. It led to the first direct negotiations with the North Vietnamese in May. According to Rostow, it was his knowledge of *Johnson's intention* to seek a bombing halt that was key to his support—it was not some sudden epiphany on Rostow's part on the merits of pursuing peace.[75]

There was little questioning about the positive progress of the war on Rostow's part, either at the time or thereafter. In fact, the relevant sections of Rostow's *Diffusion of Power* and *Concept and Controversy* read as if the post-Tet period were a lost opportunity for escalation and victory. According to Schandler, "Rusk and Rostow never reexamined their original premises [in support of military action] either in light of changing circumstances or in the light of the demonstrated failure or inadequacies of the policies being pursued."[76] In the final analysis, it was Clifford, not Rostow, who had brokered the process in a new direction after Tet and pushed his associates, including Johnson, to reexamine the fundamentals of their earlier policies. Honest brokerage was not the strong suit of this NSC advisor, and the effects of its absence on policy were notable.

II: Jimmy Carter: Zbigniew Brzezinski

Although Carter's transition to the presidency in 1976 and early 1977 was fraught with error and delay, his choice of Zbigniew Brzezinski as NSC advisor came as no surprise.[77] On December 3, Carter announced his first two cabinet choices: Cyrus Vance as secretary of state and Bert Lance, an old friend and Georgia banker, as director of the Office of Management and Budget (OMB). Vance—who had served as secretary of the army under Kennedy and deputy secretary of defense under Johnson—was a consummate Washington insider and member of the foreign policy establishment. On December 14, eleven days later, the next round of appointments was unveiled. Finally on December 16, Brzezinski's appointment was revealed. Brzezinski—the son of Polish émigrés and whose father had served in the pre–World War II Polish diplomatic corps[78]—was a professor of political science at Columbia University and a Soviet studies specialist. He had been an early supporter of Carter's candidacy and was his chief campaign adviser on foreign policy. They had met in 1973, and Brzezinski was instrumental in obtaining Carter's membership on the Trilateral Commission, of which he was executive director.[79] During the campaign, according to Carter, "I was an eager student and took full advantage of what Brzezinski had to offer . . . he was able to express complicated ideas simply. We got to know each other quite well."[80]

THE CARTER NATIONAL SECURITY PROCESS

With respect to the organization of his decision making, Carter had broadly envisioned the White House staff as serving a coordinating rather than a policy-making role. One of his aims was to avoid any semblance of the White House-centered policy process of the Nixon years. There would be no White House chief of staff like Haldeman or Haig or a powerful NSC advisor in the Kissinger mold. Carter also took office with the hope that his cabinet would serve as his chief source of policy information and advice. He invested much personal effort in its selection. Yet during the transition to office, little had been done to think about how to put the goal of cabinet government into practice.[81]

It was Carter's initial hope that Vance would be the administration's chief foreign policy spokesman and his chief policy adviser (although it was Brzezinski's view at the time that Carter himself expected to take the lead role in making foreign policy and that the NSC advisor would be "an initiator of policy as well as its coordinator"[82]). Whatever Carter's initial expectations, signs of a more active role for Brzezinski as NSC advisor began to emerge early on. Brzezinski was given cabinet rank—a first for an NSC advisor—and he attended its meetings.[83] He also came to the NSC advisor position with clear policy views. His views differed from Kissinger's—Brzezinski saw the Soviet Union as a declining power rather than an adversary that required détente, for example—but they were still a potential source of advocacy at odds with mere coordination.[84] Carter, moreover, had been warned that Brzezinski held strong policy views. He received "high recommendations," but "a few of the people who knew him well cautioned me that Zbig might be aggressive and ambitious," and that he "might not be adequately deferential to the secretary of state." [85] Furthermore, as Mulcahy notes, "To have expected Brzezinski to take a back seat in foreign policy making . . . was to have asked him to become a different person."[86] Another sign of possible danger was that Brzezinski appointed as staff secretary, the position that General Goodpaster had once held, the administrative director of the institute he headed at Columbia University.[87] But Carter was not deterred.

By and large, Carter's foreign and national security policy making operated within a clearly defined and orderly system, yet it too was beset with organizational problems that had consequences on policy decisions and outcomes. That system had been developed by Brzezinski during the transition (as head of its national security transition team, even before his own appointment or that of Vance was finalized). His view, as he relates in his memoirs, was that there were three models: a Nixon-Kissinger model of a strong president and NSC advisor but a weak secretary of state; an Eisenhower-Dulles model of a strong secretary of state but a weaker NSC advisor and president; and a more balanced "team" arrangement. He assumed that Carter wanted the third, although he recognized that Carter might "naturally gravitate toward the first model," but "in view of the Kissinger legacy he would find it hard to admit it."[88] In late December, he presented Carter with a plan that largely replicated the elaborate committee structure that had existed under Kissinger. But the proposal also had a crucial difference: the secretaries of state and defense, rather than the NSC advisor, were the lead chairmen of key groups. Carter rejected the plan preferring a simpler structure.

In early January, Brzezinski presented a new plan to Carter. It created two committees: a Policy Review Committee (PRC), usually to be chaired by the secretary of state or another cabinet member as appropriate, and a Special Coordinating Committee (SCC) to be chaired by Brzezinski himself.[89] The latter would deal with "crosscutting issues," arms control, intelligence activities, and crisis management. Brzezinski also proposed and Carter approved a procedure for organizing NSC paperwork. Brzezinski and his staff would prepare and organize most of the staff work, including the preparation of presidential review memoranda (PRMs), as well as gathering information for PRC or SCC meetings, preparing agendas, and coordinating the paper flow. If principals agreed on policy recommendations, Brzezinski would submit a presidential directive (PD) to Carter for approval. If no recommendations were forthcoming, Brzezinski, drawing on his own notes or those of his staff, would prepare a summary report for Carter, and the matter would be taken up at the presidential level.[90] It was an orderly process, but one that would create difficulties and reveal the increasingly powerful role of Brzezinski as an advocate and not just a coordinator. The new system was approved by Carter shortly before his inauguration without consultation with Vance or Harold Brown, who had been tapped for Defense.[91] According to Vance, "[I] opposed this arrangement from the beginning, and I said so to the president."[92]

BRZEZINSKI: TILTING THE PROCESS?

One important question about the new setup was whether the PRC or the SCC would be the dominant body. The former would have reinforced Carter's hope for cabinet dominance. But it was the latter that would have the upper hand in practice. Brzezinski's strong views, compared to Vance's more diplomatic and cautious stances, tended to tilt action away from the PRC, which Vance chaired, to Brzezinski's SCC. The latter ended up dealing with policy decisions that were more than just "special" or crisis oriented. As Brzezinski himself notes, "during the early phases of the Carter administration, the PRC met more frequently. . . . In time, however, the SCC became more active. I used the SCC to shape our policy toward the Persian Gulf, on European security issues, on strategic matters, as well as in determining our response to Soviet aggression. Moreover, right from the very start . . . the SCC was the central organ for shaping our SALT policy."[93] The PRC essentially functioned as the long-range back burner, and when issues were moved to Brzezinski's front burner, existing PRC plans could change. Plus, it was up to Brzezinski to decide what issues belonged in which venue: what was crosscutting or of a crisis nature was up to him.

Not only was the SCC's policy menu large, given that the full National Security Council rarely met, it became the most important game in town. As Colin Campbell notes, with few NSC meetings, and as "the ascendancy of the SCC in relation to the PRC intensified an 'escalator' process [occurred] whereby cabinet secretaries felt bound to attend the SCC even if a deputy would do just as well."[94]

Brzezinski could manipulate the process—especially by exploiting who got to attend what kind of meeting. As Moens notes, by 1979 as his power grew, Brzezinski "would quickly change PRC sessions into NSC sessions by bringing in the president, merely to oust the assistant secretaries (from State) whose opinions he did not cherish."[95] OMB Director Bert Lance, a nonstatutory member of the NSC, recalls that Brzezinski would try to keep him out of meetings by calling a "principals meeting" on short notice and at times, in Lance's view, when he knew the OMB director could not attend. Nor, since they were for principals only, could Lance send a deputy in his place. Finally, Lance confronted Brzezinski, and told him if he could not be there, his deputy would, whether or not Brzezinski approved. "If you don't like it," Lance told him, "I suggest you go talk to the president about it and see what he says. I'm telling you this is the way it's going to be." There were no more conflicts between NSC meetings and other meetings Lance had to attend, he reports.[96] (It was a short-lived victory on Lance's part. In late September 1977 he was forced to resign due to charges of mismanagement and corruption at the Georgia bank he had run; he was eventually acquitted of the charges.)

What transpired during meetings may also have worked to the detriment of the process. Vance was not alone in his concerns about Brzezinski's operations and his ability to put his thumb on the policy scale. Attorney General Griffin Bell, whom Carter asked to attend NSC meetings as a nonstatutory member, recalls that Brzezinski imposed an order on the proceedings that took me by surprise. He would always summarize the sessions, and the six or so points he would glean from the discussions often seemed a highly personal view, especially when it came to resolution of problems. This prevented a free flow of ideas to the president in the national security area.[97]

Nor may meetings of Brzezinski's SCC have been that effective. Colin Campbell found among the respondents for his study of the Carter presidency the view that the SCC "increasingly pandered to the president's preoccupations rather than presenting arm's-length preparations of stances and initiatives."[98]

What happened after meetings may also have been problematic. Vance was particularly concerned that participants were kept in the dark about what had actually been decided, since neither the PDs nor Brzezinski's summaries to Carter were circulated back to members; "this meant that the national security advisor had the power to interpret the thrust of discussion or frame the policy recommendations of department principals." Carter, however, backed Brzezinski and was worried about leaks if documents were widely circulated. He did, however, tell Vance he could come to the White House and look at the drafts if he wanted. "Given the enormous pressure on our time," Vance reports, "this was not realistic."[99]

Vance also notes in his memoirs that he made a mistake in not pressing his objections more forcefully with Carter: "The summaries often did not reflect adequately the complexity of the discussion or the full range of participants' views." Vance often found discrepancies in the documents he did see, "occasionally serious ones," and sometimes "had to go back to the president to clarify my views and to get the matter straightened out." Upon leaving office, one of the pieces of advice Vance gave his successor, Sen. Edmund Muskie (D-ME), was that he insist on reviewing NSC-prepared summaries and directives in draft form before they were forwarded to the president.[100]

Vance and others could rely on informal channels to get their views across to the president. One of these for Vance was his nightly report, which went directly to Carter for his evening reading. According to Vance, "I used this document to raise policy issues directly and quickly."[101] But as with other back-channel efforts, policy issues were raised without the input—and maybe the support—of the other principals. Vance was left to maneuver alone.

INFORMAL PROCESSES

Starting in June 1977, often in lieu of formal NSC meetings, Carter began to hold weekly breakfasts on Fridays with Vance, Brown, Brzezinski, and Vice President Walter Mondale (attendance would later expand) to resolve key policy disputes as well as to discuss broader foreign policy matters. Carter seems to have enjoyed the smaller, collegial setting. Each brought items of concern to the table, although as Carter notes, "We didn't have a prepared agenda ahead of time. . . . I would ordinarily cover all of the issues myself and then I would ask for additional ones. . . . At the conclusion of it, Brzezinski would read the decisions we had made or things that were postponed. . . . I think primarily the fact that we could actually make some decisions there was what made it attractive."[102] The meeting, in Carter's view, allowed him "to minimize misunderstandings among this high-level group. . . . This became my favorite meeting of the week, even when the subjects discussed were disagreeable."[103]

The breakfast was preceded, however, by a lunch the day before where Vance, Brown, and Brzezinski would hash over the matters to be taken up the next day. According to Vance, these lunches became "somewhat routinized" with a "complex and too lengthy agenda negotiated in advance by the staffs."[104]

It is interesting to note that Carter thought his Friday breakfasts "didn't have a prepared agenda ahead of time."[105] Yet clearly much had gone on at the luncheon the day before. Furthermore, even Vance concedes that if agreement was reached among the three principals, "it would be extremely difficult for another point of view to prevail."[106] According to Defense Secretary Brown, the "first couple of years the Thursday lunches were very informal. We just talked about things." Yet, over time, in Brown's view, the force of bureaucracy set in: "staffs—the NSC staff, Defense, State—began to see them as a way of getting issues resolved that they had been unable to resolve at a staff level. And so a big agenda began to be created and we actually resolved things, but we also lost something. We lost the free interplay and it became more than it had been—a staff driven exercise."[107]

The subsequent Friday breakfasts with Carter, not unlike Johnson's Tuesday lunches, were beset by a certain casualness in procedures. As even Brzezinski came to recognize, "there was some disadvantage in the casual way some decisions were made and interpreted. For example, each participant would write down for himself the president's decisions as guidance for implementation." This practice persisted until the spring of 1980, when Carter finally had Brzezinski prepare a summary document, following a misinterpretation over a U.N. vote on the status of Jerusalem.[108]

Effects on Policy

Although Vance and Brzezinski eventually came into conflict, particularly as Brzezinski later became a more visible and outspoken advocate, during the first months of the Carter presidency consensus seemed to prevail. Both had reservations about Carter's "deep cuts" proposal in strategic arms talks with the Soviets (Mondale and Brown favored Carter's position—which the Soviets quickly rejected). But on most other matters, as Moens points out in his study of Carter's foreign policy decision making, they "rarely disagreed."

The negative result, according to Moens, was that they "did not put the difficult (dissenting) questions on the table. . . . To make matters worse, the consensus more often than not was along the lines of Carter's initial policy beliefs." As a result, Carter "was not fully aware of the limits of his ideals." Moreover, where a John Kennedy could learn from his mistakes in the Bay of Pigs fiasco, "Carter does not seem to have learned anything from his early setbacks. SALT II, human rights, the neutron bomb fiasco . . . are all examples of this lack of self-criticism."[109]

Rather than multiple advocacy and honest brokerage, according to Moens, a lack of substantive disagreement persisted in key national security areas that would require Brzezinski's own policy advocacy to fill the breach. In particular, normalization of relations with China, dealing with the Shah of Iran, and intervention in the Ogaden War in the horn of Africa were areas of more active policy efforts on his part. Similar problems may also have been present in the areas of "human rights, American policy toward Eastern Europe, several aspects of the Middle East negotiations, and American policy toward Angola, Rhodesia, and Zaire."[110]

Similarly, as Robert McFarlane later noted,

President Carter's system was initially designed with multiple channels of access to the president and a relatively weak NSC. As the administration progressed, however, it became apparent that such an arrangement was too open and disjointed for effective policy making. The administration suffered from charges that its policy making apparatus was in disarray. . . . In the face of these problems, the president moved to strengthen his NSC and the role of his NSA [national security advisor].[111]

Brzezinski as NSC Advisor

At least initially, Brzezinski did not think he would serve in an advocacy capacity as Kissinger had done. According to one early profile of him, "Prior to taking over the NSC staff, he said he would give the president advice only when asked and that he did not visualize himself as a policy maker. He saw his role, he said, as being mainly that of an operational line officer."[112] In Brzezinski's own words at the time of his appointment as NSC advisor, "I see my job essentially as heading the operational staff of the president, helping him integrate policy, but above all helping him to facilitate the process of decision making in which he will closely consult with his principal cabinet members." Policy advice would be tendered and recommendations made only "if I am asked."[113]

Although Brzezinski may have started out as a more neutral coordinator, he quickly became a policy advocate. By October 1977, he acknowledged to one reporter that "I think the president probably concedes the fact he obtains *unsolicited* advice—and disagreement—from me."[114] Even earlier in the new administration, he put together a lengthy memorandum outlining major foreign policy objectives, a timetable for their consideration, and target dates for their achievement. According to Brzezinski, it "emerged as a basic document and guided what we did, particularly in the initial phase."[115]

Moens, in part, views Brzezinski's increasing policy advocacy as a needed antidote to the consensus-prone deliberations among the principals.[116] In his view, Brzezinski became a counterweight, in effect, offering his own policy views, which breached the consensus and widened the range of options. Yet, given the tilt that Brzezinski was able to exercise over the process, it was hardly a level playing field. Moreover, Brzezinski's advocacy was not simply that of a devil's advocate, arguing in favor of unpopular or neglected policy options. Rather, he was a *committed* advocate, pressing his own policy views. According to Brzezinski,

> By the spring and summer of 1978, some substantial differences on policy had arisen. Although Cy [Vance] and I both tried to confine them to our in-house discussions, the varying viewpoints filtered down to the bureaucracy, became increasingly the object of interagency conflicts and of gossip, and then started to leak out. This was the case, first over the issue of the Soviet-Cuban role in the African horn, and the likely impact of that on SALT, then came the China question, and in the final year and a half we differed over on how to respond to the Iranian crisis.[117]

According to Inderfurth and Johnson, these "disagreements reflected a fundamental policy difference: a more cooperative approach advocated by Vance and a more competitive (critics said, confrontational) approach advanced by Brzezinski."[118] More colloquially, in the view of Vance's assistant secretary of public affairs, Hodding Carter, Brzezinski was "like a rat terrier," shaking "himself off after a losing encounter. . . nipping at Vance's ankles."[119]

President Carter, moreover, was also sometimes resentful of Brzezinski's increasing responsibilities as NSC advisor. According to Brzezinski, "Whenever I tried to relieve him of excessive detail, Carter would show real uneasiness, and I even felt some suspicion, that I was usurping his authority." On one occasion, Brzezinski complained that Carter had not informed him about a change in a scheduled seven-power conference to one with only five powers and about messages that had been sent to the Soviet Union's foreign minister without Brzezinski's knowledge. Carter "got real furious," according to Brzezinski, "He told me in an icy fashion that I just wanted to be involved in everything." Brzezinski protested that he was just doing his job of policy coordination, but Carter "gave me a rather silent and icy stare."[120]

Yet, at the same time, Carter appreciated at least some of Brzezinski's advocacy and his policy views, even when, in Carter's mind, his NSC advisor was off base. As he notes in his memoirs, "To me, Zbigniew Brzezinski was interesting. He would probe constantly for new ways to accomplish a goal, sometimes wanting to pursue a path that might be ill-advised—but always thinking. We had many arguments . . . often disagreeing strongly and fundamentally—but we still got along well."[121] Elsewhere Carter observes that "Zbig's more provocative attitude was compatible with what I thought the National Security Advisor ought to do, giving me a whole range of new ideas and letting me sift through them to see if they are good or bad." Carter "enjoyed being around him" and was his "eager student." He recognized, even before taking office, "Zbig's strengths and some of his possible weaknesses." He would put together "a constant barrage of new ideas and suggestions," although "ninety percent of them . . . would have to be rejected. Sometimes maybe fifty percent of them . . . would have some essence or benefit that if modified were good and some of them had to be rejected outright."[122]

Part of Carter's appreciation of what Brzezinski was doing may have stemmed from his increasing dissatisfaction with the input he was receiving from State. Its personnel was "highly qualified," and "its advice was generally sound." But "I rarely received innovative ideas from its staff members about how to modify existing policy in order to meet changing conditions." As for Vance, "In many ways, [he] mirrored the character of the organization he led . . . [and was] extremely loyal to his subordinates, and protective of the State Department and its status and heritage."[123] By contrast, a strong NSC advisor enabled Carter—just at it had enabled Kennedy, Johnson, and Nixon—to control foreign and national security from the White House.

BEYOND BROKERAGE AND ADVOCACY

In addition to advocacy, Brzezinski also took on other roles as NSC advisor. He pressed the administration's policy aims in briefings of members of Congress, especially over the controversial Panama Canal Treaty.[124] In 1978, Brzezinski reestablished a congressional liaison unit within the NSC staff (as Kissinger had done during his tenure as NSC advisor). He placed a young aide who had been his former student at Columbia and was then the chief legislative assistant to Sen. Edmund Muskie in charge of it—her name was Madeleine Albright. Albright later recalled that her appointment caused some initial consternation with the White House's congressional affairs staff, who wondered why Brzezinski needed his own liaison to Congress. However, matters were satisfactorily worked out and good relations established. Her efforts were directed more at interagency and strategic coordination on matters pertaining to Congress rather than direct lobbying.[125]

As for the public face of the administration's foreign policy, Carter's initial hope was that Vance would be the chief public spokesman.[126] But Vance was somewhat uncomfortable in that capacity. According to Carter, "Vance was not particularly inclined to assume this task on a sustained basis; it is time-consuming and not always pleasant."[127] As a result, especially from 1978 on, Brzezinski filled the breach and became a more visible public and media figure. But even before that, Brzezinski had established a press office to handle his relations to the media, and he put a reporter from *Time* magazine, Jerrold L. Schecter, in charge of it.[128]

Brzezinski's public efforts sometimes created tensions with the Carter domestic staff, both in his failure to factor in domestic political repercussions (top Carter aide Hamilton Jordan warned that decisions were being made in a "political vacuum") and in the sometimes inconsistent statements made by Brzezinski and Vance.[129] In his memoirs, Vance notes that Brzezinski's public appearances violated what he thought had been an agreement that only he and Carter would define "foreign policy publicly."[130] Yet Carter counters in his memoirs, "Almost without exception, Zbig had been speaking with my approval and in consonance with my established and known policy. The underlying State Department objection was that Brzezinski had spoken at all."[131] That neither Carter nor Brzezinski had bothered to notify—or perhaps mollify—Vance remains something of a management mystery. Carter later claimed that he "monitored" Brzezinski's public appearances.[132] Nor was he bothered by Brzezinski's requests to meet with the press, make speeches, or appear on talk shows; indeed, according to Carter, "there were many times when I told him to go ahead and do it."[133] In Brzezinski's recollection, it was Carter who instigated his greater role as a spokesman: Carter "wasn't satisfied with Vance's ability to articulate and to present the case . . . the nuances weren't quite right"[134]

In general, it was Carter's view that, with "one or two exceptions," Brzezinski never publicly "promulgate[d] an issue that was contrary to my basic policy." (According to Carter, Brzezinski "went too far . . . once concerning the Soviet Union and China as related to Vietnam and the invasion of Afghanistan.") But Carter recognized that *how* Brzezinski came across could be problematic:

> When Zbig would say something, though, because of his appearance, because of his attitude, his statement, which Cy [Vance] could have made in a non-provocative way, became provocative. The press not only assumed that this was a contest between Cy and Zbig and that Zbig had won, but also that Zbig was speaking contrary to my desires and, in effect, betraying me. I recognized that then and I recognize it now.[135]

There was one big merit in the NSC advisor's public visibility. As Carter notes in his memoirs, there was on Brzezinski's part a "willingness to serve as a lightning rod—to take the blame for unpopular decisions made by others."[136]

Brzezinski also engaged in diplomatic negotiations, most notably in final normalization of relations with the People's Republic of China. After a failed Vance visit to Beijing in August 1977, Brzezinski arranged through Michael Oksenberg—his chief NSC Asia staffer and, before that, a China specialist at the University of Michigan—to have himself invited for a visit. Vance opposed the trip, but Brzezinski maneuvered and "badgered"—his word—Carter to be sent, and he was.[137] As had befallen Kissinger on his trips to China, Brzezinski's efforts generated tension with the State Department, especially concerning its effects on U.S.-Soviet relations and the SALT II treaty.[138]

In 1977, he also was an important conduit to the negotiators at what would become the SALT II talks. According to Rothkopf, he "shepherded the process closely and even went so far as having Bill Hyland, working for the NSC, oversee the delivery of the negotiation instructions to en-sure that they did not get into the hands of the State Department until the instant of their departure."[139] Unfortunately, State's views may have been more realistic. The White House had proposed deep cuts, for which the Soviets were unprepared. It would take until June 1979 to work out an agreement (although by that point, Soviet foreign policy, especially in Afghanistan, would make ratification by the Senate impossible).

With the fall of the Shah Reza Pahlavi's regime in Iran, Brzezinski be-came directly involved in determining where he would seek exile.[140] Later, he played an active role in attempts to free the U.S. hostages and in planning the failed rescue attempt of them in April 1980. His SCC was the focal point of the administration's policy deliberations. At one point, before the Shah's fall, Brzezinski even developed his own back-channel to the Iranians through its ambassador, Ardeshir Zahedi. The back-channel was shut down when Vance complained to Carter.[141]

Yet in Carter's view, Brzezinski was effective: "If Zbig said, I'd like to go to Taiwan or China or Germany, which he did a couple of times a week, I'd say, hell no, you're not going, you're going to stay here. He was always want-ing to go somewhere as an emissary and very seldom did I let him do it. But when he went, he did a good job."[142] Yet Carter was also aware of the costs of Brzezinski's missions: "Whenever Zbig went anywhere or said anything, it created tremors in the State Department. Vance was extremely protective of the State Department."[143]

NSC STAFF EFFECTIVENESS

Although Brzezinski was often at loggerheads with State and Defense, most evidence indicates that he assembled and then utilized a reasonably effective NSC staff. According to Leslie Denand, who served as special assistant to the NSC advisor in both the Ford and Carter presidencies, "I think the NSC staff in the Carter administration got off to a quick start with some very, very bright people, and did good work, and good work had a tendency to reach the President."[144] Brzezinski especially sought staff with diverse policy views: "I did very deliberately [want] to have a very catholic staff . . . it never bothered me to have people disagree with me."[145]

Unlike Kissinger, who often kept his staff in the dark and limited their contact with Nixon, Brzezinski held weekly meetings in order to, in his words, "report to the staff in full on my dealings with the president and on presidential business, so that vicariously, if not directly, they have a sense of engagement with a man for whom they are working so hard."[146] And,

"I made a point of sharing with staff a great deal about my relationship with the President."[147] According to one NSC staff member, "Kissinger was a tyrant with his staff." By contrast, "Zbig wants people to be personally responsible and deeply involved." Unlike Kissinger's strong efforts to cut off staff contact with the president, "He gets the staff people to meet with the president—that was unheard of before."[148] Brzezinski especially understood the long hours they put in on the job: "I wanted them to feel involved with the President."[149]

At the same time and likely as a result of Brzezinski's expansive role as NSC advisor, some NSC staff members perceived themselves as overextended. According to one, "We have too big a plate and can't do justice to all the issues, particularly in view of the role they want us to play."[150]

But Brzezinski was attentive to organizational dynamics. According to Madeleine Albright, despite some "we" and "they" tensions between the NSC staff and their counterparts at State, Brzezinski tried hard to foster a unified effort: "I think on the whole there were many staff meetings in which Zbig would make it very clear that he didn't like the 'we' and 'they' kind of thing, and I think all of us were aware that certain people were 'they.'"[151]

Carter's Shortcomings

Brzezinski did at times take on some brokerage activities in an attempt to improve Carter's decision making. He found Carter to be "impatient" as a decision maker. There were a number of cases "in which he would make decisions ahead of the NSC coordinating process, prompting me to complain to him."[152] Yet Carter was generally stubborn in his ways, self-confidently assured of the rightness of his policy views and disengaged from examining weaknesses in the deliberative process. According to Brzezinski, Carter "didn't use people well at times, and certainly didn't know how to discipline them." Even on his own NSC staff, he encountered difficulties: "I managed to ease out four or five people and each time it was a battle to get it done."[153] It took Carter until the summer of 1979 to shake up his cabinet, and he resisted appointing and empowering a "staff coordinator" to bring order until early 1978 (and it was not until 1979 that he would accept using the title "chief of staff").

On paper, the national security process appeared open and effective. But in practice, without presidential vigilance, it often operated less than effectively. Bureaucratic competition was especially sharp. Part of the difficulty can be traced to Brzezinski's activities. Part too had its source in what was needed to make the Carter system work, but often proved lacking: a sense of teamwork and collegiality. According to Anthony Lake, then directing the State Department's policy-planning staff, Carter's "flexible system . . . depended on collegiality if it was to work smoothly." But its organization and the actions of those who participated in it "had the effect of undercutting collegiality, as people competed in weekly meetings to decide which agency would take the lead at which meeting."[154] According to Inderfurth and Johnson, "the president never settled the differences between Vance (and his successor, Edmund Muskie) and Brzezinski. The president was unable to impose teamwork on his most senior advisers or make a consistent choice between the fundamental policy approaches and alternatives they offered."[155]

The rivalries within his foreign policy team thus persisted, and they culminated in the April 1980 resignation of Vance as secretary of state. In large part, Vance's resignation was caused by and is emblematic of those tensions, especially his feeling that he had been deliberately excluded by Brzezinski from the final deliberations leading to the hostage rescue attempt. But problems were not confined to Vance. Muskie was to complain, shortly after replacing Vance, that he had learned about the administration's decision to alter aspects of its nuclear war strategy—which Brzezinski had orchestrated—only after reading a newspaper article on it.[156] In short, as Crabb and Mulcahy conclude, "the irony is that although Carter entered office pledged to oppose the Kissinger model of foreign policy making, the actual result was the concentration of nearly as much power in the White House as had been the case in the Nixon administration."[157] At the center of that concentration, of course, was Zbigniew Brzezinski.

III. Bill Clinton: Anthony Lake and Samuel Berger

Unlike the revolving door NSC advisors of the Reagan years, Bill Clinton enjoyed comparable stability over his two terms as president. During the first term, Anthony ("Tony") Lake held the position, while through the second term the NSC advisor was Samuel R. ("Sandy") Berger. Both had strong credentials for the position.

Lake—a graduate of Harvard with a doctorate in international affairs from Princeton—had initially joined the Foreign Service in 1962 as an assistant to Ambassador Henry Cabot Lodge in South Vietnam. He held a number of diplomatic assignments there before becoming a top assistant to Henry Kissinger in 1969. As we saw, Lake was highly regarded by Kissinger, but Lake resigned in protest over the Cambodia incursion. During the Carter years, Lake returned to government, serving in the important post of director of policy planning at State. During the Reagan years, he taught at Mount Holyoke College. In the 1992 campaign, he served as one of Clinton's chief foreign policy advisers.

Berger—a graduate of Cornell with a law degree from Harvard—came to know Clinton when both were working for the presidential campaign of Sen. George McGovern in 1972; they stayed in touch over the ensuing years. During Clinton's first term as governor of Arkansas, Berger introduced him to Democratic Party power broker Pamela Harriman and secured him a place on the board of her political action committee. A sign of his closeness to Clinton: Berger was among the small circle of friends who Clinton called down to Little Rock in July 1987 to consider a presidential bid (Harriman and Berger also organized a dinner party following Clinton's disastrous speech at the 1988 Democratic convention).[158] In the mid-1970s Berger served in a variety of positions, including work as a special assistant to New York Mayor John Lindsay and on the legislative staffs of Sen. Harold Hughes (D-IA) and Rep. Joseph Resnick (D-NY). From 1977 to 1980, he was Lake's deputy director of policy planning at State. During the Reagan years, Berger was a member of the prestigious Washington law firm of Hogan & Hartson—former Arkansas Sen. J. William Fulbright was a senior partner and mentor—and a key member its international law practice. In the 1992 campaign, Berger too signed on with his old friend Clinton and served as his senior foreign policy adviser. He enlisted three other Carter-era foreign policy experts: Lake, Madeleine Albright, and Richard Holbrooke. According to Clinton, "All would play important roles in the years ahead," and during the campaign "they helped me cross the threshold of understanding and competence in foreign affairs."[159]

During Clinton's postelection transition to office, Berger was selected to head up the team for foreign and national security policy. In selecting a NSC advisor, Clinton was torn between Lake and Berger. Both, according to Clinton, "had done a great job educating and advising me on foreign policy. Tony was a little older and Sandy had worked for him in the Carter State Department, but I had known Sandy longer and better. In the end the matter was resolved when Sandy came to me and suggested that I appoint Tony national security advisor and make him the deputy."[160]

Clinton presented his foreign policy team as a group on December 22—ten days after his economic team was announced. In addition to Lake's appointment, Warren Christopher, as secretary of state, finally got the position for which he had been passed over during the Carter administration.[161]

Christopher brought experience as a deputy attorney general (under Johnson), deputy secretary of state (under Carter), as well as service on several government commissions, head of Clinton's vice presidential selection process, and codirector of the 1992 transition. The choice of defense secretary proved more difficult, but Clinton settled on Rep. Les Aspin (D-WI), the chairman of the House Armed Services Committee. The final member of the team was Madeleine Albright as U.N. Ambassador, a position that would once again carry cabinet rank. Albright proved to be a major player in the policy process.

THE CLINTON NATIONAL SECURITY PROCESS

Although other aspects of Clinton's 1992 transition proved problematic, Berger, Lake, and the rest of the foreign policy team hit the ground running in preparing for its organization. The nomenclature changed from the George H. W. Bush years (just as it had in earlier new presidencies). National Security Reviews (NSR) became Presidential Review Directives (PRD) and National Security Directives (NSD) became Presidential Decision Directives (PDD). But the structure for decision making was similar—the "Scowcroft model" had survived an interparty transition to power.

On January 21, 1993, Clinton signed PDD-2, putting the new national security arrangements in place (interestingly, PDD-1 came first: it established the National Economic Council, NEC). PDD-2 enlarged the nonstatutory membership of the National Security Council to include the secretary of the treasury, the U.N. Ambassador, the NSC advisor, the White House chief of staff, and the director of the new National Economic Council (NEC). However, the real policy-making structure of the "Scowcroft model" was kept intact: the serious policy work would continue in the principals' committee, and the deputies' committee would continue to provide interagency coordination below the principals' level and serve as the conduit upwards for policy working groups—the latter now called Interagency Working Groups (IWGs) and chaired by representatives from either departments, the NSC staff, or the NEC.[162]

But there was one important organizational change. Although administrations going back to the Ford presidency had often had some kind of economic policy group, Clinton had emphasized the importance of economic issues during the campaign and sought to institutionalize their importance by creating a National Economic Council (NEC). Headed by respected Wall Street investment banker Robert Rubin, it played an important role over the first years of the Clinton presidency. Under Clinton, however, foreign and not just domestic economic policy fell under its purview. Rubin was made a member of the NSC, and he and his NEC staff were included in meetings involving international economic issues.

In the days following the inauguration, the Clinton NSC staff ordered up twenty-nine studies of foreign policy issues, especially four studies dealing with the most pressing problems in Haiti, Somalia, Iraq, and the Balkans. Reports indicated that the administration hoped to avoid the mistakes of hasty decisions made by other new presidencies and to give Clinton a set of broad strategies to deal with foreign problems rather than piecemeal, tactical responses that might lead to policy fiascoes.[163] It was an elusive hope.

Once in office, Lake, Christopher, and Aspin met for lunch every Wednesday in Lake's West Wing office. Lake established a close relationship with press spokesman and communication chief, George Stephanopoulos, and kept him informed of foreign policy developments (Lake did the same with press secretary Dee Dee Myers, when Stephanopoulos became "senior adviser" in the spring 1993 staff shake-up).[164] Lake and Stephanopoulos talked every morning before Chief of Staff Thomas ("Mac") McLarty's senior staff meeting, which Lake attended (not the usual practice for an NSC advisor). Lake met with Clinton every morning; Vice President Al Gore, Berger, and Leon Fuerth (Gore's representative on the NSC staff) also often attended. The meeting usually lasted fifteen minutes and covered items Lake wanted to bring to the president's attention. During the rest of the day, Lake had direct access to the president and often popped into his office several times a day as the situation merited.

Lake as NSC Advisor

The organizational structure, informal meetings, and day-to-day relationships among the principals, as well as Lake's relationship to others on the White House staff, *seemed* propitious. So too did Lake's conception of his job. According to a 1995 profile on Lake in the *New York Times Magazine*, it was Lake's view that the more policy-prolific NSC advisors, like Kissinger and Brzezinski, sometimes failed to give the president a full range of policy options. In contrast, "he sought the quieter broker style exemplified by . . . Brent Scowcroft." At the same time, Lake recognized that "pure brokerage" was an impossibility. While his primary responsibility was to "make sure the president is getting all points of view," those views also included his own.[165] According to Clinton, "He gives me consistently good advice and he gives me advice that's different from his on the big questions."[166]

Lake also recognized the delicate balance between serving as broker and as personal adviser to the president. Those two activities "can come into tension."[167] Being an honest broker, according to Lake, is the "hardest thing about the job, if you have strong views."[168]

Early in his tenure, some accounts indicated that Lake, in the interest of collegiality among the principals, was too prone to seek consensus. According to Vincent Auger, Lake (and Berger among the deputies) "preferred to reach an agreed *recommendation*" to be presented to Clinton. If no consensus emerged they "tended to 'walk the issue back' to a point where everyone could agree . . . a very time consuming process."[169] In Lake's own view, however, his conception of the job changed over time:

> My view of it actually changed over the course of that four years, which led to some tension with my colleagues. When I came in, my model was the British civil servant who stays in the background and is almost strictly an honest broker and offers advice from time to time. That's what I tried to do for the first nine to ten months and it wasn't working. I had to be both honest broker and policy advocate.[170]

He became more assertive in his views, "because it helps move issues to a resolution."[171] The change was urged by Colin Powell, shortly before he left his position as JCS chairman.[172] Lake would, in his own words, still "stay behind the scenes," "achieve consensus," and "make sure that my colleagues' views had a fair hearing." But he became "less hesitant in voicing my own views, even if it prevented consensus or put me at odds with them."[173]

Lake was a strong advocate, for example, of the eastward expansion of NATO.[174] By 1994, Lake and the NSC staff (plus Rubin's NEC) also sought to weaken the linkage that State favored between China's status as a "most favored nation" in trade policy and its improvements in human rights.[175] Lake was strongly involved in urging the approval of visas to Northern Ireland's Sinn Fein leaders—despite the opposition of the British government—in hopes of fostering some measure of peaceful inclusion and accommodation, and then more active engagement in the peace process. The process was rocky—with fits, starts, and disappointments—but it did eventually lead to the power-sharing arrangements of the 1998 Good Friday Agreement.[176] Early in the new administration, Lake was also a strong advocate in finding some middle ground over the role of gays and lesbians in the military, especially "to move on and get this issue out of the way."[177] More generally, as Lake himself relates, "We were having problems on Bosnia and Haiti, and I was very interested in Northern Ireland and I did become more aggressive in trying to bring clarity to our policies . . . to become more engaged and aggressive in the direction I thought we had to go."[178] But he still sought to embrace the honest broker role: "I tried at the same time to absolutely be an honest broker, because if that doesn't happen the whole system collapses. I am positive I never blocked any information or access by anybody else. But, as I said, I did become more involved in expressing my own views."[179]

Lake recognized the difficulty of balancing brokerage and his increasing policy advocacy:

> How did I try to reconcile it? It is sometimes hard; no department is going to like being pushed by the NSC staff on an issue. I understood this, but on NATO enlargement or Northern Ireland, Haiti or Bosnia, where we had to overcome some resistance from some of the departments, that's always going to leave a bad taste no matter how much you try to do it right. So you try to make it better by, one, holding both a lot of principals' meetings and even more informal meetings so that we are all talking it out, which is why I had not just the principals' meetings—a lot of them—but also then two sets of informal meetings with my colleagues over breakfast and lunch usually every week, in which the ground rule was not to make formal decisions but simply to talk things through.[180]

He also took care in what transpired in his private meetings with Clinton, not using them as occasions to press for a decision in the direction that the NSC advisor favored as Kissinger had done:

> It could be very tempting on the very morning when you are meeting with the president to use that to make decisions. At least in my mind I was trying to make those implementation meetings on decisions that had already been made: "You want me to be doing this, you want me to be doing that" . . . and then teeing up policy discussions, saying "you are going to have to have a meeting on this or a meeting on that." And certainly giving my advice but never letting that come to a final policy decision.[181]

This, too, in his mind helped him "reconcile" brokerage and advocacy.[182]

But others fault Lake—the "later Lake" most likely—for not attempting to balance those conflicting roles well. Rothkopf, in his book *Running the World*, tells of one senior administration official who had worked with both Lake and Berger who likened their respective work ways to the style of two different college professors. One professor—Lake—asks questions of the students already knowing the answer, and "if they don't get [the right answer], dismisses them." Another professor—Berger—wants "to hear what the students have to say and take that into consideration as the discussion develops. . . . Sandy was always more inclined to open up the process and hear people."[183] Interestingly, this characterization is in line with Albright's recollections in her memoirs:

> When I did speak up, I was unnerved by the manner of Tony Lake, who chaired the meetings [of the principals]. . . . I resented it when he drummed his fingers on the table while I spoke or looked at his watch. This puzzled me because I certainly did not monopolize the meetings, and more often than not my views accorded with his. I often thought we should arrange to talk prior to meetings, but that was not Tony's style. I wasn't sure gender played any role, but I did resent being treated as though I were one of his students.[184]

Furthermore, as she notes in her memoirs, when she proposed using force in Bosnia, "Tony Lake never let me finish my argument."[185] In Albright's view, it was Secretary of State Christopher—her boss when she was U.N. ambassador—who was more open to dissent. He was a "team player," but "when I didn't fully agree with him, he urged me to say what I thought."[186]

Another high-level official who was apparently unhappy with Lake was Treasury Secretary Lloyd Bentsen, a former senator from Texas and the Democrat's vice presidential candidate in 1988. Bentsen resigned in December 1994—he had not really expected to stay on beyond two years. However, any doubts about that were removed, as Rothkopf relates, by his frustrations that "he was constantly being cut out of the interagency process by Lake"— according to interviews with Chief of Staff McLarty and Bentsen's successor, Robert Rubin of the NEC.[187]

Finally, if campaign adviser Dick Morris is to be believed, even Clinton was sometimes concerned about the recommendations he was receiving. "I never get other options; I never get other information," Clinton reportedly told Morris.[188]

LAKE: BEYOND BROKERAGE

On other facets of the NSC advisor's role, Lake was more limited in his activities. He was initially cautious concerning his public visibility. According to Inderfurth and Johnson, "Lake attempted to take the adviser's role out of the limelight."[189] Such was Lake's success that in a *New York Times* photograph of him standing next to Clinton, he was labeled "unidentified."[190]

According to the White House's history of the NSC, "Lake initially maintained a low public profile, avoiding public appearances and television interviews, so as not to upstage the Secretary of State as Kissinger had done in the Nixon administration."[191] In Lake's own view, the NSC advisor "should be strictly an inside operator." [192] When, after nine months on the job, he delivered his first public address, aides joked that "Garbo talks."[193]

In September 1993, however, in response to criticism that the Clinton administration had not adequately explained its foreign policy, Lake began to appear as a public speaker.[194] Lake was concerned that he "didn't want to seem to be competing with the secretary of state." But in retrospect, "I now believe it was a mistake. . . . the president needs all the help he can get in explaining his policies to the nation."[195] Yet Lake remained cautious: "[I tried] being less visible publicly. So that when I went to China or when I was doing the North Ireland stuff, or going to Haiti or whatever, I always tried to do it without press attention." So too in other in contexts: "inevitably in Washington, which is super-charged politically, anytime a national security advisor is speaking publicly it is going to end up in a political context."[196]

As for a concern for politics, Lake later conceded that Clinton factored politics into his foreign policy decision making, especially as Bosnia "was starting to damage him at home. And there is no question that for political reasons [Dick] Morris urged the president to act." But in general, in Lake's view, Clinton "recognized that the best politics is usually to find the best policy."[197]

As for political calculation in his own advice to Clinton, it was Lake's view that the NSC staff "needs to resist taking up that mantle." At the early morning senior staff meeting, Lake engaged in "almost daily battle" with the political staff, especially Deputy Chief of Staff Harold Ickes, "over the relative weight to be given political considerations when they conflicted with our substantive goals." Some of the political advisers would look at Lake "as if I had just fallen off the turnip truck, when I would argue for a policy that might entail some short-term political pain."[198] Moreover, in public statements according to Lake, the NSC advisor "should avoid taking partisan positions. It can diminish his or her credibility, and only adds to the distrust and division between the Executive and Congress."[199] And, "If the national security advisor is perceived as being political or, worse, offering advice to the president on political grounds, it shakes confidence in the administration, which in itself is bad politics."[200] For Lake, staying out of politics also enabled him to deal with serving as an honest broker and expressing his own policy views: "Another thing I think you can do to be an honest broker, while having views and even pushing them, is to keep, as much as possible, the NSC out of politics."[201]

With respect to diplomatic activity, Lake was also cautious. He recognized that the "secretary of state should be the chief diplomatic officer of the United States government." Yet on some occasions, "it can be more effective for the White House to do it. And sometimes I had a particular interest." On Bosnia, for example, "they needed to hear directly from the White House that the president had made a decision about what we were going to do." "In those cases," according to Lake, efforts were undertaken, "without burning the bridge, turning it into a Vance and Brzezinski, Kissinger and Rogers." [202]

When he undertook a mission abroad, "I almost invariably took along a State Department person and often a Defense Department person. I would always coordinate in advance and I never went without both Secretary Christopher's knowledge and his approval." Yet Lake also concedes, "Sometimes, frankly, that took a while."[203]

Lake also was aware of and sought to tamp down the traditional rivalry between the NSC staff and the State Department. As the NSC's history notes, "During the Carter years, Lake had witnessed the negative effects of bureaucratic infighting and squabbling" between Vance and Brzezinski. Under Clinton, "Lake was effective in maintaining cordial relations with Secretary of State Warren M. Christopher and in developing an atmosphere of cooperation and collegiality." [204] The us-versus-them tensions within previous administrations were on both their minds and agendas. According to Lake,

> I remember more than once telling them [the NSC staff] to avoid the trap . . . both Christopher and I remember this very much from the Carter administration of course. . . . I do remember telling folks at staff meetings, "We must not let this happen." Christopher and I tried to head it off. [205]

But there could be occasional flare-ups, such as when media speculation occurred in 1994 that Clinton was thinking about replacing one or both of them. Each side thought the other was planting negative stories. According to Lake,

> I remember going to some of Christopher's public relations people once, public affairs people, who were also kind of friends, and I called it the Treaty of Guadeloupe-Hidalgo, my favorite name for a treaty, telling them that we should knock it off on each side because if we don't and we go to war, the White House will win.[206]

By September 1994, other reports emerged of some degree of conflict between Lake and Christopher, particularly over policy in Haiti, as well as
concern on the part of the NSC staff that State was incapable of producing
quality policy papers.[207] Lake and Assistant Secretary of State Richard Holbrooke, once close friends, also came into conflict over the negotiations that
would eventually lead to the Dayton Accords settlement in Bosnia (discussed
further below).

Problems in Process

Accounts of Lake's record in another facet of the broker's job—not just seeing
that relevant policy options are on the table, but making sure that broader
processes of deliberation works effectively to produce them—seems mixed.
But this seems much more Clinton's doing than Lake's. According to one account, "the administration's foreign policy is derided almost everywhere for
being ad hoc, episodic, unsteady, easily reversed." In the view of Kissinger,
"Almost everywhere the administration gets engaged, it recoils before the
consequences."[208] One immediate difficulty Lake had to cope with was Clinton's campaign promise to reduce the size of the White House staff by 25
percent. For Lake, that meant operating with leaner resources: a reduction
in staff size from 179 to 143 (the latter included about 60 professionals).[209]
Most importantly, Lake had to cope with the hopelessly informal and un-
disciplined nature of Clinton's own decision making. As Lake himself notes,
"Clinton was not noted for his discipline. Meetings went on and on. So in
that sense it was sometimes messy." But continued use of the "Scowcroft
model" on the national security side did bring some order in his view: "The
process itself, the principals, the deputies, the working groups, etc., I think
was pretty orderly with the exception of NATO enlargement, which was a
violation of the system because we were so busy on many other things."[210]

Although the NSC structure and Lake's role as a close adviser to the
president continued in some ways the process that had been present under
Bush and Scowcroft, there was one crucial difference: the level of interest and
participation in foreign policy making by the president himself. As Elizabeth
Drew points out, although he was briefed regularly by Lake, "Unlike every
President since Truman, Clinton had no regularly scheduled meetings with
his foreign policy team."[211] The president was informed of the principals'
deliberations but only when necessary, according to one report: "We don't
want to take up his time," one senior official explained.[212] Some participants
complained of their lack of access to the president. According to one report,
CIA Director James Woolsey, "had such trouble getting on Clinton's sched-

ule that he called upon retired Admiral William Crowe [a Clinton supporter and former chairman of the JCS] . . . to bring something up with the President."[213] Defense Secretary Aspin also complained of how little he got to see the president. According to Fred Barnes, "Face time with Clinton became a rare occurrence for Aspin."[214]

Like George H. W. Bush, Clinton did not view the formal structure of NSC meetings as the chief arena for his foreign policy deliberations. Clinton only chaired eight meetings of the NSC from January through October 1993. These meetings were usually convened after a crisis developed or, in the words of one administration insider, "when the needle has pushed him over into the red alert zone." And they tended to focus on public presentation of the administration's response "rather than fundamental elements of the crisis itself."[215] Colin Powell, who remained as JCS chair through September 1993, likened meetings that Clinton attended to "graduate-student bull sessions" and "think-tank seminars."[216] Nor was Clinton prone to convene informal venues for deliberation (as he did in domestic policy and as Bush Sr. did in foreign policy). According to Auger, during the first two years, "persistent efforts by Lake and Christopher to get the president to commit to weekly meetings with his foreign policy advisers were repeatedly rebuffed." Even Lake's daily meeting "was often shortened or canceled."[217]

Policy was largely threshed out below the presidential level in the principals' committee, of which Christopher, Aspin, Lake, Albright, Woolsey, and Powell (and his successors) were members. Berger, Lake's deputy, and Fuerth, Gore's representative, also attended. When Clinton attended a meeting, which did not occur regularly, Chief of Staff McLarty and Vice President Gore also came along. As had Scowcroft, Lake presided over the meetings of the principals. And, according to Christopher, "almost all major foreign policy issues were taken up" by the group, and "the usual formal product of a meeting was a set of recommendations to the president."[218] Lake's weekly lunches with Christopher and Aspin (and, later, Aspin's successor William Perry) were another venue for informal policy discussion, as were the weekly breakfasts the three held along with Albright and JCS Chairman Gen. John Shalikashvili.[219]

Some observers have noted flaws at lower levels of the process. According to Auger, NSC staff members reported that meetings were lengthy and often no decisions were taken; days later "participants would reconvene to rehash the issue."[220] The IWG on Bosnia policy in 1993 was characterized by several participants as "group therapy—an existential debate over what is the role of America, etc."[221]

The IWGs also "quickly became large and unwieldy," some overlapped in their responsibilities and produced conflicting recommendations. Higher-level NSC officials "were reluctant to 'butt heads' to resolve differences . . . . The problem was merely bucked up the organizational hierarchy . . . where the issue would be reworked from scratch." There was a "backlog of issues" and a "pattern of postponed and rescheduled" deputies' meetings.[222] In 1993, review of the administration's Somalia policy was one of those issues that was stuck in the queue. According to Auger, "NSC staffers said that the performance of the deputies' committee in this instance was not unusual and that the problem continued well into 1994."[223]

Several of the key principals did have the advantage of having worked together before, but they still operated in a system in which Clinton was the key decision maker and at its center. His initial disinterest in foreign policy notwithstanding, Clinton had personally approved every top-level appointee at Defense and State. Yet when his advisers met with the president, "the meetings sometimes meandered as the President was bombarded with conflicting advice and took time to make up his mind. The division within the foreign policy group contributed to a division in the mind of a President who had few strong instincts on foreign policy questions."[224] Even as late as May 1993, when it was clear that foreign policy would take up more of his attention than he had anticipated, Clinton still voiced concerns that it was taking up too much of his time: "I felt really badly because I don't want to spend any more time on [Bosnia] than is absolutely necessary, because what I got elected to do was to let America look at our own problems."[225]

Nor were any of the principals prepared to offer a broader vision that Clinton might embrace. Both Lake and Christopher were suited to serving a president who was prepared to take the lead. Yet as Leslie Gelb noted during the transition, although Lake, Christopher, and Aspin were highly experienced problem solvers, "None of the trio seeks limelight, and all will fit comfortably with Mr. Clinton's plan to make policy in the White House." Christopher, in particular, "is not a policy maker and has no known policy agenda. . . . He thinks case by case. But he can take any policy paper and find its flaws and make it viable."[226] Christopher's skills were as a negotiator not a foreign policy architect. According to one subordinate, "he's a good fielder, but a lousy hitter."[227] Aspin was viewed as disorganized and not very skilled as a bureaucratic infighter. Even Clinton once described Aspin as a man with "1,000 brilliant questions," but few answers.[228] According to David Broder, "all three of them seem to indulge, if not encourage, Clinton's penchant for talking issues to death." The result, according to Rep. Lee Hamilton (D-IN), a leading foreign policy expert in Congress, was that "our policy has not been as well-defined, well-articulated, and well-formulated as it should be."[229]

Some changes were made in personnel. Defense Secretary Aspin proved to be a poor manager at the Pentagon, and some in the Pentagon felt alienated from him. His resignation ("requested" according to Lake)[230] was announced in December 1993, and he was replaced by his deputy, William J. Perry. Perry was seen as a more competent manager. CIA Director Woolsey was not seen as a team player. Unlike his predecessors, Clinton chose not to receive a daily oral briefing from the CIA director or his representative, preferring to read the daily intelligence report instead.[231] Woolsey lasted until the end of 1995 and was replaced by John Deutch, deputy secretary of defense.

Policy: Difficulties in Somalia and Haiti

Clinton had hoped that foreign policy issues would not preoccupy his presidency as they had his predecessor. Domestic and economic issues would take center stage. At best, as he stated, "foreign policy will come into play as it affects the economy." Yet in a post–cold war era, Clinton could not escape the press of world affairs, his own hoped-for agenda notwithstanding. Even during the transition, Clinton encountered a series of vexing foreign policy problems in Bosnia, Haiti, Somalia, North Korea, Iraq, and Russia. Clinton's problems were compounded by his own lack of foreign policy experience and that his party had been out of power for twelve years, a period in which the world scene had radically been transformed.

Somalia and Haiti especially posed early challenges.[232] Both episodes were plagued with intelligence failures and poor decision making.[233] In 1993, George H. W. Bush's humanitarian mission to aid Somalia degenerated—under Clinton's watch—into an embarrassing and bloody military mission. On October 3 and 4, in an attempt to capture Mohammed Aideed, one of the Somali warlords, eighteen U.S. soldiers were killed and their bodies dragged through the streets of Mogadishu. The grisly event was captured by television cameras and led to public and congressional calls for the United States to withdraw its forces, a policy that Clinton announced on October 7.[234] Unlike Bosnia, Somalia had not even been on the administration's front burner of pressing issues. Policy had been handled by the second-level deputies' committee, and reports indicated that Clinton and his top aides had not convened to discuss Somalia until after the events of October 3.[235]

Both Lake and Berger later came to regard Somalia as the low point of the White House's foreign policy efforts during Clinton's tenure.[236] As Lake later explained:

> The problem was that we inherited this war, which saved hundreds of thousands of lives, and I am not sorry that Bush went in. But it did not have a defined end, it did not have a defined purpose. So by February or March as I recall, we were starting to give it one and the idea was to try to figure out a way to leave behind a Somalia that was not going to have a new famine, where we would face the same choice again. Once the ambush of the Pakistani troops happened, it became changed over to too much of a preoccupation with Aideed and others. In each case it became almost a matter of implementation rather than setting a policy. . . . When we did try to fix it, after I had talked to Bob Oakley and others and started to push the U.N. to look at this in more of a political context not a military one, which we were doing by September before the Blackhawk incident, it was too late.[237]

With respect to Haiti, during the campaign, Clinton had criticized the Bush policy of repatriating Haitian "boat people" rather than allow them asylum in the United States. But during the transition, he was forced to reverse his position following reports that Haitians in large numbers were preparing rafts and other makeshift devices to leave the island pending Clinton's change in policy. By the fall, Clinton thought he had worked out an accord with the nation's military junta to restore to power the democratically elected government of Jean-Bertrand Aristide by October 31. But on October 11, just days after the Somalia disaster, a U.S. navy vessel carrying 200 military advisers and engineers sailed into Port-au-Prince harbor only to be met by a rag-tag mob of demonstrators sent there by the Haitian government. Instead of docking, the ship turned back. It was a major embarrassment to the administration.

According to Lake, there was "little—in retrospect too little—debate in our meetings about whether to use force to compel . . . compliance. Instead we ordered the ship's withdrawal, announced new sanctions against the regime, and ordered . . . warships to patrol off Haiti's shores. It was a terrible humiliation."[238]And, "We pulled the ship back in part because we had not prepared properly to react forcefully if the permission we had been given to land was revoked. For that, I was at fault."[239]

The episode painfully demonstrated that the Haitian military was not prepared to live up to its agreement to restore Aristide. But more troubling were reports indicating that the administration was aware of the deteriorating situation but saw no danger signs in sending in the lightly armed military team. As Meena Bose points out, "intelligence reports either did not reach the most influential officials, or failed to have an effect."[240]

Later, Lake took the lead in finding a more forceful means of resolving the impasse in Haiti. He personally negotiated with the exiled Aristide and pressed hard against State's view that sanctions were the only means of removing the military junta. Finally in September 1994, a year after the failed mission, he won Clinton's support.[241]

A larger contingent of U.S. forces was assembled and the threat of force led to the collapse of the military government; U.S. and later U.N. peacekeeping forces were then dispatched.[242] However, Haiti remained—and remains—a near intractable problem.

BOSNIA, MOST INTRACTABLE

If Haiti was near intractable, Bosnia was most intractable. Deliberations on what to do there illustrate a number of the problems in decision making in this presidency. Bosnia was another of the few foreign policy issues where Clinton had taken a stand during the campaign when he criticized the Bush administration's inaction and pledged to do something about Serbia's "ethnic cleansing" in the region. Yet it was not clear what course the administration would take once Clinton was in office. Clinton's three chief advisers held somewhat different views. Aspin was for doing as little as possible, Lake pushed for strong action, while Christopher took a number of different positions. The NSC's first presidential review directive (PRD-1) was on Bosnia, a clear sign of its importance.

Yet the administration struggled to find a workable policy. Early agreement was reached to stiffen economic sanctions against Serbia, call for the U.N. to authorize a no-fly zone over Bosnia, and drop food supplies by parachute to the Bosnian Muslims. But the decision "was made rather casually and, given its importance, received little public notice."[243]

Although Clinton and Christopher both thought the administration should take a tougher stance toward the Bosnian Serbs, the principals found it difficult to formulate a policy. In late March and through April, the situation in Bosnia worsened, especially following an assault on the Muslim enclave of Srebrenica. A series of meetings were convened and a number of options were discussed, but Clinton and his advisers could not reach a decision. At the same time, returning to the Bush administration policy of doing nothing had essentially been foreclosed. As Elizabeth Drew observed,

"By saying so often that something must be done to stop the ethnic cleansing, Clinton got himself in a corner. Whatever his misgivings, doing nothing wasn't an option."[244]

By late April, following a series of meetings among the principals with the Joint Chiefs and congressional leaders, a decision was reached, dubbed "lift and strike." Essentially it was a proposal to force the parties to accept a cease-fire by lifting the existing arms embargo—thus providing the Bosnian Muslims with arms to give them more of a level playing field with the Bosnian Serbs—coupled with air strikes against the Serbs if they took advantage of the situation before the arms reached the Muslims.[245]

Christopher was then dispatched to sell the proposal to the NATO allies, who were firmly against lifting the arms embargo. Not only were Britain and France against it, Clinton began to have second thoughts. At one point, following a meeting with the president, Aspin called Lake and told him that Clinton was "going South on this policy. His heart isn't in it. We have a problem here. We're out there pushing a policy that the President's not comfortable with. He's not on board."[246] As Christopher later stated, when he returned to Washington, "it became evident that there had been a sea change in attitudes during the week I had been away. No one else argued in support of pursuing the lift and strike options with our allies. . . . The President reportedly had been reading books on Balkan history that presented a grim picture of prospects for reconciliation."[247]

In May, a strategy of containment rather than intervention was adopted, with 300 U.S. troops sent to Macedonia as part of a U.N. force, thus indicating that the United States was prepared to do something. In late May, in part to head off a Russian-led solution to the crisis, the United States took the lead in crafting an allied policy of protecting Bosnian Muslim "safe areas," by force if necessary. The United States, however, would not provide ground troops if needed, but would undertake any air strikes or logistical support.

While Christopher thought the situation workable, Lake did not think the Bosnia problem would go away. It will be back, he warned.[248] But Clinton had avoided a policy fiasco that might have ensued if he had sent U.S. troops. Yet the threat of air strikes remained just that: some European allies, especially France, balked at the use of force, and the terms of an August 1993 NATO agreement prevented the United States from acting unilaterally.[249] It was only as the Serbian siege of Sarajevo intensified that the allies agreed to act with real force.

At a NATO summit in January 1994, according to Lake, "the president's personal diplomacy helped gain the ultimatum": allied agreement to air strikes against the Bosnian Serbs, especially to relieve Sarajevo, which eventually led to a cease-fire agreement. "It worked," Lake notes, "and while Bosnia remained a cancer on our foreign policy and topic A on our agenda, the situation there eased somewhat until the autumn of 1994."[250] But Lake was growing increasingly frustrated with the policy-making process on Bosnia within the administration and the reticence of NATO allies to such a point that he seriously considered resigning.[251] Nor was the cease-fire successful, serious breaches continued; NATO and U.N. response was fitful and largely ineffective.

BOSNIA: THE MERITS OF ADVOCACY ... AND BROKERAGE

It would not be until the summer of 1995, as Christopher recalls, that "the President decided that the United States should take a stronger hand, diplomatically and militarily."[252] At that point, Lake and his NSC staff took the lead in developing a new approach to Bosnia. After gaining Clinton's approval, he initially tried to enlist State and Defense in the effort, but they "offered a lot of resistance." As a result, Lake and his staff worked out what they termed an "Endgame Strategy" on their own, which Lake took to Clinton without letting the other principals see it. As Woodward notes, "Lake was supposed to be the honest broker. . . . But Bosnia was too important, and Lake decided to violate his own rules for the first time."[253] Lake and his staff prepared a seven-point plan, the central elements of which were a 51–49 geographic division of Bosnia (51 percent to the Bosnian Muslims and Croats, 49 percent to the Bosnian Serbs) and their coexistence under a federation but with significant political power allocated to each entity. In the interim the Bosnian Serbs would be threatened with air strikes and the lifting of the arms embargo if they did not negotiate, and the Croats and Bosnian Muslims were threatened with abandonment if they failed to do likewise.

As Lake explains, he took a very active role in proposing a new plan:

> It was partly because of substantive views, and that State and Defense were not in favor of as an aggressive policy. And we needed to get it done. And secondly because the formal processes were simply taking too long. I said at a luncheon, "Look, let's put a deadline on it; everybody come in with their view of what we ought to do, put it together and bring it before the president. And let's not do endless reviews on it." Then the president was at least presented with everyone's views and all of the papers, and then I pushed for my point of view.[254]

But in Lake's view, his advocacy did not stand alone, brokerage was also present: "It was a case of honest broker in the sense that everybody's views were there but I certainly was pushing as hard as I could and in every way I could."[255]

In late July and early August, the plan was discussed among the principals and with Clinton's strong backing their objections were overcome. Lake was then secretly dispatched to Europe to sell it to the allies, a mission that proved successful.[256] Lake's plan eventually led to the Dayton Accords in December 1995. The latter proved to be a diplomatic success, especially due to the persistent negotiating efforts of Assistant Secretary of State Richard Holbrooke and the periodic intervention of Secretary of State Christopher.[257]

Lake's advocacy—and its link to eventual policy success—is notable. But it was advocacy that came to the fore under special circumstances: an inability among the principals to come to agreement, a president ready for a more aggressive posture, and a security situation in Bosnia that was deteriorating. Although Lake shrewdly got Clinton on board early for his plan, Lake also invited the other principals to offer their own ideas when he presented his plan to them—brokerage remained despite Lake's own advocacy. An interdepartmental working group under Berger's chairmanship was established to produce concrete policy alternatives, which were then brought to the principals and the president for consideration—a sound deliberative policy process ensued. Lake also made sure there were no ambiguities concerning U.S. policy, once the president had made a decision.[258] As Ivo Daalder notes, Lake was clearly acting as a "true policy entrepreneur." But Bosnia was different from the advocacy undertaken by other NSC advisors. Lake had tried the normal interagency process but with little success, and he was acting in response to Clinton's request for a new course "rather than to subvert the president's will." Advocacy, moreover, did not eclipse brokerage, according to Daalder, "Lake drew clear lines between his role as advocate in the policy formulation stage, his role as honest broker in the policy decision stage, and his role as enabler [but not direct negotiator, that was Holbrooke's job] during the policy implementation stage."[259]

Although success eventually came in Bosnia, the early Clinton track record was not good there or elsewhere. In testimony before the Senate Foreign Relations Committee in November 1993, Warren Christopher conceded that Bosnia, Haiti, and Somalia were "difficult situations" where "things have not gone exactly as we planned."[260] According to another account, Clinton's "first-term foreign policy owed more to improvisation than vision . . . sometimes averting disaster, sometimes not."[261]

But the administration was also not without other successes. Secretary of State Christopher played a major diplomatic role in securing the October 27, 1994, agreement between Israel and Jordan ending four decades of hostility.[262] Treasury took the lead in arranging a financial aid package to stave off an economic crisis in Mexico. NATO expansion was achieved despite Russian objections. The administration pushed hard to arrange a settlement in Northern Ireland. Moreover, while Clinton was always attentive to the political implications of his foreign policy choices, several of these efforts were initially unpopular or politically risky. In the end, while politics was factored in, so too was good policy.

BERGER AS NSC ADVISOR

During Clinton's second term, Berger was more active, more of a central force than Lake had been, upping "the energy level of the adviser's position."[263] According to another account, Berger's methodical and hard-working approach to the job made him, according to several administration officials, "the dominant figure in setting second-term foreign policy."[264] This is echoed by another senior official outside the White House: Berger was "by far the most dominant entity in foreign policy making in this administration." Yet that official also offered a bit of a warning, adding that the White House was "too controlling."[265]

At least initially, however, Berger faced more competition from his secretary of state than Lake had experienced with Warren Christopher. Secretary of State Albright, Christopher's replacement in the second term, had an important impact in a number of areas. Most notable was her eventual success in persuading Clinton and others in the administration to take a hard military stand against Serbia's ethnic cleansing efforts in Kosovo, a position that was at odds with Berger's more cautious posture.[266] She also was an active force in Middle East negotiations. As Albright relates in her memoirs, Berger saw her as a starting pitcher who lasted until the "eighth inning, then turned the ball over to the relief pitcher—President Clinton."[267]

Yet, later on, Albright's influence appeared to wane. Six months after the Kosovo crisis in 1999, a *New York Times* account of the Berger-Albright relationship notes that Berger's proximity to the Oval Office and his long personal relationship with Clinton "effectively eclipsed" Albright. This may just be misleading "insider baseball." But Berger took the lead role in gaining China's entry to the World Trade Organization (against a more cautious, human rights concerned State Department), the unsuccessful attempt to gain Senate ratification of a nuclear test ban treaty, and, increasingly, U.S.

policy toward Russia. Berger's "presence has been unrelenting."[268] According to another *New York Times* account, while Albright played a major role in NATO expansion, she was less a factor in other key issues of the second term, including relations with China and attempts to broker a settlement in Northern Ireland.[269] In the view of Ivo Daalder of the Brookings Institution, Albright "remains a participant in the process. But her weight as secretary of state in the determination of foreign policy appears less than at any time in the Clinton administration." [270]

There were some differences in Berger's role as NSC advisor compared to Lake's. According to one account, Berger had an "obsession with finding a consensus among top officials"—not unlike Lake. But he was also skilled "as a hands-on manager."[271]

Another account noted that administration officials felt that Lake was "inscrutable," and "not giving their views a fair hearing with Clinton. No such complaints have yet been heard of Berger."[272] In Berger's view, the NSC advisor should try to "clear the underbrush" and bring the principals, if possible, to a consensus at "the highest common denominator." But "if there was no consensus at a fairly high level, it was better to bring the president two starkly different points of view."[273]

Berger also at least paid lip service to an honest broker's concern with the quality of the deliberative process. The job entails, he held, personal advice to the president, but the NSC advisor also acts as the "foreign policy chief of staff." Unlike cabinet officers, the NSC advisor has a "unique focus," attentive to "how the president would be best served in decision making, what he needs to know in addition to what he wants to know and how to keep the process moving in a direction he wants it to move. . . . You can try to tee up a decision for him in a way that does not put him in a box."[274]

According to James Steinberg, Berger's deputy NSC advisor, the principals' committee "became somewhat more of a focus for big decision making than it had before . . . the principals did a somewhat better job in the second term in using the principals' committee to provide a framework . . . for policy guidance."[275]

Berger was aided in his efforts by a closer relationship with Clinton than Lake had enjoyed. Berger had known him the longest of any White House official in the second term. According to Daalder, Berger "instinctively understands Mr. Clinton's needs better than anyone else."[276] According to one White House aide, "The president really likes Sandy and respects him. They have a strong bond in the way they interact."[277]

Better interaction also extended to the other principals. According to

Albright, "The national security team is a very close team, and we see each other and talk to each other constantly."[278] A direct phone link was set up between her office and Berger's, and according to Albright, "on some days might be used a half dozen times or more."

The "ABC" club—Albright, Berger, and (Defense Secretary and former GOP senator William) Cohen—regularly met for lunch on Monday. According to Albright, these "sessions were useful in coordinating policy, breaking logjams, and clearing the air."[279] A larger breakfast meeting with the other principals—including CIA director George Tenet, Fuerth (Gore's chief foreign policy adviser), the U.N. ambassador, and the JCS chairman—was held weekly on Wednesday.[280] Relations between Berger and Albright were also no doubt helped by the fact that they had been friends prior to the Clinton presidency. Furthermore, "one reason our foreign policy teamed functioned well," according to Albright, was that "despite small problems we all actually liked one another and often got together socially."[281]

In Albright's view, "Sandy is the glue that holds us together. In meetings, he walks everyone through what's going on. He asks hard questions, presses the points. He puts everyone through their paces."[282] Even if Albright's impact in the foreign policy process was at times limited—or shared with other principals such as Berger or Treasury Secretary Rubin—Berger made sure she remained in close contact. According to Jamie Rubin, her press spokesman, "The key to their working relationship is the phone." They spoke to each "more than two stockbrokers in a market upsurge or crash."[283]

In her memoirs, Albright does note that although historically the relationship between the NSC advisor and the secretary of state "has been tense," in comparison with her predecessors "we worked together well." Still, her relationship with Berger and his deputy Steinberg "was far from trouble free." [284] While she "found Sandy to be fair . . . I sometimes became irritated by what I saw as the NSC's attempts to micromanage." Problems arose "when Sandy and I tried to occupy each other's spaces. . . . Although the NSC's job was supposed to be limited to coordinating the actions and policies of the departments, proximity to the president sometimes tempted Sandy and his staff to assume an operational role." Given Albright's past NSC staff service under Brzezinski, she was in a tough position to object: "when I complained, Sandy—who had been in the State Department at that time—said he was doing only what Brzezinski had done." Yet when all was said and done, according to Albright, both knew that "we were going to sink or swim together. Neither of us would emerge a hero if our foreign policy flopped. We both felt an obligation to submerge any personal irritations and work together."[285]

Clinton may also have been more attentive to foreign policy deliberations with his principals during Berger's tenure, perhaps as thoughts of his presidential legacy began to loom during his second term. According to Albright, "The president was in every meeting that we wanted to have with him. He was focused. There's some people who say that he compartmentalizes . . . [but] he worked with us closely, and I felt that he was always available and always there."[286] Albright also notes that she had regular one-on-one meetings with Clinton.[287]

BERGER: BEYOND BROKERAGE

Berger also differed from Lake on other facets of the NSC advisor's job. Berger had better political antennae than Lake, another good fit with Clinton. His pre-Clinton experience was more political than Lake's academic background. In the run-up to the 1996 election, he was a participant in the weekly political strategy sessions convened by the Clintons with top White House aides and campaign advisers. According to Dick Morris, who was brought on board as a key political adviser to the reelection campaign, Berger (then still Lake's deputy) was "more a political creature, with a long track record in campaigns . . . [he] tried to thrust a sense of political reality into NSC deliberations."[288] Such was his wider acumen, that he was even twice mentioned as a possible contender to be White House chief of staff, although that job went to Erskine Bowles and then John Podesta.[289] Berger's sense of the political environment surrounding decision making was especially acute at the time of the Kosovo crisis: he was more cautious than Albright about military intervention, both with respect to creating support with Congress and gaining public approval.[290] It should be noted, however, that Morris felt that Berger's "political perspectives weren't always right." But, in Morris' view, "at least he tried."[291]

Berger was also more deeply involved in congressional lobbying than was Lake. As his deputy NSC advisor recalls, "The list of phone calls and meetings that Sandy [Berger] gets from our legislative people . . . would never have happened with Tony [Lake]. Some days, Sandy is given a list of six or eight follow-up actions to pursue, in terms of talking to particular members or going up to the Hill . . . From the outset, he has seen his role, vis-à-vis Congress very differently. He's much more proactive, much more engaged." As a result, "we've accomplished substantially more than we might have, even with a Congress controlled by the other party. I think it's made a real difference."[292]

Berger recognized that the NSC advisor should largely stay out of the role of implementing policy, especially in the conduct of diplomatic negotiations. In his view, "it is an unusual circumstance when the national security adviser should be the principal negotiator or diplomat." He did travel to Moscow before the summit meeting between Clinton and Yeltsin in order to "get some closure before the meeting. And because of a configuration of authority in the Kremlin, it was appropriate in that circumstance that I go." Also, there may be occasions, in his view, when "you want to engage at the highest levels less obtrusively." In general, however, "it is better to have the secretary of state in that role."[293]

But Berger was certainly a more visible public spokesman for the Clinton White House. According to Inderfurth and Johnson, "within two weeks of his tenure, Berger had already equaled the number of appearances on Sunday morning television talk shows that Lake had made during his four years in office."[294] One early profile piece on Berger in the *New York Times* noted that his job is not just "statecraft but stagecraft. And a principal goal of the staging is to convince skeptics that Clinton has big ideas about the world and is capable of implementing them."[295] Here, Berger's past no doubt aided his efforts—he had been a speechwriter for Sen. George McGovern during the 1972 presidential campaign as well as for Secretaries of State Vance and Muskie when he served as Lake's deputy at State during the Carter years.[296]

EFFECTS ON POLICY

Iraq, North Korea, Russia, and China posed continuing challenges to the Clinton presidency, but Clinton enjoyed less success than his two immediate predecessors. Even his attempt to deal with terrorism in the aftermath of the bombing of two U.S. embassies in Africa was fraught with intelligence and communication failures. One of the targets, a pharmaceutical factory in Sudan, appeared on subsequent investigation to have been less conclusively linked to the bombings: it was a decision to retaliate based on surmise rather than hard evidence.[297]

The Balkans remained a problem throughout Clinton's presidency, starting with Bosnia in 1993, under Lake, and culminating in Kosovo in 1999, under Berger. At times the administration was indecisive and unsure of its goals. In the Kosovo crisis, the administration was taken to task for its poor contingency planning, limited military options, and unclear "exit" strategy (by chance or luck, the United States and its NATO allies managed to avoid a full-blown invasion of Serbia; after seventy-eight days of air strikes, the Serbian government capitulated).[298] In the view of Michael Mandelbaum, a respected foreign policy expert, the war was a "perfect failure." The political consequences of the war "were the opposite of what NATO's political leaders intended," "virtually all the major political effects were unplanned, unanticipated, and unwelcome," and the war itself "was the unintended consequence of a gross error in political judgment."[299] As Brent Scowcroft noted at the time, "It's a bad strategy. And it is the job of the National Security Council to explore what happens, not if everything goes right, but what if everything goes wrong."[300] According to another account, "Critics say the Kosovo war could have been avoided in the first place through more farsighted diplomacy. Once the war began, many military experts said Clinton failed to see that the air campaign would not work in a short period of time."[301]

Poor strategy could also crop up at home: 1999 also saw the failure of the Senate to ratify a comprehensive test ban treaty, as well as public demonstrations in Seattle against a conference of the World Trade Organization, an area in which Clinton had done little to prepare public opinion.[302] With respect to the test ban treaty, even Lake notes that the administration "failed to lay the groundwork with skeptical (and sometimes hostile) Republican senators." The 51–48 vote "was the first time the Senate had rejected an international accord of this magnitude since the Treaty of Versailles."[303] Other critics have faulted the administration's response to the rise of Osama Bin Laden's terrorist activities. Opportunities to "take out" Bin Laden arose, but the administration was overly cautious.

Yet in the view of some, notably Berger and Albright, the second term was marked by some success. In Berger's view, the Clinton administration was able to move from an inherited agenda to its own: "enlarging NATO and embracing new democracies, peace in Northern Ireland, the peace process in the Middle East, trying to build up a stronger relationship with China based on openness, and trying to work with Russia. So, in some ways, as time went on, the agenda shifted from what we inherited in this post–Cold War period to what we were building."[304] Berger also played a central role in successful negotiations with the leadership of the Republican Senate in the 1997 ratification of the Chemical Weapons Convention.[305] The unsettled international context they confronted also needs to be taken into account in measuring their degree of success: like the Bush Sr. administration, the Clinton team faced the unsure and uncharted waters of post–cold war geopolitics.

Yet underlying problems remained. Organizational issues appear less problematic in this presidency, especially after its somewhat erratic start. The "Scowcroft model" was essentially carried over from the George H. W. Bush years. The crucial difference was personnel. And, from our perspective, how they defined their roles mattered, especially given a president who was often detached from the details of foreign and national security policy and the process through which it took shape.

IV. George W. Bush: Stephen Hadley

On January 26, 2005, Stephen Hadley succeeded Condoleezza Rice as national security advisor upon her confirmation as secretary of state. Hadley came well prepared for the job. He received his undergraduate degree from Cornell University and then his law degree from Yale. After a stint in the navy, he began his governmental career in 1972 as an analyst for the comptroller of the Defense Department. From 1974 until the end of the Ford administration he was a member of the NSC staff under Kissinger then Scowcroft.

Hadley returned to the private practice of law and was later, during the Clinton interregnum, a member of Scowcroft's international consulting firm. During the Reagan years he served on several advisory boards, but his most important service was as counsel to the Tower Commission's investigation of Iran-Contra—an interesting assignment given its relevance to the role of the NSC advisor, Hadley's prior connection to Scowcroft, and his future job. In the George H. W. Bush administration, Hadley served as assistant secretary of defense for international security policy, a position that involved him heavily in nuclear defense issues, arms control policy, and NATO and Western European matters. During the 2000 presidential election, he was one of the "Vulcans" that Rice organized to advise Bush on foreign and national security issues, and he worked with her during the 2000 Bush-Cheney transition. His efforts and past experience led to his appointment as her deputy NSC advisor for the duration of Bush's first term.

Assessing his role as deputy NSC advisor and then as Rice's successor is not an easy or simple task. His tenure in the deputy position presents a mixed picture. Hadley, like Rice among the principals, faced a room full of heavyweights as chair of the deputies' committee: in his case, it was Deputy Secretary of Defense Paul Wolfowitz—his former boss at Defense during the George H. W. Bush years—and Richard Armitage from State most notably. According to one participant, one of Hadley's tasks is "reining in some of the right-wing ideologues who can get the president in trouble [read: likely Wolfowitz, not Armitage]. He's methodical. He runs meetings like an orchestra conductor. But when they are over, he's quietly tossed some pretty extreme ideas overboard." He also served, in Rice's words, as her "alter ego. I can sometimes jump from A to F. He backs me up to B and C, makes me think through implications."[306] (Interestingly, Hadley's activities—if this account is correct—indicate his own incipient brokerage role now as deputy, a well as the applicability of the role at other points in the policy-making process.)

But other accounts discerned problems. Hadley's efforts in the deputies' committee were characterized by some as exhibiting some of the same "dysfunction" that dogged Rice among the principals. According to one account, "Decisions go unmade at the deadlocked deputies' meetings or get kicked back or ignored by the president's principals, his top advisers."[307] Even basic participation may have been a problem: at lower-level interagency meetings, "the Defense Department sometimes doesn't even bother to show up."[308] Other problems were discerned as well. Fair coordination may have been a problem, according to one account: "one senior official told of 'fairly regular' instances in which, after a deputies' meetings, notes would be adjusted on the basis of comments that appeared to come from the Department of Defense." On one occasion, a Defense official tried to amend conclusions "that had been collectively reached by the group. Hadley obliged."[309] The chief cause of problems, however, may have originated elsewhere. According to James Risen, Rumsfeld was a prime source of his subordinates' behavior at the deputies' meetings and other lower-level groups: within the NSC staff a strong belief developed that "Rumsfeld had told his aides at the Pentagon that they too could ignore directions from the NSC."[310] Nor was President Bush willing to ride herd on his tough-minded, tough-acting, and bureaucratically skilled defense secretary.

Hadley did, as we saw in chapter 6, take his concerns about the lack of coordination between the CIA and the military during the early phases of the war in Afghanistan to Rumsfeld directly and with positive result.[311] Hadley also was concerned about the quality of their deliberations; the deputies' committee, in his view, was not on top of what was transpiring in the early efforts against the Taliban.[312]

Yet it was the war with Iraq that was most problematic. Hadley's deputies' group did not adequately vet the intelligence concerning Saddam Hussein's possession of weapons of mass destruction, as well as other Iraqi actions that were part of the administration's case for war. Most damning was the insertion of the infamous sixteen words in Bush's 2003 State of the Union address concerning Iraq's attempts to purchase uranium in Africa—what was supposed to be a definitive signal of its continuing efforts to develop nuclear weapons, but it ultimately proved erroneous. Subsequent investigation revealed that CIA Director George Tenet had personally alerted Hadley to prevent a similar reference in Bush's October 7, 2002, speech, a major address in Cincinnati on the rationale for war against Iraq.[313] Moreover, Hadley had received two memos from the CIA in October warning against claims about uranium purchases. On July 22, 2003, Hadley accepted blame for not remembering the CIA's counsel during the drafting of the State of the Union address; he also reportedly offered the president his resignation, which was quickly rejected.[314]

As NSC advisor in Bush's second term, Hadley faced a different and, over time, less difficult cast of characters than had Rice. Rice herself, of course, replaced Colin Powell at State in 2005, thus creating a closer bond between the NSC advisor and staff and the State Department than had existed in the first term. That Hadley had been Rice's deputy at the NSC undoubtedly helped keep relations with State smooth and cooperative—just as it had when Scowcroft replaced Kissinger as NSC advisor (and, with respect to Defense, when Powell had followed Carlucci).[315]

Second-level departmental officials who had often clashed with each other and with the NSC advisor and the NSC staff—such as Wolfowitz and Armitage—had also departed at the start of the second term. After the 2006 midterm election, Rumsfeld was gone at Defense, replaced by Robert Gates. Gates was a veteran of the more cooperative and collegial George H. W. Bush foreign policy team, where he had served as Scowcroft's respected deputy and then as CIA director. With Rumsfeld gone as a key ally, Vice President Cheney's dominant role also lessened a bit.

Throughout the Bush presidency, Hadley exhibited a much lower public profile than either Rice or most of her predecessors. Information about Hadley's tenure as NSC advisor was more tightly held than in the past. Media stories and other accounts of its inner workings were fewer. Those that did appear described him as low-key and somewhat self-effacing. He did not revel in the media limelight and often had to be strongly encouraged by other White House officials to appear on the Sunday morning news programs; he was a competent voice but no Condi Rice.[316] As deputy NSC advisor, he appeared on television precisely twice.[317] On his first overseas trip in the fall of 2005, he was accompanied by just one reporter.[318] "My approach is going to be more offstage," he told one reporter, "Condi has established herself as an articulator of the president's policies. . . . It's very important that she carry that out and there not be competing voices or any sense of possible competition."[319]

Another factor that may have ameliorated tense relations with State was the apparent absence of Hadley's attempt to foster his own clearly articulated policy agenda. According to one account, "he is so relentlessly low-profile that it is difficult to get a fix on his views. Even his admirers have a hard time assessing his performance."[320] Zbigniew Brzezinski saw his successor as "straightforward . . . But there's a kind of bureaucratic regularity to him."[321] But unlike Brzezinski, Hadley did not use his position to bulldoze through his own policy views. Rather, as he himself put it, he was "an honest broker . . . somebody who is not pushing a particular policy view."[322]

Reports also indicated that during the time Rumsfeld remained at Defense, Hadley was more inclined to push back against the defense secretary's policy efforts than Rice had been.[323] According to Bob Woodward's account in *State of Denial*, Hadley had also been an early voice urging Rumsfeld's replacement.[324] But Woodward also notes that some were disappointed with Hadley's performance, Scowcroft most notably: "Hadley would not stand up to anyone—not to Cheney or Rice, and certainly not to Rumsfeld."[325]

Yet Hadley operated with a deft hand, according to one account, in tamping down the principals' "grudge matches" of the first term.[326] Some reports also signaled that the tensions of the first term had abated and that the interagency process was working more effectively. According to Hadley, "At the end of the day, people are comfortable with the decisions the president makes, and you don't have reports of fighting . . . [that] you had in the past."[327] And it was Hadley, not the hard-line Cheney in his efforts, who proved the more successful negotiator in lobbying Republican senators such as John McCain (R-AZ) and Lindsey Graham (R-SC) to come to a compromise agreement with the White House on the treatment of terrorist detainees.[328]

Hadley does not appear to have been as strongly a personal counselor to the president as was Rice when she was NSC advisor. Part of this may reflect Rice's continuing close relationship to Bush and a more assertive policy role as secretary of state. Part also may reflect Hadley's relationship to Rice, his deference to her on policy matters, and the absence on his part of a more full-blown policy vision of a Kissinger or Brzezinski. Yet, at times Hadley was a major player behind the scenes, and therein lies a tale that may yet unfold when more is known about this administration's inner workings and its pattern of counsel.

But some things are known. One of the most important of his efforts was devising the policy of a military surge in Iraq in late 2006 and early 2007. It was in great measure the product of Hadley, his then deputy J. D. Crouch II, and the NSC staff rather than the generals at the Pentagon, who mostly preferred the status quo.[329] The change in strategy was the result of a more careful vetting process than had occurred in the earlier decision to go to war.

According to one account, while it was unclear to many when, how, or why Bush decided to invade Iraq in 2003, "no such confusion clouds how the surge of 2007 was hatched."[330] Discontent with the progress of the war led to greater consultation with outside experts on counterinsurgency, with retired military officers, as well as a more thorough interagency review process, led by Crouch.[331] Increased cooperation with the Sunnis and their increasing hostility to local Al Qaeda forces—the so-called "Sunni Awakening"—boded well. Yet advice was mixed; the effort particularly departed from the advice of the bipartisan Iraq Study Group, led by former Secretary of State James Baker and former Rep. Lee Hamilton (D-IN). In the end, the president decided a major effort was called for. The surge of 30,000 additional U.S. troops (five new combat brigades) proved politically controversial. Yet as months passed, violence decreased in Iraq. Whether it will lead to a peaceful and democratic Iraq remains an open question.

Hadley presents an interesting case study of a modern NSC advisor who embraced the role of honest broker but whose public visibility and diplomatic efforts were much less frequent than his modern predecessors. Nor was he (apparently) a strong policy advocate, continually concerned with putting his imprint on the administration's policies. The latter may reflect the unique role of Secretary of State Rice in the second term, as well as Hadley's prior relationship to her. For some critics, Hadley was too deferential, and the NSC advisor's unique perspective in offering the president a different policy vision from those of the other principals fell too much by the wayside. Ivo Daalder regarded him as too "subservient" to Rice, and unable to act as an honest broker.[332] Hadley's role in the Iraq surge, however, belies an important measure of this. Yet in other policy areas, was more policy initiative needed? As Hadley himself put it, "The president is someone who believes strongly in the chain of command. Our goal is not to get in the way of that structure. We are staff. We are not line. We do not run programs. We don't run agencies. We don't run the military. We don't run operations."[333] The "running" part is right. But is the bit about getting "in the way of structure" too limited as far as policy advice, properly tendered, is concerned?

Alternatively, what transpired during Bush's second term may reflect another reality: an NSC advisor just as active as his predecessors on the policy front but one more adept at operating behind the scenes. That would be an interesting part of the story indeed. The historical evidence and policy verdict, unfortunately, remain pending.

Notes

Introduction

1. Some of the works that have focused on individual roles include Jean A. Garrison's analysis of the "games" advisors play (Garrison, *Games Advisors Play*), Daniel E. Ponder's discussion of policy "directors," "facilitators," and "monitors" (Ponder, *Good Advice*), the typologies developed for the role of the national security advisor (Crabb and Mulcahy, *Presidents and Foreign Policy Making,* 316–340; Crabb and Mulcahy, *American National Security,* 175–191) and for the role of chief of staff (Cohen, "George Bush's Vicar of the West Wing," 39–44; Cohen, "From the Fabulous Baker Boys to the Master of Disaster"; Cohen, Dolan, and Rosati, "A Place at the Table"), and my own normative analysis of advisors' role responsibilities (Burke, "Responsibilities of Presidents and Advisers"). Roger Porter's analysis of the Economic Policy Board during the Ford administration, while largely about George's organizational theory of multiple advocacy, also discusses the place of the honest broker role within it (Porter, *Presidential Decision Making,* 26–29, 241–252), as does Alexander Moens's application of the multiple advocacy model to Carter's foreign policy decision making (Moens, *Foreign Policy under Carter,* 8–28, 51–57, 168–183) and Meena Bose's analysis of multiple advocacy in Eisenhower's and Kennedy's national security policy making (Bose, *Shaping and Signaling Presidential Policy,* 9, 12, 110).

2. I am indebted to Philip Zelikow for pointing this out to me (Burke telephone interview with Philip Zelikow, December 21, 2007).

3. See George, "The Case for Multiple Advocacy in Making Foreign Policy"; Destler, "Comment"; George, *Multiple Advocacy;* and George, *Presidential Decisionmaking in Foreign Policy.*

4. George, *Presidential Decisionmaking in Foreign Policy,* 195–96.

5. Ibid., 201–6.

6. Porter, 214–15.

7. Daalder and Destler, eds., "The Role of the National Security Adviser," 1.

8. "Transcript of Bush and Sununu Remarks at News Conference," *New York Times,* November 17, 1988.

9. See Burke, *Presidential Transitions,* 166–69.

10. Burke telephone interview with Clay Johnson, September 20, 2001.

11. The formal title of the NSC advisor has changed over time. From the Eisenhower through the Johnson presidencies the title was "special assistant to the president for national security affairs." During the Nixon presidency it changed to "assistant to the president for national security affairs," which it has remained ever since. Some lists of NSC advisors include the Truman-era executive assistants; others begin with Robert Cutler's appointment to the position in March 1953.

The reader should also note that there is no common agreement whether the correct spelling of the title is NSC "advisor" or "adviser." In part this reflects the informal nature of the title, as well as differences among dictionaries over which is the preferred spelling. In their memoirs, Nixon, Kissinger, Carter, Brzezinski, and McFarlane use "adviser," while Reagan, Bush and Scowcroft, and Clinton prefer "advisor." The *New York Times* and the *Washington Post* also use "adviser." The White House uses "advisor," although a history of the National Security Council on the White House's own Web site uses "adviser" as has, since its creation by law in 1946, the White House's Council of Economic Advisers. I follow the White House's lead and use "advisor," although I do so with some trepidation. William Safire, the learned arbiter on these matters, after his usual thoughtful consideration of the question opines: "Amid this babble, a voice of cool authority is needed. My advice: in this devolutionary political era, don't knuckle under to any White House spelling diktat" (Safire, "On Language," 18).

12. Crabb and Mulcahy, *American National Security,* 177.

13. Cutler, *No Time for Rest,* 315.

14. Porter, 26.

15. See Destler, "National Security Management," 579–580.

16. Daalder and Destler, eds., "The Role of the National Security Adviser," 51, emphasis added.

17. Ibid., 76.

18. Ibid., 5.

19. Burke telephone interview with Anthony Lake, November 1, 2007.

20. Burke telephone interview with Gen. Brent Scowcroft, November 15, 2007.

21. Kissinger, *White House Years,* 30.

22. George, *Presidential Decisionmaking in Foreign Policy,* 126–28, 191–208, 236; George, "The Case for Multiple Advocacy in Making Foreign Policy," 771–72.

23. Greenstein and Immerman, "Effective National Security Advising," 342.

24. Bose, *Shaping and Signaling Presidential Policy.*

25. Porter, 214–17, 241–47.

26. Cohen, "From the Fabulous Baker Boys to the Master of Disaster," 466.

27. Burke and Greenstein, *How Presidents Test Reality,* 31–35, 257, 286–89; Bose, *Shaping and Signaling Presidential Policy,* 12–13.

28. Burke and Greenstein, 55.

29. Ibid., 289.

30. Janis, *Groupthink,* 244; Janis, *Crucial Decisions,* 30–31; Herek, Janis, and Huth, "Decision Making During International Crisis," 204–5.

31. "Higher symptom scores were related to more unfavorable immediate outcomes for U.S. vital interests (r = .64, p = .002), and to more unfavorable immediate outcomes for international conflict (r = .62, p = .002)" (Herek, Janis, and Huth, "Decision Making during International Crises," 261).

32. Ibid., 212.

33. Haney, *Organizing for Foreign Policy Crises,* 86, 90–93, 107. Of the six decision-making tasks in each Eisenhower-era case, only the 1956 Suez process received a rating of "poor" for its development of "monitoring, implementation, and contingency plans." Poor scores were much more frequent for the cases in the other administrations.

34. Destler, "National Security Management," 583.

35. Tower, Muskie, and Scowcroft, *Tower Commission Report,* 62–63.

36. Ibid., 90.

37. George, "The Case for Multiple Advocacy in Making Foreign Policy," 783.

38. George, *Presidential Decisionmaking in Foreign Policy,* 196–97.

39. George, "The Case for Multiple Advocacy in Making Foreign Policy," 784.

40. Ibid., 99.

Chapter 1

1. On pre–World War II issues dealing with military unification, see Hammond, *Organizing for Defense,* 10–106.

2. Falk, "The National Security Council Under Truman, Eisenhower, and Kennedy," 403; also see Souers, "Policy Formulation for National Security," 532–34. Both Army Chief of Staff George Marshall and Secretary of the Navy James Forrestal were early proponents of better coordination (albeit with markedly different views). Marshall was in contact with Prime Minster Churchill as early as 1943 regarding the operations of the British war cabinet, and Marshall circulated materials Churchill provided on its operations to Roosevelt and others in the administration (see Sander, "Truman and the National Security Council," 369–372). On issues dealing with military unification during World War II and through the 1947 act, see Hammond, *Organizing for Defense,* 107–226; Herspring, *The Pentagon and the Presidency,* 23–62; and Caraley, *The Politics of Military Unification.*

3. James S. Lay Jr., "Administration of the National Security Council," January 19, 1953, White House Office, Office of Special Assistant for National Security, Special Assistant Series, Administration Subseries, Eisenhower Library. This memorandum was sent to Robert Cutler during the Eisenhower transition.

4. Anderson, "The President and National Security," 43.

5. On the political and legislative history of the 1947 act, see the three-volume report of the subcommittee headed by Sen. Henry Jackson, especially the essay in volume 2 by James S. Lay and Robert H. Johnson, "The Organizational History of the National Security Council (Unites States Senate, Subcommittee on National Policy Machinery, Committee on Government Operations, *Organizing for National Security*). Also see Nelson, "National Security I," 233–34; Nelson, "President Truman and the Evolution of the National Security Council," 360–370; Sander, "Truman and the National Security Council," 369–384; and Zegart, *Flawed by Design,* 79. The report prepared by Forrestal associate Ferdinand Eberstadt had a major impact on the subsequent structure of the NSC—although its functions were quite different from what Forrestal and Eberstadt initially envisioned. Eberstadt was influential, however, in calling for the creation of a "National Security Council," as well as the establishment of the CIA under the 1947 act (Caraley, 40–41).

6. Nelson, "President Truman and the Evolution of the National Security Council," 362–63; also see Sander, 374–77.

7. Sander, 380.

8. In the original 1947 act, in addition to the three service secretaries and the secretaries of defense and state, the chair of the National Security Resources Board was designated a statutory member. Late in the drafting of the 1947 act, the president was also given the power to designate additional members of the NSC when he felt necessary (although the act stated that they were only eligible for inclusion if they held an office confirmed by the Senate); by 1949, the treasury secretary was regularly attending NSC meetings. In the 1949 reorganization (which had as its impetus recommendations by the first Hoover Commission), the executive secretary and staff were formally incorporated as part of the Executive Office of the President. In 1951, the Mutual Security Act also made the director of mutual security a statutory member of the NSC. Truman's appointee was Averill Harriman. In 1953, the National Security Resources Board was abolished and replaced by the Office of Defense Mobilization, whose chair was made a statutory member of the council. In addition, the director of the Foreign Operations Administration was made a member of the council, but later when the Foreign Operations Administration was reorganized as the International Cooperation Administration, the director of the latter was not made a statutory member.

The Chairman of the Joint Chiefs of Staff and the Director of the CIA are statutory *advisers* to the NSC.

9. The role of policy formation was embodied in the report to Forrestal by Ferdinand Eberstadt (the influential Eberstadt Report). James S. Lay Jr., "Administration of the National Security Council," January 19, 1953, White House Office, Office of Special Assistant for National Security, Special Assistant Series, Administration Subseries, Eisenhower Library.

10. Nelson, "President Truman and the Evolution of the National Security Council," 363; for a more detailed analysis, see Sander, 378–380.

11. On the BOB's efforts, see Nelson, "President Truman and the Evolution of the National Security Council," 363–66; and Sander, 382–85.

12. Nelson, "President Truman and the Evolution of the National Security Council," 366, emphasis added.

13. Souers, "Policy Formulation for National Security," 536.

14. According to a August 8, 1947, memorandum from BOB Director James Webb to Truman, selective attendance at meetings "would assure the advisory nature of the Council's actions and guard against its becoming an operating body with the President pressed to resolve spot issues" (quoted in Nelson, "President Truman and the Evolution of the National Security Council," 366).

15. National Security Council, "History of the National Security Council."

16. Inderfurth and Johnson, "Early Years," 27; in Falk's count, Truman attended eleven of fifty-six meetings (Falk, "The National Security Council Under Truman, Eisenhower, and Kennedy," 406).

17. National Security Council, "History of the National Security Council."

18. Destler, "National Security Management," 575.

19. The choice of Souers was yet another ironic twist of bureaucratic fate for Forrestal, since the latter had recommended him—presumably banking on his institutional loyalty as a naval officer—to Truman for the post. Forrestal and Souers also had come to know each other during their prewar years in the financial world, and Souers had served on the group drafting the Eberstadt Report (see Sander, 385).

20. Souers, 537.

21. According to Elmer Staats, Souers was also well known to Truman even before his presidency (Elmer Staats Oral History, July 13, 1964, Kennedy Library, 7).

22. Nelson, "President Truman and the Evolution of the National Security Council," 367.

23. Ibid., 368.

24. On the early organization of the staff, see Souers, 537–38; and Lay, "National Security Council's Role in the U.S. Security and Peace Program," 37–39. In 1949, the NSC staff budget was $200,000 with a full staff of thirty-one (including clerical), half of whom according to Souers were on detail from other departments (Souers, 538).

25. Souers, 538–39. Also see Nelson, "President Truman and the Evolution of the National Security Council," 368–371; and Falk, 408.

26. James S. Lay Jr., "Administration of the National Security Council," January 19, 1953, White House Office, Office of Special Assistant for National Security, Special Assistant Series, Administration Subseries, Eisenhower Library.

27. National Security Council, "History of the National Security Council."

28. Millis, *Arms and the State,* 223.

29. Nelson, "The Evolution of the National Security State Ubiquitous and Endless," 270.

30. Elmer Staats Oral History, July 13, 1964, Kennedy Library, 7. Staats had a long

and distinguished governmental career. He was deputy director of the Bureau of the Budget under Truman, served four years as executive director of the OCB, eventually returning to the deputy position at the BOB through the remainder of the Eisenhower presidency, and continued until 1966 when he became comptroller general of the United States, serving until 1981.

31. James S. Lay Jr., "Administration of the National Security Council," January 19, 1953, White House Office, Office of Special Assistant for National Security, Special Assistant Series, Administration Subseries, Eisenhower Library.

32. Ibid.

33. Falk, 413.

34. Souers, 536.

35. Nelson, "President Truman and the Evolution of the National Security Council," 372.

36. In 1956, Cutler wrote of Lay, he is "a man of keen, analytical intelligence and impeccable nonpartisanship. He, his deputy and the other nine 'think people' on the staff are scrupulously non-political and non-policymaking" (Cutler, "The Development of the National Security Council," 455).

37. Falk, 415.

38. The memorandum from Truman to Lay is contained in Lay's January 1953 report to Cutler (James S. Lay Jr., "Administration of the National Security Council," January 19, 1953). On Lay as head of the senior staff, see Clark and Legere, *The President and the Management of National Security,* 59.

39. Nelson, "President Truman and the Evolution of the National Security Council," 373; also see Falk, 414–15.

40. Souers, 543.

41. Cutler had served as deputy to Gordon Gray and often attended meetings on Gray's behalf; Gray succeeded Cutler as NSC advisor in June 1958 (Gordon Gray Oral History, June 25, 1975, Eisenhower Library, 12).

42. Cutler, *No Time for Rest,* 292.

43. Among those consulted were officials from the Truman years (Allan Dulles, Gordon Gray, James Lay, Paul Nitze, Sidney Souers), foreign policy notables (Robert Lovett, George Marshall, Charles Bohlen), academics (Harvard's W. Y. Elliott), and others, such as Ferdinand Ebertsadt, who had been involved in national security planning (Bowie and Immerman, *Waging Peace,* 87; also see 308–310).

44. Nelson, "National Security I," 246.

45. Cutler, *No Time for Rest,* 299. Cutler's meeting with Eisenhower may have occurred the week before since in Cutler's files there is letter from Eisenhower to Cutler on March 17, 1953, indicating approval of his report and its circulation to members of the NSC (Memorandum from the President to Robert Cutler, March 17, 1953, White House Office, Office of Special Assistant for National Security, Special Assistant Series, Administration Subseries, Eisenhower Library). Cutler's March 16 report and Eisenhower's March 17 letter are also reproduced in *Foreign Relations of the United States,* Vol. 2, *National Security Affairs,* 244–258.

46. NSC Study, "General George C. Marshall," February 19, 1953, White House Office, Office of Special Assistant for National Security, Special Assistant Series, Administration Subseries, Eisenhower Library.

47. Ibid.

48. Eisenhower had proposed such individuals as Governors Allan Shivers of Texas, Dan Thornton of Colorado, Earl Warren of California as well as other "persons of stature" such as his friends newspaper publisher Roy Roberts, Harry Bullis, the chairman of General

Mills, and Charles Thomas, the head of Monsanto (NSC Study, "The President," February 9, 1953, White House Office, Office of Special Assistant for National Security, Special Assistant Series, Administration Subseries, Eisenhower Library). The memo also indicates that Eisenhower thought that Cutler's title should be "Director to Executive Officer" because it would "command respectful attention of big shots when telephoned or visited." Eisenhower also thought that the title of "Director and Special Assistant to the President for NSC Affairs" might also work if Cutler "thought there was value in the White House link" (Note: this is a February 16 addendum to the February 9, 1953, document).

49. NSC Study, "General George C. Marshall," February 19, 1953.

50. Nelson, "National Security," 246.

51. Memorandum from Robert Cutler to the President, "Recommendations Regarding the National Security Council," March 16, 1953, White House Office, Office of Special Assistant for National Security, Special Assistant Series, Administration Subseries, Eisenhower Library.

52. Ibid.

53. Ibid., emphasis added.

54. Ibid. On the internal operations of the Planning Board, see Bowie and Immerman, 91–92.

55. Gordon Gray Oral History, June 25, 1975, Eisenhower Library, 18.

56. Bowie and Immerman, 89.

57. See Eisenhower, *Mandate for Change,* 131–32. The Director of the U.S. Information Agency was also added as a nonstatutory member.

58. Cutler, *No Time for Rest,* 299.

59. On the Jackson Committee and its work, see Bowie and Immerman, 93–95. As Bowie and Immerman note, the OCB was the weaker part of the Eisenhower national security system: "Over the subsequent months and years the administration continually tinkered with the OCB's organization and functions; still, its performance never met the president's expectations. But the OCB's important contribution to America's national security was never questioned, and Eisenhower and his advisers viewed his successor's decision to dismantle it as a grave mistake" (95). On problems with the Truman-era PSB and the subsequent development of the OCB also see Elmer Staats Oral History, July 13, 1964, Kennedy Library, 8–10.

60. NSC Study, "General George C. Marshall," February 19, 1953.

61. The most widely available report of the Jackson subcommittee [its formal title was Senate Committee on Government Operations, Subcommittee on National Policy Machinery] is Jackson, ed., *The National Security Council.* For other criticisms of the Eisenhower NSC machinery (including analysis of the Jackson subcommittee), see Falk, 423–29; Nelson, "National Security I," 252–55; Hammond, "The National Security Council as a Device for Interdepartmental Coordination," 903–910; Hammond, *Organizing for Defense,* 357–370; Bowie and Immerman, 94–95; and Brands, "The Age of Vulnerability," 966–974.

62. Schlesinger, "Effective National Security Advising," 351.

63. Henry, *Presidential Transitions,* 617–18.

64. Cutler, *No Time for Rest,* 300. Copyright © Robert Cutler. By permission, Little Brown & Co.

65. Cutler, "The Development of the National Security Council," 442. However, as Dillon Anderson, who followed Cutler's first stint at NSC advisor, notes, "corporate" does not mean that the NSC operated "in a corporate way as a Board of Directors; nor does it conduct operations or issue directives" (Anderson, "The President and National Security," 43).

66. Memorandum of Discussion at the 166th Meeting of the National Security Council, Tuesday, October 13, 1953, *Foreign Relations of the United States,* Vol. 2, *National Security Affairs,* 535.

67. Henderson, "Advice and Decision," 157.

68. Robert Cutler, "Report to the President: Operations of the National Security Council, January 1953–April 1955," April 1, 1955, White House Office, Office of Special Assistant for National Security, Special Assistant Series, Chronological Subseries, Eisenhower Library.

69. Karl G. Harr Jr., Columbia University Oral History, April 27, 1967, Eisenhower Library, 8.

70. Cutler, *No Time for Rest,* 296.

71. Cutler, "The Development of the National Security Council," 446.

72. Cutler, *No Time for Rest,* 301.

73. Ibid., 302, 304.

74. Ibid., 304–5.

75. See, for example, Neustadt, *Presidential Power,* 229; and Hammond, "The National Security Council as a Device for Interdepartmental Coordination," 904.

76. Cutler, "The Development of the National Security Council," 443, emphasis added.

77. Robert Cutler, "Report to the President: Operations of the National Security Council, January 1953–April 1955," April 1, 1955.

78. Cutler, *No Time for Rest,* 305; also see Brownell, *Advising Ike,* 292.

79. Henderson, "Advice and Decision," 161. In his absence, Vice President Nixon presided, unlike in the Truman years when the secretary of state would preside in the president's absence.

80. Cutler, *No Time for Rest,* 305.

81. Cutler, "The Development of the National Security Council," 443.

82. Kinnard, *President Eisenhower and Strategy Management,* 15–16.

83. Elmer Staats Oral History, June 11, 1980, Eisenhower Library, 16.

84. Dillon Anderson, Columbia University Oral History, December 30, 1969, Eisenhower Library, 37, 38, 65.

85. Brownell, 292–3.

86. Cutler, *No Time for Rest,* 302, emphasis added.

87. Ibid., 304–305. Gordon Gray, who as assistant secretary of defense for International Security Affairs from 1955–1957 attended NSC meetings with Defense Secretary Wilson as his backup and chief premeeting briefer, later recalled that "it was not always easy to brief him . . . . He would take a 'trip around the world,' as he expressed it. We'd get on some subject and then he's get in some reminiscence about General Motors or something else . . . frequently he would go to a National Security Council meeting not fully briefed about the issues which were coming up" (Gordon Gray Oral History, June 25, 1975, Eisenhower Library, 3, 4).

88. Cutler, *No Time for Rest,* 306.

89. Ibid., 403–4 n.8; also see Cutler, "The Development of the National Security Council," 446–47.

90. Cutler, "The Development of the National Security Council," 448.

91. Ibid., 449. As Cutler recounts, the OCB members met on Wednesdays at the State Department for a "skimpy lunch." Only the members were present "to discuss and settle (if possible) most secret and 'p' factor matters." They then adjourned for a longer meeting with their deputies present. According to Cutler, "The need and potential utility of some impartial mechanism or small group continuously to check on policy *performance* became more apparent every year" (Cutler, *No Time for Rest,* 313, emphasis in original).

92. Cutler, "The Development of the National Security Council," 450; also see Anderson, "The President and National Security," 45; and Harr, "Eisenhower's Approach to National Security Decisionmaking," 93–101.

93. Karl G. Harr Jr., Columbia University Oral History, April 27, 1967, Eisenhower Library, 25, 28.

94. Cutler, *No Time for Rest*, 298; also see Cutler, "The Development of the National Security Council," 452–53.

95. Robert Cutler, "Attendance at National Security Council Meetings," November 30, 1954 (revised March 30, 1955), White House Office, Office of Special Assistant for National Security, Special Assistant Series, Administration Subseries, Eisenhower Library. As Cutler notes in the memo, only the secretaries of state and defense were permitted to bring along one "observer" each, and that by express presidential permission.

96. Robert Cutler, "Report to the President: Operations of the National Security Council, January 1953–April 1955," April 1, 1955.

97. But Cutler also noted—in response to this and other criticisms—that "to say this, however, is not to say that [the Hoover Commission task force] . . . has correctly analyzed the *cause* for the deficiencies, suggested the correct *cure* for the deficiencies, or grasped the *continuing progress* being made toward improvement within the existing structure." (Robert Cutler, "Memorandum with Reference to Proposed Report by Hoover Commission Task Force on 'Procurement' Relative to National Security Mechanism," March 25, 1955, White House Office, Office of Special Assistant for National Security, Special Assistant Series, Chronological Subseries, Eisenhower Library, emphasis in original).

98. Ibid.

99. Executive Order 10700 brought the OCB within NSC control; it was signed on February 25, 1957, and was scheduled to take effect on July 1, 1957.

100. Cutler, *No Time for Rest*, 348; also see Nelson, "The 'Top of Policy Hill,'" 322.

101. Robert Cutler, "Basis on which the NSC Mechanism Can Effectively Serve the President," January 7, 1957, White House Office, Office of Special Assistant for National Security, Special Assistant Series, Administration Subseries, Eisenhower Library.

102. Memorandum from Robert Cutler to the President, "Interim Report on Organization of the NSC Mechanism," March 20, 1957, White House Office, Office of Special Assistant for National Security, Special Assistant Series, Administration Subseries, Eisenhower Library. Cutler followed the interim report with a full report on July 1, 1957, which included a lengthy section on the OCB; "The Structure and Functions of the National Security Council," July 1, 1957, White House Office, Office of Special Assistant for National Security, Special Assistant Series, Administration Subseries, Eisenhower Library.

103. See Gordon Gray, "Memorandum of Meeting with President," January 7, 1960, White House Office, Office of Special Assistant for National Security, Special Assistant Series, Presidential Subseries, Eisenhower Library.

104. Gordon Gray, "Memorandum of Meeting with Mr. Bundy," January 19, 1961, Eisenhower Papers, Presidential Transition Series, Eisenhower Library. For a more negative assessment of the OCB, see Clark and Legere, 65–67.

105. According to Eisenhower, the OCB "functioned fairly well. However, I came finally to believe that this work could have been better done by a highly competent and trusted official with a small staff of his own, rather than by a committee whose members had to handle the task on a part-time basis" (Eisenhower, *Waging Peace*, 634).

106. Cutler, *No Time for Rest*, 315. Cutler's term as special assistant for national security affairs officially began on March 23, 1953; before that—as he was planning the new NSC system—his title was Administrative Assistant to the president, without specific duties (Cutler, *No Time for Rest*, 403 n.6).

107. Ibid.

108. Ibid., 316.

109. Ibid., 315.

110. Eisenhower, *Mandate for Change,* 270–71.

111. Cutler, *No Time for Rest,* 295, emphasis added.

112. Leviero, "'Untouchable, Unreachable, and Unquotable.'"

113. Lubell, "Mystery Man of the White House."

114. Cutler, *No Time for Rest,* 318–19.

115. Adams, *Firsthand Report,* 140–41. The issue was resolved by Vice President Nixon, who contacted McCarthy, and explained to him that he was being used as a tool of the Democrats to embarrass the administration. McCarthy quickly had his letter retrieved before it was "officially received" at the White House, thus preventing the need for an official reply.

116. Bose, *Shaping and Signaling Presidential Policy,* 19; also see Bose, 29–41; and Bowie and Immerman, 123–146 for discussion of Project Solarium.

117. Bose, *Shaping and Signaling Presidential Policy,* 30, 33.

118. On the JCS study, see Bose, *Shaping and Signaling Presidential Policy,* 34–36.

119. Cutler, *No Time for Rest,* 295.

120. Cutler, "The Development of the National Security Council," 458.

121. Ibid., 457.

122. Ibid., 458.

123. Also see Nelson, "The 'Top of Policy Hill,'" 320–22.

124. Ibid., 318; Nelson, "The Importance of Foreign Policy Process," 113; National Security Council, "History of the National Security Council, 1947–1997"; Harr, "Eisenhower's Approach to National Security Decisionmaking," 111; Henderson, "Advice and Decision," 170.

125. Cutler, *No Time for Rest,* 306.

126. Burke and Greenstein, 55.

127. Cutler, *No Time for Rest,* 295. Goodpaster recounts similar experiences in his role as staff secretary, see Goodpaster, "Organizing the White House," 66.

128. Greenstein, *The Hidden-Hand Presidency,* 148. According to Anna Kasten Nelson, "The Eisenhower style was a continuing mix of formal procedure with informal meetings of conversation" (Nelson, "The 'Top of Policy Hill,'" 312, also see 324).

129. Henderson, "Advice and Decision," 171–72. Among them were Dillon Anderson, James Black (head of Pacific Gas and Electric), Gene Holman (chairman of Standard Oil of New Kersey), Dean Mallot, (president of Cornell University), and Charles Thomas (head of Monsanto and member of the Manhattan Project); Joseph Dodge, a Detroit banker, joined the group in 1954 after serving as director of the Bureau of the Budget. According to Dillon Anderson, the effort "didn't pan out. Theoretically it was a good idea to have some people around who were not burdened daily with administrative responsibilities and did not have to live with loyalties back in their Departments, and didn't have to live with the feeling that the Secretary had let them down if he agreed with the other Secretaries. He wanted to get away from that. On paper it's a better idea perhaps than in practice, because I think he had good people. . . . I just don't think it came through as—quite as he had thought it would" (Dillon Anderson, Columbia University Oral History, December 20, 1969, Eisenhower Library, 33).

Another important consultative body established during the Eisenhower presidency was directed at oversight on intelligence gathering. As Richard Best notes, in a Congressional Research Service report, "In 1956, President Eisenhower, partly in response to recommendations of the second Hoover Commission on the Organization of the Executive Branch of

Government, also established the Board of Consultants on Foreign Intelligence Activities in the Executive Office. This board was established by Executive Order 10656 and was tasked to provide the President with independent evaluations of the U.S. foreign intelligence effort. The Board of Consultants lapsed at the end of the Eisenhower Administration, but a similar body, the President's Foreign Intelligence Advisory Board (PFIAB), was created by President Kennedy after the Bay of Pigs failure. PFIAB was itself abolished in 1977, but was resurrected during the Reagan Administration in 1981. Members are selected by the President and serve at his discretion" (Best, "The National Security Council,"10).

130. The Gaither Committee moved from civil defense to a broader, more critical study of military preparedness. Its work was leaked to the press, and its findings ran counter to administration policies. Cutler had approved the broader study, which he later regretted; see Cutler, *No Time for Rest,* 336–37, 354–55.

131. Bose, *Shaping and Signaling Presidential Policy,* 102–3.

132. Burke and Greenstein, 37.

133. Cutler, "The Development of the National Security Council," 453–54. Also see his final report to Eisenhower where he raises this issue, again argues against their attendance at NSC meetings, and also notes (page 5) the occasions when outside consultants have been used (Robert Cutler, "Report to the President: Operations of the National Security Council, January 1953–April 1955," April 1, 1955).

134. Kinnard, 16. On the origins and operations of the staff secretariat, see Goodpaster, "Organizing the Presidency," 65–66; and Clark and Legere, 61–62.

135. Neil H. McElroy, Columbia University Oral History, May 8, 1967, Eisenhower Library, 28.

136. Gordon Gray Oral History, June 25, 1975, Eisenhower Library, 7, 8; Goodpaster has similar recollections (Goodpaster, "Organizing the Presidency," 80; Goodpaster Oral History, June 11, 1980, Eisenhower Library, 64: "I don't remember anything dropping between us").

137. Anderson was centrally involved in the infamous fight, at the Republican state convention at Mineral Wells, with the Taft forces over the composition of the Texas delegation to the 1952 national convention (on the Mineral Wells contest, see Brownell, 112–14). As result of this and further campaign activities, he became acquainted with Eisenhower's top political advisers such as Henry Cabot Lodge, Herbert Brownell, Gov. Sinclair Weeks of Massachusetts, William Rogers, and Cutler.

138. Anderson, "The President and National Security," 45.

139. See Henderson, "Advice and Decision," 161–170.

140. Dillon Anderson, Columbia University Oral History, December 30, 1969, Eisenhower Library, 69–70.

141. In 1954, while still serving as president of UNC, Gray served as chair of the Personnel Security Board of the Atomic Energy Commission; the board's most notable activity was the security investigation of J. Robert Oppenheimer.

142. Gordon Gray Oral History, June 25, 1975, Eisenhower Library, 2, 4.

143. Daalder and Destler, eds., "The Nixon Administration National Security Council," 6–7.

144. Nelson, "The 'Top of Policy Hill,'" 323.

145. Gordon Gray Oral History, June 11, 1980, Eisenhower Library, 7.

146. Gordon Gray letter to John S. D. Eisenhower, October 18, 1961, Gordon Gray Papers, Eisenhower Library.

147. Nelson, "The Importance of Foreign Policy Process," 122; also see Nelson, "National Security I," 252.

148. With respect to Cutler's substantive vision, as Lubell noted in 1954, Cutler "has

never been responsible for basic judgments. Always others set the objectives with Cutler contributing his terrific energy and ability to organize and simplify the most bewildering details. In short—and this is undoubtedly how he, himself, would have it—Cutler is not likely to become either the star or the author of the play. Those functions remain for Eisenhower himself. In Cutler, however, the President has found a stage manager who can put whatever play is written into production for that is worth" (Lubell, "Mystery Man of the White House," 81).

149. Gordon Gray Oral History, June 11, 1980, Eisenhower Library, 39.

150. Gordon Gray, Memorandum for the Record, December 2, 1957, Gordon Gray Papers, Eisenhower Library.

151. Ibid., November 24, 1959.

152. Greenstein and Immerman, 342. According to Bowie and Immerman, Cutler and his Eisenhower-era successors "effectively if imperfectly promoted multiple advocacy by playing role that closely approximated Alexander George's model 'custodian manager'" (257).

153. Bose, *Shaping and Signaling Presidential Policy,* 37. A summary account of the meeting can be found in Memorandum of Discussion at the 165th Meeting of the National Security Council, Wednesday, October 7, 1953, *Foreign Relations of the United States,* Vol. 2, *National Security Affairs,* 514–535.

154. Burke and Greenstein, 55; also see Haney, 90–93.

155. Memorandum of Discussion at the 166th Meeting of the National Security Council, Wednesday, October 7, 1953, *Foreign Relations of the United States,* Vol. 2, *National Security Affairs,* 520.

156. Bowie and Immerman, 101.

157. Ibid., 142, 143. Bowie and Immerman note that "Cutler's critique was in part within his mandate" as NSC advisor, especially his role in making sure planning papers "presented contested issues" and reflected "divergent views." But they also contend that Cutler may have become an advocate for particular policies in his critique, as well as violating his own operating norms that Planning Board members "express and stand by their honest views" (143).

158. Cutler, *No Time for Rest,* 305.

159. Memorandum of Discussion at the 166th Meeting of the National Security Council, Tuesday, October 13, 1953, *Foreign Relations of the United States,* Vol. 2, *National Security Affairs,* 547.

160. Brands, "The Age of Vulnerability," 979.

161. Adams, 388.

162. Dillon Anderson letter to Richard Nixon, September 3, 1968, Gordon Gray Papers, Eisenhower Library. For an excellent analysis of Eisenhower's general national security strategy, see Bowie and Immerman.

163. R. C. Cutler, "The Use of the NSC Mechanism: Korea, Vietnam, Lebanon," March 1968, Gordon Gray Papers, Eisenhower Library.

164. Ibid. In the margins of the document, Eisenhower also noted that "there were many split views brought forth at the NSC." Furthermore, as Cutler notes in his memoirs, even more important than "*what* is planned is that the planners *become accustomed* to working and thinking together on hard problems; enabling them—when put to the ultimate test—to arrive more surely at a reasonable plan or policy" (Cutler, *No Time for Rest,* 296–97, emphasis in original). Similar points are also made in his final report to the president at the end of his first stint as NSC advisor in April 1955: "Every so often history takes charge. Then there is no time for papers to be properly staffed through the Planning Board and decisions must flow from oral discussion. That Council members have been trained in the customary Council procedure serves to condition them for crash problems which must be

decided without the usual background material," (Robert Cutler, "Report to the President: Operations of the National Security Council, January 1953–April 1955," April 1, 1955). Brownell also makes the same point about the impact on crisis management. Members of the team "became accustomed to working with each other." Prior planning "enabled those persons involved in the policy process to draw on knowledge and information acquired earlier that would be useful in responding to any immediate and pressing crises at hand" (293).

165. Bose, *Shaping and Signaling Presidential Policy*, 103.

166. Letter from Eisenhower to Dillon Anderson, April 5, 1967, Gordon Gray Papers, Eisenhower Library.

167. Letter from Eisenhower to Gordon Gray, May 10, 1967, Gordon Gray Papers, Eisenhower Library.

168. Robert Cutler, "Memorandum for Mr. Lay," August 6, 1957, White House Office, Office of Special Assistant for National Security, Special Assistant Series, Administration Subseries, Eisenhower Library.

169. Cutler, *No Time for Rest*, 314.

170. Ibid.

171. Gordon Gray Oral History, June 25, 1975, Eisenhower Library, 6.

172. Lord, *The Presidency and the Management of National Security*, 87, emphasis added.

173. Greenstein and Immerman, 343.

174. Ibid., 344.

175. Henderson, "Advice and Decision," 159.

176. Clark and Legere, 64.

177. Greenstein and Immerman, 345.

178. Nelson, "The Importance of Foreign Policy Process," 125.

179. Nelson, "National Security I," 250, emphasis added.

180. Mark J. White notes, however, that Wilson had substantive concerns about the administration's policy of supporting the Diem regime after the partition of Vietnam (see White, *Against the President*, 137–168).

181. Eisenhower's third secretary of defense from June 1959 until January 1961 was Thomas S. Gates Jr. Gates also lacked pre-Eisenhower defense experience—he had been an investment banker and the president of the University of Pennsylvania. But he had served during the Eisenhower years as undersecretary then secretary of the navy.

Chapter 2

1. Preston, *The War Council*, 244.

2. Bundy's father, Harvey Bundy, had served as Stimson's assistant secretary of state during the Hoover administration, and he once again returned to Washington to serve Stimson when he became secretary of war under FDR.

3. McGeorge Bundy, "Letter to the Jackson Subcommittee," 82–84.

4. Jackson, xiii. The official title of the position, "Special Assistant to the President for National Security Affairs," was carried over from the Eisenhower administration.

5. See Eisenhower, "Account of My December 6th 1960 Meeting with President-Elect Kennedy," Whitman Diary, Ann Whitman File, Eisenhower Library, also Smith, *Organizational History of the National Security Council*, 13–14, 49–50.

6. Bundy, *Danger and Survival*, 354.

7. Smith, *Organizational History of the National Security Council*, 6. Moreover, as Smith points out, in his last year in office Eisenhower directed "that a substantial portion of the

time of the Council during 1960 be spent in discussing major national security problems facing the United States now and in the future"; eight reports were prepared by the Planning Board for the NSC's consideration (1).

8. Sorensen, *Kennedy,* 281.

9. Smith, *Organizational History of the National Security Council,* 17.

10. National Security Council, "History of the National Security Council"; also see Dickinson, "The Institutionalization of the National Security Staff," 7. Determining the size of the NSC staff is not, however, an easy matter. A number of staff members are detailees from other agencies, departments, and the military, and separating policy-making positions from administrative or staff positions can be difficult. Rusk, for example, notes that Bundy "had perhaps a staff of a dozen people" (Rusk, *As I Saw It,* 518). Dickinson has attempted to estimate the number of professional staff members as a subset of the budgeted positions drawn from the Federal Civilian Workforce Statistics. For Eisenhower the average is fourteen professional, forty-two budgeted; for JFK/LBJ: twelve professional, forty-five budgeted; for Nixon: fifty professional, seventy-five budgeted; for Ford: forty-five professional, eighty-four budgeted; for Reagan: thirty-five professional, sixty-two budgeted ("The Institutionalization of the National Security Staff," 24).

11. On NSAMs and Bundy's role, see Smith, *Organizational History of the National Security Council,* 23.

12. Preston, *War Council,* 41.

13. Sorensen, *Kennedy,* 287.

14. Schlesinger, *A Thousand Days,* 426, 406.

15. Dean Rusk Oral History, July 28, 1969, Johnson Library, 26.

16. Inderfurth and Johnson, "Transformation," 66.

17. Bird, *Color of Truth,* 186; Destler, *Presidents, Bureaucrats, and Foreign Policy,* 101.

18. Morris, *Uncertain Greatness,* 77.

19. Bird, 188; also see Preston, *War Council,* 43; and Destler, *Presidents, Bureaucrats, and Foreign Policy,* 101.

20. Bird, 188–89.

21. Rothkopf, *Running the World,* 90.

22. Memorandum from McGeorge Bundy to the President, May 16, 1961, President's Office Files, Staff Memoranda-Bundy, Kennedy Library. Clifton was military aide Chester "Ted" Clifton.

23. Smith, *Organizational History of the National Security Council,* 12.

24. Nelson, "The Evolution of the National Security State Ubiquitous and Endless," 283. Kissinger later secured a spacious suite on the first floor of the White House, just down the hall from the Oval Office.

25. On the use of task forces, see Smith, *Organizational History of the National Security Council,* 21–22.

26. Inderfurth and Johnson, "Transformation," 66.

27. Preston, *War Council,* 42.

28. Rothkopf, 85.

29. Memorandum from McGeorge Bundy to the President, May 16, 1961, President's Office Files, Staff Memoranda-Bundy, Kennedy Library, emphasis in original.

30. A memo from Bundy to the president on June 22, 1961, listed the participants as Walt Rostow, Ralph Dungan, Arthur Schlesinger Jr., Chester Clifton, Bromley Smith, Carl Kaysen, Robert Komer, Charles Johnson, Roger Johnson, Samuel Belk, and Tazewell Shepard (Memorandum from McGeorge Bundy to the President, June 22, 1961, National Security Files, Departments and Agencies, Kennedy Library).

31. On Taylor's role, see "Memorandum of Meeting in the President's Office—Discussion of Role of General Taylor," June 29, 1961, National Security Files, Meetings and Memoranda, Kennedy Library.

32. Memorandum from McGeorge Bundy to the President, June 22, 1961, National Security Files, Departments and Agencies, Kennedy Library.

33. Elmer Staats Oral History, July 13, 1964, Kennedy Library, 20.

34. Reeves, *President Kennedy,* 53.

35. At the bottom of the memo, Bundy left a line for Kennedy's approval. NSC record of action #2438 shows Kennedy's approval of the proposal (Memorandum from McGeorge Bundy to the President, October 10, 1961, National Security Files, Meetings and Memoranda, Kennedy Library).

36. On the 1962 meetings, see NSC meetings 497–507, National Security Files, Meetings and Memoranda; on the 1963 meetings, see NSC meetings 508–519, National Security Files, Meetings and Memoranda, Kennedy Library.

37. Not until a week had passed after the missiles were discovered and his options were clear in his mind did Kennedy give the group a formal designation and legal sanction to carry out instructions. He called it the Executive Committee of the National Security Council, or ExCom (Frankel, *High Noon in the Cold War,* 77–78).

38. "National Security Council, Record of Action, Standing Group Meeting," January 5, 1962, National Security Files, Meetings and Memoranda, Kennedy Library. In attendance were Undersecretary of State for Political Affairs George McGhee, Deputy Undersecretary of Defense Roswell Gilpatric, CIA Director John McCone, NSC Executive Secretary Bromley Smith, and McGeorge Bundy.

39. Smith, *Organizational History of the National Security Council,* 51.

40. Memorandum from McGeorge Bundy to the President, April 2 1963, National Security Files, Meetings and Memoranda, Kennedy Library. It is also worth noting that Robert Kennedy had expressed his own concerns to his brother about the need for a better decision process. At the end of a memo calling for more meetings to discuss Cuba and South American policy, the attorney general noted that: "PS: I think this kind of effort should be applied to other problems as well. The best minds (*me) in Government should be utilized in finding solutions to these major problems. They should be available in times other than deep crisis and emergencies as is now the case. You talk to McNamara but mostly on Defense matters, you talk to Dillon but primarily on financial questions, Dave Bell on AID matters, etc. These men should be sitting down and thinking of some of the problems facing us in a broader context. I think you could get a good deal more out of what is available in Government than you are at the present time"(Memorandum from Robert Kennedy to the President, March 14, 1963, Latin America Folder, Subject Files 1961–1964, Sorensen Papers, Kennedy Library).

41. On the records of the first meeting of the group, see "National Security Council Standing Group, Records of Actions," April 16, 1963, National Security Files, Meetings and Memoranda, Kennedy Library.

42. Smith, *Organizational History of the National Security Council,* 53.

43. See, for example, Memorandum from David Klein to McGeorge Bundy, "Subject: NSC Standing Group Meeting—Discussions of East-West Trade Policy," September 7, 1963, National Security Files, Meetings and Memoranda, Kennedy Library. Other records for the Standing Groups' meetings are available in the National Security Files at the Kennedy Library.

44. "The basis of the problem was a request by the Department of State for an evaluation of the following possible military courses of action in Cuba. A. U.S. unilateral action

with U.S. Air, Naval, and Army forces. B. Invasion by a U.S. trained and supported volunteer Army composed of Cubans and other anti-Castro Latin Americans. C. Invasion by a combination of A and B above. . . . Courses of action A and C are the only courses which assure success" (Staff Study Prepared by the Department of Defense, January 16, 1961, *Foreign Relations of the United States,* Vol. 10, *Cuba, 1961–1962,* http://www.state.gov/www/about_state/history/frusX/16_30.html); a published copy of the Cuba *Foreign Relations* volume is also available.

45. Ironically, according to a paper prepared by Bissell for the CIA on March 15, 1961, the swampy nature of the site was explicitly touted as one of its advantages over other sites then under consideration: "The area selected is located at the head of a well protected deep water estuary on the south coast of Cuba. It is almost surrounded by swamps impenetrable to infantry in any numbers and entirely impenetrable to vehicles, except along two narrow and easily defended approaches" (*Foreign Relations of the United States,* Vol. 10, *Cuba, 1961–1962,* http://www.state.gov/www/about_state/history/frusX/61_75.html).

46. See Smith, *Organizational History of the National Security Council,* 35.

47. Rothkopf, 83.

48. Memorandum of Meeting with President Kennedy, February 8, 1961, *Foreign Relations of the United States,* Vol. 10, *Cuba, 1961–1962,* http://www.state.gov/www/about_state/history/frusX/16_30.html.

49. Memorandum from McGeorge Bundy to the President, March 15, 1961, National Security Files, Countries Series, Cuba, General, 1/61–4/61, Kennedy Library.

50. Janis, *Groupthink,* 14–47; Sorensen, *Kennedy,* 304–5; Schlesinger, *A Thousand Days,* 258, 295. Alexander George offers an interesting assessment of the success of deliberations based on Kennedy's and Khrushchev's incentive to avoid war (see George, "The Cuban Missile Crisis").

51. Janis, *Groupthink,* 19–26.

52. Sorensen, *Kennedy,* 305, 304. For a more recent analysis that stresses the newness of the administration as a primary source of error, see Stern, "Probing the Plausibility of Newgroup Syndrome."

53. Maxwell Taylor Oral History, April 12, 1964, Kennedy Library, 9.

54. Ibid., 10, emphasis added.

55. McGeorge Bundy interview with the Taylor committee, May 4, 1961, National Security Files, Paramilitary Study Group, 4, Kennedy Library, emphasis added.

56. Janis, *Groupthink,* 19, emphasis added.

57. Ibid.

58. Memorandum of Telephone Conversation between McGeorge Bundy and Dean Rusk, February 3, 1961, *Foreign Relations of the United States,* Vol. 10, *Cuba, 1961–1962,* http://www.state.gov/www/about_state/history/frusX/11_45.html, emphasis added.

59. Memorandum From McGeorge Bundy to the President, February 8, 1961, President's Office Files, Countries Series, Cuba, Security, 1961, Kennedy Library, emphasis added.

60. Memorandum from McGeorge Bundy to the President, February 18, 1961, *Foreign Relations of the United States,* Vol. 10, *Cuba, 1961–1962,* http://www.state.gov/www/about_state/history/frusX/45_60.html emphasis added.

61. Bird, 195.

62. Rothkopf, 89; Higgins, *The Perfect Failure,* 111; Schlesinger, *A Thousand Days,* 252. According to Mann, "I did this because I did not wish to leave the impression that I would not support whatever the President decided to do." According to one account, "This meeting was held in the State Department and Senator Fulbright was also present. Senator

Fulbright spoke out against the plan. The President again indicated his preference for an operation which would infiltrate the force in units of 200–250 and then develop them through a build up. Colonel Hawkins from CIA expressed the belief that landing small groups would merely serve to alert Castro and they would be eliminated one by one. He indicated that a group of 200 was below the critical number able to defend themselves. *Mr. Rusk expressed opposition to the plan* but Mr. Berle and Mr. Mann expressed general approval. Mr. McNamara also expressed approval of the general concept. The President indicated that he still wished to make the operation appear as an internal uprising and wished to consider the matter further the next morning" (Editorial Note 80, Meeting of April 4, 1961, *Foreign Relations of the United States*, Vol. 10, *Cuba, 1961–1962*, http://www.state.gov/www/about_state/history/frusX/76_90.html, emphasis added). According to Schlesinger, "Kennedy once again wanted to know what could be done in the way of quiet infiltration as against the beachhead assault." And Berle "wanted the men to be put into Cuba but did not insist on a major production." As they were leaving the room, Kennedy called Schlesinger back and asked for his opinion; Schlesinger said he opposed the plan. Returning to his office he began to compose his lengthy April 5 memorandum to Kennedy (Schlesinger, *A Thousand Days*, 252).

63. Higgins, 83.

64. Ibid., 85.

65. Memorandum from McGeorge Bundy to General Maxwell Taylor, May 4, 1961, Paramilitary Study Group, National Security Files, Kennedy Library.

66. Maxwell Taylor Oral History, April 12, 1964, Kennedy Library, 9.

67. Dallek, *An Unfinished Life*, 368.

68. Hersh, *The Dark Side of Camelot*, 202.

69. Ibid., 219; Bird, 200.

70. Bird, 197.

71. Janis, *Groupthink*, 25.

72. Memorandum from President Kennedy to McGeorge Bundy, February 4, 1961, President's Office Files, Staff Memoranda-Bundy, Kennedy Library.

73. Memorandum from President Kennedy to McGeorge Bundy, February 5, 1961, President's Office Files, Staff Memoranda-Bundy, Kennedy Library.

74. Memorandum of Meeting with President, February 8, 1961, *Foreign Relations of the United States*, Vol. 10, *Cuba, 1961–1962*, http://www.state.gov/www/about_state/history/frusX/31_45.html.

75. Editorial Note 59, Meeting of March 11, 1961, *Foreign Relations of the United States*, Vol. 10, *Cuba, 1961–1962*, http://www.state.gov/www/about_state/history/frusX/46_60.html.

76. Dallek, *An Unfinished Life*, 360; Memorandum from McGeorge Bundy to the President, March 15, 1961, National Security Files, Countries Series, Cuba, General, 1/61–4/61, Kennedy Library.

77. Dallek, *An Unfinished Life*, 360; also see Editorial Note 66, Meeting of March 16, 1961, *Foreign Relations of the United States*, Vol. 10, *Cuba, 1961–1962*, http://www.state.gov/www/about_state/history/frusX/61_75.html.

78. Janis, *Groupthink*, 23.

79. Ibid., 24.

80. According to Schlesinger, "As you know, there is great pressure within the government in favor of a drastic decision with regard to Cuba. . . . However, as soon as one begins to broaden the focus beyond Cuba to include the hemisphere and the rest of the world, the arguments against this decision begin to gain force" (Memorandum from Arthur Schlesinger

Jr. to President Kennedy, February 11, 1961, *Foreign Relations of the United States,* Vol. 10, *Cuba, 1961–1962,* http://www.state.gov/www/about_state/history/frusX/31_45.html). On March 15, Schlesinger wrote Kennedy, in reference to a recent meeting of the principals, "I had the impression that the military aspects of the problem had received more thoughtful attention than the political aspects. It did not seem to me that the political risks had been adequately assessed or that convincing plans had been laid to minimize them. For example, it was not clear that anyone had thought through the question of our public response if the operation should be undertaken. Do we take the public position that it is a spontaneous Cuban enterprise? Do you say in your press conference, for example, that the U.S. had nothing to do with it? Do we swear this in the United Nations? What happens then when Castro produces a couple of prisoners who testify that they were armed, trained and briefed by Americans? Do we continue to deny this? or change our original story?" "I should add that there seems to me a slight danger of our being rushed into something because CIA has on its hands a band of people it doesn't quite know what to do with. When you were out of the room, Allen Dulles said, 'Don't forget that we have a disposal problem. If we have to take these men out of Guatemala, we will have to transfer them to the U.S., and we can't have them wandering around the country telling everyone what they have been doing.' Obviously this is a genuine problem, but it can't be permitted to govern U.S. policy" (Memorandum from Arthur Schlesinger Jr. to President Kennedy, March 15, 1961, *Foreign Relations of the United States,* Vol. 10, *Cuba, 1961–1962,* http://www.state.gov/www/about_state/history/frusX/61_75.html).

On April 5, Schlesinger wrote Kennedy, "When you asked me after the meeting yesterday what I thought about the Cuban proposal, I am afraid that I did not give a properly ordered answer. My brief answer is that I am in favor of a continuation and expansion of the present approach to Cuba—i.e., quiet infiltration of anti-Castro exiles into Cuba and subsequent support through air drops. The beachhead operation, with the landing and recognition of the provisional government, would represent, however, a change of phase in our Cuban policy. If entirely successful, it would have the highly beneficial result of getting rid of the Castro regime. If we could achieve this by a swift, surgical stroke, I would be for it. But in present circumstances the operation seems to me to involve many hazards; and on balance—and despite the intelligence and responsibility with which the case for the action has been presented—I am against it." Schlesinger then outlined the "hazards" of the invasion plan, going on to note that these "hazards would be outweighed, in my judgment, by the advantage of getting rid of Castro a) if the operation could be swift and surgical; b) if support were forthcoming from our allies, both in Latin America and in Europe; c) if the danger to the US were visible and overwhelming. Conditions (a) and (b) seem doubtful. Of (c), it can only be said that it is not self-evident to many people (including the Chairman of the Senate Foreign Relations Committee)." But towards the end of the memo, Schlesinger does concede that, "On balance, I think that the risks of the operation slightly outweigh the risks of abandonment. These latter risks would be mitigated somewhat if we could manage a partial rather than a total abandonment (i.e., if we could put the men into Cuba quietly)" (Memorandum from Arthur Schlesinger Jr. to President Kennedy, April 5, 1961, *Foreign Relations of the United States,* Vol. 10, *Cuba, 1961–1962,* http://www.state.gov/www/about_state/history/frusX/76_90.html). In Dallek's view, the downward revisions in the CIA plan muted Schlesinger's objections (Dallek, *An Unfinished Life,* 360). In Schlesinger's view, he was a "college professor, fresh to government" potentially interposing his "unassisted judgment . . . against that of august figures" (Smith, *Organizational History of the National Security Council,* 35).

81. Janis, *Groupthink,* 38.

82. Ibid.; also see Schlesinger, *A Thousand Days,* 257.

83. Rusk, 209–211; also see Dean Rusk Oral History, January 2, 1970, Part 2, Johnson Library, 6, where he notes his own concerns about the plan but also those of Vice President Johnson. According to Dallek, Rusk did have some reservations, but they were lodged as "muted protests" (Dallek, *An Unfinished Life,* 361). At an early meeting of the principals on February 8, 1961, for example, "Secretary Rusk stated that without careful—and successful—diplomatic preparation such an operation could have grave effects upon the U.S. position in Latin America and at the U.N. . . . Both Mr. Rusk and Mr. Berle [head of the task force on Latin American affairs] believed that no present decision on the proposed invasion was necessary, *but both made clear their conviction that U.S. policy should not be driven to drastic and irrevocable choice by the urgencies, however real, of a single battalion of men*" (Memorandum of Meeting with President Kennedy, February 8, 1961, *Foreign Relations of the United States,* Vol. 10, *Cuba 1961–1962,* http://www.state.gov/www/about_state/history/frusX/31_45.html, emphasis added). Rusk was also reported to be in dissent at the April 4 meeting, which Fulbright had attended (see Editorial Note 80, Meeting of April 4, 1961, *Foreign Relations of the United States,* Vol. 10, *Cuba, 1961–1962,* http://www.state.gov/www/about_state/history/frusX/76_90.html).

84. Memorandum from Chester Bowles to Dean Rusk, March 31, 1961, *Foreign Relations of the United States,* Vol. 10, *Cuba, 1961–1962,* http://www.state.gov/www/about_state/history/frusX/61_75.html.

85. Janis, *Groupthink,* 41; also see Schlesinger, *A Thousand Days,* 250–51.

86. Rusk, 209.

87. White, 196–97.

88. Rusk, 209.

89. Memorandum from the Joint Chiefs of Staff to Robert McNamara, January 27, 1961, *Foreign Relations of the United States,* Vol. 10, *Cuba, 1961–1962,* http://www.state.gov/www/about_state/history/frusX/16_30.html.

90. Memorandum of Conversation, January 22, 1961, *Foreign Relations of the United States,* V01.10, *Cuba, 1961–1962,* http://www.state.gov/www/about_state/history/frusX/16_30.html, emphasis added.

91. Editorial Note 66, Meeting of March 16, 1961, Meeting, *Foreign Relations of the United States,* Vol. 10, *Cuba, 1961–1962,* http://www.state.gov/www/about_state/history/frusX/61_75.html, emphasis added.

92. Dallek, *An Unfinished Life,* 361.

93. Janis, *Groupthink,* 43.

94. Ibid., 41.

95. Schlesinger, *A Thousand Days,* 259.

96. May and Zelikow, *The Kennedy Tapes,* 28. On Eisenhower's continued criticism of the Kennedy NSC system, which was relayed to Kennedy through CIA Director John McCone (who regularly briefed Eisenhower), see Smith, *Organizational History of the National Security Council,* 49–50.

97. See Smith, *Organizational History of the National Security Council,* 37–38.

98. Frankel, 29.

99. Stern, *Avoiding 'The Final Failure,'* 69.

100. ExCom transcript, 11:50 A.M. meeting, October 16, 1961, in May and Zelikow, 62.

101. Ibid., 63.

102. Ibid., 70.

103. Stern, *Avoiding 'The Final Failure,'* 71.

104. Frankel, 84.

105. Stern, *Avoiding 'The Final Failure,'* 81.

106. ExCom transcript, 6:30 P.M. meeting, October 16, 1961, in May and Zelikow, 94 (emphasis in original); Stern, *Avoiding 'The Final Failure,'* 83.

107. Stern, *Avoiding 'The Final Failure,'* 79.

108. Ibid., 87.

109. Bundy's comments about sabotage actions reveal another facet of his role as NSC advisor. He was the de facto chair of the secret Special Group Augmented (SGA), which had replaced the Eisenhower-era 5412 Committee and oversaw covert operations. Operation Mongoose, which planned a covert sabotage effort in Cuba culminating in a popular uprising against Castro, was led by the legendary Gen. Edward Landsdale, who reported to Bundy and the SGA. The uprising, in turn, would be aided by U.S. military intervention (see Bird, 242–44, also 223–25).

110. Bird, 231.

111. Stern, *Avoiding 'The Final Failure,'* 92.

112. Kennedy personal dictation transcript, near midnight, October 18, 1961, in May and Zelikow, 172.

113. Bundy, *Danger and Survival,* 400.

114. Bird, 232.

115. Frankel, 99.

116. Bird, 232.

117. Stern, *Avoiding 'The Final Failure,'* 42.

118. Bird, 233.

119. May and Zelikow, 693.

120. Ibid., 42.

121. Stern, *Avoiding 'The Final Failure,'* 87.

122. Frankel, 84.

123. Bundy, *Danger and Survival,* 392.

124. Ibid., 400.

125. Bird, 233.

126. The memorandum can be found in Bird, 234.

127. Bundy would later applaud the merits of ExCom deliberations without Kennedy present. In reflecting on JFK's sometime absence due to other duties, Bundy notes, "In twenty-one months he had learned what we have seen repeatedly in this history, that in structured meetings counsel to the president is often constrained" (Bundy, *Danger and Survival,* 397). According to Stern, the willingness of ExCom members "to express critical points of view was often directly affected by whether or not JFK was present. The character of the discussions, as described in the narrative, changed dramatically when the President left the room" (Stern, *Averting 'The Final Failure,'* 416).

128. Stern, *Averting 'The Final Failure,'* 421.

129. Ibid., 417.

130. Ibid., 418, emphasis in original.

131. Ibid., emphasis in original.

132. Ibid., 419, emphasis in original.

133. Ibid., 420–21, emphasis in original.

134. Ibid., emphasis in original.

135. How explicit was the trade of the Turkish missiles as part of the deal to resolve the crisis remains a matter of some contention. At a 1989 conference on the missile crisis,

Dobrynin complained that, in fact, there had been an explicit trade. Sorensen also acknowledged at the conference that he had edited out reference to an explicit trade in Robert Kennedy's diaries and in Kennedy's book *Thirteen Days;* see Bird, 238–39.

136. Bundy, *Danger and Survival,* 400.

137. Ibid.

138. May and Zelikow, 189.

139. Bundy, *Danger and Survival,* 400.

140. May and Zelikow, 202. During the first week of the crisis, as he had during the Bay of Pigs deliberations, Rusk did not take a clear position. He realized the missiles needed to be removed, but "I didn't commit myself to any policy line or join any task force at first, although I consulted with all. . . . As secretary of state I felt I should hold myself in reserve and hear all points of view before giving my recommendation to the president." "I intentionally took no position at first because I did not think that was my appropriate role." Yet on Saturday, October 20th, Kennedy asked Rusk as the senior member to begin the meeting with his recommendation; Rusk briefly listed his reasons in favor a naval blockade—or "quarantine," as he preferred to call it (Rusk, 231–34).

141. Janis, *Groupthink,* 141.

142. Bundy, *Danger and Survival,* 459.

143. Frankel, 99.

144. Ibid., 77–78.

145. Ibid., 78. On the other hand, as Stern observes, "Kennedy's management of the ExCom discussions was subtle and understated, but remarkably effective" (Stern, *Averting 'The Final Failure,'* 416).

146. Stern, *Averting 'The Final Failure,'* 294, also 422; also see Hersh, *Dark Side of Camelot,* 364.

147. These were generally dictated by President Kennedy to his secretary, Evelyn Lincoln. Some can be found in Dictation Notes, President's Office File, Staff Memoranda, Kennedy Library.

148. Memorandum from President Kennedy to McGeorge Bundy, August 7, 1961, President's Office Files, Staff Memoranda-Bundy, Kennedy Library.

149. Ibid., August 21, 1961.

150. Ibid.

151. Ibid., April 14, 1961.

152. Ibid., July 10, 1961.

153. National Security Council, "History of the National Security Council."

154. Burke and Greenstein, 182. Rusk, it should be noted, presents a more positive view. The Tuesday lunches offered a more comfortable setting for Johnson, and the participants "knew how to keep their mouths shut," unlike in the larger NSC. It was a "full discussion," but "each of us took notes." If there were differences, "we would frequently compare notes afterwards," taking any disputes to LBJ "for clarification. But that seldom occurred because usually it would be quite clear at the table itself as to what was being decided" (Dean Rusk Oral History, July 28, 1969, Johnson Library, 22–23).

155. Burke and Greenstein, 183, 258.

156. Ibid., 258.

157. Preston, *War Council,* 51.

158. National Security Council, "History of the National Security Council."

159. Burke and Greenstein, 259.

160. Fortas, "Portrait of a Friend," 8–10.

161. Dean Rusk Oral History, July 28, 1969, Johnson Library, 37.

162. But Rusk also notes that once a decision was made "he expected them to comply,"

and he "was always impatient with those who were trying to build, on the record, a record of dissent." Rusk also notes Johnson's "deep feelings" and "glandular reactions" about his policies and programs (Dean Rusk Oral History, July 28, 1969, Johnson Library, 5).

163. Burke and Greenstein, 140–41.

164. See Ibid., 124–26, 161–73, 205–213, 216–229, 260.

165. Ibid., 257.

166. Preston, *War Council,* 155, 157. It should also be noted that Bundy was cautious at the time of the second attack in the Gulf of Tonkin. He urged Johnson "to think it over" and not react quickly. Johnson, without consulting many of his advisers, was determined to act quickly: "I didn't ask you that. I told you to help me get organized," he snapped back at Bundy. According to Bundy, "I was just a messenger boy. And he made sure I stayed that way" (Bird, 289).

167. Preston, *War Council,* 52.

168. Ibid., 158.

169. George Ball, "How Valid Are the Assumptions Underlying Our Viet-Nam Policies?," October 5, 1964, National Security Files, Country File-Vietnam; also see Ball, *The Past Has Another Pattern,* 380, 383, 392; and Burke and Greenstein, 171–72. Ball would have ample opportunity over the ensuing months to express his views (which were trenchant and insightful), yet some observers have concluded that his dissent became so routine and predictable that Ball might be regarded as a "domesticated dissenter," one whose activities come to serve a symbolic purpose and bolstering the defense that all sides had been heard. For a fuller scholarly account of Ball's dissenting role in Johnson's Vietnam deliberations, see White, 251–314. Rusk regarded Ball as a "devil's advocate" for the antiwar position, assigned that role by Johnson himself, and "it may be that George Ball convinced himself in the process" (Dean Rusk Oral History, September 26, 1969, Part 1, Johnson Library, 34).

170. Preston, *War Council,* 6–7.

171. Memorandum from McGeorge Bundy to the President, May 31, 1965, White House Central Files, Publicity, Johnson Library.

172. Memorandum from McGeorge Bundy to the President, May 5, 1965, McGeorge Bundy Memos to the President, Johnson Library.

173. Memorandum from McGeorge Bundy to the President, March 6, 1965, McGeorge Bundy Memos to the President, Johnson Library.

174. Memorandum from McGeorge Bundy to the President, January 27, 1965, National Security File, Memos to the President, Johnson Library. According to Preston, "While direct, Bundy's memo was neither manipulative nor an inaccurate assessment" (Preston, *War Council,* 167). Bird notes that Bundy's language "must have alarmed a president so insecure in his reputation for handling foreign policy. . . . Clearly, Mac was pushing his president" (Bird, 304).

175. Burke and Greenstein, 127.

176. Rusk, 447. According to Rusk, "I did not participate in this decision authorizing the first retaliatory bombing attacks. . . . Although I had some reservations about the bombing raids, I did not oppose them" (447); also see Dean Rusk Oral History, September 26, 1969, Part 1, Johnson Library, 22–23. On February 23, Rusk also wrote Johnson that he favored the stationing of a marine battalion at DaNang if the security situation called for it (448).

177. Summary notes of the 554th NSC meeting, February 1, 1965, National Security Files, NSC Meetings File, Johnson Library.

178. The policy developed out of a Vietnam Working Group, led by William Bundy, which had been working since November (see Bird, 291–97; and Preston, *War Council,* 160–64).

179. See Burke and Greenstein, 130–33.

180. Ibid., 143.

181. Bird, 306.

182. Preston, *War Council*, 175, 176. Bird echoes these reports, but notes that "Others in the room saw Bundy at his coolest" (306).

183. Humphrey, *The Education of a Public Man*, 483. On Humphrey's exclusion from the principals, see Burke and Greenstein, 154, 168, 184.

184. See Preston, *War Council*, 180; and Burke and Greenstein, 154–55.

185. Memorandum from McGeorge Bundy to the President, "Subject: Vietnam Decisions," February 16, 1965, McGeorge Bundy Memos to the President, Johnson Library. On February 27, the State Department issued a white paper on the new policy.

186. Ball, 389.

187. Burke and Greenstein, 162.

188. Ibid., 125, 175–77. Taylor was an early advocate of an air campaign, but as troops began to be introduced, he began to argue in favor of a "coastal enclave" strategy rather than Westmoreland's preference for offensive search-and-destroy operations.

189. Memorandum from McGeorge Bundy to the President, April 14, 1965, NSC History, Deployment of Forces, Johnson Library, emphasis in original.

190. See Burke and Greenstein, 180–81.

191. Memorandum from McGeorge Bundy to the President, March 26, 1965, NSC History, Deployment of Forces, Johnson Library.

192. Summary Notes of the 550th NSC Meeting, March 26, 1965, NSC Meetings File, Johnson Library.

193. Taylor, *Swords and Plowshares*, 341.

194. Kahin, *Intervention*, 319; also see Burke and Greenstein, 185–86.

195. Preston, *War Council*, 191–95. Earlier, Bundy had also been highly tolerant of aide Michael Forrestal's pessimistic assessments of the situation in South Vietnam. Forrestal also warned Bundy that he was not consulting widely enough (See Bird, 279–283).

196. Preston, *War Council*, 191–95. Bundy had been forewarned of the limits of bombing the North. A war games exercise in 1964, SIGMA II-64, had indicated that it was unlikely to break the will of the enemy. Bundy, however, according to one participant had "brushed off the results" (Bird, 277). In early summer 1965, Bundy was also apparently becoming either concerned about his standing with Johnson or disillusioned with his job that he contacted the president of Harvard to inquire about returning to the faculty (Bird, 325).

197. See Burke and Greenstein, 214–15.

198. Memorandum from McGeorge Bundy to the President, July 1, 1965, 8:20 P.M., NSC History, Deployment of Forces, Johnson Library; Burke and Greenstein, 205–8. Several hours earlier, Bundy also urged that discussion of Ball's memo occur in only the smallest of groups; Rusk and McNamara "feel that it is exceedingly dangerous to have this possibility reported in a wider circle" (Memorandum from McGeorge Bundy to the President, July 1, 1965, 5:50 P.M., McGeorge Bundy Memos to the President, Johnson Library). Rusk later noted that "our gradual response was not working. . . . I put my reservations aside" and advised LBJ to send an additional 100,000 troops (Rusk, 450).

199. Memorandum from McGeorge Bundy to the Secretary of Defense, June 30, 1965, NSC Meeting File, Deployment of Forces, Johnson Library.

200. Memorandum from McGeorge Bundy to the President, July 19, 1965, National Security File, Country File, Vietnam, Johnson Library, emphasis added.

201. See Burke and Greenstein, 214–16.

202. Chester Cooper Notes, 2:30–5:30 Meeting, July 21, 1965, Meeting Notes File, Johnson Library. The meeting notes are also reproduced in *Foreign Relations of the United States, 1964–1968,* Vol. 3, *Vietnam, June–December 1965,* http://www.state.gov/www/about_state/history/vol_iii/070.html; also see Preston, *War Council,* 206; Bird, 339; and White, 312.

203. Jack Valenti Notes, Noon–2:15 Meeting, July 22, 1965, Meeting Notes File, Johnson Library. The meeting notes are also reproduced in *Foreign Relations of the United States, 1964–1968,* Vol. 3, *Vietnam, June–December 1965,* http://www.state.gov/www/about_state/history/vol_iii/070.html.

204. They are too numerous to detail here, but see Burke and Greenstein, 232–38. Bird characterizes the process as a "charade" (337).

205. By November, 1965, Westmoreland estimated he would need 410,000 troops on the ground by July 1966 (Bird, 340).

206. Destler, "National Security Management," 582; Zegart, 241. Bundy's average number of yearly entries was thirty-nine; his successor Walt Rostow was close at thirty-five.

207. Bird, 320.

208. *Preston, War Council,* 197–98; on Bundy and the college teach-ins also see Bird, 318–323.

209. Bird, 321–22.

210. Preston, *War Council,* 183.

211. On Bundy's press contacts, see Bird, 101–5, 272–73, 274, 278, 300, 310, 314–16, 327–29.

212. Ibid., 300.

213. Ibid., 297, 298.

214. The episode may also have been the occasion of failed brokerage on Bundy's part. According to Morton Halperin, the U.S. ambassador in Santo Domingo "received strong hints from Washington that it would like him to report that a rebel victory would lead to a pro-Communist government." The message was conveyed through a telephone call from Rusk and McNamara, "who both asked him if he did not agree with this judgment which had been reached in Washington." The ambassador, who favored U.S. intervention, "was quick to pick up on the cue and report that there was danger of Communists coming to power" (Halperin, *Bureaucratic Politics and Foreign Policy,* 164).

215. Rusk, 375.

216. Preston, *War Council,* 200–201. On the lack of deliberation on sending troops and the questionable assumption that a Castro-ite coup was in the offing, see Bird, 324–25. On the administration's position see Dean Rusk Oral History, January 2, 1970, Part 2, Johnson Library, 15–26.

217. Preston, *War Council,* 53.

218. Andrew Goodpaster Oral History, June 11, 1980. Eisenhower Library, 66.

219. Smith, *Organizational History of the National Security Council,* 18.

220. Bromley Smith Oral History, July 29, 1969, Johnson Library, 15.

221. Fortas, "Portrait of a Friend," 8–10.

222. Dean Rusk Oral History, July 28, 1969, Johnson Library, 8–9.

223. Ball, 173; for similar comments by others in the administration, see Preston, *War Council,* 51.

224. Rusk, 518–19. In a letter to Dean Acheson, Rusk told him that he never felt Bundy was "causing problems for the intimate triangle of the president, the Secretary of State and the Secretary of Defense" (Preston, *War Council,* 51–52).

Chapter 3

1. Hitchens, *The Trial of Henry Kissinger*, x, emphasis added.

2. Elliot Richardson Oral History, May 31, 1988, Nixon Presidential Materials Project, National Archives, College Park, Md., 2.

3. Daalder and Destler, eds., "The Nixon Administration National Security Council," 46. The quote is from Richard Solomon, an NSC staffer who later served in high-level positions in the State Department.

4. Allen, Oral History, 6–8; Kissinger, *White House Years*, 10.

5. According to Allen, "Kissinger, on his own, volunteered information to us through a spy, a former student, that he had in the Paris peace talks, who would call him and debrief, and Kissinger called me from pay phones and we spoke in German . . . he offloaded mostly every night what had happened in Paris" (Allen, Oral History, 11). According to Kissinger, for both political camps, he would "answer specific questions on foreign policy, but I would not offer general advice or volunteer suggestions." He also notes that he never took up campaign manager John Mitchell's suggestion that he "call a certain Mr. Haldeman if I ever received any hard information" about what any preelection moves the Johnson administration was undertaking concerning Vietnam negotiations (Kissinger, *White House Years*, 10). No mention is made of telephone calls to Allen. Haldeman later recalled that Kissinger passed information on the Vietnam peace talks to John Mitchell (H. R. Haldeman Oral History, August 13, 1987, Nixon Presidential Materials Project, National Archives, College Park, Md., 22).

6. Kissinger, *White House Years*, 11–12, 15. It was the second time that Kissinger had met Nixon, the first occurred in 1967 at a Christmas party hosted by Clare Boothe Luce (Kissinger, *White House Years*, 8).

7. Nixon, *RN*, 341.

8. H. R. Haldeman Oral History, August 13, 1987, 44.

9. Kissinger, *White House Years*, 41; also see Isaacson, *Kissinger*, 136; and Dallek, *Nixon and Kissinger*, 80.

10. Goodpaster, Eisenhower's former staff secretary, was on temporary leave from his position as deputy commander in Saigon in order to work on the Nixon transition. In the third volume of his memoirs, Kissinger especially singles out Goodpaster as the "architect" of the new system, as well as an important source in recommending that the NSC advisor rather than departmental representatives (especially State) chair key committees (Kissinger, *Years of Renewal*, 75). Roger Morris, however, regards Halperin—who was then at the Defense Department's Office of International Security Affairs—as the key force in drafting the new plan and with Goodpaster in more of an after-the-fact approval role (Morris, *Uncertain Greatness*, 78–84).

11. Kissinger, *White House Years*, 43; Burke telephone interview with Harold Saunders, January 3, 2008.

12. Kissinger, *White House Years*, 43; Kissinger, *Years of Renewal*, 75–76; also see Morris, *Uncertain Greatness*, 80–81; Prados, *Keeper of the Keys*, 263, 266–67; and Rothkopf, 115–18.

13. Rothkopf, 120. For a list of NSSMs through early October 1971, see Leacacos, "Kissinger's Apparat," 93. Fifty-five NSSMs were ordered by Kissinger in the administration's first 100 days. Morris points out that the NSSMs trailed off to only eight in the first four months of 1970. In part this reflected that basic national security policies were now set, but also that "increasingly the most important decisions were to be taken outside the NSC" (Morris, *Uncertain Greatness*, 92).

14. Isaacson, 155.

15. Kissinger, *White House Years,* 44; also see Morris, *Uncertain Greatness,* 86–91.

16. Kissinger, *White House Years,* 44. Kissinger also provides an interesting account of Nixon's indecisiveness in personally pressing the issue against Rogers's and Laird's opposition by his delay in signing NSDM 2, which put the organizational changes into effect. Nixon finally signed it on January 19, and it was formally put into effect shortly after his inauguration. According to Kissinger, NSDM 2 encompassed all the changes Kissinger had proposed, except that Nixon wanted the CIA director to be removed from NSC meetings—an exclusion that Laird and Kissinger eventually got Nixon to rescind (see Kissinger, *White House Years,* 44–47). Morris notes that a reduced CIA role was in Halperin's original plan (Morris, *Uncertain Greatness,* 81, 88). Statutorially, however, the CIA director is an adviser to the NSC.

17. H. R. Haldeman Oral History, August 13, 1987.

18. Audio Cassette, Diaries of H. R. Haldeman, November 21, 1972, Nixon Presidential Materials Project, National Archives, College Park, Md. Nixon's comment does not appear in Haldeman's published version of his diaries.

19. Allen, Oral History, 19.

20. Daalder and Destler, eds., "The Nixon Administration National Security Council," 4.

21. Isaacson, 154, 156.

22. Strober and Strober, *Nixon,* 86.

23. Daalder and Destler, eds., "The Nixon Administration National Security Council," 33.

24. Morris, *Uncertain Greatness,* 81.

25. Isaacson, 203–4.

26. Daalder and Destler, eds., "The Nixon Administration National Security Council," 33.

27. Hyland, *Mortal Rivals,* 7.

28. Rush, "An Ambassador's Perspective," 347–48.

29. Handwritten Diaries of H. R. Haldeman, June 4, 1969, Nixon Presidential Materials Project, National Archives, College Park, Md.; also see Haldeman, *Haldeman Diaries,* 63. The Haldeman "diaries" at the National Archives in College Park, Md., consist of seven written journals from the start of the Nixon presidency to December 2, 1970. At that point Haldeman began dictating his daily notes on audio cassettes. His published version of the diaries is a selective compilation of many of the more interesting daily entries. There are also some discrepancies between the published version and the archival records.

30. Ehrlichman, "The White House and Policy-Making," 127.

31. Kissinger, *White House Years,* 45.

32. Scowcroft, "Ford as President and His Foreign Policy," 312.

33. Daalder and Destler, eds., "The Nixon Administration National Security Council," 3.

34. Ibid., 32.

35. Prados, 277.

36. Strober and Strober, *Nixon,* 123.

37. Daalder and Destler, eds., "The Nixon Administration National Security Council," 13.

38. Isaacson, 189.

39. Ibid., 185.

40. Hyland, 7. According to Hyland, Nixon had a high regard for Kissinger's staff and

even suggested that they all be outfitted with blue blazers with the NSC insignia on the breast pocket. "This idea died, to our great relief," Hyland reports (7).

41. Strober and Strober, *Nixon,* 423.

42. Audio Cassette, Diaries of H. R. Haldeman, July 12, 1971; also see Haldeman, *Haldeman Diaries,* 318.

43. Kissinger's efforts even got territorial. He was able to move his office from the basement of the White House near the Situation Room to more coveted quarters on the first floor of the West Wing, where the NSC advisor has been housed ever since (Prados, 280). According to Robert Odle Jr., a White House staff member, Kissinger was even able to gain access to a bathroom on the first floor of the West Wing that was attached exclusively to the office of Bryce Harlow. Once, when Harlow was away, Kissinger convinced Haldeman to wall up the entrance to the bathroom from Harlow's office and install in its place a door to the corridor that would permit Kissinger, Haldeman, and Harlow to use it (Strober and Strober, *Nixon,* 86).

44. Prados, 281–82.

45. Daalder and Destler, eds., "The Bush Administration National Security Council," 42.

46. Prados, 281.

47. Isaacson, 189.

48. Handwritten Diaries of H. R. Haldeman, October 13, 1969; also see Haldeman, *Haldeman Diaries,* 99.

49. Audio Cassette, Diaries of H. R. Haldeman, July 24, 1971; also see Haldeman, *Haldeman Diaries,* 330; Dallek, *Nixon and Kissinger,* 329; Ehrlichman, *Witness to Power,* 295.

50. See Allen, Oral History, 7, 13.

51. See Prados, 277–281; and Isaacson, 183–89.

52. Burke telephone interview with Harold Saunders, January 3, 2008. Saunders served on the NSC staff or in the State Department through the Carter administration.

53. Prados, 283.

54. Daalder and Destler, eds., "The Nixon Administration National Security Council," 13; also see Isaacson, 189.

55. Prados, 282. Other counts differ. According to Isaacson, by 1971 the staff had doubled to 46 professionals and 105 administrative personnel (Isaacson, 204). Another count placed the size of the staff at 120 in early 1971 (Leacacos, "Kissinger's Apparat," 85).

56. Isaacson, 188.

57. Prados, 283.

58. Allen, Oral History, 13–14.

59. Sonnenfeldt, "Reconstructing the Nixon Foreign Policy," 320.

60. Burke telephone interview with Harold Saunders, January 3, 2008.

61. Ibid.

62. Daalder and Destler, eds., "The Nixon Administration National Security Council," 2.

63. Burke telephone interview with Harold Saunders, January 3, 2008.

64. Daalder and Destler, eds., "The Nixon Administration National Security Council," 7.

65. Ibid., 14.

66. Ibid., 17.

67. Rothkopf, 115. But Rothkopf also quotes Schlesinger as saying that some of them were reminiscent of the more favorable Operation Solarium exercise under Eisenhower (120).

68. Leacacos, "Kissinger's Apparat," 91.

69. Ibid., 86, 87, 88.

70. Burke telephone interview with Harold Saunders, January 3, 2008.

71. Allen, Oral History, 13.

72. Handwritten Diaries of H. R. Haldeman, June 24, 1970; also see Haldeman, *Haldeman Diaries,* 177.

73. Ehrlichman, "The White House and Policy-Making," 124.

74. Ibid., 127. Interestingly, Kissinger notes in his own memoirs—here in criticism of a State Department-dominated NSC process, that "the typical department will present two absurd alternatives as straw men bracketing its preferred option—which usually appears in the middle position. A totally ignorant decision-maker could easily satisfy his departments by blindly choosing Option 2 of any three choices they submit to him" (Kissinger, *White House Years,* 43).

75. Strober and Strober, *Nixon,* 120.

76. Ibid., 127.

77. Woodward, "Ford Disagreed With Bush About Invading Iraq."

78. Isaacson, 147–48; Ehrlichman, *Witness to Power,* 209.

79. Daalder and Destler, eds., "The Nixon Administration National Security Council," 6.

80. Sonnenfeldt, "Reconstructing the Nixon Foreign Policy," 318.

81. Rush, "An Ambassador's Perspective," 347.

82. Engel, "Where a Future President Learned About the World," 54.

83. On Rogers's appointment, see Dallek, *Nixon and Kissinger,* 83.

84. Quoted in Sorensen, "The President and the Secretary of State," 232.

85. Strober and Strober, *Nixon,* 135; Rush, "An Ambassador's Perspective," 337–38.

86. Strober and Strober, *Nixon,* 95.

87. Kissinger, *White House Years,* 26, 31, 589, 887.

88. Prados, 296; Isaacson, 262.

89. Isaacson, 265.

90. Ibid., 265–66.

91. There appears to be some evidence that this can be traced back to Nixon rather than just being a Kissinger initiative. An April 20, 1970, Haldeman diary entry states: Nixon "wants to set up back channel to issue orders to military not through the Secretary of Defense . . . [Nixon] will personally take over responsibility for war in Cambodia" (Handwritten Diaries of H. R. Haldeman, April 20, 1970; also see Haldeman, *Haldeman Diaries,* 152).

92. Prados, 298.

93. H. R. Haldeman Oral History, August 13, 1987.

94. Handwritten Diaries of H. R. Haldeman, August 29, 1969; also see Haldeman, *Haldeman Diaries,* 83.

95. Ibid., March 10, 1970; also see Haldeman, *Haldeman Diaries,* 136.

96. Ibid., June 23, 1970; also see Haldeman, *Haldeman Diaries,* 176.

97. Ibid., July 13, 1970; also see Haldeman, *Haldeman Diaries,* 18–82.

98. Ibid., July 15, 1970; also see Haldeman, *Haldeman Diaries,* 182.

99. Ibid., August 6, 1970; also see Haldeman, *Haldeman Diaries,* 186.

100. Ibid., September 10, 1970; also see Haldeman, *Haldeman Diaries,* 192.

101. Audio Cassette, Diaries of H. R. Haldeman, November 11, 1971; also see Haldeman, *Haldeman Diaries,* 372.

102. Handwritten Diaries of H. R. Haldeman, January 22, 1970; also see Haldeman, *Haldeman Diaries,* 122.

103. Audio Cassette, Diaries of H. R. Haldeman, November 11, 1971; also see Haldeman, *Haldeman Diaries,* 372.

104. Handwritten Diaries of H. R. Haldeman, October 9, 1969; also see Haldeman, *Haldeman Diaries,* 97.

105. Ibid., October 11, 1969; also see Haldeman, *Haldeman Diaries,* 99.

106. Ibid., October 13, 1969; also see Haldeman, *Haldeman Diaries,* 99.

107. Ibid., October 15, 1969; also see Haldeman, *Haldeman Diaries,* 100.

108. Ibid., October 27, 1969, emphasis added; also see Haldeman, *Haldeman Diaries,* 103.

109. Ehrlichman, *Witness to Power,* 297; on Ehrlichman's view of Kissinger's fued with Rogers, see 296–300.

110. Handwritten Diaries of H. R. Haldeman, October 16, 1969; also see Haldeman, *Haldeman Diaries,* 100.

111. Ibid., February 10, 1970; also see Haldeman, *Haldeman Diaries,* 127.

112. Ibid., January 19, 1970; also see Haldeman, *Haldeman Diaries,* 122.

113. Ibid., March 9, 1970; also see Haldeman, *Haldeman Diaries,* 135.

114. Audio Cassette, Diaries of H. R. Haldeman, October 13, 1971; also see Haldeman, *Haldeman Diaries,* 364.

115. Dallek, *Nixon and Kissinger,* 350–51.

116. Audio Cassette, Diaries of H. R. Haldeman, December 22, 1971; also see Haldeman, *Haldeman Diaries,* 386. On the spy incident also see Dallek, *Nixon and Kissinger,* 350–51; Issacson, 380–85; and Ehrlichman, *Witness to Power,* 303–9.

117. Handwritten Diaries of H. R. Haldeman, April 1, 1970; also see Haldeman, *Haldeman Diaries,* 145.

118. Audio Cassette, Diaries of H. R. Haldeman, November 20, 1972; also see Haldeman, *Haldeman Diaries,* 539.

119. Ibid., January 7, 1973; also see Haldeman, *Haldeman Diaries,* 562. Isaacson particularly links Nixon's concerns about his and Kissinger's papers to Kissinger's leaks to reporters in late 1972 about their policy differences and Kissinger's difficulties in dealing with Nixon (Isaacson, 475). Berman links it to Nixon's concern that Kissinger would take all the public credit for a successful negotiation with North Vietnam or pass the blame if the effort proved unsuccessful (Berman, *No Peace, No Honor,* 222–23).

120. Isaacson, 231–32.

121. Strober and Strober, *Nixon,* 124.

122. Prados, 283.

123. Rush, "An Ambassador's Perspective," 337.

124. Audio Cassette, Diaries of H. R. Haldeman, March 17, 1973; also see Haldeman, *Haldeman Diaries,* 589; also see Isaacson, 352.

125. H. R. Haldeman Oral History, August 13, 1987, 153.

126. Woodward, "Ford Disagreed With Bush About Invading Iraq."

127. Handwritten Diaries of H. R. Haldeman, January 14, 1970; also see Haldeman, *Haldeman Diaries,* 121.

128. Dallek, *Nixon and Kissinger,* 122, 142.

129. Handwritten Diaries of H. R. Haldeman, June 29, 1970; also see Haldeman, *Haldeman Diaries,* 178; and Ehrlichman, *Witness to Power,* 311.

130. Audio Cassette, Diaries of H. R. Haldeman, July 10, 1971; also see Haldeman, *Haldeman Diaries,* 317. On Nixon's concerns about the China trip also see Dallek, *Nixon and Kissinger,* 298–99.

131. Audio Cassette, Diaries of H. R. Haldeman, July 13, 1971; also see Haldeman, *Haldeman Diaries,* 319.

132. Ibid., August 11, 1971; also see Haldeman, *Haldeman Diaries,* 339.

133. Ibid., September 14, 1971; also see Haldeman, *Haldeman Diaries,* 356.

134. Isaacson, 350.

135. Ibid., 341, 346.

136. Audio Cassette, Diaries of H. R. Haldeman, December 14, 1972; also see Haldeman, *Haldeman Diaries,* 555.

137. Haldeman, *The Ends of Power,* 94–95; also see Audio Cassette, Diaries of H. R. Haldeman, December 13, 1972; and Haldeman, *Haldeman Diaries,* 554.

138. Audio Cassette, Diaries of H. R. Haldeman, October 8, 1971; also see Haldeman, *Haldeman Diaries,* 365.

139. Ibid., February 15, 1973; also see Haldeman, *Haldeman Diaries,* 579. Nixon later met with then NSC aide Brent Scowcroft, who informed him that it was his error that he was not informed of the communiqué.

140. Audio Cassette, Diaries of H. R. Haldeman, March 19, 1973; also see Haldeman, *Haldeman Diaries,* 589.

141. Prados, 283; Rothkopf, 139.

142. Allen, Oral History, 16.

143. Handwritten Diaries of H. R. Haldeman, June 16, 1969; also see Haldeman, *Haldeman Diaries,* 69. Yet, as Dallek documents, Kissinger's initial efforts at dealing with leaks came from Nixon himself, one month into the new presidency (Dallek, *Nixon and Kissinger,* 122).

144. Major leaks began early, in May 1969, with *New York Times* articles on the bombing of North Vietnamese sanctuaries in Cambodia and the shooting down of a reconnaissance plane near Korea, an event reminiscent of the North Korean seizure of the USS *Pueblo* the year before. Kissinger immediately contacted FBI Director J. Edgar Hoover (Haldeman, *The Ends of Power,* 100–104). Those leaks, in turn, began the process of FBI phone taps on NSC staff members, starting with Kissinger aide Morton Halperin. According to Prados, Kissinger spoke with Hoover four times on the day before the taps were installed (Prados, 271–72). When news of the wiretaps became public, Halperin filed a civil suit against Nixon and Kissinger. In 1992, Halperin ended his lawsuit against Kissinger in return for a formal apology (see Stolberg, "Kissinger's Appearance Revives Memories of Vietnam Era"). Kissinger also sent a letter of formal apology to Anthony Lake, which Lake hung in his study (Burke telephone interview with Anthony Lake, November 1, 2007). Others on the NSC staff who were tapped included Helmut Sonnenfeldt, Richard L. Sneider, Daniel I. Davidson, Winston Lord, and Richard M. Moose (Prados, 281); in all there were seventeen FBI wiretaps, thirteen on government officials, four on journalists. The program went on for twenty-one months until February 1971, although some taps were in place for much shorter periods (Isaacson, 217). For a fuller discussion, see Isaacson, 212–227; Dallek, *Nixon and Kissinger,* 123–24; and Morris, *Uncertain Greatness,* 157–161. On its broader relations to Watergate, see Isaacson, 227. According to Haldeman, it was "All this for nothing. The leakers were never discovered" (Haldeman, *The Ends of Power,* 104).

145. Haldeman, *The Ends of Power,* 104.

146. Ehrlichman, *Witness to Power,* 300–302.

147. Haldeman, *The Ends of Power,* 110, also 111–13. Also see Isaacson, 329–330; and Dallek, *Nixon and Kissinger,* 309–312.

148. Haldeman, *The Ends of Power,* 194–95; also see Ehrlichman, *Witness to Power,* 311. Dallek partially takes a more benign view and attributes the resumption of taping to Kissinger being behind in sending the president memos, but he does note that one motivation on Nixon's part may have been to prevent Kissinger from taking credit for foreign policy initiatives (Dallek, *Nixon and Kissinger,* 247).

149. See Ehrlichman, *Witness to Power,* 302–9.

150. Isaacson, 201–2; Dallek, *Nixon and Kissinger,* 155.

151. Isaacson, 194.

152. Burke telephone interview with Harold Saunders, January 3, 2008.

153. Ibid.

154. Ibid.

155. Ibid.

156. Allen, Oral History, 13.

157. Prados, 281.

158. Sonnenfeldt, "Reconstructing the Nixon Foreign Policy," 323.

159. Prados, 285–86.

160. Ibid., 296, 297; also see Morris, *Uncertain Greatness* 174; Isaacson, 263; and Berman, *No Peace, No Honor,* 74–76.

161. Nixon, *RN,* 589.

162. Ibid., 587.

163. Ibid., 592. For Kissinger's version of his meeting with Brezhnev, see *White House Years,* 1154–64.

164. Audio Cassette, Diaries of H. R. Haldeman, April 22, 1972; also see Haldeman, *Haldeman Diaries,* 444. For more detail of the events, see Isaacson, 410–13; and Dallek, *Nixon and Kissinger,* 375–381.

165. Isaacson, 414.

166. Audio Cassette, Diaries of H. R. Haldeman, February 6, 1973; also see Haldeman, *Haldeman Diaries,* 575.

167. Ehrlichman, *Witness to Power,* 311, emphasis in original.

168. Allen, Oral History, 22.

169. Strober and Strober, *Nixon,* 135.

170. Burke telephone interview with Harold Saunders, January 3, 2008.

171. Strober and Strober, *Nixon,* 94.

172. On the Rogers plan, see Dallek, *Nixon and Kissinger,* 171–79, 219–223, 271–76, 357.

173. See Ehrlichman, *Witness to Power,* 298–99.

174. Handwritten Diaries of H. R. Haldeman, March 10, 1970; also see Haldeman, *Haldeman Diaries,* 136.

175. Ibid., March 17, 1970; also see Haldeman, *Haldeman Diaries,* 139.

176. Ibid., March 18, 1970, emphasis added; also see Haldeman, *Haldeman Diaries,* 139.

177. Ibid., August 16, 1970; also see Haldeman, *Haldeman Diaries,* 189.

178. Ibid., August 17, 1970, emphasis added; also see Haldeman, *Haldeman Diaries,* 189.

179. Ibid., August 18, 1970; also see Haldeman, *Haldeman Diaries,* 190.

180. Ibid., September 21, 1970, emphasis added; also see Haldeman, *Haldeman Diaries,* 196.

181. Burke telephone interview with Harold Saunders, January 3, 2008.

182. Dallek, *Nixon and Kissinger,* 109–110; Prados, 286–87.

183. Daalder and Destler, eds., "The Nixon Administration National Security Council," 8.

184. Rothkopf, 127.

185. Isaacson, 208–9.

186. Kissinger, *Years of Upheaval,* 263–64.

187. See Prados, 326; and Isaacson, 429–436.

188. Hyland, 43.

189. Isaacson, 318.

190. Smith, *Doubletalk,* 170; Isaacson, 319–321.

191. Kissinger, *White House Years,* 542.

192. Isaacson, 321. For Kissinger's more benign view see Kissinger, *White House Years,* 542.

193. Smith, *Doubletalk,* 147.

194. Isaacson, 321–22.

195. Smith, *Doubletalk,* 228; also see Hersh, *Price of Power,* 342.

196. Isaacson, 324.

197. Daalder and Destler, eds., "The Nixon Administration National Security Council," 28.

198. Hersh, *Price of Power,* 342; Prados, 287.

199. Smith, *Doubletalk,* 233.

200. Ibid., 225.

201. Ibid., 109–110.

202. Isaacson, 432. Dallek also notes that the SALT agreement was "flawed. It did nothing to inhibit the 'MIRV explosion,' which produced a huge expansion in the number of warheads on both sides over the next decade" (Dallek, *Nixon and Kissinger,* 398). According to chief arms negotiator Gerard Smith, Kissinger's back-channel efforts with Dobrynin in 1970 and 1971 "followed an entirely different procedure from that which governed the delegation. There were no building blocks, no analytic work, no strategic analysis in the agencies concerned. There were no Verification Panel or National Security Council discussions. There were no consultations with congressional committees or with allies" (Smith, *Doubletalk,* 225).

203. Jimmy Carter Oral History, Miller Center of Public Affairs Oral History Project, November 29, 1982, Carter Library, 58.

204. Rothkopf, 127.

205. Dallek, *Nixon and Kissinger,* 293.

206. Audio Cassette, Diaries of H. R. Haldeman, June 28, 1971; also see Haldeman, *Haldeman Diaries,* 307.

207. Daalder and Destler, eds., "The Nixon Administration National Security Council," 44.

208. Ibid., 46; also see Rothkopf, 133.

209. Daalder and Destler, eds., "The Nixon Administration National Security Council," 27–28; also see Rothkopf, 136. Dallek has a more positive account of Kissinger's efforts, particularly in finessing differences with the Chinese (Dallek, *Nixon and Kissinger,* 332–33).

210. Daalder and Destler, eds., "The Nixon Administration National Security Council," 27.

211. Strober and Strober, *Nixon,* 136; also see Isaacson, 405.

212. Isaacson, 405.

213. Ibid., 245.

214. Ibid., 397.

215. Kissinger, *White House Years,* 1349.

216. Ehrlichman, *Witness to Power,* 312 ; also see Dallek, *Nixon and Kissinger,* 407, 415, 421, who also notes that Nixon was worried about the negative political implications of a settlement before Election Day.

217. Audio Cassette, Diaries of H. R. Haldeman, September 28, 1972; also see Haldeman, *Haldeman Diaries,* 510. For an alternative interpretation stressing the better bargaining position for a deal before the election, see Isaacson, 440–41.

218. But Dallek also notes that Kissinger was reluctant in the role of "political operative" during the 1972 election and resisted press briefings for partisan purposes. He told reporters that he did not raise funds for the Nixon campaign and was careful not to direct public criticism at Sen. George McGovern, the Democratic nominee (Dallek, *Nixon and Kissinger,* 400).

219. Ehrlichman, *Witness to Power,* 314.

220. Audio Cassette, Diaries of H. R. Haldeman, November 29, 1972; also see Haldeman, *Haldeman Diaries,* 545–46.

221. Ibid., December 10, 1972; also see Haldeman, *Haldeman Diaries,* 442.

222. Dallek, *Nixon and Kissinger,* 421.

223. Audio Cassette, Diaries of H. R. Haldeman, January 13, 1973; also see Haldeman, *Haldeman Diaries,* 568.

224. Berman, *No Peace, No Honor,* 223.

225. Ehrlichman, *Witness to Power,* 314.

226. Dallek, *Nixon and Kissinger,* 470. For an excellent, archivally rich, and extended account of Nixon and Kissinger on the Vietnam War, see Berman, *No Peace, No Honor.*

227. Dallek, *Nixon and Kissinger,* 230.

228. See Prados, 307–8; 402–6; and Dallek, *Nixon and Kissinger,* 229–230.

229. Audio Cassette, Diaries of H. R. Haldeman, September 8, 1971; also see Haldeman, *Haldeman Diaries,* 351.

230. Berman, *No Peace, No Honor,* 159.

231. Ibid., 188–89.

232. Audio Cassette, Diaries of H. R. Haldeman, November 20, 1972. Nixon's comment does not appear in Haldeman's published version of his diaries.

233. Ibid., November 21, 1972. Nixon's comments do not appear in Haldeman's published version of his diaries.

234. Ibid., April 28, 1971; also see Haldeman, *Haldeman Diaries,* 282. One wonders whether Nixon realized his pun. Also, according to Dallek, after floating some names, it was Kissinger who persuaded Nixon to select him as the secret envoy (Dallek, *Nixon and Kissinger,* 289).

235. Ibid., December 28, 1970; also see Haldeman, *Haldeman Diaries,* 226.

236. Ibid., May 13, 1971; also see Haldeman, *Haldeman Diaries,* 286.

237. Ibid., May 18, 1971; also see Haldeman, *Haldeman Diaries,* 287.

238. Ibid., May 19, 1971, emphasis added; also see Haldeman, *Haldeman Diaries,* 289.

239. Ibid., July, 21, 1971, emphasis added; also see Haldeman, *Haldeman Diaries,* 325.

240. Ibid., November 21, 1972, emphasis added; also see Haldeman, *Haldeman Diaries,* 541.

241. Rush, "An Ambassador's Perspective," 349. Rush was offered the position, but Rogers did not want to resign at that point for fear of being perceived as being forced out by Kissinger. By May 1973, Kissinger not Rush was appointed secretary of state. On this episode, see Rush, 340–41.

242. Dallek, *Nixon and Kissinger,* 619.

243. Rothkopf, 110.

244. Both Winston Lord and William Colby, director of the CIA, are clear on this (see Strober and Strober, *Nixon,* 100, 130).

245. Sonnenfeldt, "Reconstructing the Nixon Foreign Policy," 320.

246. Morris, *Uncertain Greatness,* 3.

247. Memorandum from the President to Haldeman, Ehrlichman, and Kissinger, March 2, 1970, White House Special Files, Staff Members' Office Files—Haldeman, Nixon Presidential Materials Project, National Archives, College Park, Md.

248. Strober and Strober, *Nixon,* 124.

249. Audio Cassette, Diaries of H. R. Haldeman, March 2, 1971, emphasis added; also see Haldeman, *Haldeman Diaries,* 253.

250. Isaacson, 140.

251. Stolberg, "Kissinger's Appearance Revives Memories of Vietnam Era."

252. Woodward, "Ford Disagreed With Bush About Invading Iraq."

253. Rothkopf, 115.

254. Kissinger, "Domestic Structure and Foreign Policy," 527.

Chapter 4

1. According to Kissinger, "We were flying on Air Force One, and I saw Scowcroft disagreeing with Haldeman, and Haldeman very imperiously tried to insist on his point of view, but Scowcroft disagreed with him, and he was a terrier who had got hold of someone's leg and wouldn't let go. In his polite and mild manner, he insisted on his view, which was correct. It was some procedural matter, but he was challenging Haldeman at the height of Haldeman's power" (Goldberg, "Breaking Ranks," 63).

2. Callahan, "Honest Broker," 29.

3. Goldberg, "Breaking Ranks," 63.

4. Rothkopf, 154.

5. National Security Council, "History of the National Security Council."

6. Isaacson, 557.

7. Ford, *A Time to Heal,* 149.

8. Kissinger, *Years of Renewal,* 189.

9. Burke telephone interview with Harold Saunders, January 3, 2008.

10. Burke telephone interview with Gen. Brent Scowcroft, November 15, 2007.

11. Daalder and Destler, eds., "The Role of the National Security Adviser," 11.

12. Burke telephone interview with Gen. Brent Scowcroft, November 15, 2007.

13. Burke telephone interview with Harold Saunders, January 3, 2008.

14. Ibid.

15. Isaacson, 493.

16. Ibid., 576.

17. Audio Cassette, Diaries of H. R. Haldeman, January 7, 1973.

18. Isaacson, 661.

19. McFarlane and Smardz, *Special Trust,* 157; also see Cannon, *Time and Change,* 266, 331; and Ford, 121, 129.

20. Ford, 326.

21. Scowcroft, "Ford as President and His Foreign Policy," 312.

22. Kissinger, *Years of Renewal,* 837.

23. Ibid., 183.

24. Burke telephone interview with Gen. Brent Scowcroft, November 15, 2007.

25. Prados, 376.

26. Kissinger, *Years of Renewal,* 183–84.

27. Ibid., 437.

28. National Security Council, "History of the National Security Council."

29. Burke telephone interview with Gen. Brent Scowcroft, November 15, 2007.

30. Ibid., emphasis added.

31. Callahan, "Honest Broker," 29.

32. National Security Council, "History of the National Security Council." One interesting organizational change, which was pondered by not carried out, was examined by an extensive White House Study Project undertaken in December 1976. It proposed moving the NSC advisor and staff "out of the White House office and setting it up as an Executive Office function in the same manner as OMB." The proposal was odd, given that statutorily the NSC staff was already a unit in the EOP (White House Study Project, December 7, 1976, White House Staff Files, White House Operations, Cheney, Ford Library).

33. For example, from August 1974, when Ford assumed the presidency, through early March 1975, Ford convened nine meetings of the NSC and ten meetings of the cabinet (Memorandum from James E. Connor to Donald Rumsfeld, "Presidential Meetings with the Cabinet and NSC From August 9, 1974 to the Present," March 12, 1975, White House Staff Files, James Connor, Staff Secretary Files, Ford Library).

34. Callahan, "Honest Broker," 29.

35. Daalder and Destler, eds., "The Bush Administration National Security Council," 3.

36. Scowcroft, "Ford as President and His Foreign Policy," 311.

37. Ibid.

38. Kissinger, *Years of Renewal,* 949.

39. Burke telephone interview with Gen. Brent Scowcroft, November 15, 2007.

40. Ibid.

41. Isaacson, 698–99; also see Ford, 398.

42. Ford, 404.

43. Ibid., 298.

44. Greene, *The Presidency of Gerald R. Ford,* 185.

45. Isaacson, 702–3.

46. DeFrank, *Write It When I'm Gone,* 91.

47. Greene, *Presidency of Gerald R. Ford,* 161.

48. Ford, 280.

49. Greene, *Presidency of Gerald R. Ford,* 147; Prados, 370.

50. Greene, *Presidency of Gerald R. Ford,* 149–150.

51. Ibid., 150.

52. Prados, 367.

53. Ibid., 375.

54. Rothkopf, 154.

55. Bush and Scowcroft, *A World Transformed,* 17.

56. Daalder and Destler, eds., "The Role of the National Security Adviser," 58.

57. Bush and Scowcroft, 17–18.

58. Bush and Scowcroft, 19 (emphasis added). Scowcroft notes that his appointment came as a surprise and that he would have preferred serving as secretary of defense since he had already served as NSC advisor. But he was aware of Sen. John Tower's (R-TX) aspirations for the job and he immediately accepted (20).

59. The initial JCS chairman until October 1 was Adm. William Crowe.

60. Daalder and Destler, eds., "The Role of the National Security Adviser," 58.

61. Bush and Scowcroft, 36.

62. Baker, *The Politics of Diplomacy,* 21–22.

63. Cheney, "The Bush Presidency," 9–10.

64. Bush and Scowcroft, 25.

65. Rothkopf, 266.

66. Baker, *Politics of Diplomacy,* 22.

67. Burke telephone interview with Gen. Brent Scowcroft, November 15, 2007.

68. Callahan, "The Honest Broker," 30.

69. Burke telephone interview with Gen. Brent Scowcroft, November 15, 2007.

70. Bush and Scowcroft, 31.

71. Burke telephone interview with Gen. Brent Scowcroft, November 15, 2007.

72. Bush and Scowcroft, 35.

73. Ibid.

74. Ibid.

75. Callahan, "The Honest Broker," 30.

76. Ibid., 32.

77. Baker, *Politics of Diplomacy,* 25.

78. Daalder and Destler, eds., "The Bush Administration National Security Council," 35–36.

79. Ibid., 36.

80. Burke telephone interview with Gen. Brent Scowcroft, November 15, 2007.

81. *Tower Commission Report,* 9–11, 91.

82. Mulcahy, "The Bush Administration and National Security Policy Making," 5.

83. Burke telephone interview with Gen. Brent Scowcroft, November 15, 2007.

84. Goldberg, "Breaking Ranks," 56.

85. Daalder and Destler, eds., "The Role of The National Security Adviser," 16.

86. Burke telephone interview with Gen. Brent Scowcroft, November 15, 2007.

87. Daalder and Destler, eds., "The Role of the National Security Adviser," 6.

88. Ibid., 9.

89. Hoffman, "Politics of Timidity."

90. Rosenthal, "National Security Adviser Redefines Role."

91. Burke telephone interview with Gen. Brent Scowcroft, November 15, 2007.

92. Ibid.

93. Ibid.

94. Ibid.

95. Ibid.

96. Daalder and Destler, eds., "The Role of the National Security Adviser," 58.

97. In addition to the recommendations embodied in the *Tower Commission Report,* which were largely Scowcroft's handiwork, he "drew up a model for reform of the NSC system," which he gave to Carlucci and Powell (Burke telephone interview with Gen. Brent Scowcroft, November 15, 2007).

98. Callahan, "Honest Broker," 31. As Gates later noted, sometimes it was the number three person in the department who was on the committee, since the number two person was usually tasked with managing departmental affairs. Thus Robert Kimmitt, the undersecretary of state for political affairs usually attended instead of Deputy Secretary of State Lawrence Eagleburger, while Paul Wolfowitz, undersecretary of defense for policy, attended for Defense rather than Donald J. Atwood, undersecretary of defense (See Rothkopf, 266–67).

99. Daalder and Destler, eds., "The Bush Administration National Security Council," 4.

100. Burke telephone interview with Philip Zelikow, December 21, 2007.

101. Ibid.

102. Gates, "Intelligence in the Reagan and Bush Presidencies," 154–55.

103. Burke telephone interview with Gen. Brent Scowcroft, November 15, 2007.

104. Prados, 549.

105. Bush and Scowcroft, 40, 53.

106. Prados, 549–550.

107. Baker, *Politics of Diplomacy*, 68.

108. Morrison, "Retooling the Security Machinery," 1425.

109. Daalder and Destler, eds., "The Bush National Security Council," 12.

110. Daalder and Destler, eds., "The Role of the National Security Adviser," 20; also see Rothkopf, 273–74.

111. Daalder and Destler, eds., "The Role of the National Security Adviser," 26–27.

112. Bolton, "The Making of Foreign Policy in the Bush Administration," 118; also see Scowcroft's comments in Bush and Scowcroft, 61.

113. Bolton, 110.

114. Baker, *Politics of Diplomacy*, 67.

115. Mulford, "The Bush Presidency and International Economic Issues," 131–33.

116. See Bolton, 110–114.

117. Bush and Scowcroft, 42.

118. Ibid., 45.

119. Baker, *Politics of Diplomacy*, 25.

120. Burke telephone interview with Gen. Brent Scowcroft, November 15, 2007.

121. Bush and Scowcroft, 43–45; Painton and Duffy, "Brent Scowcroft," 24.

122. Baker, *Politics of Diplomacy*, 84–85, 93.

123. Daalder and Destler, "The Bush Administration National Security Council," 6.

124. The proposed reduction was 20 percent for each side, but that worked out at roughly 325,000 troops from the Soviet Union versus 30,000 U.S. forces to be removed.

125. See Bush and Scowcroft, 79–85; and Baker, *Politics of Diplomacy*, 92–96.

126. Bush and Scowcroft, 211. The agreed position was mutual reduction to 195,000 in the central zone (Germany and Eastern Europe), coupled with 30,000 U.S. troops elsewhere in Europe, for a total of 195,000 Soviet troops versus 225,000 U.S. troops. On Soviet acceptance, see Baker, *Politics of Diplomacy*, 212–13.

127. Bush and Scowcroft, 245.

128. Ibid., 155. On the various views of the principals see 154–55; and Baker, *Politics of Diplomacy*, 168–170.

129. Beschloss and Talbott, *At the Highest Levels*, 93–94. According to their account, Baker and Bush were most enthusiastic about a meeting, while Scowcroft still had reservations. As Scowcroft recollects, Bush took the lead saying it was time for a meeting. Bush "put it in that way he has when his mind is made up. Neither Baker nor I remonstrated with him. Baker had never been as negative as I about an early Gorbachev meeting, and I no longer felt so strongly about it" (Bush and Scowcroft, 129).

130. Bush and Scowcroft, 173.

131. Judis, "Statecraft and Scowcroft," 20.

132. Rothkopf, 280; also see 283–85 on subsequent Bush arms reduction efforts.

133. Bush and Scowcroft, 193.

134. Ibid., 188.

135. Melanson, "George Bush's Search for a Post-Cold War Grand Strategy," 158.

136. According to Baker, two-plus-four had been developed in a memo by State's policy planning staff and presented to him by Dennis Ross and Robert Zoellick (see Baker, *Politics of Diplomacy*, 198–99).

137. Bush and Scowcroft, 235.

138. Ibid., 243.

139. Baker, *Politics of Diplomacy*, 208–216. Baker does note that there may have been continued NSC opposition to the plan: "During the back and forth about whether [German Chancellor Helmut] Kohl had really approved of what we were doing, it became obvious to me that NSC staff were not only opposed to Two-plus-Four, but working on the President to decline to approve it, even though I'd convinced London, Paris, and Moscow to go along, and the Germans too, were on board." Baker then notes that he had given a memo on the plan to President Bush, had consulted with Robert Blackwill, the NSC special assistant for European Affairs, and that a letter he had sent Kohl had been cleared by the NSC staff. Baker then made his third call of the day to Bush, telling him of the success of the negotiations, but noting that "frankly it was more difficult than it had to be, just because some there were biased against the Two-plus-Four idea." "George Bush was his usual magnanimous self and told me he understood my point" (Baker, *Politics of Diplomacy*, 215–16).

140. Bush and Scowcroft, 299, 300.

141. Beschloss and Talbott, 470.

142. Walsh, "Bush's Man with the Hawk's Eye View," 28; also see Judis, "Statecraft and Scowcroft."

143. Judis, "Statecraft and Scowcroft," 21.

144. Bush and Scowcroft, 516.

145. Ibid., 520, 521. On Scowcroft's care in how Bush initially publicly responded to news of the coup, see Beschloss and Talbott, 422.

146. Judis, "Statecraft and Scowcroft," 20.

147. Baker, *Politics of Diplomacy*, 109.

148. Bush and Scowcroft, 110–11.

149. Bush and Scowcroft, 174; Greene, *The Presidency of George Bush*, 95. Scowcroft decided to notify the press of his visit at the last minute on his arrival in Beijing. It proved to be a mistake since CNN was on hand, making the trip seem more secret than it was. According to the *New York Times*, "Administration aides said that the trip was being kept secret at Beijing's request, apparently because the Chinese wanted to make certain that it appeared the Americans were coming to them on Chinese terms and not the other way around" (Friedman, "China Trip Seeks to Alter Americans' Perceptions").

150. Brinkley, "The Bush Administration and Panama," 178.

151. Daalder and Destler, eds., "The Bush Administration National Security Council," 4.

152. Drew, "Letter from Washington," 100.

153. Hoffman, "Politics of Timidity."

154. Greene, *Presidency of George Bush*, 103.

155. Burke telephone interview with Gen. Brent Scowcroft, November 15, 2007.

156. Baker, *Politics of Diplomacy*, 186.

157. Ibid., 188–89.

158. Broder and Healy, "Panama Operation Hurt by Critical Intelligence Gaps."

159. Brinkley, "The Bush Administration and Panama," 181.

160. For an analysis of whether Saddam's invasion of Kuwait could have been prevented by more vigilant U.S. action and clearer signals that an invasion would not stand, see Berman and Jentleson, "Bush and the Post-Cold-War World," 118–121. According to Scowcroft, in light of Arab negotiations then underway with Saddam, there were no threats to intervene in large measure because the Arab allies viewed such as counterproductive (Bush and Scowcroft, 313).

161. Schwarzkopf's analysis was that Iraq "was poised to launch a punitive but limited strike into Kuwait" (Woodward, *The Commanders*, 209).

162. Woodward, *Commanders*, 221–22.

163. Bush and Scowcroft, 311.

164. According to the *Wall Street Journal*'s account, the day before the invasion, aides from the NSC staff, State, the Pentagon and other agencies "met throughout the day to evaluate growing intelligence indications that an invasion was imminent, administration officials say. By about 6 P.M., the signs of an invasion were so strong that Mr. Scowcroft and Richard Haass, the top NSC Middle East analyst, went to the presidential residence to tell Mr. Bush. While they were there, officials say, Mr. Scowcroft got a call informing him that fighting had begun. By about 8:45 P.M., Mr. Scowcroft called back Mr. Bush to confirm that a full-fledged invasion, not a simple border skirmish, was under way. By that time, officials say, Mr. Scowcroft was sitting in the White House's West Wing, overseeing a meeting of officials from several government agencies linked by closed-circuit television. One official recalls him already beginning to jot down notes for phone calls Mr. Bush should make to other world leaders, which Mr. Bush subsequently made by the dozen" (Seib, "Scowcroft, Once Obscured by Other Bush Aides, Emerges as Influential Player in Mideast Crisis").

165. Bush and Scowcroft, 313. According to Woodward, Scowcroft "pressed for more actions that would demonstrate that the United States was taking the Iraq invasion seriously." He immediately drafted a plan to freeze Iraqi assets. He also proposed that a squadron of F-15 fighters—about twenty-four planes—be sent to Saudi Arabia. Asked about sending ground forces, Scowcroft replied that he wanted something moved quickly but that would not be "an immediate visible presence" (Woodward, *Commanders,* 223–24).

166. Bush and Scowcroft, 318.

167. Ibid.

168. Ibid., 324.

169. Rosenthal, "Scowcroft and Gates."

170. Woodward, *Commanders,* 245.

171. Bush and Scowcroft, 327–28; Woodward, *Commanders,* 247–253.

172. Bush and Scowcroft, 332–33, emphasis in original. In his memoirs, Baker discusses the statement and in his view it indicated that Bush was not immediately prepared to go to war. The aim was "to undo Iraq's aggression." But as he notes, "What the president's statement did not reveal was how he would go about doing that" (Baker, *Politics of Diplomacy,* 276–77).

173. Bush and Scowcroft, 335.

174. Woodward and Atkinson, "Launching Operation Desert Shield."

175. Pfiffner, "Presidential Policy-Making and the Gulf War," 4.

176. Woodward, *Commanders,* 259–260.

177. Haass, "Oral History: The Gulf War."

178. Bush and Scowcroft, 382.

179. Ibid., 353–54. Baker was also in dissent in late August over a unilateral embargo of Iraq versus one with U.N. sanction. According to Scowcroft, there was a sharp internal debate. Gates, Cheney, and Scowcroft urged action; Baker, however, convinced Bush not to move unilaterally (Bush and Scowcroft, 352).

180. Bush and Scowcroft, 361; Scowcroft, Sununu, and Baker felt it would be counterproductive, play into Iraq propaganda, and provoke radicals in the region.

181. Woodward, *Commanders,* 284.

182. Painton and Duffy, "Brent Scowcroft," 24.

183. Woodward, *Commanders,* 285, 301–2.

184. Scowcroft, "Oral History: The Gulf War."

185. Woodward, *Commanders,* 41–42, 302–3.

186. Baker, *Politics of Diplomacy,* 301. Elsewhere Baker notes, "I was not concerned that

[sanctions] weren't being given a fair shot, I think they were given a fair shot and I concluded fairly early on that Saddam would starve everybody in Iraq before he would back down and that we weren't going to be able to do it through economic sanctions. That's not to say I didn't defend the policy . . . of using economic sanctions because I think it was an appropriate policy to put in place before we resorted to force" (Baker, "Oral History: The Gulf War").

187. Baker, *Politics of Diplomacy*, 302.

188. Powell, "Oral History: The Gulf War."

189. Bush and Scowcroft, 381.

190. Scowcroft, "Oral History: The Gulf War."

191. Woodward, *Commanders*, 318–320.

192. Bush and Scowcroft, 121–22; on Baker's concerns that the announcement was premature, without appropriate congressional and coalition briefings, see Baker, *Politics of Diplomacy*, 330. Yet, according to Baker, the White House feared that there would be leaks from the Pentagon.

193. Bush and Scowcroft, 384, 387.

194. Goldberg, "Breaking Ranks," 52.

195. Powell, "Oral History: The Gulf War."

196. Bush and Scowcroft, 393–96. According to Scowcroft, "Jim Baker as I recall said, 'Why don't I take a trip around to the members of the Security Council—to the countries they represent—and see what the mood is toward the Security Council passing authorization for the use of force.' We did not know what it was going to be. Jim went around to all the members of the Security Council—all but two I think—and had extensive discussion and he came back he said, 'Hey, I think we can get a resolution through the Security Council.' So we decided to do that before we went to the Congress because we were not all sure that we could get the Congress to support it" (Burke telephone interview with Gen. Brent Scowcroft, November 15, 2007). Scowcroft also became concerned about Bush's rhetoric, particularly treatment of U.S. embassy personnel in Kuwait, as Bush campaigned before the midterm elections. Bush was becoming emotionally involved, according to Scowcroft, so he and Gates began to accompany him on his travels (Bush and Scowcroft, 389).

197. Burke telephone interview with Gen. Brent Scowcroft, November 15, 2007.

198. Ibid., emphasis added.

199. Bush and Scowcroft, 432–33.

200. Yetiv, "The Agent-Structure Question in Theory," 139–140.

201. Rothkopf, 297–98.

202. Greene, *Presidency of George Bush*, 130.

203. Ibid., 135.

204. Bush and Scowcroft, 489.

205. Greene, *Presidency of George Bush*, 136.

206. Judis, "Statecraft and Scowcroft," 21.

207. Bush and Scowcroft, 565.

208. Ibid., 487.

209. Hoffman, "Zip My Lips," and Dowd, "Basking in Power's Glow."

Chapter 5

1. Cannon, *President Reagan*, 310.

2. On the cabinet councils, see Burke, *Presidential Transitions*, 144–151; and Burke, *The Institutional Presidency*, 143–150.

3. The nomenclature of the paper trail also changed—a seemingly endemic occurrence in each new administration. The Carter-era PRMs became National Security Study Documents (NSSDs), while the PDs were labeled National Security Decision Directives (NSDDs). On the SIGs, NSSDs and NSDDs, see McFarlane, Sanders, and Shull, "The National Security Council," 266–69.

4. Writing in 1986, Colin Campbell observes that "only the SIG on intelligence remains active. The Crisis Preplanning Group chaired by the NSC staff director for policy development coordinates the administration's management of major foreign policy emergencies. The Strategic Arms Control group headed by the assistant to the president for national security affairs [the NSC advisor] has supplanted the SIG on defense. And the Economics Policy Council has absorbed the entire case load of the SIG on International Economic Policy" (Campbell, *Managing the Presidency,* 43).

5. For further analysis see Burke, *Presidential Transitions,* 161–62.

6. Regan, *For the Record,* 268.

7. Weinberger, Oral History, 34.

8. According to Richard Allen, Reagan would even go beyond the several pages that Allen might highlight for him to read and instead read the whole document. This led to some tension with Michael Deaver, who told Allen to cut the material by 75 percent, presumably at the behest of Nancy Reagan, whom Deaver often served as an enforcer in her efforts to protect her husband from overwork. Allen refused, but after "I left, they went back to one page memos" (Allen, Oral History, 66).

9. Anderson, *Revolution,* 219.

10. Regan, 188.

11. Reagan, *An American Life,* 296, 253.

12. Ibid., 511.

13. Burke, *Presidential Transitions,* 97.

14. The other two were Martin Anderson for domestic and economic issues and Caspar Weinberger for budget matters. All three served in the Nixon administration and all had long been associated with the president-elect (Burke, *Presidential Transitions,* 98).

15. Burke, *Presidential Transitions,* 102; Baker, *Work Hard, Study . . . and Keep Out of Politics!,* 139.

16. See Oberdorfer, "Reagan Aides See Power Grab"; and Cannon, "Pitfall for Strong Men." Although Haig did not get to see Reagan, he met with Meese, Baker, and Deaver, who subjected it to, as Haig later phrased it, a "dogged critique." In his version of the episode, Haig claims that his memo—National Security Decision Directive 1—had already been worked out by State, Defense, and the NSC, and had been reviewed by Weinberger, Casey, and Allen (Haig, *Caveat,* 74, 76); McFarlane, then Haig's counselor at State, backs up Haig's account (McFarlane, *Special Trust,* 172–73). Also see Mulcahy, "The Secretary of State and the National Security Adviser," 287–89; and Baker, *Work Hard, Study . . . and Keep Out of Politics!,* 140–41.

17. The agreement also called for the creation of the three main senior interdepartmental groups (SIGs) and the working groups under them.

18. According to Allen, it was he who suggested that Bush be tapped instead of Haig (Allen, Oral History, 50). As it turned out, the group, titled the Special Situations Group, only met once.

19. Prados, 452.

20. Ibid., 463–64.

21. McFarlane and Smardz, *Special Trust,* 194. McFarlane claims it was the same piece of paper that Haig had presented in January 1981. Allen notes that it "didn't really matter. . . .

We were making decisions, we knew how to make decisions" (Allen, Oral History, 50).

22. Hedrick Smith, "A Scaled Down Version of the Security Adviser's Task."

23. Inderfurth and Johnson, "Transformation," 75.

24. Mulcahy, "The Secretary of State and the National Security Adviser," 291.

25. Allen, Oral History, 48. In mid-June, Allen was appointed the chair of a committee—because "nobody else wanted it"—set up to coordinate a strategy for the approval of the sale of AWACS surveillance planes to Saudi Arabia; the proposed sale was controversial with some members of Congress and had been opposed by the Israelis (Allen, Oral History, 55, also 50–51).

26. Allen, Oral History, 48.

27. Hedrick Smith, "A Scaled Down Version of the Security Adviser's Task." Allen did have someone who received press calls, but he did not have "a press officer who was a press spokesman for the NSC, and I thought that was right thing to do." Allen also did not have his own congressional relations unit and worked through the White House's congressional affairs office (Allen, Oral History, 49).

28. Bock, *The White House Staff and the National Security Assistant,* 157.

29. Hedrick Smith, "A Scaled Down Version of the Security Adviser's Task."

30. Rothkopf, 222.

31. Cannon, *President Reagan,* 189.

32. Allen, Oral History, 49.

33. McFarlane and Smardz, 173.

34. Ibid., 174.

35. Gelb, "Foreign Policy System Criticized by U.S. Aides."

36. Ibid.

37. Ibid.

38. Inderfurth and Johnson, "Transformation," 76. Allen, however, notes a more active role: "Every paper that went to the President passed through my turnstile, and I had the opportunity to top it with a memorandum or do whatever I wanted to it" (Allen, Oral History, 56).

39. Haig, 85.

40. Gelb, "Foreign Policy System Criticized by U.S. Aides;" also see Gwertzman, "Haig Charges a Reagan Aide is Undermining Him."

41. Allen, Oral History, 52–54. In his oral history, Allen also notes how there was some pressure on him to resign when the scandal story broke, but he refused to do so until he was cleared.

42. Meese, *With Reagan,* 85, emphasis added.

43. Allen, Oral History, 54.

44. On Clark's largely successful service as deputy secretary of state, see Kengor and Doerner, *The Judge,* 117–140.

45. Kengor and Doerner, 145–46.

46. Morris, *Dutch,* 456.

47. Ibid., 455.

48. National Security Council, "History of the National Security Council."

49. Prados, 464.

50. Morris, *Dutch,* 456.

51. Kengor and Doerner, 149.

52. Prados, 464.

53. See Prados, 465.

54. Kengor and Doerner, 157.

55. National Security Council, "History of the National Security Council"; also see McFarlane and Smardz, 196–99.

56. McFarlane and Smardz, 195–96; also see McFarlane, Sanders, and Shull, "The National Security Council," 270–71.

57. Kengor and Doerner, 197–202; also see McFarlane and Smardz, 219–235.

58. Bock, 162; also see Kengor and Doerner, 194–95.

59. Inderfurth and Johnson, "Transformation," 76.

60. Weinberger, Oral History, 20.

61. See Mulcahy, "The Secretary of State and the National Security Adviser," 292; also see McFarlane and Smardz, 204; and Kengor and Doerner, 181, 183. According to Gelb, "Unlike Mr. Haig who seeks the limelight, 'Judge' Clark is always careful to insure that it is his boss, the president, who gets the credit for making foreign policy" (Gelb, "Haig-Clark Feuds Emerging over Foreign Policy").

62. Weisman, "Haig Resigns Over Foreign Policy Course."

63. National Security Council, "History of the National Security Council."

64. McFarlane and Smardz, 199.

65. Kengor and Doerner, 152.

66. McFarlane and Smardz, 199.

67. Weinberger, Oral History, 19.

68. Strober and Strober, *The Reagan Presidency,* 88.

69. Shultz, *Turmoil and Triumph,* 164–67, 269–270, 306–8, 316–19, 321–22.

70. Morris, *Dutch,* 488.

71. Shultz, 317.

72. Shultz, Oral History, 14.

73. Morris, *Dutch,* 489; Kengor and Doerner, 237–241.

74. Morris, *Dutch,* 499.

75. Shultz, 319.

76. Strober and Strober, *Reagan Presidency,* 88.

77. See Bock, 162–64.

78. Ibid., 163.

79. Baker, *Politics of Diplomacy,* 26.

80. Kengor and Doerner, 247–250.

81. Baker, *Work Hard, Study . . . and Keep Out of Politics!,* 193–95; also see Cannon, *President Reagan,* 423–27. For Clark's view, see Kengor and Doerner, 153–56.

82. McFarlane and Smardz, 254–55.

83. Baker, *Politics of Diplomacy,* 26–27.

84. Others who had concerns besides Clark were Meese, Weinberger, and Casey. See Clark's account of the episode in Strober and Strober, *Reagan Presidency,* 90; for Baker's view see Baker, *Work Hard, Study . . . and Keep Out of Politics!,* 199–202; for McFarlane's see McFarlane and Smardz, 259–260; on Shultz's role and account, see Shultz, *Turmoil and Triumph,* 319–321; also see Morris, *Dutch,* 499–500.

85. Baker, *Politics of Diplomacy,* 26–27.

86. Baker, *Work Hard, Study . . . and Keep Out of Politics!,* 193, also 204–5.

87. Morris, *Dutch,* 500; also see Deaver, *Behind the Scenes,* 129–130.

88. Nelson, "The Evolution of the National Security State Ubiquitous and Endless," 289.

89. Abshire, *Saving the Reagan Presidency,* 59.

90. Strober and Strober, *Reagan Presidency,* 443; McFarlane and Smardz, 323.

91. Rothkopf, 236.

92. McFarlane and Smardz, 323.

93. Ibid., 286–87.

94. Ibid., 270–71.

95. Ibid., 273.

96. Rothkopf, 236.

97. McFarlane and Smardz, 279–80.

98. Ibid., 281, 282.

99. Ibid., 281; also see McFarlane, Sanders, and Shull, "The National Security Council," 269.

100. McFarlane, Sanders, and Shull, "The National Security Council," 265.

101. Weinberger, *In the Arena,* 299.

102. Abshire, 59. McFarlane's system also played a positive role in dealing with the threat to energy supplies during the Iran-Iraq war; see McFarlane, Sanders, and Shull, "The National Security Council," 271–73.

103. McFarlane and Smardz, 276–77.

104. National Security Council, "History of the National Security Council."

105. Rothkopf, 231; also see McFarlane and Smardz, 243–254.

106. Inouye-Hamilton Committee, "Congress and the NSC," 334; also see McFarlane and Smardz, 243.

107. Shultz, 659–660, 798.

108. Weinberger, Oral History, 19.

109. See McFarlane and Smardz, 17–20, 23–25.

110. McFarlane and Smardz, 19; also see Shultz, 793. According to Shultz, McFarlane told him he was "turning it [the Ledeen effort] off entirely. . . . I was troubled by McFarlane's tendency to dissemble when it served his purpose."

111. Abshire, 141–42; also see Wallison, *Ronald Reagan,* 178.

112. McFarlane and Smardz, 327–28. According to Peter J. Wallison, White House legal counsel during Regan's tenure as chief of staff, Poindexter did not report through Regan and the latter's authority over Poindexter was tenuous at best; Poindexter would ask to see the president through Regan but only as a matter of courtesy. Wallison would discover this when, in his efforts as legal counsel, he began looking into issues surrounding Iran-Contra and found Poindexter uncooperative. Poindexter had "the same access to the President as his predecessor . . . This meant that he reported to the President and not the chief of staff" (162).

113. Shultz, 690, 798.

114. See *Tower Commission Report,* 254–351.

115. Ibid., 337; McFarlane and Smardz, 54–66.

116. *Tower Commission Report,* 337; McFarlane and Smardz, 66.

117. *Tower Commission Report,* 295.

118. Ibid., 281–82.

119. Inderfurth and Johnson, "Transformation," 77.

120. Schneider, "Poindexter at the Security Council."

121. Prados, 507.

122. Campbell, *Managing the Presidency,* 43.

123. Schneider, "Poindexter at the Security Council."

124. Shultz, 826–27.

125. See Abshire, 68–143.

126. Shultz, 831.

127. McFarlane and Smardz, 105.

128. Powell, *My American Journey,* 309.

129. Schneider, "Poindexter at the Security Council."

130. Baker, *Work Hard, Study . . . and Keep Out of Politics!,* 203.

131. Strober and Strober, *Reagan Presidency,* 413.

132. Shultz, 815–16, emphasis in original; also see Powell, 305.

133. Powell, 305; Weinberger, 349.

134. Weinberger, 349.

135. Weinberger, Oral History, 19.

136. *Tower Commission Report,* 25.

137. According to the Tower Commission, Donald Regan, who was at the hospital meeting, testified to them that "the matter was discussed for 20 to 25 minutes, with the President asking quite a few questions. He recalled the President then saying "'yes, go ahead. Open it up" (*Tower Commission Report,* 26). Yet in his memoirs, Regan states, "There is nothing in my notes or in my memory to suggest that the idea of swapping arms for hostages was mentioned by either man on this occasion" (21).

138. Regan, 6, 20–21.

139. McFarlane and Smardz, 27.

140. *Tower Commission Report,* 26. Yet, Reagan would remember the hospital meeting—or at least parts of it—when interviewed by White House legal counsel Peter Wallison: Reagan "did remember McFarlane coming to see him when he was in the hospital, and telling him that the Iranians wanted to open negotiations. He said he thought this was a fine idea. Regan then asked whether the President remembered saying he did not want to ship weapons when we didn't know who we were dealing with, and the President again said he had no recollection of this" (Wallison, 226).

141. McFarlane and Smardz, 28.

142. Shultz, 796.

143. Weinberger, 350.

144. McFarlane and Smardz, 29.

145. Ibid.; also see Abshire, 61.

146. McFarlane and Smardz, 31.

147. Abshire, 62.

148. McFarlane and Smardz, 34. The Tower Commission also relates Reagan's approval in a narrative that is close to what McFarlane provides in his memoirs, based on his testimony at the time (*Tower Commission Report,* 27). Wallison notes that the date of the August 3 meeting first appears in McFarlane's memoirs, "long after the various investigations had ended" (244).

149. *Tower Commission Report,* 28–29. The Tower Commission also notes that when Reagan learned of the actual shipments in September, according to Don Regan, he "decided to 'leave it alone'" (28). Wallison also notes that Reagan told him, in January 1987, that he had no recollection of approving the shipments following the August meetings (226, also see 243–46).

150. According to Wallison, the White House legal counsel, "Regan—who attended virtually all the President's morning briefings with the national security advisor—recalled that the President was 'surprised' to learn of the shipment" (172, also see 178). Weinberger relates in his memoirs that he thought the arms-for-hostages deal had been stopped, only to find in the late fall of 1985 some odd cable traffic relating to the operation that had been mistakenly routed to him. He then demanded a meeting of the principals with the president (Weinberger, 350–51). The Tower Commission quotes Regan as saying that in August the president "expressed concern with any one-for-one swap of arms for hostages and indicated 'we should go slow on this but develop contact'" (28).

151. *Tower Commission Report,* 27. Not only is what had been decided unclear, how it may have been decided was problematic. According to the Tower Commission, the deliberative process was "murky": "Most NSC principals apparently had an opportunity to discuss the request with the President in and around the first two weeks of August. There clearly was a series of meetings with one or more of the principals in attendance. In addition, a number of the participants seem to recall a single meeting at which all the principals were present. White House records, however, show no meetings of the NSC principals in August scheduled for the purpose of discussing this issue. Other evidence suggests that there were meetings of the NSC principals in August at which the issue could have been discussed" (26–27).

152. The first shipment of 100 TOW antitank missiles by Israel took place on August 20, 1985; an additional 408 missiles were shipped on September 14. A request for more sophisticated weapons from Iran led to the November shipment of 80 HAWK missiles (Abshire, 62; also see *Tower Commission Report,* 438–443).

153. Strober and Strober, *Reagan Presidency,* 404.

154. McFarlane and Smardz, 46.

155. Shultz, 799. Weinberger's recollection of the December 7 meeting is similar (Weinberger, 351).

156. Shultz, 800

157. Rothkopf, 244.

158. McFarlane and Smardz, 86.

159. Ibid., 80–82.

160. Ibid., 87–88.

161. Shultz, 828, emphasis in the original; Prados describes this exchange as "heated" (533).

162. McFarlane and Smardz, 102.

163. Prados, 515.

164. Under the terms of the Foreign Assistance Act of 1961, a presidential "finding" is required when the CIA is using appropriated funds to conduct operations in foreign countries (beyond its normal intelligence gathering activities) and such activities are deemed to be in interest of the national security. Findings are then usually disclosed to the intelligence committees of the House and the Senate. According to the *Tower Commission Report,* it is not clear if Reagan actually signed the finding (177). However, the original document, which Poindexter had destroyed, may have had Reagan's signature, while the document available to the Tower Commission may have been an unsigned copy.

165. Inouye-Hamilton Committee, "Congress and the NSC," 321. Tower Commission investigators would later find a copy of the document (*Tower Commision Report,* 177).

166. Strober and Strober, *Reagan Presidency,* 478.

167. Shultz, 803.

168. Reagan, 512.

169. Strober and Strober, *Reagan Presidency,* 445.

170. Shultz, 803.

171. Ibid. In Weinberger's recollection, this was the first time that Reagan "gave me the clear impression that he had approved the idea" (Weinberger, 351).

172. *Tower Commission Report,* 67.

173. On the changes, see *Tower Commission Report,* 219, 228–29.

174. Schneider, "Poindexter at the Security Council."

175. Inouye-Hamilton Committee, "Congress and the NSC," 326.

176. Ibid., 325. Poindexter later said that did not tell "the vice president, or Bill

Casey—and I don't think Ollie [North] did either. I didn't tell my superiors because I knew that if it ever leaked out it was going to be very controversial. I wanted the president to have some deniability, which he had." "The highest level of sign-off on the diversion was me" (Strober and Strober, *Reagan Presidency*, 508).

177. Strober and Strober, *Reagan Presidency*, 496. In Meese's view, Casey probably wasn't knowledgeable about the diversion because "Bill Casey was smart—so smart that he would know the political downsides of this, the dangers involved" (Strober and Strober, *Reagan Presidency*, 499–500).

178. Schneider, "Poindexter at the Security Council."

179. Strober and Strober, *Reagan Presidency*, 486.

180. Ibid., 513.

181. Schneider, "Poindexter at the Security Council."

182. *Tower Commission Report*, 62–63.

183. Ibid., 81.

184. Ibid.

185. Ibid., 62–63.

186. Ibid., 79–80.

187. Strober and Strober, *Reagan Presidency*, 476.

188. Burke telephone interview with Gen. Brent Scowcroft, November 15, 2008.

189. After leaving the deputy defense secretary slot, Carlucci headed a commission on foreign aid, as well as serving as a principal member of the Packard Commission on Defense Management.

190. Carlucci, Oral History, 24.

191. Powell, 310–11.

192. Powell replaced Peter Rodman, who had initially served as Carlucci's deputy.

193. Bamford, "Carlucci and the NSC."

194. Kirschten, "Competent Manager," 469, 474.

195. Burke telephone interview with Gen. Brent Scowcroft, November 15, 2007.

196. Powell, 335.

197. Kirschten, 474.

198. National Journal, "NSC's Powell," 478.

199. Carlucci, Oral History, 38.

200. Shultz, 903–4.

201. Ibid., 907.

202. Ibid., 908.

203. Ibid. Shultz later noted that Carlucci as NSC advisor "was a very honorable person, but what Frank wants to do is run things. He was an ambassador running his embassy and he was running this and that. The idea of a national security adviser who didn't run anything was hard for him. He kept trying to run things and I kept after him about that. So we had a lot of tension. But when Cap resigned as Secretary of Defense, I was a strong supporter of Frank to be Secretary of Defense, because that's what he wants to do, so let him. There's plenty of things to run over at the Defense Department. That'll keep him occupied" (Shultz, Oral History, 17).

204. Carlucci, Oral History, 38.

205. National Security Council, "History of the National Security Council." According to one estimate, Carlucci quickly replaced twenty-four of the NSC's fifty-nine professional staff members (Bamford, "Carlucci and the NSC"). Carlucci puts the figure at 60 percent, but notes that many of them were on detail from regular agencies (Carlucci, Oral History, 38).

206. DeYoung, *Soldier*, 158.

207. Bamford, "Carlucci and the NSC."

208. Shultz, 877, 903.

209. Ibid., 924.

210. Carlucci, Oral History, 22–23.

211. Ibid., 11.

212. Kirschten, "Competent Manager," 472; also see Carlucci, Oral History, 39.

213. Carlucci, Oral History, 39.

214. National Journal, "NSC's Powell," 478.

215. Shultz, 990–91.

216. National Security Council, "History of the National Security Council."

217. Powell, 343–44.

218. Shultz, Oral History, 14–15.

219. Carlucci, Oral History, 29.

220. Ibid., 47.

221. Shultz, Oral History, 14–15.

222. Ibid., 17.

223. Powell, 332.

224. Daalder and Destler, eds, "The Role of the National Security Adviser," 51.

225. DeYoung, 163.

226. Ibid., 164.

227. Ibid.

228. Ibid., 165.

229. National Security Council, "History of the National Security Council."

230. Powell, 393.

231. Ibid., 334.

232. Ibid., 349.

233. Shultz, Oral History, 29.

Chapter 6

1. Sciolino, "Compulsion to Achieve."

2. Due to space limitations, I will not explore the issue of the administration's response to the terrorist threat and Al Qaeda before September 11. Some analysis can be found in Moens, *The Foreign Policy of George W. Bush,* 87–123. Richard A. Clarke, the chief anti-terrorism adviser in the Clinton administration and for a time under Bush, is highly critical of Rice's efforts pre–September 11 (see Clarke, *Against All Enemies,* 229–232, 234–38). In his memoirs, Tenet notes that he had a weekly private meeting with Rice and that in almost every meeting, especially in the spring and summer of 2001, "terrorism was high on the agenda." But he, like Clarke, notes the slowness in developing a new antiterrorism policy during that period. Tenet also has an interesting account of his concerns—and the response to them—when intelligence reports surfaced in July 2001 of an impending Al Qaeda attack. (Tenet, *At the Center of the Storm,* 144–45, 152–160); also see Bumiller, *Condoleezza Rice,* 141–163.

3. Greenstein, *The Presidential Difference,* 281.

4. Heclo, "The Political Ethos of George W. Bush," 46.

5. Carney, "Why Bush Doesn't Like Homework," 46–47.

6. Kettl, *Team Bush,* 150.

7. On Bush's use of both collegial and formal patterns of advising, see Burke, "From

Success to Failure?" 176–77; on problems in its formal operations with respect to Iraq, see 177–192; on problems with its collegial deliberations, see 192–99.

8. Woodward, *Bush at War,* 144. These and other quotes are reprinted with permission of Simon & Schuster Adult Publishing Group from *Bush at War* by Bob Woodward. Copyright 2002 by Bob Woodward.

9. Thomas and Wolffe, "Bush in the Bubble," 37.

10. Harris and Balz, "First 100 Days Go By in a Blitz."

11. Rothkopf, 401.

12. Thomas and Wolffe, 37.

13. Kumar, "Recruiting and Organizing the White House Staff." Clay Johnson had been Bush's gubernatorial chief of staff, the head of his preelection transition effort, the executive director of the transition, the head of the White House personnel office, and then deputy director of OMB.

14. Kessler, *A Matter of Character,* 177.

15. See, for example, Moens, *Foreign Policy of George W. Bush,* 133–140; and Tenet, 171, 180, 235.

16. McManus and Gerstenzang, "Bush Takes CEO Role in Waging War." Similarly, in the view of journalist Frank Bruni, "Aides said he was asking more questions in . . . meetings, grilling his advisers with more requests for explanations and often demanding to talk not only to the deputy from an administration agency who was giving him a briefing but to the head of the agency" (Bruni, *Ambling into History,* 248). Once decisions were made, strategy determined, and plans set, Bush did not micromanage the effort, as Lyndon Johnson had done during Vietnam. According to Chief of Staff Card, "He gets consulted, but consistent with how does that tactic help us achieve the overall mission. He isn't saying 'I want eight more tanks here,' [or] 'Why are you taking this division up this road.'" In the view of another aide, "He does not and will not micro-manage the plan. Instead, what he does is pepper people with questions to ascertain how the plan is going and to get the latest details and the latest information" (Balz and Allen "CEO Bush Takes Over Management of Message").

17. Balz and Allen "CEO Bush Takes Over Management of Message."

18. Kessler, *A Matter of Character,* 184.

19. Tenet, 235.

20. Leiby, "Breaking Ranks"; also see DeYoung, 518.

21. Campbell, "Unrestrained Ideological Entrepreneurship in the Bush II Advisory System," 97.

22. Balz and Neel, "For Bush, Questions, Clues, and Contradiction."

23. See ibid.

24. Suskind, *The Price of Loyalty,* 126, 293.

25. Thomas and Wolffe, 37.

26. See, for example, Baker, "A President Besieged and Isolated, Yet at Ease."

27. Not only were few outside "Wise Men" brought in as a reality check—as has occurred from time to time in previous presidencies—but discordant voices from even within the Bush political family were sidelined. Brent Scowcroft, George H. W. Bush's trusted NSC advisor, raised concerns about the administration's Iraq policy and his fears that Bush had been "mesmerized" by Israeli Prime Minister Ariel Sharon. Yet, as one account (of a number) has noted, "Scowcroft was ostracized by the White House and fired from the one small assignment he had been given, the chairmanship of the President's Foreign Intelligence Advisory Board" (Risen, *State of War,* 222).

28. McGeary, "Odd Man Out," 29.

29. Thomas, "The Quiet Power of Condi Rice," 29.

30. See Bumiller, *Condoleezza Rice,* 136–38. Cheney did receive a consolation prize: the directive specified that he would preside at meetings of the NSC in the president's absence and at the president's direction.

31. Allen, "Bush Taps Rice for Security Adviser."

32. Bumiller, *Condoleezza Rice,* 135.

33. Thomas, "The Quiet Power of Condi Rice," 28.

34. However, in the view of David Rothkopf, Rice "could not be more effective" precisely because of her closeness to Bush (Kessler and Ricks, "Rice's NSC Tenure Complicates New Post"). The issue remains open. It is not clear what she privately advised Bush and if she was able to successfully mix brokerage and advocacy in a way that not only fit this president's comfort level but served effective decision making.

35. See Pfiffner, "President George W. Bush and His War Cabinet," 12; and Warshaw, "The Political Lens of the President's War Cabinet for the War in Afghanistan," 11–12.

36. Thomas, "The 12 Year Itch," 64.

37. Bumiller, "In the New Bush Cabinet, Loyalty Trumps Celebrity."

38. Thomas, "The 12 Year Itch," 64–65.

39. Thomas, "The Quiet Power of Condi Rice," 28; also see Kessler and Slevin, "Rice Fails to Repair Rifts"; and Woodward, *Plan of Attack,* 175–76, 415. (These and other quotes are reprinted with permission of Simon & Schuster Adult Publishing Group from *Plan of Attack* by Bob Woodward. Copyright 2004 by Bob Woodward.) DeYoung especially notes Deputy Secretary of State Richard Armitage's use of the word "dysfunctional," and also its use by one former Republican cabinet official (477). Feith points out that the representatives from State were often at fault through passivity and delaying efforts (Feith, *War and Decision,* 250). Feith is also negative in his overall assessment of the interagency decision-making process: clarity was lacking, and disagreements were often unresolved and not brought to the president's attention (245).

40. See Sanger, "Missile Shield Point Man Does Not Shy From Tough Fight."

41. De Young, 335, 398, 477–78; Rothkopf, 414.

42. Thomas, "The Quiet Power of Condi Rice," 28.

43. See Burke, *Becoming President,* 170; Sanger and Tyler, "Wartime Forges a United Front for Bush Aides;" and Weisman, "What Rift?"

44. Thomas, "The 12 Year Itch," 64; also see Kessler and Slevin, "Rice Fails to Repair Rifts."

45. Ignatius, "A Foreign Policy Out of Focus."

46. Kessler and Slevin, "Rice Fails to Repair Rifts."

47. Kessler and Ricks, "Rice's NSC Tenure Complicates New Post." But Rice also has her defenders. As James Mann observes, Rice was a central and effective player: "She had quietly played at least as significant a role as any of the others. She had been the prime mover behind the drafting of a new National Security Strategy that laid the framework for a preventive war. She had served as the White House coordinator and as the president's closest adviser, throughout the entire Iraq operation. And she had emerged after the war as the principal spokesman for the administration's expansive vision of its mission in the Middle East" (Mann, *Rise of the Vulcans,* 367).

48. Purdom, "From Behind the Scenes to State Front."

49. Ignatius, "A Foreign Policy Out of Focus."

50. Starobin, "On Her Own."

51. Allen, "Rice is Named Secretary of State."

52. Bumiller, "A Partner in Shaping an Assertive Foreign Policy."

53. Kessler and Ricks, "Rice's NSC Tenure Complicates New Post."

54. Kessler and Slevin, "Rice Fails to Repair Rifts." According to Risen, "Rice, who was supposed to be managing the interagency policy process, seemed either unwilling or unable to rein in Rumsfeld, so the defense secretary simply got away with pursuing his own foreign policy." "Early on," Rumsfeld made it clear that "he worked for George W. Bush, not Condoleezza Rice" (Risen, *State of War,* 161, 163). The problem with Rumsfeld was apparently severe: "Time and again in the Bush administration, Rumsfeld simply ignored decisions made by the president in front of his war cabinet, according to senior administration officials. . . . Rumsfeld succeeded by using a passive-aggressive style in which he would raise an unending series of questions and concerns about a proposal without flatly stating his opposition to it. If a decision went against him in one meeting, he and his aides would simply arrange another meeting with a different group of administration officials and would repeat the process until the Pentagon view prevailed. Rumsfeld succeeded by wearing out his bureaucratic foes, and by refusing to take no for an answer." Powell, by contrast, was at a disadvantage since he "made the mistake of playing by the rules" (Risen, *State of War,* 161–62).

55. Calabresi, "Condi Gets Her Shot."

56. DeYoung, 417.

57. Ibid., 478.

58. Thomas, "The Quiet Power of Condi Rice," 28.

59. Elliott and Calabresi, "Is Condi the Problem?" 37.

60. Suskind, 256.

61. Hughes, *Ten Minutes from Normal,* 282.

62. Thomas, "The Quiet Power of Condi Rice," 26; Bumiller, *Condoleezza Rice,* 190.

63. See Thomas, "The Quiet Power of Condi Rice," 28–29; and Lemann, "Without a Doubt," 167.

64. Kessler, "Rice Goes from Inside to the Front."

65. Kessler and Slevin, "Rice Fails to Repair Rifts."

66. Lemann, "Without a Doubt," 167.

67. Ibid.

68. Allen and Lane, "Rice Helped Shape Bush Decision on Admissions."

69. Lemann, "Without a Doubt," 177–78.

70. See Burke, *Becoming President,* 74–80, 117–120.

71. See Babington, "Democrats Criticize Rice Over Iraq War"; Kessler, "Rice is Closer to Final Vote of Senate"; and Bumiller, *Condoleezza Rice,* 252–53. Sens. Barbara Boxer (D-CA) and John Kerry (D-MA) voted against her in the Foreign Relations Committee. She was finally confirmed as secretary of state on January 26 by a vote of 85–13, the largest margin against a nominee to State since 1825, when Henry Clay was approved by 27–24, in the aftermath of the "corrupt bargain" of the 1824 election of John Quincy Adams.

72. Kessler, "Rice Hitting the Road to Speak"; also see Bumiller, *Condoleezza Rice,* 244–47.

73. Kessler, "Rice Hitting the Road to Speak."

74. Perlez, "Rice on the Front Line Foreign Policy War."

75. See Kessler, "Rice Goes from Inside to the Front"; and Starobin, "On Her Own," 273.

76. Kessler, "Rice Goes from Inside to the Front."

77. Woodward, *Bush at War,* 254.

78. Ibid., 30.

79. Ibid., 254.

80. Pfiffner, "National Security Policymaking and the Bush War Cabinet," 86.

81. Woodward, *Bush at War,* 85–86.

82. Ibid., 182–83.

83. Moens, *Foreign Policy of George W. Bush,* 133.

84. Woodward, *Bush at War,* 149.

85. Rice's realistic assessment of the Taliban also runs counter to one of Irving Janis's signs of groupthink: a tendency for policy makers to underestimate the skills and abilities of the adversary.

86. Woodward, *Bush at War,* 275.

87. See Kagan and Kristol, "A Winning Strategy"; and Sammon, *Fighting Back,* 289–296, 315.

88. Woodward, *Bush at War,* 244.

89. Ibid., 245.

90. Ibid., 112.

91. Ibid., 225.

92. They wanted to add the words "continue to" harbor terrorists to the text of the speech (see Woodward, *Bush at War,* 105).

93. Woodward, *Bush at War,* 82–83.

94. Ibid., 179.

95. Ibid., 129, 213, 233. It should also be noted that not all of Rice's efforts met with success. At a meeting of the NSC on October 9, 2001, Rice asked if the Northern Alliance was getting divergent and confusing advice from different foreign governments. "No one answered," according to Woodward. The group then went on to discuss other terrorist groups (Woodward, *Bush at War,* 215).

96. Ibid., 160, 307.

97. Ibid., 236.

98. Ibid., 195.

99. Ibid., 157–58.

100. Ibid., 162.

101. Ibid., 158.

102. Ibid., 167–68.

103. Ibid., 256–58, 260–63; also see Moens, *Foreign Policy of George W. Bush,* 144.

104. Woodward, *Bush at War,* 258.

105. Moens, *Foreign Policy of George W. Bush,* 144.

106. Woodward, *Bush at War,* 144.

107. Ibid., 158.

108. Ibid.

109. Ibid., 256.

110. John McLaughlin, deputy director of the CIA, recalled one of then candidate Bush's daily CIA briefings. McLaughlin had just begun when Bush started asking questions, and the session lasted four hours. According to McLaughlin, "If this guy is elected, the briefer better be ready to be interactive" (Woodward, *Bush at War,* 161).

111. Woodward, *Bush at War,* 62–63.

112. Ibid., 136.

113. On February 13, 2001, the seventeenth day of Bush's new presidency, Rice had chaired a meeting of the principals that began a review of Iraq policy (DeYoung, 315–17; Woodward, *Plan of Attack,* 13). Treasury Secretary O'Neill dates the first meeting on Iraq to January 30, 2001 (Suskind, 70–75). By the summer of 2001, the deputies group was nearing completion of a new plan; but with the events of September 11, it was never presented

to the president (Woodward, *Plan of Attack,* 22). On pre–September 11 planning on Iraq, also see Moens, *Foreign Policy of George W. Bush,* 70–75; and Feith, 199–212.

114. Sammon, 232–33; Moens, *Foreign Policy of George W. Bush,* 164; Tenet, 306–7. According to Bumiller (*Condoleezza Rice,* 166), Rice said that "Don [Rumsfeld] didn't offer an opinion about Iraq."

115. Woodward, *Bush at War,* 87.

116. Ibid., 91.

117. Woodward, *Plan of Attack,* 26.

118. Bumiller, *Condoleezza Rice,* 171. Rumsfeld tried to bring the CIA into the early planning process, telling the president, "It's particularly important that I talk to [CIA Director] George Tenet." "Fine," Bush relied, but not now, at a later date. In a later interview with Woodward, Bush could not recall if he had talked to Cheney about his instructions to Rumsfeld (Woodward, *Plan of Attack,* 3–4). Other accounts note that military planning had been ordered as early as September 17, 2001. On that day, a three- page, "Top Secret" document was signed by President Bush outlining a plan for going to war in Afghanistan as part of the global war on terror; it also directed the Pentagon to begin planning military options against Iraq (Kessler, "U.S. Decision on Iraq has Puzzling Past"; also see Pfiffner, "National Security Policymaking and the Bush War Cabinet," 89–90; and Fallows, "Blind into Baghdad," 56).

119. Woodward, *Plan of Attack,* 2–4.

120. Ibid., 3.

121. Ibid., 30 emphasis added.

122. Ibid., 3.

123. According to James Fallows, "The three known exceptions to this pattern actually underscore the limits on top-level talks. One was the discussions at Camp David just after 9/11: they led to 'Afghanistan first,' which delayed rather than forestalled the concentration on Iraq. The second was Colin Powell's 'You break it, you've bought it' warning to the president in the summer of 2002; far from leading to serious questions about the war, it did not even persuade the administration to use the postwar plans devised by the State Department, the Army, and the CIA. The third was a long memo from Rumsfeld to Bush a few months before the war began, when a campaign against Iraq was a foregone conclusion. . . . its only apparent effect was that Bush called in his military commanders to look at the war plans" (Fallows, "Bush's Lost Year," 79).

124. Tenet, 305, also see 308.

125. Woodward, *Plan of Attack,* 416. When Woodward asked Rumsfeld about it, Rumsfeld replied that he agreed with the president's decision, but added, "Whether there ever was a formal moment where he asked me . . . I can't recall it." According to Woodward, Bush later told him that "he had not asked Rumsfeld" (Woodward, *Plan of Attack,* 416).

126. Ibid., 251.

127. Ibid., 272; According to Powell, there was never "a moment when we all made our recommendations and [Bush] made a decision." The president made the decision for war "in his own mind, by himself" (DeYoung, 429).

128. Ibid., 66.

129. Ibid., 249–250. Stephen Hadley and I. Lewis Libby, Cheney's chief of staff and key foreign policy adviser, were assigned the task. Both were lawyers by training, and, as part of their work, they visited the CIA. Libby then presented the case on January 25, 2003, to Rice, Hadley, Richard Armitage (Powell's deputy), Paul Wolfowitz (Rumsfeld's deputy), White House Communications Director Dan Bartlett, speechwriter Michael Gerson, Karl Rove, and Karen Hughes (who had left the White House but was still serving as an informal

adviser). Although some were impressed, according to Woodward, Armitage thought the case "overreaching and hyperbole," and Hughes said "it didn't work" as a public relations effort. However, it became the basis for Powell's presentation before the U.N. (Woodward, *Plan of Attack,* 290).

130. Tenet, 360–64.

131. Woodward, *Plan of Attack,* 87; Bumiller, *Condoleezza Rice,* 174; but see Frum, *The Right Man,* 237–338. Although the axis of evil line reference had been presumably vetted by the State Department, after the speech, according to Woodward, "Powell was surprised by the intense focus on the line, and soon realized it might turn into a to-do list for some time to come" (Woodward, *Plan of Attack,* 94).

132. Woodward, *Plan of Attack,* 126. Rice had raised the same issue at a December 28, 2001, briefing of the principals by Franks, and both she and Card did so again at another briefing by Franks on September 6, 2002, (Woodward, *Plan of Attack,* 64, 173).

133. Ibid., 133.

134. Ibid., 208.

135. Ibid., 388.

136. According to Woodward's account, Bush told him that Saddam was showing no signs of compliance and that he had made his mind up for war. Powell reminded him again of their August conversation, especially about "owning this place." "Powell wasn't sure whether Bush had fully understood the meaning and consequences of total ownership." The president, however, made it clear he had made his decision: "this was not a discussion, but the president informing one of his cabinet members of his decision. The fork in the road had been reached and Bush had chosen war." "Are you with me on this?" Bush asked him. "I think I have to do this. I want you with me." White House records indicate it was a twelve minute meeting (Woodward, *Plan of Attack,* 269–270; also see DeYoung, 429).

137. Woodward, *Plan of Attack,* 266–69.

138. As Woodward observes, "In his first months as secretary of state, Powell had never really closed the personal loop with Bush, never established a comfort level—the natural, at-ease state of closeness both had with others. There existed a distance between these two affable men—a wariness—as if they were stalking each other from afar, never sitting down and having it out, whatever the 'it' was" (Woodward, *Bush at War,* 13).

139. DeYoung, 401–3; Woodward, *Plan of Attack,* 149–150. In Woodward's account, Powell laid out his concerns, including the instability war might cause in the Middle East and the problems to be confronted in Iraq following the war: "You need to understand not just a military timeline but the other things that are going to be facing you." According to Woodward, Powell "did not feel the downsides had been brought out in sufficient, gory detail." "The president listened, asked some questions but did not push back that much. Finally, he looked at Powell. 'What should I do? What else can I do?'" At that point, Powell laid out his own plan for taking the issue to the United Nations (150–52). It is also important to note that Powell was not dead set against regime change in Iraq. As Moens observes, "there is no evidence that Powell ever opposed regime change in Iraq, as the question for him was not 'whether' but 'how' and 'when.' Clearly, this leaves considerable daylight between Cheney and Powell, but it is not about continuing the existing policy versus regime change" (Moens, *Foreign Policy of George W. Bush,* 169; also see Feith, 247–49).

140. Woodward, *Plan of Attack,* 220.

141. Ibid., 227. In crafting the resolution Powell gained an ally in Rice who agreed on the need to compromise to gain the support of the U.N. Security Council. Recalcitrance was not "worth it" in her view; "Let's not hang on ceremony here." One of the key issues in the negotiations, especially with France, hung on a single word. The French insisted on a

false declaration by Iraq *and* a failure to cooperate as triggers for a "material breach" of the resolution. Administration hard liners (and, initially, Powell) pressed for *or* rather than *and,* which would have made the case much easier; a false declaration by Saddam (which they presumed would occur) would then be the pretext for war (Woodward, *Plan of Attack,* 222–25). The administration also thought it had avoided the need for a second resolution by the U.N. following a presumed Iraqi "material breach." Powell and Rice ended up conceding on the issue—*and* prevailed. Powell thought he had bested the French in the negotiations by securing a tough resolution, which eventually passed the Security Council by a unanimous 15–0 (including Syria) vote on November 8, 2002. As it turned out, the words of the resolution would prove more significant than its seeming toughness and unanimity seemed initially to suggest. Iraq's declaration of December 7 that it possessed no WMD was not sufficient as a casus belli, as Cheney and others had once hoped. The outcome would turn now on the weapons inspection process and the perception of (the *and* in the resolution) Iraqi cooperation, and both in turn would bring the Security Council back in for a second round of deliberations (see also Moens, *Foreign Policy of George W. Bush,* 181–82).

142. Woodward, *Plan of Attack,* 173.

143. Ibid., 251.

144. Lemann, "How it Came to War," 39; also see Bumiller, "A Partner in Shaping an Assertive Foreign Policy"; Bumiller, *Condoleezza Rice,* 185; Frum, 197–201; and Hughes, 282–83. Meetings were held in the spring of 2002, according to Haass, and "my staff would come back to me and report that there's something in the air here. So there was a sense that it was gathering momentum, but it was hard to put down." When Colin Powell had his August 2002 meetings with Bush, where he successfully pressed the case to secure a U.N. resolution, "the agenda was not whether Iraq, but how" (Lemann, "How It Came to War," 39). According to another account, when administration officials were asked "to recall how and when the president decided to invade Iraq, they had a hard time picking out one turning point." In the view of one State Department official, "We never had a decisive moment. It was like water dripping" (Thomas, "The 12 Year Itch," 62).

145. See Hersh, "The Stovepipe"; Hosenball, Isikoff, and Thomas, "Cheney's Lone Path to War"; Ackerman and Judis "The Selling of the Iraq War"; Pfiffner, "Did President Bush Mislead the Country in his Arguments for War with Iraq?" 41–42; and Pollack, "Spies, Lies, and Weapons," 88. According to Feith, many of the accounts—especially Hersh's—attributing the "stovepipe" to his Office of Special Plans are inaccurate. He had created a very small Policy Counterrorism Evaluation Group after 9/11, but he argues that it was hardly a separate intelligence operation, had a staff of only one after April 2002, and was not a part of OSP (Feith, 116–17; also see 294).

146. See Ackerman and Judis, "The Selling of the Iraq War"; and Ackerman and Judis, "The Operator." According to Hersh, "In the view of many CIA analysts and operatives, [Tenet] was too eager to endear himself to the administration's hawks and improve his standing with the President and the Vice President. Some CIA analysts were constantly being urged by the Vice-President's office to provide worst-case assessments on Iraqi weapons issues. 'They got pounded on, day after day,' one senior Bush administration official told me, and received no consistent backup from Tenet and his senior staff. 'Pretty soon you say, F**k it.' And they began to provide the intelligence that was wanted" (Hersh, "The Stovepipe," 80). However, the July 2004 report of the Senate Intelligence Committee contains testimony from a number of CIA analysts disputing charges that they had been "pressured" (Senate Intelligence Committee, *Report of the Select Committee on Intelligence,* 357–363, 445–46, but also see 455–59). Tenet also disputes the pressure claim in his memoirs, but notes that some analysts felt pressured and contacted the CIA's ombudsman, who felt the

matter was "hurt feelings" not politicization of intelligence (Tenet, 344–45). Another important treatment of this issue, defending the administration, can be found in Feith, 263–273.

147. Pfiffner, "Did President Bush Mislead the Country in his Arguments for War with Iraq?" 44.

148. See Pfiffner, "Did President Bush Mislead the Country in his Arguments for War with Iraq?"; Pfiffner, "Intelligence and Decision Making before the War with Iraq"; Ackerman and Judis, "The Selling of the Iraq War"; Stone, "Were Qaeda-Iraq Links Exaggerated?"; Pollack, "Spies Lies, and Weapons"; and Barstow, Broad, and Gerth, "How the White House Embraced Disputed Arms Intelligence." On areas of Iraqi non-compliance with U.N. resolutions, see Moens, *Foreign Policy of George W. Bush,* 190. Tenet has an interesting discussion of how the majority of agency representatives felt that the aluminum tubes were for nuclear purposes (Tenet, 324–25) and on the poor intelligence on mobile weapons labs (376–383). For a defense of the administration's position, see Kessler, *A Matter of Character,* 196–205.

149. Hersh, "The Stovepipe," 80–87. One might also defend Cheney's and Rumsfeld's efforts as Stephen Cambone did at his confirmation hearings as undersecretary of defense for intelligence on February 27, 2003, when he noted that the "consumers" of intelligence should question how the analysts "arrived at those conclusions and what the sources of information were" (Federal Document Clearing House, "U.S. Armed Services Committee," 10). Similarly, as Kenneth Pollack notes, "no policymaker should accept intelligence estimates unquestioningly. While I was at the NSC, I regularly challenged analysts as to why they believed what they did . . . Any official who does less is derelict in his or her duty" (Pollack, "Spies, Lies, and Weapons," 88). But by the same token, this approach places more burden on top policy makers, especially through the brokerage of the NSC advisor, to make sure that the "consumers" have got it right. Problems also carried over into the administration's public presentation of its case for war, especially when France, Russia, and Germany began to balk at intervention in early 2003. As Moens points out, "The Bush team did what many decision makers have done in similar cases; they started to bolster their arguments. The UN would no longer authorize war so they had to make the strongest indictment of Iraq and proceed to war with few allies. Bush and his advisers . . . began to make the case more compelling than the information at hand could support. As political scientist Alexander George has pointed out, such bolstering typically leads to distortions in information" (Moens, *Foreign Policy of George W. Bush,* 188; also see George, *Presidential Decisionmaking in Foreign Policy,* 1980, 38). For a critique of the principals' assessment of intelligence information, as well as Cheney's and Rumsfeld's stovepiping, see Pillar, "Intelligence, Policy, and the War in Iraq." According to Pillar, then the CIA national intelligence officer for the Near East and South Asia, the administration turned the standard intelligence model "upside down. The administration used intelligence not to inform decision-making but to justify a decision already made" (17).

150. See Gordon and Trainor, *Cobra II,* 125–26.

151. Fallows, "Bush's Lost Year," 79.

152. On Powell's problems with some of the intelligence, see De Young, 439–446; Tenet, 372–383; and Woodward, *Plan of Attack,* 298–301. Ironically, Powell and his staff had based his U.N. speech on the NIE, believing it more reliable than information they had been provided for the speech from Douglas Feith's Special Plans operation in the Pentagon and from the vice president's staff. Material from both of the latter, according to one Powell aide, "was unsourced, a lot of it was just out of newspapers . . . it was nuts" (Bamford, *A Pretext for War,* 368–69; also see DeYoung, 445). As for the NIE, it had been produced, at

the request of Democrats in the Senate, in nineteen days, rather than the usual six months or plus (Bumiller, *Condoleezza Rice,* 194). For his part, Feith notes in retrospect the CIA's lack of adequate human intelligence in Iraq but its failure to make that more widely known to policy makers: "I recall no intelligence official ever confessing the inadequacy of the intelligence sources to the Deputies Committee at the time" (Feith, 260).

153. Woodward, *Plan of Attack,* 295. In mid-November, Powell had mused privately to his chief of staff about what would happen when we "have troops on the ground in Iraq and search it from one end to the other—and find nothing" (DeYoung, 424).

154. Woodward, *Plan of Attack,* 286. On March 16, 2003, an article appeared in the *Washington Post* under Walter Pincus's byline titled "U.S. Lacks Specifics on Banned Arms." Woodward worked on it and, in his view, based on some Bush administration sources, the evidence against the Saddam regime was "pretty thin": "Several of these sources, I know, did voice their reservations within their various organizations but they also did not have enough to robustly challenge the conclusions that had been already reached. I have no evidence that the reservations of these particular sources reached the president" (Woodward, *Plan of Attack,* 356).

155. Risen, *State of War,* 121–22.

156. It should be noted that in his 2003 State of the Union address, President Bush claimed, based on British intelligence, only that Iraq *had sought* to purchase the uranium. It should also be noted that the uranium purchase issue may still be an open question. As Kessler notes, "the British House of Commons Intelligence and Security Committee [the Butler Committee] reviewed the MI6 intelligence about the Niger claim and concluded in September 2003 that, based on the information MI6 gathered [which was not based on the forged documents], the finding was 'reasonable.'" MI6 was also "justified in continuing to claim that the intelligence was credible" (Kessler, *A Matter of Character,* 199). The Butler Committee also found that Bush's statement in the 2003 State of the Union Address "was well-founded" (Butler Committee, "Review of Intelligence on Weapons of Mass Destruction," 123).

157. On the October speech see Tenet, 450–51. In his memoirs, Tenet also notes a January 6, 2003, meeting with Rice and Hadley where one of his CIA aides noted that the nuclear case was weak. At a later meeting Hadley asked for more material on Iraq's efforts to obtain nuclear weapons, which the CIA then provided. Tenet then argues NSC officials took some material on uranium purchases out of context, which eventually found its way into the State of the Union speech (371). Tenet later notes in his memoirs that the internal CIA vetting process of the State of the Union speech had broken down and that he had failed "to fully study the speech myself" (459; also see 449–475 where Tenet devotes a full chapter to the episode).

158. Sanger and Miller, "National Security Aide Says He's to Blame for Speech Error."

159. Cooper, "Pinning the Line on the Man," 31; Pfiffner, "Did President Bush Mislead the Country in his Arguments for War with Iraq?" 32–33.

160. Interestingly, Tenet notes in his memoirs that many of the dissents by a range of agencies were not in the footnotes or endnotes but in colored boxes interspersed throughout the document—some sixteen pages in total of the ninety-page report. It is not clear, however, where the uranium dissent appeared (Tenet, 327; also see 324–339 for a fuller discussion of the NIE).

161. Milbank and Allen, "Iraq Flap Shakes Rice's Image"; also see Milbank and Priest, "Warning in Iraq Report Unread"; and Sanger and Miller, "National Security Aide Says He's to Blame for Speech Error."

162. Allen, "President Assails Iraq War Skeptics"; Sanger, "Bush Aides Deny Effort to Slant Data on Iraq Arms."

163. The best analysis of intelligence failures on Iraq can be found in the report of the Robb-Silverman Commission, appointed under President Bush's executive order (Commission on the Intelligence Capabilities of the United States Regarding Weapons of Mass Destruction 2005, 3–11, 45–249). It is also important to note that the reports of the postwar Iraq Survey Group, while not finding the actual presence of WMD, a nuclear capability, and other evidence that the Bush administration had alleged in its case for war, still concluded that Iraq had been in violation of U.N. Resolutions 1441 and 687. In inspector David Kay's preliminary report, delivered to congressional intelligence committees on October 2, 2003, he indicated that his team had found equipment and activities never declared to the U.N. inspectors, covert research on biological warfare agents, signs that Iraq was exploring chemical weapons programs, design work on prohibited missiles, and an ongoing interest in developing a future nuclear capability (see Risen and Miller, "No Illicit Arms Found in Iraq"; Kagan and Kristol, "The Right War for the Wrong Reasons"; and Pollack, "Spies, Lies, and Weapons," 81). Similar points were made in inspector Charles Duelfer's (Kay's successor) report to Congress a year later. Duelfer noted that Saddam sought to preserve "the capability to reconstitute weapons of mass destruction when the [U.N.] sanctions were lifted" but he had made no "concerted effort to restart programs." The report also indicated that Saddam had used the U.N.'s oil-for-food program's vouchers to buy influence in a number of different countries with the aim of getting the sanctions lifted (Jehl, "U.S. Reports Finds Iraqis Eliminated Arms in 90's"; Priest and Pincus, "U.S. 'Almost All Wrong' on Weapons"; also see Feith's analysis of the report, 326–331). Tenet has a very interesting account of the Kay and Duelfer missions, especially of difficulties with Kay (Tenet, 401–415). Saddam's top military commanders also believed that Iraq possessed WMD and that they would use them in case of attack, according to a classified 2005 U.S. military report. According to one account, Saddam "was so secretive and kept information so compartmentalized that his top military leaders were stunned when he told them three months before the war that he had no weapons of mass destruction" (Gordon and Trainor, "Even as U.S. Invaded, Hussein Saw Iraqi Unrest as Top Threat"; also see Gordon and Trainor, *Cobra II,* 118–120).

164. Pincus, "White House Backs Off Claim on Iraqi Buy."

165. Pincus, "Tenet Says He Didn't Know about Claim."

166. Pincus, "White House Faulted on Uranium Claim." Some positive developments did come out of the controversy: a CIA officer was assigned to participate in the speech-writing process.

167. Mufson, "Forget WMD"; Pfiffner, "Did President Bush Mislead the Country in his Arguments for War with Iraq?" 33; emphasis added. Yet as Tenet notes, he had raised the issue in a meeting on January 6, 2003 (371). Tenet also notes a late December 2002 meeting of two of his key deputies with Rice where they went over the case against Iraq. Rice interrupted one of them asking, "if you are saying these are *assertions,* we need to know this. We can't send troops to war based on assertions." She asked about levels of confidence in the assessment that Saddam had chemical weapons. "What's high confidence, ninety percent?" she asked. "That's about right," was the reply. Rice: "That's a heck of a lot lower than we're getting from reading the PDB [president's daily briefing]." "The weakest case was nuclear," the CIA representative noted. Rice, turning to Tenet's deputy, John McLaughlin: "You (the intelligence community) have gotten the president way out on a limb on this." McLaughlin later related the conversation to Tenet: "We've got *them* out on a limb?" (Tenet, 369–371, emphases in original). Whoever got whom out on the limb is of interest, but more so is that the weakness in some of the intelligence *had directly* been presented to Rice. Moreover, it elicited no apparent further reaction on her part.

168. Pfiffner, "Did President Bush Mislead the Country in his Arguments for War with Iraq?" 33.

169. Pincus, "Deutch Sees Consequences in Failed Arms Search."

170. Priest, "House Probers Conclude Iraq War Data Was Weak"; Hulse and Sanger, "New Criticism on Prewar Use of Intelligence."

171. Kessler and Priest, "Iraq Data Not Old."

172. Fallows, "Blind Into Baghdad," 54.

173. O'Hanlon, "Iraq Without a Plan," 33.

174. Woodward, *Plan of Attack,* 180.

175. O'Hanlon, "Iraq Without a Plan," 41.

176. Woodward, *Plan of Attack,* 55.

177. Ibid., 133.

178. Ibid., 148. Franks noted that there would be 265,000 troops in the country, but over time that might be drawn down to 50,000, roughly eighteen months after the end of combat (i.e., November 2004). On Franks's strategy, in addition to his memoirs (Franks, *American Soldier*), see Ackerman, "Vision Impaired"; Barnes, "The Commander"; and Boyer, "The New War Machine." Three pages of what is apparently a later version of the Phase IV plan are reproduced in Scarborough (*Rumsfeld's War,* 180–82).

179. Franks, 393.

180. Woodward, *Plan of Attack,* 152.

181. Ibid., 259. Indeed, as late as March 16, 2003, on the eve of the invasion, Cheney still maintained that "I really do believe we will be greeted as liberators" (McGeary, "3 Flawed Assumptions,"60).

182. Woodward, *Plan of Attack,* 276.

183. An excerpt from the thirty-eight page study can be found in Gordon, "Faulty Intelligence Misled Troops at War's Start." In other respects, as Gordon notes, the report "was less prescient": it feared "score-settling among ethnic groups" rather than the emergence of an insurgency (the latter only briefly noted), and it "underestimated the fragile state of Iraq's infrastructure"; (also see Tenet, 423–27). In May 2007, as part of the Senate Select Committee's investigation of prewar intelligence, the gist of two NIC assessments in January 2003 were made public: "Principal Challenges in Post-Saddam Iraq," and "Regional Consequences of Regime Change in Iraq." Both painted a sober picture of difficulties in a postwar Iraq (see Walter Pincus, "Assessments Made in 2003 Foretold Situation in Iraq"). In August 2002, the CIA also circulated an intelligence analysis that described possible chaos in a postwar Iraq (see Pincus, "Before War, CIA Warned of Negative Outcomes").

184. Bender, "CIA Warned Administration of Postwar Guerilla Peril."

185. O'Hanlon "Iraq Without a Plan," 33–37; also see Fallows, "Blind into Baghdad," 63–64.

186. Fallows, "Blind into Baghdad," 68.

187. See Brinkley and Schmitt, "Iraqi Leaders Say U.S. Was Warned of Disorder."

188. Gordon, "The Strategy to Secure Iraq Did Not Foresee a 2nd War"; also see Fallows, "Blind into Baghdad,"64–65, 73

189. Woodward, *Plan of Attack,* 282.

190. Fallows, "Blind into Baghdad," 56–58.

191. Woodward, *Plan of Attack,* 283.

192. Some accounts of the incident suggest that Rumsfeld was responding to Cheney's pressure to fire Warrick. Another account faults Rice's inability to resolve the matter more effectively: "Some of Powell's key lieutenants, who had gone along with the president's decision to give the Pentagon the principal postwar role, were frustrated by the Defense Depart-

ment's refusal to include them—and then Rice's unwillingness to intercede" (Kessler and Slevin, "Rice Fails to Repair Rifts"). Feith presents an interesting account from Rumsfeld's perspective, noting his concern over the large numbers of State and Agency for International Development personnel proposed by Garner for positions in ORHA and the need for more rigor in the selection process (Feith, 377–78, 386–89).

193. "Powell couldn't believe the silliness" (Woodward, *Plan of Attack*, 283–284); also see Schmitt and Brinkley, "State Department Foresaw Trouble Now Plaguing Iraq"; Packer, "War After the War," 62; Jehl and Sanger, "New to the Job"; and Fallows, "Blind into Baghdad," 72. Gordon and Trainor note, however, limits in State's study. It was "of uneven quality," and "proposed some good ideas but was far short of a viable plan" (Gordon and Trainor, *Cobra II*, 159). Feith emphasizes that it was largely concept papers, not a postwar plan. Moreover, it was not really a State Department project, but one largely produced by Iraqi "externals" under State sponsorship, and it had never undergone any interagency vetting (Feith, 376–77).

194. Rieff, "Who Botched the Occupation?"; Fallows, "Blind into Baghdad," 72. Feith notes, however, that neither he nor other senior leaders in the Pentagon were hostile to the project and that they never told Garner to ignore it (Feith, 376, 378).

195. On the OSP, see Feith, 117, 293–94, 386; Scarborough, 40–43; and Moens, *Foreign Policy of George W. Bush*, 183–84. The Defense Department had been given authority over postwar Iraq in January 2003, under National Security Presidential Directive No. 24, signed by the president.

196. As Woodward notes, "It was a different way of doing things . . . because the State Department would be directly subordinate to Defense" (Woodward, *Plan of Attack*, 282; also see Feith, 315–17, 347).

197. Moens, *Foreign Policy of George W. Bush*, 195–96.

198. Feith, 317–19, 347–350, 435; also see Packer, *War After the War*, 62.

199. Packer, 62.

200. Ibid.

201. Woodward, *Plan of Attack*, 329; Feith, 402–9. Interestingly, given his comments that his job was only there to analyze and advise, Feith notes that Bush approved his proposal for an Iraq Interim Authority (408–9).

202. Ibid., 343. Feith notes in his memoirs that he was presenting Garner's plans and used his slides, and he presented the pros and cons (Feith, 367).

203. O'Hanlon, "Iraq Without a Plan," 37–38. O'Hanlon also faults General Franks's Phase IV planning: "One need only consult the Third Infantry Division's after action report, which reads: 'higher headquarters did not provide [us] with a plan for Phase IV. As a result, Third Infantry Division transitioned into Phase IV in the absence of guidance'" (O'Hanlon, "Iraq Without a Plan," 36). "There was no plan for oversight and reconstruction, even after the division arrived in Baghdad" (Brinkley and Schmitt, "Iraqi Leaders Say U.S. Was Warned of Disorder"; also see Rieff, "Who Botched the Occupation," 44). Moreover, according to O'Hanlon, "A broader Department of Defense report on the war similarly observed that 'late formation of Department of Defense [Phase IV] organizations limited time available for the deployment of detailed plans and pre-deployment coordination'" (O'Hanlon, "Iraq Without a Plan," 36). Further: "While Franks himself always cautioned that this stage of the operation could take years, it was ultimately assumed that much of the regular Iraqi army would survive and be available to play a large role in keeping postwar order" (O'Hanlon, "Iraq Without a Plan," 37). Rumsfeld's efforts to pare down the size of U.S. forces won an ally in Franks. They were right about combat operations, but not prepared for the postwar situation that developed. As O'Hanlon notes, Bremer later viewed this

as a mistake and argued that "the single most important change . . . would have been having more troops in Iraq at the beginning and throughout." Bremer later claimed to have "raised this issue a number of times with our government" (O'Hanlon, "Iraq Without a Plan," 39). As for General Franks, he had warned Rumsfeld of the need to focus on the postwar period more, but, in Woodward's words, "Rumsfeld and the others had been focused on the war." As for Powell, as war planning occurred over sixteenth months, he "felt that the easier the war looked, the less Rumsfeld, the Pentagon and Franks had worried about the aftermath" (Woodward, *Plan of Attack,* 413, 414). In General Franks's view, "I wish some things had been done differently. I wish Don Rumsfeld and Colin Powell had forced the Defense and State Departments to work more closely together" (Franks, 544). As for Feith, a May 2005 profile of Feith in the *New Yorker* indicates that Feith did consider the "possibility that the invasion and its aftermath could be disastrous," and that concerns were forwarded to the president, the latter notably in Rumsfeld's October 2002 "parade of horribles" memo, discussed at an NSC meeting. According to Feith, "Instead of saying, 'How can we conceal from the President those things that would make him reluctant?,' we decided we had to go to him before he makes such an important decision with a list of all those things that could go wrong." Likewise, Feith sent a memo to General Franks, who was in charge of postwar planning, arguing that "'we're going to have major law-and-order problems after the war. . . . I wrote a memo anticipating problems'" (Goldberg, "Anticipating Problems," 40–41). On Rumsfeld's "parade of horribles" memo, see Feith, 332–34; on Feith's own memo, see 362–66; on his view that their planning was cautious and sober, not one of rosy scenarios, as many critics charged, see 409–410, 415.

204. Barry and Thomas, "The Unbuilding of Iraq," 37.

205. Gordon, "The Strategy to Secure Iraq Did Not Foresee a 2nd War." A December 2004 study by the Defense Science Board, an independent advisory body to the secretary of defense, on the general topic of postconflict stabilization and reconstruction concluded that stabilization of disordered nations might require 20 troops per 1000 population [the ratio was 6:1000 for Iraq], that reconstruction and stabilization should be a "core competency" of both State and Defense, that the State Department should be "the locus for this reconstruction integration," and that "certain critical capabilities require preparation years in advance" (Defense Science Board, *To and From Hostilities,* viii, ix, xvii). As Gordon and Trainor point out with respect to these troop projections and parallels for Iraq, "The implicit question was whether Iraq would be more like the Balkans or Afghanistan. The NSC briefing made clear that in one key respect Iraq had more in common with the Balkans than Afghanistan": dense urban areas requiring more troops. Yet no alarm bells sounded: "Hadley seemed to take comfort in the Afghan parallel. At the White House, the briefing never prompted any second-guessing of Rumsfeld's position" (104).

206. Gordon, "The Strategy to Secure Iraq Did Not Foresee a 2nd War."

207. It should be noted that Rice might have found an ally in Powell (and vice versa). According to Woodward, Powell had several back-channel phone conversations with Franks about his concerns with the leanness of the troop commitment (Woodward, *Plan of Attack,* 80). Powell had also raised concerns about Franks's war plan at an NSC meeting in early September 2002 (see Franks, 394–97). But Powell was also cautious: "When Bush on the eve of war pointedly asked each of his senior advisers if they had any problems with the war plan, Powell raised no objection. A senior State Department official said Powell did not recommend a larger force" (Kessler and Pincus, "Advisers Split as War Unfolds").

208. According to then Secretary of the Army Thomas White, "Our working budgetary assumption was that 90 days after completion of the operation, we would withdraw the first 50,000, and then every 30 days we'd take out another 50,000 until everybody was back"

(Gordon, "The Strategy to Secure Iraq Did Not Foresee a 2nd War"). On April 16, 2003, General Franks was so optimistic that he "flew to Baghdad and instructed his commanders to draw up plans to begin pulling out" (Gordon, "The Strategy to Secure Iraq Did Not Foresee a 2nd War").

209. Woodward, *Plan of Attack,* 322. On Miller's difficulties with Defense, especially see Gordon and Trainor, *Cobra II,* 148–49. According to a *Time* magazine account, Rice also established other interagency working groups, but they too experienced difficulty: "Rice's working groups failed on two counts. First, they never succeeded in getting State and the Pentagon on the same page." Second, "the Rice group responsible for postwar planning led by Elliott Abrams [from the NSC] and Robin Cleveland [from OMB] woefully underestimated the cost of reconstructing Iraq" (Elliott, "So, What Went Wrong?" 35). According to another *Time* account, "The process never got much traction. Both Defense and State had their planning operations on Iraq (looking at very different things in very different ways), and according to one participant, Pentagon officials regularly skipped meetings of Rice's group that was planning for postwar Iraq" (Elliott and Calabresi, "Is Condi the Problem?" 37).

210. Woodward, *Plan of Attack,* 281; Franks, 362. At other points in his memoirs, Franks is a bit more diplomatic yet still highly critical. In contrast to one member of the Pentagon staff that Franks regards as "one of the brightest, most energetic officers I knew," "Doug Feith was another matter. . . . [Feith] was a theorist whose ideas were often impractical; among some uniformed officers in the Building, he had a reputation for confusing abstract memoranda with results in the field. My dealings with him had left me ambivalent: I liked him personally, but I wasn't convinced that the Secretary was always well-served by his advice" (Franks, 330). On Feith's view of Franks, see Feith, 288–292.

211. Gordon, "Debate Lingering on Decision to Dissolve Iraqi Military."

212. According to Anderson, "the origins of the decree have never been clarified" (Anderson, "Out on the Street," 73; also see Fallows, "Blind into Baghdad," 74). In Bremer's view and Feith's, there was no Iraqi army left to deal with (Fallows, "Blind into Baghdad," 74; Feith, 432). According to Bremer, moreover, "I don't have any second thoughts about disbanding the army. Neither did the secretary of defense, and he's my boss" (Filkins, "Bremer Pushes Iraq on Difficult Path to Self-Rule"; also see Barnes, "The Essential Bremer"; and Barnes, "Our Man in Baghdad"). Interestingly, "restructuring an Iraqi military" was the second item listed under "key tasks" in Franks's Phase IV plan; the first dealt with identifying, securing, and destroying WMD (Scarborough, 181), and use of the Iraqi army was featured in Feith's own prewar briefing (Feith, 366–68). Many were kept in the dark about what Bremer was up to. According to one report, Powell was kept in the dark about that decision, and Rice "had nothing to do" with it. For Powell and his aides, the decision "demonstrated the administration's tendency to make important decisions without consulting key officials."

The report also noted that Powell and Rice were not told in advance of the decision to disband the Iraqi army, and that "as he was preparing to leave office, Mr. Powell told Mr. Bush that the national security process was broken" (Gordon and Trainor, "After Invasion, Point Man for Iraq was Shunted Aside"). Not only may Powell and Rice have been out of the loop regarding the Iraqi army, so too may have been the president. According to another report, the decision to disband "may have been made without President Bush's advance knowledge, according to a senior White House source. The well-placed source said he is virtually certain that the president did not know of the decision before it was taken." Disbanding the army, moreover, "contradicted the recommendations of the [NSC's] interagency planning group," which Bush *had* been briefed on (Risen, *State of War,* 3, 133). The JCS was also out of the loop on disbanding the army, as were top U.S. officers in the region such as Gen. John Abizaid, Frank's deputy, and Gen. David McKernan, Frank's chief military planner in the field, at least according to some accounts (Gordon and Trainor, *Cobra II,* 476, 482–85). In September 2007, following reports that Bush had given an interview in which he stated that he had not authorized a change in policy, Bremer wrote an op-ed piece in the *New York Times.* In it, Bremer defended his actions and outlined his efforts at wider consultation. According to Bremer, General Abazaid favored the option of building a new army "open to both vetted members of the old army and new recruits," rather than recalling back into service the old Iraqi army. Bremer also said that Rumsfeld had forwarded a memo to the other principals, including Rice and Powell, indicating that remnants of the Saddam regime would be eliminated. Bremer sent a memo proposing a new army to Wolfowitz, William J. Haynes (Defense Department's general counsel), Feith, and Franks. Bremer notes that he briefed Rumsfeld several times and received "detailed comments" on a draft order from both the JSC and the Office of the Secretary of Defense, and the announcement of the decision to disband was coordinated with DiRita. No one raised objections, according to Bremer. On May 22, 2003, Bremer sent President Bush a memo on his de-Baathification policy which included statements about the dissolution of the military, followed by a video conference. According to Bremer, the next day Bush sent him a note, thanking him and stating that "you have my full support and confidence" (Bremer, "How I Didn't Dismantle Iraq's Army"). Subsequent accounts of Bremer's op-ed noted that his plan to disband the army was only mentioned fleetingly in Bremer's letter; according to one, "the letters, combined with Mr. Bush's comments, suggest confusion within the administration about what quickly proved to be a decision with explosive repercussions" (Andrews, "Envoy's Letter Counters Bush on Dismantling the Iraq Army"). A related issue is whether Bremer had been too severe in his de-Baathification efforts (see Anderson, "Out on the Street"). In testimony before the Senate Foreign Relations Committee on May 18, 2004, even Paul Wolfowitz conceded that point, as well as generally acknowledging that planning had erred in assuming "that we'd have basically more stable security conditions than we've encountered" (Wright and Ricks, "U.S. Faces Growing Fear of Failure"); in a press briefing on July 23, 2003, he stated that "some important assumptions turned out to underestimate the problem" (Mann, 360). Tenet was also concerned about Bremer's early decisions (Tenet, 426–430). Feith offers an interesting defense of Bremer's de-Baathification policy (427–431).

213. Bumiller, "A Partner in Shaping an Assertive Foreign Policy."

214. Slevin and Allen, "Rice to Lead Effort to Speed Iraqi Aid"; also see Allen, "Iraq Shake-up Skipped Rumsfeld."

215. Sanger and Shanker, "Rumsfeld Quick To Dismiss Talk of Reduced Role in Iraq Policy." According to Feith, Rumsfeld sent a sharp memo to Chief of Staff Card telling him that he had been advised of the change in the memo itself but had not been consulted beforehand (Feith, 470).

216. The prospects of Rice's ability to ride herd over the NSC's deliberations were also enhanced, after the Iraq war, with the August 2003 appointment of Robert Blackwill, once Rice's boss in the Bush Sr. NSC staff, to the new NSC post of coordinator of strategic planning, a position designed to achieve better cohesion and long-range planning (see Wright, "Foreign Policy Guru Tapped to Aid Rice"). Blackwill had been a member of Rice's "Vulcans" (Bush's foreign affairs advisory group) during the 2000 election and transition, then had served a stint as U.S. ambassador to India. Also see Bumiller, *Condoleezza Rice,* 224–25.

217. Gordon, "The Strategy to Secure Iraq Did Not Foresee a 2nd War."

218. Tenet, 447–48.

219. Burke e-mail correspondence with Prof. Scott Sagan of Stanford University, January 31, 2008.

220. Jehl and Sanger, "New to the Job."

221. Milbank, "Down to the Nuts and Bolts at NSC."

222. Jehl and Sanger, "New to the Job."

223. But part of the problem was also the apparent lack of commitment by some of the other principals in making the system work. According to one administration insider, "early on, Defense Secretary Rumsfeld admonished his deputies that he alone would speak for the Pentagon in interagency debates. . . . That stance effectively gutted the traditional security council process" (Ignatius, "A Foreign Policy Out of Focus").

224. Moens, *Foreign Policy of George W. Bush,* 200.

225. Bumiller, *Condoleezza Rice,* 219.

226. Purdom, "From Behind the Scenes to Stage Front."

227. Thomas, "The Quiet Power of Condi Rice," 29.

228. Ibid.

229. Hughes, 282.

230. See Burke, *Becoming President,* 108–112, 219–221; and Moens, *Foreign Policy of George W. Bush,* 59–60.

231. Ignatius, "A Foreign Policy Out of Focus."

Conclusions

1. Rockman, "America's Departments of State," 925. Also see Brzezinski's discussion of the superiority of a "presidential" system to a "secretarial" one (Brzezinski, *Power and Principle,* 533–38).

2. Burke, *Institutional Presidency,* 24–52.

3. Burke telephone interview with Anthony Lake, November 1, 2007.

4. This emphasis on the role of the NSC advisor is not to suggest that it is all that matters in developing effective decision making. The organization and structure of decision-making processes are consequential, as are the nature and degree of presidential management of their inner workings (see Burke, *Institutional Presidency,* 53–116). Some administrations have sought deliberate organizational strategies for balancing White House and departmental impact on the policy process, such as the cabinet council systems in the Reagan and George H. W. Bush presidencies or the differing organizational arrangements in the national security apparatus below the level of the full Council or the principals. Appointments also matter. Whether at the cabinet level or among key members of the White House staff (including the NSC advisor), the impact of personality, skill, and ability among the principals has been consequential. Secretaries of state and defense have varied in the influence they are able to exert on the policy process, some have been stronger (George Shultz and Caspar Weinberger under Reagan, Donald Rumsfeld under George W. Bush) others have been weaker (Cyrus Vance under Carter, Warren Christopher under Clinton).

5. See Lord, 4–33.

6. Ibid., 23.

7. Greenstein and Immerman, 343, 344.

8. Ibid.

9. Lord, 97.

10. George, "The Case for Multiple Advocacy in Making Foreign Policy," 783.

11. Other possibilities for introducing brokerage but with some structural modifications

deserve further attention than can be given here. For example, Destler has also proposed that the NSC advisor return to the model of the executive secretary's coordinator role in the Truman NSC, with the secretary of state as the president's chief policy adviser: "eliminate the job of assistant for national security affairs and place the facilitator in a position a notch lower, such as the currently vacant post of executive secretary of the NSC" (Destler, "National Security Management," 587). He also has proposed abolishing the post in favor of a state department-dominated foreign policy process (Destler, "A Job that Doesn't Work," 87). Moens argues that presidents will always need an in-house foreign policy adviser. He suggests that the NSC advisor fulfill that role, but that, like Destler, the executive secretary's position be recast as process manager (Moens, *Foreign Policy under Carter,* 181–82).

12. Burke telephone interview with Anthony Lake, November 1, 2007.

13. Destler, "National Security Advice to U.S. President," 170–71; also see Moens, *Foreign Policy under Carter,* 24.

14. See Moens, *Foreign Policy under Carter,* 20; and Porter, 216.

15. Porter, 217; but see Moens, *Foreign Policy under Carter,* 176–77.

16. Sisco, "Ford, Kissinger and the Nixon-Ford Foreign Policy," 330.

17. Burke telephone interview with Gen. Brent Scowcroft, November 15, 2007.

18. Daalder and Destler, "The Role of the National Security Adviser," 2. For Carlucci, that right of appeal also extended to Reagan's decisions. On arms control matters, for example, Carlucci once told Reagan, "There are disagreements between George and Cap on a number of issues. And you're going to have to decide. I have to give each of them the right to appeal to you if they disagree with your decision." According to Carlucci, "By and large they would accept it," although on several occasions they did appeal (Carlucci, Oral History, 33).

19. Daalder and Destler, "The Role of the National Security Adviser," 51.

20. Burke telephone interview with Anthony Lake, November 1, 2007.

21. Rostow, *Diffusion of Power,* 364–65.

22. Mulcahy, "Walt Rostow as NSC Adviser," 232.

23. The practice of having the CIA director or his designate personally brief the president on a daily basis began under Truman (Nelson, "The Evolution of the National Security State Ubiquitous and Endless," 275).

24. *Tower Commission Report,* 90–91.

25. Destler, "National Security Management," 577.

26. *Tower Commission Report,* 11.

27. Lord, 94.

28. See Destler, "National Security Management," 582; and Zegart, 241–42.

29. George, "The Case for Multiple Advocacy in Foreign Policy," 783.

30. Porter, 216.

31. *Tower Commission Report,* 91.

32. Cutler, *No Time for Rest,* 295; for a brief discussion of Cutler's occasional speaking activities, usually to government-related audiences, see 355.

33. Carlucci, Oral History, 39.

34. Burke telephone interview with Anthony Lake, November 1, 2007.

35. Daalder and Destler, "The Role of the National Security Adviser," 14.

36. Ibid., 80.

37. Burke telephone interview with Gen. Brent Scowcroft, November 15, 2007.

38. Bromley Smith Oral History, July 29, 1969, Johnson Library, 35.

39. Daalder and Destler, "The Role of the National Security Adviser," 6.

40. In Allen's case it was probably a result of the peculiar organizational setting in which he was enmeshed: a reporting line through Ed Meese and a communications and media-staging operation headed by Michael Deaver.

41. *Tower Commission Report,* 11.

42. Lake, *6 Nightmares,* 262.

43. Burke telephone interview with Anthony Lake, November 1, 2007.

44. *Tower Commission Report,* 91.

45. Newmann, *Managing National Security Policy,* 7.

46. Burke telephone interview with Harold Saunders, January 3, 2008.

47. Cohen, Dolan, and Rosati, "A Place at the Table," 134, 136.

48. Daalder and Destler, "The Role of the National Security Adviser," 16.

49. George, "The Case for Multiple Advocacy in Making Foreign Policy," 783.

50. *Tower Commission Report,* 92.

51. Carlucci, Oral History, 37.

52. Isaacson, 509.

53. Smith, *Doubletalk,* 242, emphasis added.

54. As noted in chapter 1, the OCB was initially chaired by the undersecretary of state rather than the NSC advisor. But over time the NSC advisor's role became more significant largely because of his perceived neutrality. As Carnes Lord notes, "Eisenhower became increasingly dissatisfied with [its] interagency performance. . . . In 1957, the National Security Adviser was given formal membership in the [OCB], and the OCB was integrated into the NSC staff; in 1960, the National Security Adviser was made chairman of the OCB, in recognition of the need for a presiding official who would be seen to be impartial in adjudicating agency disagreements" (Lord, 71).

55. *Tower Commission Report,* 92, emphasis added; also see Lord, 104–5.

56. Daalder and Destler, "The Role of the National Security Adviser," 46.

57. Burke telephone interview with Anthony Lake, November 1, 2007.

58. Daalder and Destler, "The Role of the National Security Adviser," 6.

59. Burke telephone interview with Anthony Lake, November 1, 2007.

60. See Hermann and Preston, "Presidents, Advisers, and Foreign Policy"; Haney, 113–14; Burke, *Institutional Presidency,* 218–221; and Kowert, *Groupthink or Deadlock,* 154.

61. Daalder and Destler, "The Role of the National Security Adviser," 52.

62. *Tower Commission Report,* 88.

63. Scowcroft, "Ford as President and His Foreign Policy," 312.

64. As former NSC Executive Secretary Bromley Smith notes, "The whole art of staff work is to figure out how one thinks the president wants to work and then try to adapt the machinery. . . . You quickly can adapt the machinery to his needs and requirements" (Bromley Smith Oral History, July 29, 1969, Johnson Library, 29).

65. Bose, *Shaping and Signaling Presidential Policy,* 105.

66. Lord, 86.

67. Bowie and Immerman, 259.

68. Woodward, *Bush at War,* 167–68.

69. Burke, *Institutional Presidency,* 180–82, 192–96.

70. Bose, *Shaping and Signaling Presidential Policy,* 109–110.

71. Moens, *Foreign Policy under Carter,* 169–170.

72. Bose, *Shaping and Signaling Presidential Policy,* 102.

73. Kowert, 24.

74. Ibid., 155.

75. Bowie and Immerman, 256.

76. See Johnson, *Managing the White House;* George, *Presidential Decisionmaking in Foreign Policy,* 145–168; Burke and Greenstein, 5–7, 274–289; Haney, 5–9; and Burke, *Institutional Presidency,* 53–89.

77. See Burke, *Institutional Presidency,* 53–89; and Preston, *The President and His Inner Circle,* 257–59.

78. See Burke, *Institutional Presidency,* 91–97; and Bose, *Shaping and Signaling Presidential Policy,* 101–2.

79. Hult and Walcott, *Empowering the White House;* Walcott and Hult, "White House Structure and Decision Making."

80. Janis, *Groupthink,* 2–13, 242–76.

81. Herek, Janis, and Huth, "Decision Making during International Crises," 204–5; Janis, *Groupthink,* 244; Janis, *Crucial Decisions,* 30–31.

82. Haney, 125.

83. Burke, *Institutional Presidency,* 53–89.

84. Burke telephone interview with Anthony Lake, November 1, 2007.

85. Burke telephone interview with Gen. Brent Scowcroft, November 15, 2007.

86. Lord, 97.

87. Sisco, "Ford, Kissinger and the Nixon-Ford Foreign Policy," 331.

88. Burke telephone interview with Gen. Brent Scowcroft, November 15, 2007.

89. Ibid.

90. Ibid.

91. Destler, "Comment," 787.

92. Rockman, "America's Departments of State," 923.

93. Hall, "The 'Custodial Manager' of the Policy-Making Process," 149; also see Lord, 169–175.

94. George, *Presidential Decisionmaking in Foreign Policy,* 195, 206.

95. Porter, 216.

96. *Tower Commission Report,* 88, 92.

97. Daalder and Destler, "The Role of the National Security Adviser," 14.

98. Ibid., 53.

99. Popkin, "The Art of Managing the White House," 6.

100. Cohen, "From the Fabulous Baker Boys to the Master of Disaster," 467.

101. Porter; Herek, Janis, and Huth, "Decision Making during International Crises"; Burke and Greenstein, *How Presidents Test Reality;* Moens, *Foreign Policy under Carter;* Haney, *Organizing for Foreign Policy Crises;* Bose, *Shaping and Signaling Presidential Policy.*

102. Pfiffner, "Did President Bush Mislead the Country in his Arguments for War with Iraq?" 45, emphasis added.

103. *Tower Commission Report,* 88.

Appendix B

1. Bird, 348,

2. Komer would be sent to South Vietnam as deputy to the U.S. military command and placed in charge of the pacification program—"Operation Phoenix."

3. Berman, *Lyndon Johnson's War,* 21.

4. Before the war, Rostow taught briefly at Columbia University.

5. On Rostow's early life and career, see Rostow, *Concept and Controversy,* 1–95. It is interesting that two of Rostow's works, *Concept and Controversy* and *Diffusion of Power,*

are partially autobiographical, but also richly descriptive and analytic on broader issues of economic and political development.

6. Kennedy's slogan "New Frontier" was adapted, in part from Rostow's notion of "new peaceful frontiers" in his book *Stages of Economic Growth* (Mulcahy, "Walt Rostow as National Security Adviser," 225).

7. On Rostow's NSC staff then State Department service, see Rostow, *Diffusion of Power,* 168–170.

8. Mulcahy, "Walt Rostow as National Security Adviser," 225; Schlesinger, *A Thousand Days,* 445.

9. Bird, 186.

10. Bird, 348.

11. Berman, *Lyndon Johnson's War,* 21.

12. Mulcahy, "Walt Rostow as National Security Adviser, 226; Halberstam, *Best and the Brightest,* 627.

13. Destler, *Presidents, Bureaucrats, and Foreign Policy,* 107.

14. Rostow, *Diffusion of Power,* 358–59. On the strengths and weaknesses of the Tuesday lunches, see Mulcahy, "Rethinking Groupthink," 239–243; Bromley Smith Oral History, July 29, 1969, Johnson Library, 22–28; and Smith, *Organizational History of the National Security Council,* 63.

15. Bromley Smith Oral History, July 29, 1969, Johnson Library, 23.

16. On the use of NSC meetings during this period, see Rostow, *Diffusion of Power,* 360–63; Mulcahy, "Rethinking Groupthink," 238–39; Bromley Smith Oral History, July 29, 1969, Johnson Library, 20–22; and Smith, *Organizational History of the National Security Council,* 65.

17. Bromley Smith Oral History, July 29, 1969, Johnson Library, 21.

18. Inderfurth and Johnson, "Transformation," 67.

19. Burke telephone interview with Harold Saunders, January 3, 2008.

20. Rostow, *Diffusion of Power,* 362.

21. According to Inderfurth and Johnson, "the SIG framework never became a very effective method for interagency coordination" ("Transformation," 67). Also see Destler, *Presidents, Bureaucrats, and Foreign Policy,* 104–5. According to Roger Morris, the SIGs and the IRGs "became merely rubber stamps for the process of passing on consensus memoranda, brokered by inter-agency vetos" (Morris, *Uncertain Greatness,* 75). According to Bromley Smith, then the executive secretary of the NSC, representatives from State "began sending papers from the [SIG] directly to the president, shorting out the secretary·of state . . . it was not a satisfactory procedure." Rostow "had to pick up the ball and put questions in shape so the president could deal with them" (Bromley Smith Oral History, July 29, 1969, Johnson Library, 19–20).

22. Burke telephone interview with Harold Saunders, January 3, 2008.

23. Ibid.

24. Dean Rusk Oral History, July 28, 1969, Johnson Library, 28. Rusk also felt Rostow did a good job in arranging for him to see LBJ when Rusk felt it was needed or to "put them in his evening reading and get a notation back as to the President's wishes" (26).

25. Bromley Smith Oral History, July 29, 1969, Johnson Library, 31.

26. Rostow, *Diffusion of Power,* 364–65.

27. Prados, 239.

28. Mulcahy, "Walt Rostow as NSC Adviser," 231; Clark and Legere, 83.

29. Destler, *Presidents, Bureaucrats, and Foreign Policy,* 108.

30. Mulcahy, "Walt Rostow as NSC Adviser," 232.

31. Prados, 239.

32. Mulcahy, "Walt Rostow as NSC Adviser," 227.

33. Inderfurth and Johnson, "Transformation," 67.

34. Morris, *Uncertain Greatness*, 77.

35. Berman, *Lyndon Johnson's War*, 22.

36. Ibid., 31.

37. Memorandum from Rostow to the President, March 22, 1967, *Foreign Relations of the United States*, Vol. 5, *Vietnam, 1967*, http://www.state.gov/r/pa/ho/frus/johnsonlb/v/13143.htm.

38. Berman, *Lyndon Johnson's War*, 29–30.

39. Ibid., 86–87.

40. Ibid., 163.

41. Memorandum from Rostow to the President, February 5, 1968, *Foreign Relations of the United States*, Vol. 6, *Vietnam, January–August 1968*, http://www.state.gov/r/pa/ho/frus/johnsonlb/vi/13690.htm; also see Rostow, *Diffusion of Power*, 466–67.

42. Rostow devotes a number of pages in *Concept and Controversy* to this issue, including comments after the war by North Vietnamese officials on the effects it might have had. But he was not able to sell the operation to Johnson, Rusk, and McNamara (see Rostow, *Concept and Controversy*, 299–302).

43. Berman, *Lyndon Johnson's War*, 48–49.

44. Memorandum from Rostow to the President, May 19, 1967, *Foreign Relations of the United States*, Vol. 5, *Vietnam, 1967*, http://www.state.gov/r/pa/ho/frus/johnsonlb/v/13148.htm.

45. Rostow's comments are part of a lengthy set of notes from the meeting; see Memorandum from the President's Assistant (Jones) to the President, November 2, 1967, *Foreign Relations of the United States*, Vol. 5, *Vietnam, 1967*, http://www.state.gov/r/pa/ho/frus/johnsonlb/v/13161.htm. On the wise men's meetings and their positions on Vietnam, see Berman, *Lyndon Johnson's War*, 96–104; and Schandler, *Lyndon Johnson and Vietnam*, 256–65.

46. Memorandum from Rostow to the President, November 2, 1967; for Rostow's summary of the view of the wise men, see Memorandum from Rostow to the President, November 3, 1967; Johnson also asked Rostow to explicitly compare the current views of McNamara and McGeorge Bundy, which can be found in Memorandum from Rostow to the President, November 4, 1967, all in *Foreign Relations of the United States*, Vol. 5, *Vietnam, 1967*, http://www.state.gov/r/pa/ho/frus/johnsonlb/v/13161.htm.

47. Berman, *Lyndon Johnson's War*, 84–85.

48. Memorandum from William J. Jorden to Walt Rostow and press secretary George Christian, August 31, 1967, *Foreign Relations of the United States*, Vol. 5, *Vietnam, 1967*, http://www.state.gov/r/pa/ho/frus/johnsonlb/v/13157.htm.

49. Prados, 250, 253.

50. Schandler, 83–84. Westmoreland and Bunker thought such an effort unwise and might indicate that they were panicking.

51. Ibid., 178; also see Rostow, *Diffusion of Power*, 520.

52. Berman, *Lyndon Johnson's War*, 57, emphasis added.

53. *Foreign Relations of the United States*, Vol. 5, *Vietnam, 1967*, http://www.state.gov/r/pa/ho/frus/johnsonlb/v/13155.htm.

54. Berman, *Lyndon Johnson's War*, 80.

55. Ibid., 117.

56. Miller, *Lyndon*, 413.

57. Memorandum from Rostow to the President, January 19, 1967, *Foreign Relations of the United States,* Vol. 5, *Vietnam, 1967,* http://www.state.gov/r/pa/ho/frus/johnsonlb/v/13137.htm.

58. Schandler, 257. Rostow's comments are from a 1972 article in *Esquire* magazine, "Aftermath, Losing Big" 12.

59. Schandler, 79–80; also see Rostow, *Diffusion of Power,* 462–64.

60. Rostow, *Concept and Controversy,* 303, 304. On his critique of how the war was being fought, see *Diffusion of Power,* 510–525.

61. Daalder and Destler, eds, "The Role of the National Security Adviser," 4.

62. Brinkley, *Dean Acheson,* 256–59.

63. See, for example, McPherson "Notes of Meeting," February 27, 1968, also Rostow Memorandum for the Record (to the President), February 29, 1968, *Foreign Relations of the United States,* Vol. 6, *Vietnam, January-August 1968,* http://www.state.gov/r/pa/ho/frus/johnsonlb/vi/13694.htm; also Berman, *Lyndon Johnson's War,* 191.

64. Schandler, 118. Rostow states much the same in *Diffusion of Power,* 520.

65. Schandler, 139.

66. On his critique of Clifford, who essentially had no plan in Rostow's view, see Schandler, 243.

67. Memorandum from Rostow to the President, March 6, 1968, and Memorandum from Rostow to Johnson, March 21, 1968, *Foreign Relations of the United States,* Vol. 6, *Vietnam, January-August 1968,* http://www.state.gov/r/pa/ho/frus/johnsonlb/vi/13698.htm; also see Berman, *Lyndon Johnson's War,* 182, 166, 192.

68. Berman, *Lyndon Johnson's War,* 159.

69. Schandler, 299. Since January 1968, Rostow had been part of a special committee at the undersecretary level that had been exploring options should peace talks materialize (Schandler, 181).

70. For Clifford's account of his efforts, see his memoirs, *Counsel to the President,* 496–526.

71. Schandler, 262. It is interesting to speculate what their response would have been had they known Johnson was not going to seek reelection.

72. Ibid., 260–61.

73. Clifford, 513; also see Bird, 368.

74. Schandler, 274.

75. "Nevertheless, as it became clear that Johnson leaned to Rusk's proposition—to try to induce negotiation by a bombing halt at the 20th parallel—I had less and less reserve about its timing" (Rostow, *Diffusion of Power,* 521); also see Schandler, 277. Clark Clifford notes that that White House counsel Harry McPherson had an important role in selling Johnson on the bombing halt, and Clifford regarded him as his "silent partner" (485).

76. Schandler, 325.

77. On the Carter transition, see Burke, *Presidential Transitions,* 17–54.

78. His father's last position had been consul general in Montreal, where Brzezinski earned his undergraduate degree at McGill University before attending Harvard for his doctorate.

79. On the Trilateral Commission, its work, and Carter's role, see Brzezinski, 5–6; Brzezinski Miller Center Oral History, February 18, 1982, Carter Library, 58–59; and Nelson, "The Evolution of the National Security State Ubiquitous and Endless," 287.

80. Carter, *Keeping Faith,* 51; Brzezinski Miller Center Oral History, February 18, 1992, Carter Library, 58–60.

81. Burke, *Presidential Transitions,* 32–33.

82. Brzezinski Miller Center Oral History, February 18, 1982, Carter Library, 62.

83. Brzezinski later recalled that full meetings of the cabinet, "were just awful . . . two hours of wasted time [on Monday mornings]. I started bringing the Monday morning new issues of *Time, Newsweek,* and *U.S. News and World Report* to cabinet meetings. . . . so I always had these magazines on my knees . . . and I read three magazines in these two hours because it was a waste of time. After a while we had cabinet meetings every two weeks, and then after a while I think we had them on the average maybe once a month or so" (Brzezinski, Miller Center Oral History, February 18, 1982, Carter Library, 64).

84. On the differences between Brzezinski and Kissinger, see Andrianopoulos, *Kissinger and Brzezinski.*

85. Carter, 52.

86. Mulcahy, "The Secretary of State and the National Security Adviser," 282.

87. Brzezinski, 76.

88. Ibid., 10.

89. In addition to the two principal committees, there were also lower-level, interdepartmental groups, chaired by senior agency officials, to deal with matters not requiring the attention of the SCC or PRC. Also, Vance usually chaired most PRC meetings, although a few were chaired by the secretary of defense, and a couple by the secretary of the treasury (Brzezinski, 59, Brzezinski Miller Center Oral History, February 18, 1982, Carter Library, 62–64).

90. On the development of the NSC system, see Brzezinski, 10, 58–63.

91. Brzezinski Miller Center Oral History, February 18, 1982, Carter Library, 63, 67.

92. Vance, *Hard Choices,* 37; also see Brzezinski, 62–63.

93. Brzezinski, 66.

94. Campbell, *Managing the Presidency,* 66.

95. Moens, *Foreign Policy under Carter,* 54, 62.

96. Lance, *The Truth of the Matter,* 107.

97. Bell, *Taking Care of the Law,* 39.

98. Campbell, *Managing the Presidency,* 66.

99. Vance, 37.

100. Ibid., 37–38. Muskie apparently followed his advice. On this whole issue of meeting reports, also see Brzezinski, Miller Center Oral History, February 18, 1982, Carter Library, 74.

101. Vance, 39.

102. Carter, Miller Center Oral History, November 29, 1982, Carter Library, 32.

103. Carter, 56.

104. Vance, 39.

105. Hargrove, *Carter as President,* 26.

106. Vance, 39.

107. Moens, *Foreign Policy Under Carter,* 40.

108. Brzezinski, 68.

109. Moens, *Foreign Policy Under Carter,* 48, 84.

110. Ibid., 48.

111. McFarlane, "The National Security Council," 264.

112. Bonafede, "Zbigniew Brzezinski," 194.

113. Gelb, "Brzezinski Says He'll Give Advice to Carter Only When he Asks for It."

114. Bonafede, "Zbigniew Brzezinski," 195 (emphasis added).

115. Brzezinski reviewed the document at the end of the administration and found seven of the ten major objectives had been achieved (Brzezinski Miller Center Oral History, February 18, 1982, Carter Library, 67).

116. Moens, *Foreign Policy Under Carter,* 172.

117. Brzezinski, 38.

118. Inderfurth and Johnson, "Transformation," 73.

119. Hodding Carter, "How Jimmy Carter's Foreign Policy Bit the Dust."

120. Brzezinski, 71.

121. Carter, 54.

122. Carter, Miller Center Oral History, November 29, 1982, Carter Library, 39.

123. Carter, 52.

124. Carter, Miller Center Oral History, November 29, 1982, Carter Library, 28; also see Brzezinski Miller Center Oral History, February 18, 1982, Carter Library, 66.

125. Albright, in Brzezinski Miller Center Oral History, February 18, 1982, Carter Library, 10–13. Her interview is part of the Brzezinski Oral History.

126. Carter, 54.

127. Ibid.

128. Brzezinski, 77–78.

129. Bock, 136, 145.

130. Vance, 35.

131. Moreover, according to Carter, Brzezinski was "always ready and willing to explain our position on international matters, analyze a basic strategic relationship, or comment on a current event. He and I recognized the problems generated within the State Department when he spoke out on an issue, and he did so much less frequently than would have been the case had he followed his natural inclinations. There were periods when we would agree that he refrain from making any public statements" (Carter, *Keeping Faith,* 53, 54).

132. Carter, Miller Center Oral History, November 29, 1982, Carter Library, 39.

133. Ibid., 40.

134. Brzezinski Miller Center Oral History, February 18, 1982, Carter Library, 65.

135. Carter, Miller Center Oral History, November 29, 1982, Carter Library, 40.

136. Carter, 54.

137. Brzezinski, 205–6.

138. Ibid., 219–220.

139. Rothkopf, 183.

140. According to Carter, he suspected some premeeting politicking on Brzezinski's part, when because of his medial condition the Shah sought exile in the United States: Vice President Mondale "was inclined to bring the Shah in. I think Brzezinski would work on Fritz privately and then sometimes Fritz would agree with him in a session. But Vance and I were very strongly opposed to it" (Carter, Miller Center Oral History, November 29, 1982, Carter Library, 37).

141. Vance, 328; Brzezinksi, 359–360, But Brzezinski also notes that he did not have daily contact with Zahedi as reported (370).

142. Carter, Miller Center Oral History, November 29, 1982, Carter Library, 40.

143. Ibid., 41.

144. Denand, in Brzezinski Miller Center Oral History, February 18, 1982, Carter Library, 21. Denand's interview is part of the Brzezinski Oral History.

145. Brzezinski Miller Center Oral History, February 18, 1982, Carter Library, 82.

146. Bonafede, "Zbigniew Brzezinski," 199.

147. Brzezinski Miller Center Oral History, February 18, 1982, Carter Library, 82.

148. Bonafede, "Zbigniew Brzezinski," 200.

149. Brzezinski Miller Center Oral History, February 18, 1982, Carter Library, 82.

150. Bonafede, "Zbigniew Brzezinski," 199.

151. Albright, in Brzezinski Miller Center Oral History, February 18, 1982, Carter Library, 18.

152. Brzezinski, 71.

153. Brzezinski, Miller Center Oral History, February 18, 1982, Carter Library, 91.

154. Lake, "Carter's Foreign Policy: Success Abroad, Failure at Home," 149.

155. Inderfurth and Johnson, "Transformation," 74.

156. Mulcahy, "The Secretary of State and the National Security Adviser," 285.

157. Crabb and Mulcahy, *American National Security,* 158, 161.

158. Clinton, *My Life,* 290, 333; Apple, "A Domestic Sort with Global Worries."

159. Clinton, 383.

160. Ibid., 455–56.

161. Although Clinton had considered others for State—including Colin Powell and Sen. Sam Nunn (D-GA)—the choice of Christopher came as no surprise. Secretary of defense proved more difficult. Powell was again considered, as was Rep. David McCurdy (D-OK). Sam Nunn was again a leading candidate, but he told Clinton he already had enough involvement in defense matters and wanted to do other things.

162. National Security Council, "History of the National Security Council;" also see Auger, "The National Security Council System After the Cold War," 52–54.

163. Oberdorfer, "Balkans, Haiti, Iraq, and Somalia Head NSC Policy Study List."

164. Myers's relationship to Lake started out rocky: no one bothered to inform the press secretary of the June 1993 bombing of Iraq in retaliation for the assassination plot against former President Bush during his Kuwait visit. But later, according to Birnbaum, their relationship improved: "the two had struck up a working relationship that allowed them to remain in steady and largely informal contact during the course of the day." Lake saw to it that Myers was present in some of the important meetings. According to Birnbaum, "unlike other men in the White House," as a former professor at Mt. Holyoke, "he was accustomed to dealing with women in the normal course of business" (Birnbaum, *Madhouse,* 164, 168–69).

165. DeParle, "The Man Inside Bill Clinton's Foreign Policy," 37.

166. Ibid., 46.

167. Ibid., 37.

168. Burke telephone interview with Anthony Lake, November 1, 2007.

169. Auger, "The National Security Council System After the Cold War," 62, emphasis in original; also see Sciolino, "3 Players Seek a Director for Foreign Policy Story."

170. Burke telephone interview with Anthony Lake, November 1, 2007.

171. DeParle, "The Man Inside Bill Clinton's Foreign Policy," 37.

172. Lake, *6 Nightmares,* 131.

173. Ibid., 131–32.

174. According to Goldgeier, the author of several works on NATO expansion during the Clinton years, Lake was initially one of "few key people" who wanted to see rapid expansion take place. "Lake encouraged the president to make statements supporting expansion and then used those statements to direct the [NSC] staff to develop a plan and a timetable for putting these ideas into action." Yet Goldgeier also argues that the decision process "was not at all clearcut." Many of those he interviewed could not put their finger on the point when a decision had been made. Moreover, "These interpretations vary so widely because the president and his top advisers did not make a formal decision about a timetable or process for expansion until long after Clinton had started saying NATO would enlarge" (Goldgeier, "NATO Expansion," 340, 352; also see Goldgeier, *Not Whether But When,* 11, 38–39, 44, 152–55, 159, for more extended analysis of what Goldgeier term's Lake's role as a key "policy entrepreneur"; on problems in the decision-making process, especially concerns from Defense and the Joints Chiefs about what had been decided, see 163–66).

175. See Rothkopf, 351–53.

176. See Lake, *6 Nightmares,* 118–128. For a comprehensive analysis of the administration's Northern Ireland policy, see Lynch, *Turf War,* especially 32, 48–50, 92–98, 114–17, 121–27, 136–37 on Lake's involvement and that of Nancy Soderberg, who held the then number three position on the NSC staff as "staff director."

177. Lake, "Frontline Interview," 4.

178. Burke telephone interview with Anthony Lake, November 1, 2007.

179. Ibid.

180. Ibid.

181. Ibid.

182. Ibid.

183. Rothkopf, 346.

184. Albright, *Madame Secretary,* 166.

185. Ibid., 383.

186. Ibid., 132.

187. Rothkopf, 358.

188. Morris, *Behind the Oval Office,* 246.

189. Inderfurth and Johnson, "National Security Advisers," 178; also see Heilbrunn, "Lake Inferior," 34.

190. DeParle, "The Man Inside Bill Clinton's Foreign Policy," 34

191. National Security Council, "History of the National Security Council."

192. Marcus, "Anthony Lake's Secretive Mission."

193. Ibid.

194. National Security Council, "History of the National Security Council."

195. Lake, *6 Nightmares,* 262.

196. Burke telephone interview with Anthony Lake, November 1, 2007.

197. Lake, *6 Nightmares,* 261.

198. Ibid., 259; on Dick Morris's efforts (frustrated, in his view, by Lake) to inject more political calculation into foreign policy decisions, see Morris, *Behind the Oval Office,* 244–47. According to Morris, "Whenever I came too close to NSC issues, the foreign policy staff honked like geese in a pond, warning one another of an approaching dog. Tony Lake, deeply idealistic but highly territorial, thought political advice was unchaste" (245).

199. Lake, *6 Nightmares,* 261, 262.

200. Burke telephone interview with Anthony Lake, November 1, 2007.

201. Ibid.

202. Ibid.

203. Ibid.

204. National Security Council, "History of the National Security Council."

205. As Lake further notes, "Because if it looks like there is a House of York and a House of Lancaster, then reporters will immediately start playing the traditional game of going to folks at the State Department and saying, 'Here's what the NSC says is happening' and at the State Department, the testosterone will flow and the State Department officials will on background say, 'No, here's what is happening' and then they will take it back to the NSC staffer and the NSC staffer will fight back, and it gets out of control" (Burke telephone interview with Anthony Lake, November 1, 2007).

206. Burke telephone interview with Anthony Lake, November 1, 2007. Other accounts indicate the confrontation took place at the Waldorf-Astoria Hotel and involved Christopher's chief of staff, Tom Donilon, and White House press secretary Michael McCurry (DeParle, "The Man Inside Bill Clinton's Foreign Policy," 57).

207. Sciolino, "2 Key Advisers in a Bitter Duel on U.S. Foreign Policy." According to Elizabeth Drew, despite his professorial, courteous, and somewhat reserved demeanor, "Lake was in fact a tough, highly competitive man, emotional and quite at home with four-letter words" (Drew, *On the Edge,* 140).

208. DeParle, "The Man Inside Bill Clinton's Foreign Policy," 38.

209. Rothkopf, 322; also see Burke, *Presidential Transitions,* 305, 309, 339–340; Auger, "The National Security System After the Cold War," 55.

210. Burke telephone interview with Anthony Lake, November 1, 2007.

211. Drew, *On the Edge,* 144.

212. McManus, "Clinton Defers to Aides on Foreign Policy."

213. Drew, *On the Edge,* 153.

214. Barnes, "You're Fired," 12.

215. Hoagland, "Flaws and Fissures in Foreign Policy."

216. Powell, 576.

217. Auger, "The National Security Council System After the Cold War," 68.

218. Christopher, *In the Stream of History,* 129–130.

219. Daalder, *Getting to Dayton,* 71.

220. Auger, "The National Security Council System After the Cold War," 62.

221. Drew, *On the Edge,* 150.

222. Auger, "The National Security Council System After the Cold War," 60.

223. Ibid.

224. Drew, *On the Edge,* 145.

225. McAllister, "Secretary of Shhhhh!" 33.

226. Gelb, "Clinton's Security Trio."

227. McAllister, "Secretary of Shhhhh!" 33.

228. Barnes, "You're Fired," 12

229. Broder, "Wobbling Dangerously."

230. Lake, *6 Nightmares,* 130.

231. Balz and Woodward, "America's Road to War."

232. Rwanda might also be added to the list. In 1994, when racial strife broke out in Rwanda, an estimated one million people died in the ensuing violence. Yet the White House took no action. It was "one of the greatest regrets of my presidency," Clinton notes in his memoirs (553).

233. Bose, "Priorities and Policy Making," 5.

234. The troops were scheduled to leave by March 31, 1994.

235. Bose, "Priorities and Policy Making," 5.

236. Berger, "*Frontline* Interview," 6.

237. Burke telephone interview with Anthony Lake, November 1, 2007.

238. Lake, *6 Nightmares,* 131.

239. Ibid., 260.

240. Bose, "Priorities and Policy Making," 6.

241. For an inside account, see Lake, *6 Nightmares,* 132–141.

242. In September 1994, 19,600 U.S. troops were initially introduced, and in March 1995 a U.N. commander took over, with the U.S. providing 2,400 of the 6,000 U.N. force. The U.N. force was withdrawn a year later.

243. Drew, *On the Edge,* 146.

244. Ibid., 153.

245. The effort sought to bring the warring parties (especially the Bosnian Serbs) to agreement on the Vance-Owens plan, which had been developed by U.N. negotiators Cyrus

Vance and David Owens. Some in the Clinton inner circle felt that the plan rewarded Bosnian Serb aggression by moving Bosnian Muslims into enclaves and dividing the nation into autonomous provinces. Yet, Vance-Owens had the support of the European Union and a U.S. alternative to the plan might led to charges that the United States had aborted the then still ongoing peace process as well as greater responsibility by the United States rather than the European allies to devise a solution to the crisis (see Daalder, *Getting to Dayton,* 10–19).

246. Drew, *On the Edge,* 157.

247. Christopher, *In the Stream of History,* 347.

248. Drew, *On the Edge,* 163.

249. In fact, both a NATO and a U.N. agreement were required for any air strikes.

250. Lake, *6 Nightmares,* 132. Daalder's account of the February 1994 cease-fire agreement presents a more complex narrative in which Clinton's efforts at the January 1994 NATO meeting are less central as the impetus for the eventual cease-fire; but they did provide an opening for proponents of stronger intervention, such as Lake and Albright, to move the administration in a more forceful posture (see Daalder, *Getting to Dayton,* 23–26). For Lake's account of events in Bosnia in the fall of 1994 through 1995, see Lake, *6 Nightmares,* 142–151.

251. Daalder, *Getting to Dayton,* 84; Rothkopf, 366.

252. Christopher, *In the Stream of History,* 347.

253. Woodward, *The Choice,* 258–59.

254. Burke telephone interview with Anthony Lake, November 1, 2007.

255. Ibid.

256. Lake, *6 Nightmares,* 146–150; also see Christopher, *Chances of a Lifetime,* 255; and Woodward, *The Choice,* 260–68.

257. See Christopher, *Chances of a Lifetime,* 255–271. Some 20,000 U.S. troops would be sent as part of the NATO peacekeeping force in Bosnia. The last contingent left nine years later, in December 2004; there were no military personnel killed due to hostile action.

258. For an excellent account of the deliberative process, see Daalder, *Getting to Dayton,* 90–114.

259. Ibid., 172.

260. Sciolino, "Christopher Spells out New Priorities."

261. Harris, "As Clinton Adviser, Berger Combines Stagecraft with Statecraft."

262. See Christopher, *Chances of a Lifetime,* 212–226.

263. Inderfurth and Johnson, "National Security Advisers," 178.

264. Harris, "As Clinton Adviser, Berger Combines Stagecraft with Statecraft."

265. Harris, "Berger's Caution Has Shaped Role of U.S. in War."

266. As Albright notes in her memoirs, Berger was opposed to a more aggressive stand: "You can't just talk about bombing in the middle of Europe. What target would you hit? What would you do the day after? It is irresponsible to keep making threatening statements outside of some coherent plan. The way you people talk at the State Department about bombing, you sound like lunatics" (Albright, *Madame Secretary,* 383).

267. Albright, *Madame Secretary,* 318.

268. Perlez, "With Berger in Catbird Seat, Albright's Star Dims."

269. Erlanger, "Albright, a Bold Voice Abroad, Finds Her Role Limited at Home."

270. Perlez, "With Berger in Catbird Seat, Albright's Star Dims."

271. Ibid.

272. Harris, "As Clinton Adviser, Berger Combines Stagecraft with Statecraft."

273. Forum on the Role of the National Security Adviser, 146.

274. Ibid., 142, 146.

275. Daalder and Destler, eds., "The Clinton Administration National Security Council," 17.

276. Perlez, "With Berger in Catbird Seat, Albright's Star Dims."

277. *National Journal,* "Samuel Berger," 1176.

278. Albright, "*Frontline* Interview," 9.

279. Albright, *Madame Secretary,* 349.

280. Harris, "Berger's Caution Has Shaped Role of U.S. in War"; Albright, *Madame Secretary,* 349.

281. Albright, *Madame Secretary,* 349.

282. Ahrens, "The Reluctant Warrior."

283. Ibid.

284. Albright, *Madame Secretary,* 348.

285. Ibid., 348–49.

286. Albright, "*Frontline* Interview," 8.

287. Albright, *Madame Secretary,* 348.

288. Morris, *Behind the Oval Office,* 245–46.

289. *National Journal,* "Samuel Berger," 1175–76.

290. Harris, "Berger's Caution Has Shaped Role of U.S. in War."

291. Morris, *Behind the Oval Office,* 246.

292. Daalder and Destler, eds., "The Clinton Administration National Security Council," 19.

293. Forum on the Role of the National Security Adviser, 151–52.

294. Inderfurth and Johnson, "National Security Advisers," 179; *National Journal,* "Samuel Berger," 1175–76.

295. Harris, "As Clinton Adviser, Berger Combines Stagecraft with Statecraft."

296. *National Journal,* "Samuel Berger," 1175.

297. Weiner and Risen, "Decision to Strike Factory in Sudan Based on Surmise;" also see Hersh, "The Missiles of August"; and Risen, "To Bomb Sudan Plant or Not: A Year Later, Debates Rankle." That the attack took place near the time of Clinton's grand jury testimony on the Lewinsky scandal and his admission of a relationship to her also generated some criticisms if not suspicions, see Guliotta and Eilperin, "Tough Response Appeals to Critics of President." The timing of a set of air strikes on Iraq—as the House of Representatives began to undertake its vote on Mr. Clinton's impeachment in December of 1998—raised similar questions.

298. Sciolino and Bronner, "How a President Distracted by Scandal, Entered Balkan War"; also see Weiner and Perlez, "How Clinton Approved the Strikes on Belgrade"; Myers and Schmitt, "War's Conduct Creates Tensions Among Chiefs"; and Steven Erlanger, "NATO Was Closer to Ground War in Kosovo Than Is Widely Realized."

299. Mandelbaum, "A Perfect Failure," 2.

300. Harris, "Berger's Caution Has Shaped Role of U.S. in War."

301. Harris, "In Handling of Crisis, a Different President."

302. According to one account, "White House miscalculation led to talks without a focus" (Sanger, "The Shipwreck in Seattle").

303. Lake, *6 Nightmares,* 239, 240.

304. Berger, "*Frontline* Interview," 8.

305. *National Journal,* "Samuel Berger," 1175.

306. Sanger, "Missile Shield Point Man Does Not Shy From Tough Fight."

307. Thomas, "The Quiet Power of Condi Rice," 28; also see Kessler and Slevin, "Rice Fails to Repair Rifts"; Woodward, *Plan of Attack,* 175–76, 415; and Robbins, "New Security Post Lifts Hadley's Profile." DeYoung especially notes Deputy Secretary of State Richard Armitage's use of the word "dysfunctional," and also that term's use by one former Republican cabinet official (477).

308. Thomas, "The 12 Year Itch," 64–65.

309. Rothkopf, 414; also see De Young, 335, 398, 477–78; and Kessler, "For New National Security Adviser, a Mixed Record."

310. Risen, *State of War,* 161, 163.

311. Woodward, *Bush at War,* 112.

312. Ibid., 225.

313. On the October speech see Tenet, 450–51. In his memoirs, Tenet also notes a January 6, 2003, meeting with Rice and Hadley where one of his CIA aides noted that the nuclear case was weak. At a later meeting Hadley asked for more material on Iraq's efforts to obtain nuclear weapons, which the CIA then provided, and from which Tenet then argues NSC officials took some material on uranium purchases out of context, eventually finding their way into the State of the Union speech (371). Tenet later notes in his memoirs that the internal CIA vetting process of the State of the Union speech had broken down and that he had failed "to fully study the speech myself" (459; also see 449–75 where Tenet devotes a full chapter to the episode).

314. Sanger and Miller, "National Security Aide Says He's to Blame for Speech Error"; also see Kessler, "For New National Security Adviser, a Mixed Record."

315. The one exception to this pattern—although its symmetry is a bit different— occurred when Clark, who had been Haig's deputy at State, moved over to the NSC advisor position. Clark, as we saw, initially tried to keep relations with Haig civil and effective, but Haig had difficulties and battled with whoever occupied whatever White House position— whether NSC advisor or chief of staff.

316. Stolberg, "Quiet Bush Aide Seeks Iraq Czar, Creating a Stir."

317. Robbins, "New Security Post Lifts Hadley's Profile."

318. Baker, "The Security Adviser Who Wants the Role, Not the Stage."

319. Ibid. Yet as Dana Milbank notes, Hadley was the "invisible man of the Bush presidency. . . . Hadley has had a leading role in the foreign-policy adventures of the past eight years—and yet he leaves no fingerprints," (Milbank, "The Man Who Wasn't There, Still Here").

320. Stolberg, "Quiet Bush Aide Seeks Iraq Czar, Creating a Stir."

321. Ibid.

322. Ibid.; also see Robbins, "New Security Post Lifts Hadley's Profile."

323. Stolberg, "Quiet Bush Aide Seeks Iraq Czar, Creating a Stir."

324. Woodward, *State of Denial,* 364, 368.

325. Ibid., 419.

326. Baker, "The Security Adviser Who Wants the Role, Not the Stage."

327. Baker, "Bush Aide to Leave No. 2 National Security Post."

328. Baker, "The Security Adviser Who Wants the Role, Not the Stage."

329. Hadley was succeeded as deputy NSC advisor by J. D. Crouch II. Crouch was apparently more hawkish in his views than others in the administration; he favored a harder line toward North Korea and Iran than was ultimately pursued. Yet despite his strong views, reports indicated that he ran the interagency process well and was something of an honest broker. According to Undersecretary of Defense Eric S. Edelman, "While not disguising his views or pretending he didn't have any, he managed to be incredibly fair and objective and ran an even-handed process that gave everybody a chance to put their oar in the water" (Baker, "The Security Adviser Who Wants the Role, Not the Stage"). Crouch's successor was James F. Jeffrey, who took over in August 2007. Jeffrey was a career foreign service officer who had held a variety assignments relating to Europe and the Middle East. Most notable was his prior work as deputy assistant secretary of state for the Near East and senior adviser on Iraq to the secretary of state.

330. Duffy and Kukis, "Why the Surge Worked," 30.

331. See Barnes, "How Bush Decided on the Surge," 24–25; and Baker, "Bush Aide to Leave No. 2 National Security Post."

332. Efron, "So, What's Not to Like About Amiable Advisor?"

333. Baker, "The Security Adviser Who Wants the Role, Not the Stage."

Bibliography

Books

Abshire, David M. *Saving the Reagan Presidency.* College Station: Texas A&M University Press, 2005.

Adams, Sherman. *Firsthand Report: The Story of the Eisenhower Administration.* New York: Harper & Brothers, 1961.

Albright, Madeleine, with Bill Woodward. *Madame Secretary: A Memoir.* New York: Miramax, 2003.

Ambrose, Stephen E. *Nixon: The Triumph of a Politician, 1962–1972.* New York: Simon & Schuster, 1989.

Anderson, Martin. *Revolution: The Reagan Legacy.* Stanford, Calif.; Hoover Institution Press, 1990.

Andrianopoulos, Gerry Argyris. *Kissinger and Brzezinski: The NSC and the Struggle for Control of US National Security Policy.* New York: St. Martin's Press, 1991.

Baker, James A. III. *The Politics of Diplomacy.* New York: G. P. Putnam's Sons, 1995.

———. *Work Hard, Study . . . and Keep Out of Politics!: Adventures and Lessons from an Unexpected Life.* New York: G. P. Putnam's Sons, 2006.

Ball, George W. *The Past Has Another Pattern.* New York: Norton, 1982.

Bamford, James. *A Pretext for War: 9/11: Iraq and the Abuse of America's Intelligence Agencies.* New York: Doubleday, 2004.

Bell, Griffin B. *Taking Care of the Law.* New York: Wm. Morrow, 1982.

Berman, Larry. *Lyndon Johnson's War: The Road to Stalemate in Vietnam.* New York: Norton: 1989.

———. *No Peace, No Honor: Nixon, Kissinger, and Betrayal in Vietnam.* New York: Free Press, 2001.

Beschloss, Michael R., and Strobe Talbott. *At the Highest Levels: The Inside Story of the End of the Cold War.* Boston: Little, Brown, 1993.

Bird, Kai. *The Color of Truth: McGeorge Bundy and William Bundy: Brothers in Arms.* New York: Simon & Schuster, 1998.

Birnbaum, Jeffrey H. *Madhouse: The Private Turmoil of Working for the President.* New York: Random House, 1996.

Bock, Joseph G. *The White House Staff and the National Security Assistant: Friendship and Friction at the Water's Edge.* New York: Greenwood, 1987.

Bose, Meena. *Shaping and Signaling Presidential Policy: The National Security Decision Making of Eisenhower and Kennedy.* College Station: Texas A&M University Press, 1998.

Bowie, Robert R., and Richard H. Immerman. *Waging Peace: How Eisenhower Shaped an Enduring Cold War Strategy.* New York: Oxford University Press, 1998.

Bremer, L. Paul III. *My Year in Iraq: The Struggle to Build a Future of Hope.* New York: Simon & Schuster, 2006.

Brinkley, Douglas. *Dean Acheson: The Cold War Years, 1953–1971.* New Haven: Yale University Press, 1992.

Brownell, Herbert, with John P. Burke. *Advising Ike: The Memoirs of Attorney General Herbert Brownell.* Lawrence: University Press of Kansas, 1993.

Bruni, Frank. *Ambling into History: The Unlikely Odyssey of George W. Bush.* New York: HarperCollins, 2002.

Brzezinski, Zbigniew. *Power and Principle: Memoirs of the National Security Adviser, 1977–1981.* New York: Farrar, Strauss, and Giroux, 1983.

Bumiller, Elisabeth. *Condoleezza Rice: An American Life.* New York: Random House, 2007.

Bundy, McGeorge, ed. *The Pattern of Responsibility.* Boston: Houghton Mifflin, 1952.

———. *Danger and Survival: Choices About the Bomb in the First Fifty Years.* New York: Random House, 1988.

Burke, John P. *Presidential Transitions: From Politics to Practice.* Boulder, Colo.: Lynne Rienner, 2000.

———. *The Institutional Presidency: Organizing and Managing the White House from FDR to Clinton.* Baltimore: Johns Hopkins University Press, 2000.

———. *Becoming President: The Bush Transition, 2000–2003.* Boulder, Colo.: Lynne Rienner, 2004.

Burke, John P., and Fred I. Greenstein, with Larry Berman and Richard Immerman. *How Presidents Test Reality: Decisions on Vietnam, 1954 and 1965.* New York: Russell Sage, 1989.

Bush, George H. W., and Brent Scowcroft. *A World Transformed.* New York: Knopf, 1998.

Campbell, Colin. *Managing the Presidency: Carter, Reagan, and the Search for Executive Harmony.* Pittsburgh, Pa.: University of Pittsburgh Press, 1986.

Cannon, James. *Time and Chance: Gerald Ford's Appointment with History.* New York: HarperCollins, 1994.

Cannon, Lou. *President Reagan: The Role of a Lifetime.* New York: Simon & Schuster 1991.

Caraley, Demetrios. *The Politics of Military Unification: A Study of Conflict and the Policy Process.* New York: Columbia University Press, 1966.

Carter, Jimmy. *Keeping Faith: Memoirs of a President.* New York: Bantam Books, 1982.

Christopher, Warren. *In the Stream of History: Shaping Foreign Policy for a New Era.* Stanford, Calif.: Stanford University Press, 1998.

———. *Chances of a Lifetime.* New York: Scribner, 2001.

Clark, Keith C., and Laurence Legere, eds. *The President and the Management of National Security: A Report by the Institute for Defense Analysis.* New York: Praeger, 1969.

Clarke, Richard A. *Against All Enemies: Inside America's War on Terror.* New York: Free Press, 2004.

Clifford, Clark, with Richard Holbrooke. *Counsel to the President: A Memoir.* New York: Doubleday, 1991.

Clinton, Bill. *My Life.* New York: Knopf, 2004.

Crabb, Cecil V., and Kevin Mulcahy. *Presidents and Foreign Policy Making: From FDR to Reagan.* Baton Rouge: Louisiana State University Press, 1986.

———. *American National Security: A Presidential Perspective.* Pacific Grove, Calif.: Brooks/Cole, 1991.

Cutler, Robert. *No Time for Rest.* Boston: Little, Brown, 1965.

Daalder, Ivo H. *Getting to Dayton: The Making of America's Bosnia Policy.* Washington, D.C.: Brookings Institution, 2000.

Dallek, Robert. *An Unfinished Life: John F. Kennedy, 1917–1963.* Boston: Little, Brown, 2003.

———. *Nixon and Kissinger: Partners in Power.* New York: HarperCollins, 2007.

Deaver, Michael K., with Mickey Herskowitz. *Behind the Scenes.* New York: Wm. Morrow, 1987.

DeFrank, Thomas M. *Write It When I'm Gone: Remarkable Off-the-Record Conversations with Gerald R. Ford.* New York: G. P. Putnam's Sons, 2007.

Destler, I. M. *Presidents, Bureaucrats, and Foreign Policy.* Princeton, N.J.: Princeton University Press, 1972.

DeYoung, Karen. *Soldier: The Life of Colin Powell.* New York: Knopf, 2006.

Drew, Elizabeth. *On the Edge.* New York: Simon & Schuster, 1994.

Ehrlichman, John. *Witness to Power: The Nixon Years.* New York: Simon & Schuster, 1982.

Eisenhower, Dwight D. *Mandate for Change, 1953–1956.* Garden City, N.Y.: Doubleday, 1963.

———. *Waging Peace.* Garden City, N.Y.: Doubleday, 1965.

Federal Document Clearing House. *U.S. Senate Armed Services Committee Hold Hearings on Nominations, February 27, 2003.* Washington, D.C.: Federal Document Clearing House, 2003.

Feith, Douglas J. *War and Decision: Inside the Pentagon at the Dawn of the War on Terrorism.* New York: Harper, 2008.

Ford, Gerald R. *A Time to Heal: The Autobiography of Gerald R. Ford.* New York: Harper & Row, 1979.

Foreign Relations of the United States, Vol. 2, *National Security Affairs,* Part 1. Washington, D.C.: Government Printing Office, 1984.

Foreign Relations of the United States, Vol. 4, *Vietnam, 1966.* Washington, D.C.: Government Printing Office, 1998.

Foreign Relations of the United States, Vol. 5, *Vietnam, 1967.* Washington, D.C.: Government Printing Office, 2002.

Foreign Relations of the United States, Vol. 6, *Vietnam, January–August 1968.* Washington, D.C.: Government Printing Office, 2002.

Foreign Relations of the United States, Vol. 10, *Cuba, 1961–1962.* Washington, D.C.: Government Printing Office, 1997.

Frankel, Max. *High Noon in the Cold War: Kennedy, Khrushchev, and the Cuban Missile Crisis.* New York: Ballantine, 2004.

Franks, Tommy. *American Soldier.* New York: Regan Books, 2004.

Freedman, Lawrence. *Kennedy's Wars: Berlin, Cuba, Laos, and Vietnam.* New York: Oxford University Press, 2000.

Frum, David. *The Right Man: The Surprise Presidency of George W. Bush.* New York: Random House, 2003.

Garrison, Jean A. *Games Advisors Play: Foreign Policy in the Nixon and Carter Administrations.* College Station: Texas A&M University Press, 1999.

George, Alexander L. *Presidential Decisionmaking in Foreign Policy: The Effective Use of Information and Advice.* Boulder, Colo.: Westview, 1980.

Goldgeier, James M. *Not Whether But When: The U.S. Decision to Enlarge NATO.* Washington, D.C.: Brookings Institution, 1999.

Gordon, Michael R., and Bernard Trainor. *Cobra II: The Inside Story of the Invasion of Iraq.* New York: Pantheon, 2006.

Greene, John Robert. *The Presidency of Gerald R. Ford.* Lawrence: University Press of Kansas, 1995.

———. *The Presidency of George Bush.* Lawrence: University Press of Kansas, 2000.

Greenstein, Fred I. *The Hidden-Hand Presidency: Eisenhower as Leader.* New York: Basic Books, 1982.

———. *The Presidential Difference: Leadership Style from FDR to George W. Bush.* Princeton, N.J.: Princeton University Press, 2004.

Haig, Alexander. *Caveat: Realism, Reagan and Foreign Policy.* New York: Macmillan, 1984.

Halberstam, David. *The Best and the Brightest.* New York: Penguin, 1972.

Haldeman, H. R. *The Ends of Power.* New York: New York Times Books, 1978.

—. *The Haldeman Diaries: Inside the Nixon White House.* New York: Putnam, 1994.

Halperin, Morton H. *Bureaucratic Politics and Foreign Policy.* Washington, D.C.: Brookings Institution, 1974.

Hammond, Paul Y. *Organizing for Defense: The American Military Establishment in the Twentieth Century.* Princeton, N.J.: Princeton University Press, 1961.

Haney, Patrick J. *Organizing for Foreign Policy Crises: Presidents, Advisers, and the Management of Decision Making.* Ann Arbor: University of Michigan Press, 1997.

Hargrove, Erwin C. *Jimmy Carter as President: Leadership and the Politics of the Public Good.* Baton Rouge: Louisiana State University Press, 1988.

Henry, Laurin L. *Presidential Transitions.* Washington, D.C.: Brookings Institution, 1960.

Hersh, Seymour M. *The Price of Power: Kissinger in the Nixon White House.* New York: Simon & Schuster, 1983.

—. *The Dark Side of Camelot.* Boston: Little, Brown, 1997.

Herspring, Dale R. *The Pentagon and the Presidency: Civil-Military Relations from FDR to George W. Bush.* Lawrence: University Press of Kansas, 2005.

Higgins, Trumbull. *The Perfect Failure: Kennedy, Eisenhower, and the CIA at the Bay of Pigs.* New York: Norton, 1987.

Hitchens, Christopher. *The Trial of Henry Kissinger.* New York: Verso, 2001.

Hughes, Karen. *Ten Minutes from Normal.* New York: Viking, 2004.

Humphrey, Hubert H. *The Education of a Public Man: My Life and Politics.* Garden City, N.Y.: Doubleday, 1976.

Hyland, William. *Mortal Rivals: Superpower Relations from Nixon to Reagan.* New York: Random House, 1987.

Isaacson, Walter. *Kissinger: A Biography.* New York: Simon & Schuster, 1992.

Jackson, Henry M., ed. *The National Security Council: Jackson Subcommittee Papers on Policy-Making at the Presidential Level.* New York: Praeger, 1965.

Janis, Irving L. *Groupthink: Psychological Studies of Policy Decisions and Fiascoes.* Boston: Houghton Mifflin, 1982.

—. *Crucial Decisions: Leadership in Policymaking and Crisis Management.* New York: Free Press, 1989.

Kahin, George McT. *Intervention: How America Became Involved in Vietnam.* New York: Knopf, 1986.

Kengor, Paul, and Patricia Clark Doerner. *The Judge: William P. Clark, Ronald Reagan's Top Hand.* San Francisco: Ignatius Press, 2007.

Kessler, Glenn. *The Confidante: Condoleezza Rice and the Creation of the Bush Legacy.* New York: St. Martin's Press, 2007.

Kessler, Ronald. *A Matter of Character: Inside the White House of George W. Bush.* New York: Sentinel, 2004.

Kettl, Donald F. *Team Bush: Leadership Lessons from the Bush White House.* New York: McGraw-Hill, 2003.

Kinnard, Douglas. *President Eisenhower and Strategy Management: A Study in Defense Politics.* Lexington: University Press of Kentucky, 1977.

Kissinger, Henry. *The White House Years.* Boston: Little, Brown, 1979.

—. *Years of Upheaval.* Boston: Little, Brown, 1982.

—. *Years of Renewal.* New York: Simon & Schuster, 1999.

Kowert, Paul A. *Groupthink or Deadlock: When Do Leaders Learn from Their Advisors?* Albany: SUNY Press, 2002.

Lake, Anthony. *6 Nightmares.* Boston: Little, Brown, 2000.

Lance, Bert. *The Truth of the Matter: My Life In and Out of Politics.* New York: Summit Books, 1991.

Lord, Carnes. *The Presidency and the Management of National Security.* New York: Free Press, 1988.

Lynch, Timothy J. *Turf War: The Clinton Administration and Northern Ireland.* Burlington, Vt.: Ashgate, 2004.

Mabry, Marcus. *Twice as Good: Condoleezza Rice and Her Rise to Power.* New York: Modern Times, 2007.

Mann, James. *Rise of the Vulcans: The History of Bush's War Cabinet.* New York: Viking, 2004.

May, Ernest R., and Philip D. Zelikow. *The Kennedy Tapes: Inside the White House During the Cuban Missile Crisis.* Cambridge, Mass.: Harvard University Press, 1997.

McFarlane, Robert C., and Zofia Smardz. *Special Trust.* New York: Cadell & Davies, 1994.

Meese, Edwin. *With Reagan: The Inside Story.* Washington, D.C.: Regnery Gateway, 1992.

Miller, Merle. *Lyndon: An Oral Biography.* New York: G. P. Putnam's Sons, 1980.

Millis, Walter, with Harvey C. Mansfield and Harold Stein, *Arms and the State: Civil-Military Elements in National Policy.* New York: Twentieth Century Fund, 1958.

Moens, Alexander. *Foreign Policy under Carter: Testing Multiple Advocacy Decision Making.* Boulder, Colo.: Westview, 1990.

———. *The Foreign Policy of George W. Bush: Values, Strategy and Vision.* Burlington, Vt.: Ashgate, 2004.

Morris, Dick. *Behind the Oval Office.* New York: Random House, 1997.

Morris, Edmund. *Dutch: A Memoir of Ronald Reagan.* New York: Random House, 1999.

Morris, Roger. *Uncertain Greatness: Henry Kissinger and American Foreign Policy.* New York: Harper & Row, 1977.

Neustadt, Richard E. *Presidential Power and the Modern Presidents: The Politics of Leadership From Roosevelt to Reagan.* New York: Macmillan, 1990.

Newmann, William W. *Managing National Security Policy: The President and the Process.* Pittsburgh, Pa.: University of Pittsburgh Press, 2003.

Nixon, Richard M. *RN: The Memoirs of Richard Nixon.* New York: Grosset & Dunlap, 1978.

Ponder, Daniel E. *Good Advice: Information and Policy Making in the White House.* College Station: Texas A&M University Press, 2000.

Porter, Roger B. *Presidential Decision Making: The Economic Policy Board.* Cambridge, Mass.: Cambridge University Press, 1980.

Powell, Colin, with Joseph E. Persico. *My American Journey.* New York: Random House, 1995.

Prados, John. *Keepers of the Keys: A History of the National Security Council from Truman to Bush.* New York: William Morrow, 1991.

Preston, Andrew. *The War Council: McGeorge Bundy, the NSC, and Vietnam.* Cambridge, Mass.: Harvard University Press, 2006.

Preston, Thomas. *The President and His Inner Circle: Leadership Styles and the Advisory Process in Foreign Affairs.* New York: Columbia University Press, 2001.

Reagan, Ronald. *An American Life.* New York: Simon & Schuster, 1990.

Reeves, Richard. *President Kennedy: Profile of Power.* New York: Simon & Schuster, 1993.

Regan, Donald T. *For the Record: From Wall Street to Washington.* San Diego: Harcourt Brace Jovanovich, 1988.

Risen, James. *State of War: The Secret History of the CIA and the Bush Administration.* New York: Free Press, 2006.

Rostow, W. W. *Diffusion of Power: An Essay on Recent History.* New York: Macmillan, 1972.

———. *Concept and Controversy: Sixty Years of Taking Ideas to Market.* Austin: University of Texas Press, 2003.

Rothkopf, David. *Running the World: The Inside Story of the National Security Council and the Architects of American Power.* New York: Public Affairs, 2005.

Rusk, Dean. *As I Saw It.* New York: Norton, 1990.

Sammon, Bill. *Fighting Back: The War on Terrorism from Inside the Bush White House.* Washington, D.C.: Regnery 2002.

Scarborough, Rowan. *Rumsfeld's War: The Untold Story of America's Anti-terrorist Commander.* Washington, D.C.: Regnery, 2004.

Schandler, Herbert Y. *Lyndon Johnson and Vietnam: The Unmaking of a President.* Princeton, N.J.: Princeton University Press, 1977.

Schlesinger, Arthur Jr. *A Thousand Days: John F. Kennedy in the White House.* Boston: Houghton Mifflin, 1965.

Senate Intelligence Committee. *Report of the Select Committee on Intelligence on the U.S. Intelligence Community's Prewar Intelligence Assessments on Iraq, July 7, 2004.* Washington, D.C.: Government Printing Office, 2004.

Shultz, George P. *Turmoil and Triumph: My Years as Secretary of State.* New York: Scribner's, 1993.

Smith, Bromley K. *Organizational History of the National Security Council during the Kennedy and Johnson Administrations.* Washington, D.C.: National Security Council, 1988.

Smith, Gerard. *Doubletalk: The Story of the First Strategic Arms Limitation Talks.* Garden City, N.Y.: Doubleday, 1980.

Sorensen, Theodore. *Decision-Making in the White House: The Olive Branch and the Arrows.* New York: Columbia University Press, 1963.

———. *Kennedy.* New York: Harper & Row, 1965.

Stern, Sheldon M. *Averting the 'Final Failure': John F. Kennedy and the Secret Cuban Missile Crisis Meetings.* Stanford, Calif.: Stanford University Press, 2003.

Strober, Deborah Hart, and Gerald S. Strober. *The Reagan Presidency: An Oral History of the Era.* Washington, D.C.: Brassey's, 2003.

———. *Nixon: An Oral History of His Presidency.* New York: HarperCollins, 1994.

Suskind, Ron. *The Price of Loyalty: George W. Bush, the White House, and the Education of Paul O'Neill.* New York: Simon & Schuster, 2004.

Taylor, Maxwell D. *Swords and Plowshares.* New York: Norton, 1972.

Tenet, George. *At the Center of the Storm: My Years at the CIA.* New York: HarperCollins, 2007.

Tower, John, Edmund Muskie, and Brent Scowcroft. *The Tower Commission Report: The Full Text of the President's Special Review Board.* New York: Random House, 1987.

United States Senate, Subcommittee on National Policy Machinery, Committee on Government Operations. *Organizing for National Security,* 3 vols. Washington D.C.: Government Printing Office, 1961.

Vance, Cyrus. *Hard Choices: Critical Years in America's Foreign Policy.* New York: Simon & Schuster, 1983.

Wallison, Peter J. *Ronald Reagan: The Power of Conviction and the Success of His Presidency.* Boulder, Colo.: Westview, 2003.

Weinberger, Caspar W. *In the Arena: A Memoir of the Twentieth Century.* Washington, D.C.: Regnery, 2001.

White, Mark J. *Against the President: Dissent and Decision-Making in the White House.* Chicago: Ivan R. Dee, 2007.

Woodward, Bob. *The Commanders.* New York: Simon & Schuster, 1991.

———. *The Choice.* New York: Simon & Schuster, 1996.

———. *Bush at War.* New York: Simon & Schuster, 2002.

———. *Plan of Attack.* New York: Simon & Schuster, 2004.

———. *State of Denial: Bush at War, Part III.* New York: Simon & Schuster, 2006.

Zegart, Amy B. *Flawed by Design: The Evolution of the CIA, JCS, and NSC.* Stanford, Calif.: Stanford University Press, 1999.

Book Chapters, Articles, Other Sources

Ackerman, Spencer. "Vision Impaired, Tommy Franks's Big Mistakes." *New Republic,* August 30, 2004, 18–23.

Ackerman, Spencer, and John B. Judis. "The Selling of the Iraq War: The First Casualty." *New Republic,* June 30, 2003, 14–25.

———. "The Operator." *New Republic,* September 22, 2003, 18–29.

Ahrens, Frank. "The Reluctant Warrior: National Security Adviser Sandy Berger, a Onetime Dove Who Has Learned the Value of Claws." *New York Times,* February 24, 1998.

Albright, Madeleine. "*Frontline* Interview: The Clinton Years." November 2000. http://www.pbs.org/wgbh/pages/frontline/shows/clinton/interviews/albright.

Allen, Mike. "Bush Taps Rice for Security Adviser." *Washington Post,* December 18, 2000.

———. "President Assails Iraq War Skeptics." *Washington Post,* June 18, 2003.

———. "Iraq Shake-up Skipped Rumsfeld." *Washington Post,* October 8, 2003.

———. "Rice is Named Secretary of State." *Washington Post,* November 17, 2004.

Allen, Mike, and Charles Lane. "Rice Helped Shape Bush Decision on Admissions." *Washington Post,* January 17, 2003.

Allen, Richard V. Oral History, Ronald Reagan Oral History Project, Miller Center of Public Affairs, University of Virginia, May 28, 2002. http://www.webstorage3.mcpa.virginia.edu/poh/transcripts/ohp_2002_0528_allen.pdf.

Anderson, Dillon. "The President and National Security." *Atlantic Monthly,* January 1956, 42–46.

Anderson, Jon Lee. "Out on the Street." *New Yorker,* November, 15, 2004, 72–79.

Andrews, Edmund L. "Envoy's Letter Counters Bush on Dismantling the Iraq Army." *New York Times,* September 4, 2007.

Apple, R. W. Jr. "A Domestic Sort with Global Worries." *New York Times,* August 25, 1999.

Auger, Vincent A. "The National Security Council After the Cold War." In *U.S. Foreign Policy After the Cold War,* edited by Randall B. Ripley and James M. Lindsay, 42–73. Pittsburgh, Pa.: University of Pittsburgh Press, 1997.

Babington, Charles. "Democrats Criticize Rice over Iraq War." *Washington Post,* January 26, 2005.

Baker, James A. III. "Oral History: The Gulf War." *Frontline,* January 9, 1996. http://www.pbs.org/wgbh/pages/frontline/gulf/oral/baker/1.html.

Baker, Peter. "The Security Adviser Who Wants the Role, Not the Stage." *Washington Post,* January 29, 2006.

———. "Bush Aide to Leave No. 2 National Security Post." *Washington Post,* May 5, 2007.

———. "A President Besieged and Isolated, Yet at Ease." *Washington Post,* July 2, 2007.

Balz, Dan, and Mike Allen. "CEO Bush Takes Over Management of Message." *Washington Post,* March 28, 2003.

Balz, Dan, and Terry Neel. "For Bush, Questions, Clues, and Contradiction." *Washington Post,* October 22, 2000.

Balz, Dan, and Bob Woodward. "America's Road to War." *Washington Post,* January 27, 2002.

Bamford, James. "Carlucci and the NSC." *New York Times Magazine,* January 18, 1987, 16ff.

Barnes, Fred. "You're Fired." *New Republic*, January 10, 1994, 12–14.

———. "The Commander." *Weekly Standard*, June 2, 2003, 22–25.

———. "The Essential Bremer." *Weekly Standard*, April 12, 2004, 11–12.

———. "Our Man in Baghdad." *Weekly Standard*, July 26, 2004, 21–23.

———. "How Bush Decided on the Surge." *Weekly Standard*, February 4, 2008, 20–27.

Barry, John, and Evan Thomas. "The Unbuilding of Iraq." *Newsweek*, October 6, 2003, 33–37.

Barstow, David, William Broad, and Jeff Gerth. "How the White House Embraced Disputed Arms Intelligence." *New York Times*, October 3, 2004.

Bender, Bryan. "CIA Warned Administration of Postwar Guerilla Peril." *Boston Globe*, August 10, 2003.

Berger, Samuel. "*Frontline* Interview: The Clinton Years." November 2000. http://www.pbs .org/wgbh/pages/frontline/shows/clinton/interviews/berger.

Berman, Larry, and Bruce W. Jentleson. "Bush and the Post-Cold-War World." In *Bush Presidency First Appraisals*, edited by Colin Campbell and Bert A. Rockman, 93–128. Chatham, N.J.: Chatham House, 1991.

Best, Richard A. Jr. "The National Security Council: An Organizational Assessment," Congressional Research Service Report for Congress, April 21, 2008. http://www.fas.org/sgp/ crs/natsec/RL30840.pdf.

Bolton, John R. "The Making of Foreign Policy in the Bush Administration." In *The Bush Presidency: Ten Intimate Perspectives*, Part 1, edited by Kenneth W. Thomson, 107–125. Lanham, Md.: University Press of America, 1997.

Bonafede, Dom. "Zbigniew Brzezinski." In *Fateful Decisions: Inside the National Security Council*, edited by Karl F. Inderfurth and Loch K. Johnson, 194–202. New York: Oxford University Press, 2004.

Bose, Meena, "Priorities and Policy Making: The Use of Force in the Clinton Administration, 1993–1998." PRG Report 21 (2, 1999): 4–7.

Boyer, Peter. "The New War Machine." *New Yorker*, June 30, 2003, 55–71.

Brands, H. W. "The Age of Vulnerability: Eisenhower and the National Insecurity State." *American Historical Review* 94 (4, 1989): 963–989.

Bremer, L. Paul. "How I Didn't Dismantle Iraq's Army." *New York Times*, September 6, 2007.

Brinkley, Douglas G. "The Bush Administration and Panama." In *From Cold War to New World Order: The Foreign Policy of George H.W. Bush*, edited by Meena Bose and Rosanna Perotti, 175–183. Westport, Conn.: Greenwood Press, 2002.

Brinkley, Joel, and Eric Schmitt. "Iraqi Leaders Say U.S. Was Warned of Disorder after Hussein, but Little Was Done." *New York Times*, November 30, 2003.

Broder, David. "Wobbling Dangerously." *Washington Post*, October 13, 1993.

Broder, John, and Melissa Healy. "Panama Operation Hurt by Critical Intelligence Gaps." *Los Angeles Times*, December 24, 1989.

Bumiller, Elisabeth. "A Partner in Shaping an Assertive Foreign Policy." *New York Times*, January 7, 2004.

———. "In the New Bush Cabinet, Loyalty Trumps Celebrity." *New York Times*, November 22, 2004.

Bundy, McGeorge. "Letter to the Jackson Subcommittee." In *Fateful Decisions: Inside the National Security Council*, edited by Karl F. Inderfurth and Loch K. Johnson, 81–84. New York: Oxford University Press, 2004.

Burke, John P. "Responsibilities of Presidents and Advisers." *Journal of Politics* 46 (3, 1984): 818–845.

———. "The Neutral/Honest Broker Role in Foreign Policy Decision Making: A Reassessment." *Presidential Studies Quarterly* 35 (2, 2005): 229–258.

———. "Condoleezza Rice as NSC Advisor: A Case Study of the Honest Broker Role." *Presidential Studies Quarterly* 35 (3, 2005): 554–575.

———. "From Success to Failure? Iraq and the Organization of George W. Bush's Decision Making." In *The Polarized Presidency of George W. Bush,* edited by George C. Edwards III and Desmond S. King, 173–211. New York: Oxford University Press, 2007.

Butler Committee. "Review of Intelligence on Weapons of Mass Destruction." July 14, 2004. http://www.butlerreview.org.uk.

Calabresi, Massimo. "Condi Gets Her Shot." *Washington Post,* November 29, 2004.

Callahan, David. "Honest Broker: Brent Scowcroft in the Bush White House." *Foreign Service Journal,* 69 (2, 1992): 27–32.

Campbell, Colin. "Unrestrained Ideological Entrepreneurship in the Bush II Advisory System." In *The George W. Bush Presidency: Appraisals and Prospects,* 73–104. Washington, D.C.: CQ Press, 2004.

Cannon, Lou. "Pitfall for Strong Men." *Washington Post,* March 26, 1981.

Carlucci, Frank. Oral History, Ronald Reagan Oral History Project, Miller Center of Public Affairs, University of Virginia, August 28, 2001. http://www.webstorage3.mcpa.virginia.edu/poh/transcripts/ohp_2001_0828_carlucci.pdf.

Carney, James. "Why Bush Doesn't Like Homework." *Time,* November 15, 1999, 46–50.

Carter, Hodding. "How Jimmy Carter's Foreign Policy Bit the Dust." *Washington Post,* January 5, 1987.

Cheney, Richard. "The Bush Presidency." In *The Bush Presidency: Ten Intimate Perspectives,* Part 2, edited by Kenneth W. Thomson, 3–24. Lanham, Md.: University Press of America, 1998.

Cohen, David B. "George Bush's Vicar of the West Wing: John Sununu as White House Chief of Staff." *Congress & the Presidency* 24 (1, 1997): 37–59

———. "From the Fabulous Baker Boys to the Master of Disaster: The White House Chief of Staff in the Reagan and G. H. W. Bush Administrations." *Presidential Studies Quarterly* 32 (3, 2002): 463–483.

Cohen, David B., Chris J. Dolan, and Jerel A. Rosati. "A Place at the Table: The Emerging Foreign Policy Roles of the White House Chief of Staff." *Congress & the Presidency* 29 (2, 2002): 119–149.

Commission on the Intelligence Capabilities of the United States Regarding Weapons of Mass Destruction. "Report to the President of the United States." March 31, 2005. http://www.wmd.gov/report.

Cooper, Matthew, "Pinning the Line on the Man," *Time,* July 28, 2003, 31.

Cutler, Robert, "The Development of the National Security Council," *Foreign Affairs* 34 (3, 1956): 441–458.

Daalder, Ivo H., and I. M. Destler, eds. "The Nixon Administration National Security Council." *The National Security Council Project: Oral History Roundtables.* Washington, D.C.: Center for International and Security Studies and The Brookings Institution, 1998. http://www.cissm.umd.edu/papers/files/Nixon.pdf.

———. "The Bush Administration National Security Council." *The National Security Council Project: Oral History Roundtables.* Washington, D.C.: Center for International and Security Studies and The Brookings Institution, 1999. http://www.cissm.umd.edu/papers/files/Bush.pdf.

———. "The Role of the National Security Adviser." *The National Security Council Project: Oral History Roundtables.* Washington, D.C.: Center for International and Security

Studies and The Brookings Institution, 1999. http://www.brookings.edu/fp/research/projects/nsc/transcripts/19991025.htm.

———. "The Clinton Administration National Security Council." The National Security Council Project: Oral History Roundtables, Washington, D.C.: Center for International and Security Studies and The Brookings Institution, 2000. http://www.cissm.umd.edu/papers/files/Clinton.pdf.

Defense Science Board. "Transition to and from Hostilities." U.S. Department of Defense, Office of the Undersecretary of Defense for Acquisition, Technology, and Logistics, December 2004. http://www.acq.osd.mil/dsb/reports/2004-12-DSB_SS_Report_Final.pdf.

DeParle, Jason. "The Man Inside Bill Clinton's Foreign Policy." New York Times Magazine, August 20, 1995, 33ff.

Destler, I. M. "Comment: Multiple Advocacy, Some 'Limits and Costs.'" American Political Science Review 66 (3, 1972): 786–790.

———. "National Security Advice to U.S. Presidents: Some Lessons from Thirty Years." World Politics 29 (2, 1977): 143–176.

———. "A Job that Doesn't Work." Foreign Policy 38 (2, 1980): 80–88.

———. "National Security Management: What Presidents Have Wrought." Political Science Quarterly 95 (4, 1980–81): 573–588.

Dickinson, Matthew J. "The Institutionalization of the National Security Staff, 1949–2001." Paper prepared for delivery at the 2003 Annual Meeting of the American Political Science Association, Philadelphia, Pa.

Dowd, Maureen. "Basking in Power's Glow." New York Times, December 31, 1989.

Drew, Elizabeth. "Letter from Washington." New Yorker, October 30, 1989, 100–109.

Duffy, Michael, and Mark Kukis. "Why the Surge Worked." Time, February 11, 2008, 28–33.

Efron, Sonni. "So, What's Not to Like about Amiable Advisor?" Los Angeles Times, June 6, 2005.

Ehrlichman, John D. "The White House and Policy-Making." In The Nixon Presidency: Twenty-Two Intimate Perspectives, edited by Kenneth W. Thompson, 119–148. Lanham, Md.: University Press of America, 1987.

Elliott, Michael. "So, What Went Wrong?" Time, September 28, 2003, 31–39.

Elliott, Michael, and Massimo Calabresi. "Is Condi the Problem?" Time, April 5, 2004, 32–37.

Engel, Jeffrey A. "Where a Future President Learned About the World." Newsweek, December 31, 2007, 54–55.

Erlanger, Steven. "Albright, a Bold Voice Abroad, Finds Her Role Limited at Home." New York Times, September 1, 1998.

———. "NATO Was Closer to Ground War in Kosovo Than Is Widely Realized." New York Times, November 7, 1999.

Falk, Stanley L. "The National Security Council Under Truman, Eisenhower, and Kennedy." Political Science Quarterly 79 (3, 1964): 403–434.

Fallows, James. "Blind into Baghdad." Atlantic Monthly, January/February 2004, 52–74.

———. "Bush's Lost Year." Atlantic Monthly, October 2004, 68–84.

Filkins, Dexter. "Bremer Pushes Iraq on Difficult Path to Self-Rule." New York Times, March 21, 2004.

Fortas, Abe. "Portrait of a Friend." In The Johnson Presidency: Twenty Intimate Portraits, edited by Kenneth W. Thompson, 8–10. Lanham, Md.: University Press of America, 1986.

"Forum on the Role of the National Security Adviser." In Fateful Decisions: Inside the National Security Council, edited by Karl F. Inderfurth and Loch K. Johnson, 141–157. New York: Oxford University Press, 2004.

Friedman, Thomas. "China Trip Seeks to Alter Americans' Perceptions." *New York Times,* December 10, 1989.

———. "Baker Seen as Balance to Bush." *New York Times,* November 3, 1990.

Gates, Robert M. "Intelligence in the Reagan and Bush Presidencies." In *The Bush Presidency: Ten Intimate Perspectives,* Part 1, edited by Kenneth W. Thomson, 143–161. Lanham, Md: University Press of America, 1997.

Gelb, Leslie, H. "Brzezinski Says He'll Give Advice to Carter Only When He Asks for It." *New York Times,* December 17, 1976.

———. "Foreign Policy System Criticized by U.S. Aides." *New York Times,* October 19, 1981.

———. "Haig-Clark Feuds Emerging over Foreign Policy." *New York Times,* June 22, 1982.

———. "Clinton's Security Trio." New York Times, December 20, 1992.

George, Alexander L. "The Case for Multiple Advocacy in Making Foreign Policy." *American Political Science Review* 66 (3, 1972): 751–785.

———. "Rejoinder to 'Comment' by I. M. Destler." *American Political Science Review* 66 (3, 1972): 791–795.

———. "Multiple Advocacy." *U.S. Commission on the Organization of the Government for the Conduct of Foreign Policy, Appendices,* Vol. 2. Washington, D.C.: Government Printing Office, 1975, 94–99.

———. "The Cuban Missile Crisis." In *Avoiding War: Problems of Crisis Management,* edited by Alexander L. George, 222–268. Boulder, Colo.: Westview, 1991.

Goldberg, Jeffrey. "Anticipating Problems." *New Yorker,* May 9, 2005, 40–41.

———. "Breaking Ranks: What Turned Brent Scowcroft Against the Bush Administration?" *New Yorker,* October 31, 2005, 55–65.

Goldgeier, James M. "NATO Expansion: The Anatomy of a Decision." In *The Domestic Source of American Foreign Policy: Insights and Evidence,* 5th ed., edited by Eugene R. Wittkopf and James M. McCormick, 339–354. Lanham. Md.: Rowman & Littlefield, 2008.

Goodpaster, Andrew J. "Organizing the White House." In *The Eisenhower Presidency: Eleven Intimate Perspectives,* edited by Kenneth W. Thompson, 63–88. Lanham, Md.: University Press of America, 1984.

Gordon, Michael R. "The Strategy to Secure Iraq did not Foresee a 2nd War." *New York Times,* October 19, 2004.

———. "Faulty Intelligence Misled Troops at War's Start." *New York Times,* October 20, 2004.

———. "Debate Lingering on Decision to Dissolve Iraqi Military." *New York Times,* October 21, 2004.

Gordon, Michael R., and Bernard Trainor. "Even as U.S. Invaded, Hussein Saw Iraqi Unrest as Top Threat." *New York Times,* March 12, 2006.

———. "After Invasion, Point Man for Iraq was Shunted Aside." *New York Times,* March 13, 2006.

Greenstein, Fred I., and Richard H. Immerman. "Effective National Security Advising: Recovering the Eisenhower Legacy." *Political Science Quarterly* 115 (3, 2000): 335–345.

Guliotta, Guy, and Juliet Eilperin. "Tough Response Appeals to Critics of President." *Washington Post,* August 21, 1998.

Gwertzman, Bernard. "Haig Charges a Reagan Aide is Undermining Him." *New York Times,* November 4, 1981.

Haass, Richard. "Oral History: The Gulf War." *Frontline,* January 9, 1996. http://www.pbs.org/wgbh/pages/frontline/gulf/oral/haass/1.html.

Hall, David K. "The 'Custodial Manager' of the Policy-Making Process." In *Decisions of the*

Highest Order: Perspectives on the National Security Council, edited by Karl F. Inderfurth and Loch K. Johnson, 146–154. Pacific Grove, Calif.: Brooks/Cole, 1988.

Hammond, Paul Y. "The National Security Council as a Device for Interdepartmental Coordination: An Interpretation and Appraisal." *American Political Science Review* 54 (4, 1960): 899–910.

Harr, Karl G. Jr. "Eisenhower's Approach to National Security Decisionmaking." In *The Eisenhower Presidency: Eleven Intimate Perspectives,* edited by Kenneth W. Thompson, 89–112. Lanham, Md.: University Press of America, 1984.

Harris, John. "As Clinton Adviser, Berger Combines Stagecraft with Statecraft." *Washington Post,* July 7, 1997.

———. "Berger's Caution Has Shaped Role of U.S. in War." *Washington Post,* May 16, 1999.

———. "In Handling of Crisis, a Different President." *Washington Post,* June 8, 1999.

Harris, John, and Dan Balz. "First 100 Days Go By in a Blitz." *Washington Post,* April 29, 2001.

Heclo, Hugh. "The Political Ethos of George W. Bush." In *The George W. Bush Presidency: An Early Assessment,* edited by Fred I. Greenstein, 17–50. Baltimore: Johns Hopkins University Press, 2003.

Heilbrunn, Jacob. "Lake Inferior." *New Republic,* September 20, 1993, 29–35.

Henderson, Phillip G. "Advice and Decision: The Eisenhower National Security Council Reappraised." In *The Presidency and National Security,* edited by R. Gordon Hoxie, 153–185. New York: Center for the Study of the Presidency, 1984.

Herek, Gregory M., Irving L. Janis, and Paul Huth. "Decision Making during International Crises: Is Quality of Process Related to Outcome?" *Journal of Conflict Resolution* 31 (2, 1987): 203–226.

Hermann, Margaret, and Thomas Preston. "Presidents, Advisers, and Foreign Policy: The Effects of Leadership Style on Executive Arrangements." *Political Psychology* 15 (1, 1994): 75–96.

Hersh, Seymour M. "The Missiles of August." New Yorker, October 12, 1998, 34–41.

———. "The Stovepipe." *New Yorker,* October 27, 2003, 77–87.

Hoagland, Jim. "Flaws and Fissures in Foreign Policy." *Washington Post,* October 31, 1993.

Hoffman, David. "The Politics of Timidity." *Washington Post, National Weekly Edition,* October 23–29, 1989.

———. "Zip My Lips: George Bush's Penchant for Secret Decisions" *Washington Post,* January 7, 1990.

Hosenball, Mark, Michael Isikoff, and Evan Thomas. "Cheney's Lone Path to War." *Newsweek,* November 17, 2003, 35–40.

Hulse, Carl, and David E. Sanger. "New Criticism on Prewar Use of Intelligence." *New York Times,* September 29, 2003.

Ignatius, David. "A Foreign Policy Out of Focus." *Washington Post,* September 2, 2003.

Inderfurth, Karl F., and Loch K. Johnson, "Early Years." In *Fateful Decisions: Inside the National Security Council,* edited by Karl F. Inderfurth and Loch K. Johnson, 27–33. New York: Oxford University Press, 2004.

———. "National Security Advisers: Profiles." In *Fateful Decisions: Inside the National Security Council,* edited by Karl F. Inderfurth and Loch K. Johnson, 173–182. New York: Oxford University Press, 2004.

———. "Transformation." In *Fateful Decisions: Inside the National Security Council,* edited by Karl F. Inderfurth and Loch K. Johnson, 63–79. New York: Oxford University Press, 2004.

Inouye-Hamilton Committee. "Congress and the NSC." In *Fateful Decisions: Inside the*

National Security Council, edited by Karl F. Inderfurth and Loch K. Johnson, 316–334. New York: Oxford University Press, 2004.

Jehl, Douglas. "U.S. Report Finds Iraqis Eliminated Illicit Arms in 90's." *New York Times,* October 7, 2004.

Jehl, Douglas, and David E. Sanger. "New to the Job, Rice Focused on More Traditional Fears." *New York Times,* April 5, 2004.

Judis, John B. "Statecraft and Scowcroft." *New Republic,* February 24, 1992, 18–21.

Kagan, Robert, and William Kristol. "A Winning Strategy." *Weekly Standard,* November 26, 2001, 20–25.

———. "The Right War for the Wrong Reasons." *Weekly Standard,* February 23, 2004, 20–28.

Kessler, Glenn. "U.S. Decision on Iraq Has Puzzling Past." *Washington Post,* January 12, 2003.

———. "Rice Hitting the Road to Speak." *Washington Post,* October 20, 2004.

———. "For New National Security Adviser, a Mixed Record." *Washington Post,* November 17, 2004.

———. "Rice Goes from Inside to the Front." *Washington Post,* January 17, 2005.

———. "Rice is Closer to Final Vote of Senate." *Washington Post,* January 20, 2005.

Kessler, Glenn, and Walter Pincus. "Advisers Split as War Unfolds." *Washington Post,* March 31, 2003.

Kessler, Glenn, and Dana Priest. "Iraq Data Not Old, Bush Aides Insist." *Washington Post,* September 29, 2003.

Kessler, Glenn, and Peter Slevin. "Rice Fails to Repair Rifts, Officials Say." *Washington Post,* October 12, 2003.

Kessler, Glenn, and Thomas E. Ricks. "Rice's NSC Tenure Complicates New Post." *Washington Post,* November 16, 2004.

Kirschten, Dick. "Competent Manager." *National Journal,* February 28, 1987, 468–479.

Kissinger, Henry A. "Domestic Structure and Foreign Policy." *Daedalus* 95 (2, 1966): 503–529.

Kumar, Martha. "Recruiting and Organizing the White House Staff." *PS: Political Science and Politics* 35 (1, 2002): 35–40.

Lake, Anthony. "Carter's Foreign Policy: Success Abroad, Failure at Home." In *The Carter Presidency: Fourteen Intimate Perspectives of Jimmy Carter,* edited by Kenneth W. Thompson, 145–158. Lanham, Md.: University Press of America, 1990.

———. "*Frontline* Interview: The Clinton Years." November 2000. http://www.pbs.org/wgbh/pages/frontline/shows/clinton/interviews/lake.

Lauter, David. "Brent Scowcroft: The Man Behind the President." *Los Angeles Times,* October 14, 1990.

Lay, James S. Jr. "National Security Council's Role in the U.S. Security and Peace Program" *World Affairs* 115 (2, 1952): 37–39.

Leacacos, John P. "Kissinger's Apparat." In *Fateful Decisions: Inside the National Security Council,* edited by Karl F. Inderfurth and Loch K. Johnson, 85–93. New York: Oxford University Press, 2004.

Leiby, Richard. "Breaking Ranks." *Washington Post,* January 19, 2006.

Lemann, Nicholas. "Without a Doubt." *New Yorker,* October 14, 2002, 164–179.

———. "How It Came to War." *New Yorker,* March 31, 2003, 36–40.

Leviero, Anthony. "'Untouchable, Unreachable, and Unquotable.'" *New York Times Magazine,* January 30, 1955, 12ff.

Lubell, Samuel. "Mystery Man of the White House." *Saturday Evening Post,* February 6, 1954, 6ff.

Mandelbaum, Michael. "A Perfect Failure: NATO's War Against Yugoslavia." *Foreign Relations,* 78 (5, 1999): 2–8.

Marcus, Ruth. "Anthony Lake's Secretive Mission." *Washington Post,* December 20, 1993.

McAllister, J. F. O. "Secretary of Shhhhh!" *Time,* June 7, 1993, 32–33.

McFarlane, Robert C., with Richard Saunders and Thomas C. Shull. "The National Security Council: Organization for Policy Making." In *The Presidency and National Security Policy,* edited by R. Gordon Hoxie, 261–273. New York: Center for the Study of the Presidency, 1984.

McGeary, Johanna. "Odd Man Out" *Time,* September 10, 2001, 24–32.

———. "3 Flawed Assumptions." *Time,* April 7, 2003, 58–62.

McManus, Doyle. "Clinton Defers to Aides on Foreign Policy." *Los Angeles Times,* February 14, 1993.

McManus, Doyle, and James Gerstenzang. "Bush Takes CEO Role in Waging War." *Los Angeles Times,* September 23, 2001.

Melanson, Richard A. "George Bush's Search for a Post-Cold War Grand Strategy." In *The Bush Presidency: Ten Intimate Perspectives Part II,* edited by Kenneth W. Thomson, 151–166. Lanham, Md.: University Press of America, 1998.

Milbank, Dana. "Down to the Nuts and Bolts at NSC." *Washington Post,* July 25, 2001.

———. "The Man Who Wasn't There, Still Here." *Washington Post,* May 29, 2008.

Milbank, Dana, and Mike Allen. "Iraq Flap Shakes Rice's Image." *Washington Post,* July 27, 2003.

Milbank, Dana, and Dana Priest. "Warning in Iraq Report Unread." *Washington Post,* July 20, 2003.

Morrison, David. "Retooling the Security Machinery." *National Journal,* June 10, 1989, 1425.

Mufson, Steven. "Forget WMD, What's an NIE?" *Washington Post,* July 20, 2003.

Mulcahy, Kevin, V. "The Secretary of State and the National Security Adviser: Foreign Policymaking in the Carter and Reagan Presidencies." *Presidential Studies Quarterly* 16 (2, 1986): 280–299.

———. "The Bush Administration and National Security Policy Making: A Preliminary Assessment." Paper prepared for delivery at the 1990 Annual Meeting of the American Political Science Association, San Francisco, Calif.

———. "Walt Rostow as National Security Adviser, 1966–69." *Presidential Studies Quarterly* 25 (2, 1995): 223–236.

———. "Rethinking Groupthink: Walt Rostow and the National Security Advisory Process in the Johnson Administration." *Presidential Studies Quarterly* 25 (2, 1995): 237–250.

Mulford, David C. "The Bush Presidency and International Economic Issues." In *The Bush Presidency: Ten Intimate Perspectives,* Part 1, edited by Kenneth W. Thompson, 127–139. Lanham, Md.: University Press of America, 1997.

Myers, Steven, and Eric Schmitt. "War's Conduct Creates Tensions Among Chiefs." *New York Times,* May 30, 1999.

National Journal. "NSC's Powell: Carlucci's Alter Ego." February 28, 1987.

———. "Samuel Berger: The Washington 100." June 14, 1997, 1175–76.

National Security Council. "History of the National Security Council, 1947–1997." http://www.whitehouse.gov/nsc/history.html.

Nelson, Anna Kasten. "National Security I: Inventing a Process (1945–1961)." In *The Illusion of Presidential Government,* edited by Hugh Heclo and Lester M. Salamon, 229–262. Boulder, Colo.: Westview, 1981.

———. "The 'Top of Policy Hill': President Eisenhower and the National Security Council." *Diplomatic History* 7 (4, 1983): 307–26.

———. "President Truman and the Evolution of the National Security Council." *Journal of American History* 7 (2, 1985): 360–378.

———. "The Importance of Foreign Policy Process: Eisenhower and the National Security Council." In *Eisenhower: A Centenary Assessment,* edited by Gunter Bischof and Stephen E. Ambrose, 111–125. Baton Rouge: Louisiana State University Press, 1995.

———. "The Evolution of the National Security State Ubiquitous and Endless." In *The Long War: A New History of U.S. National Security Policy Since World War II,* edited by Andrew J. Bacevich, 265–301. New York; Columbia University Press, 2007.

O'Hanlon, Michael E. "Iraq Without a Plan." *Policy Review* 128 (December 2004/January 2005): 33–45

Oberdorfer, Don. "Reagan Aides See Power Grab: Haig Starts Fast and Strong." *Washington Post,* February 8, 1981.

———. "Balkans, Haiti, Iraq, and Somalia Head NSC Policy Study List." *Washington Post,* January 31, 1993.

Packer, George. "War After the War." *New Yorker,* November 24, 2003, 58–85.

Painton, Priscilla, and Michael Duffy. "Brent Scowcroft: Mr. Behind-the-Scenes." *Time,* October 7, 1991, 24.

Perlez, Jane. "With Berger in Catbird Seat, Albright's Star Dims." *New York Times,* December 14, 1999.

———. "Rice on the Front Line Foreign Policy War." *New York Times,* August 19, 2001.

Pfiffner, James P. "Presidential Policy-Making and the Gulf War." In *The Presidency and the Gulf War,* edited by Marcia Whicker, James P. Pfiffner, and Raymond Moore, 3–23. Westport, Conn.: Praeger, 1993.

———. "President George W. Bush and His War Cabinet." Paper presented at the conference on "The Presidency, Congress, and the War on Terrorism," University of Florida, February 7, 2003.

———. "Did President Bush Mislead the Country in his Arguments for War with Iraq?" *Presidential Studies Quarterly* 34 (1, 2004): 25–46.

———. "National Security Policymaking and the Bush War Cabinet." In *Transforming the American Polity: The Presidency of George W. Bush and the War on Terrorism,* edited by Richard S. Conley, 84–100. Upper Saddle River, N.J.: Pearson Prentice Hall 2005.

———. "Intelligence and Decision Making before the War with Iraq." In *The Polarized Presidency of George W. Bush,* edited by George C. Edwards III and Desmond S. King, 213–242. New York: Oxford University Press, 2007.

Pillar, Paul R. "Intelligence, Policy, and the War in Iraq." *Foreign Affairs* 85 (2, 2006): 15–27.

Pincus, Walter. "White House Backs Off Claim on Iraqi Buy." *Washington Post,* July 8, 2003.

———. "Tenet Says He Didn't Know about Claim." *Washington Post,* July 17, 2003.

———. Deutch Sees Consequences in Failed Search for Arms." *Washington Post,* July 25, 2003.

———. "White House Faulted on Uranium Claim." *Washington Post,* December 24, 2003.

———. "Assessments Made in 2003 Foretold Situation in Iraq." *Washington Post,* May 20, 2007.

———. "Before War, CIA Warned of Negative Outcomes." *Washington Post,* June 3, 2007.

Pollack, Kenneth M. "Spies, Lies, and Weapons: What Went Wrong?" *Atlantic Monthly,* January/February 2004, 78–92.

Popkin, Samuel L. "The Art of Managing the White House." In *Chief of Staff: Twenty-Five Years of Managing the Presidency,* edited by Samuel Kernell and Samuel L. Popkin, 1–12. Los Angeles: University of California Press, 1986.

Powell, Colin. "Oral History: The Gulf War." *Frontline,* January 9, 1996. http://www.pbs.org/wgbh/pages/frontline/gulf/oral/powell/1.html.

Priest, Dana. "House Probers Conclude Iraq War Data Was Weak." *Washington Post,* September 28, 2003.

Priest, Dana, and Walter Pincus. "U.S. 'Almost All Wrong' on Weapons." *Washington Post,* October 7, 2004.

Purdom, Todd. "From Behind the Scenes to Stage Front." *New York Times,* November 16, 2004.

Rieff, David. "Who Botched the Occupation? Blueprint for a Mess." *New York Times Magazine,* November 2, 2003, 28ff.

Risen, James. "To Bomb Sudan Plant or Not: A Year Later, Debates Rankle." *New York Times,* October 27, 1999.

Risen, James, and Judith Miller. "No Illicit Arms Found in Iraq, U.S. Inspector Tells Congress." *New York Times,* October 3, 2003.

Robbins, Carla Anne. "New Security Post Lifts Hadley's Profile." *Wall Street Journal,* January 13, 2005.

Rockman, Bert A. "America's Departments of State: Irregular and Regular Syndromes of Policy Making." *American Political Science Review* 75 (4, 1981): 911–927.

———. "The Presidency and Bureaucratic Change After the Cold War." In *U.S. Foreign Policy After the Cold War,* edited by Randall B. Ripley and James M. Lindsay, 21–41. Pittsburgh, Pa.: University of Pittsburgh Press, 1997.

Rosenthal, Andrew. "National Security Adviser Redefines Role." *New York Times,* November 3, 1989.

———. "Scowcroft and Gates: A Team Rivals Baker." *New York Times,* February 21, 1991.

Rostow, W. W. "Aftermath, Losing Big: A Reply." *Esquire,* December 1972, 10–12.

Rush, Kenneth. "An Ambassador's Perspective." In *The Nixon Presidency: Twenty-Two Intimate Perspectives,* edited by Kenneth W. Thompson, 335–358. Lanham, Md.: University Press of America, 1987.

Safire, William. "On Language; The Goldilocks Recovery." *New York Times Magazine,* January 29, 1995, 18.

Sander, Alfred D. "Truman and the National Security Council: 1945–1947." *Journal of American History* 59 (2, 1972), 369–388.

Sanger, David E. "The Shipwreck in Seattle." *New York Times,* December 5, 1999.

———. "Missile Shield Point Man Does Not Shy From Tough Fight." *New York Times,* February 16, 2001.

———. "Bush Aides Deny Effort to Slant Data on Iraq Arms." *New York Times,* June 9, 2003.

Sanger, David E., and Patrick E. Tyler. "Wartime Forges a United Front for Bush Aides." *New York Times,* December 22, 2001.

Sanger, David, and Judith Miller. "National Security Aide Says He's to Blame for Speech Error." *New York Times,* July 23, 2003.

Sanger, David, and Thom Shanker. "Rumsfeld Quick To Dismiss Talk of Reduced Role in Iraq Policy." *New York Times,* October 9, 2003.

Schlesinger, Arthur Jr. "Effective National Security Advising: A Most Dubious Precedent." *Political Science Quarterly* 115 (3, 2000): 347–351.

Schmitt, Eric, and Joel Brinkley. "State Department Foresaw Trouble Now Plaguing Iraq." *New York Times,* October 19, 2003.

Schneider, Keith. "Poindexter at the Security Council: A Quick and Troubled Reign." *New York Times,* January 11, 1987.

Sciolino, Elaine. "Compulsion to Achieve." *New York Times,* December 18, 2000.

———. "3 Players Seek a Director for Foreign Policy Story." *New York Times,* November 8, 1993.

———. "2 Key Advisers in a Bitter Duel on U.S. Foreign Policy." *New York Times,* September 24, 1994.

———. Christopher Spells out New Priorities." *New York Times,* Nov. 5, 1993.

Sciolino, Elaine, and Ethan Bronner. "How a President Distracted by Scandal, Entered Balkan War." *New York Times,* April 18, 1999.

Scowcroft, Brent. "Ford as President and his Foreign Policy." In *The Ford Presidency: Twenty-Two Intimate Perspectives of Gerald R. Ford,* edited by Kenneth W. Thompson, 309–318. Lanham, Md.: University Press of America, 1988.

———. "Oral History: The Gulf War," *Frontline,* January 9, 1996. http://www.pbs.org/wgbh/pages/frontline/gulf/oral/scowcroft/1.html.

Seib, Gerald F. "Scowcroft, Once Obscured by Other Bush Aides, Emerges as Influential Player in Mideast Crisis." *Wall Street Journal,* October 17, 1990.

Shultz, George. Oral History, Ronald Reagan Oral History Project, Miller Center of Public Affairs, University of Virginia, December 18, 2002. http://www.webstorage3.mcpa.virginia.edu/poh/transcripts/ohp_2002_1218_shultz.pdf.

Sisco, Joseph J. "Ford, Kissinger and the Nixon-Ford Foreign Policy." In *The Ford Presidency: Twenty-Two Intimate Perspectives of Gerald R. Ford,* edited by Kenneth W. Thompson, 319–332. Lanham, Md.: University Press of America, 1988.

Slevin, Peter, and Mike Allen. "Rice to Lead Effort to Speed Iraqi Aid." *Washington Post,* October 7, 2003.

Smith, Hedrick. "A Scaled Down Version of the Security Adviser's Task." *New York Times,* March 4, 1981.

Sonnenfeldt, Helmut. "Reconstructing the Nixon Foreign Policy." In *The Nixon Presidency: Twenty-Two Intimate Perspectives,* edited by Kenneth W. Thompson, 315–334. Lanham, Md.: University Press of America, 1987.

Sorensen, Theodore. "The President and the Secretary of State." *Foreign Affairs* 66 (2, 1987–88): 231–248.

Souers, Sidney W. "Policy Formulation for National Security." *American Political Science Review* 43 (3, 1949): 534–43.

Starobin, Paul. "On Her Own." *National Journal,* January 29, 2005, 266–73.

Stern, Eric K. "Probing the Plausibility of Newgroup Syndrome: Kennedy and the Bay of Pigs." In *Beyond Groupthink: Political Group Dynamics and Foreign Policy-Making,* edited by Paul 't Hart, Eric K. Stern, and Bengt Sundelius, 153–189. Ann Arbor: University of Michigan Press, 1997.

Stolberg, Sheryl Gay. "Kissinger's Appearance Revives Memories of Vietnam Era." *New York Times,* January 2, 2007.

———. "Quiet Bush Aide Seeks Iraq Czar, Creating a Stir." *New York Times,* April 30, 2007.

Stone, Peter H. "Were Qaeda-Iraq Links Exaggerated?" *National Journal,* August 9, 2003, 2569–70.

Thomas, Evan. "The Quiet Power of Condi Rice." *Newsweek,* December 16, 2002, 25–34.

———. "The 12 Year Itch." *Newsweek,* March 31, 2003, 54–65.

Thomas, Evan, and Richard Wolffe. "Bush in the Bubble." *Newsweek,* December 19, 2005, 29–39.

Walcott, Charles E., and Karen M. Hult. "White House Structure and Decision Making: Elaborating the Standard Model." *Presidential Studies Quarterly* 35 (2, 2005): 303–18.

Walsh, Kenneth T. "Bush's Man with the Hawk's Eye View." *U.S. News & World Report,* October 7, 1991, 28–29.

Warshaw, Shirley Anne. "The Political Lens of the President's War Cabinet for the War in Afghanistan." Paper presented at the conference on "The Presidency, Congress, and the War on Terrorism," University of Florida, February 7, 2003.

Weinberger, Caspar. Oral History, Ronald Reagan Oral History Project, Miller Center of Public Affairs, University of Virginia, November 19, 2002. http://www.webstorage3. mcpa.virginia.edu/poh/transcripts/ohp_2002_1119_weinberger.pdf.

Weiner, Tim, and Jane Perlez. "How Clinton Approved the Strikes on Belgrade." *New York Times,* April 4, 1999.

Weiner, Tim, and James Risen. "Decision to Strike Factory in Sudan Based on Surmise." *New York Times,* September 21, 1998.

Weisman, Steven. "Haig Resigns Over Foreign Policy Course." *New York Times,* June 26, 1982.

———. "What Rift?" *New York Times,* June 1, 2003.

Wright, Robin. "Foreign Policy Guru Tapped to Aid Rice." *Washington Post,* December 23, 2003.

Wright, Robin, and Thomas E. Ricks. "U.S. Faces Growing Fear of Failure." *Washington Post,* May 19, 2004.

Woodward, Bob. "Ford Disagreed With Bush About Invading Iraq." *Washington Post,* December 28, 2006.

Woodward, Bob, and Rick Atkinson. "Launching Operation Desert Shield." *Washington Post,* National Weekly Edition, September 3–9, 1990, 8–10.

Yetiv, Steve A. "The Agent-Structure Question in Theory: President Bush's Role during the Persian Gulf Crisis." In *From Cold War to New World Order: The Foreign Policy of George H. W. Bush,* edited by Meena Bose and Rosanna Perotti, 137–150. Westport, Conn.: Greenwood Press, 2002.

Index

"Quis custodiet ipsos custodes?"
"Who will be guarding the guardians?"
—Juvenal

The U.S. president's decisions on national security and foreign policy reverberate around the world. The National Security Council (NSC) and the national security advisor are central to the decision making process. But how was the role of the national security advisor originally understood, and how has that understanding changed over time? Above all, how has the changing role of the national security advisor affected executive decisions and the implementation of policy?

Now, presidential scholar John P. Burke systematically and thoroughly addresses these questions. In *Honest Broker?*, he reviews the office of national security advisor from its inception during the Eisenhower presidency to its latest iteration in the White House of George W. Bush. He explores the ways in which the original conception of the national security advisor—as an "honest broker" who, rather than directly advocate for any certain policy direction, was instead charged with overseeing the fairness, completeness, and accuracy of the policymaking process—has evolved over time. In six case studies he then analyzes the implications of certain pivotal changes in the advisor's role, providing thoughtful and sometimes critical reflections on how these changes square with the role of "honest broker."

Finally, Burke offers some prescriptive consideration of how the definition of the national security advisor's role relates to effective presidential decision making and the crucial issues of American national security. *Honest Broker?* will be an important resource for scholars, students, political leaders, and general readers interested in the U.S. presidency, foreign policy, and national security.

JOHN P. BURKE is a professor of political science at the University of Vermont in Burlington. He has written seven books and is a former winner of the American Political Science Association's Richard Neustadt Award for the best book on the American Presidency. His Ph.D. is from Princeton University.

Joseph V. Hughes Jr. and Holly O. Hughes Series
on the Presidency and Leadership

TEXAS A&M UNIVERSITY PRESS • COLLEGE STATION
www.tamu.edu/upress

$29.95

ISBN-13: 978-1-60344-102-
ISBN-10: 1-60344-102-6

52995

9 781603 441025